RECOGNITION AND ENFORCEMENT OF JUDGMENTS IN CIVIL AND COMMERCIAL MATTERS

This collection offers a study of the regimes for the recognition and enforcement of foreign commercial judgments in 15 Asian jurisdictions: mainland China, Hong Kong, Taiwan, Japan, Korea, Malaysia, Singapore, Thailand, Vietnam, Cambodia, Myanmar, the Philippines, Indonesia, Sri Lanka and India.

For practising lawyers, the book is intended as a practical guide to current law and procedures for enforcing judgments in the selected jurisdictions. However, it does not stop at describing current law and practice. Of interest to academics and students, it also analyses the common principles of the enforcement regimes across the jurisdictions, and identifies what should be regarded as the norm for enforcement in Asian countries for the purpose of attracting foreign direct investment and catalysing rapid economic development.

In light of the common principles identified, the book explores how laws in Asia may generally be improved to enable judgments to be more readily enforced, while ensuring that legitimate concerns over indirect jurisdiction, due process and domestic public policy are respected and addressed. With this in mind, the book discusses the potential impact that the adoption of the 2005 Hague Convention on Choice of Court Agreements might have on Asian jurisdictions; it also considers the potential impact of the 2019 Hague Convention on the Recognition and Enforcement of Foreign Judgments in Civil or Commercial Matters.

This timely book argues that it is imperative to adopt a uniform system for the recognition and enforcement of judgments throughout Asia if there is to be traction for the enhanced crossborder commerce that is expected to result from endeavours such as the ASEAN Economic Community (AEC), the Belt and Road Initiative (BRI), CPTPP (also known as TPP-11), and RCEP.

Volume 1 in the series Studies in Private International Law – Asia

Studies in Private International Law – Asia

General Editor: Anselmo Reyes
Advisory Editor: Paul Beaumont

Much has been written about private international law in the EU and the US. Less is known about the conflict of laws in Asia. Thus, little attention has been paid so far to the modernisation of private international law codes and rules that has been taking place over the last decade all over Asia. That trend continues. Now is the time to take stock of those reforms that have already taken place and suggest further improvements for the future.

Published under the celebrated series *Studies in Private International Law*, this monograph sub-series provides a forum for discussion and analysis of private international law in Asia. The series is not solely a survey of jurisdictions for practitioners. Comprising in-depth thematic and country-specific studies, each volume considers the private international law of Asian countries from a variety of perspectives. An underlying assumption is that private international law in different jurisdictions follow broad discernible patterns. Each volume in this sub-series highlights those patterns and discusses how rules in different Asian jurisdictions are either converging with, or diverging from, the patterns identified. Such an analytical framework will assist academics, judges, lawyers and legislators to envisage ways in which laws affecting cross-border relationships can be harmonised across jurisdictions and be made more responsive to the needs of citizens in Asia and elsewhere.

Recognition and Enforcement of Judgments in Civil and Commercial Matters

Edited by
Anselmo Reyes

•HART•
OXFORD • LONDON • NEW YORK • NEW DELHI • SYDNEY

HART PUBLISHING

Bloomsbury Publishing Plc

Kemp House, Chawley Park, Cumnor Hill, Oxford, OX2 9PH, UK

First published in Great Britain 2019

A catalogue record for this book is available from the British Library.

Library of Congress Cataloging-in-Publication data

Names: Reyes, Anselmo, editor.

Title: Recognition and enforcement of judgments in civil and commercial matters / edited by Anselmo Reyes

Description: Oxford ; New York Hart 2019. | Series: Studies in private international law – Asia volume 1 | Includes bibliographical references and index.

Identifiers: LCCN 2019027741 (print) | LCCN 2019027742 (ebook) | ISBN 9781509924257 (hardback) | ISBN 9781509924271 (Epub)

Subjects: LCSH: Judgments, Foreign—East Asia. | Judgments, Foreign—Southeast Asia | Judgments, Foreign—South Asia.

Classification: LCC KNC474 .R43 2019 (print) | LCC KNC474 (ebook) | DDC 347.5/077—dc23

LC record available at https://lccn.loc.gov/2019027741

LC ebook record available at https://lccn.loc.gov/2019027742

ISBN: HB: 978-1-50992-425-7
ePDF: 978-1-50992-426-4
ePub: 978-1-50992-427-1

Typeset by Compuscript Ltd, Shannon

UPDATE

As anticipated in the text, the 2019 Hague Convention on the Recognition and Enforcement of Foreign Judgments in Civil or Commercial Matters[1] was adopted on 2 July 2019 by the 22nd Diplomatic Session of the Hague Conference on Private International Law. The 2019 Convention will come into effect after 12 months from the time when two states become party. The 2019 Convention is essentially similar, with only minor differences, to the 2018 Draft Hague Convention discussed here and does not affect the analysis in this book.

The main differences between the 2019 Hague Convention and the 2018 Draft Hague Convention are as follows: Article 2(1)(g) deletes the word 'transboundary' which appeared before 'marine pollution' in the draft; Articles 2(1)(l)–(p) (exclusion of privacy, IP, activities of armed forces, law enforcement activities, and anti-trust matters) which appeared in brackets in the draft have been adopted, with the addition of Article 2(1)(q) (exclusion of sovereign debt); Article 4(4) on recognition or enforcement when a judgment is subject to review in the state of origin has been simplified; Article 4 did not adopt the provisions on common courts found in the draft; Article 5(1)(h) refers to a judgment that has ruled on 'a lease of immovable property' (as opposed to 'a tenancy of immovable property' in the draft) being eligible for recognition and enforcement; Article 5(3) qualifies that Article 5(1) does not apply to a judgment that 'ruled on a residential lease of immovable property (tenancy) or ruled on the registration of immovable property' unless given by the court of the state where the property is situated; Article 6 (stating that a judgment on rights *in rem* in immovable property will only be recognised and enforced if the property is situated in the state of origin) adopts Article 6(b) (but not Articles 6(a) and 6(c)) of the draft; Article 11 of the draft dealing with non-monetary remedies in IP matters has not been adopted; Article 19 on judgments pertaining to a state adopts Article 20 of the draft but in modified form; Article 29 on the establishment of relations pursuant to the 2019 Hague Convention did not appear in the draft.

Anselmo Reyes
Kyoto
3 July 2019

[1] For the text, see www.hcch.net/en/instruments/conventions/full-text/?cid=137. Articles 1 to 10 of the 2019 Hague Convention correspond to Articles 1 to 10 of the draft. Articles 11 to 28 correspond to Articles 12 to 29 of the draft. Article 29 was not in the draft. Articles 30 to 32 correspond to Articles 30 to 32 of the draft.

ACKNOWLEDGEMENTS

Numerous persons have been involved in the production of this book. I hope that they will not mind if I do not mention them all by name and confine myself here to acknowledging the assistance and advice of ten individuals. Naoshi Takasugi, Romesh Weeramantry, Anton Cooray, Yeo Tiong Min, Adeline Chong, Mark Fisher, Catherine Shen, Ho Ching Him and Li Pak Hei all generously helped out in different ways at critical junctures when this work encountered difficulties. My special thanks go to my research assistant, Wilson Lui, for his meticulous editing of the text and footnotes in every chapter. But for his efforts this book would not have been possible.

Anselmo Reyes
Kyoto
1 April 2019

TABLE OF CONTENTS

Update v
Acknowledgements vii
List of Contributors xi
List of Cases xiii
List of Legislative Materials xxv

1. *Introduction: Towards a System for the Recognition and Enforcement of Judgments* 1
Anselmo Reyes

2. *China* 31
Weixia Gu

3. *Hong Kong* 51
James Y P Wong

4. *Taiwan* 85
Fuldien Li and Yen-Te Wu

5. *Japan* 97
Kazuaki Nishioka

6. *South Korea* 119
Unho Lee

7. *Singapore* 141
Kenny Chng

8. *Malaysia* 163
Sitpah Selvaratnam

9. *Vietnam* 179
Nguyen Ngoc Minh, Tran Ha Han and Nguyen Thi Thu Trang

10. *Cambodia* 201
Alex Larkin and Potim Yun

11. *Myanmar* 209
Zaw Thura

12. *The Philippines* 223
Arvin A Jo and Jocelyn P Cruz

13. *Indonesia* 243
Afifah Kusumadara

14. *Thailand* 259
Akawat Laowonsiri

15. *Sri Lanka* 271
Kankani Tantri Chitrasiri, Sajini Fernando and Aslesha Weerasekara

16. *India* 291
Sai Ramani Garimella

17. *Conclusion: Towards an Asia of Judgments without Borders* 309
Anselmo Reyes

Bibliography 327
Index 339

LIST OF CONTRIBUTORS

Kankani Tantri Chitrasiri is a retired Justice of the Supreme Court of Sri Lanka and presently the Parliamentary Commissioner for Administration (Ombudsman) of Sri Lanka.

Kenny Chng is an Assistant Professor at the School of Law of Singapore Management University.

Jocelyn P Cruz is an Assistant Professor in the Department of Commercial Law of the Ramon V Del Rosario College of Business at De La Salle University in the Philippines.

Sajini Fernando is a Sri Lankan attorney.

Sai Ramani Garimella is an Assistant Professor at the Faculty of Legal Studies of South Asian University in India.

Weixia Gu is an Associate Professor at the Law Faculty of the University of Hong Kong.

Arvin A Jo is an Assistant Professor in the Department of Commercial Law of the Ramon V Del Rosario College of Business at De La Salle University in the Philippines.

Afifah Kusumadara is a Lecturer at the Law Faculty of Brawijaya University in Indonesia.

Akawat Laowonsiri is a Lecturer at the Law Faculty of Thammasat University in Thailand.

Alex Larkin is a Senior Counsel at the firm of PYT & Associates (a member of VDB Loi) in Cambodia.

Unho Lee is a Lecturer at the International Trade Department of Pusan National University and a Research Fellow at the Law Faculty of Kyushu University.

Fuldien Li is a Professor at the Chinese Culture University College of Law in Taipei and Chairperson of the Chinese Arbitration Association in Taiwan.

Nguyen Ngoc Minh is a Partner at the firm of Dzungsrt & Associates in Vietnam.

Nguyen Thi Thu Trang is a Counsel at the firm of Dzungsrt & Associates in Vietnam.

Kazuaki Nishioka is a Post-Doctoral Research Fellow at the Law Faculty of Zurich University.

Anselmo Reyes is an International Judge of the Singapore International Commercial Court and a member of the International Commercial Expert Committee of the China International Commercial Court. He is presently a Guest Professor at the Law Faculty of Doshisha University in Kyoto.

Sitpah Selvaratnam is a Partner at the firm of Tommy Thomas in Malaysia.

Zaw Thura is a Judge of the Union of Myanmar and an Assistant Director of the Law and Procedure Department in the Office of the Union Judiciary Supervision of the Supreme Court of the Union.

Tran Ha Han is a Senior Associate at the firm of Dzungsrt & Associates in Vietnam.

Asiesha Weerasekara is a Sri Lankan attorney.

James Y P Wong is an Associate at Dentons Hong Kong LLP.

Yen-Te Wu is a Professor at the Chinese Culture University College of Law in Taipei.

Potim Yun is a Partner at the firm of PYT & Associates (a member of VDB Loi) in Cambodia.

LIST OF CASES

Cambodia

Case No 131/003/2007 of 26 June 2007, Decision No 092/003/2007 CC.D of 10 July 2007 (Constitutional Council) 202

Canada

Beals v Saldanha [2003] 3 SCR 416 160
Boardwalk Regency Corp v Maalouf (1992) 88 DLR (4th) 612 (Ont CA) 156
Leaton Leather & Trading Co Ltd v Ngai Tak Kong (1997) 147 DLR (4th) 1377 63

China

Gezhouba Sanlian Industrial Co Ltd v Robinson Helicopter Co Inc (2001) (Hubei Provincial High Court) 44–45
Gomi Akira v Dalian Fari Seafood Ltd (Application of Gomi Akira (Japanese Citizen) to Chinese Court for Recognition and Enforcement of Japanese Judicial Decision) (1996) 1 *Supreme People's Court Gazette* 29 (Dalian Intermediate People's Court) 43
Hou Yijun v Hou Kelis (Henan Zhengzhou Intermediate People's Court) 36
Kolma Group AG v Jiangsu Textile Industry (Group) Import and Export Co Ltd (2016) Su-01 Xie Wai Ren Civil Judgment (Nanjing Intermediate People's Court) 44–45, 311
Liu Li v Tao Li and Tong Wu (2015) Yue Wuhan Zhong Min Shang Wai Chu Zi No 00026 (30 June 2017) (Hubei Wuhan Intermediate People's Court) 44–45
Schneider Electric Industries SAS v Wenzhou Fly-Dragon Electrical Co Ltd (2005) Wen Min San Chu Zi No 155 (Zhejiang Wenzhou Intermediate People's Court) 41
Spring Comm v Piao Zonggen (2011) Shen Zhong Fa Min Yi Chu Zi No 45 (30 September 2011) (Guangdong Shenzhen Intermediate People's Court) 127
Wang Qingfang's Application for the Recognition of An American Adoption Judgment (2006) Er Zhong Min Te Zi No 10319 (Beijing Municipality Intermediate People's Court No 2) 43

England and Wales

Adams v Cape Industries plc [1990] Ch 433 .... 63, 151, 157, 160
Bozson v Altrincham Urban District Council [1903] 1 KB 547 (CA) 279

British South Africa Co v Companhia de Moçambique [1893] AC 602 (HL) 75, 216
Carl Zeiss Stiftung v Rayner & Keeler Ltd [1967] 1 AC 853 150
Coin Controls Ltd v Suzo International (UK) Ltd [1999] Ch 33 75
ED&F Man (Sugar) Ltd v Haryanto (No 2) [1991] 1 Lloyd's Rep 429 (CA) 64
Emanuel v Symon [1908] 1 KB 302 .... 278, 321
Godard v Gray (1870) LR 6 QB 139 148
Henderson v Henderson (1843) 3 Hare 100 148
Israel Discount Bank of New York v Hadjipateras [1984] 1 WLR 137 156
Johnson v Gore Wood & Co [2002] 2 AC 1 148
Nouvion v Freeman (1889) 15 App Cas 1 ....65, 69
Owens Bank Ltd v Bracco [1992] 2 AC 443 155
Philip Alexander Securities & Futures Ltd v Bamberger [1997] ILPr 73 64
Plastus Kreativ AB v Minnesota Mining and Manufacturing Co [1995] RPC 438 75
Re Lines Bros [1983] Ch 1 74
Re Overseas Aviation Engineering (GB) Ltd [1963] Ch 24 71
Sadler v Robins [1808] 1 Camp 253 279
Showlag v Mansour [1995] 1 AC 431 157
Sirdar Gudyal Singh v The Rajah of Faridkote [1894] AC 670 293
Spiliada Maritime Corp v Cansulex Ltd (The Spiliada) [1987] AC 460 ....22, 141
Vervaeke v Smith [1983] 1 AC 145 (HL) 64
Vizcaya Partners Ltd v Picard [2016] 3 All ER 181 151

France

Cass le civ, Simitch [1985] Rev crit DIP 369 (French Supreme Court) 267

Germany

German Züblin International Co Ltd v Wuxi Walker General Engineering Rubber Co Ltd doc no 20 S Ch 13/04 (18 May 2006) (Berlin Court of Appeal) 44

Hong Kong

Anthony Wee Soon Kim v UBS AG Hong Kong Branch [2006] 2 HKC 1 55
Anthony Wee Soon Kim v UBS AG Hong Kong Branch CACV 96/2006 (5 November 2007) 55
Bank of China Ltd v Yang Fan [2016] 3 HKLRD 7 68–69
CEF New Asia Co Ltd v Wong Kwong Yiu, John [1999] 3 HKLRD 697 59
Chen Li Hung v Ting Lei Miao (2000) 3 HKCFAR 9 ....59, 67
Cheung Koon Ping v Muneyoshi Michiyoshi [1994] 3 HKC 563 73
Chiyu Banking Corp Ltd v Chan Tin Kwun [1996] 2 HKLR 395 67–69
Compania Sud Americana De Vapores SA v Hin-Pro International Logistics Ltd DCCJ 3986/2014 (17 November 2015) 70

Cova Enterprises Ltd v Ruddy Tjanaka [2004] 1 HKLRD 199 66
Democratic Republic of Congo v FG Hemisphere Associates LLC (2011) 14 HKCFAR 95 67
DX v LN FCMC 7870/2014 (30 November 2015) 76
Esquel Enterprises Ltd v TAL Apparel Ltd [2006] 2 HKLRD 363 75
Fabiano Hotels Ltd v Profitmax Holdings Inc [2017] 6 HKC 414 67
Korea Data Systems Co Ltd v Jay Tien Chiang [2001] 3 HKC 239 ....65, 67
Ku Chia Chun v Ting Lei Miao [1999] 1 HKLRD 123 59
Lam Chit Man v Cheung Shun Lin [2001–2003] HKCLRT 243 (CA) 65, 68–69
Lam Chit Man v Lam Chi To [2001–2003] HKCLRT 141 (CA) 65, 68
Lee Yau Wing v Lee Shui Kwan [2007] 2 HKLRD 749 68–69
Nintendo of America Inc v Bung Enterprises Ltd [2000] 2 HKC 629 ....67, 70
Prime Credit Leasing Sdn Bhd v Tan Cho Lung Raymond [2006] 4 HKLRD 741 60
Tan Tay Cuan v Ng Chi Hung [2001] HKLRD (Yrbk) 195 68
The '*Hua Tian Long*' [2010] 3 HKLRD 611 67
Westpac New Zealand Ltd v Gao Hui [2009] 4 HKC 373 70
Wu Wei v Liu Yi Ping HCA 1452/2004 (30 January 2009) 68
Yick Tat Development Co v Yung Chung Yiu HCA 1590/2007 (17 March 2011) 66

India

ABC Laminart Pvt Ltd v AP Agencies, Salem [1989] 2 SCR 1; [1989] AIR SC 1239 301
Abdul Rahman v Cassim & Sons [1933] AIR PC 58 279
ABN v Satish Dayalal Choksi [1990] AIR Bom 170 300
Achal Ram v Kazim Hussain Khan (1905) ILR 27 All 271 291
Angile Insulations v Davy Ashmore India Ltd [1995] 4 SCC 153; [1995] AIR SC 1766 302
Bharat Heavy Electricals v Electricity Generation Incorporations [2017] CS (Comm) 190/2017 (Delhi High Court) 302, 321
BMIC Ltd v Chinnakannan Sivasankaran [2016] Execution Petition No 6 of 2016 (Madras High Court) 303, 306
Chormal Balchand Firm v Kasturi Chand Seraoji [1938] AIR Cal 511 301
Dr Devika Damji Shah v Rashmi Mukesh Shah (2012) 114(5) Bom LR 2757 (Bombay High Court) 297
Dr V Ravi Chandran v Union of India [2010] 1 SCC 174 303
Duggamma v Ganeshayya [1964] ILR Kar 609; [1965] AIR Kant 97 305
Gajanan Sheshadri Pandharpurkar v Shantabai [1939] AIR Bom 374 299
Gurdas Mann v Mohinder Singh Brar [1993] AIR P&H 92 299
Hakam Chand v Gammon India Ltd [1971] 1 SCC 286; [1971] AIR SC 740 302
Hanil Era Textiles Ltd v Puromatic Filters (P) Ltd [2004] 4 SCC 671; [2004] AIR SC 2432 302
Hindupur v Bellur (2015) SCC OnLine Del 7484 300
Kevin George Vaz v Cotton Textiles Exports [2006] 5 Bom CR 555 297
Kumarina Investment Ltd v Digital Media Convergence Ltd (2010) SCC Online TDSAT 641 302
Lalji Raja and Sons v Firm Hansraj Nathuram [1971] 3 SCR 815; [1971] AIR SC 974 301

M/S Alcon Electronics Pvt Ltd v Celem SA of Fos 34320 Roujan, France [2017] 2 SCC 253; [2017] AIR SC 1 303
M/S Rite Approach Group Ltd v M/S Rosoboronexport Ltd [2007] 2 Arb LR 443 (Delhi); (2007) 139 DLT 55; [2007] AIR Delhi 145....................304
Maloji Rao Narsingh Rao v Sankar Saran [1955] AIR 1955 All 490 (Allahabad High Court)....................298
Marine Geotechnics LLC v Coastal Marine Construction & Engineering Ltd [2014] 2 Bom CR 769 298
Middle East Bank Ltd v Rajendra Singh Sethia [1991] AIR Cal 335 299
Modi Entertainment Network v WSG Cricket Pte Ltd [2003] AIR SCW 733.............. 302, 321
Panchpakesa Iyer v K N Husain [1934] AIR Mad 145 299
Patel Roadways v Prasad Trading Co [1991] 3 SCR 391; [1992] AIR SC 1514....................302
Ram Coomar Condoo v Chunder Canto Mookerjee (1876) ILR 2 Cal 233 291
Ramanathan Chettyar v Kalimuthu Pillay (1912) 18 Ind Cas 189 301
RMV Vellachi Achi v RMA Ramanatha Chettiar [1973] AIR Mad 141....................301
S P Chengalvaraya Naidu v Jagannath [1994] 1 SCC 1; [1994] AIR SC 853....................300
Sankaran Govindam v Lakshmi Bharathi [1975] 1 SCR 57; [1974] AIR SC 1764....................300
Satya v Teja Singh [1975] 2 SCR 97....................300
Shalig Ram v Firm Daulatram Kundanmal [1963] 2 SCR 574; [1967] AIR SC 739....................301
Shin Satellite Public Co Ltd v Jain Studios Ltd (2006) 2 SCC 628....................303
State Bank of India v Dr Vijay Mallya [2018] EWHC 1084 (Comm)....................304
Sumikin Bussan International (Hong Kong) Ltd v King Shing Enterprises Ltd (in liq) [2008] 5 Bom CR 464....................297
Super General Co v Suresh Thonikkadavu Veedu [2017] CRP No 506/2016 (D) (21 February 2017) (Kerala High Court)....................297
Surya Vadanan v State of Tamil Nadu [2015] AIR SC 2243....................303
The Andhra Bank Ltd v R Srinivasan [1962] 3 SCR 391; [1962] AIR SC 232....................301
Trilochan Choudhury v Dayanidhi Patra [1961] AIR Ori 158....................299
Union of India v Competition Commission of India [2012] AIR Del 66 (Delhi High Court)....................305
Y Narasimha Rao v Y Venkata Lakshmi [1991] 2 SCR 821; [1991] 3 SCC 451 294

Indonesia

Bankers Trust Co v PT Jakarta International Hotel and Development Tbk No 46/Pdt.G/1999 (9 December 1999) (South Jakarta District Court)....................254
Bankers Trust Co v PT Mayora Indah Tbk No 46/Pdt.G/1999 (9 December 1999) (South Jakarta District Court)....................254
Karaha Bodas Co LLC v Perusahaan Pertambangan Minyak dan Gas Bumi Negara (Pertamina) Nos 001 and 002/Pdt/Arb.Int/1999/PN.JKT.PST and 002/Pdt.P/2000/PN.JKT.PST (3 February 2000) (Central Jakarta District Court)....................254
No 258/Pdt.P/2007/PN.JAK.SEL (25 September 2007) (South Jakarta District Court)....244
PT Nizwar v Navigation Maritime Bulgare No 2944K/PDT/1983 (20 August 1984) (Supreme Court) 254

PT Perusahaan Listrik Negara (PLN) v PT Paiton Energy No 517/Pdt.G/1999/PN.JKT.PST (13 December 1999) (Central Jakarta District Court)....254
PT Tempo v PT Roche Indonesia No 454/Pdt.G/1999/PN.JAK.SEL (South Jakarta District Court, 25 January 2000)....254

Japan

Judgment of Mito District Court, Ryuugasaki Branch, 29 October 1999, 1034 *Hanrei Taimuzu* 270....107
Judgment of Mito District Court, Shimozuma Branch, 5 November 2012, 2012WLJPCA11056005....113
Judgment of Nagoya District Court, 6 February 1987, 1236 *Hanrei Jiho* 113....104, 106–07
Judgment of Nagoya District Court, 24 November 1999, 1068 *Hanrei Taimuzu* 234....107
Judgment of Nagoya District Court, Toyohashi Branch, Heisei 23(Wa) No 561 (29 November 2012)....135
Judgment of Nagoya High Court, 17 May 2013, 2013WLJPCA05176005....113
Judgment of Osaka District Court, 22 December 1977, 361 *Hanrei Taimuzu* 127....111
Judgment of Osaka District Court, 17 January 1996, 956 *Hanrei Taimuzu* 286....107
Judgment of Osaka High Court, 9 April 2003, 1141 *Hanrei Taimuzu* 270....108
Judgment of the Supreme Court, 7 June 1983, 37-5 *Minshu* 611....107
Judgment of the Supreme Court, 26 February 1985, 37-6 *Katei Saiban Geppo* 25....104
Judgment of the Supreme Court, 11 July 1997, 51-6 *Minshu* 2573....110
Judgment of the Supreme Court, 11 September 1997, 51-6 *Minshu* 2573....102
Judgment of the Supreme Court, 28 April 1998, 52-3 *Minshu* 853....101, 104–09
Judgment of the Supreme Court, 26 September 2002, 56-8 *Minshu* 1551....106
Judgment of the Supreme Court, 23 March 2007, 61-2 *Minshu* 619....110
Judgment of the Supreme Court, 24 April 2014, 68-4 *Minshu* 329....104, 106
Judgment of Tokyo District Court, 4 July 1960, unreported....108
Judgment of Tokyo District Court, 20 July 1960, 11-7 *Kaminshu* 1522....108
Judgment of Tokyo District Court, 13 November 1967, 215 *Hanrei Taimuzu* 173....107
Judgment of Tokyo District Court, 6 September 1968, 242 *Hanrei Taimuzu* 263....107
Judgment of Tokyo District Court, 24 October 1970, 259 *Hanrei Taimuzu* 254....107
Judgment of Tokyo District Court, 21 December 1976, 870 *Hanrei Jiho* 96....109
Judgment of Tokyo District Court, 11 November 1988, 1315 *Hanrei Jiho* 95....109
Judgment of Tokyo District Court, 26 March 1990, 857 *Kin'yu Shoji Hanrei* 39....109
Judgment of Tokyo District Court, 18 February 1991, 760 *Hanrei Taimuzu* 250....107
Judgment of Tokyo District Court, 16 December 1991, 794 *Hanrei Taimuzu* 246....107
Judgment of Tokyo District Court, 30 January 1992, 45-9 *Katei Saiban Geppo* 45....107
Judgment of Tokyo District Court, 14 January 1994, 1509 *Hanrei Jiho* 96....104, 106–07, 111
Judgment of Tokyo District Court, 31 January 1994, 1509 *Hanrei Jiho* 101....104, 107
Judgment of Tokyo District Court, 29 May 1995, 904 *Hanrei Taimuzu* 202....107
Judgment of Tokyo District Court, 2 September 1996, 1608 *Hanrei Jiho* 130....107
Judgment of Tokyo District Court, 24 February 1998, 995 *Hanrei Taimuzu* 271....107
Judgment of Tokyo District Court, 25 February 1998, 972 *Hanrei Taimuzu* 258....104, 107

Judgment of Tokyo District Court, 9 September 2003, 2003WLJPCA09090007 111
Judgment of Tokyo District Court, 19 January 2006, 1229 *Hanrei Taimuzu* 334 107
Judgment of Tokyo District Court, 29 January 2008, 2008WLJPCA01298006 107
Judgment of Tokyo District Court, 19 February 2008, 2008WLJPCA02198003 107
Judgment of Tokyo District Court, 12 February 2009, 2068 *Hanrei Jiho* 95 111
Judgment of Tokyo District Court, 28 March 2011, 1351 *Hanrei Taimuzu* 241 107
Judgment of Tokyo District Court, 13 December 2013, 2013WLJPCA12138015 111
Judgment of Tokyo District Court, 8 January 2014, 2014WLJPCA01088001 107
Judgment of Tokyo District Court, 20 March 2015, 1422 *Hanrei Taimuzu* 348 108
Judgment of Tokyo District Court, 29 January 2016, 2313 *Hanrei Jiho* 67 107
Judgment of Tokyo District Court, Hachioji Branch, 8 December 1997, 976 *Hanrei Taimuzu* 235 107
Judgment of Tokyo District Court, Hachioji Branch, 13 February 1998, 987 *Hanrei Taimuzu* 282 .... 106–07, 111
Judgment of Tokyo High Court, 27 February 1990, 1344 *Hanrei Jiho* 139 111
Judgment of Tokyo High Court, 28 June 1993, 1471 *Hanrei Jiho* 89 102
Judgment of Tokyo High Court, 15 November 1993, 46-6 *Katei Saiban Geppo* 47 .... 107, 110
Judgment of Tokyo High Court, 24 September 2015, 2305 *Hanrei Jiho* 68 110
Judgment of Tokyo High Court, 25 November 2015, 2015WLJPCA11256007 108
Judgment of Yokohama District Court, 30 March 1999, 1696 *Hanrei Jiho* 120 107

Malaysia

Amos William Dawe v Development & Commercial Bank (Ltd) Bhd [1981] 1 MLJ 230 (FC) 175
Bank of New Zealand v Wong Kee Tat [1990] 2 MLJ 435 (HC) 169–70
Banque Nasionale De Paris v Wuan Swee May [2000] 3 MLJ 587 (HC) 171
Charles Priya Marie v Koshy Cherian [2010] 6 CLJ 693 (HC) 169, 174
Commerzbank (South East Asia) Ltd v Dennis Ling Li Kuang [2000] 2 CLJ 57 (HC) 171
Commerzbank (South East Asia Ltd) v Tow Kong Liang [2011] 3 CLJ 127 (CA) 171
Excelmore Trading Pte Ltd v Excelmore Classics Sdn Bhd [1996] 1 LNS 392 (HC) 169
Fortune Hong Kong Trading Ltd v Cosco Feoso (Singapore) Pte Ltd [2000] 2 SLR 717 (CA) 171
Goodness For Import And Export v Phillip Morris Brands Sarl [2016] 5 MLJ 171 170
Ho Hong Bank Ltd v Ho Kai Neo [1932] 1 MLJ 76 164
Hua Daily News Bhd v Tan Thien Chien & Ors [1986] 2 MLJ 107 (SC) 173
International Factors Leasing Pte Ltd v Winds Cruises Pte Ltd [1999] 4 MLJ 165 (HC) 172
Issar Singh v Samund Singh (1941) 10 MLJ (FMSR) 28 175
Juara Aspirasi (M) Sdn Bhd v Tan Soon Ping [2012] 1 MLJ 50 (CA) 173
Jupiters Ltd (trading as Conrad International Treasury Casino) v Gan Kok Beng [2007] 7 MLJ 228 (HC) 171
KS Das v P Suppiah [1988] 2 MLJ 445 (SC) 169
Kuah Tian Nam v Lee Siok Poh [2009] 1 LNS 703 (HC) 175

Lim Kang Hai v Lim Chik Lock [2013] 1 LNS 539 (HC) 175
Malayan Banking Bhd v Ng Man Heng [2005] 1 MLJ 470 (HC) 170
Malayan Banking Bhd v Paxelent Corporation Bhd [2007] 3 CLJ 247 (HC)....................169
Maril-Rionebel (M) Sdn Bhd v Perdana Merchant Bankers Bhd and other Appeals [2001] 4 MLJ 187 (CA)....................173
Marina Bay Sands Pte Ltd v Ng Kong Seong [2016] 1 LNS 1007 (HC)....................171
Marina Bay Sands Pte Ltd v Wong Kar Hin [2017] 1 LNS 680 (HC)....................171
Metrowangsa Asset Management Sdn Bhd v Ahmad b Hj Hassan [2005] 1 MLJ 654 174
PNG Oxygen Ltd v Lim Kok Chuan [2018] 1 LNS 237 (HC) 173–74
Re Raju Jayaraman Kerpaya ex p Associated Asian Securities (Pte) Ltd [1999] 5 CLJ 23 (HC)....................172
Saeed U Khan v Lee Kok Hooi [2001] 5 MLJ 416 (HC) 172
Siti Nur Aishah bt Ishak v Golden Plus Holdings Bhd [2017] 3 MLJ 701 170
Standard Chartered Bank (Singapore) Ltd v Pioneer Smith (M) Sdn Bhd [2015] 7 CLJ 677 (HC) 171
Tankam and Shina Tamby v RMKA Mootoopalany Chetty [1899] 6 SSLR 11 164
The Aspinall Curzon Ltd v Khoo Teng Hock [1991] 2 MLJ 484 (HC).................... 171, 174
The Bank of East Asia Ltd Singapore Branch v Axis Incorporation Bhd (No 1) [2009] 6 MLJ 587 (HC)....................172
The Bank of East Asia Ltd Singapore Branch v Axis Incorporation Bhd (No 2) [2009] 6 MLJ 564 (HC)....................172
The Ritz Hotel Casino Ltd v Seri Osu Hj Sukam [2005] 3 CLJ 390 (HC)....................171
United Malayan Banking Corp Bhd v Soo Lean Tooi [1984] 1 MLJ 47 (HC)....................170
Wong Teck Lim v Sim Lim Finance Ltd [2001] 2 CLJ 685 (CA)....................170
Zhang Jing v Ng Fong Yong [2014] 10 CLJ 841 (HC)....................169

Myanmar

A N Abdul Rahiman v J M Mahomed Ali Rowther (1928) 6 AIR (Rangoon) 552....................217
C Burn v D T Keymer (1913) 7 *Lower Burma Rulings* 56....................217
K B Walker v Gladys P Walker [1935] AIR (Rangoon) 284 212
Mohamed Khan v Damayanthi Parekh [1952] *Burma Law Reports* 356 216
SPS Chokkappa Chetty v ISPSRM Raman Chetty (1917) 9 *Lower Burma Rulings* 103.......215
SPSN Kasivisvanathan Chettiar v SS Khrishnappa Chettiar [1951] *Burma Law Reports* 399 217
Steel Brothers & Co Ltd v Y A Ganny Sons and Two [1965] *Burma Law Reports* 449 (CC) 215, 318
VAS Arogya Odeyar v VR RM N S Sathappa Chettiar [1951] *Burma Law Reports* 211 (HC).................... 214–15

Netherlands

NJ 2004, 615, LJN: AF7005 (27 June 2003) (Supreme Court of the Netherlands) 253

Philippines

Asiavest Merchant Bankers v Court of Appeals GR No 110263 (2001) 232
Bank of the Philippine Islands Securities v Guevara GR No 167052 (2015)................... 237–38
Boudard v Tait GR No L-45193 (1939)..............................231
Fujuki v Marinay GR No 196049 (2013) 233
Hang Lung Bank Ltd v Saulog GR No 73765 (1991) 228–29
Hongkong and Shanghai Banking v Sherman GR No 72494 (1989)..............................236
Ingenohl v Olsen GR No L-22288 (1925) 224, 227, 233–35, 239
Johnston v Compagnie Generale Transatlantique 242 NY 381 (1926)..............................226
Mijares v Ranada GR No 139325 (2005) 224, 227, 229, 234–35, 237
Nagarmull v Binalbagan-Isabela Sugar Co GR No L-22470 (1970) 234–35
Northwest Orient Airlines v Court of Appeals GR No 112573 (1995)..............................230
Oil and Natural Gas Commission v Court of Appeals GR No 114323 (1998) 226
Pakistan International Airlines v Ople GR No 61594 (1990).............................. 236–37
Philippine Aluminum Wheels v FASGI Enterprises GR No 137378 (2000)..............................232
Philsec Investment v Court of Appeals GR No 103493 (1997) 239
Re Consolidation of Intellectual Property Courts with Commerical Courts, Supreme Court of the Philippines Administrative Matter No 03-03-03-SC..............................227
St Aviation Services Co Pte Ltd v Grand International Airways Inc, GR No 140288 (2006) 225

Singapore

Alberto Justo Rodriguez Licea v Curacao Drydock Co Inc [2015] 4 SLR 172......... 149, 153–54
Bank of India v Trans Continental Commodity Merchants Ltd [1986] 2 MLJ 342..............................171
Ching Mun Fong (exrx of the estate of Tan Geok Tee, decd) v Liu Cho Chit [2000] 1 SLR(R) 53..............................148
Eleven Gesellschaft Zur Entwicklung Und Vermarktung Von Netzwerktechonologien MBH v Boxsentry Pte Ltd [2014] SGHC 210 150
Ermgassen & Co Ltd v Sixcap Financials Pte Ltd [2018] SGHCR 8 146
Giant Light Metal Technology (Kunshan) Co Ltd v Aksa Far East Pte Ltd [2014] 2 SLR 545 ....44, 147, 149–50, 152–53
Goh Nellie v Goh Lian Teck [2007] 1 SLR(R) 453 150
Henry v Geoprosco International Ltd [1976] QB 726 152
Hong Pian Tee v Les Placements Germain Gauthier Inc [2002] 1 SLR(R) 515.......... 142, 146, 148–50, 154–55
Humpuss Sea Transport Pte Ltd (in compulsory liquidation) v PT Humpuss Intermoda Transportasi TBK [2016] 5 SLR 1322.............................. 148–50, 153
JIO Minerals FZC v Mineral Enterprises Ltd [2011] 1 SLR 391 141
JM Lyon & Co v Meyer & Goldenberg (1891) 1 SSLR 19 173–74
Kader Nina Merican v Kader Meydin (1876) 1 SSLR 3..............................173
Kwa Ban Cheong v Kuah Boon Sek [2003] 3 SLR(R) 644 148
Liao Eng Kiat v Burswood Nominees Ltd [2004] 4 SLR(R) 690.............................. 155–56

Man Financial (S) Pte Ltd (formerly known as E D & F Man International (S) Pte Ltd) v Wong Bark Chuan David [2008] 1 SLR 663 ... 141
Manharlal Trikamdas Mody v Sumikin Bussan International (HK) Ltd [2014] 3 SLR 1161 ... 148, 150
Murakami Takako (exrx of the estate of Takashi Murakami Suroso, decd) v Wiryadi Louise Maria [2007] 4 SLR(R) 565 ... 148, 150, 159
Pattni v Ali [2007] 2 AC 85 ... 158
Poh Soon Kiat v Desert Palace Inc (trading as Caesars Palace) [2010] 1 SLR 1129 ... 149, 155–56
Ralli v Angullia (1917) 15 SSLR 33 (Straits Settlements CA) ... 171, 173–74
Shi Wen Yue v Shi Minjiu [2016] SGHCR 8 ... 146
Sun-Line (Management) Ltd v Canpotex Shipping Services Ltd [1985–1986] SLR(R) 695 ... 151
The Bunga Melati 5 [2011] 4 SLR 1017 (HC) ... 150
The Bunga Melati 5 [2012] 4 SLR 546 (CA) ... 148, 150
The Republic of the Philippines v Maler Foundation and other appeals [2014] 1 SLR 1389 ... 154
The Vasiliy Golovnin [2007] 4 SLR(R) 277 ... 148
United Malayan Banking Corp Bhd v Khoo Boo Hor [1995] 3 SLR(R) 839 ... 151
United Overseas Bank Ltd v Tjong Tjui Njuk [1987] SLR(R) 275; [1987] 2 MLJ 295 ... 151, 170
Westacre Investments Inc v The State-Owned Company Yugoimport SDPR (also known as Jugoimport-SDPR) [2009] 2 SLR(R) 166 ... 144, 158
William Jacks & Co (Singapore) Pte Ltd v Nelson Honey & Marketing (NZ) Ltd [2015] SGHCR 21 ... 151
WSG Nimbus Pte Ltd v Board of Control for Cricket in Sri Lanka [2002] 1 SLR(R) 1088 ... 146, 152, 156
Yong Tet Miaw v MBF Finance Bhd [1992] 2 SLR(R) 549 ... 153

South Korea

Seoul Central District Court Decision 2006Gahap89560 (23 August 2007) ... 134
Seoul Central District Court Decision 2015Gahap534482 (9 June 2017) ... 127
Seoul District Court Decision 99Gahap26523 (5 November 1999) ... 127, 132
Seoul District Court Eastern Branch Decision 93Gahap19069 (10 February 1995) ... 129
Seoul District Court Southern Branch Decision 99Gahap14496 (20 October 2000) ... 129
Seoul District Court Western Branch Decision 2009Gahap6806 (14 December 2010) ... 127
Seoul High Court Decision 2007Na122966 (6 March 2009) ... 131
Seoul High Court Decision 2013Na2012912 (12 March 2015) ... 131
Seoul High Court Decision 2017Na2009518 (17 November 2017) ... 127
Supreme Court Decision 2000Da35795 (8 December 2000) ... 130
Supreme Court Decision 2002Da59788 (22 January 2005) ... 123
Supreme Court Decision 2002Da74213 (28 October 2004) ... 126, 128
Supreme Court Decision 2004Du11275 (24 March 2006) ... 137
Supreme Court Decision 2008Da31089 (22 July 2010) ... 131

Supreme Court Decision 2009Da19093 (28 April 2011) 134
Supreme Court Decision 2009Da22549 (24 May 2012) 130
Supreme Court Decision 2009Da25944 (11 June 2009) 131
Supreme Court Decision 2009Da68620 (24 May 2012) 130
Supreme Court Decision 2009Da68910 (29 April 2010) 122, 133
Supreme Court Decision 2009Ma1600 (25 March 2010) 122, 130
Supreme Court Decision 2010Da18355 (15 July 2010) 124, 136
Supreme Court Decision 2012Da23832 (30 May 2017) 126
Supreme Court Decision 2012Meu66 (15 February 2013) 126
Supreme Court Decision 2015Da1284 (15 October 2015) 129
Supreme Court Decision 2015Da207747 (28 January 2016) 129, 131
Supreme Court Decision 2017Da288757 (26 April 2018) 127
Supreme Court Decision 71Da1393 (22 October 1971) 126
Supreme Court Decision 85Daka1767 (28 April 1987) 127
Supreme Court Decision 93Da39607 (21 November 1995) 136
Supreme Court Decision 93Meu1051 (10 May 1994) 130
Supreme Court Decision 96Da20093 (9 September 1997) 125, 138
Supreme Court Decision 98Da35037 (9 June 2000) 124
Supreme Court Established Rule for Family Relation Register No 173 (10 December 2007) 132
Supreme Court Established Rule for Family Relation Register No 419 (8 January 2015) 132
Supreme Court Order Ja2009Ma1600 (25 March 2010) 122, 130
Supreme Court Order Ja80Ma403 (26 September 1980) 125
Suwon District Court Pyeongtaek Branch Decision 2007Gahap1076 (24 April 2009) 129

Sri Lanka

Associated Newspapers of Ceylon Limited v Prins Gunasekera [2000] 2 Sri LR 323 276
Bulankulama v Secretary of Industrial Development [2000] 3 Sri LR 243 (the *Eppawala Phosphate Mining* case) 283–84
Cornel & Co Ltd v Mitsui and Co Ltd [2000] 1 Sri LR 57 275
Denoon v Northway [1883] 5 SCC 133 280
Fernando v Chittambaram Chettiar [1949] 49 NLR 217 279
Lalwani v Indian Overseas Bank [1998] 2 Sri LR 197 276
Nallaratnam Singarasa v Attorney General SC Spl (LA) No 182/99 (SC) (15 September 2006) 284
Narayanaswami v Marimuttupillai [1949] XLI CLW 12 277
Sepala Ekanayake v Attorney General [1988] 1 Sri LR 46 284
Shamji Gordhandas & Co v Ramanathan & Co [1917] 20 NLR 129 .... 278, 280
Siriwardene v Air Ceylon Ltd [1982] 2 Sri LR 544 279
Suhada Gamlath, Secretary to the Ministry of Justice and Law Reform v Kristina Ivasauskaite-Rosairo No (PHC) APN 3/2010 (CA Revision) (1 June 2011) 286

Ruhunu Ware Pvt Ltd v Freight Links International and Direx Corp 288
Vaitalingam v Murugesu [1931] 34 NLR 79 278
Watte Gedera Wijebanda v Conservator General of Forests [2009] 1 Sri LR 337 283
Weragama v Eksath Lanka Wathu Kamkaru Samithiya [1994] 1 Sri LR 293 283
Worman & Co v Noorbhai 15 NLR 355 278

Taiwan

Chongshangtzu No 525 (2006) 89
Chungshang-geng (2) tzu No 27 (2010) 90
Kangtzu No 46 (1930) 89
Shang-geng (1) tzu No 81 (2008) 90
Taikangtzu No 185 (2008) 88
Taikangtzu No 1004 (2015) 87
Taishangtzu No 2579 (1996) 86
Taishangtzu No 372 (1998) 89
Taishangtzu No 1118 (1998) 86
Taishangtzu No 109 (2008) 86, 88
Taishangtzu No 552 (2011) 89
Taishangtzu No 1367 (2013) 89, 91
Taishangtzu No 2213 (2014) 90
Taishangtzu No 1998 (2015) 93
Taishangtzu No 2198 (2015) 93
Taishangtzu No 232 (2016) 87
Zonsutzu No 561 (2014) 94

Thailand

No 2351/2548 (Central Juvenile and Family Court) 265
SCJ 45/2524 (Supreme Court) 269
SCJ 585/2461 (Supreme Court) 262, 264–68, 320
SCJ 937/2476 (Supreme Court) 266
SCJ 3882/2549 (Supreme Court) 266
SCJ 6565/2544 (Supreme Court) 266, 269
SCJ 15066/2555 (Supreme Court) 265

United States

Hilton v Guyot 159 US 113 (1895) 42, 224–25
In Re Union Carbide Corp Gas Plant Disaster [1986] 634 F Supp 842 (SDNY) 305
Sahu v Union Carbide Corp [2008] No 06-5694-cv (2d Cir) (3 November 2008) 305

Vietnam

Decision No 133/2010/QDST-HN (26 January 2010) (People's Court of Ho Chi Minh City)....198
Decision No 302/2011/QD-TDC-DSST (22 June 2011) (People's Court of Ho Chi Minh City)....198
Judgment No 02/2005/KT-ST (22 August 2005) (People's Court of Khanh Hoa)....182

LIST OF LEGISLATIVE MATERIALS

International Instruments

1927 Convention on the Execution of Foreign Arbitral Awards (Geneva Convention)..........101
1929 Convention for the Unification of Certain Rules Relating to International Carriage by Air (Warsaw Convention)..........100
1951 Convention Relating to the Status of Refugees..........100–01
1954 Hague Convention on Civil Procedure..........100
1956 Hague Convention on the Law Applicable to Maintenance Obligations towards Children..........100
1958 Convention on the Recognition and Enforcement of Foreign Arbitral Awards (1958 New York Convention)..........24, 27, 47, 91, 101, 121, 144, 176, 182, 200, 226–27, 249, 252, 254–55, 257, 310, 325
1960 Convention on Third Party Liability in the Field of Nuclear Energy (as amended in 1964, 1982 and 2004)..........64, 78
1961 Hague Apostille Convention..........225, 230
1961 Hague Convention Abolishing the Requirement of Legalisation for Foreign Public Documents..........100, 120
1961 Hague Convention on the Conflicts of Laws Relating to the Form of Testamentary Dispositions..........100
1965 Hague Convention on the Service Abroad of Judicial and Extrajudicial Documents in Civil or Commercial Matters (1965 Hague Service Abroad Convention)..........41, 100, 121, 131, 285
Art 10(a)..........109
1965 ICSID Convention..........101, 252, 257
1969 International Convention on Civil Liability for Oil Pollution Damage (as amended by the 1992 Protocol)..........64, 77
1970 Hague Convention for the Suppression of Unlawful Seizure of Aircraft..........284
1970 Hague Convention on the Taking of Evidence Abroad in Civil or Commercial Matters..........121, 285
1971 Hague Convention on the Recognition and Enforcement of Foreign Judgments in Civil and Commercial Matters..........5, 11, 13, 16, 18–20, 22–23, 25, 97, 195–96, 199, 225, 252, 295
Art 1..........6–7, 196
Art 2..........6
Art 3..........6
Art 4..........6–7
Art 5..........6–7
Arts 6–8..........7

Art 6 ... 7
Art 7 ... 7
Art 8 ... 7
Arts 9–12 ... 7
Art 9 ... 7
Art 10 ... 7–8
Art 11 ... 8
Art 12 ... 8
Arts 13–19 ... 8
Art 13 ... 197–98
Art 14 ... 8
Arts 20–23 ... 8
Art 20 ... 23
Art 21 ... 8, 23
1971 International Convention on the Establishment of an International Fund for Compensation for Oil Pollution Damage
Art 8 ... 261
1973 Hague Convention of the Law Applicable to Maintenance Obligations ... 100
1973 Convention on International Trade in Endangered Species of Wild Fauna and Flora ... 282
1974 United Nations Convention on a Code of Conduct for Liner Conferences ... 64, 78
1980 Hague Convention on the Civil Aspects of International Child Abduction ... 100, 121, 261, 285
1982 United Nations Convention on the Law of the Sea ... 282
1985 UNCITRAL Model Law on International Commercial Arbitration
Art 1(1), fn 2 ... 3, 29, 211
1989 United Nations Convention on the Rights of the Child ... 261
1992 Convention on Biological Diversity ... 282
1992 International Convention on Civil Liability for Oil Pollution Damage (Civil Liability Convention) ... 101, 105
Art X ... 261
Art X(1) ... 102
Art X(2) ... 102
1992 International Convention on the Establishment of an International Fund for Compensation for Oil Pollution Damage (Establishment Convention) ... 101, 105
Art 8 ... 102
1993 Hague Convention on Protection of Children and Co-operation in Respect of Intercountry Adoption ... 261, 285
1997 Convention on Supplementary Compensation for Nuclear Damage (Nuclear Damage Convention) ... 101, 105
Art 13(5) ... 102
Art 13(5)(c) ... 102
Art 13(6) ... 102
1999 Convention for the Unification of Certain Rules for International Carriage by Air (Montreal Convention) ... 101
2001 International Convention on Civil Liability for Bunker Oil Pollution Damage ... 64, 77

2004 United Nations Convention on Jurisdictional Immunities of States and Their Property 101
2005 Hague Convention on Choice of Court Agreements (2005 Hague Convention) 5–6, 16, 18–20, 23, 28, 31, 41, 47–49, 51, 53, 55, 80–81, 83, 97, 116, 121, 137–38, 142, 166, 176, 185, 195–96, 199, 203, 207, 221, 225, 241, 253–57, 263, 269, 295, 308–09, 311, 325
Art 1 9
Art 2 .... 9, 46, 252
Art 2(2) 11, 46
Arts 2(2)(a)–2(2)(p) 306
Art 2(3) 10–11
Art 2(4) 10–11
Art 3 .... 9, 11
Art 3(c) 9
Arts 5–7 9
Art 5(1) 10, 12
Art 5(2) 10, 13
Art 6 40
Arts 8–15 9
Art 8 40
Art 8(2) 11
Art 8(3) 11
Art 8(4) 11
Art 9 10
Art 10 10
Art 15 11
Art 19 306
Art 20 .... 11, 312, 321, 323
Art 21 11
Art 23 146
2015 Hague Principles on Choice of Law in International Commercial Contracts 5, 308
2018 Hague Convention on the Recognition and Enforcement of Judgments in Civil and Commercial Matters (draft) (2018 Draft) 6, 16, 18–20, 22–23, 49, 53, 81, 83–84, 161
Art 2(1) 11
Arts 2(1)(l)–(p) v
Art 2(2) 11
Art 2(3) 10
Art 2(4) 11
Art 4 11
Art 4(1) 11
Art 4(2) 11
Art 4(3) 11
Art 5(1) 12

Art 5(2) 13
Art 6(a) v
Art 6(b) v
Art 6(c) v
Art 7(1) 13
Art 8 14
Art 9 14
Art 11 v
Arts 13–16 14
Art 14(1) 14
Art 18 14
Art 19 14
Art 20 v
2019 Hague Convention on the Recognition and Enforcement of Foreign Judgments in Civil or Commercial Matters v
Art 2(1)(g) v
Arts 2(1)(l)–(p) v
Art 2(1)(q) v
Art 4 v
Art 4(4) v
Art 5(1) v
Art 5(1)(h) v
Art 5(3) v
Art 6 v
Art 19 v
Art 29 v
ASEAN Comprehensive Investment Agreement (ACIA) 269, 315
Art 13 241
Art 13(1)(f) 241
ASEAN Framework Agreement on Services (AFAS) 269
Art 9 262
ASEAN Trade in Goods Agreement (ATIGA) 269
Berne Convention for the Protection of Literary and Artistic Works
Art 33 193
Brussels Convention 53
Brussels I Regulation 53
Brussels II Regulation 53
Framework Agreement on the ASEAN Investment Area
Art 12 262
ICC Uniform Customs and Practice for Documentary Credits (UCP 500) 182
International Covenant on Civil and Political Rights 262
Art 2 284
Art 14 263
Paris Convention for the Protection of Industrial Property 239
Art 28 193
Rome Convention 53
Rome I Regulation 53

Rome II Regulation 53
Statute of the Hague Conference on Private International Law (Hague Statute)
Art 1 5
Supplementary Protocol to the 1971 Hague Convention 5–6, 20
Art 1 8
Art 2 8
Art 4 8
Art 5 9
Trade-Related Aspects of Intellectual Property Rights Agreement (TRIPS Agreement) 282
Art 64 193

Bilateral Treaties and Agreements

Agreement between China and Laos (the China–Laos Treaty) 39
Agreement between Japan and the Republic of Korea Concerning the Settlement of Problems in Regard to Property and Claims and Economic Cooperation (1965) 130
Agreement between the Republic of India and the Islamic Republic of Afghanistan on Juridical and Judicial Cooperation in Civil and Commercial Matters for the Service of Summons, Judicial Documents, Commission and Execution of Judgments and Arbitral Awards (2016)
Art 16 296
Art 17 296
Agreement between the Republic of India and the United Arab Emirates on Juridical and Judicial Cooperation in Civil and Commercial Matters for the Service of Summons, Judicial Documents, Judicial Commissions, Execution of Judgments and Arbitral Awards (1999) 297
Agreement between Vietnam and Algeria
Art 18(2) 186
Agreement between Vietnam and Bulgaria
Art 47 186
Art 48(2) 187
Art 54(c) 186
Agreement between Vietnam and Cambodia
Art 20 186
Art 21 186
Agreement between Vietnam and Cuba
Art 46 186
Art 47 186
Agreement between Vietnam and Czechoslovakia
Art 47(1)(b) 186
Agreement between Vietnam and France
Art 21(1) 186
Art 21(5) 186
Agreement between Vietnam and Hungary
Art 51(2) 186
Art 55(2) 186

Agreement between Vietnam and Kazakhstan
Art 24(1) ... 186
Art 25(i) ... 186
Art 27(1) ... 186
Agreement between Vietnam and Mongolia
Art 43 ... 186
Agreement between Vietnam and North Korea
Art 30(1)(2) ... 186
Agreement between Vietnam and Laos
Art 44(1) ... 186
Art 45(2) ... 186
Agreement between Vietnam and Poland
Art 45(a) ... 186
Agreement between Vietnam and the Russian Federation
Art 35 ... 194
Art 52(2) ... 186
Art 53(2) ... 194
Agreement between Vietnam and Ukraine
Art 42(1) ... 187
Agreement between Vietnam Economic and Cultural Office in Taipei and Taipei Economic and Cultural Office in Vietnam ... 87, 185
Art 19 ... 186
Agreement between Vietnam and Belarus
Art 57(2) ... 186
Agreement between Vietnam and China (the China–Vietnam Treaty)
Art 17(1) ... 194
Art 18 ... 39
Art 18(1) ... 194
Art 18(2) ... 194
Agreement on Judicial Cooperation between the Republic of Indonesia and the Kingdom of Thailand (1978) ... 256
Agreement on Mutual Judicial Assistance in Civil Matters between the Kingdom of Cambodia and the Socialist Republic of Vietnam (2013) (the Cambodia–Vietnam Treaty) ... 201, 207
Art 21 ... 206
Art 22 ... 203–04
Art 23 ... 203
Art 24 ... 204
Arrangement on Reciprocal Recognition and Enforcement of Civil Judgments in Matrimonial and Family Cases by the Courts of the Mainland and of the Hong Kong Special Administrative Region (20 June 2017) ... 79
Arrangement on Reciprocal Recognition and Enforcement of Judgments in Civil and Commercial Matters by the Courts of the Mainland and of the Hong Kong Special Administrative Region (18 January 2019) ... 79, 81
Art 1 ... 82
Art 2 ... 82

Art 3 ... 82
Art 4 ... 82
Art 5 ... 82
Art 11 ... 82
Art 12 ... 82
Art 13 ... 82
Art 15 ... 82
Art 17 ... 83
Art 18 ... 83
Art 24 ... 83
Arrangement on Reciprocal Recognition and Enforcement of Judgments in Civil and Commercial Matters by the Courts of the Mainland and of the Hong Kong Special Administrative Region Pursuant to Choice of Court Agreements between Parties Concerned (2006, 2008) ... 79
Bilateral Agreement between Vietnam and the United States of America (2000)
Chapter II ... 193
Consular Convention between Japan and the United Kingdom ... 109
Convention for the Extension of Hong Kong Territory (1898) ... 52
Convention of Peking (1860) ... 52
Treaty between the Republic of Azerbaijan and the Republic of India on Legal and Judicial Cooperation in Civil and Commercial Matters (2013)
Art 14 ... 296
Art 17 ... 296
Treaty of Nanking (1842) ... 52
Treaty on Judicial Assistance in Civil and Commercial Matters between Australia and the Republic of Korea (1999) ... 127

Primary Legislation, Secondary Legislation and Other Materials

Australia

Foreign Judgments Act 1991 ... 93, 127
Foreign Judgments Regulations (Statutory Rules No 321 of 1992) ... 127
Statutory Rules No 334 of 1999 ... 127

California

Business and Professions Code ... 90
Code of Civil Procedure ... 122, 224
Civil Execution Act (former)
Arts 1132–34 ... 122

Cambodia

Civil Code (2007)
Art 1 ... 202
Art 354 ... 202

Civil Procedure Code (2006) 202
Art 199 204–07
Art 199(c) 204–05, 207
Art 199(d) 204, 206
Art 352(2) 205
Art 352(3) 204–06
Art 352(4) 204
Book 6
Chapter 2 206
Chapter 3 206
Chapter 4 206
Constitution of the Kingdom of Cambodia
Art 44 203
Paris Peace Accords (Agreements on a Comprehensive Political Settlement of the Cambodia Conflict) 202
Royal Kram No NS/RKM/0714/018 on the Promulgation of the Law approving the Agreement on Mutual Judicial Assistance in Civil Matters between the Kingdom of Cambodia and the Socialist Republic of Vietnam (17 July 2014) 203
Sub-decree on Recognition of Private Ownership of Cambodian Citizens No 25 (22 April 1989) 201

China

1991 Civil Procedure Law
Art 268 43
1992 Maritime Law 34
1995 Negotiable Instruments Law 34
1995 Civil Aviation Law 34
2008 Chinese Anti-Monopoly Law 37
2012 Civil Procedure Law (CPL)
Art 3 37
Art 5 42
Arts 19–21 312
Art 25 312
Art 33 39
Art 34 312
Art 280 35
Art 281 .... 35–36, 40
Art 282 .... 35–36, 40, 42
2012 Supreme People's Court (SPC) Interpretation of the 2010 Law
Art 1 36–37
Art 10 35
2015 SPC Interpretation of the 2012 CPL (The Interpretation of the Supreme People's Court on the Application of the Civil Procedure Law of the People's Republic of China) (2015 Interpretation)
Art 306 40

Art 533 ... 36
Art 544 ... 42
Act on Application of Foreign Law ... 33
General Principles of Civil Law (GPCL) ... 33–34
Law on the Application of Laws over Foreign-related Civil Relation (2010 Law) ... 34–35
Tang Code ... 33

England and Wales

Administration of Justice Act 1920 ... 164
Civil Jurisdiction and Judgments Act 1982
s 35 ... 53
Foreign Limitation Periods Act 1984 ... 53
Judgment Extension Act 1868 ... 164
Judgments Act 1838 ... 303
State Immunity Act 1978 ... 67
Subordinate Courts Act 1948 ... 165
Statute of George III (1800) ... 164

Hong Kong

Application of English Law Ordinance (Cap 88) ... 52
Arbitration Ordinance (Cap 609)
Part 11A ... 76
Bankruptcy Ordinance (Cap 6)
s 6 ... 74
s 6A ... 74
Basic Law ... 53, 79
Art 8 ... 52
Bunker Oil Pollution (Liability and Compensation) Ordinance (Cap 605) ... 64
s 21 ... 77
Companies (Winding Up and Miscellaneous Provisions) Ordinance (Cap 32)
s 178(3) ... 74
Foreign Judgments (Reciprocal Enforcement) Ordinance (Cap 319) ... 54, 59, 64, 78, 312
long title ... 80
s 2(2) ... 62
s 3 ... 80–81
s 3(2) ... 62
s 3(3) ... 62
s 4(1) ... 62
s 4(2) ... 62
s 5 ... 287
s 6 ... 63
s 6(1)(a)(iii) ... 63
s 6(2) ... 61, 66
s 6(2)(a)(i) ... 61
s 6(2)(a)(ii) ... 61

s 6(2)(a)(iii) 61
s 6(2)(a)(iv) 61
s 6(2)(a)(v) 61
s 6(2)(b) 61
s 6(2)(c) 61
s 6(3) 61
s 11 80
Foreign Judgments (Reciprocal Enforcement) Order (Cap 319A) 60
s 4 62
Sch 1 .... 59, 62, 79
Sch 2 .... 59, 62, 79
Foreign Judgments (Restriction on Recognition and Enforcement) Ordinance (Cap 46) 55
s 3 63–64
s 3(3) 63
s 4 62
High Court Ordinance (Cap 4)
s 20A 72
s 21B 75
s 21C 71
s 21D(1) 71–72
s 21L 73
Mainland Judgments in Matrimonial and Family Cases (Reciprocal Recognition and Enforcement) Bill 83
Mainland Judgments (Reciprocal Enforcement) Ordinance (Cap 597) 54–55, 68, 79, 82–83
s 2 56
s 3(2) 56
s 5(2) 56
s 6(1) 57
s 6(2) 57
s 7 57
ss 9–13 57
s 10 57
s 11 57
s 12 57
s 14 57
s 16 57
s 17 58
s 18(1) 58
s 19 58
s 20 58
Sch 1 56
Merchant Shipping (Liability and Compensation for Oil Pollution) Ordinance (Cap 414)
long title 78
s 18 78
s 18(2) 64

s 27 ... 78
s 27(3) ... 64
Merchant Shipping (Liner Conferences) Ordinance (Cap 482) ... 78
Sch 1, pt 1, cl I ... 64
Nuclear Material (Liability for Carriage) Ordinance (Cap 479)
s 10(4) ... 64
s 10(5) ... 78
s 10(6) ... 78
Practice Direction SL1.1 (High Court) ... 54
Rules of the High Court (Cap 4A) (RHC)
Ord 11
rr 1(1)(a)–(p) ... 22
r 1(1)(d) ... 21
Ord 14 ... 28
Ord 44A ... 75
Ord 45 ... 75
Ord 48 ... 74
Ord 49 ... 72
Ord 49B ... 74
Ord 50 ... 75
Ord 51 ... 73
Ord 71
r 41 ... 65
r 42 ... 65
Supreme Court Ordinance (Cap 4) (former)
s 5 ... 52

India

Act of Settlement 1781 ... 293
Charter of 1774 ... 293
Code of Civil Procedure (CPC) ... 322
s 2 ... 295
s 2(2) ... 294
s 2(9) ... 294
s 13 ... 294, 300, 303–05, 308
s 13(a) ... 299
s 13(b) ... 299
s 13(c) ... 299
s 13(d) ... 299–300, 307
s 13(e) ... 300
s 29(c) ... 297
s 44A ... 294–95, 297–98, 303–05, 307
s 44A, *explanation I* ... 295, 298
s 44A, *explanation II* ... 295
Ord 38
r 5 ... 304

Commercial Courts Act 2015 307
Competition Act 2002
s 53N 305
Indian Contract Act 1872
s 28 301
Ministry of Law Amended Notification No GSR 201 (13 March 1958) 296
Ministry of Law Justice and Company Affairs Notification No F12(1)/98-Judl (23 November 2000) 297
Ministry of Law Notification No SRO 183 (18 January 1956) 296
Ministry of Law Notification No SRO 399 (1 March 1953) 296
Ministry of Law Notification No SRO 1959 (2 March 1954) 296
Ministry of Law Notification No SRO 3282 (15 October 1957) 296
Ministry of Law Notification No F12(3)/68J (31 July 1968) 296
Ministry of Law Notification No F12(4)/68J (17 June 1968) 296
Ministry of Law Notification No GSR 1720 (26 September 1970) 296
Ministry of Law Notification No GSR 2096 (18 November 1968) 296
Ministry of Law Notification No SRO 4 (3 January 1956) 296
Regulating Act 1773 293
Regulation of 1793 293

Indonesia

Act No 1 of 1974 on Marriage (Marriage Act) 247, 249–50
Act No 1 of 2004 concerning State Treasury
Art 50 256
Act No 4 of 1996 on Mortgage (Mortgage Act) 250
Act No 5 of 1960 concerning Basic Regulations on Agrarian Principles (Basic Agrarian Act) 247–48, 250
Act No 7 of 1989, as amended by Act No 3 of 2006 and as amended by Act No 50 of 2009, on Religious Court (Religious Court Act) 249
Act No 8 of 1999 concerning Consumer Protection 250
Act No 11 of 2006 on the Governing of Aceh 245
Act No 12 of 2006 (Citizenship Act) 247
Act No 13 of 2003 concerning Manpower (Labour Act) 250
Act No 23 of 2006, as amended by the Act No 24 of 2013, on Population Administration 249
Act No 24 of 2000 on Treaties 248, 254
Act No 25 of 2007 on Capital Investment (Investment Act) 247
Act No 30 of 1999 on Arbitration and Alternative Dispute Resolution (Arbitration Act)
Art 66(b), *elucidation* 250
Art 69 255
Bill on Indonesian private international law (2014) 247, 252
Civil Code (*Burgerlijk Wetboek voor Nederlandsch-Indie*) (1846) (BW)
Art 439 245
Art 1868 244
Art 1870 244
Art 1902 244

Code of Civil Procedure (*Reglement op de Rechtvordering*)
Arts 54–57 251
Code of Indonesian Private International Law 246
Code of Procedure for Areas Outside Java and Madura) (*Rechtsreglement Buitengewesten*)
Art 191(1) 251
Commercial Code (*Wetboek van Koophandel voor Nederlandsch-Indie*) (1847)
Art 724 243
Art 724(5) 243
Constitution
Art 11 254
Art 26 247
Dutch Colonial Constitution (*Indische Staatsregeling*) (IS) (1926)
Art 131 246
Art 163 246
General Provisions of Legislation for the Dutch East Indies (*Algemene Bepalingen van Wetgeving voor Nederlandsch Indie*) (AB) (1847)
Art 3 246
Art 4 246
Art 11 246
Art 12 246
Art 15 246
Art 16 246–49
Art 17 246–49
Art 18(1) 246–49
Government Regulation No 54 of 2007 249
Joint Decree between the Chief Justice of the Supreme Court and the Minister of Religious Affairs No 07/KMA/1985 and No 25 of 1985 245
President Instruction No 1 of 1991 on the Dissemination of the Compilation of Islamic Law 245
Presidential Decree No 34 of 1981 .... 249, 254
Qanun Aceh No 8 of 2014 on Basic Islamic Sharia 245
Reglement op de Burgerlijke Rechtsvordering (Rv)
Art 431 .... 251, 255
Art 436 .... 243–45, 249, 251–53, 255–57, 319–20
Art 436(2) 251
Art 436(3) 251
Renewed Indonesian Code (*Het Herziene Indonesisch Reglement*)
Art 180(1) 251
Supreme Court Regulation No 1 of 1990 on Recognition and Enforcement of Foreign Arbitral Awards 249, 254
Supreme Court Regulation (*Surat Edaran Mahkamah Agung*) No 3 of 2000 and No 4 of 2001 on *Putusan Serta Merta (Uitvoerbaar bij voorraad) dan Provisionil* [Judgment with Immediate Execution and Provisional Judgment] 251
Transitional Provisions of Indonesian Constitution (1945)
Art II 243, 245, 247, 248

Japan

Act on Civil Jurisdiction of Japan with respect to a Foreign State etc (Act No 24 of 24 April 2009)....101
Act on General Rules for Application of Laws (*Ho no tekiyou ni kansuru tsuu soku hou*) (AGR).... 98–99
Act on Implementation of Convention on the Civil Aspects of International Child Abduction....100
Act on Recognition of and Assistance for Foreign Insolvency Proceedings (Act No 129 of 29 November 2000)....103
Act on Special Provisions Concerning Civil Procedure Attendant upon Implementation of the Convention on Civil Procedure and Another Convention....100
Act on the Law Applicable to the Form of Wills....100
Act on the Law Applicable to the Obligation of Support....100
Arbitration Act.... 100, 121, 250
Check Act
Arts 76–81....100
Constitution
Art 20....98
Art 41....97
Art 65....97
Art 89....98
Code of Civil Procedure (1890)....100
Code of Civil Procedure (Act No 109 of 26 June 1996, as amended) (CCP).... 100, 102
Arts 3-2–3-11....99
Art 3-3(11)....114
Art 3-5....114
Art 3-5(2).... 114–15
Art 3-5(3)....113
Art 3-9.... 106–07
Art 110(1)(iii)....108
Art 118....97, 101, 103–04, 107–08, 110–17
Art 118(i)....105
Art 118(ii).... 108–09
Art 118(iii).... 110, 115
Art 118(iv)....107
Civil Execution Act (Act No 4 of 1979, as amended) (CEA)....99–100, 104
Art 22(6).... 97, 103, 112
Art 24....97, 101, 103, 112, 117
Art 24(1).... 101, 112
Art 24(2)....113
Art 24(3)....113
Art 24(4)....113
Arts 43–167(16)....113
Arts 168–179....113
Domestic Relations Case Procedure Act....100

Horei ... 33, 98
Intellectual Property Basic Act
Art 2(2) ... 113
Negotiable Instrument Act
Arts 88–94 ... 100
Personal Status Litigation Act ... 100
Statute of Limitation ... 130

Malaysia

Civil Law Act 1956 ... 164
Courts of Judicature Act 1964
s 22 ... 165
s 23 ... 165, 170, 173
s 23(1) ... 170
s 24 ... 165
Employment Act 1955
s 83 ... 175
Employment (Procedure-Reciprocal Provisions) Regulations 1957 (revised 1983) (PU(A) 334/1983) ... 175
r 5 ... 176
r 6 ... 176
Federal Constitution
Art 121(1) ... 165
Foreign Judgments (Reciprocal Enactment) Act 1933 ... 164
Insolvency Act 1967
s 104 ... 175
Judgments (Reciprocity) Enactment 1922 (Johor) ... 164
Maintenance Orders (Facilitation for Enforcement) Act 1949 (Maintenance Act) ... 174
s 3 ... 174
s 6 ... 174
ss 6(1)–6(7) ... 174
Sch ... 174
Merchant Shipping (Liability and Compensation for Oil and Bunker Oil Pollution) Act 1994 (MSO-Oil Pollution Act)
s 24 ... 176
Second Sch ... 176
Practice Direction 6 of 2013 ... 165
Practice Direction 7 of 2013 ... 165
Probate and Administration Act 1959
Part IV ... 175
s 52 ... 175
PU(B) 2/1989 ... 175
Reciprocal Enforcement of Judgments Act 1958 (REJA) ... 163–65, 173, 315
First Sch ... 166, 170, 174, 177–78, 314
s 2 ... 166–67
s 3(2) ... 166, 168

s 3(3) 166, 169
s 3(4) 169
s 4(1) 167
s 4(1), *proviso (a)* 166
s 4(1), *proviso (b)* 167, 171
s 4(2) 167–68
s 4(3) 168
s 4(4) 168
s 4(5) 168
s 5(1)(a)(ii) 167
s 5(1)(a)(iii) 167
s 5(1)(a)(iv) 167
s 5(1)(a)(v) 167
s 5(1)(a)(vi) 167
s 5(1)(b) 167
s 5(2) 167, 170, 176
s 5(2)(a) 167
s 5(2)(a)(i) 169
s 5(2)(a)(ii) 170
s 5(2)(a)(iii) 170
s 5(2)(a)(iv) 170
s 5(2)(a)(v) 170
s 5(2)(b) 167
s 5(2)(c) 170
s 5(3) 167, 176
s 6(1) 169
s 7 172
s 8 172
s 9(1) 168
Reciprocal Enforcement of Judgments (Application of Section 9) Order 1994, PU(A) 73/1994 169
Reciprocal Enforcement of Judgments (Extension of Part II) Order 2000, PU(A) 122/2000 169
Rules of Court 2012
Ord 11 173
Ord 46
r 2(1)(a) 173
Ord 47 173
Ord 49 173
Ord 50 173
Ord 52 173
Ord 67 165
r 3(1) 167
r 3(2) 168
r 3(3) 168
r 3(4) 168

r 5(1) ... 168
r 5(2) ... 168, 172
r 5(3) ... 172
r 5(7) ... 168
r 6 ... 168
r 9(1) ... 172
r 10(2) ... 168
Ord 70
r 12(11) ... 174
Rules of the High Court 1980
Ord 65 ... 171

Myanmar

Code of Civil Procedure (Amendment) Act 1937 (India Act VIII of 1937) ... 219
Code of Civil Procedure (Amendment) Act 1956
s 1(2) ... 219
Civil Procedure Code (India Act V of 1908) (CPC) ... 210
s 2(5) ... 211
s 2(6) ... 211
s 10 ... 212
s 13 ... 211–18
s 14 ... 211–16
ss 15–24 ... 214, 216
s 15 ... 214
s 16 ... 214–16
s 16, *proviso* ... 216
s 17 ... 214
s 18 ... 214
s 19 ... 214
s 20 ... 214
s 20, *explanation II* ... 215
s 21 ... 214
s 22 ... 214
s 23 ... 214
s 24 ... 214
ss 36–74 ... 220
s 44A ... 219–21
s 47 ... 219
s 48 ... 221
s 121 ... 212
s 151 ... 215–16
First Sch (Rules of Procedure)
Ord XIII
r 10 ... 213
Ord XV ... 211–14, 218–21

Ord XXI
rr 1–103 220
Ord XL
rr 1–5....... 221
Constitution (1947)
Art 2 209
Art 5 209
Art 6 209
Art 7 209
Arts 133–53....... 209
Art 141 209
Chapter VIII....... 209
Constitution (1974)....... 209
Constitution (2011)
Arts 293–336....... 210
Chapter VI....... 210
Limitation Act (India Act IX of 1908)
First Sch 221
para 117....... 221
para 183....... 221
SLORC Declaration 6/88 (24 September 1988)....... 210
State Revolutionary Council Declaration 14/62 (7 March 1962)....... 210

Netherlands

Dutch Code of Civil Procedure
Art 431 .... 251, 253, 320

Philippines

An Act to Ordain and Institute the Civil Code of the Philippines, Republic Act No 386 (1950) (Civil Code)
Art 15 224
Art 16 224
Art 17 224
Art 17(3) 235–36
Code of Civil Procedure (1914)....... 224, 226–27
Codigo Civil (Spain)....... 224
Art 11(a) 236
Art 171 236
Competition Act (Republic Act No 10667) (21 July 2015) (Competition Law)
s 3....... 240
s 4(k)(2) 240
Constitution of the Republic of the Philippines (1987)
Art VIII, s 5(5)....... 226
Intellectual Property Code of the Philippines (IP Law) (1997)....... 240, 282, 307
s 3....... 239

Judiciary Reorganization Act of 1980 (Batas Pambansa Blg 129)
s 19 ... 229
Revised Rules on Evidence, as Amended per Supreme Court Resolution Adopted on 14 March 1989 (1989) (Rules of Evidence)
r 131 ... 230
s 3 ... 231
r 132
ss 24–25 ... 231
s 24 ... 225, 230
Rules of Civil Procedure (Rules of Court) (1997)
r 4, ss 1–2 ... 228
r 39, s 48 ... 226

Singapore

Choice of Court Agreements Act (Act 14 of 2016) (CCAA) ... 143–44, 148
s 2 ... 145
s 2(1) ... 145
s 2(2) ... 151
s 9 ... 142
s 9(1)(a) ... 142
s 9(1)(b) ... 142
s 9(2)(d) ... 142
s 10 ... 145
s 10(2) ... 146
s 13 ... 145
s 13(1) ... 145
s 13(2) ... 145
s 14(a) ... 145
s 14(b) ... 145
s 14(c) ... 145
s 15(1) ... 146
s 15(1)(a) ... 146
s 16 ... 146
s 19 ... 145
Reciprocal Enforcement of Commonwealth Judgments Act (Cap 264, 1985 rev ed) (RECJA) ... 145, 147, 152, 159, 161
s 2(1) ... 144, 153
s 2A ... 142, 146
s 3(1) ... 144, 158
s 3(2) ... 144
s 3(2)(b) ... 151
s 3(2)(c) ... 151, 157
s 3(2)(d) ... 155
s 3(2)(e) ... 150

s 3(2)(f) 154, 156–58
s 3(3) 143
s 3(3)(a) 153
s 3(5) 143
s 4(1)(a) 144
Reciprocal Enforcement of Foreign Judgments Act (Cap 265, 2001 rev ed)
(REFJA) 145, 147–48, 161
s 2(1) 144, 153
s 2A 142, 146
s 3(2) 144
s 3(2)(b) 153–54
s 4(3)(a) 158
s 4(4) 143
s 4(4)(a) 153
s 4(4)(c) 153
s 4(7) 153
s 5(1)(a)(iii) 157
s 5(1)(a)(iv) 155
s 5(1)(a)(v) 156
s 5(1)(b) 157
s 5(2)(a)(i) 152, 158
s 5(2)(a)(ii) 158
s 5(2)(a)(iii) 151, 158
s 5(2)(a)(iv) 151
s 5(2)(a)(v) 151
s 5(2)(b) 159
s 5(3)(b) 158
s 6(1) 150
s 7(1) 142–43
Supreme Court of Judicature Act (Cap 322, 2007 rev ed)
s 18D(1)(a) 321
s 18F 151
Supreme Court of Judicature Act (Cap 322, s 80, 2014 rev ed) Rules of Court
Ord 14 313
Ord 47 149
Ord 48 149
Ord 49 149
Ord 51 149
Ord 67 144
Ord 110
r 1(2)(a) 321
r 1(2)(b) 321
r 7 310
r 7(1)(a) 321
r 8(2) 321

Sri Lanka

Civil Aspects of International Child Abduction Act (No 10 of 2001) 285
s 3 286
s 9 286
s 15(2) 286
Civil Procedure Code of 1889 (No 2 of 1889) (as amended) (CPC) 280
s 5 277
s 9 277
s 187 281
s 188 281
s 189 279
s 225 281
s 226 281
s 227 281
s 228 281
s 229 281
s 233 281
s 237 281
s 240 281
s 754(1) 279
Code of Intellectual Property Act (No 52 of 1979) 275, 282
Companies Act (No 17 of 1982)
s 31 275
s 51 275
s 131 275
s 210 275
s 211 275
Companies Act (No 7 of 2007) 275, 282
Constitution of the Democratic Socialist Republic of Sri Lanka (Constitution of Sri Lanka)
Art 14A 273
Art 27(14) 283
Art 27(15) 283
Art 28(f) 283
Art 29 283
Art 33(h) 283
Art 41A(1) 273
Art 41B 273
Sch 272
Art 41C 273
Sch 272
Art 140 283
Art 154P 274
Art 154P(4)(b) 283

Art 157 .... 284, 286
13th Amendment (1987) 274
19th Amendment (2015) 272–73
Debt Recovery (Special Provisions) Act (No 2 of 1990) 274
Enforcement of Foreign Judgments Ordinance (No 4 of 1937) (Enforcement of Foreign Judgments Ordinance) 271, 273, 277
s 2 275
s 4 287
Gazette No 2112/33 (28 February 2019) 274
High Court of the Provinces (Special Provisions) Act (No 10 of 1996) 274
s 2 282
High Court of the Provinces (Special Provisions) Act (No 19 of 1990) 274
High Court of the Provinces (Special Provisions) Act (No 54 of 2006)
s 5A 274
s 5C 274
Intellectual Property Act (No 36 of 2003) (IP Act) 282
Judicature Act (No 2 of 1978) (Judicature Act)
s 9 274
s 19 274
s 30 273
Mutual Assistance in Civil and Commercial Matters Act (No 39 of 2000)
preamble 285
s 2 285
s 16 285
National Environmental Act (No 47 of 1980) (as amended)
Part IV 282
Reciprocal Enforcement of Judgments Ordinance (No 41 of 1921) 271, 273, 320
s 3 276
s 3(1) 276
s 3(2) 276
s 3(2)(b) 276
s 5 287
s 6 275
Right to Information Act (No 12 of 2016) 273

South Korea

Act on Special Cases Concerning Remote Video Trials
Art 3 140
Act on the Protection, etc. of Fixed-term and Part-time Workers Amendment (2014)
Art 13(2) 129
Act on the Use, etc. of Electronic Documents in Civil Litigation, etc.
Art 6(1) 139
Art 8 139

Arbitration Act
Art 39 (pre-amended) ... 121
Civil Code (1958) ... 120
Civil Execution Act (CEA)
Art 26 ... 119, 121–22
Art 26(1) ... 121
Art 26(2) ... 133
Art 27 ... 119, 121–22
Art 27(1) ... 123, 128
Art 27(2) ... 133
Art 28(1) ... 133
Art 39(1) ... 133–34
Art 49 ... 134
Art 61(1) ... 134
Art 70 ... 134
Art 74 ... 134
Arts 78–171 ... 134
Arts 188–222 ... 134
Arts 223–51 ... 134
Civil Procedure Act (CPA) ... 137–39
Arts 2–40 ... 123
Art 2 ... 123–24
Art 3 ... 123
Art 5(1) ... 123
Art 5(2) ... 124
Art 11 ... 133
Art 12 ... 124
Art 18 ... 136
Art 20 ... 135
Art 30 ... 125
Art 31 ... 134
Art 217 ... 119, 121–22, 132
Art 217(1) ... 122, 132–33
Art 217(1)-1 ... 123
Art 217(1)-2 ... 131
Art 217(1)-3 ... 128–29
Art 217(1)-4 ... 126
Art 217(2) ... 122, 132
Art 217 *bis* ... 119, 122
Art 217 *bis* (1) ... 129, 132
Art 264(1) ... 132
Art 451(1) ... 128
Art 451(1)(6) ... 128

Art 451(1)(7) ... 128
Art 451(2) ... 128
Civil Procedure Code (1960) ... 120
Commercial Code (1962) ... 120
Company Reorganisation Act (former) ... 130
Conflict of Laws Act (1962) ... 120
Constitution ... 119–20
Criminal Code (1953) ... 120
Criminal Procedure Code (1954) ... 120
Fair Transactions in Subcontracting Act Amendment (2011)
Art 35 ... 129
Monopoly Regulation and Fair Trade Act (FTA) ... 136
Art 2 (pre-amended) ... 137
Art 2–2 ... 137
Art 56(1) ... 137
Art 57 ... 137
Private International Law Act (PILA) (2001) ... 137
Art 2 ... 124
Art 2(1) ... 123
Art 10 ... 129
Art 32(4) ... 129
Chapter I ... 120
Chapter II ... 120
Chapter III ... 120
Chapter IV ... 120
Chapter V ... 120
Chapter VI ... 120
Chapter VII ... 120
Chapter VIII ... 120
Chapter IX ... 120
Private International Law Act Amendment Proposal (2018) ... 119
Art 2(1) ... 123
Art 3 ... 120
Art 3(1) ... 123
Art 3(3) ... 123
Art 4 ... 120
Art 4(1) ... 124
Art 4(2) ... 124
Art 5 ... 120
Art 6 ... 120
Art 7 ... 120
Art 8 ... 120, 124, 314
Art 8(1) ... 125
Art 8(2) ... 124
Art 8(3) ... 124

Art 8(4) ... 124
Art 8(5) ... 125
Art 9 ... 120, 125
Art 10 ... 120
Art 10(1) ... 125
Art 10(1)-3 ... 135
Art 10(1)-4 ... 135
Art 10(2) ... 125
Art 11 ... 120
Art 12 ... 120
Art 14 ... 120
Art 15 ... 120
Arts 24–25 ... 120
Art 33 ... 120
Arts 39–40 ... 120
Art 39 ... 135
Art 40 ... 135
Art 40(1) ... 135
Art 42 ... 120
Art 45 ... 120
Arts 57–63 ... 120
Art 77 ... 120
Art 80 ... 120
Arts 90–94 ... 120
Chapter I ... 120
Chapters II–X ... 120
Chapter II ... 120
Chapter IV ... 120
Chapter V ... 120
Chapter VI ... 120
Chapter VII ... 120
Chapter VIII ... 120
Chapter IX ... 120
Chapter X ... 120
Rules on the Use, etc. of Electronic Documents in Civil Litigation, etc.
r 4 ... 139
r 10 ... 139
r 30(1) ... 139
r 30(2) ... 139
Uniform Foreign Money-Judgments Recognition Act (UFMJRA) ... 126

Taiwan

Act Governing Relations between the People of Taiwan and Mainland China
Art 74 ... 91

Act Governing the Choice of Law in Civil Matters Involving Foreign Elements ... 87–88, 93
Arbitration Law
Art 37(1) ... 91
Art 47(2) ... 91
Chapter 7 ... 91
Civil Code
Art 72 ... 89
Art 930 ... 89
Code of Civil Procedure
Art 1 ... 88
Art 2 ... 88
Art 12 ... 94
Art 15 ... 88, 94
Art 15(1) ... 88
Art 21 ... 88
Art 24 ... 313
Art 402 ... 85–87, 89, 92–94
Art 402(1) ... 91, 94
Art 402(2) ... 87, 89, 91, 93
Art 402(3) ... 86, 89–90
Art 402(4) ... 87, 91
Code of Civil Procedure (Korea)
Art 217 ... 121
Compulsory Enforcement Act
Art 4(1) ... 86, 92
Art 4(1)(1) ... 87
Family Act
Art 52(1) ... 93
Law in Supporting Foreign Courts on Consigned Cases ... 88–89

Thailand

Civil Liability for Oil Pollution Damage Act BE 2560 (2017)
s 36 ... 261
Civil Procedure Act RE 127 (BE 2451, 1908)
s 50 ... 262
Civil Procedure Code ... 259–60, 264, 267
Conflict of Laws Act BE 2481 (1938) (1938 Act) ... 259–60, 265
s 3 ... 264
s 5 ... 261
Requirement of Contributions to the International Fund for Compensation to the International Fund for Compensation for Oil Pollution Damage Caused by Ships Act BE 2560 (2017)
s 34 ... 261

United States

Alien Torts Claims Act 305
Trading with the Enemy Act 233, 235

Vietnam

Circular No 11/TATC (12 July 1974)
  Part IV 181
Civil Code (1995) 181
Civil Code (2005) 181
Civil Code (2015) 181
  Art 1 183
  Art 3(4) 195
  Art 664 182
  Art 666 182
  Art 679 193
  Part 5 182
Civil Procedure Code (2004) 181
Civil Procedure Code (2015) (CPC) 179, 181, 200
  Art 2(3) 182
  Art 27(5) 183
  Art 29(9) 183
  Art 30(2) 193
  Art 31(4) 183
  Art 33(3) 183
  Art 37(1)(b) 183
  Art 39(2)(d) 183
  Art 423 183
  Art 423(1)(a) 183
  Art 423(1)(b) 190
  Art 425 197
  Art 432–43 198
  Art 432 199
  Art 432(1) 187
  Art 434 187
  Art 436 188
  Art 437 189
  Art 439 .... 189–90, 198
  Art 439(4) 193–94
  Art 440 .... 189–90, 316
  Art 440(1) 194, 316
  Art 440(2) 193–94, 316
  Art 440(2)(a)–(c) 316
  Art 442 189
  Art 443 189

Art 444–46 ... 198
Art 447–50 ... 198
Art 469 ... 190, 316
Art 469(1)(dd) ... 193–94
Art 470 ... 186, 190, 316
Art 470(1) ... 316
Art 470(1)(a) ... 194
Art 470(1)(c) ... 317
Art 470(2) ... 316
Art 472 ... 196
Art 481 ... 199
Chapter XXXIV ... 183
Chapter XXXV ... 188, 198
Chapter XXXVI ... 188
Part 8 ... 182
Commerical Law (2005)
Art 3 ... 183
Decree No 116/2005/ND-CP
Chapter III ... 195
Hoang Viet laws and regulations (Gia Long Code) (1815)
Art 195 ... 181
Joint Circular No 04/TTLN (24 July 1993) ... 181
Labour Code (2012) ... 182
Art 3 ... 183
Law on Competition (2004)
Art 58 ... 195
Chapter 5 ... 195
Law on Enforcement of Civil Judgments (2008) ... 179, 188
Law on Environmental Protection (2014)
Art 161(4) ... 194
Law on Investment (2014)
Art 14 ... 196
Law on Marriage and Family (2014) ... 182
Art 3 ... 183
Law on Organisation of People's Courts (2014) ... 182
Law on Treaties (2016)
Art 6(1) ... 184
Maritime Code (2015)
Art 5(2) ... 182
Ordinance on Recognition and Enforcement of Civil Judgments and Decisions of Foreign Courts (1993) ... 181
Resolution No 01/2014/NQ-HDTP of the Council of Judges of the Supreme People's Court Guiding the Implementation of Certain Provisions of the 2010 Law on Commercial Arbitration (Resolution No 01)
Art 14(2)(dd) ... 191

Washington

Revised Code of Washington
s 4.28.180 131
Superior Court Civil Rules
r 4 131

1

Introduction: Towards a System for the Recognition and Enforcement of Judgments

ANSELMO REYES

I. Purpose

Judges, lawyers and legal academics, let alone judges and lawyers in Asia, are not generally familiar with the law and procedures involved in the recognition and enforcement of foreign judgments. That may be for a variety of reasons, including that the subject does not usually form part of the standard law school curriculum. While some may vaguely know how domestic judgments are enforced, most are uncertain what happens when it comes to enforcing a foreign judgment in their country. The question typically arises when a defendant fails to pay a money judgment rendered in a foreign jurisdiction and the plaintiff comes before the court in the defendant's home country with a view to enforcing the judgment against the defendant's assets there. It may be that, in a majority of cases, commercial parties honour judgments against them, if only to maintain a good business relationship. But, in the small percentage of cases where commercial judgments are not met, it becomes important for plaintiffs to know how to convert judicial determinations in their favour into hard cash. The principal purpose of this book is to plug the knowledge gap by sketching out the law for recognition and enforcement of general civil and commercial judgments in a number of Asian jurisdictions and to examine the rationale underlying that law in general terms.

This book accordingly will describe in the next 15 chapters the extent to which, and the processes by which, an equivalent number of Asian jurisdictions recognise and enforce foreign judgments in general civil and commercial matters. The Asian jurisdictions are China, Hong Kong, Taiwan, Japan, South Korea, Singapore, Malaysia, Vietnam, Cambodia, Myanmar, Philippines, Indonesia, Thailand, Sri Lanka and India. Information on the systems of recognition and enforcement in each jurisdiction has been provided in the chapter corresponding to that place or country. Readers may consult a relevant chapter for practical guidance in relation to a country or place. But the chapters do not stop at communicating information. They are more ambitious. The specialist authors of each chapter were further invited to assess the system in his or her assigned jurisdiction and suggest how that regime might be improved for the future. Each chapter is therefore also an attempt at persuasion. The chapters invite governments, legislators, judges, lawyers, academics, and other stakeholders in the 15 jurisdictions to consider reforms to their laws and procedures for the recognition and enforcement of foreign judgments.

The purpose of this Introduction and the Conclusion at the end of this book is to provide background and context, especially for non-specialist readers with little or no prior knowledge of the law relating to recognition and enforcement of foreign judgments. The Introduction and Conclusion are respectively intended to foreshadow and pull together key themes that run throughout the 15 jurisdiction chapters. This Introduction will attempt to answer the question: If a state[1] was to put together a rudimentary but workable system for the recognition and enforcement of judgments, what might that system (and the underlying reasons for it) be? The Conclusion will consider whether, in practical terms, the rudimentary system posited in this Introduction is or is not already in place among the 15 jurisdictions considered. If the basic system is not already in place, the Conclusion will suggest what needs to be done to implement the rudimentary system across the board in all jurisdictions. Between them, the Introduction and Conclusion are supposed to (1) provide a general framework for the recognition and enforcement of foreign judgments; (2) offer a simple yardstick (namely, the rudimentary system) against which individual regimes for recognition and enforcement may be evaluated; and (3) support proposals for reform put forward in each jurisdiction chapter.

The book looks forward to a time, one hopes sooner rather than later, when judgments in general civil or commercial disputes will be portable, in the sense of being readily recognised and enforced, across borders in Asia. Currently, as will be seen from the 15 jurisdiction chapters, a region so envisaged remains a work in progress, with some Asian countries having already developed sophisticated and efficient regimes for recognition and enforcement, but others not just yet. It is hoped that this book will contribute towards the realisation of the aspiration.

II. Preliminary Matters

This chapter has so far been referring compendiously to the 'recognition and enforcement' of judgments. It might be asked whether there is any need to do that. Why not just use 'recognition' or 'enforcement', but not both? The reason is that, although related, 'recognition' and 'enforcement' are not the same. They are not synonyms. A court may 'recognise' a judgment (for instance, in order to determine whether a party is estopped by *res judicata* from re-litigating a matter or issue that has been decided by a court elsewhere), even though no one is seeking to 'enforce' that judgment against assets within the court's jurisdiction. Some judgments (for instance, a decision dismissing a claim) may by their nature be capable of recognition, but not enforcement. In some countries, 'recognition' may be automatic. Provided that a judgment meets certain criteria, it will be entitled to recognition in an

[1] The word 'state' is used here in the private international law sense. Under private international law, the Hong Kong Special Administrative Region of the People's Republic of China is treated as a 'state', although it is part of a country (namely, China). Mainland China would be another 'state' for the purposes of private international law. Similarly, from a private international law perspective, although a single country, the US is treated as comprising 50 'states' and one federal 'state'.

enforcing state without need to undergo any process. In contrast, before a foreign judgment can be enforced against a defendant's assets within an enforcing state, it will normally have to be 'recognised' by the enforcing state through some formal process. That will typically entail the foreign judgment being in essence converted into a judgment or decree of the enforcing state, by undergoing a process of registration in the enforcing state or through the enforcing state issuing its own judgment expressly recognising the foreign decision for the purposes of enforcement.

Before considering the question to be tackled in this Introduction, it is useful to make explicit a limitation and an assumption underpinning this book. It will also be convenient to say something about the Hague Conference on Private international Law and its work as that will be integral not just to this Introduction and the Conclusion, but to the entirety of this book.

A. Limitation to General Civil and Commercial Matters

The limitation to the present exercise is that the discussion here will concentrate on the recognition and enforcement of judgments in general civil and commercial matters. That is because when it comes to judgments relating to other civil matters (such as the status of a person, family issues, marriage, divorce, the well-being of a child, succession, inheritance, consumer transactions and employment) numerous factors come into play, so that a state may have legitimate reasons for refusing to recognise or enforce such types of civil judgments. Since there are a plethora of social, cultural, religious and other considerations that states may take into account when considering whether to recognise or enforce civil judgments dealing with status, family, employment, consumer issues and like matters of a non-commercial nature, it would be impractical to put forward a meaningful one-size fits all regime for the recognition and enforcement of judgments in those matters. In contrast, in the case of judgments resolving disputes arising out of general civil and commercial matters, especially commercial contracts freely negotiated at arm's length between two businesses (often situated in different countries), the range of factors to be taken into account when considering whether to recognise or enforce is typically more limited. The relevant principles are therefore more readily enumerated and analysed.

This begs the question of what is meant by a 'commercial matter'. The contributors to the jurisdiction chapters were asked to discuss whether their law had a specific understanding of 'commercial matters', distinguishing that expression from 'non-commercial civil matters'. It will be seen, however, that many of the jurisdictions do not distinguish in their statutes or jurisprudence between 'commercial' and other civil matters.[2] Accordingly, for convenience, this exposition will simply adopt the non-exhaustive definition of 'commercial' in footnote 2 to Article 1(1) of the UNCITRAL Model Law on International Commercial Arbitration:

> Relationships of a commercial nature include, but are not limited to, the following transactions: any trade transaction for the supply or exchange of goods or services; distribution agreement;

[2] Given the lack of a formal distinction between judgments in 'commercial' and other civil matters, chapter contributors have referred to judgments in a variety of civil matters as illustrations of how a court in their assigned jurisdiction is likely to handle foreign judgments in commercial matters.

commercial representation or agency; factoring; leasing; construction of works; consulting; engineering; licensing; investment; financing; banking; insurance; exploitation agreement or concession; joint venture and other forms of industrial or business cooperation; carriage of goods or passengers by air, sea, rail or road.

The definition is wide. It is hoped that the jurisdictions considered here will, whether formally or informally, at least classify most (if not all) contracts falling within the scope of the definition as being 'commercial' in nature when considering whether to recognise or enforce judgments.

B. Assumption that Increased Recognition and Enforcement are Economically Beneficial

The assumption underlying the exercise here is that it would be beneficial for a state to recognise and enforce foreign judgments in general civil and commercial matters. The basic argument may be readily summarised: An investor A from State X will be reluctant to enter into a cross-border commercial relationship (if at all) with a national B of State Y, if it will be difficult or impossible to enforce a judgment in A's favour from (say) the court of a neutral third-party state against B's assets in State Y. On the other hand, if it is relatively straightforward to enforce foreign judgments against assets in State Y, more investors from State X and other states will be willing to invest in State Y, thereby boosting foreign direct investment (FDI) within State Y and leading to a rise in State Y's GDP. From the viewpoint of State X whose nationals may wish to export to markets abroad (including in State Y), State X cannot expect judgments of its courts to be recognised against nationals in (say) State Y, unless State X is equally willing to recognise the judgments of the courts of State Y. To facilitate trade with State Y and elsewhere, State X should therefore be prepared to recognise judgments of the courts of State Y and elsewhere. The correctness of the basic argument is taken for granted. There is no attempt to marshall empirical evidence here in its support. Nor is there any attempt to rehearse the pros and cons of the opening up and globalisation of a state's economy that is likely to result from a state's greater recognition and enforcement of foreign commercial judgments. A rise in FDI and GDP are simply presumed to be to the overall benefit of a state's citizens.[3]

[3] The author has not in fact been able to find any empirical study establishing a correlation between FDI and liberalisation of a country's laws on the recognition and enforcement of foreign judgments. The closest that the author has found is an analysis of the likely extra cost in enforcing English judgments relating to financial contracts within the EU following a 'hard' Brexit. The study suggests that the UK's departure from the liberal regime for the recognition and enforcement of judgments among EU countries will lead to a significantly greater cost for commercial enterprises seeking to enforce English judgments in the EU. It may possibly be inferred from this that the converse will likewise be true. In other words, being part of a liberal regime for the recognition and enforcement of judgments should decrease the cost of doing business among the members of that regime and so attract investors to establish themselves within such states. See Philips Jacobs, 'Auswirkungen des Brexits auf internationale Finanzierungsverträge' Londoner Kreis Research Paper Series 2018 No 1, London Kreis, available online: www.londoner-kreis.org/deutsch/wp-content/uploads/sites/2/2018/06/20180608_LK_NO1_Studie_zu_Auswirkungen_von_Brexit_Vertragsrecht_vF.pdf.

C. The Hague Conference, its Conventions, and the Judgments Project

The Hague Conference on Private International Law first met as a series of conferences in The Hague from 1893 onwards. It became an inter-governmental body with legal personality in international law in 1955. As at 1 March 2019, it had 83 members (82 states and one Regional Economic Integration Organisation (REIO)).[4] It has two Regional Offices, one for Latin America based in Buenos Aires and the other for the Asia Pacific based in Hong Kong. The Hague Conference's objective is 'the progressive unification of the rules of private international law'.[5] It aims to achieve this by promulgating multilateral conventions (known as Hague Conventions) dealing with various aspects of the conflict of laws. Although African states remain under-represented in the Hague Conference, it currently has a sufficiently large number of members from civil and common law jurisdictions, so that its more recent instruments do not merely reflect one or other of common law or civil law practice but are a considered amalgam of both traditions. This is even more so, because since 2005 the Hague Conference has operated on the basis of consensus, as opposed to majority vote, in the adoption of conventions and other instruments. The Hague Conference has to date produced 39 Hague Conventions and one soft law instrument.[6] Of these, three conventions directly concern the recognition and enforcement of judgments in civil and commercial matters. Those three are the 1971 Hague Convention on the Recognition and Enforcement of Foreign Judgments in Civil and Commercial Matters, the Supplementary Protocol to the 1971 Hague Convention and the 2005 Hague Convention on Choice of Court Agreements.

The Hague Conference's Judgments Project started in 1992.[7] The Project's original intention had been to produce a double convention that would (1) harmonise the grounds for a state to claim direct jurisdiction in civil and commercial cases; and (2) provide for the recognition and enforcement of civil and commercial judgments. But the Project found it hard to reconcile common and civil law approaches to direct jurisdiction. Consequently, apart from the 2005 Hague Choice of Court Agreements Convention, no multilateral instrument has so far been produced by the Judgments Project. In 2012, the Judgments Project decided temporarily to set aside work on an instrument on direct jurisdiction and to focus on a convention dealing solely with the recognition and enforcement of judgments in civil and commercial matters. It is hoped that the fruits of that decision, a draft Hague Convention on the Recognition and Enforcement of Judgments in Civil and Commercial Matters, will be

[4] The REIO is the European Union (EU). Of the countries covered here, the following are members of the Hague Conference (with year of membership in brackets): Japan (1957), China (1987), South Korea (1997), Sri Lanka (2001), Malaysia (2002), India (2008), the Philippines (2010), Vietnam (2013), and Singapore (2014).

[5] Statute of the Hague Conference on Private International Law (Hague Statute), Art 1.

[6] One of the 39 Conventions is the Hague Statute. The soft law instrument is the 2015 Hague Principles on Choice of Law in International Commercial Contracts. Of the 40 instruments that the Hague Conference has produced, only about half are relevant to today's conditions, the others having been superseded or become obsolete with the passage of time.

[7] On the Judgments Project, see www.hcch.net/en/projects/legislative-projects/judgments. On the problems encountered in drafting a double convention, see Guangjian Tu, *A Study on a Global Jurisdiction and Judgments Convention* (Hong Kong, Sweet & Maxwell, 2009).

ready for adoption by the 22nd Diplomatic Session of the Hague Conference in June 2019. At the time of writing this chapter, the latest draft of the proposed convention is that prepared by the Special Commission of the Judgments Project in May 2018. That document will be referred to here as the '2018 Draft'.[8]

It is instructive to compare the texts of the 1971 and 2005 Hague Conventions and the 2018 Draft with a view to seeing, in general terms, in what ways they are similar. The next sections will summarise the key articles of those documents. The summaries, however, are limited to the purposes of this chapter and should not be taken as an exhaustive account of the provisions in the three documents.

i. The 1971 Hague Convention and the Supplementary Protocol[9]

Article 1 of the 1971 Hague Convention excludes the following matters from its scope: (1) the status or capacity of persons or questions of family law; (2) the existence or constitution of legal persons or the powers of their officers; (3) maintenance obligations; (4) succession; (5) bankruptcy, compositions or analogous proceedings; (6) social security; (7) damage or injury in nuclear matters; and (8) the payment of customs duty, tax or penalty. By Article 2 the Convention applies to decisions whether styled by a rendering court[10] as a 'judgment', 'order' or 'writ of execution'. But Article 2 further excludes provisional measures and the decisions of administrative tribunals from the Convention's ambit. Article 3 provides that the Convention will apply regardless of the nationalities of the parties to a judgment.

Article 4 sets out the basis rule: A judgment *shall* be entitled to recognition and enforcement if: (1) the relevant court had jurisdiction within the terms of the Convention to render the decision; (2) the decision is 'no longer subject to ordinary forms of review' in the originating state; and (3) the decision is enforceable in the originating state. Article 5 deals with the converse: A judgment *may* be refused recognition or enforcement if (1) that would be 'manifestly incompatible with the public policy' of the enforcing state; (2) the judgment resulted from a lack of due process; (3) a party had 'no adequate opportunity fairly to present [one's] case'; (4) the decision was obtained by procedural (that is, extrinsic) fraud; or (5) proceedings between the same parties on the same facts and for the same purpose either (a) are pending in the enforcing state having been commenced therefore before the relevant proceedings in the originating state, (b) have resulted in a decision by a court of the enforcing state or (c) have resulted in a decision by a court of some other state which would be entitled to recognition and enforcement under the law of the enforcing state.

[8] It is by no means certain that the 22nd Diplomatic Session will approve the 2018 Draft, either in its present form or at all. There remains a lack of consensus over parts of the draft text (presently appearing there in brackets). Disagreements are especially apparent in relation to the recognition and enforcement of judgments concerning intellectual property. Even if the text of the 2018 Draft is not ultimately approved, that should not affect the analysis here, as any convention that is finally adopted is only likely to differ from the 2018 Draft in matters of degree or emphasis, with the substantial thrust being the same.

[9] For the text of the 1971 Hague Convention, see www.hcch.net.en/instruments/conventions/full-text?cid=78. For the text of the Supplementary Protocol, see www.hcch.net.en/instruments/conventions/full-text/?cid=79.

[10] In this book, the expressions 'rendering court' or 'originating court' will be used interchangeably to describe the court whose judgments are to be enforced in another jurisdiction (the 'enforcing state'). The state in which the rendering court is situated will be designated as the 'rendering state' or the 'originating state'. The expression 'enforcing court' will be used to describe the court of the enforcing state where the judgment of a rendering court is sought to be enforced.

Articles 6 to 8 qualify the basic principles in Articles 4 and 5. By Article 6, a default judgment (that is, one obtained in the absence of a party) shall not be recognised or enforced, unless the party in default received proper notice of the foreign proceedings, in accordance with the law of the originating state, in sufficient time to enable that party to defend one's self. By Article 7 recognition or enforcement are not to be refused solely because the originating state has applied a law other than that which would be applied under the private international law rules of the enforcing state.[11] Article 8 stresses that, '[w]ithout prejudice to such review as is required by the terms of the preceding Articles, there shall be no review of the merits of the decision rendered by the court of origin'.

Articles 9 to 12 deal with the question of when a rendering court is to be regarded as having jurisdiction to decide a case. In assessing jurisdiction, an enforcing court 'shall be bound by the findings of fact on which that court based its jurisdiction, unless the decision was rendered by default' (Article 9). Article 10 sets out the situations in which a rendering court will be treated as having jurisdiction. These situations will be referred to as grounds of 'indirect jurisdiction' or 'international jurisdiction'. They are 'indirect' in the sense that the court in the enforcing state is determining from the list of grounds in Article 10 whether the court in the originating state had jurisdiction to hear a case and deliver a decision in respect of it. This is to be distinguished from the situation where a court in some state assesses whether it has jurisdiction ('direct jurisdiction') to hear a case under the laws of that state. Under Article 10, there will be indirect jurisdiction in the following circumstances:

(1) if the defendant had, at the time when the proceedings were instituted, his habitual residence in the State of origin, or, if the defendant is not a natural person, its seat, its place of incorporation or its principal place of business in that State;
(2) if the defendant had, in the State of origin, at the time when the proceedings were instituted, a commercial, industrial or other business establishment, or a branch office, and was cited there in proceedings arising from business transacted by such establishment or branch office;
(3) if the action had as its object the determination of an issue relating to immovable property situated in the State of origin;
(4) in the case of injuries to the person or damage to tangible property, if the facts which occasioned the damage occurred in the territory of the State of origin, and if the author of the injury or damage was present in that territory at the time when those facts occurred;
(5) if, by a written agreement or by an oral agreement confirmed in writing within a reasonable time, the parties agreed to submit to the jurisdiction of the court of origin disputes which have arisen or which may arise in respect of a specific legal relationship, unless the law of the State addressed would not permit such an agreement because of the subject matter of the dispute;
(6) if the defendant has argued the merits without challenging the jurisdiction of the court or making reservations thereon; nevertheless such jurisdiction shall not be recognised if the defendant has argued the merits in order to resist the seizure of property or to obtain its release, or if the recognition of this jurisdiction would be contrary to the law of the State addressed because of the subject matter of the dispute;

[11] There is a proviso to Art 7: 'Nevertheless, recognition or enforcement may be refused if, to reach its decision, the court of the State of origin had to decide a question relating either to the status or the capacity of a party or to his rights in other matters excluded from this Convention by sub-paragraphs (1)–(4) of the second paragraph of Article 1, and has reached a result different from that which would have followed from the application to that question of the rules of private international law of the State addressed'.

(7) if the person against whom recognition or enforcement is sought was the plaintiff in the proceedings in the court of origin and was unsuccessful in those proceedings, unless the recognition of this jurisdiction would be contrary to the law of the State addressed because of the subject matter of the dispute.

Article 11 specifies when a rendering court will be treated as having had indirect jurisdiction to deal with a counterclaim. There is such indirect jurisdiction: (a) if, had the counterclaim been brought as the principal claim, the rendering court would have had indirect jurisdiction under the situations set out in (1) to (6) above or (b) if the counterclaim arises out of a contract which forms the basis of the principal claim (being a principal claim over which the rendering court has indirect jurisdiction under Article 10). Article 12 identifies exceptions to Article 10. By Article 12, a rendering court will not have jurisdiction if, under the law of the enforcing state or by agreement of the parties: (1) the courts of the enforcing state have exclusive jurisdiction over the subject matter of the action; (2) the courts of some other state have exclusive jurisdiction over the subject matter; or (3) an arbitral tribunal has exclusive jurisdiction over the subject matter.

Articles 13 to 19 deal with procedures for recognition and enforcement in an enforcing state. Of these, Article 14 is the most relevant here. That provides for the law of the enforcing state to govern procedures for recognition and enforcement. It also stipulates that if a judgment 'contains provisions which can be dissociated', then 'any one or more of these may be separately recognised or enforced'. Thus, it is possible for a judgment falling within the scope of the Convention to be recognised only in part, if such part is severable from the rest of the judgment.

Articles 20 to 23 cover the situation where Contracting States to the Convention have concluded a Supplementary Agreement with each other. Of these, the most important provision is Article 21 which states:

> Decisions rendered in a Contracting State shall not be recognised or enforced in another Contracting State in accordance with the provisions of the preceding Articles unless the two States, being Parties to this Convention, have concluded a Supplementary Agreement to this effect.

Thus, even when a state ratifies or accedes to the 1971 Hague Convention, the instrument will not be operative as between that state and another Contracting State until both have concluded a Supplementary Agreement enabling the 1971 Convention to take effect as between them. The need for multiple Supplementary Agreements between Contracting States may explain why the 1971 Hague Convention has failed to attract parties. The Convention came into effect in 1979. But, at present, there are only five Contracting States to the Convention (Albania, Cyprus, Kuwait, the Netherlands and Portugal).

The Supplementary Protocol to the 1971 Hague Convention entered into force in 1979. But there are to date only four parties to it (Cyprus, Kuwait, the Netherlands and Portugal). It applies to foreign judgments rendered against a person having a domicile or habitual residence in a Contracting State (Article 1). In such situation, by Article 2, recognition and enforcement are to be refused at the request of the person against whom a judgment is directed (the defendant), where the relevant decision was based on one of the grounds of indirect jurisdiction specified in Article 4 of the Supplementary Protocol. Those grounds are:

(a) the presence in the territory of the State of origin of property belonging to the defendant, or the seizure by the plaintiff of property situated there, unless:

- the action is brought to assert proprietary or possessory rights in that property, or arises from another issue relating to such property,
- the property constitutes the security for a debt which is the subject matter of the action;

(b) the nationality of the plaintiff;
(c) the domicile, habitual residence or ordinary residence of the plaintiff within the territory of the State of origin unless the assumption of jurisdiction on such a ground is permitted by way of an exception made on account of the particular subject matter of a class of contracts;
(d) the fact that the defendant carried on business within the territory of the State of origin, unless the action arises from that business;
(e) service of a writ upon the defendant within the territory of the State of origin during his temporary presence there;
(f) a unilateral specification of the forum by the plaintiff, particularly in an invoice.

Article 5 defines the domicile or habitual residence of a legal person (for instance, a corporation) as the place 'where it has its seat, its place of incorporation, or its principal place of business'.

ii. The 2005 Hague Convention[12]

The 2005 Hague Convention came into force in 2015. As at 1 March 2019, there were 32 parties (including one REIO (the EU)). The US, the Ukraine and China signed the Convention in 2009, 2016 and 2017 respectively, but have yet to ratify or accede to it. The Convention applies 'in international cases to exclusive choice of court agreements concluded in civil or commercial matters' (Article 1).[13] An 'exclusive choice of court agreement' is an agreement[14] whereby the court of a Contracting State is designated as the exclusive forum for deciding disputes which have arisen or may arise in connection with a particular legal relationship (Article 3). The Convention has two key components. The first component (essentially Chapter II (Articles 5 to 7)) ensures that the court designated by the parties in an exclusive choice of court agreement (and no other court) will hear a dispute arising out of the particular legal relationship. The second component (essentially Chapter III (Articles 8 to 15)) ensures that the judgment of the designated court will be recognised and enforced in all other Contracting States, save only in limited and narrowly defined circumstances.

By Article 2, the Convention is not applicable where a choice of court agreement: (1) has been entered into by an individual acting as a 'consumer' (that is, 'acting primarily for personal, family or household purposes'); or (2) is contained in an employment contract. In addition, the instrument does apply in any of a long list of matters: (1) the status and legal capacity of natural persons; (2) maintenance obligations; (3) other family law matters, including matrimonial property regimes; (4) wills and succession; (5) insolvency, composition and analogous matters; (6) carriage of passengers and goods; (7) marine pollution, limitation of liability for maritime claims, general average, and emergency towage and salvage; (8) antitrust or competition matters; (9) liability for nuclear damage; (10) personal injury claims; (11) tort or delict claims for damage to tangible property; (12) rights *in rem* in immovable property and tenancies of immovable property; (13) the validity, nullity or

[12] For the text, see www.hcch.net/en/instruments/conventions/specialised-sections/choice-of-court.
[13] 'Commercial matters' are not defined in the Convention.
[14] The agreement must be 'concluded or documented (i) in writing; or (ii) by any other means of communication which renders information accessible so as to be usable for subsequent reference' (Art 3(c)).

dissolution of legal persons, and the validity of decisions of their organs; (14) the validity of intellectual property rights (IPRs) other than copyright and related rights; (15) the infringement of IPRs other than copyright and related rights, except where infringement proceedings are brought for breach of a contract between the parties relating to such rights or could have been brought for breach of that contract; and (16) the validity of entries in public registers. There is, however, a proviso to the exclusions in Article 2(3):

> [P]roceedings are not excluded … where a matter … arises merely as a preliminary question and not as an object of the proceedings. In particular, the mere fact that a matter … arises by way of defence does not exclude proceedings from the Convention, if that matter is not an object of the proceedings.

The Convention expressly does not apply to arbitration and related proceedings (Article 2(4)). Article 7 further excludes interim measures from the scope of the Convention. Article 10, on the other hand, qualifies the exclusions in Article 2, so that if an excluded matter merely arises as a preliminary question, a ruling on that question shall not be refused recognition or enforcement.

By Article 5(1), the designated court will have jurisdiction to decide disputes covered by the parties' choice of court agreement, unless that agreement is null and void under the law of the state in which the designated court is situated. Moreover, the designated court 'shall not decline to exercise jurisdiction on the ground that the dispute should be decided in a court of another State' (Article 5(2)). By Article 6, except in narrow circumstances, non-designated courts in Contracting States shall decline to exercise jurisdiction over disputes falling within the parties' choice of court agreement.

The court of a Contracting State *may* only refuse to recognise and enforce the judgment of the designated court in the limited situations where (Article 9):

> (a) the agreement was null and void under the law of the State of the chosen court, unless the chosen court has determined that the agreement is valid;
> (b) a party lacked the capacity to conclude the agreement under the law of the requested State;
> (c) the document which instituted the proceedings or an equivalent document, including the essential elements of the claim,
>   (i) was not notified to the defendant in sufficient time and in such a way as to enable him to arrange for his defence, unless the defendant entered an appearance and presented his case without contesting notification in the court of origin, provided that the law of the State of origin permitted notification to be contested; or
>   (ii) was notified to the defendant in the requested State in a manner that is incompatible with fundamental principles of the requested State concerning service of documents;
> (d) the judgment was obtained by fraud in connection with a matter of procedure;
> (e) recognition or enforcement would be manifestly incompatible with the public policy of the requested State, including situations where the specific proceedings leading to the judgment were incompatible with fundamental principles of procedural fairness of that State;
> (f) the judgment is inconsistent with a judgment given in the requested State in a dispute between the same parties; or
> (g) the judgment is inconsistent with an earlier judgment given in another State between the same parties on the same cause of action, provided that the earlier judgment fulfils the conditions necessary for its recognition in the requested State.

Apart from the grounds in Article 9, there is to be no review of the merits of a judgment. A judgment shall be recognised provided that it is effective and enforceable in the originating state (Article 8(3)). An enforcing court will be bound by the findings of fact of the designated court, unless the judgment is one obtained by default (Article 8(2)). Recognition may be delayed, if the judgment is being reviewed in the originating state or if the time limit for a review has not yet expired (Article 8(4)). Where parts of a judgment are severable, then it may be recognised and enforced only as to part (Article 15).

Article 20 should be noted, as it can apply where parties have chosen the court of a neutral third-party state having no connection with the parties or the subject matter of a dispute, as the forum for the resolution of disputes under a commercial contract. Article 20 provides that a state can

> declare that its courts may refuse to recognise or enforce a judgment … if the parties were resident in the requested State, and the relationship of the parties and all other elements relevant to the dispute … were connected only with the requested State.

In addition, Article 21 stipulates that, where a Contracting State 'has a strong interest in not applying this Convention to a specific matter', it can so declare. But the declaration should be 'no broader than necessary and … the specific matter excluded is clearly and precisely defined'.

iii. The 2018 Draft[15]

On the assumption that the 2018 Draft is adopted in its current form and ignoring wording marked out in brackets, it will not apply to judgments dealing with a number of excluded matters (Article 2(1)): (1) revenue, customs or administrative matters; (2) status and legal capacity of natural persons; (3) maintenance obligations; (4) family law matters, including matrimonial property regimes; (5) wills and succession; (6) insolvency, composition, resolution of financial institutions, and analogous matters; (7) carriage of passengers and goods; (8) marine pollution, limitation of liability for maritime claims, general average, and emergency towage and salvage; (9) liability for nuclear damage; (10) validity, nullity or dissolution of legal persons or associations of natural or legal persons, and validity of decisions of their organs; (11) validity of entries in public registers; and (12) defamation.[16] Article 2(2) contains a proviso similar to Article 2(3) of the 2005 Hague Convention on the position where an excluded matter has arisen as a preliminary or incidental question in the proceedings before the rendering court. Article 2(4) of the 2018 Draft excludes arbitration-related proceedings. It will be seen that, although longer, there is overlap among matters excluded from the 2018 Draft and the 1971 and 2005 Hague Conventions.

The basic rule is found in Article 4. Judgments of a Contracting State are to be recognised and enforced in other Contracting States (Article 4(1)), provided that the judgments are effective and enforceable in the originating state (Article 4(3)). There is to be no review of the merits (Article 4(2)). Where a judgment is subject to review in the originating state, the enforcing court may (1) provisionally recognise or enforce the judgment subject to security being put up; (2) delay a decision on recognition or enforcement; or (3) refuse recognition or enforcement without prejudice to a later application.

[15] For the text, see assets.hcch.net/docs/9faf15e1-9c36-4e57-8d56-12a7d895faac.pdf.

[16] There remains a debate over whether judgments relating to the following matters (currently set out in brackets in the 2018 Draft) should also be excluded: privacy, IPRs, activities of armed forces, law enforcement activities and antitrust (competition).

Article 5(1) sets out grounds of indirect jurisdiction. To be eligible for recognition and enforcement, a judgment must meet at least one of the grounds in Article 5(1). Those grounds are:

(a) the person against whom recognition or enforcement is sought was habitually resident in the State of origin at the time that person became a party to the proceedings in the court of origin;
(b) the natural person against whom recognition or enforcement is sought had his or her principal place of business in the State of origin at the time that person became a party to the proceedings in the court of origin and the claim on which the judgment is based arose out of the activities of that business;
(c) the person against whom recognition or enforcement is sought is the person that brought the claim, other than a counterclaim, on which the judgment is based;
(d) the defendant maintained a branch, agency, or other establishment without separate legal personality in the State of origin at the time that person became a party to the proceedings in the court of origin, and the claim on which the judgment is based arose out of the activities of that branch, agency, or establishment;
(e) the defendant expressly consented to the jurisdiction of the court of origin in the course of the proceedings in which the judgment was given;
(f) the defendant argued on the merits before the court of origin without contesting jurisdiction within the timeframe provided in the law of the State of origin, unless it is evident that an objection to jurisdiction or to the exercise of jurisdiction would not have succeeded under that law;
(g) the judgment ruled on a contractual obligation and it was given in the State in which performance of that obligation took place, or should have taken place, in accordance with
    (i) the parties' agreement, or
    (ii) the law applicable to the contract, in the absence of an agreed place of performance, unless the defendant's activities in relation to the transaction clearly did not constitute a purposeful and substantial connection to that State;
(h) the judgment ruled on a tenancy of immovable property and it was given in the State in which the property is situated;
(i) the judgment ruled against the defendant on a contractual obligation secured by a right *in rem* in immovable property located in the State of origin, if the contractual claim was brought together with a claim against the same defendant relating to that right *in rem*;
(j) the judgment ruled on a non-contractual obligation arising from death, physical injury, damage to or loss of tangible property, and the act or omission directly causing such harm occurred in the State of origin, irrespective of where that harm occurred;
(k) the judgment concerns the validity, construction, effects, administration or variation of a trust created voluntarily and evidenced in writing, and—
    (i) at the time the proceedings were instituted, the State of origin was designated in the trust instrument as a State in which disputes about such matters are to be determined; or
    (ii) at the time the proceedings were instituted, the State of origin was expressly or impliedly designated in the trust instrument as the State in which the principal place of administration of the trust is situated.

    This sub-paragraph only applies to judgments regarding internal aspects of a trust between persons who are or were within the trust relationship;
(l) the judgment ruled on a counterclaim—
    (i) to the extent that it was in favour of the counterclaimant, provided that the counterclaim arose out of the same transaction or occurrence as the claim;

(ii) to the extent that it was against the counterclaimant, unless the law of the State of origin required the counterclaim to be filed in order to avoid preclusion;

(m) the judgment was given by a court designated in an agreement concluded or documented in writing or by any other means of communication which renders information accessible so as to be usable for subsequent reference, other than an exclusive choice of court agreement.[17]

Article 5(2) deals with the situation where recognition or enforcement is sought against someone who dealt as a consumer or against an employee in connection with an employment contract.

It will be seen that, although much longer than the list of indirect jurisdiction grounds in the 1971 Hague Convention, there is overlap between the grounds in the 2018 Draft and the 1971 Hague Convention. In particular, there will be indirect jurisdiction under both instruments where:

1. The person against whom recognition or enforcement is sought (the defendant) was substantially present in the originating state, because: (a) the defendant was habitually resident in the originating state at the time of the proceedings before the rendering court or (b) had a principal place of business or an establishment without separate legal personality in the originating state at that time and the claim underlying the judgment arose out of the business activities of such place or establishment;
2. the defendant submitted to the jurisdiction of the rendering court by: (a) bringing the claim there, (b) expressly consenting to that jurisdiction, (c) arguing the case on the merits before the rendering court without contesting jurisdiction, or (d) agreeing to that jurisdiction by an exclusive choice of court agreement;
3. the judgment deals with the title to immoveable property situated in the originating state;
4. the judgment deals with damage (death, physical injury, loss of tangible property) for breach of a non-contractual obligation and the act that gave rise to the damage occurred in the originating state, regardless of where the damage was actually suffered; or,
5. the judgment is in favour of a counterclaiming party and the counterclaim arises out of the same transaction or occurrence as the claim.

It follows from the 2018 Draft and the 1971 Hague Convention acknowledging indirect jurisdiction where parties have designated a court as the exclusive forum for the resolution of their disputes, that both documents are compatible with the 2005 Hague Convention.

Article 7(1) sets out the narrow grounds for which recognition or enforcement may be refused. Leaving aside ground (g) in the Draft (relating to IPRs over which there is presently no consensus), the grounds for refusal are:

(a) the document which instituted the proceedings or an equivalent document, including a statement of the essential elements of the claim—

(i) was not notified to the defendant in sufficient time and in such a way as to enable him to arrange for his defence, unless the defendant entered an appearance and presented

[17] An 'exclusive choice of court agreement' is defined in Art 5(1)(m) of the 2018 Draft Convention as 'an agreement concluded by two or more parties that designates, for the purpose of deciding disputes which have arisen or may arise in connection with a particular legal relationship, the courts of one State or one or more specific courts of one State to the exclusion of the jurisdiction of any other courts'.

his case without contesting notification in the court of origin, provided that the law of the State of origin permitted notification to be contested; or

(ii) was notified to the defendant in the requested State in a manner that is incompatible with fundamental principles of the requested State concerning service of documents;

(b) the judgment was obtained by fraud;

(c) recognition or enforcement would be manifestly incompatible with the public policy of the requested State, including situations where the specific proceedings leading to the judgment were incompatible with fundamental principles of procedural fairness of that State and situations involving infringements of security or sovereignty of that State;

(d) the proceedings in the court of origin were contrary to an agreement, or a designation in a trust instrument, under which the dispute in question was to be determined in a court other than the court of origin;

(e) the judgment is inconsistent with a judgment given in the requested State in a dispute between the same parties; or

(f) the judgment is inconsistent with an earlier judgment given in another State between the same parties on the same subject matter, provided that the earlier judgment fulfils the conditions necessary for its recognition in the requested State.

Although there are differences in wording and emphasis, the grounds for refusal in the 2018 Draft are broadly similar to the grounds for refusal in the 1971 and 2005 Conventions. Those grounds are roughly: (1) a lack of due process (including inadequate notice of the proceedings before the rendering court such that the defendant was not afforded a reasonable opportunity to present a defence); (2) extrinsic (procedural) fraud; (3) incompatibility with public policy; (4) *res judicata*, that is, inconsistency with a judgment of the enforcing state or an earlier judgment in a third-party state which would be recognised in the enforcing state; and (5) breach of an agreement to litigate a dispute before a designated court such that the rendering court lacked jurisdiction to determine the matter before it. Article 8 further provides that a ruling on a preliminary question will not be recognised or enforced. Article 9 envisages the possibility of partial recognition or enforcement where parts of a judgment are severable.

Articles 13 to 16 deal with the procedures for obtaining recognition and enforcement in an enforcing state. Article 14(1) such procedures are to be governed by the law of the enforcing state.

Article 18 allows a state to declare that its courts *may* refuse to recognise or enforce a judgment 'if the parties were resident in the requested State, and the relationship of the parties and all other elements relevant to the dispute, other than the location of the court of origin, were connected only with the requested State'. Article 19 additionally permits a state with 'a strong interest in not applying this Convention to a specific matter' to make a declaration accordingly, but the declaration should be 'no broader than necessary' and the exclusion has to be precisely defined.

iv. Common Elements in the 1971 and 2005 Conventions and the 2018 Draft

From the foregoing survey, it will have been noticed that the formats of the three instruments are similar. It is submitted that there are at least the following common elements: (1) a list of excluded matters; (2) a requirement that a judgment be final and conclusive in the sense of no longer being subject to review or appeal; (3) a list of grounds of indirect jurisdiction; and (4) a list of grounds for refusal of recognition and enforcement.

The excluded matters largely have the effect that the three instruments are most likely to apply in commercial matters, as opposed to matters concerning (for example) a person's status, family, succession, inheritance consumer matters and employment. That a judgment must be final precludes recognition and enforcement of merely interlocutory or interim judgments that typically are limited to maintaining a status quo, pending a conclusive determination by the rendering court on a matter. An interlocutory decision ordering some interim measure is subject to change so that, if recognised and enforced elsewhere, there will have to be back-tracking if the rendering court ultimately decides against the party in whose favour the interim measure was granted. The same difficulty arises where a rendering court's decision remains subject to appeal, such that it may be quashed or varied by an appellate court. The grounds of indirect jurisdiction are largely based on (1) the defendant's habitual residence or (insofar as closely connected with the claim being brought in the rendering court) the place where the defendant has its principal place of business or some sort of establishment, branch or agency; (2) the defendant's submission to the rendering court's jurisdiction either by (a) express agreement (as exemplified, for instance, in an exclusive choice of court agreement), (b) contesting the claim before the rendering court on the merits without challenging jurisdiction, or (c) itself invoking the rendering court's jurisdiction by bringing a related counterclaim; or (3) the claim relates to title to immovable property situated in the originating state. The grounds for refusal typically involve an assessment of: (1) whether the rendering court had indirect jurisdiction; (2) whether there has been a denial of due process (including procedural fraud in the obtaining of the judgment); (3) whether recognition or enforcement would be contrary to the public policy of the enforcing state; and (4) whether there is some sort of *res judicata* (for example, because of a contrary prior judgment in the enforcing state or a judgment in some other state that the enforcing state would recognise). There is an indication in the three Hague documents that: (1) judgments may be recognised in part, provided that such part is severable; and (2) even if a judgment involves a determination of an excluded matter, the judgment may still be recognised if the excluded matter only arose as a preliminary question requiring decision in order to arrive at a determination on some principal non-excluded issue before the rendering court.

There is a further element that is common to the three Hague documents. None of the instruments come into effect unless states sign up to them. Ratification or accession to any of the three instruments functions as an agreement with all other parties to the document to recognise and enforce each other's judgments in accordance with the terms of the document. The system of recognition and enforcement envisaged under any of the three documents hinges on the agreement of Contracting States to accord reciprocal treatment to judgments falling within the terms of the relevant instrument. Accordingly, a requirement of reciprocity can also be characterised as a common element to all three instruments.

The next section will examine the extent to which the common elements identified above can be essential ingredients to a simple, but effective legal regime for the recognition and enforcement of judgments.

III. Towards a Rudimentary System[18]

A country can establish a system for the recognition and enforcement of civil and commercial judgments by entering into bilateral treaties with states whose nationals and corporations the country would like to attract as investors. In that way, bespoke terms for the mutual recognition and enforcement of judgments can be worked out case-by-case between the country and the states with which it would like to deal. The terms may or may not mirror some or all of the terms of the 1971 and 2005 Hague Conventions and the 2018 Draft. The difficulty with this method is that it would likely take too long. Treaties are time-consuming to negotiate. Having been negotiated, they still have to be signed and ratified by each party. Consider, for example, the 60+ countries that form part of China's Belt and Road Initiative (BRI), if the objective was to create a network of bilateral regimes for the mutual recognition and enforcement of judgments among the countries in the BRI, that would mean that each country would have to negotiate and enter into some 60 treaties. That would be a Herculean task and provide little benefit to the BRI in the near or medium term. In fact, few of the 15 Asian states countries covered here have actually entered into a significant number of bilateral treaties for the mutual recognition and enforcement of judgments. Many have not entered into any agreements to that effect at all.

An alternative to bilateral treaties would be to sign up to the 1971 and 2005 Hague Conventions and, on the assumption that it is adopted by the Diplomatic Council of the Hague Conference at some point, the forthcoming Hague Convention on the Recognition and Enforcement of Judgments in Civil and Commercial Matters. The difficulty with this as a strategy is that the 1971 Hague Convention presently only has five parties and, in any event, will not come into operation in a Contracting State unless it enters into a Supplementary Agreement with another Contracting State. Thus, if the 1971 Hague Convention is to give rise to a widespread network of mutual recognition and enforcement, it will have to attract many more signatories and those states will have to negotiate Supplementary Agreements with each other. The 2005 Hague Convention is available for accession and would undoubtedly be an excellent first step towards establishing a regime for the mutual recognition and enforcement of judgments. But its scope is limited to the situation where commercial parties enter into exclusive choice of court agreements designating the court of a Contracting State as the forum to resolve their disputes. It is hoped that the forthcoming Hague Convention will plug the gap. Nonetheless, even if promulgated in 2019, it will take time before a sufficient number of states sign up to it. Typically, countries adopt a 'wait-and-see' attitude with new conventions and do not come on board until a number of other states have done so. The jurisdictions discussed in this book (with the possible exception of Singapore which has been actively taking part in the discussions on the 2018 Draft) currently have no plans to sign up to the forthcoming convention.

Another method, one that may not be as time-consuming as entering into bilateral treaties, would be for judiciaries in different countries to enter into Memorandums of Guidance (MOGs) with one another, setting out in a non-legally binding document the criteria and procedures that a judiciary will apply when considering whether to recognise a

[18] See generally Béligh Elbalti, 'Spontaneous Harmonization and the Liberalization of the Recognition and Enforcement of Foreign Judgments' (2014) 16 *Japanese Yearbook of Private International Law* 264.

judgment rendered by another judiciary. This method may be faster, because the MOGs are purely informal, being solely for the purpose of communicating information to members of the public interested in having a judgment recognised or enforced by the court of one or other party to an MOG. MOGs can therefore be entered into as between judiciaries on an administrative basis without need for government or legislative intervention or approval. Nonetheless, the process of entering into bilateral MOGs will still take time and their non-binding nature means that there is no guarantee that the MOG will be adhered to by a relevant court. The latter will still have to apply the law in its jurisdiction, including when that law is different from what is stated in the MOG. The existence of MOGs may thus be insufficiently reassuring to the foreign investors which a country is seeking to attract. Still, insofar as reciprocity is a requirement for recognition and enforcement of a judgment, MOGs may be useful evidence of reciprocity as between the states of the judicial parties to them. An MOG shows one court's willingness, subject to the conditions laid down in the MOG, to recognise and enforce a decision of a court in another country.

The quickest and most efficient way to establish a system for the recognition and enforcement of civil and commercial judgments may be to look at one's own laws and procedures and to develop them to some internationally acceptable standard (for instance, as evidenced by the three Hague instruments). If it is accepted that a relatively liberal regime of recognition and enforcement of civil and commercial judgments is likely to encourage FDI, the delays inherent in negotiating bilateral treaties or MOGs are something that a country can ill afford in economic terms. If the goal is to attract FDI as soon as possible, a country cannot only rely on the negotiation of bilateral treaties or MOGs. It is therefore submitted that the common elements of the three Hague documents identified in the previous section can serve as a starting point for assessing whether the law in one's jurisdiction offers a simple, but workable regime for the recognition and enforcement of general civil and commercial judgments. The remainder of this section will consider each of the common elements more closely with a view to identifying a minimum system that would be advisable for a country to adopt into its laws.

A. Excluded Matters

The excluded matters in the three Hague documents essentially narrow down the foreign decisions that are likely to be recognised and enforced to judgments of a commercial nature. The exclusions can in effect be treated as defining what are not to be considered commercial matters. It is suggested that such negative definition of 'commercial matters' is consonant with the positive, non-exhaustive definition of 'commercial matters' adopted here as found in footnote 2 to Article 1(1) of the UNCITRAL Model Law. A basic regime should at least recognise and enforce money judgments rendered by a foreign court in general civil and commercial matters so defined. It would also be desirable to recognise at least certain types of non-money judgment (such as where a claim has been dismissed in an originating state, in order to prevent a losing plaintiff from re-litigating the same matter against the same defendant in the enforcing state). It may be more difficult to recognise civil and commercial judgments ordering specific performance or final injunctions. At least in common law jurisdictions, specific performance and injunctions qualify as equitable relief and are thus subject to the court's discretion. It may be a step too far for an enforcing state, especially one in a common law jurisdiction, automatically to recognise a final order for specific performance or an injunction by an originating court, as that may entail the judge in the enforcing court abdicating its discretion as to the appropriateness of such relief in the circumstances of a case. At best, perhaps, in the case of non-monetary judgments, the enforcing court might recognise (and consider itself bound by) the originating court's findings of fact. Then, the enforcing court might take into account the fact that the originating court ordered non-monetary relief as a relevant factor when considering whether (as a matter of the enforcing court's discretion) to order an analogous remedy. In practice, the scenario just described will probably rarely arise. It is a maxim of equity in common law jurisdictions that specific performance and injunctions will not be awarded where damages are an adequate remedy or where there will be a need constantly to supervise whether an order for specific performance or injunction is being obeyed. Accordingly, since in most general civil and commercial disputes monetary compensation or damages are likely to be an adequate remedy, the question of granting specific performance or an injunction should not normally arise.

The contributors to the 15 jurisdiction chapters were invited to comment on the likely approach their country would take to the recognition or enforcement of judgments on four matters falling among the exclusions to the 1971 and 2005 Hague Conventions and the 2018 Draft. The four special cases are (1) judgments relating to IPRs; (2) judgments relating to land situate in the enforcing state or elsewhere; (3) judgments relating to environmental damage sustained in the enforcing state or elsewhere; and (4) judgments relating to antitrust (competition). The court of an enforcing state may be unwilling to enforce such judgments because such decisions can adversely affect the rights and liabilities of third parties within the enforcing state, not just the parties to the judgment. For instance, a foreign judgment declaring that title to land situate in an enforcing state is vested in the plaintiff, might affect the security interest of third parties protected by a public register in the enforcing state. Recognition of the foreign judgment in such case could prejudice the holders of those security interests without their having had a chance to defend their rights against the plaintiff's claim. However, one technique to get around this, as is apparent from the three Hague instruments, would be to analyse the nature of the original claim sought to be enforced by a judgment. Assume that title to land or the validity of an IPR registration in an enforcing state, are dealt with in a rendering court's judgment as a preliminary or incidental question to a substantive determination of the rights of the plaintiff and defendant as between themselves. In such circumstances, an enforcing state may recognise the rendering court's judgment, because the latter only touches on the rights and liabilities of the parties to the judgment. The rendering court's judgment does not impinge on the rights, liabilities or interests of others.

B. Finality

As already discussed above, there will be problems where a judgment is prematurely recognised because the same is not final or conclusive. An enforcing court may find itself having to rescind a previous decision to recognise or enforce an interlocutory judgment or a first instance decision that has been appealed against or which is subject to the possibility of appeal. Therefore, it would make sense for a basic system to require that judgments be final and conclusive in the sense of no longer being subject to review or appeal. A corollary is that a judgment must be enforceable and operative in the originating state, if it is to be recognised and enforced in the enforcing state. If the rendering court has set aside or nullified its judgment, then there would be nothing to recognise and enforce in an enforcing state.

This does not mean that a court cannot take into account the existence of an interlocutory order by a foreign court when deciding whether to grant (say) interim relief in aid of the foreign proceedings. For example, consider the case where a court in State X grants an anti-suit injunction ordering a defendant not to initiate or continue proceedings in State Y, pending the final determination of the plaintiff's claim before the court of State X. The court of State X may not recognise the injunction because it is merely interlocutory and not final. But, if the plaintiff applies to the court in State Y for a stay of proceedings begun there by the defendant, the court in State Y may wish to consider the grant of an injunction in State X as a factor to take into account when itself independently deciding whether to grant a stay of the proceedings in State Y. This, of course, assumes that the law of State Y allows the court there to grant stays, injunctions or other relief in aid of proceedings abroad.

C. Indirect Jurisdiction

If a defendant is to be held bound by a judgment rendered against him or her in a foreign country, the enforcing court must have some assurance that it was reasonable and fair to expect the defendant to appear and defend proceedings in that foreign country. To take an extreme case, suppose that a plaintiff chooses to sue a defendant in State X which has no connection whatsoever with the parties or the subject matter of a dispute. Why should a defendant who is resident or based in a place other than State X be expected to take the trouble to defend itself in the State X proceedings? If the plaintiff, having proved the claim in State X, should obtain a judgment from the court of State X in default of the defendant's appearance, why would it be fair for a court in some other country where the defendant has assets to recognise and enforce the State X judgment? The requirement of indirect jurisdiction ensures that there is a link between the state where a judgment was obtained and either the defendant or the subject matter of a dispute, otherwise it would be unfair and unreasonable for the defendant to be put to the trouble and expense of appearing in the originating state to defend himself or herself.

Indirect jurisdiction is also referred to as 'international jurisdiction' because it involves the identification of internationally accepted grounds for a court to assume jurisdiction over a defendant or an action. The difficulty, however, is in determining precisely what are internationally accepted grounds of assuming jurisdiction and what are not. It is evident from the 1971 and 2005 Hague Conventions and the 2018 Draft that, apart from a small number of grounds, there is no consensus as to what grounds of indirect jurisdiction are accepted internationally. It appears that, at a minimum, a rendering court is generally accepted as having indirect jurisdiction: (1) if the state in which the court is situated is the habitual residence of the defendant; (2) if the state in which the court is situated is the place where the defendant has a principal place of business or an establishment, branch or agency, provided that such place of business, establishment, branch or agency was closely connected to the claim; (3) if the defendant has submitted to the court's jurisdiction (a) by express agreement, (b) by defending the claim on the merits without challenging jurisdiction, or

(c) by invoking the court's jurisdiction by bringing a counterclaim related to the claim; (4) if the claim relates to title in immovable property within the state of the rendering court; and (5) if the claim relates to a non-contractual obligation and the act that gave rise to the damage (death, personal injury, damage to property) occurred in the state of the rendering court. There may be other grounds. But as can be seen from the Supplementary Protocol to the 1971 Hague Convention, those grounds especially when based on the plaintiff's nationality, residence or domicile or on the fact that fortuitously the defendant was temporarily present within the territory of the rendering court or happens to have assets there, may be insufficient bases on which to claim indirect jurisdiction. It does not seem that such other grounds are widely accepted internationally.

If damages or money is due from a defendant to a plaintiff, it should be reasonably foreseeable that the plaintiff will seek the defendant out in the latter's habitual residence in order to claim payment. The defendant cannot seriously complain about having to defend against a claim for damages or monies due or owing in his or her home jurisdiction. Similarly, there should be indirect jurisdiction in the case where a defendant has a place of business, but only if that place of business has some connection with a claim, as opposed to simply being a place where fortuitously a defendant happens to transact unrelated business or has assets.

Where the defendant has submitted to a court's jurisdiction, it can hardly complain about a judgment being rendered against it. We have seen that under the 2005 Hague Convention and the 2018 Draft, a country is allowed to declare that where: (1) both parties to an action are resident in an enforcing state; and (2) the action has no connection with the rendering state, but is closely connected with the enforcing state, then the court of the enforcing state may refuse to recognise the judgment of the rendering court. This would be despite the parties having by a choice of court agreement designated the court of the rendering state as the exclusive jurisdiction for the determination of their commercial disputes. It is submitted that this basis for refusal of recognition is not at heart a question of indirect jurisdiction. It is instead better classified as an application of the public policy ground for refusal. The rendering court has indirect jurisdiction as a result of the parties' submission to it by express agreement. The question before the enforcing court is whether to refuse recognition on public policy grounds, because (for instance) the agreement offends against the mandatory jurisdiction of the court of the enforcing state as stipulated in the latter state's laws. It is submitted that, if the enforcing court's decision in the matter would be similar to that of the rendering court, the enforcing court should refrain from exercising its discretion not to recognise and enforce the foreign judgment. In other words, in those circumstances, it should not be contrary to public policy to enforce what the enforcing court would have decided in any case. On the contrary, the matter being commercial in nature, it would more conducive to public policy to give full vent to the principle of party autonomy.

Where a defendant unsuccessfully challenges the jurisdiction of the rendering court and then opts not to defend the case there on the merits, can he or she subsequently resist recognition and enforcement in another state on the ground of a lack of indirect jurisdiction? In that case, the minimal grounds of indirect jurisdiction discussed here would not be met. The defendant has not defended the case on the merits before the rendering court. He or she simply queried the rendering court's jurisdiction but failed to persuade the rendering court of a lack of jurisdiction. Consequently, on the basic principles here, the enforcing court would not be able to find indirect jurisdiction by voluntary submission to the jurisdiction of the rendering court. If there is to be recognition, it will be necessary to found indirect jurisdiction on some other ground.

Where title to land is concerned, it makes sense that the court where the land is situated should have indirect jurisdiction. An adjudication on the title to land will often affect not just the immediate parties to a dispute, but also potentially involve third parties who may have interests (for example, mortgages, charges or other security interests) in the land. Consequently, the court in the place where the land is situated would be in a better position to take account of (and strike an appropriate balance among) the competing interests in the land. Further, the court's decision can lead to the rectification of any public registry in the enforcing state relating to the land in dispute.

The last ground of indirect jurisdiction put forward here as a minimum requirement for a basic system of recognition echoes a perennial conundrum among law students. If A in State A commits a wrong which affects B in State B, which state's court will have indirect jurisdiction over the matter: the court of the state where the wrong was committed (State A) or the court of the state where the damage occurred (State B) or the courts of both states? In line with the principle that a plaintiff should seek out his or her defendant, it would seem to make sense for the court of State A to claim jurisdiction on the basis that, having committed the wrong in State A, the defendant A should reasonably have anticipated being sued there by plaintiff B. In practice, such a rule may possibly be too narrow in today's world. Consider the situation where A in State A commits a serious environmental wrong which adversely affects numerous persons (many of whom have only limited income) in State B. It may be that the court of State B will assert jurisdiction in such case, especially given the scale of the calamity in State B. In those circumstances, under the minimal rules proposed here, the judgment of State B against A will not be recognised in State A due to a lack of indirect jurisdiction. But one might ask whether it would be reasonable to expect all those harmed in State B by A's environmental tort, to bring their action in State A.

In many common law jurisdictions, the court can claim exorbitant jurisdiction over a third party not present or resident within the territory, if that third party is a 'proper or necessary party' to proceedings that have been commenced against a defendant.[19] A judgment rendered against such third party would not be eligible for recognition or enforcement under the minimum grounds of indirect jurisdiction proposed here. That would be the case even though the rendering court may well be a forum which is closely linked to the subject matter of the action and even though the third party was joined to the proceedings to ensure that he or she would be bound by the findings of the court. This is unfortunate. The joinder of the third party is supposed to reduce the risk of contradictory findings by different courts, where one set of defendants is sued in one country and another set of defendants in the same matter are sued elsewhere only because they do not happen to be habitually resident or have a relevant place of business within the territory of the rendering court. However, the present state of international law appears to be that jurisdiction based solely on a third party being a 'proper or necessary party' is not yet a generally accepted ground of indirect jurisdiction.

[19] See, for example, in Hong Kong, Rules of the High Court (Cap 4A) (RHC), Ord 11, r 1(1)(d). Provisions similar to Ord 11, r 1(1)(d) are often cited in support of arguments that the joinder of third parties in international commercial litigation is more straightforward than the joinder in international commercial arbitration of third parties who are not privy to an arbitration agreement.

In a recent paper,[20] Professor Brand has argued that the 2018 Draft should, in the alternative, put forward only four (as opposed to 13) grounds of indirect jurisdiction. Those four grounds would allow indirect jurisdiction where:

(a) the person against whom recognition or enforcement is sought was habitually resident in the State of origin at the time that person became a party to the proceedings in the court of origin;
(b) the person against whom recognition or enforcement is sought is the person that brought the claim on which the judgment is based;
(c) the defendant expressly consented to the jurisdiction of the court of origin either prior to or in the course of the proceedings in which the judgment was given; or
(d) the dispute in the State of origin was based on facts which would have satisfied a basis of direct jurisdiction available in the State addressed.[21]

Grounds (a), (b) and (c) are similar to the minimum ground proposed above and already feature in the 1971 Hague Convention and the 2018 Draft. Ground (d) is new. It encapsulates a mirror principle whereby grounds for indirect jurisdiction should be the same as the grounds for direct jurisdiction applied by a country.[22] Professor Brand observes that ground (d) would make it unnecessary to have all the other grounds of indirect jurisdiction in the 2018 Draft. Further, ground (d) would address what Professor Brand calls the 'jurisdiction gap problem'.[23] That gap arises because many countries discriminate against foreign judgments. They do so by applying narrow grounds of indirect jurisdiction when it comes to recognition of foreign judgments but apply wide-ranging grounds of direct jurisdiction (including claims to exorbitant jurisdiction) in relation to cases initiated before their own courts. Of the Asian countries covered in this book, Professor Brand suggests[24] that Japan and South Korea apply the same grounds for direct and indirect jurisdiction, while Indonesia[25] applies narrower grounds of indirect jurisdiction than it relies on to assert direct jurisdiction.

[20] Ronald A Brand, 'The Circulation of Judgments under the Draft Hague Convention' University of Pittsburgh School Law Legal Studies Research Paper Series Working Paper No 2019-02 (February 2019), University of Pittsburgh School of Law, available online: papers.ssrn.com/sol3/papers.cfm?abstract_id=3334647. Professor Brand is a member of the US delegation to the Special Commission of the judgments Project working on the 2018 Draft.

[21] ibid, 17.

[22] The mirror principle is itself not without difficulty. Many common law states are able to assert extra-territorial jurisdiction in a wide range of situations (see, for example, in the case of Hong Kong, the situations listed in RHC, Ord 11, rr 1(1)(a)–(p)). However, common law states also typically apply a doctrine of *forum non conveniens*. See eg *Spiliada Maritime Corp v Cansulex Ltd* [1987] AC 460. Thus, notwithstanding that a case is one where the court can assert exorbitant jurisdiction, it may decline to do so upon the application of a defendant, on the ground that the court is not an appropriate or convenient forum for the trial of the case on grounds of fairness, cost and efficiency. Suppose that a defendant applied for a stay of proceedings in the rendering state on the basis of *forum non conveniens*, but the court there rejected the application and proceeded to determine the case on the merits. Even though the enforcing state may have a similar basis as the rendering court for asserting direct jurisdiction over the case (that is, if the action had been brought before the enforcing court in the first instance), could the defendant still submit in enforcement proceedings that there was a lack of indirect jurisdiction because the rendering court ought to have declined jurisdiction on the ground of *forum non conveniens*? If there is scope for such a challenge to indirect jurisdiction in proceedings for recognition and enforcement, what principles should an enforcing court apply in deciding the challenge?

[23] See Brand (n 20) 22.

[24] See Brand (n 20) 23.

[25] As the Indonesian chapter here highlights, Indonesia does not recognise foreign judgments, but at best may treat them as presumptive evidence of a party's rights in domestic proceedings.

It remains to be seen whether ground (d) will be adopted by the Diplomatic Council of the Hague Conference later this year.[26] If a country were to adopt the mirror principle in ground (d), it would mean that a common law court which can claim direct jurisdiction over a third party as a 'proper or necessary' party to ongoing litigation, would be obliged to find indirect jurisdiction in respect of a judgment rendered by a foreign court against a third party on a similar basis.

D. Grounds for Refusal

The four grounds for refusal identified as common elements in the three Hague documents are: (1) lacked of indirect jurisdiction; (2) denial of due process (including procedural fraud in the obtaining of the judgment); (3) incompatibility with public policy; and (4) the existence of prior *res judicata*.

Indirect jurisdiction has already been considered. As for due process, one test that emerges from a consideration of the 1971 and 2005 Hague Conventions and the 2018 Draft is that a defendant must have had a fair or reasonable opportunity to present its case before the rendering court. That will usually at least entail receiving proper notice of the proceedings before the rendering court in accordance with the procedural rules of that court. But clearly there is more to the due process requirement. For instance, where a judgment was obtained by fraud, then plainly there would be a lack of due process. It should be noted, however, that the focus is on fraud in the obtaining of the judgment, that is, extrinsic fraud. The due process ground should not be a pretext for reviewing the substantive merits of a case under the guise of investigating whether (say), contrary to the rendering court's findings, a plaintiff fraudulently induced a defendant to enter into a contract. The three Hague documents are adamant that the enforcing court is bound by the findings of the rendering court and there should be no review of the substantive merits of a case. A difficulty is that, apart from the situations of fraud and a lack of sufficient notice pursuant to the procedural rules of the originating state, judges in different countries may have differing views on what does or does not constitute due process. Indeed, different persons may reasonably disagree with one another over whether due process has been followed in a given situation. It is suggested that, unless there has been an egregious failing by the rendering court to afford a defendant with an opportunity to be heard, enforcing courts should refrain from finding a lack of due process and refusing recognition on that basis. If the question is merely one over which different judges might reasonably differ as to whether there has been due process, then that is not a situation where an enforcing court should find a lack of due process calling for the refusal of recognition.[27]

[26] Professor Brand (n 20) 33 also proposes a mechanism similar to that in Art 21 of the 1971 Hague Convention to address what he calls the problem of 'mutual trust'. He observes, in this connection, that 'countries may be hesitant to ratify a judgments convention which allows any other country to join and automatically receive reciprocal benefits'. He suggests that it may consequently be beneficial for the Hague Conference to put forward alternative Conventions for states to choose between, one along the lines of the current 2018 Draft and the other along the lines of his proposal of four grounds of indirect jurisdiction and a bilateral mechanism similar to that of Art 20 in the 1971 Hague Convention.

[27] For a discussion of due process and its abuse in the context of international commercial arbitration, see Lucy Reed, 'Ab(use) of Due Process: Sword vs Shield' (2017) 33(3) *Arbitration International* 361. It is submitted that Professor Reed's observations are equally pertinent to the recognition and enforcement of commercial judgments.

The public policy ground may be invoked where, for instance, the mandatory law of an enforcing state confers exclusive jurisdiction on the courts of tribunals of the state in a particular matter or requires that such matter be determined in a way contrary to the decision reached by the originating court. But situations of exclusive jurisdiction or overriding legislation just described are less likely to arise in purely commercial matters where the principle of party autonomy should normally prevail and parties be left free to agree the forum for the resolution of their dispute and the governing law to be applied to the same. Otherwise, it is submitted that the public policy ground should as a general principle only be invoked where recognition and enforcement of a foreign judgment would be repugnant to the fundamental legal, social, cultural, or religious norms of an enforcing state. This would assimilate the public policy ground for refusal in the case of judgments with the public policy ground for refusal in the case of foreign arbitral awards under the 1958 New York Convention. There does not seem to be a good reason why the scope of the public policy ground should differ when it comes to the treatment of foreign judgments and foreign arbitral awards in commercial matters. This means that not every mistake in the application by a foreign court of the law of the enforcing state or every failure of a foreign court to apply such law should qualify as a reason for invoking the public policy ground to refuse recognition and enforcement. Any court, even the courts of an originating state, may apply its law wrongly at first instance or on appeal or fail to apply its law at all in a situation where application is required. But it is not every situation where a court does so that enforcement of the resulting decision would be repugnant to the fundamental norms of the relevant state. Provided that there has been due process and a court has acted in good faith (as opposed to fraudulently), the possibility of any court getting the facts or law wrong is simply part of the litigation risk implicit in any commercial dispute. Mere error in the law by an originating state should not operate as a pretext for an enforcing court to review the merits of a judgment or refuse recognition and enforcement.

A difficulty is that the law of a country may not have a concept of 'public policy'. Thus, the law of such country might, instead of referring to a matter being 'contrary to public policy' prefer the use of an expression such as 'contrary to the fundamental principles' of that country's laws. 'Public policy' is treated as equivalent to the 'fundamental principles' of the country's laws. Vietnam (as can be seen from its chapter in this book) is an example of such a state. In that situation, it may be tempting for the court of such country to treat any mistake in the application of its laws by a rendering court as contrary to 'public policy'. The reasoning would be that, since all principles of a country's laws must in a sense be 'fundamental', a mistake in the application of any of the country's laws must be 'contrary to the fundamental principles' of the country's laws. It is submitted that this would be too broad a view to take of the 'public policy' ground for refusing recognition, especially in a commercial matter. For the reasons set out previously in relation to mistake of law, it is suggested that there should only be a refusal to recognise a foreign judgment when to do so would be repugnant to the social order or fabric of a state.

There may be utility in distinguishing, at least for the purposes of analysis, between international and domestic public policy. International public policy refers to ensuring that due process has been observed in the obtaining of a judgment in the enforcing state. It largely goes to procedure and has been discussed above as a separate ground for refusal.

On the other hand, domestic public policy involves those situations where recognition of a foreign judgment would be repugnant because the substance of a judgment or its effect are objectionable and run against the grain of a state's fundamental legal, social, cultural or religious norms. For instance, recognition may have the effect of sanctioning a violation of substantive human rights which the originating state is committed to upholding. In such circumstance, given genuine and serious concerns of domestic policy, it may be that exceptionally an originating court is entitled to review the substantive merits of a decision.

Res judicata also makes sense as a ground for refusing recognition. If a previous judgment by the court in the enforcing state has already dealt with the same issues as between the same parties, it would be in the public interest for there to be an end to litigation.[28] If the outcome of a foreign judgment is the same as that previously made by the court of the enforcing state, there would be no point to recognising the foreign judgment. If the foreign judgment is not the same, recognition would lead to contradictory enforceable decisions. That would be highly undesirable. Similarly, if there previously was a decision between the same parties on the same matter in some state and the court of the enforcing state was bound to recognise that prior judgment, recognition of a later contradictory decision made in some other state could lead to the situation of incompatible judgments being potentially enforceable in a state.

The 1971 Hague Convention suggests that a foreign judgment should not be recognised if it is between the same parties and on the same matter as a pending case commenced in an enforcing state before the proceedings giving rise to the foreign judgment. But this situation is not straightforward. On the one hand, it would be a waste of time and resources for the identical action to be litigated in two different places. But there may be a problem where there is a jurisdiction gap between two states, X and Y. Consider the case where the court of State X accepts only limited grounds of indirect jurisdiction, but invokes a plethora of grounds of direct jurisdiction in relation to actions before it. Suppose further that the judiciary of State X has a reputation of taking years to resolve cases. In such case, there may be a race among the parties to establish jurisdiction in the state most favourable to them. The plaintiff will want to establish its claim in State Y which has the reputation of providing speedy decisions. The defendant will have an interest in commencing proceedings in State X, typically artificially creating a cause of action by seeking a declaration of non-liability to the plaintiff (that is, a negative declaration). The defendant's action in State X would consequently be a 'torpedo' action, calculated to postpone the day when the defendant will have to honour any contractual commitment to the plaintiff. If the earlier commencement of proceedings in an enforcing state is to be a ground for the refusal of

[28] There are at least two types of *res judicata*. There is cause of action *res judicata* where parties are estopped from re-litigating a matter because their rights and obligations towards each other have been finally and conclusively determined as between them in a judgment. But there can also be *res judicata* on a discrete issue (also known as issue estoppel). Where an issue has been finally and conclusively determined in a prior judgment, a court subsequently hearing a different dispute in which the same issue arises may have to decide whether or not it will recognise the previous court's finding on the issue as binding for the purposes of determining the dispute before it.

recognition, safeguards (such as the ground not being applicable where the action in the enforcing state is only seeking a negative declaration) will have to be put in place to prevent abuse.

E. Reciprocity[29]

It will be seen from the succeeding jurisdiction chapters that a number of Asian countries require evidence of reciprocity, before they will enforce a judgment from another state. Such evidence is to establish that an originating state accords reciprocal treatment to an enforcing state, such that the former will enforce the judgments of the latter. One way to establish reciprocity would therefore be to point to a bilateral treaty or multilateral convention to which the originating and enforcing states are party, whereby the courts of one are bound to recognise and enforce the judgments of the other in defined circumstances. Where there is no such instrument, it may be possible to establish reciprocity by pointing to (1) a past case where the court of the originating state recognised the decision of the enforcing state or (2) to a provision in the law of the originating state that would have the effect of leading to the recognition by the originating state of the enforcing state's judgments. Sometimes the absence of reciprocity is shown by pointing to a past case where the court of the originating state has refused recognition of an enforcing state's judgment. It may sometimes also be argued that, in the absence of any reported past case wherein a court of the originating state has recognised the judgment of an enforcing state, there is no evidence of reciprocity. But these last two approaches are of questionable validity, insofar as they are used to demonstrate a lack of reciprocity. On the first approach, as we have seen, courts may refuse recognition on a variety of internationally accepted grounds: lack of finality, absence of indirect jurisdiction, failure to observe due process or incompatibility with public policy. The mere fact that a state has previously refused recognition of a state's judgment, cannot therefore establish an absence of reciprocity without more. Where in the past an originating state has explicitly refused recognition of an enforcing state's judgment on the basis of a lack of reciprocity, that does not mean that over time the position has remained the same. There may be only a few reported cases in a given country dealing with the recognition and enforcement of judgments generally, let alone cases dealing with the recognition and enforcement of judgments from a specific originating state. Accordingly, it is submitted that a reported case decided 10 years ago can hardly be a guide to the current position on reciprocity in a given state. The position may have evolved over time as the judiciary of a state has developed, but there simply has not been a case involving the specific enforcing state to show that views in the originating state have changed. On the second approach, the problem if both originating and enforcing state adopt the same stance on reciprocity is that one ends up in a chicken-and-egg deadlock. One country will not regard the other as according reciprocal treatment unless and until the other actually does so in a specific case. The other country adopts the same attitude. Both will be perpetually waiting for the other to make the first move.

[29] For an exhaustive discussion of reciprocity, see Béligh Elbalti, 'Reciprocity and the Recognition and Enforcement of Foreign Judgments: A Lot of Bark But Not Much Bite' (2017) 13(1) *Journal of Private International Law* 184.

It is submitted that a better approach to reciprocity, insofar as it is regarded as a pre-requisite for the recognition and enforcement of judgments, is to presume reciprocity in the absence of proof to the contrary. This is the approach advocated in the Nanning Statement of the 2nd China–ASEAN Justice Forum adopted on 8 June 2017.[30]

But should reciprocity even be a requirement? Superficially, a condition of reciprocity may seem attractive: Why should I recognise your judgments, if you do not recognise mine? Looked at more closely, the requirement might be better characterised as retaliatory in nature. It does not make logical sense in this global day and age to refuse recognition, not because of anything wrong about a judgment, but because of a failure between the originating and enforcing states to achieve agreement on reciprocal treatment. As will be seen from the chapter on the Philippines, it is possible to dispense with reciprocity as a requirement altogether and abide instead by a principle of comity. Comity means that the judgments of a sovereign state should be accorded due respect so that, subject to meeting requirements of finality, due process, indirect jurisdiction and compatibility with public policy, judgments should be recognised and enforced as a matter of course.

Possibly as a result of the 1958 New York Convention in relation to the recognition and enforcement of foreign arbitral awards,[31] we have grown accustomed to thinking that recognition and enforcement requires a treaty or convention or at least evidence of reciprocal treatment. But, in contrast to a judgment, an arbitral award is merely a piece of paper. In the absence of a treaty or convention such as the 1958 New York Convention, it is not apparent why one state should treat an award as having any effect at all across borders. A judgment is not a mere piece of paper. It is the manifestation of an official act of the judicial arm of a sovereign state. As such, pursuant to the doctrine of comity, it should be treated

[30] See Art VII of the Statement:

> Regional cross-border transactions and investments require a judicial safeguard based on appropriate mutual recognition and enforcement of judicial judgments among countries in the region. Subject to their domestic laws, Supreme Courts of participating countries will keep good faith in interpreting domestic laws, try to avoid unnecessary parallel proceedings, and consider facilitating the appropriate mutual recognition and enforcement of civil or commercial judgments among different jurisdictions. If two countries have not been bound by any international treaty on mutual recognition and enforcement of foreign civil or commercial judgments, both countries may, subject to their domestic laws, presume the existence of their reciprocal relationship, when it comes to the judicial procedure of recognizing or enforcing such judgments made by courts of the other country, provided that the courts of the other country had not refused to recognize or enforce such judgments on the ground of lack of reciprocity.

The Statement reflects a consensus reached among attendees. Participants in the Forum included Chief Justice Zhou Qiang of the Supreme People's Court of China, Vice-President You Ottara of the Supreme Court of Cambodia, Deputy Chief Justice Takdir Rahmadi of the Supreme Court of Indonesia, President Khamphane Sitthidampha the People's Supreme Court of Laos; Chief Judge Tan Sri Richard Malanjum of the High Court of Sabah and Sarawak and Justice of the Federal Court of Malaysia, Chief Justice Htun Htun Oo of the Union of Myanmar; Justice Andres B Reyes Jr of the Court of Appeal of the Philippines, Justice Steven Chong of the Court of Appeal of the Supreme Court of Singapore, President Veerapol Tungsuwan of the Supreme Court of Thailand, Deputy Chief Justice Nguyen Van Thuan of the Supreme People's Court of Viet Nam, Deputy ASEAN Secretary-General AKP Mochtan, Chief Justice Sayed Yousuf Halem of Afghanistan, Justice Hasan Foez Siddique of the Appellate Division of the Supreme Court of Bangladesh, Justice Hari Krishna Karki of Nepal, Chief Justice Main Saqib Nisar of Pakistan, and Chief Justice Wewage Priyasath Gerad of Sri Lanka. The text is available online: www.chinajusticeobserver.com/nanning-statement-of-the-2nd-china-asean-justice-forum.

[31] The 1958 New York Convention, which as at 1 March 2019 had 159 parties, is one of the most successful international instruments ever.

with due respect by all sovereign states enjoying good relations with the originating state.[32] In those premises, there would not be a need to resort to reciprocity as a pre-condition to recognition. In conferences on the 2005 Hague Convention that the author has attended, the concern has been expressed that a liberalised regime for the recognition and enforcement of commercial judgments such as that envisaged by the 2005 Hague Convention would constitute an encroachment on a country's sovereignty. However, it is unclear why this should be so. Given a principle of comity, foreign judgments should in the ordinary course of events be treated with deference and recognised. If there is something about a foreign judgment that is contrary to an enforcing states' public policy, that state has the discretion to refuse recognition in the public interest. Since the state retains ultimate control over whether to recognise and enforce a judgment in the public interest, it is difficult to understand why in practical terms basing a regime for the recognition and enforcement of judgments on comity should be regarded as tantamount to a surrender of sovereignty.

F. Procedures

The three Hague instruments set out simple procedures for the recognition and enforcement of judgments within their scope (requiring, for example, a minimum number of documents and dispensing with any need for legalisation).

In broad terms, countries may adopt three basic procedures. First, in particular where a country has entered into a treaty or convention with another country,[33] there may be a system of registration before a court or competent authority in the enforcing state, as a result of which a foreign judgment is made enforceable in the same way as a domestic judgment. The relevant court or competent authority simply checks that the conditions for recognition and enforcement mentioned in a treaty, convention or code of civil procedure have been met. This procedure is intended to be speedy and inexpensive. Second, a plaintiff may bring an action in the originating state based on the debt to which the judgment gives rise. This route is usually available in many common law states. The plaintiff sues the judgment debtor in domestic proceedings in debt claiming the amount due and owing under the foreign judgment. This procedure is then combined with an application for summary judgment[34] on the basis that there is no defence against the claim based on the foreign judgment. The enforcing court simply considers whether the foreign judgment should be recognised applying similar criteria to those discussed above (finality, indirect jurisdiction, due process and compatibility with public policy). Upon recognition, the foreign judgment constitutes a *res judicata* and the defendant in the domestic proceedings is not entitled to look behind the findings of the foreign judgment and re-litigate the issues previously

[32] For a historical study of comity as a principle of private international law, see Joel R Paul, 'The Transformation of International Comity' (2008) 71 *Law and Contemporary Problems* 19, available online: scholarship.law.duke.edu/cgi/viewcontent.cgi?article=1477&context=lcp.

[33] Typically, where there is a treaty or convention between two states, legislation in an enforcing state will provide that the registration procedure must be used for the recognition and enforcement of a judgment by the court of a party to the treaty or convention.

[34] The summary judgment procedure means that there will be no full-blown trial where live witnesses are heard and their evidence is tested by cross-examination. See, for example, in Hong Kong, the summary judgment procedure in RHC Ord 14.

ventilated in the originating state. Given the possibility of a resort to a summary judgment procedure, this method of enforcement may be as speedy and cost-effective as the registration procedure. Third, a plaintiff starts fresh proceedings in the enforcing state against the defendant and uses the foreign judgment as evidence in support of the plaintiff's claim. This is not as effective as the second method because it is open to the defendant to contest the correctness of the foreign judgment, not just in terms of the criteria discussed above, but also substantively. In effect, this third approach can give rise to a complete re-hearing of the matters decided by the originating court.

It is submitted that only the first and second approaches described above qualify as appropriate procedures for the recognition and enforcement of judgments. The third method is not genuinely one for the recognition and enforcement of a foreign judgment, because it permits the originating court's judgment to be re-opened and re-argued. The third method does not address the underlying principle that there should be an end to disputes and a party should not be compelled to re-litigate that which has already been decided. The third method also has a high risk of resulting in different outcomes in different states.

IV. Summary

A minimal no-frills, but workable system for the recognition and enforcement of judgments would at least have the following features:

1. Application to judgments of a general civil and commercial nature, 'commercial' being broadly defined along the lines in footnote 2 to Article 1(1) of the UNCITRAL Model Law on International Commercial Arbitration.
2. A requirement that to be recognised a judgment must be final and conclusive. The judgment must at least be one for the payment of money. It may also be a good idea to provide for the recognition of judgments dismissing a plaintiff's claim. The judgment must be enforceable and effective in the originating state.
3. At least the following as grounds of indirect jurisdiction:
    - (a) The state in which the rendering court is situated was the habitual residence of the defendant at the start of the foreign proceedings.
    - (b) The state in which the rendering court is situated is the place where the defendant had a principal place of business or an establishment, branch or agency at the start of the foreign proceedings, provided that such place of business, establishment, branch or agency was closely connected to the claim.
    - (c) The defendant submitted to the court's jurisdiction:
        - (i) by express agreement,
        - (ii) by defending the claim on the merits without challenging jurisdiction, or
        - (iii) by invoking the court's jurisdiction by bringing a counterclaim related to the claim.
    - (d) The claim concerns title to immovable property located within the state of the rendering court.
    - (e) The claim concerns a non-contractual obligation and the act that gave rise to the damage (death, personal injury, damage to property) occurred in the state of the rendering court.

Additionally, consideration should be given to a ground of indirect jurisdiction based on the mirror principle as advocated by Professor Brand.[35]

4. A requirement that to be recognised (a) a judgment should not have been obtained by fraud and (b) due process must have been observed in obtaining the judgment, in that the defendant had sufficient notice of the proceedings in accordance with the laws of the enforcing state, as well as a reasonable opportunity to defend itself against the plaintiff's claim.
5. The following grounds for refusal of recognition and enforcement:

   (a) lack of indirect jurisdiction;
   (b) denial of due process (including procedural fraud in the obtaining of the judgment);
   (c) incompatibility with public policy; and
   (d) the existence of prior *res judicata*.

   Apart from an evaluation whether or not the foregoing grounds of refusal have or have not been made out, there should be no review of the substantive merits of a foreign judgment. Where a foreign judgment is severable, it may be recognised and enforced only in part, if the remainder falls foul of one or other ground of refusal.
6. As an optional requirement, evidence of reciprocal treatment between the originating and enforcing states, with reciprocity being presumed in the absence of evidence to the contrary. However, consideration might be given to simply applying a principle of comity, rather than reciprocity.
7. A simple, cost-effective recognition and enforcement procedure whereby a foreign judgment is recognised following (a) a registration procedure or (b) summary proceedings in a domestic action commenced in the enforcing state by the plaintiff against the defendant on the basis of the debt arising from the foreign judgment.

[35] See Brand (n 20).

2

China

WEIXIA GU*

I. Introduction

The unparalleled economic growth of the People's Republic of China has resulted in a paradigm shift in its legal regime. Once a closed market to the world, China now faces an unprecedented surge of international business and movement of global capital into its domestic market in light of its immense economic growth in the past 40 years. As a result of this growth, the internationalism of business in China requires the domestic courts to accommodate private international law practices such as allowing foreign judgments to be recognised and enforced in the domestic courts: a clear indicator of globalisation[1] and the development of China's economy.

An important step China has taken in the past few years is to improve efficiency in recognising and enforcing foreign judgments. Specifically, the salient shift to a more liberal application of the reciprocity principle, the signing of the 2005 Hague Choice of Court Convention (2005 Hague Convention) and the growing number of bilateral treaties on judicial assistance are clear indicators of China's recent willingness to improve commercial certainty for the parties involved, to promote fairness for both domestic and foreign litigants, and to ensure the global movement of judgments, resulting in increased investor confidence and further economic growth in China.

This chapter will analyse current theory and practice with respect to the recognition and enforcement of foreign civil and commercial judgments in China.[2] There are three regimes that will be analysed: (1) the existing Sino-bilateral judicial assistance treaties on civil and commercial matters; (2) in the absence of a bilateral treaty, the application by the Chinese courts of the principle of 'reciprocity' while taking account of procedural and substantive concerns specific to China; and (3) the potential impact of the 2005 Hague Convention signed by the Chinese government in September 2017.

* Research for this chapter has been supported by Hong Kong Government Research Grants Council General Research Fund (Project Numbers: HKU 17617416 and 17602218). Edward Chin is acknowledged for his research assistance.

[1] Wenliang Zhang, 'Sino-Foreign Recognition and Enforcement of Judgments: A Promising "Follow-Suit" Model?' (2017) 16 *Chinese Journal of International Law* 515, 515.

[2] This does not include Special Administrative Regions (SARs) such as Hong Kong and Macau, which have a different legal tradition. This chapter will restrict itself to a discussion of laws relating to the Chinese mainland without any reference to any of the SARs.

II. Background

A. Promotion of Economic Prosperity

In 2018 China celebrated the 40th anniversary of reform and opening-up. China's economic growth over the past 40 years has been impressive. China, a unitary state with the second largest economy in the world, has a civil law system which integrates socialist values and communist principles. Once a closed society and market, it now engages in many billions of dollars' worth of trade per year. Data from the World Bank showed that China's GDP per capita was US$7,077.77 in 2013 and grew to US$8,826.99 in 2017.[3] It is not surprising that China has become one of the world's fastest and largest emerging markets, with manufacturing, services and agriculture as the main industries fuelling the Chinese economy.

An increase in international trade and economic prosperity will inevitably lead to disputes. The free flow of judgments between China and the rest of the world will ensure commercial certainty and predictability in cross-border business and trade. More importantly, this will ensure any Chinese-led initiatives will be viewed favourably due to China's commitment to ensuring that international litigation will be dealt with fairly and justly.

This is especially important as China engages in the Belt and Road Initiative (BRI), in which China has invested billions of dollars in infrastructure projects throughout Eurasia.[4] The purpose of the BRI is as much promoting economic integration between China and Eurasia as counterbalancing China's diplomatic relations with the United States.[5] From China's perspective, the best way forward is continued economic growth and development achieved through stronger economic ties with Asia and Europe. To attain this China-led economic prosperity, China must ensure the smooth functioning of international trade and development, including inevitably its ability to deal with foreign judgments.

B. Development of Private International Law in China

A brief historic review of the development of private international law in China can be divided into three phases: first, pre-1978; second, from 1978 to China's accession to the WTO in 2001; and third, from 2001 onwards.

i. Pre-1978

Chinese scholars have argued that private international law rules have existed since the seventh century, ie the Tang Dynasty, where international trade existed between China

[3] The World Bank, 'GDP Per Capital (Current US$)' (*The World Bank*), available online: data.worldbank.org/indicator/NY.GDP.PCAP.CD?locations=CN.

[4] This initiative focuses on two routes: one by land and one by sea. These routes connect China, Russia, India, several European countries and other south Asian countries. The BRI also led to the formation of the Asian Infrastructure Investment Bank, a multilateral financial institution created to address the financial needs of this initiative. The way forward is to ensure a robust set of laws and rule governing how China will interact with the rest of the world.

[5] Peter Ferdinand, 'Westward Ho – The China Dream and "One Belt, One Road": Chinese Foreign Policy Under Xi Jinping' (2016) 92(4) *International Affairs* 941.

and East Asia. The Tang Code (primary legislation of the Tang Dynasty) illustrated China's early attempt to codify rules to govern cross-border trade relationships with foreign parties. However, subsequent dynasties, such as the Ming and Qing Dynasties, pursued a closed-door policy towards global trade, adopting the principle of 'strict territoriality' where all cases, regardless of their foreign elements, were decided according to Chinese law at that time.[6]

After the fall of the Qing Dynasty, the Republic of China (ROC) was established in 1911. In the same year, the law known as the Act on Application of Foreign Law was promulgated. This new law was inspired by the then Japanese private international law regime (known as the *Hōrei*) and was considered to be one of the most comprehensive regimes at that time.[7] But Japanese legal norms were found to be incompatible with the then Chinese society,[8] so that the Act was rarely applied in practice.[9] Some socio-political issues were also noted during this period. The new ROC was weak and the transition from its imperial past to Asia's first republic created much difficulty. Internally, China was in a state of uncertainty, facing political tensions within its inner political circle, namely, the Nationalist Party (*Kuomintang*) and the Communist Party. Externally, China had to deal with unequal treaties signed during China's imperial time with respect to foreign powers. Leading scholars from the ROC legacy, such as Professor Ma Han Bao (Herbert Ma), stated that the adoption of the law was more of symbolic significance rather than having actual impact in China or improving its foreign trade and policy.[10] In 1949, after many years of civil war, the People's Republic of China replaced the ROC in mainland China. All previous laws, including the Act on Application of Foreign Law, were abrogated. Between 1968 and 1978, the Cultural Revolution created further uncertainty in the law. Anti-foreign and anti-western sentiment dominated most of this period and led to a dismantling of the then legal structure.

ii. From 1978 to 2001

It was not until 1978, when the Cultural Revolution ended, that China reintroduced private international law back into its legislative agenda. The General Principles of Civil Law (GPCL) was enacted in 1986. It contained nine provisions on private international law.[11] However, the GPCL did not address the overwhelming need for more rules in the field. Moreover, foreign-related procedures and international judicial cooperation, such as recognition and enforcement of foreign judgments, were largely left unregulated.[12] The founder of private international law study in China post-1978, Professor Han Depei at

[6] Jin Huang, *Guoji Sifa [Private International Law]* (Beijing, Beijing Law Press, 2005) 165.

[7] Zhengxin Huo, *Guoji Sifa [Private International Law]* 2nd edn (Beijing, Foreign Trade University Press, 2015) 78; Qingjun Xu, 'The Codification of Conflicts of Laws in China: A Long Way to Go' (2017) 65(4) *The American Journal of Comparative Law* 919, 926.

[8] Juan Shen, *Guoji Sifa [Private International Law]* (Beijing, China Social Science Press, 2006) 43; Guangjian Tu, *Private International Law in China* (Singapore, Springer, 2016) 1.

[9] Yicheng Ruan, 'Zhongguo Guoji Sifa Zhidu De Jianli' [The Establishment of the Chinese Private International Law System] in Hanbao Ma (ed), *Guoji Sifa Lunwen Xuanji* (Taipei, Wu-nan Book, 1984).

[10] Hanbao Ma, *Guoji Sifa: Zhonglun Gelun* 3rd edn (Taipei, San Min, 2014) 24.

[11] Xu (n 7) 927.

[12] Zheng Sophia Tang, Yongping Xiao and Zhengxin Huo, *Conflict of Laws in the People's Republic of China* (Cheltenham, Edward Elgar, 2010) 12.

Wuhan University, argued that the pre-2010 regime had some major defects.[13] First, statutes in this area were incomplete. Second, laws and rules were out of date. Third, there were inconsistencies among regulations. Fourth, the regime lacked a consistent legislative framework.[14] But Chinese government officials at the time viewed a lack of private international law rules as beneficial to governance, due to a prevailing mistrust of international trade and foreign parties.[15]

iii. Post-2001

In the face of strong dissent, economic development in China paved the way for further development of private international law in China during this period. China's accession to the WTO in 2001 was a turning point when the authorities recognised that the GPCL's private international law rules could not meet new conditions and there was a need for additional laws to regulate foreign civil relations.[16] This led to the drafting of a comprehensive code devoted to the conflict of laws.[17] On 28 October 2010, the first Chinese statute on private international law was adopted. Officially known as the Law on the Application of Laws over Foreign-related Civil Relation (the '2010 Law'), it contained 52 provisions on the governing law in different civil relations having foreign elements (more specifically known as 'applicable law' rules). Although there were still deficiencies, the 2010 Law created a basic framework for conflict of laws rules in China. It was an important step towards ensuring that China met its obligation under the WTO and ensured a measure of certainty in the law applicable to foreign relations. China's most prominent private international law scholar today, Professor Huang Jin at China University of Political Science and Law, commented that this was 'the climax of modernising the Chinese conflicts system'.[18]

C. Sources of Private International Law

i. The 2010 Conflict of Laws Code and the 2012 Judicial Interpretation

The 2010 Law has become the major source of private international law in China. It covers, inter alia, applicable law rules with respect to cross-border marriage, succession, contract, property and intellectual property. There are other laws containing applicable law rules, which remain in force. These include the 1992 Maritime Law, the 1995 Negotiable Instruments Law, and the 1995 Civil Aviation Law. They work in tandem with the 2010 Law.

[13] Depei Han, *Guoji Sifa [Private International Law]* (Beijing, China Higher Education Press, 2000).

[14] ibid, 17.

[15] Tung-Pi Chen, 'Private International Law of the People's Republic of China: An Overview' 35(3) *American Journal of Comparative Law* (1987) 445, 446.

[16] Jie (Jeanne) Huang, 'The Partially Modernized Chinese Conflicts System: Achievements and Challenges – Review of Zheng Sophia Tang, Yongping Xiao, and Zhengxin Huo, Conflict of Laws in the People's Republic of China' (2017) 13(3) *Journal of Private International Law* 633, 634. See also Lutz-Christian Wolff, 'China's Private International Investment Law: One-Way Street into PRC Law?' (2008) 56 *American Journal of Comparative Law* 1039, 1045.

[17] Xu (n 7) 929.

[18] ibid.

In 2012 the Supreme People's Court (SPC) issued a judicial interpretation on the 2010 Law (the '2012 Interpretation'). The 2012 Interpretation, consisting of 21 provisions, had two primary goals.[19] First, it clarified existing rules to facilitate implementation in actual judicial practice. Second, it provided additional rules that were discussed during the drafting of the 2010 Law but were not implemented in the 2010 Law.[20] Leading Chinese private international law scholars, such as Huang, have emphasised that the modernisation of China's private international law is not only for pragmatic ends;[21] but is more for the protection of the national judicial sovereignty.[22] This is illustrated by Article 10 of the 2012 Interpretation in which certain matters are precluded from contractual agreements such as those relating to antitrust and financial securities. Although the 2010 Law has significantly changed the regulatory landscape of applicable laws in China, not all commentators are convinced that it is a finished product.[23] Scholars such as Tang, Xiao and Huo have argued that complete modernisation can only occur when three policy changes are made.[24] First, China's policy should move from a sovereignty-oriented to an efficiency-oriented approach. Second, there should be an elimination of local protectionism in adjudication and legislation involving conflict of laws issues. Finally, there needs to be a balance of interest between internationalism and nationalism.[25]

ii. The 2012 Civil Procedure Law and the 2015 Judicial Interpretation

China's Civil Procedure Law (CPL) has become another important source of the private international law landscape, particularly with respect to procedural matters with a foreign element, such as the recognition and enforcement of foreign judgments. The CPL was first promulgated in 1991 and its most recent comprehensive amendment was introduced in 2012.

The statutory basis for the recognition and enforcement of foreign judgments is contained in Articles 281 and 282 of the 2012 CPL. Article 281 states that a party who seeks to have a foreign judgment recognised and enforced in China can apply to the Intermediate People's Court where the judgment debtor is domiciled or the property to be enforced against is located. Alternatively, the foreign court can request the relevant Chinese court to recognise and enforce the judgment.[26] On the other hand, the law also allows domestic Chinese parties, either by themselves or through the Chinese court, to apply to foreign courts for the recognition and enforcement of Chinese judgments in that foreign jurisdiction.[27] Article 282 further states that, subject to the court and Chinese national, social and public interest, the relevant Chinese court will recognise and enforce a legally effective judgment from a foreign country, either on the basis of (1) an international treaty or convention

[19] Huang (n 16) 635.
[20] ibid.
[21] Tang, Xiao and Huo (n 12) 400.
[22] ibid. See also Huang (n 16) 635.
[23] Tang, Xiao and Huo (n 12) 400.
[24] ibid, 403–04.
[25] ibid.
[26] CPL, Art 281.
[27] CPL, Art 280.

concluded with or acceded to by China or (2) the principle of reciprocity. Where either criterion is met, the Chinese court will recognise and enforce a foreign judgment.[28] In terms of limitation, the 2015 SPC Interpretation of the 2012 CPL (the '2015 Interpretation') sets a period of two years.[29] The time limit for the enforcement application will be calculated from the date when a People's Court recognises a foreign judgment.[30] Although Articles 281 and 282 of the CPL provide the basis of recognition and enforcement, Chinese courts are not always consistent in their application. For example, in *Hou Yijun v Hou Kelis*, the Henan Zhengzhou Intermediate People's Court applied Articles 281 and 282, but ignored a China-Romania Treaty concluded in 1991.[31] This has led some commentators to doubt the pragmatism of the CPL regime. In some instances, it has been considered challenging and unpredictable.[32]

In addition, pursuant to Article 533 of the 2015 Interpretation, there is some guidance as to when the Chinese court should refuse to recognise and enforce a foreign judgment. This will be discussed below.

D. Basic Overview of Court System

The Chinese court system consists of four levels. That is, from top to bottom: the SPC, the provincial-level High People's Court, the city-level Intermediate People's Court, and the district-level Basic People's Court. In most domestic cases, the Basic People's Court is the court of first instance for most disputes. However, important cases with a foreign element usually go to the Intermediate People's Court.[33] This does not exclude the Basic People's Court from hearing less complex foreign-related cases.

Each Chinese court is divided into a number of different chambers. Each chamber has a different function. The most important chamber with respect to the recognition and enforcement of foreign judgment is Civil Division Number 4. Civil Division Number 4 (*min si ting*) specialises in cases with foreign elements.[34]

In terms of what constitutes a foreign element in China, five scenarios have been laid down in Article 1 of the 2012 Interpretation. The first is where one or both parties are non-Chinese nationals, stateless persons, or foreign enterprises or organisations. The second is where a relevant individual's or company's habitual residence is not in China. The third is where the subject matter of a dispute is located outside China. The fourth is where the facts that have caused the formation, alteration or termination of a legal relationship occur outside China. The fifth covers any other situations that may be considered as having a

[28] CPL, Art 282.

[29] The Interpretation of the Supreme People's Court on the Application of the Civil Procedure Law of the People's Republic of China, adopted at the 36th session of the Judicial Committee of the Supreme People's Court on 18 December 2014 (the 2015 Interpretation), is promulgated for implementation on 4 February 2015.

[30] 2015 Interpretation, Art 547.

[31] See Tang, Xiao and Huo (n 12) 148, fn 29.

[32] Peter Yuen and John Choong, 'The Enforcement of Domestic and Foreign Court Judgments in the PRC' in Michael J Moser (ed), *Dispute Resolution in China* (New York, JurisNet, 2012) 381.

[33] 2015 Interpretation, Art 1.

[34] Weixia Gu, 'Courts in China: Judiciary in the Economic and Societal Transition' in Jiunn-Rong Yeh and Wen-Chen Chang (eds), *Asian Courts in Context* (Cambridge, Cambridge University Press, 2014) 491.

foreign element.[35] Chinese jurisprudence treats cases relating to Hong Kong, Macau and Taiwan as cases having a foreign element.

The SPC, apart from assuming the role of apex court, can also provide guidance to lower level courts, such as by issuing judicial interpretations on the application of certain laws. All forms of SPC interpretations are legally binding. Although Chinese courts do not adopt the common law principle of precedent, cases decided by the SPC and provincial high courts (particularly of economically developed regions) are regarded as highly persuasive.

E. Civil and Commercial Matters

In the past, China did not distinguish between its various branches of laws. Civil and commercial matters did not come into the forefront of discussion until just a few decades ago.[36] Chinese legislation, such as the CPL, does not define civil or commercial matters. However, Article 3 of the CPL discusses the scope of civil actions. It states that the CPL '[applies] to civil actions accepted by a People's Court regarding property or personal relationships between citizens, legal persons, and other organizations',[37] noting that governmental bodies or institutions are precluded.

Commercial matters, on the other hand, are not defined or discussed in the CPL. Professor Albert Chen has argued that China's development of a socialist market economy contributed to the development of a concept of commercial law closely relating to civil law practice in China, and there is a general consensus among academics and practitioners that there has been a fusion between civil and commercial law.[38] It is for this reason that there is only a Civil Code rather than separate codes for civil and commercial matters. More specifically, the Civil Code lays a foundation for commercial matters, in which special principles are applied. For example, the Securities Law and the Company Law are both commercial law statutes, but the CPL is still applicable to both. International arbitration disputes are also categorised as commercial matters.

There has been some debate as to whether commercial matters are part of private law or whether they are part of private law but contain public law elements.[39] This is important in context of the recognition and enforcement of foreign judgments. For example, competition law matters involve both commercial law and public law considerations. Although the author has not been able to locate any cases on the recognition and enforcement of foreign competition law judgments in China, it is likely that the Chinese courts will refuse to recognise and enforce any foreign judgment with a public law element by virtue of the public policy exception, as the public law element of such foreign judgment may be viewed as subject to the exclusive power of the Chinese authorities and Chinese law (for instance, the 2008 Chinese Anti-Monopoly Law).

[35] 2012 Interpretation, Art 1.

[36] Albert Chen, *An Introduction to the Legal System of the People's Republic of China* (Hong Kong, LexisNexis, 2011) 314.

[37] CPL, Art 3.

[38] Chen (n 36) 317.

[39] Haocai Luo and Wanzhong Sun (eds), *Yushi Jujin de Zhongguo Faxue [The Developing Legal Science of China]* (Beijing, Chinese Legal System Press, 2001); Chen (n 36) 317.

III. Recognition and Enforcement under Treaties or Similar Arrangements

A. Bilateral Treaties on Recognition and Enforcement

One of the primary channels a party can apply for recognition and enforcement of a foreign judgment through is a bilateral judicial assistance treaty on judgment recognition and enforcement concluded between China and a foreign state. The procedures are typically set out in the treaty, which is binding on courts once it has been ratified by China and appropriately integrated into Chinese domestic law. Thus, once it is established that there is a relevant and effective bilateral treaty, a judgment covered by the treaty is prima facie recognisable and enforceable.

To date, China has signed 39 bilateral treaties which contain arrangements for judgment recognition and enforcement, out of which 37 have been ratified by the Chinese legislature. A full list of these treaties can be found on the Chinese Ministry of Foreign Affairs' website.[40] According to Tsang's empirical study, a sizeable number of China's trading partner countries have been negotiating or have entered into bilateral treaty arrangements with China.[41] Tsang further contends that it is likely that the bilateral treaty regime will exceed the reciprocity regime (discussed below) in importance, because each treaty is unique and may take into consideration a country's special relationship with China.[42] However, there are political, economic, legal and cultural differences that exist between China and foreign countries, which ultimately make this unlikely to happen.[43] This may explain why China has not concluded bilateral enforcement treaties with its largest trading partners, such as the United States, Germany and Japan.[44] In contrast, the majority of bilateral treaties that China has so far concluded are with developing countries. There may be several reasons for this. For example, developing countries may view China's economic growth as beneficial to their economy, whereas developed countries may view China as a major rival and formal bilateral treaties as a hindrance to future negotiations.

As at 31 December 2016, there were 2,846 enforcement cases in China, of which only one per cent were under bilateral treaties.[45] France, one of the few major trading partners in the West which has a long standing bilateral treaty with China, had only one judgment enforcement case in China at the end of 2016.[46] In terms of why bilateral treaty regimes are not as effective as should be, Tsang contends that Chinese judges may not be aware of the existence of certain bilateral treaties.[47] Even if they are aware, problems may still arise.

[40] The Ministry of Foreign Affairs, 'The Present Situation of China's Judicial Assistance and Extradition Treaties' (*Ministry of Foreign Affairs*, February 2018), available online: www.fmprc.gov.cn/web/ziliao_674904/tytj_674911/wgdwdjdsfhzty_674917/t1215630.shtml.

[41] King Fung (Dicky) Tsang, 'Chinese Bilateral Judgment Enforcement Treaties' (2017) 40(1) *Loyola of Los Angeles International and Comparative Law Review* 1, 10.

[42] ibid.

[43] ibid.

[44] Michael J Moser and Friven Yeoh, 'Arbitrating China Business Disputes' in Michael J Moser (ed), *Dispute Resolution in China* (New York, JurisNet, 2012) 4.

[45] Tsang (n 41) 10.

[46] ibid.

[47] ibid, 32.

When an enforcement action is brought, the Chinese court will have to look at a relevant treaty, the terms of which are bespoke. The outcome of similar scenarios may differ because of differences in bilateral treaties. As a result, the more bilateral treaties China enters into, the more likely that inconsistency may occur in the courts' approach. This will make judgment enforcement through the treaty regime less predictable. In the long run, the author submits that a principled approach should be preferred.

i. *Common Elements*

There are several common elements (grounds of refusal) that the Chinese courts will consider prior to recognising and enforcing a foreign judgment under a bilateral treaty (or, for that matter, on the basis of the principle of reciprocity). Generally, these elements are (1) indirect jurisdiction of the rendering court; (2) finality of the foreign judgment; (3) due process and public policy; and (4) due service of legal documents.[48]

a. Indirect Jurisdiction of the Rendering Court

A typical bilateral treaty with China provides that the court issuing the foreign judgment must be competent (the 'competence clause'). A treaty can take one or more of three approaches in this respect:

1. The treaty will expressly provide detailed jurisdictional grounds that must be satisfied.
2. The treaty may restrict recognition or enforcement to the extent that a judgment of a foreign court is deemed to infringe the exclusive jurisdiction of the Chinese court.
3. The judgment rendering state must have jurisdiction to hear the case according to the law of the enforcing state.[49]

The China–Vietnam Treaty and China–Laos Treaty adopt the first approach.[50] Article 18 of the China–Vietnam treaty is illustrative of a competence clause, setting out different scenarios in which the rendering court will be treated as having competence to hear a case.[51] The second approach concerns the direct jurisdiction of the Chinese courts. The CPL specifies three matters which are reserved to the exclusive jurisdiction of the Chinese courts: (1) disputes arising out of the immovable property in China; (2) disputes arising out of port operations in China; and (3) disputes relating to succession and inheritance where the major portion of an estate is in China.[52] The purpose of a competent jurisdiction requirement is to ensure that a state's sovereignty is taken into account when determining whether to recognise and enforce a judgment. For example, immovable property is the exclusive jurisdiction of the Chinese courts in that territorial integrity is concerned. Foreign courts will not have jurisdiction to hear such disputes, and it would be beyond their competence

[48] A good overview of these factors can be found in Yujun Guo, 'Country Report: The People's Republic of China' in Adeline Chong (ed), *Recognition and Enforcement of Foreign Judgments in Asia* (Singapore, Asian Business Law Institute, 2017) 52–55.
[49] ibid.
[50] ibid.
[51] See eg the China–Vietnam Treaty at www.npc.gov.cn/wxzl/gongbao/2001-01/03/content_5007132.htm.
[52] CPL, Art 33.

to do so. The rationale behind this is to ensure that the foreign court has jurisdiction to adjudicate a dispute without infringing upon the jurisdiction of an enforcing state (ie here, the Chinese courts). If the jurisdictional grounds are not satisfied by the rendering court, the Chinese court may refuse recognition and enforcement of the foreign judgment. In this regard, Articles 6 and 8 of the 2005 Hague Convention have created a framework. Article 6 sets out the obligations of a court which the parties have not designated as the forum in which to resolve their disputes, while Article 8 identifies formal criteria for the recognition and enforcement of a judgment by the parties' designated court.[53] In the past, difficulties in determining which court has jurisdiction have created unnecessary delays and cost and impeded the free flow of international judgments. Now, by virtue of the 2005 Hague Convention which China signed in September 2017, international standards for evaluating indirect jurisdiction have been made clear and Chinese domestic law could benefit from the same once the 2005 Hague Convention is ratified.

b. Finality of the Foreign Judgment

The judgment to be recognised and enforced must be final, conclusive and enforceable in the state that issued it. This means that there is no possible chance of re-litigation within that state or anywhere else.[54] A number of treaties have this requirement. In cases where a treaty is silent, Article 306 of the 2015 CPL Interpretation provides guidance on the matter, stating that a foreign judgment that is subject to appeal will not be recognised and enforced in China as it may be inconsistent with a later ruling in the originating jurisdiction. 'Finality' entails a conclusive determination of litigants' substantive rights and obligations. As such, interim injunctive relief granted by a foreign court are unlikely to be recognised in China.

c. Due Process and Public Policy

The Chinese courts will refuse to recognise or enforce any judgment that is contrary to China's domestic public policy, including on issues such as sovereignty, security, and social and public interest.[55] Although it is provided in the law, it is generally observed that public policy defences are rarely used in recognition and enforcement cases in China.[56] It also should be noted that public policy includes both procedural and substantive matters. A substantive matter would be the infringement or violation of morality and justice of China.[57] On the other hand, a procedural matter would be the lack of a fair hearing or lack of civil capacity among the parties. These may overlap with the 'due process' criterion.[58]

d. Proper Service of Legal Documents

Proper service of the legal document is another common element adopted by Chinese courts and judges. This element may be included in a bilateral treaty. In the absence of

[53] The 2005 Hague Convention, Arts 6, 8.
[54] Tsang (n 41) 30.
[55] CPL (2012), Arts 281 and 282.
[56] Guo (n 48) 68.
[57] Guo (n 48) 53–54.
[58] Tang, Xiao and Huo (n 12) 158.

express provision in the treaty, the relevant People's Court may apply the 1965 Hague Service Abroad Convention of which China is a party. In *Schneider Electric Industries SAS v Wenzhou Fly-Dragon Electrical Co Ltd*,[59] the Wenzhou Intermediate People's Court refused recognition and enforcement of a French judgment due to improper method of service. In that case, service of legal documents was done 'by way of post', which is prohibited under Chinese law, as well as contrary to the 1965 Hague Convention and the bilateral treaty between France and China. After surveying several leading cases, Zhang concluded that the 'due service requirement' has been the court's paramount concern, as opposed to special attention being paid to the principle of reciprocity.[60]

B. The 2005 Hague Convention

On 12 September 2017 China signed the 2005 Hague Convention on Choice of Court Agreements. So far, it has not yet come into effect in China as it has not yet been ratified. The 2005 Hague Convention and its impact on China will be discussed in detail below.

IV. Recognition and Enforcement in the Absence of Treaties or Similar Arrangements

In the absence of bilateral treaties, a foreign judgment will be recognised and enforced by applying domestic law. Tang, Xiao and Huo argue that there are three approaches to whether Chinese courts will give effect to such judgments.[61] The first approach is that the Chinese court may simply disregard the foreign judgment. The second approach (also known as the 'principle of reciprocity') is that the Chinese court may recognise a foreign judgment if the rendering court is one that has previously recognised Chinese judgments before. The third approach is that the Chinese courts may recognise the foreign judgment if it meets certain procedural and substantive standards.[62] Among the three approaches, the second approach on 'reciprocity' is the most predominant alongside that of bilateral treaties.[63] This approach can further be broken down into de facto and de jure reciprocity which will be analysed subsequently. The third approach is simply the application of the various grounds of refusal that a court can take into consideration (see section III.A.i above). This section will thus focus on the second approach. Specifically, this section will discuss the development of reciprocity in China. It will then look critically at the paradigm shift by the People's Court as to how the principle of reciprocity is to be applied as evidenced by the recent Nanning Statement in 2017, specifically how the courts are moving away from a strict application of de facto reciprocity to a more pragmatic and liberal recourse to de jure reciprocity.

[59] Zhejiang Wenzhou Intermediate People's Court Decision *Schneider Electric Industries SAS v Wenzhou Fly-Dragon Electrical Co Ltd* (2005) Wen Min San Chu Zi No 155.

[60] Wenliang Zhang, 'Recognition and Enforcement of Foreign Judgments in China: A Call for Special Attention to Both the "Due Service Requirement" and the "Principle of Reciprocity"' (2013) 12(1) *Chinese Journal of International Law* 143.

[61] Tang, Xiao and Huo (n 12).

[62] ibid, 161.

[63] Zhang (n 1) 519.

A. Recognition and Enforcement

Prior to a discussion of reciprocity, the difference between recognition and enforcement should be noted. Recognition means giving effect to a foreign court's decision. Thus, recognition will have the effect of finality (or *res judicata*), as if the foreign judgment has been converted into a decision of the domestic court. Enforcement, on the other hand, is the process of compelling a party to comply with the rights and obligations arising out of the foreign judgment.[64] In China, Chinese courts must first recognise a foreign judgment prior to enforcing the same.

i. Development of the Principle of Reciprocity

Reciprocity is the concept whereby 'the judgment rendered in a foreign country is allowed the same effect only as the courts of that country allow the judgment of the country in which the judgment in question is sought to be executed'.[65] The 2015 CPL Interpretation provides that reciprocity is a prerequisite for all foreign judgments seeking recognition and enforcement in China, except for those arising out of divorce proceedings.[66] Elbati has argued that China has one of the most restrictive reciprocity systems in the world.[67] As will be discussed below, in the absence of a bilateral treaty, the courts regularly deny the recognition of foreign judgments based on this principle.[68] The current statutory basis for the principle of reciprocity can be found in Articles 5 and 282 of the 2012 CPL. Article 5 states that '[w]here a foreign court imposes restrictions on civil litigation rights on any [Chinese citizen or organisation], China has a right to apply the principle of reciprocity to the litigant of that foreign country'. Article 282 states that '[h]aving received an application or a request for recognition and enforcement of a legally effective judgment or ruling of a foreign court, a People's Court shall review such judgment or ruling … in accordance with the principle of reciprocity …' Chen argues that the development of the reciprocity principle in China is mainly concerned with two sources: (1) sovereignty and the mutual cooperation of states of different economic and social background; and (2) the historical basis of the principle.[69] As Chen points out, '[t]he denial of recognition of the legal system amounts to a denial of a country's entire political order'.[70]

Therefore, for the first source, when conducting international relations with a foreign state, China expects foreign states to recognise her socialist ideology of ownership and trade arrangement. Only then will China feel obligated to engage in international cooperation where mutual recognition of commercial relationship and system of ownership is acknowledged by a foreign state.[71] The second source is historically rooted in the oppression of

[64] Tang, Xiao and Huo (n 12) 161.
[65] *Hilton v Guyot* 159 US 113 (1895), 227.
[66] 2015 Interpretation, Art 544.
[67] Béligh Elbalti, 'Reciprocity and the Recognition and Enforcement of Foreign Judgments: A Lot of Bark but Not Much Bite' (2017) 13(1) *Journal of Private International Law* 184, 201.
[68] ibid, 201.
[69] Chen (n 15) 457.
[70] ibid.
[71] ibid.

China by foreign powers and the forcing of China to enter into unequal treaties. Resentment and bitterness over that experience has led China to adopt the concept of equality and mutual benefit.[72] This is rooted in the need for the concept of reciprocity in China and is perceived to be necessary for continued cooperation not only with Western countries, but also countries involved in the Belt and Road Initiative.

B. Application of the Principle of Reciprocity

There are two approaches in applying reciprocity – de facto and de jure reciprocity. Thus far, the Chinese courts have only applied de facto reciprocity in the absence of a bilateral treaty or agreement.

i. De Facto Reciprocity

De facto reciprocity is where an enforcing court will only recognise and enforce judgments of rendering states that have previously factually recognised and enforced the judgments of the enforcing state. Since the notion of reciprocity was first introduced by the 1982 CPL (For Trial Implementation), Chinese courts have taken a conservative approach in the application of that concept. In almost all cases, the People's Court required 'actual precedents demonstrating that the foreign state had recognised and enforced Chinese judgments in the past' before it considered recognising and enforcing the foreign state's judgment.[73] In the famous *Gomi Akira* case, the Dalian Intermediate People's Court refused to recognise and enforce a Japanese judgment involving payment of a debt, on the basis of the absence of a treaty or a reciprocal relationship between Japan and China according to the then Article 268 of the 1991 CPL. This was because, as Japan had not recognised or enforced any previous Chinese judgments, the court concluded that there was no reciprocity between China and Japan.[74] In *Wang Qing Fang*, the Beijing No.2 Intermediate People's Court rejected an application for recognition and enforcement of an American judgment in China on the sole basis of an absence of de facto reciprocity.[75] These illustrate that, in the absence of a treaty, the Chinese court used not to consider other factors when determining recognition and enforcement of foreign judgments. Once it had been determined that there was no de facto reciprocity, an application would fail without further analysis. De facto reciprocity became a 'factual obstacle' to the recognition and enforcement of foreign judgments and most applications were declined.[76] Zhang points out that there have only been three cases in which foreign judgments have been recognised on the basis of reciprocity, all of which are de facto reciprocity cases and all of which have been decided within the last five or so years.[77]

[72] ibid.

[73] Tang, Xiao and Huo (n 12) 162.

[74] *Gomi Akira v Dalian Fari Seafood Ltd* (Application of Gomi Akira (Japanese Citizen) to Chinese Court for Recognition and Enforcement of Japanese Judicial Decision) (1996) 1 *Supreme People's Court Gazette* 29.

[75] Beijing Municipality Intermediate People's Court No 2 Decision *Wang Qingfang's Application for the Recognition of An American Adoption Judgment* (2006) Er Zhong Min Te Zi No 10319.

[76] Tang, Xiao and Huo (n 12) 164.

[77] Zhang (n 1) 521. See also Zhang (n 1) fn 29.

Comparing this to the 2,817 cases (as at 31 December 2016) in which judgments have been recognised on the basis of treaty reciprocity,[78] this would mean that, until recently, there has only been a slim chance of succeeding on the ground of de facto reciprocity. Consequently, de facto reciprocity has been regarded by many scholars as 'the most difficult and controversial hurdle to overcome in recognising and enforcing foreign judgments in China'.[79]

Among the critics, Elbalti has argued that there is no requirement in the CPL that the rendering state must have actually recognised Chinese judgments before the Chinese court can recognise and enforce the rendering state's judgments.[80] He has suggested that the Chinese court has been taking a narrow approach of its own accord without statutory mandate. This restrictive application of the reciprocity can cause what Zhang has referred to as a 'bad-to-worse' circle or a vicious cycle where it will almost be impossible to establish reciprocity between China and foreign states in the future.[81] An example of this has been the China-Japan recognition and enforcement feud, where Japanese and Chinese courts have taken turns refusing to recognise each other's judgments.[82] Like China, Japan also has a reciprocity requirement, thereby making it difficult for Japan to take the first step in recognising a Chinese judgment. Instead, the Chinese and Japanese courts have taken retaliatory positions, where neither has been able to break the deadlock. It may be that the 'first-step' gesture of recognising a judgment will only happen in countries with a more commercially-oriented mindset such as those in the West, as many Asian countries may insist on 'saving face'.[83] The author's view is that de facto reciprocity is not a logically feasible approach, given China's economic 'rise' as neither China nor the relevant foreign state will gain any commercial advantage from retaliatory judicial acts.

But the rigidity of de facto reciprocity has been gradually softening in China today as some foreign courts have taken the initiative in recognising and enforcing Chinese judgments.[84] Correspondingly, Chinese courts have been responsive to such positive gestures and they have reciprocated by also recognising and enforcing foreign judgments. This may be seen in the 2016 case of *Kolma v SUTEX Group*,[85] wherein the Nanjing Intermediate People's Court accepted that there was reciprocity between China and Singapore, as the Singapore High Court had recognised a Chinese judgment in the 2014 case of *Giant Light Metal Technology (Kunshan) v Aksa Far East*.[86] In 2017, in *Liu Li v Tao Li and Tong Wu*,[87] the Wuhan Intermediate People's Court recognised and enforced a Los Angeles court judgment on the basis that the District Court of California had previously recognised and enforced a Chinese judgment (that is, *Gezhouba Sanlian Industrial Co Ltd v Robinson*

[78] Tsang (n 41) 30.
[79] Zhang (n 1) 535.
[80] Elbalti (n 67) 184.
[81] Zhang (n 1) 521.
[82] ibid, 542.
[83] See eg the Berlin Court of Appeal Decision *German Züblin International Co Ltd v Wuxi Walker General Engineering Rubber Co Ltd* doc no 20 S Ch 13/04 (18 May 2006).
[84] Tang, Xiao and Huo (n 12) 163.
[85] Nanjing Intermediate People's Court Decision *Kolma Group AG v Jiangsu Textile Industry (Group) Import and Export Co Ltd* (2016) Su-01 Xie Wai Ren Civil Judgment.
[86] *Giant Light Metal Technology (Kunshan) v Aksa Far East* [2014] 2 SLR 545 (Singapore HC).
[87] Hubei Wuhan Intermediate People's Court Decision *Liu Li v Tao Li and Tong Wu* (2015) Yue Wuhan Zhong Min Shang Wai Chu Zi No 00026 (30 June 2017).

Helicopter Co Inc, a 2001 decision of the Hubei Provincial High Court). Both *Kolma* and *Liu Li* illustrate that the Chinese courts are willing to 'follow suit' once foreign courts have taken the first step in recognising and enforcing a Chinese judgment.[88] As will be further analysed, the judicial attitude towards reciprocity has been liberalised even further over the last couple of years. This may be attributable, at least in part, to the launch of the Belt and Road Initiative by the Chinese government.

ii. *De Jure Reciprocity*

The main difference between de facto and de jure reciprocity is that the latter reciprocity does not require previous actual precedent.[89] De jure reciprocity requires only a likelihood that the rendering court will recognise and enforce Chinese judgments.[90] A likelihood of recognition and enforcement can be assumed in the absence of evidence to the contrary. Thus, where a foreign rendering court has not refused the recognition and enforcement of a Chinese judgment in the past, reciprocity may be presumed and the judgment of the rendering court can be recognised and enforced. De jure reciprocity is consequently more flexible. It is also in line with China's current open economic policy and expansive market needs. It promotes amicable relationships with foreign courts and strengthens economic stability, thereby serving the interest of greater economic integration among the countries of the Belt and Road Initiative.

The less restrictive approach is particularly important in light of China's relationship with the Association of Southeast Asian Nations (ASEAN), the 10 members of which are within the scope of China's Belt and Road Initiative. Enhanced business resulting from market liberalisation will inevitably lead to an increase in commercial disputes among nationals of China and ASEAN states.[91] In this regard, on 8 June 2017, the Nanning Statement was issued at the 2nd China–ASEAN Justice Forum. Amongst other things, under Article VII of the Statement, Chinese and ASEAN judges affirmed that:

> If two countries have not been bound by an international treaty on mutual recognition and enforcement of foreign civil or commercial judgments, both countries may, subject to their domestic laws, presume the existence of their reciprocal relationship, when it comes to the judicial procedure of recognising or enforcing such judgments made by courts of the other country, provided that the courts of the other country had not refused to recognise or enforce such judgments on the ground of lack of reciprocity.[92]

The Statement is not legally binding and subject to domestic law. But it is an endorsement of the de jure reciprocity approach. It is not only beneficial to mutual business cooperation among China and ASEAN nations. It can also be regarded as indicative of a regional or possibly global trend to a more generous application of the reciprocity principle. Thus, foreign jurisdictions (for instance, Germany, New Zealand and Israel) have most

[88] See Zhang (n 1).
[89] Tang, Xiao and Huo (n 12) 162.
[90] ibid.
[91] Anselmo Reyes, 'ASEAN and The Hague Conventions' (2014) 22(1) *Asia Pacific Law Review* 25, 26.
[92] Nanning Statement of the 2nd China–ASEAN Justice Forum, Art VII.

recently applied de jure reciprocity to recognise and enforce Chinese civil and commercial judgments.[93] However, since the Nanning Statement, there has been no known case of de jure reciprocity having been applied by the Chinese Court.

V. Special Cases

The recognition and enforcement of a judgment may not be possible in all commercial and civil matters, as some matters may fall within the public policy exception. For example, although a foreign judgment for the payment of damages consequent upon a cartel agreement may be commercial in nature, it may also give rise to public policy issues. Thus, it may be difficult for the Chinese court to recognise and enforce judgments dealing with questions of competition law.

Another example would be a foreign judgment for the payment of compensation in respect of an alleged infringement of an intellectual property right (IPR). Since IPRs rights will typically have a territorial foundation (for example, trademark and patent)[94] so that the ownership and content of an IPR will be governed by the country in which the IPR has been registered, public policy concerns may arise where it is sought to enforce a foreign judgment dealing with the ownership and content of an IPR registered in the enforcing state. So far, however, the recognition and enforcement across borders of judgments relating to IPRs has not featured to any significant extent in Chinese academic literature.

Under Article 2 of the 2005 Hague Convention, the instrument 'shall not apply to … the validity of intellectual property rights other than copyright or related rights'.[95] Judgments relating to trademark and patent infringement are thus excluded. In broad terms, copyright arises from the creation of a particular work and the right so arising is not registered.[96] According to Brand and Herrup, 'related rights', in the context of the 2005 Hague Convention, means the 'rights in a specific use of an existing work by someone other than the original author, and which use make an additional contribution to the exiting work'.[97] Brand and Herrup give the example of an author writing a song and a vocalist singing that song.[98] The writing of the song will give rise to copyright in the lyricist, while the vocalist singing the song will be considered as having a 'related right'.[99] It is perfectly feasible, in the author's view, for a foreign judgment dealing with copyright and related rights to obtain recognition and enforcement in China. There is no public register of copyright in China that will need to be rectified or modified in light of any such judgment. The judgment will simply deal with the rights of the claimant and respondent as between themselves. It is difficult to see how third parties will be affected or how a 'public' element can arise. Of course, the foreign judgment must meet all the requirements set by Chinese domestic law for recognition and enforcement (including reciprocity).

[93] See Zhang (n 1) 521.
[94] The 2005 Hague Convention, Art 2(2).
[95] ibid.
[96] Ronald A Brand and Paul M Herrup, *The 2005 Hague Convention on Choice of Court Agreement: Commentary and Documents* (New York, Cambridge University Press, 2008) 68.
[97] ibid.
[98] ibid.
[99] ibid.

VI. The Future

A. Ratification of the 2005 Hague Convention

As previously mentioned, China has only signed, but not yet ratified the 2005 Hague Convention. There are currently no obstacles that might hinder ratification, as the instrument is in line with China's political and economic interest. Academics have suggested that the 2005 Hague Convention would bring more certainty in comparison with the current recognition and enforcement regime in China.[100] The following is a list of distinct advantages advocated by Chinese mainstream private international law scholars that China will obtain once the 2005 Hague Convention is ratified.[101]

First, China will have more influence in international litigation. As an early member of the 2005 Hague Convention, China will be able to influence the future direction of its application. China will have 'first-mover's advantage'. Test cases will go before the Chinese courts, so that other Contracting States and potential litigants will be able to refer to these cases as possible future precedents. China will be able to shape how the Convention may be applied in practice, promoting the legitimacy and competence of the Chinese courts, as many countries still view Chinese jurisprudence with suspicion.[102] Second, China will enjoy reciprocity in relation to states with which China presently does not have a bilateral treaty relationship. Thus, accession will help to grow China's potential business partners, and will indirectly benefit China's economy. Obviously, it will be conducive to China's Belt and Road Initiative. With China's entry into the 2005 Hague Convention, it will be likely that Belt and Road nations will follow suit, in order to partner with China in the development of their respective economies. In addition, China's economic 'rise' requires international portability of Chinese judgments and vice versa. Third, it will make international commercial litigation equally important as the current international commercial arbitration regime. Thus, it will not only promote the current arbitration regime in China, but it will also give litigants another option for the resolution of their international commercial disputes. The 2005 Hague Convention may be viewed as a cross-border enforcement instrument parallel to the 1958 New York Convention. However, in comparison to the 1958 New York Convention, the 2005 Hague Convention still has a limited number of Contracting States. As at 1 April 2019, there are only 32 Contracting States (including the EU as a Regional Economic Integration Organisation (REIO)) to the 2005 Hague Convention and it has entered into force only within the EU (including Denmark), in Mexico, Montenegro and Singapore. The fact that China has signed the 2005 Hague Convention shows China's commitment towards making the process of recognising and enforcing foreign judgments more efficient.

[100] Guangjian Tu, 'The Hague Choice of Court Convention: A Chinese Perspective' (2007) 55(2) *The American Journal of Comparative Law* 347, 365.

[101] See Yongping Xiao, 'Pizhun Xuanze Fayuan Xieyi Gongyue de Libi Fenxi Ji Woguo de Duice' [An Analysis of Ratifying the Convention on Choice of Court Agreements and China's Way to Deal with it] (2017) 1(5) *Wuhan University International Law Review* 1 for a detailed account.

[102] Huang Zhang, 'International Jurisdiction under the 2005 Hague Convention on Choice of Court Agreements: Implications for China' (2017) 47 *Hong Kong Law Journal* 555, 581.

B. Domestic Reform

The recognition and enforcement of foreign judgments has been much debated among Chinese academics even prior to China's signature of the 2005 Hague Convention. In April 2016, Chinese private international law academics gathered at the Wuhan University Institute of International Law and jointly proposed a Model Law on Recognition and Enforcement of Foreign Judgments in China to address deficiencies in the existing regulatory framework.[103] The Model Law was drafted in broader terms than the 2005 Hague Convention.

First, it does not require a choice of court agreement as a precondition to seeking recognition and enforcement. Second, in addition to applying to all judgments by a foreign court in civil and commercial matters, it also applies to civil damages in criminal cases, but excludes administrative matters.[104] Under the Model Law, the effect of recognition and enforcement would be the same as if the judgment had been rendered by the Chinese court, ie *res judicata*. Third, it consolidates the grounds for refusal to recognise and enforce a foreign judgment along lines similar to those listed in section III.A.i discussed above.[105]

In particular, the Model Law also deals with reciprocity. It suggests that, where China does not have a bilateral treaty with a rendering state, the Chinese court should examine whether there is an existing reciprocal relationship.[106] In this respect, it adopts de jure reciprocity and states:

> If the applicant who advocates the reciprocal relationship proves that the foreign court has the likelihood of recognising and enforcing the judgment of the court of the People's Republic of China based on its legal provisions or judicial practice, the People's Court may presume that there is a reciprocal relationship.[107]

The Model Law reflects closely the spirit of the 2005 Hague Convention and complements it. Moreover, it takes into consideration the local Chinese context and hence suits China's judicial practice. The Model Law has been submitted to the SPC for consideration. It is expected that the SPC will publish judicial interpretations on recognition and enforcement of foreign judgments in the not too distant future and that those will likely build upon the Model Law.

The principle of reciprocity was intended to reflect comity among nations. Currently, in practice, the Chinese courts have used reciprocity as a retaliatory mechanism to punish foreign courts for not recognising and enforcing Chinese judgments.[108] Reciprocity is now moving in the right direction in China. However, the biggest obstacle may still lie in the judicial attitude by individual Chinese courts. Although there have been important steps

[103] Wuhan University Institute of International Law, 'Model Law on Recognition and Enforcement of Foreign Judgments in China' (Model Law), presented in the 2nd China Private International Law Society Research Committee Seminar in the National Justice and Chinese International Civil Procedure Law Reform Forum (file with author).

[104] Model Law, Art 1.

[105] Model Law, Art 4.

[106] Model Law, Art 17.

[107] Model Law, Art 18.

[108] Tang, Xiao and Huo (n 12) 165.

towards achieving a new, more liberal reciprocity regime, the best way to resolve the issue may be through regulatory enactment, such as amending the CPL or publishing judicial interpretations of the reciprocity requirement in the CPL. Unlike common law courts, there is no binding system of precedent in China (apart from SPC judgments which are highly persuasive on all Chinese courts). The ruling of one province does not constrain a court in another province to follow suit. Defining reciprocity clearly through a regulatory enactment will ensure that the application of reciprocity will be in line with China's political and economic reality. Instead of looking at reciprocity as an overarching requirement, it should play a secondary role, ie to develop amicable relations with foreign courts.

C. Hague Judgments Project

The boldest move that China can take would be to accede to the proposed convention now being drafted by the Hague Judgment Project. The Special Commission on the Judgments Project met from 24 to 29 May 2016, which resulted in the 2018 draft Hague Judgment Convention (2018 Draft). Unlike the 2005 Hague Convention, the proposed 2018 Draft will not require a choice of court agreement as a precondition of recognition and enforcement. The proposed new convention instead seeks to 'extend the benefits of enhanced access to justice, and reduced costs and risks of cross-border dealings, to a broader range of cases'.[109] The likelihood, however, is that China will first work on accession to the 2005 Hague Convention prior to joining any further international conventions in the field, especially given the much wider scope of the proposed new convention.

VII. Conclusion

2018 marked the 40th anniversary of China's economic reform and opening to the world. Now is an opportune time to reflect upon the jurisprudential development of China's recognition and enforcement of foreign judgments and to consider pragmatic ways of improving such regime. China's economic 'rise' requires it to be more flexible when it comes to the recognition and enforcement of foreign judgments. The current bilateral treaty regime is an improved system over what preceded it. However, although each treaty can cater to each individual diplomatic relation with China, a system that relies solely on the existence of treaties would be inefficient as it requires the Chinese court to apply different standards to different cases that come before it.

China's recent signing of the 2005 Hague Convention is a positive development. Accession will bring China in line with international practice in relation to choice of court agreements. However, it will take time to realise the full extent of the benefits that the 2005 Hague Convention can deliver to China. This means that, although the judiciary has

[109] Francisco J Garcimartín Alférez and Geneviève Saumier, 'Judgments Convention: Revised Preliminary Explanatory Report' (*Hague Conference on Private International Law*, Fourth Meeting of the Special Commission on the Recognition and Enforcement of Foreign Judgments, 24–29 May 2018), available online: assets.hcch.net/docs/7cd8bc44-e2e5-46c2-8865-a151ce55e1b2.pdf.

recently been liberalising the rigid reciprocity system where recognition and enforcement of a foreign judgment does not fall within the terms of a bilateral or multilateral treaty, the time has come to acknowledge openly that the system of de facto reciprocity is contrary to China's economic interest and is in need of reform. Instead, a shift from de facto to de jure reciprocity is to be welcomed as it is in line with the spirit of international cooperation and China's out-going economic strategy. In light of economic globalisation, the Chinese court should presume reciprocity in the absence of evidence to the contrary and is encouraged to take the first step in recognising and enforcing judgments based on goodwill.

3

Hong Kong

JAMES Y P WONG

I. Overview

The private international law of Hong Kong[1] originated from English common law and statutes. Since China resumed sovereignty over Hong Kong in 1997, it has been a 'special administrative region' of China, which continues to practise capitalism and the common law system.

Hong Kong has a dual regime for the recognition and enforcement of foreign judgments: 'statutory' and 'common law'. The statutory regime enables registration of eligible judgments in mainland China (excluding Taiwan and Macau) and 15 designated countries, as well as other judgments covered by international conventions, as judgments of the Hong Kong court. These statutes give effect to various arrangements, scheme or bilateral agreement, and international conventions, which have been made by Hong Kong or its sovereign (formerly the UK and currently the People's Republic of China (PRC)). Other judgments may be recognised and enforced under the common law regime.

Hong Kong has not adopted the 2005 Hague Convention on Choice of Court Agreements, which the PRC signed in 2017. It is exploring the adoption of the forthcoming Hague Convention on the Recognition and Enforcement of Judgments in Civil and Commercial Matters, by participating in the Hague Conference and engaging in public consultations in Hong Kong.

II. Background

A. Hong Kong[2]

Hong Kong is located in the south-eastern part of China, at the mouth of the Pearl River Delta and adjacent to China's Guangdong province. It has been part of China since

[1] See Lord Collins of Mapesbury and others (eds), *Dicey, Morris & Collins* on *the Conflict of Laws* 15th edn (London, Sweet & Maxwell, 2012); Graeme Johnston and Paul Harris, *The Conflict of Laws in Hong Kong* 3rd edn (Hong Kong, Sweet & Maxwell, 2017); 'Enforcement of Judgments and Arbitral Awards Global Guide' (*Practical Law*, 2019), available online: uk.practicallaw.thomsonreuters.com/Browse/Home/International/EnforcementofJudgmentsGlobalGuide?transitionType=Default&contextData=(sc.Default)&firstPage=true&comp=pluk&bhcp=1.

[2] 'Hong Kong in Figures (Latest Figures)' (*Census and Statistics Department*, 22 February 2019), available online: www.censtatd.gov.hk/hkstat/hkif/index.jsp.

ancient times. Between 1842 and 1898, Britain acquired Hong Kong through three treaties with the then Qing Government of China.[3] On 1 July 1997, the PRC resumed sovereignty over Hong Kong. Since then, Hong Kong has been a 'Special Administrative Region' of China. It operates under the 'One Country, Two Systems' principle under the Basic Law, which is effectively the city's constitution. Hong Kong enjoys a high degree of autonomy from the PRC Government, except on matters of national defence and foreign affairs. Hong Kong practises separation of powers, with separate executive, legislative and judiciary branches. Its Government may conduct external affairs in accordance with the Basic Law. By and large, its previous social, economic and political system during colonial times has been preserved.

In 2018 Hong Kong's population was 7.4 million. The majority are ethnic Chinese, with a sizeable presence of expatriates and people of different ethnic backgrounds. While Western culture has a significant influence, many Chinese people still hold traditional Chinese culture and value. The variety of religious beliefs reflects this. The Basic Law will be effective until 30 June 2047, being 50 years from 1 July 1997. It is widely expected that the current system of Hong Kong will be extended beyond 2047, subject to suitable modifications based on the prevailing social and political conditions.

B. Sources and Development of Private International Law

As a former British colony, Hong Kong adopted English law including its private international law. These laws, together with the common law system, have been largely preserved through the handover in 1997. Since then, Hong Kong has continued to develop its private international law in accordance with the Basic Law.

In 1844, English law was formally received and applied by the Hong Kong legislature, which was established in 1843. The definitive statutory provision for the reception of English law was enacted in 1846 and re-enacted in 1873 in section 5 of the then Supreme Court Ordinance (Cap 4). This was replaced by the Application of English Law Ordinance (Cap 88) in 1966.[4] When China resumed its sovereignty in 1997, this Ordinance ceased its effect. The Basic Law preserves the laws previously in force in Hong Kong. Article 8 of the Basic Law provides:

> the laws previously in force in Hong Kong, that is, the common law, rules of equity, ordinances, subordinate legislation and customary law shall be maintained, except for any that contravene this Law, and subject to any amendment by the legislature of the Hong Kong Special Administrative Region.

Against this background, Hong Kong has continued to develop it since 1997. In adjudicating cases, the judiciary may refer to case law from other common law jurisdictions. English case law remains highly persuasive in Hong Kong courts. Notably, however, numerous statutory reforms in England over the past decades have not been incorporated in Hong Kong.

[3] The Treaty of Nanking 1842, the Convention of Peking 1860 and the Convention for the Extension of Hong Kong Territory 1898.

[4] Yash Ghai, *Hong Kong's New Constitutional Order* 2nd edn (Hong Kong, Hong Kong University Press, 1999) 362.

These include various European Conventions,[5] the Foreign Limitation Periods Act 1984 and section 35 of the Civil Jurisdiction and Judgments Act 1982.

Under the Basic Law, the Hong Kong Government may enter into bilateral arrangements with other jurisdictions. Hong Kong has concluded three arrangements with mainland China regarding mutual recognition and enforcement of judgments, apart from other arrangements with mainland China concerning various aspects of mutual legal assistance in civil and commercial matters. Representatives of the Hong Kong Department of Justice have been, as part of the PRC delegation, participating in the work of the Hague Conference, especially with regard to the 2005 Hague Convention on Choice of Court Agreements and the 2018 Draft Hague Convention on the Recognition and Enforcement of Judgments in Civil and Commercial Matters.

C. The Judicial System

Hong Kong is a common law jurisdiction under the Basic Law. It prides itself on its independent judiciary, which is free from influence from the executive and legislative branches of the Government. Hong Kong courts have the right of final adjudication, subject to the right of legislative interpretation by the Standing Committee of the PRC National People's Congress in limited circumstances.

The recognition and enforcement of foreign judgments are usually handled by the Court of First Instance of the High Court. It has unlimited jurisdiction in both civil and commercial matters. If a claim is below HK$3,000,000, it will usually be handled by the District Court, which hears civil disputes of a value over HK$75,000 but not more than HK$3,000,000 and criminal matters with its jurisdiction limited to seven years' imprisonment. There are various magistrates' courts and tribunals dealing with smaller civil claims, criminal and certain specialist matters.

The Court of Appeal of the High Court hears appeals on all civil and criminal matters from various courts and statutory bodies, including the Court of First Instance and the District Court.

The Court of Final Appeal is the highest appellate court in Hong Kong, which hears appeal from the Court of Appeal and, in exceptional cases (known as 'leapfrog' appeals), from the Court of First Instance.

D. Scope of Civil and Commercial Judgments

Under Hong Kong law, there are no exhaustive definitions for civil or commercial matters. The expression 'civil' is generally used as a notion to be distinguished from 'criminal' matters. In this wide formulation, any matters which are not criminal can be regarded as civil. These would include, for example, public law matters in judicial review proceedings, winding up and bankruptcy proceedings, and regulatory matters such as market

[5] For example, the Rome Convention, the Rome I and Rome II Regulations, the Brussels Convention, and the Brussels I and Brussels II Regulations.

misconduct proceedings. 'Commercial' matters broadly refer to cases which involve the commercial rights and interests of parties. In the High Court of Hong Kong, there is a specialist list called the 'Commercial List', which handles commercial cases. The High Court's Practice Direction SL1.1 broadly refers to the function of the list as 'to facilitate the disposal of actions involving commercial matters'. As recognised in a Government consultation paper, in the Hong Kong legal system, 'civil and commercial' judgments may include all judgments apart from criminal judgments.[6]

III. Recognition and Enforcement under Treaties or Similar Arrangements: The Statutory Regime

The statutory regime enables registration of eligible foreign judgments as judgments of the Hong Kong court. The statutes arose from various cross-border arrangements, bilateral agreements and similar schemes, which Hong Kong or its sovereign (before 1 July 1997, the UK) made at different times. As a result, several laws were enacted. When compared to the common law regime, registration of judgments under statute is more straightforward, as the procedure for registration is usually faster.

This section is divided into four sub-sections. Section A introduces the distinction between recognition and enforcement, and the concept of *res judicata*. Section B discusses the Mainland Judgments (Reciprocal Enforcement) Ordinance (Cap 597). Section C explains the Foreign Judgments (Reciprocal Enforcement) Ordinance (Cap 319). Section D refers to the international conventions applicable to Hong Kong which provide for the recognition and enforcement of foreign judgments or decisions.

A. Recognition/Enforcement and *Res Judicata*

Before discussing the enforcement regimes, it is worth mentioning the distinction between recognition and enforcement of foreign judgments under Hong Kong law, and the relevant concept of *res judicata*.

Hong Kong law distinguishes between enforcement and recognition. In broad terms, enforcement means making a claim or counterclaim based on a foreign judgment, whereas recognition means relying on a foreign judgment as a defence to a claim or as conclusive evidence of an issue in a claim.[7] Enforcement also refers to the execution or carrying out of a foreign judgment in favour of the successful party, particularly a foreign monetary judgment. Certain judgments are not capable of being enforced. These include but are not limited to a judgment granting declaratory relief, a judgment dismissing a claim, or a judgment *in rem* determining title to a foreign immovable. On the other hand, if a party merely relies on a foreign judgment to resist a claim or to prove an issue, he or she is seeking

[6] See Department of Justice, 'Proposed Arrangement Between Hong Kong and the Mainland on Reciprocal Recognition and Enforcement of Judgments in Civil and Commerical Matters: Consultation Paper' (*Department of Justice*, July 2018) para 13, available online: www.doj.gov.hk/eng/public/pdf/2018/lpdpapere.pdf.

[7] See Lord Collins of Mapesbury (n 1) vol 1 [14-002]–[14-006].

recognition, as opposed to enforcement, of that judgment. For example, a respondent in a court action may resist a claim of debt by seeking recognition of a foreign judgment which dismissed the same debt claim. By the same token, if a party to a foreign judgment attempts to re-open an issue which has been adjudicated in that judgment, the other party may seek recognition of the judgment as conclusive evidence of the same issue. It follows that, while a court must recognise a foreign judgment if it is to enforce the same, the court need not enforce every judgment which it recognises.

Under Hong Kong law, it is well-established that foreign judgments which have been recognised can give rise to issue estoppel or *res judicata*. Accordingly, the same parties cannot re-litigate the same matters which have been, or should have been, resolved in previous court (or arbitral) proceedings, including previous foreign court proceedings. Section 5 of the Foreign Judgments (Restriction on Recognition and Enforcement) Ordinance (Cap 46) provides:

> No proceedings may be brought by a person in Hong Kong on a cause of action in respect of which a judgment has been given in his favour in proceedings between the same parties, or their privies, in a court of an overseas country, unless that judgment is not enforceable or entitled to recognition in Hong Kong.

Apart from this procedural bar, the Hong Kong court has power to enforce and recognise the substantive ruling or order by a foreign court, as well as to set aside the registration of a foreign judgment, if the matter in dispute has been subject to a previous final and conclusive foreign court judgment (or arbitral award) (see sections III.B.v and III.C.iii below).

In *Anthony Wee Soon Kim v UBS AG Hong Kong Branch*,[8] Deputy High Court Judge Carlson, with whom the Court of Appeal agreed,[9] discussed the 'narrow' and 'extended' applications of the doctrine of *res judicata*. The narrow application means estoppel on issues which have been resolved in the foreign proceedings, while the extended application covers such issues which could and should have been raised by a party in the foreign proceedings but were not. This case established that the concept of *res judicata* covers matters which could and should have been raised in the previous foreign proceedings.

B. Mainland China

In July 2006, Hong Kong entered into an arrangement with the Supreme People's Court of China for the recognition and enforcement of judgments in civil and commercial matters pursuant to choice of court agreements made by the parties concerned, which was amended in February 2008.[10] The arrangement covers money judgments by a designated court of either mainland China or Hong Kong exercising jurisdiction in business-to-business arrangements pursuant to the parties' written exclusive jurisdiction clause. To give effect to the arrangement, Hong Kong enacted the Mainland Judgments (Reciprocal Enforcement) Ordinance (Cap 597), which came into effect on 1 August 2008.

[8] *Anthony Wee Soon Kim v UBS AG Hong Kong Branch* [2006] 2 HKC 1.
[9] *Anthony Wee Soon Kim v UBS AG Hong Kong Branch* CACV 96/2006 (5 November 2007) [13] (Rogers VP).
[10] The arrangement was modelled after the 2005 Hague Convention on Choice of Court Agreements.

A key feature of Cap 597 is the requirement of a written exclusive jurisdiction agreement. Such an agreement is defined in Section 3(2) of the Ordinance as

> an agreement concluded by the parties to a specified contract and specifying the courts in the Mainland or any of them as the court to determine a dispute which has arisen or may arise in connection with the specified contract to the exclusion of courts of other jurisdictions.

A 'specified contract' means 'a contract other than (a) an employment contract; and (b) a contract to which a natural person acting for personal consumption, family or other non-commercial purposes is a party' (section 2). This broadly covers commercial or business-to-business contracts.

In June 2017, the Hong Kong Government entered into a second arrangement with the PRC Government regarding the recognition and enforcement of civil judgments in matrimonial and family cases. This covers various types of matrimonial and family civil judgments, including: (1) decrees absolute of divorce, decrees absolute of nullity, maintenance orders, custody orders, etc made by the Hong Kong courts; and (2) judgments on dissolution of marriage, validity of marriage, duty to maintain the other party to a marriage, custody of a child, etc by the PRC courts. On 8 February 2019, the Department of Justice launched a public consultation to seek views on the proposed legislative bill for implementing the arrangement.

The existing regime under Cap 597 will be superseded by a new regime. On 18 January 2019, Hong Kong and the Supreme People's Court of China signed an arrangement on reciprocal recognition and enforcement of judgments in civil and commercial matters between the two places. The new arrangement will be a more comprehensive regime than this existing arrangement under Cap 597. After implementation by local legislation in both places, this new arrangement will come into effect and supersede the existing arrangement. Features of the new arrangement will be discussed in section VIII.A below.

i. *Requirements for Registration*

The Court of First Instance must, upon the application of a mainland judgment creditor accompanied by application fee, make an order that the judgment be registered under the Ordinance, upon satisfaction of the following requirements (in section 5(2)):

1. The judgment was given on or after 1 August 2008 by the parties' chosen mainland court which is a 'designated court'. 'Designated courts' include the Supreme People's Court, a Higher People's Court, an Intermediate People's Court and a recognised Basic People's Court (see Schedule 1 to the Ordinance). Alternatively, the judgment was given by another designated court to which the case was transferred from the chosen court, or which has handled the relevant appeal or retrial.
2. The relevant choice of mainland court agreement was made on or after 1 August 2008.
3. The judgment is final and conclusive between the parties. These include (a) a judgment by the Supreme People's Court; (b) a judgment against which no appeal is allowed under mainland law or no appeal has been filed prior to the expiry of the appeal period;

(c) a second instance judgment by a designated court other than a recognised primary people's court; or (d) a judgment in a retrial by a designated court of a higher level than the original court (section 6(1)).

4. The judgment is enforceable in mainland China. There is a rebuttable presumption of enforceability if a certificate is issued by the original court certifying that the judgment is final and enforcement in mainland China (section 6(2)).
5. The judgment orders the payment of a sum of money, not being taxes or other charges of a like nature or a sum in respect of a fine or other penalty.

The time limit for a judgment creditor to apply for registration is two years. The period commences from the last day of the period for performance of the judgment specified in the judgment or the effective date of the judgment (section 7).

ii. Partial Registration and Currency

If the Court of First Instance finds that only some provisions of the mainland judgment are registrable or where performance is required in stages, it will register those provisions of the judgment but not the other non-registrable provisions (sections 9 and 13). If the judgment has been partly satisfied, the Court will register the judgment for the outstanding balance (section 10). If the mainland judgment is expressed in a currency other than Hong Kong dollars, it shall be registered in Hong Kong dollars on the basis of the exchange rate prevailing at the date of registration (section 11). In addition to the judgment sum, a registered judgment will include any interest and costs certified by the original court, as well as any reasonable costs of and incidental to the registration of the judgment (section 12).

iii. Effect of Registration

Upon registration, the registered judgment will be of the same force and effect as a judgment of the Court of First Instance, with effect from the day of registration. Enforcement action can be taken on the judgment and the registered sum will carry interest (section 14).

iv. Recognition of Mainland Judgments

The Hong Kong Court will recognise any mainland judgment which would satisfy the requirements of registration, whether or not the judgment has been registered. The effect is to recognise the judgment as conclusive between its parties in any proceedings founded on the same cause of action, which judgment may be relied on by way of defence or counterclaim in any such proceedings. This does not apply to a mainland judgment which has been registered but set aside, or which has not been registered but would be liable to be set aside if registered on any ground other than that the judgment has been wholly satisfied (section 16).

v. Setting Aside of Registration

When making an order to register a mainland judgment, the Court of First Instance will specify the period within which an application to set aside the registration may be made. The Court may subsequently extend this period (section 17). The Court may, upon application by any party, set aside a registered judgment upon the satisfaction of any of the following requirements (in section 18(1)):

1. The judgment is not a mainland judgment which satisfies the requirements in section 5(2)(a) to (e) of the Ordinance (see section III.B.i above).
2. The judgment has been registered in contravention of the Ordinance.
3. The relevant choice of mainland court agreement was invalid under mainland law, unless the original court has determined that the agreement is valid.
4. The judgment has been wholly satisfied.
5. The courts in Hong Kong have exclusive jurisdiction over the case according to Hong Kong law.
6. The judgment debtor who did not appear in the original court to defend the proceedings was not summoned to appear according to mainland law, or was so summoned but was not given sufficient time to defend the proceedings according to mainland law. This provision does not apply where the judgment debtor was summoned to the original court by service through public announcement in accordance with mainland law (section 18(2)).
7. The judgment was obtained by fraud.
8. A judgment on the same cause of action between the parties to the judgment has been given by a court in Hong Kong or an arbitral award on the same cause of action between the parties has been made by an arbitral tribunal in Hong Kong.
9. A judgment on the same cause of action between the parties to the judgment has been given by a court in a place outside Hong Kong or an arbitral award on the same cause of action between the parties has been made by an arbitration tribunal in a place outside Hong Kong, and the judgment or award has already been recognised or enforced by the court in Hong Kong.
10. The enforcement of the judgment would be contrary to public policy.
11. The judgment has been reversed or otherwise set aside pursuant to an appeal or a retrial under mainland law.

If there is a pending appeal to a registered judgment or a retrial has been ordered, the Court may exercise its discretion either to set aside the registration or to adjourn the application until after such period, in order to allow sufficient time for the appeal or retrial (section 19). After a registration has been set aside, the judgment creditor cannot make a further application to register it again, except: (1) where the registration was set aside because the judgment was not enforceable at the date of application, but the judgment has since become enforceable; (2) where the registration was set aside because of a pending appeal or retrial and the appeal or retrial has been disposed of; or (3) where the registration was set aside because, despite the judgment having been partly satisfied prior to registration, the entire judgment sum had wrongly been registered as outstanding, and hence the registration was in contravention of the Ordinance. In such case, the judgment creditor may apply to register for the unpaid balance of the judgment sum (section 20).

vi. Indirect Jurisdiction

The Ordinance does not address the issue of establishing the jurisdiction of the court which gave the judgment – ie grounds of indirect jurisdiction. It is submitted that this is not necessary because indirect jurisdiction would have been established by the written exclusive jurisdiction agreement choosing a PRC court, which is a prominent requirement under the Ordinance. The exclusive jurisdiction clause would amount to the parties' prior agreement to submit to the jurisdiction of the chosen PRC court which rendered the judgment in question.

vii. Judgments in Macau, Taiwan and Unrecognised Jurisdictions

Notably, the Ordinance does not cover judgments in Macau or Taiwan. Hong Kong has not concluded any mutual arrangement or agreement with Macau or Taiwan regarding mutual recognition and enforcement of judgments. Thus, the enforcement of Macau or Taiwanese judgments is governed by the common law regime, which will be discussed in section IV below.

In relation to Taiwan, its Government of the Republic of China is not recognised by the PRC, Hong Kong's sovereign. This used to cause uncertainties as to the enforceability of Taiwanese judgments in Hong Kong.[11] The position was clarified by the Court of Final Appeal in 2000, which confirmed their enforceability in Hong Kong subject to certain conditions. In particular, the conditions are:

1. The judgments concern private, as opposed to public, rights;
2. It is in the interests of justice, the dictates of common sense and the needs of law and order; and
3. Giving them effect would not be inimical to the sovereign's interests or otherwise contrary to public policy.[12]

In that case, Bokhary PJ said that the principle does not involve recognising any unrecognised entity. It goes 'purely and simply to protecting private rights'.

In principle, these requirements apply to determining the enforceability of court judgments from any other jurisdiction whose Government is not recognised by Hong Kong's sovereign.

C. The 15 Countries Specified in Cap 319A

The Foreign Judgments (Reciprocal Enforcement) Ordinance (Cap 319) enables registration of judgments in 15 designated countries. These countries are listed in Schedules 1 and 2 to the Foreign Judgments (Reciprocal Enforcement) Order (Cap 319A). Currently, these countries are Australia, Bermuda, Brunei, India, Malaysia, New Zealand, Singapore, Sri Lanka, Belgium, France, Germany, Italy, Austria, The Netherlands and Israel.

[11] *Ku Chia Chun v Ting Lei Miao* [1999] 1 HKLRD 123; *CEF New Asia Co Ltd v Wong Kwong Yiu, John* [1999] 3 HKLRD 697.

[12] *Chen Li Hung v Ting Lei Miao* (2000) 3 HKCFAR 9.

i. Historical Background

These countries were designated by way of various Legal Notices, which were issued in the 1970s and 1990s by the then colonial Government, on the basis of reciprocity of enforcement. As the long title of the Ordinance states, the Ordinance was enacted:

> To make provision for the enforcement in the Colony of Hong Kong of judgments given in other parts of the Commonwealth and foreign countries *which afford reciprocal treatment to judgments* given in the Colony of Hong Kong, for facilitating the enforcement in such parts or countries of judgments given in the Colony of Hong Kong, and for matters connected therewith. (emphasis added)

The UK Government, Hong Kong's then sovereign, determined reciprocity as follows. Reciprocity with the Commonwealth jurisdictions was established by a Commonwealth scheme. Reciprocity with non-Commonwealth jurisdictions was established by bilateral agreements concluded between them and the UK. Since the handover and the change of sovereign, the reciprocal scheme and agreements ceased to have effect. The Hong Kong Department of Justice has since written to all the 15 jurisdictions to find out whether Hong Kong judgments can be recognised and enforced there. It has received a number of responses.[13]

Indeed, section 3 of the Ordinance empowers the Hong Kong Government to add countries to the list in Cap 319A or to delete any from it, after considering the 'substantial reciprocity of treatment'. The power and obligation to consider reciprocity falls on the executive branch of the Hong Kong Government, namely the Chief Executive in Council. In addition, section 11 empowers the Hong Kong Government to make foreign judgments unenforceable in Hong Kong if there is no reciprocity with a given jurisdiction. It states that

> if it appears to the [Chief Executive in Council] that the treatment in respect of recognition and enforcement accorded by the courts of any foreign country to judgments given in the superior courts of [Hong Kong] is substantially less favourable than that accorded by the courts of [Hong Kong] to judgments of the superior courts of that country, the [Chief Executive in Council] may by order apply this section to that country.

However, to date, there has been no executive order or legislative amendment to the above list of 15 countries, nor any public information that the Government will update the list.

Notably, from the perspective of a litigant, it is not necessary to undertake the fact-finding exercise as to whether a particular foreign jurisdiction gives reciprocal enforcement. One can apply for registration of judgments as long as the relevant jurisdiction is listed in the legislation.[14]

[13] See Law Society of Hong Kong Circular 12-883 and the correspondence between the Law Society of Hong Kong and the Department of Justice, quoted in WS Clarke, *Hong Kong Civil Court Practice: Desk Edition 2019* (Hong Kong, LexisNexis, 2019) [412]. Based on this information, the Department of Justice only received responses from some, but not all, of the 15 countries.

[14] *Prime Credit Leasing Sdn Bhd v Tan Cho Lung Raymond* [2006] 4 HKLRD 741.

ii. Indirect Jurisdiction

The grounds for establishing the jurisdiction of the rendering state are set out in section 6(2) of the Ordinance.[15] For instance, there would be a submission where a judgment debtor voluntarily appears as a respondent in the foreign court in order to contest those proceedings (section 6(2)(a)(i)). Where a judgment debtor is a party to foreign proceedings, there would likewise be a submission where he or she makes a claim or counterclaim in those proceedings (section 6(2)(a)(ii)). There would also be submission where the judgment debtor was a respondent in the foreign action and had, prior to those proceedings, agreed to submit to the jurisdiction of the foreign court on the matters in dispute (section 6(2)(a)(iii)). Another situation in which there is a submission to the foreign court would be where the judgment debtor was, at the time when the foreign proceedings were instituted, resident in or had its principal place of business as a company in the foreign country (section 6(2)(a)(iv)). Further, if the judgment debtor had an office or place of business in the foreign country and the proceedings there were in respect of a transaction effected through or at that office or place, then there would be submission to the foreign court (section 6(2)(a)(v)). Insofar as judgments in respect of immovable property or in an action *in rem* in relation to movable property, where the relevant property was at the time of the proceedings situate in the foreign country, there would be submission (section 6(2)(b)). Finally, in cases other than the foregoing, there would be submission where the jurisdiction of the original court is recognised by Hong Kong law (section 6(2)(c)).

All of the foregoing instances of submission are subject to section 6(3) of the Ordinance, which provides that the foreign court shall not be deemed to have had jurisdiction in two instances. The first is where the subject matter of the proceedings is immovable property outside the country. The second is where the judgment debtor was a person who, under the rules of public international law, was entitled to immunity from the foreign court's jurisdiction and did not submit to the jurisdiction of that court.

[15] S 6(2) provides that:

For the purposes of this section, the courts of the country of the original court shall, subject to the provisions of subsection (3), be deemed to have had jurisdiction—

(a) in the case of a judgment given in an action in personam—
  (i) if the judgment debtor, being a defendant in the original court, submitted to the jurisdiction of that court by voluntarily appearing in the proceedings; or
  (ii) if the judgment debtor was plaintiff in, or counterclaimed in, the proceedings in the original court; or
  (iii) if the judgment debtor, being a defendant in the original court, had before the commencement of the proceedings agreed, in respect of the subject matter of the proceedings, to submit to the jurisdiction of that court or of the courts of the country of that court; or
  (iv) if the judgment debtor, being a defendant in the original court, was at the time when the proceedings were instituted resident in, or being a body corporate had its principal place of business in, the country of that court; or
  (v) if the judgment debtor, being a defendant in the original court, had an office or place of business in the country of that court and the proceedings in that court were in respect of a transaction effected through or at that office or place;

(b) in the case of a judgment given in an action of which the subject matter was immovable property or in an action in rem of which the subject matter was movable property, if the property in question was at the time of the proceedings in the original court situate in the country of that court;

(c) in the case of a judgment given in an action other than any such action as is mentioned in paragraph (a) or (b), if the jurisdiction of the original court is recognised by the law of the registering court.

Notably, the above section 6(2) should be read with section 4 of the Foreign Judgments (Restriction on Recognition and Enforcement) Ordinance (Cap 46), which provides that the following steps shall not amount to submission to jurisdiction of a foreign court:

1. The person against whom judgment was given appeared in the rendering court to contest its jurisdiction.
2. He appeared in the rendering court to ask it to dismiss or stay the proceedings on the ground that the dispute in question should be submitted to arbitration or to the determination of the courts of another country.
3. He appeared in the rendering court to protect or obtain the release of property seized or threatened with seizure in the proceedings.

iii. Requirements for Registration

A judgment creditor may apply to the Court of First Instance to register a judgment from any of these countries, within six years after the judgment date. The requirements of the registration are as follows (sections 3(2) and 3(3) of Cap 319):

1. First, there must be a judgment from a 'superior court', except if the judgment is one on appeal from a court which is not a superior court. The Ordinance specifically designates certain courts in Australia as 'superior courts'. For other countries, the expression refers to courts 'having unlimited jurisdiction in civil and criminal matters' (section 4 of and Schedules 1 and 2 to Cap 319A).
2. Second, the judgment must be final and conclusive as between the parties to the judgment. A judgment is deemed to be final and conclusive even if there is a pending appeal or the judgment is subject to appeal.
3. Third, the judgment must be one for the payment of a sum of money, not being taxes or other charges of a like nature or in respect of a fine or other penalty.
4. Fourth, the judgment must have been given after the coming into operation of the order directing that the provisions of the Ordinance are to extend to the relevant foreign country.

Upon the satisfaction of these four requirements, the Hong Kong court must register the judgment as its own judgment. There are two exceptions. A judgment cannot be registered if it has been wholly satisfied. Nor can a judgment be registered if it could not be enforced by execution in the country of the original court (section 4(1)). The effect of the registration then is that a registered judgment has the same force and effect as a judgment of the Court of First Instance for the purposes of execution. Enforcement proceedings may be taken on the registered judgment. The judgment sum carries interest from the date of registration (section 4(2)).

The Ordinance expressly excludes the registration of judgments in connection with matrimonial matters, the administration of the estates of deceased persons, bankruptcy, winding up of companies, lunacy and guardianship of infants (section 2(2)).

The application for registration must be made within six years after the date of judgment, or where there is an appeal against the judgment, after the date of the last judgment given in the proceedings (section 4(1)).

iv. Grounds for Refusing Enforcement

Under section 6 of the Ordinance, the court must set aside the registration of a judgment on the following grounds:

1. The judgment is not a judgment to which the provisions of the Ordinance apply or the registration was made in contravention of any of its provisions.
2. The rendering court lacked jurisdiction (that is, indirect jurisdiction is not established).
3. The judgment debtor did not receive notice of the foreign proceedings in sufficient time to enable him or her to defend those proceedings and did not appear to defend the proceedings, even if process had been duly served on him or her under the laws of the foreign country.
4. The judgment was obtained by fraud.
5. The enforcement of the judgment is contrary to public policy of Hong Kong.
6. The rights under the judgment are not vested in the person who applied for registration.

In addition, section 3 of Foreign Judgments (Restriction on Recognition and Enforcement) Ordinance (Cap 46) provides that a foreign judgment shall not be recognised or enforced in Hong Kong if it was given in breach of an agreement for settlement of disputes between the parties. In determining the existence of any settlement agreement, the Hong Kong court is not bound by the decision of any foreign court (section 3(3)).

Further, the court may exercise its discretion to set aside a registration if the matter in dispute in the rendering court had previous to the judgment date been the subject of a final and conclusive judgment by a court having jurisdiction in the matter.

In this regard, grounds (3) and (5) above warrant further consideration. Indirect jurisdiction will be discussed further below in section IV.B.i below.

a. Reasonable Notice and the Broader Notion of Fair Procedure

Under section 6(1)(a)(iii) of the Ordinance, the registration of a foreign judgment must be set aside if the court is satisfied that there was a lack of reasonable notice of the foreign proceedings and did not appear – i.e. ground (3) above. The question of whether there was 'sufficient notice' is one of fact to be assessed by the Hong Kong court.

In common law, there is a broader notion of fair procedure, which has been suggested to apply similarly to both the statutory and common law regimes.[16] Accordingly, a foreign judgment may be impeached if it offends the notions of substantial justice in Hong Kong. These in principle covers circumstances in which a defendant contested the foreign procedures but there was procedural injustice. For example, impeachment succeeded where the terms of a default judgment misleadingly hid the existence of an obvious ground of appeal, or where a litigant in person genuinely did not know, and was not told, of his right of appeal.[17]

[16] Johnston and Harris (n 1) [9.026]–[9.028].

[17] ibid, [9.028], citing *Adams v Cape Industries plc* [1990] Ch 433 and *Leaton Leather & Trading Co Ltd v Ngai Tak Kong* (1997) 147 DLR (4th) 1377.

b. Public Policy

There is limited case law guidance on how public policy is interpreted in the context of setting aside foreign judgments. Based on English case law, it would appear that a foreign judgment obtained in violation of a Hong Kong anti-suit injunction will not be enforced. Moreover, under the principle of *res judicata*, a foreign judgment inconsistent with a previous decision of a Hong Kong court will not be enforced.[18]

D. International Conventions

There are several international conventions applicable in Hong Kong which provide for enforcement of foreign judgments. These include the 1969 International Convention on Civil Liability for Oil Pollution Damage (as amended by the 1992 Protocol), the 2001 International Convention on Civil Liability for Bunker Oil Pollution Damage and the 1960 Convention on Third Party Liability in the Field of Nuclear Energy (as amended in 1964, 1982 and 2004).[19] These Conventions provide for settlement of disputes on an international level. Hong Kong has enacted domestic laws which deal with its international obligation to recognise and enforce foreign judgments in relation to these matters.[20] The Foreign Judgments (Reciprocal Enforcement) Ordinance (Cap 319) apply to the recognition and enforcement of these foreign judgments.[21] These matters will be discussed further in section VI.C below, under the heading 'environmental wrong'.

Separately, the 1974 United Nations Convention on a Code of Conduct for Liner Conferences has been applied to Hong Kong, as it was applied to Hong Kong by the United Kingdom prior to the handover. Since 1997, the PRC has applied the Convention to Hong Kong. Accordingly, the Convention has continued to apply to Hong Kong. It was adopted in Hong Kong through the enactment of the Merchant Shipping (Liner Conferences) Ordinance (Cap 482). The 1974 Convention defines 'liner conference' as:

> a group of two or more vessel-operating carriers which provides international liner services for the carriage of cargo on a particular route or routes within specified geographical limits and which has an agreement or arrangement, whatever its nature, within the framework of which they operate under uniform or common freight rates and any other agreed conditions with respect to the provision of liner services.[22]

In essence, liner conferences are formal or informal private arrangements between carriers or between shipping lines which enable them to utilise common freight rates and

[18] ibid, [9.091], citing *Philip Alexander Securities & Futures Ltd v Bamberger* [1997] ILPr 73; *Vervaeke v Smith* [1983] 1 AC 145 (HL); *ED&F Man (Sugar) Ltd v Haryanto (No 2)* [1991] 1 Lloyd's Rep 429 (CA). By analogy with the Foreign Judgments (Restriction on Recognition and Enforcement) Ordinance (Cap 46) s 3, judgments obtained in breach of an arbitration agreement may be refused recognition and enforcement as a matter of public policy. Compare the approach in *Dickson Valora Group (Holdings) Co Ltd v Fan Ji Qian* [2019] 2 HKLRD 173.

[19] 'List of Treaties in Force and Applicable to the Hong Kong Special Administrative Region' (*Department of Justice*, 14 November 2018), available online: www.doj.gov.hk/eng/laws/interlaw.html.

[20] These include the Merchant Shipping (Liability and Compensation for Oil Pollution) Ordinance (Cap 414), the Bunker Oil Pollution (Liability and Compensation) Ordinance (Cap 605) and the Nuclear Material (Liability for Carriage) Ordinance (Cap 479).

[21] See Cap 414, ss 18(2), 27(3); Cap 605, s 21; Cap 479, s 10(4).

[22] Cap 482, sch 1, pt 1, c I.

to engage in other cooperative activities on a particular route or routes, with a view to reducing competition.[23] The Ordinance provides for the enforcement of judgments or decisions under the 1974 Convention, by way of a registration application in the High Court.[24]

IV. Recognition and Enforcement in the Absence of Treaties or Similar Arrangements: The Common Law Regime

If a foreign judgment does not fall into any of above statutes, the judgment may be enforced at common law. Under the common law regime, the court may recognise and/or enforce a foreign judgment under specific rules.

A judgment creditor seeking enforcement needs to commence a court action, claiming for the judgment debt under his judgment. Generally, it has to prove the following: (1) the rendering court had jurisdiction to adjudicate upon the cause or matter that gave rise to the judgment (that is, there was indirect jurisdiction); (2) the judgment is final and conclusive; and (3) the judgment is not impeachable according to Hong Kong conflict of law rules.[25]

The judgment debtor may resist the recognition and enforcement by establishing that one or other of the aforesaid requirements were absent. In addition, the judgment debtor may resist recognition and enforcement by showing that the judgment was procured by fraud, was obtained by unfair procedure or is offensive to public policy in Hong Kong. It will be seen that the relevant principles under the common law and statutory regimes are similar. However, the common law regime is independent and 'quite distinct'.[26]

A. A Summary Process for Enforcement

A judgment creditor may utilise the 'summary judgment' procedure in seeking enforcement of his foreign judgment. The procedure applies to court actions in Hong Kong generally, which include an action to enforce a foreign judgment.

Under this procedure, if the court considers that the defendant does not have an arguable defence against the debt claim, it may straightaway give judgment in the claimant's favour. This enables a claimant to dispense with various usual steps in court proceedings (for example, discovery, exchange of witness statements, trial) and obtain judgment speedily. The summary judgment process is thus essentially a means of obtaining recognition of a foreign judgment and enforcing the same by bringing a cause of action for debt in the Hong Kong court based on the foreign judgment. The effect of the summary judgment would then be to convert the foreign judgment into a final judgment of the Hong Kong court. A respondent may appeal against the summary judgment on the basis that it was

[23] Anila Premti, 'Liner Shipping: Is There a Way for More Competition?' (*United Nations Conference on Trade and Development*, UNCTAD Discussion Papers No 224, March 2016) 3, available online: unctad.org/en/PublicationsLibrary/osgdp2016d1_en.pdf; Clarke (n 13) [988]–[1087].

[24] See Rules of the High Court (Cap 4A), Ord 71, rrs 41, 42.

[25] Adopting the English common law rule in *Nouvion v Freeman* (1889) 15 App Cas 1, which was applied in *Korea Data Systems Co Ltd v Jay Tien Chiang* [2001] 3 HKC 239 [23].

[26] *Lam Chit Man v Lam Chi To* [2001–2003] HKCLRT 141 (CA) [11].

wrongly made. However, because the foreign judgment will typically give rise to issue estoppel or *res judicata*, the grounds upon which the respondent may resist summary judgment will be extremely limited. In particular, the court will not normally revisit the merits of the foreign judgment.

B. Grounds for Refusing Recognition and Enforcement at Common Law

This part summarises the grounds for refusing recognition or enforcement of foreign judgments at common law by reference to relevant case law.

i. Indirect Jurisdiction

The rendering court must have the jurisdiction to adjudicate on the cause giving rise to the judgment. There has been limited judicial discussion on the principles for determining jurisdiction of the rendering court (that is, indirect jurisdiction). As the rule is derived from English common law, it is submitted that English rules on indirect jurisdiction should form the starting point of an analysis[27] in relation to Hong Kong. The court should certainly have regard to the corresponding rules for establishing indirect jurisdiction under the statutory framework (that is, section 6(2) of the Foreign Judgments (Reciprocal Enforcement) Ordinance), as it would be odd if Hong Kong common law principles were radically different from the statutory ones. Accordingly, it is submitted that the principles enumerated below should apply when determining indirect jurisdiction,

For actions *in personam*, there are two main bases of indirect jurisdiction, namely submission and presence. On submission, the person against whom judgment was given must have voluntarily submitted to the jurisdiction of the rendering court by (1) agreeing to submit before the judgment was delivered; (2) participating in the court proceedings; or (3) making a claim or counterclaim in the court proceedings. In the alternative, presence in the foreign jurisdiction can be established. The person against whom judgment was given was, at the time proceedings were instituted, present in the foreign country (in the case of natural persons) or had its principal place of business there (in the case of a body corporate). Where a person merely has an office or place of business in the relevant country, such presence may be sufficient if the foreign proceedings were in respect of a transaction effected through or at that office or place of business. For actions *in rem*, the movable or immovable property in question must at the time of the proceedings have been situate in the foreign country.[28]

The recognition of jurisdiction must accord with the principles of public international law applicable in Hong Kong. For instance, where the rendering court is in a state whose Government is not recognised by the PRC Government, the judgment must relate to the private rights of parties and giving effect to the judgment must accord with the interests of

[27] Lord Collins of Mapesbury (n 1) [14R-054]–[14-117].

[28] *Cova Enterprises Ltd v Ruddy Tjanaka* [2004] 1 HKLRD 199; *Yick Tat Development Co v Yung Chung Yiu* HCA 1590/2007 (17 March 2011).

justice, the dictates of common sense and the needs of law and order.[29] Nor will Hong Kong recognise the jurisdiction of a foreign court if it gives judgment against a person who under the rules of public international law was entitled to immunity from the jurisdiction of that court and did not waive such immunity. Further, the subject matter of the judgment must not be regulated by an international convention which has been given effect in Hong Kong law, unless the jurisdictional requirements of the convention are fulfilled.

On immunity, the corresponding rules of English law, which are partly regulated by the State Immunity Act 1978, cannot be directly applied. It is submitted that instead the party seeking recognition and enforcement of a foreign judgment needs to satisfy two requirements: (1) the court giving judgment would have jurisdiction if it applied Hong Kong rules on immunity; and (2) the Hong Kong court has jurisdiction to hear the proceedings for the recognition and enforcement of that foreign judgment. For these purposes, the immunities available in Hong Kong include sovereign immunity (for which Hong Kong has adopted an 'absolute', as opposed to 'relative', approach),[30] so-called Crown immunity[31] and diplomatic immunities.

ii. Finality and Conclusiveness

As previously mentioned, the foreign judgment must be final and conclusive according to the law of the rendering court. It must be established that the judgment cannot be modified. A judgment subject to an appeal or leave to appeal will be regarded as final and conclusive, until interfered with by a higher court.[32] A default judgment which is liable to be set aside can also be final and conclusive, although its enforceability may be subject to other considerations including procedural fairness and public policy (see further below).[33]

The issue of finality and conclusiveness has been considered in a series of Hong Kong case law, which will be discussed below. The relevant principles are significant for two reasons. First, despite the mutual arrangements between Hong Kong and mainland China, there remains a large number of mainland Chinese judgments which fall outside the statutory scheme (eg in the absence of an exclusive jurisdiction agreement). The common law regime still applies. Second, the principles on finality and conclusiveness may apply similarly to judgments from other jurisdictions.

In essence, the problems with finality and conclusiveness arise from the 'protest' system (also known as the 'review' or 'trial supervision' system) under PRC law. The system enables the procuratorate to require a court to retry a case.

The question is whether the existence of such a system means that PRC judgments are inconclusive and not final. Despite consideration by the Hong Kong court in numerous

[29] *Chen Li Hung* (n 12) 21.

[30] Under the 'absolute' approach of sovereign immunity, a foreign sovereign is immune from the jurisdiction of the court, unless it waives its immunity. In contrast, the 'relative' approach only affords immunity to a foreign sovereign in exercise of its sovereign function, but not otherwise (for example, if it enters into a purely commercial contract). See *Democratic Republic of Congo v FG Hemisphere Associates LLC* (2011) 14 HKCFAR 95 and specialist texts eg Hazel Fox and Philippa Webb, *The Law of State Immunity* 3rd edn (Oxford, Oxford University Press, 2013).

[31] The '*Hua Tian Long*' [2010] 3 HKLRD 611.

[32] *Chiyu Banking Corp Ltd v Chan Tin Kwun* [1996] 2 HKLR 395; *Korea Data Systems* (n 25).

[33] *Nintendo of America Inc v Bung Enterprises Ltd* [2000] 2 HKC 629; *Fabiano Hotels Ltd v Profitmax Holdings Inc* [2017] 6 HKC 414.

cases, the position remains open.[34] This matter raises questions of public importance, which remain highly relevant despite the enactment of the Mainland Judgments (Reciprocal Enforcement) Ordinance. It applies to all PRC judgments which fall outside the scope of that Ordinance (for example, where an exclusive jurisdiction clause is absent).

In *Chiyu Banking Corporation Limited v Chan Tin Kwun* (*Chiyu*),[35] the claimant bank sought to enforce a judgment from the Fujian Intermediate People's Court. It related to the respondent's liability as a guarantor for unrepaid banking facilities. The respondent appealed to the Fujian Higher People's Court, which dismissed the appeal. The claimant petitioned to the Fujian People's Procuratorate for a retrial. The Procuratorate reported to the Supreme People's Procuratorate requesting the latter to lodge a protest. The issue was whether the invoking of the protest procedure rendered the judgment not final and conclusive. Peter Cheung J (as he then was) held that it was not final and conclusive. The reason was that the court granting the judgment, upon receiving the protest, must retry the action. The protest system is not simply an appeal process, but instead triggers a retrial which may alter the judgment. Although the judgment was not appealable and was enforceable in mainland China, it was not final and conclusive for the purpose of recognition in Hong Kong, because it was not 'final and unalterable in the court which pronounced it'. Notably, Peter Cheung J did not say that the presence of the protest procedure necessarily rendered every PRC judgment not final and conclusive. That view has been confirmed in the subsequent decision of the Court of Appeal in *Lee Yau Wing v Lee Shui Kwan*.[36]

In *Lee Yau Wing*, the claimant obtained a summary judgment in Hong Kong, based on a PRC judgment by the People's Court in Qingyuan. The respondent appealed on the ground that the PRC judgment was not final and conclusive due to the protest system. The Court of Appeal allowed the appeal and ordered the case to proceed to trial. Peter Cheung JA said that the mere existence of the trial supervision system under PRC law did not render a PRC judgment inconclusive and not final. He considered that finality should depend on the 'actual circumstances' of each case. But the Court of Appeal expressly left open the matter until fuller argument in some future case.[37]

The Court of Appeal in *Lam Chit Man v Lam Chi To* followed *Chiyu*, holding that a judgment of the Dongguan Municipality People's Court was not final and conclusive. Woo JA stated that the major reason was that neither party had submitted PRC law evidence on the protest system and thus it was not known whether the current PRC law remained the same or had been amended.[38] Subsequently, in *Lam Chit Man v Cheung Shun Lin*, the Court of Appeal reached the same conclusion by following *Chiyu*, concluding that a Shenzhen judgment was not final and conclusive. However, unlike in *Chiyu*, the claimant in *Lam Chit Man* never lodged a protest, although there was no evidence that the PRC law provided for a time limit for lodging a protest.[39]

Lam Chit Man v Cheung Shun Lin suggested that a PRC judgment is not final and conclusive because of the protest system, even if a protest has not yet been lodged. This would in

[34] *Bank of China Ltd v Yang Fan* [2016] 3 HKLRD 7.

[35] *Chiyu* (n 32).

[36] *Lee Yau Wing v Lee Shui Kwan* [2007] 2 HKLRD 749.

[37] See also *Tan Tay Cuan v Ng Chi Hung* [2001] HKLRD (Yrbk) 195; *Wu Wei v Liu Yi Ping* HCA 1452/2004 (30 January 2009).

[38] *Lam Chit Man v Lam Chi To* (n 26) [20].

[39] *Lam Chit Man v Cheung Shun Lin* [2001–2003] HKCLRT 243 (CA) [31].

principle broaden the scope of *Chiyu* by rendering all PRC judgments unenforceable in Hong Kong, due to the presence of the protest system, even if it has not been invoked. The decision should, however, be treated with circumspection, given that no PRC law evidence was filed at first instance and it was not possible properly to evaluate the current status of the protest system. More recently, in *Bank of China Ltd v Yang Fan*, Anthony To J stated that the position could have been changed, in light of 'tremendous changes' to PRC law over the past 20 years.[40] He pointed to similarities in the current PRC system and the appellate system in Hong Kong, and suggested that PRC judgments could have been final and conclusive despite the protest system.[41]

In summary, there is no rule or principle which says that all PRC judgments are inconclusive and not final due to the possible invocation of the protest system. In light of to the development of PRC law since *Chiyu*, the question should be more fully considered based on current PRC law. A practical approach to the question, with reference to current PRC law, should be adopted. Adopting a narrow interpretation of *Chiyu*, at the very least, the protest procedure must have been invoked before it could conceivably render a judgment inconclusive and not final. For instance, the complainant must have at a minimum petitioned the procuratorate for a protest to be lodged. It is unsatisfactory for the Court of Appeal in *Lam Chit Man v Cheung Shun Lin* to have concluded without more that a Shenzhen court judgment is not final and conclusive although a protest had not been lodged, simply because there was no evidence in that case that the PRC law provides for a time limit for lodging a protest.[42]

It is submitted that, going forward, the Hong Kong court should look at the question more robustly. It is a curious anomaly that, while a mainland judgment may be enforced in mainland China, it cannot be enforced in Hong Kong simply because a petition has been lodged with the procuratorate asking that the protest procedure should be applied. Given that a judgment pending appeal or a default judgment can be regarded as final and conclusive, it is hard to justify that the mere possibility of a retrial under the protest system should give rise to a contrary result. The reasoning for the proposition that 'the procuratorate and protest system is not simply an appeal process'[43] is hardly compelling and it is respectfully submitted that the Hong Kong court's analysis of the situation by reference to wording in the nineteenth century English case of *Nouvion v Freeman*[44] is artificial and impractical. Given the public importance of the matter, the question deserves fuller judicial or legislative attention. Unless and until the legislature intervenes, it is incumbent upon the court to adopt a more rigorous analysis of the law, taking as its starting point the stance propounded by Andrew Cheung CJHC in *Lee Yau Wing*.[45] The court should critically analyse the actual circumstances of each case to assess the finality and conclusiveness of the PRC judgment in question. This may require the court to assess not just what the current protest system is under PRC law, but also what steps the complainant has taken to invoke the system,

[40] *Bank of China Ltd* (n 34) [52].
[41] ibid, [53].
[42] *Lam Chit Man v Cheung Shun Lin* (n 39).
[43] *Chiyu* (n 32) 399G–H.
[44] *Nouvion* (n 25).
[45] *Lee Yau Wing* (n 36).

the approach of the procuratorate to the complaint, the nature of the complaint, the time that has elapsed since the petition and retrial (if any), and the prospects of reversal of the original judgment in any retrial. Such approach will enable the court to better assess the nature of the original PRC judgment in a realistic manner.

iii. Impeachable on Other Grounds

This is a catch-all category which enables the court to refuse to recognise or enforce a foreign judgment if it offends notions of justice in Hong Kong. This is a broad category, which includes a number of disparate principles. For example, the rendering court should have afforded the judgment debtor a reasonable opportunity to be heard (due process) and the foreign judgment should not have been obtained through procedural injustice or irregularity. The judgment debtor must at least have been given reasonable notice of the foreign proceedings so as to have had a proper opportunity to present a case.[46] The foreign judgment should not have been obtained by fraud by the party seeking to have the same recognised or enforced. Note, however, that in Hong Kong, it is a disciplinary offence for the lawyers of a party to allege fraud without compelling evidence that a fraud has been perpetrated. Thus, bare allegation of fraud without full particulars and unsupported by hard evidence is likely to be struck out by the Hong Kong court, without indemnity costs being adjudged to the judgment creditor. Finally, the enforcement of a judgment should not be contrary to Hong Kong public policy. For example, the Hong Kong court will not recognise or enforce a foreign judgment which is inconsistent with a previous judgment or order of the Hong Kong court or contrary to the principle of *res judicata*. As a matter of public policy, the Hong Kong court generally does not enforce a foreign judgment relating to foreign penal, revenue or public laws.[47]

iv. Interlocutory Judgments

Foreign interlocutory judgments or interim measures are not recognisable or enforceable in Hong Kong. The usual objection is that they are not final and conclusive between the parties, which is a requirement under both the statutory and common law regimes just described. Moreover, interlocutory judgments or orders usually do not satisfy the requirement that the judgment to be enforced needs to be for the payment of a sum of money. If, for example, a party obtains an interim injunction from a foreign court, it needs to apply afresh to the Hong Kong court for an injunction. It is not open for it to seek recognition or enforcement of the foreign interim injunction, because it is not final and conclusive.[48] However, a foreign court's costs order which is final and conclusive is enforceable, even though it is granted before the conclusion of the foreign court proceedings[49] in respect, for example, of the costs of an interlocutory hearing.

[46] *Nintendo of America Inc* (n 33).
[47] Johnston and Harris (n 1) [4.008]–[4.033], [9.080].
[48] *Westpac New Zealand Ltd v Gao Hui* [2009] 4 HKC 373.
[49] *Compania Sud Americana De Vapores SA v Hin-Pro International Logistics Ltd* DCCJ 3986/2014 (17 November 2015).

V. Enforcement Procedures and Timing

If a judgment creditor successfully enforces a foreign judgment under the statutory or common law regime, the court will make a judgment or order. This turns the foreign judgment into a Hong Kong court judgment or order, which the judgment creditor can directly enforce. If the judgment debtor does not voluntarily comply with the judgment or order (ie pay the judgment debt), there are various ways for the judgment creditor to enforce or 'execute' it. 'Execution' here means 'quite simply, the process for enforcing or giving effect to the judgment of the court'.[50]

A monetary judgment may be enforced by writ of *fieri facias*, garnishee proceedings, a charging order and the appointment of a receiver. In practice, judgment creditors often resort to insolvency proceedings to aid the debt collection process, and, in appropriate circumstances, wind up or bankrupt the judgment debtors in order to enforce the judgment debts.

The general procedures and timing required for each mode of enforcement is briefly set out below.[51]

A. Writ of *Fieri Facias*[52]

The writ of *fieri facias* (commonly known as the writ of *fi fa*) is the principal means of enforcing a monetary judgment. It requires the court bailiff to seize such of the goods, chattels and other property of the judgment debtor as are reasonably sufficient to satisfy the judgment debt together with interest and the costs of the execution. If the judgment debtor does not make payment, the goods will be sold, usually by public auction, and the proceeds of sale will be handed to the judgment creditor for satisfying the judgment, with any surplus to be returned to the judgment debtor.

Procedurally, the judgment creditor shall issue the writ of execution, in prescribed form with appropriate variations, in the High Court, and pay the prescribed fee. Upon issuance, the writ is returned to the judgment creditor, who shall deliver it to the bailiff's office in the High Court. The writ binds the property in the goods of the judgment debtor since the writ is delivered to the bailiff.[53] Upon delivery, the bailiff acquires a legal right to seize the judgment debtor's goods and property to satisfy the judgment debt stated in the writ.

It is the bailiff's duty under the writ to ascertain where the judgment debtor's goods are and to seize them. He may legally enter the judgment debtor's premises, subject to the overriding rule that he must not gain entry by force against the will of the judgment debtor. The list of property which is liable to attachment and sale is set out in section 21D(1) of the

[50] Michael Wilkinson, Eric TM Cheung and Gary Meggitt, *A Guide to Civil Procedure in Hong Kong* 6th edn (Hong Kong, LexisNexis, 2017) 865, citing *Re Overseas Aviation Engineering (GB) Ltd* [1963] Ch 24, 39 (Lord Denning MR).

[51] For details, see texts on Hong Kong civil procedure eg Camille Cameron and Elsa Kelly, *Principles and Practice of Civil Procedure in Hong Kong* 2nd edn (Hong Kong, Sweet & Maxwell, 2008) [17.01] to [17.47]; Wilkinson, Cheung and Meggitt (n 50) 865–971; Allan Leung and Douglas Clark, *Civil Litigation in Hong Kong* 5th edn (Hong Kong, Sweet & Maxwell, 2017) [12.001]–[12.090]; Clarke (n 13).

[52] Wilkinson, Cheung and Meggitt (n 50) 893–908.

[53] High Court Ordinance (Cap 4), s 21C.

High Court Ordinance (Cap 4). These include land, goods, money, bank notes, cheques, bills of exchange, promissory notes, Government stock, bonds or other securities for money, debts, shares in the capital or joint stock of any company or corporation (other than a private company) and all other property belonging to the judgment debtor. Exceptions are the judgment debtor's tools of trade and his necessary wearing apparel and bedding.

After the property is seized, the bailiff will proceed to sell the same to satisfy the judgment debt. He or she is under a duty to obtain the best price reasonably obtainable. The sale will normally be by public auction. The proceeds of the sale will be handed to the judgment creditor to satisfy the judgment debt, with any surplus to be returned to the judgment debtor.

The time required for this process may vary. If the bailiff can identify and seize liquid assets, such as bank notes or cheques, the process would be quick and straightforward. The process will be lengthened if the bailiff seizes illiquid assets such as immovable property and a public auction is required to sell them.

B. Garnishee[54]

A garnishee order enables a judgment creditor to obtain payment of the judgment debt by the seizure and attachment of debts due or accruing due to the judgment debtor from a third person. The court orders the third person (the 'garnishee') to pay direct to the judgment creditor (the 'garnishor') the debt that the garnishee owes to the judgment debtor. Third party debts include the judgment debtor's funds in bank accounts in Hong Kong, which are usual targets for garnishee applications in the Hong Kong court.

The requirements for a garnishee application include: (1) that the judgment debt must be at least HK$1,000; (2) there is a debt which is due or accruing due from the garnishee to the judgment debtor; and (3) the garnishee is in Hong Kong.

Procedurally, this is a two-stage process. First, the judgment creditor applies ex parte (ie with one party and not notifying other parties) for a provisional order known as an 'order *nisi*'. The application needs to be supported by an affidavit, which must be served on the judgment debtor and the garnishee. Second, there will be an inter partes court hearing (ie between all parties, which include the judgment creditor/garnishor, judgment debtor and the garnishee). At the hearing, the judgment debtor or garnishee may oppose the application. Upon hearing any opposition, the court will exercise its discretion and decide whether or not to grant the application and to make a final order – ie a 'garnishee order absolute'.

It generally takes six to eight weeks from the date of a garnishee application until the grant of a final order, assuming all requirements have been satisfied and there is no opposition.

C. Charging Order[55]

The judgment creditor may apply for a charging order against the judgment debtor's property, which may include land, securities, funds in court and any interest which the judgment

[54] Rules of the High Court (Cap 4A), Ord 49; Wilkinson, Cheung and Meggitt (n 50) 924–37.
[55] High Court Ordinance (Cap 4) s 20A; Wilkinson, Cheung and Meggitt (n 50) 937–54.

debtor holds beneficially or as a trustee under a trust. Usually the imposition of a charging order will make the judgment debtor pay the debt, since, for example, a charging order over land is an encumbrance on the property which affects its sale or transfer. If the debtor does not pay, the judgment creditor may enforce the charging order by obtaining an order for sale of the charged property and apply the proceeds of sale to satisfy the judgment debt.

There are three main classes of property which may be charged: (1) land, securities and funds in court; (2) the judgment debtor's beneficial interest under a trust; and (3) certain property held by the judgment debtor as a trustee. The procedures are similar to those for a garnishee order. There is a two-stage process. First, the judgment creditor needs to apply ex parte (without notice to other parties) for an order *nisi* with a supporting affidavit. The latter must be served on the judgment debtor and any other relevant party, for example, a trustee of the property (if any). Second, at the inter partes hearing (between all parties), the court will hear any opposition from the parties, and will exercise its discretion and decide whether or not to grant a final order in the application – ie a 'charging order absolute'.

The above procedure will usually take six to eight weeks from the date of application until the grant of the charging order, assuming all requirements have been satisfied and there is no opposition.

The judgment creditor may apply to enforce the charging order, primarily by an order of sale by commencing separate proceedings. The court has a discretion as to whether to order the sale of the charged property.[56]

D. Appointment of Receiver[57]

A receiver may receive money or other income arising from the judgment debtor's property, which will prevent the judgment debtor from dealing with such property to the prejudice of the judgment creditor.

A judgment creditor may apply for the appointment of receiver to a master in the High Court, pursuant to s 21L of the High Court Ordinance (Cap 4) and Order 51 of the Rules of the High Court (Cap 4A). In granting the order, the court may require the applicant to provide an undertaking in damages, for any loss and damage which the judgment debtor may incur as a result of the order. The main role of the receiver is to apply the monies received to satisfy the judgment debt. An order for appointment may include such directions as to the giving of security by the receiver, usually by guarantee. A receiver will be entitled to such proper remuneration as the court may authorise.

E. Insolvency Proceedings[58]

Judgment creditors often utilise winding up and bankruptcy procedures in aid of the enforcement of judgment debts. These are not methods of enforcement per se. But the proceedings are 'akin to execution because its purpose is to enforce, on a pari passu basis,

[56] See *Cheung Koon Ping v Muneyoshi Michiyoshi* [1994] 3 HKC 563.
[57] See Wilkinson, Cheung and Meggitt (n 50) 959–61.
[58] ibid, 969.

the payment of the admitted or proved debts of the (judgment debtor)'.[59] In practice, the mere threat of commencing insolvency proceedings often pressurises the judgment debtor to repay the judgment debt, in order to avoid a winding up or bankruptcy order.

To commence the process, the judgment creditor needs to serve a statutory demand on the judgment debtor, which requires him to repay the judgment debt within 21 days. There is a requirement that the debt is above the statutory threshold, currently at HK$10,000.[60] Within the 21-day period, the judgment debtor must either repay the debt, or oppose it with bona fide and substantial grounds. Otherwise, the judgment creditor may commence winding up proceedings (if the debtor is a company) or bankruptcy proceedings (if the debtor is a natural person).

To commence the proceedings, the judgment creditor shall petition for the winding up or bankruptcy of the judgment debtor, by issuing and presenting a winding up or bankruptcy petition in the High Court together with filing fee. Upon issuance of the petition, the court will then set the first hearing date. There is a list of procedural requirements under the winding up rules or bankruptcy rules which the petitioner shall comply with. These include advertisement of the petition in the Government Gazette and two Hong Kong newspapers (in case of winding up), filing and service of all documents on the judgment debtor and the Official Receiver, and answering any requisitions raised by the court. Upon satisfaction of all procedural requirements, the court will issue a Registrar's Certificate to signify compliance. At the first hearing date, if there is no opposition, the court will exercise its discretion and decide whether to make a winding up or bankruptcy order.

Assuming all the papers are in order and there is no opposition, it generally takes three to five months from the date of statutory demand to the grant of a winding up or bankruptcy order.

F. Other Procedures to Assist Enforcement

The principal ways of seeking enforcement of a monetary judgment have been outlined above. In addition, there are miscellaneous procedures which assist the judgment creditor to procure performance of the judgment.

A practical problem which judgment creditors face is to identify the nature and value of the judgment debtor's assets within the jurisdiction. For this purpose, a judgment creditor may seek assistance from the court by way of miscellaneous mechanisms. In particular, he may apply for 'oral examination' against the judgment debtor or its officer (if the judgment debtor is a company).[61] Under these mechanisms, the judgment debtor would be brought to the court and be examined on oath as to the whereabouts of his assets. Accordingly, the court can make appropriate orders against the judgment debtor concerning performance of the judgment.

In addition, the judgment creditor may seek a stop order or stop notice, which will enable him or her to assert an interest in any securities or funds in court before the judgment debtor takes steps to dispose of them. A stop order prohibits a person from taking certain

[59] ibid, citing *Re Lines Bros* [1983] Ch 1, 20.
[60] Bankruptcy Ordinance (Cap 6), ss 6, 6A; Companies (Winding Up and Miscellaneous Provisions) Ordinance (Cap 32), s 178(3).
[61] Rules of the High Court (Cap 4A), Ords 48, 49B.

specified steps in relation to funds in court, whereas a stop notice prohibits dealings of securities not in court.[62]

Furthermore, the judgment creditor may apply for a prohibition order, which restricts a judgment debtor from leaving Hong Kong until the judgment is satisfied. The judgment creditor needs to show that the judgment debtor is demonstrably going to escape from the jurisdiction in order to evade liability for payment of the judgment debt.[63] If there is evidence that the judgment debtor has deliberately refused to comply with a court judgment or order, the judgment creditor may commence committal proceedings and/or apply for a writ of sequestration,[64] which are processes of punishing contempt of court. These mechanisms will have a deterrence effect against, and punish a judgment debtor for, his deliberate refusal or failure to pay a judgment debt.

VI. Special Cases

As stated above, it is a requirement for the recognition and enforcement of a foreign judgment that the foreign court has jurisdiction over the matter. The Hong Kong court imposes restriction on the subject matter jurisdiction of foreign courts, for example, in respect of intellectual property matters and disputes relating to land. In determining the jurisdiction of the foreign court, there are specific requirements regarding foreign judgments which touch upon certain specific subject matters.

A. Intellectual Property

In order to be recognised and enforced, the foreign judgment should not directly relate to the grant and registration of intellectual property rights in Hong Kong. It may, however, relate to a ruling on an infringement of an intellectual property right which is to be, or has been, granted or registered in the country of the foreign court, or is otherwise within the foreign court's jurisdiction.

The *Moçambique* rule[65] (described in Section VI.B) applies by analogy in determining a court's jurisdiction in intellectual property cases. In *Esquel Enterprises Ltd v TAL Apparel Ltd*[66] the Court of Appeal followed the English cases of *Coin Controls Ltd v Suzo International (UK) Ltd*[67] and *Plastus Kreativ AB v Minnesota Mining and Manufacturing Co.*[68] Tang JA determined that the *Moçambique* rule applied to patent cases. Accordingly, if a case relates to the infringement of a foreign patent, this 'must clearly be a weighty factor' in determining jurisdiction.[69] The Hong Kong court will generally consider that it should not exercise jurisdiction over a dispute concerning foreign intellectual property rights, in particular patents, designs and trademarks registered in another country. This may in principle be extended to

[62] ibid, Ord 50.
[63] High Court Ordinance (Cap 4), s 21B; Rules of the High Court (Cap 4A), Ord 44A.
[64] Rules of the High Court (Cap 4A), Ord 45.
[65] From the case *British South Africa Co v Companhia de Moçambique* [1893] AC 602. See also s VI.B below.
[66] *Esquel Enterprises Ltd v TAL Apparel Ltd* [2006] 2 HKLRD 363.
[67] *Coin Controls Ltd v Suzo International (UK) Ltd* [1999] Ch 33.
[68] *Plastus Kreativ AB v Minnesota Mining and Manufacturing Co* [1995] RPC 438.
[69] *Esquel Enterprises* (n 66) [38].

unregistered rights such as copyright, goodwill, reputation, trade secrets, etc. The rationale for the rule is that the validity of intellectual property rights are matters of public interest and territorial in nature. Such rights should therefore be regulated and enforced by the local court. As a matter of public policy and comity, a foreign court should not interfere with the issues concerning the validity and registration of such rights. As a result, in principle, the Hong Kong court will regard a foreign court as having jurisdiction over an intellectual property right dispute, if the subject rights are related to the country of the foreign court. A foreign judgment relating to intellectual property rights outside of the relevant country may consequently not be recognised or enforced in Hong Kong.

But there are strong arguments against too strict a prohibition. For instance, the Hong Kong Arbitration Ordinance (Cap 609) was amended in 2017 to include a new Part 11A. The amendment enables parties to resolve intellectual property disputes through arbitration and arbitral awards dealing with intellectual property rights may thus be enforced in Hong Kong and will not automatically be refused recognition simply because they deal with intellectual property rights. This applies equally to awards relating to the validity and registration of intellectual property rights. Given the position in arbitration, there is little justification for foreign court judgments relating to intellectual property rights being automatically refused recognition or enforcement in Hong Kong, provided that all other factors (including submission to jurisdiction or presence in the foreign country) are satisfied. Whether or not a foreign judgment dealing with intellectual property rights is ultimately enforced in Hong Kong may depend on the question litigated. Thus, if the main question before the foreign court was whether an intellectual property right (for example, a trademark or patent) had been validly registered in Hong Kong and if the foreign court concludes that such registration was invalid and should be rectified, the Hong Kong court is unlikely to recognise that part of the foreign judgment. A public registration of intellectual property rights affects third parties whom may not have been privy to the relevant foreign court proceedings between the claimant and respondent. In those circumstances, rectification of the Hong Kong registration could potentially have adverse consequences on the third parties who would not have had an opportunity to make appropriate representations and to be heard in the foreign proceedings. In contrast, where the validity of intellectual property rights arises purely as an incidental question in the foreign proceedings (for example, as a defence to a claiming for breach of a licensing agreement where it is argued that there was no breach because a trademark or patent registration in Hong Kong was not valid), there may be a basis for the Hong Kong court to recognise the outcome of the foreign judgment on the main issue. A finding of breach or the absence of breach in relation to the licensing agreement would only be binding on the parties to the alleged licensing agreement and would not require the Hong Kong registration to be varied.

B. Land

The foreign judgment should not directly relate to land outside the country in which the rendering court is situate. Under the *Moçambique* rule as applied to Hong Kong,[70]

[70] *DX v LN* FCMC 7870/2014 (30 November 2015).

Hong Kong courts have no jurisdiction over disputes concerning title or interests in immovable property outside Hong Kong, or claims of trespass to immovable property or other claims of wrongdoing relating to damages to, entry upon or occupation of such property. There are exceptions (1) where the claim is based on a personal obligation arising between the parties; (2) in administration cases in which the claim is in connection with the administration of estates and trusts; or (3) where the issue as to title of foreign land only arises as an incidental question. Further, in some cases, the court may take jurisdiction where the facts justify it, for example if the parties have waived any objection and no third-party interest is involved. The scope of the rule is uncertain. One can see the justification for the rule, in the converse situation where a foreign court determines a question of title or interest in Hong Kong real property. Such a question should be more properly determined by the Hong Kong court and, for that reason, the Hong Kong court may not recognise a judgment purporting to decide title or interest in Hong Kong land. The force of the rule is, however, weaker if the property question only arises incidentally, that is, as one of the many issues that need to be resolved in order to determine a dispute solely affecting the parties before the foreign court. It is submitted that the question of recognition will essentially be determined as part of the Hong Kong court's assessment of the indirect jurisdiction of the foreign court.

C. Environmental Wrong

There are various international conventions relating to environment matters which apply to Hong Kong.[71] These conventions provide for dispute settlement concerning the relevant environmental wrong. Hong Kong has enacted various domestic legislations accordingly, which deal with the recognition and enforcement of those judgments or decisions. Several examples are discussed below.

The 2001 International Convention on Civil Liability for Bunker Oil Pollution Damage applies to Hong Kong. It was adopted to ensure that adequate, prompt and effective compensation is available to persons who suffer damage caused by spills of oil, when carried as fuel in ships' bunkers.[72] The Convention provides for the settlement of disputes regarding damage as a result of spills of oil from ships' bunkers. To give effect to its international obligation, Hong Kong enacted the Bunker Oil Pollution (Liability and Compensation) Ordinance (Cap 605). Section 21 of that Ordinance provides that the Foreign Judgment (Reciprocal Enforcement) Ordinance (Cap 319), except certain excluded provisions, applies to a relevant judgment given by a Member State of the Convention (except the PRC). The requirements for enforcement are: (1) the judgment must be final and conclusive; and (2) the judgment orders the payment of a sum of money other than tax, charge of a like nature, fine or other penalty.

The 1969 International Convention on Civil Liability for Oil Pollution Damage (as amended by the 1992 Protocol) also applies to Hong Kong. It provides a mechanism for

[71] See discussion in section III.C above.

[72] See 'International Convention on Civil Liability for Bunker Oil Pollution Damage (BUNKER)' (*International Maritime Organisation*), available online: www.imo.org/en/About/Conventions/ListOfConventions/Pages/International-Convention-on-Civil-Liability-for-Bunker-Oil-Pollution-Damage(BUNKER).aspx.

ensuring the payment of compensation for oil pollution damage.[73] Hong Kong has enacted the Merchant Shipping (Liability and Compensation for Oil Pollution) Ordinance (Cap 414). It provides for

> compensation for pollution caused by the discharge or escape of oil from oil-carrying ships and for the liability of shipowners; for compulsory insurance in respect of such liability; for contributions by oil importers and others to the International Fund for Compensation for Oil Pollution Damage; for the liability of the Fund in certain circumstances for such pollution; for the indemnification of shipowners by the Fund; and for incidental or related matters.[74]

Sections 18 and 27 of that Ordinance set out jurisdictional requirements of the Hong Kong courts and enables registration of foreign judgments under and in accordance with the Foreign Judgments (Reciprocal Enforcement) Ordinance (Cap 319).

Hong Kong has enacted the Nuclear Material (Liability for Carriage) Ordinance (Cap 479), in recognition of its international obligations under the 'relevant international agreement' with respect to third-party liability in the field of nuclear energy which has been applied to Hong Kong. An example is the 1960 Convention on Third Party Liability in the Field of Nuclear Energy (as amended in 1964 and 1982). Under section 10(4) of that Ordinance, the Foreign Judgments (Reciprocal Enforcement) Ordinance (Cap 319) applies to any foreign judgment which is certified by the Chief Executive of Hong Kong to be a 'relevant foreign judgment' under the Ordinance. The Ordinance gives effect to the enforceability of such a foreign judgment under the relevant international agreement.[75]

D. Breach of Competition Law

There is no rule or principle against the recognition or enforcement of foreign judgments in class actions relating as a result of breach of competition law. Similarly, as above, since competition law involves local regulations imposed by a state, the recognition and enforcement of foreign judgments relating to the breach of competition law is potentially objectionable for reasons of public policy, particularly if it involves foreign penal laws. Besides, the Merchant Shipping (Liner Conference) Ordinance (Cap 482) provides for the enforcement of 'judgments' pursuant to the 1974 United Nations Convention on a Code of Conduct for Liner Conferences 1974, which relates to reduction of competition and relates to competition law issues.

VII. Assessment of the Current Regime

Hong Kong enjoys the rule of law and the benefit of an independent judiciary. These promote the fair and efficient administration of justice, including the recognition and enforcement

[73] See 'International Convention on the Establishment of an International Fund for Compensation for Oil Pollution Damage (FUND)' (*International Maritime Organisation*), available online: www.imo.org/en/About/Conventions/ListOfConventions/Pages/International-Convention-on-the-Establishment-of-an-International-Fund-for-Compensation-for-Oil-Pollution-Damage-(FUND).aspx.

[74] Cap 414, Long Title.

[75] Nuclear Material (Liability for Carriage) Ordinance (Cap 479), s 10(6), which prevails over s 10(5) that affords substantive defence to a person against whom enforcement is sought.

of foreign judgments. Its private international law, which derived its origin from English common law and continues to evolve, provides a solid foundation for self-refinement and future development.

The current regime, as described above, is a product of political and legal developments through the city's history. This includes the former British colonial rule, China's resumption of its sovereignty, and the practice of the 'One Country, Two Systems' principle under the Basic Law. Hong Kong's unique status as a special administrative region of China offers possibilities for the city to improve its law, including on recognition and enforcement of foreign judgments.

In this regard, the major deficiency of the current regime is the lack of uniformity and clarity of the law. More particularly, the following issues will be discussed below:

1. Restrictive application of Cap 597 to cases with an exclusive jurisdiction agreement;
2. Lack of convincing justification for the selection of the 15 countries under Cap 319A, for which registration of judgments is enabled;
3. Uncertainty and lack of clarity for common law rules, which are derived from old English case law and are arguably stagnant due to legislative reforms in England; and
4. Progress of the consultation and adoption processes of the Hague Conventions.

A. Limited Application of Cap 597 to Mainland Judgments

The application of Cap 597, which enables registration of mainland Chinese judgments, is restricted to cases with an exclusive jurisdiction agreement. This requires the parties to have agreed on an exclusive choice of court agreement. This significantly restricts the coverage of the registration mechanism, which effectively requires mainland judgment creditors to pursue the common law route. As discussed above, there are problems with enforcing mainland judgments under the common law regime, including on the issue of finality and conclusiveness of mainland judgments.

Hong Kong's new arrangements with the mainland, as referred to above,[76] will alleviate these problems. These arrangements, however, need to be implemented by local legislation before they come into effect. There is currently no timeline for the process of local legislation and implementation in Hong Kong and the mainland.

B. Need for Review of the List of Countries in Cap 319A

Cap 319 enables registration of judgments in the 15 countries listed in Schedules 1 and 2 to the Foreign Judgments (Reciprocal Enforcement) Order (Cap 319A). As described above, these countries were designated by the previous colonial Government in the 1970s and 1990s, based on the then Commonwealth scheme and bilateral agreements between the UK

[76] Those are the 'Arrangement on Reciprocal Recognition and Enforcement of Civil Judgments in Matrimonial and Family Cases by the Courts of the Mainland and of the Hong Kong Special Administrative Region' (20 June 2017) and the 'Arrangement on Reciprocal Recognition and Enforcement of Judgments in Civil and Commercial Matters by the Courts of the Mainland and of the Hong Kong Special Administrative Region' (18 January 2019).

and the non-Commonwealth countries on the list.[77] Since the handover in 1997, the scheme and bilateral agreements ceased to have effect in Hong Kong. However, Cap 319 continues to have effect in Hong Kong, in respect of the list of 15 countries designated by the previous colonial Government's Legal Notices. This alone calls for a full review of the list by the current Hong Kong Government.

More importantly, since the list was finalised in 1990s, there has been development around the world on the recognition and enforcement of judgments. In the spirit of the Ordinance (as shown in its long title and various sections including sections 3 and 11), the Chief Executive in Council should review and reconsider the list from time to time, in order to fully utilise the benefits conferred by the Ordinance. This will enable registration of judgments of such foreign jurisdictions which afford substantial reciprocity of treatment to Hong Kong judgments. That will promote the mutual enforcement of judgments, for the promotion of international comity and individual justice among litigants.

C. Uncertainty and Lack of Clarity of Common Law Rules

The common law regime originated from the English common law rules. Since Hong Kong does not have a substantial body of case law on enforcing foreign judgments, the Hong Kong courts often refer to English case law in adjudicating cases. This means the laws of Hong Kong are scattered in case law in England and Hong Kong, which renders the rules uncertain and unclear.

Apart from the general problems of uncertainty with common law, there is a special problem in this area due to the substantial development of English law principles since 1997, which have not been adopted. Examples are various European Conventions concerning enforcement of foreign judgments mentioned in section II.B above. Therefore, the Hong Kong courts may need to refer to old English case law prior to such changes, in order to ascertain the common law position. Such old English common law may not necessarily reflect current social and economic situations.

In any event, reliance on English case law may not necessarily be appropriate in resolving disputes in the Hong Kong courts. This calls for consideration of a potential code which is catered for Hong Kong and takes into account the latest legal development on the law in this regard.

D. Progress on Adopting the Hague Conventions

To date, Hong Kong has not adopted the 2005 Hague Convention on Choice of Court Agreements. Following two rounds of public consultations in 2004 and 2007, the Hong Kong Government decided to take a 'wait-and-see' approach.[78] There were concerns over the

[77] Clarke (n 13) [412].

[78] In January 2014, the Hong Kong Government published a consultation paper on the then draft Hague Convention on Exclusive Choice of Court Agreements, Jurisdiction and Foreign Judgments. On 30 June 2005 the Government published another consultation paper on the 2005 Hague Convention on Choice of Court Agreements as adopted. The public's views were mixed. While some respondents (such as the judiciary and the Law

terms of the Convention, its implications to the laws in Hong Kong and the Judiciary and the number of its Member States. The Government indicated that it would keep the issue in view from time to time.[79] Meanwhile, the PRC signed the 2005 Hague Convention on 9 September 2017 without making any reservation in relation to Hong Kong. Therefore, when the PRC accedes to the 2005 Hague Convention, it should also apply to Hong Kong, unless the PRC shall in future make a reservation to exclude Hong Kong.

As regards the 2018 Draft Hague Convention on the Recognition and Enforcement of Foreign Judgments in Civil and Commercial Matters, the Hong Kong Government published a consultation paper in October 2016 in this regard. It has also been participating, as part of the PRC delegation, in the Special Commission of the Hague Conference Judgments Project in respect of the draft Convention. It is envisaged that Hong Kong will continue to take part in such work until its conclusion.

In relation to both Conventions, the progress of the consultations and/or adoption processes has been slow. Regarding the 2005 Hague Convention, it is clear from the Government's papers referred to above that the Government is adopting a 'wait-and-see' approach, in view of the concerns raised by the public. It is unclear whether the Government plans to take any steps to address or alleviate the public's concerns. Unless and until it takes active steps to deal with them, it is unclear when the Government will be able to achieve much progress in the adoption process.

In view of the above issues and problems, the next section will suggest reform and improvement to the current regime.

VIII. The Future

With regard to the above identified issues, it is suggested that the Government should: (1) implement the new comprehensive arrangement with mainland China on mutual enforcement of judgments; (2) take the initiative to review and update the list of countries for Cap 319, pursuant to its powers under section 3 of Cap 319; and (3) expedite the consultation process on the Hague Conventions, with a view to adopting these Conventions. These will be explained further below.

A. Implement the New Regime of Enforcement for PRC Judgments

On 18 January 2019,[80] the Hong Kong and PRC governments signed a new arrangement on reciprocal recognition and Enforcement of Judgments in civil and commercial matters.

Society of Hong Kong) were generally in favour of applying the 2005 Hague Convention to Hong Kong, others (such as the Hong Kong Bar Association) expressed reservation on certain terms of the 2005 Hague Convention.

[79] See the written reply by the then Secretary for Justice, Mr Rimsky Yuen SC, to the question of Mr Dennis Kwok, member of the Legislative Council: 'LCQ15: The Hague Convention on Choice of Court Agreements' (25 June 2004), available online: www.info.gov.hk/gia/general/201406/25/P201406240828.htm.

[80] Before the signing of the Arrangement, in November 2018, the Hong Kong Government published a paper on the Proposed Arrangement to the Legislative Council Panel on Administration of Justice and Legal Services: Department of Justice, 'Proposed Arrangement on Reciprocal Recognition and Enforcement of Judgments in Civil and Commercial Matters between Hong Kong and the Mainland' (*Legislative Council*, November 2018),

It provides for the establishment of a new bilateral legal mechanism for mutual recognition and enforcement. Subject to implementation by local legislation, the new mechanism will have the following features:[81]

1. It will be a more comprehensive regime than the current one (under Cap 597) for mutual recognition and enforcement of judgments in civil and commercial matters. It will apply generally to matters which are considered to be of a 'civil and commercial' nature under both Hong Kong and mainland law (Articles 1 and 2).
2. Certain judgments are expressly excluded, for instance, judicial review cases, certain family matters, succession and probate, certain intellectual property cases, marine pollution claims, bankruptcy and insolvency, determination of a natural person's right to vote, disappearance or death or legal capacity for civil acts, validity of arbitration agreement and its setting aside, recognition and enforcement of arbitral awards (Articles 3, 5 and 15). Preservation measures in mainland or anti-suit injunction or interim reliefs in Hong Kong are also excluded (Article 4).
3. Except for the above, the covered judgments will include, in the case of mainland, all legally effective judgments of the second instance, judgments of the first instance from which no appeal is allowed according to law or no appeal has been filed by the expiry of the statutory time limit for appeal, as well as the above types of judgments given in accordance with the trial supervision procedure. In the case of Hong Kong, these will include all legally effective judgments given by the Court of Final Appeal, the Court of Appeal and the Court of First instance of the High Court, the District Court, the Labour Tribunal, the Lands Tribunal, the Small Claims Tribunal or the Competition Tribunal (Article 4).
4. On jurisdiction, the court of the requested place for enforcement shall consider the original court to have jurisdiction if one of the specified conditions is satisfied and if the court of the requested place considers its courts do not have exclusive jurisdiction over the action according to its laws. The list of specified conditions include, for example, the defendant's place of residence, office or place of business, place of performance of the relevant contract, place of commission of the tort, etc (Article 11).
5. The grounds for refusal of recognition and enforcement include, for example, where the defendant was not legally summoned in the original court or was not given a reasonable opportunity to present his case, fraud, where the judgment was rendered in an action after the court of the requested place has accepted an action or given a judgment on the same dispute, the existence of a valid arbitration agreement, etc (Articles 12 and 13).
6. Both monetary relief and non-monetary reliefs will be covered. Where the judgment provides for punitive or exemplary damages, the punitive or exemplary part of the

available online: www.legco.gov.hk/yr18-19/english/panels/ajls/papers/ajls20181126cb4-230-3-e.pdf. In that paper, the Hong Kong government outlined the need for a wider statutory regime for the recognition and enforcement of PRC judgments in general. It proposed that the government enter into a further arrangement with the PRC government on the subject.

[81] The following references to specific Articles refer to those in the 'Arrangement on Reciprocal Recognition and Enforcement of Judgments in Civil and Commercial Matters by the Courts of the Mainland and of the Hong Kong Special Administrative Region' (18 January 2019). See also the Consultation Paper of the Arrangement: Department of Justice (n 6).

damages will not be recognised and enforced, save for certain exceptions in intellectual property, competition law and trade secrets cases (Articles 17 and 18).
7. A court of the requested place may, before or after accepting any application for recognition and enforcement of a judgment, impose property preservation or mandatory measures in accordance with the law of that place (Article 24).

The arrangement will take effect on a date to be announced, after both Hong Kong and mainland China have completed the necessary implementation and legislation procedures. It will supersede the current regime under Cap 597.

The new regime will provide greater clarity and certainty, with a wider scope of application than Cap 597. The Hong Kong government's continued efforts on local legislation and continued communications with the PRC authorities will be welcomed.

Separately, the Department of Justice launched a public consultation in February 2019 to seek views on the proposed 'Mainland Judgments in Matrimonial and Family Cases (Reciprocal Recognition and Enforcement) Bill', which is a welcome step towards better safeguards for families, particularly in cross-border marriages.

B. Review the List of Countries in Cap 319A

The Chief Executive in Council, or its delegate, should take the initiate to review the list of 15 countries in Cap 319A. In accordance with sections 3 and 11 of that Ordinance, it is contemplated that the list should be revised to cover countries which allow enforcement of Hong Kong judgments by registration. Therefore, the review will involve (1) a survey on the enforceability of Hong Kong judgments around the world, particularly those countries with which Hong Kong maintains a close social and economic relationship; (2) communications between Hong Kong (or the PRC Government in appropriate circumstances) and the relevant foreign jurisdictions on the reciprocal enforcement of judgments; and (3) an assessment by the Hong Kong Government on the benefits or otherwise of including a particular jurisdiction to the list.

C. Speed up Consultations on and Integration of Hague Conventions

Regarding the 2005 Hague Convention on Choice of Court Agreements, the Government should take the initiative to handle and address the public concerns expressed in the consultation process. Given that the PRC has signed the 2005 Hague Convention in 2017, the Hong Kong Government should take more active steps to deal with those concerns, with an aim to adopting the 2005 Hague Convention in future.

Regarding the 2018 Draft Hague Convention on the Recognition and Enforcement of Foreign Judgments,[82] the Government indicated that, once the 2018 Draft

[82] '2018 Draft Convention' (*Hague Conference on Private International Law*, 24–29 May 2018), available online: assets.hcch.net/docs/23b6dac3-7900-49f3-9a94-aa0ffbe0d0dd.pdf.

Hague Convention has been concluded, it will consider the question of applying that Convention to Hong Kong. Before that, it will assess the impact of its provisions on the legal system of Hong Kong and the views of interested parties.

The forthcoming convention will facilitate the recognition and enforcement of foreign judgments across the Member States. If (as one can expect) it is widely adopted across jurisdictions, Hong Kong can benefit from adopting the convention in the future, thereby promoting the mutual recognition and enforcement of judgments among states. This will foster Hong Kong's position as an international dispute resolution centre and attract foreign investment.

In February 2019, the Department of Justice published a Consultation Paper No 2, with the the 2018 Draft Hague Convention appended.[83] The paper sets out the key outstanding issues of the 2018 Draft Hague Convention and seeks comments from the interested parties.

IX. Conclusion

The dual regime for recognition and enforcement of foreign judgments has arisen from Hong Kong's unique historical background. The statutes provide relatively straightforward procedures for enforcing eligible judgments, as a result of cross-border arrangements, scheme and bilateral agreements and international conventions. The common law allows recognition and enforcement of other judgments. The relevant rules, which are derived from English common law, are flexible but tend to be uncertain. It is hoped that the Government will take the initiative to review and reform the laws, including adoption of international convention and local legislation, with a view to achieving a more unified set of rules in harmony with the international law and standards.

[83] Department of Justice, 'Consultation Paper No. 2 on 2018 Draft Convention on the Recognition and Enforcement of Foreign Judgments' (February 2019), available online: www.doj.gov.hk/eng/public/pdf/2019/consultation_ild.pdf.

4

Taiwan

FULDIEN LI AND YEN-TE WU

I. Introduction

Taiwan (or the Republic of China, ROC) follows the automatic recognition system for foreign judgments and foreign arbitral awards. The so-called 'automatic recognition system' means that the effect of any final and binding judgment rendered by a foreign court shall be recognised automatically if the judgment complies with the legal requirements of the country where the recognition is sought. Such foreign judgment is not subject to any judicial review.

II. Background

Regarding the recognition of foreign judgments in Taiwan, Article 402 of the Code of Civil Procedure provides:

> A final and binding judgment rendered by a foreign court shall be recognized, except in case of any of the following circumstances:
>
> 1. Where the foreign court lacks jurisdiction pursuant to the ROC laws;
> 2. Where a default judgment is rendered against the losing defendant, except in the case where the notice or summons of the initiation of action had been legally served in a reasonable time in the foreign country or had been served through judicial assistance provided under the ROC laws;
> 3. Where the performance ordered by such judgment or its litigation procedure is contrary to ROC public policy or morals;
> 4. Where there exists no mutual recognition between the foreign country and the ROC.
>
> The provision of the preceding paragraph shall apply mutatis mutandis to a final and binding ruling rendered by a foreign court.

A foreign judgment will be recognised unless it falls within one of the exceptions stipulated in Article 402 of the Taiwan Code of Civil Procedure. In short, the Taiwan Code of Civil Procedure adopts the principle of automatic recognition – a final and binding judgment rendered by a foreign court is prima facie equivalent to a final and binding judgment rendered by a Taiwan court. If any of the exceptional circumstances is applicable to a foreign judgment, Taiwan courts shall refuse to recognise it, even though it is a final and binding judgment rendered by a foreign court. In practice, the standard of recognising foreign judgments rests on whether these judgments fall within the exceptional circumstances stipulated in Article 402 of the Code of Civil Procedure. However, this does not mean that the merits of foreign judgments are subject to review by Taiwan courts. The factual findings and application of laws determined by a foreign court shall not be subject to adjudication by the Taiwan court.[1] According to a civil ruling by the Supreme Court,[2] the effect of any final and binding judgment rendered by a foreign court should depend on its compliance with the requirements set out in Article 402 of the Code of Civil Procedure. The doctrine of *res judicata* applies to foreign judgments. In other words, regardless of whether the factual findings and application of the law by a foreign court were erroneous or not, they are not included in the scope of consideration by the Taiwan court.

Furthermore, Article 4(1) of the Compulsory Enforcement Act governs the enforcement of foreign judgments. The three criteria in applying for recognition and enforcement of a final and binding foreign judgment are as follows: (1) a final and binding foreign judgment; (2) no exceptional circumstance arising under Article 402 of the Code of Civil Procedure; and (3) a declaratory judgment confirming the enforceability of a foreign judgment rendered by a court in Taiwan.[3]

In any case, as long as a final and binding foreign judgment meets specified requirements, its effect is automatically recognised by Taiwan courts. In terms of declaratory or constitutive foreign judgment, only if it fulfils the conditions of recognition shall its effect be recognised without any further special procedure. However, given the nature of condemnatory judgments, the realisation of payments requires state power; hence, any condemnatory judgment rendered by a foreign court is not directly enforceable in Taiwan. The enforceability of a final and binding judgment rendered by a foreign court shall only be granted after a Taiwan court reviews it and ensures that it fulfils all conditions of recognition, thereby declaring it enforceable.

III. Recognition and Enforcement in the Absence of Treaties or Similar Arrangements

Considering the difficulties in the recognition of Taiwan's unsettled status, it is unlikely that bilateral or international treaties would enable Taiwan to recognise and enforce

[1] Two civil judgments of the Supreme Court (Taishangtzu No 1118 (1998) and Taishangtzu No 109 (2008) have stressed that the prohibition of any review of the substance of foreign judgments is applied by most countries when reviewing applications for recognition of foreign judgments. With regard to the recognition of a foreign judgment and its enforcement, the court in the country of enforcement is prohibited from reviewing a foreign judgment as to its substance, including factual findings and application of laws. A foreign judgment can only be reviewed when it is unclear whether such a judgment is consistent with domestic public policy or morals. This is a statutory exception stipulated in Art 402(3) of the Code of Civil Procedure. The provision expressly states that the effect of a foreign judgment shall not be recognised when its content or litigation procedure is contrary to ROC public policy or morals.

[2] Taishangtzu No 2579 (1996).

[3] Art 4(1) of the Compulsory Enforcement Act provides:

> an application for compulsory execution under a final and binding foreign judgment shall be granted when it does not fall within any circumstances under Article 402 of the Code of Civil Procedure, and declared enforceable by ROC courts. The court where the debtor's domicile is located has jurisdiction over the proceeding with respect to the application for enforcement. In cases where the debtor is not domiciled in the ROC, the court where the property for execution is located, or where the execution is carried out, has jurisdiction.

foreign judgments. One of the few exceptions, however, is the Agreement between the Taipei Economic and Cultural Office in Vietnam and the Vietnam Economic and Cultural Office in Taipei on Judicial Assistance in Civil Matters, which was signed in 2010 as a result of increasing numbers of transnational marriages between Taiwan and Vietnam citizens. Both parties agreed that either party shall enforce civil judgments rendered by the other party on the basis of equality and reciprocity.

Nonetheless, despite the global reality of having no treaty applicable to Taiwan in terms of recognition and enforcement of foreign judgments, Taiwan courts have repeatedly recognised and enforced foreign judgments. In 1965, Article 402(2) was amended from 'serving the notice or summons of the initiation of action on the parties in a foreign country' to 'legally serving the notice or summons of the initiation of action in a foreign country within a reasonable time'. The concept of 'no mutual recognition', which is subject to Article 402(4), was also changed from 'no recognition of states in public international law' to 'no mutual recognition' of judicial decisions.

When a Taiwan court reviews an application for recognition of a foreign judgment, the court shall not recognise its effect in any case if it falls within any of the four exceptional circumstances stipulated in Article 402 of the Code of Civil Procedure. Once an application is rejected, a foreign judgment shall not be enforced through compulsory execution procedures. According to a civil judgment by the Supreme Court,[4] when a foreign judgment is filed for recognition, the court will give a simple decision without any merits review. If the other party protests the foreign judgment's recognition under Article 402 of the Code of Civil Procedure, the court will decide on whether or not the judgment falls under any of the exceptional circumstances. On the other hand, a court declaration of enforceability is required for an application for compulsory execution of a condemnatory judgment (or ruling) in accordance with the Compulsory Enforcement Act Article 4(1)(1).

The following sections elaborate on the four exceptional circumstances specified in Article 402 of the Code of Civil Procedure.

A. The Foreign Court has No Jurisdiction under Taiwan Law

Some academic theories assert that a foreign court has no jurisdiction over disputes when its judgment does not meet jurisdictional requirements under the Taiwan Code of Civil Procedure. In practice, a foreign court's lack of jurisdiction means that a Taiwan court has exclusive jurisdiction over certain matters; hence, no other court (including courts in other countries) can administer such adjudication. In this regard, most types of exclusive jurisdiction are specified in the Code of Civil Procedure. For example, in a demarcation dispute involving real property, the court where the real property is located has exclusive jurisdiction.

According to the civil ruling of the Supreme Court,[5] although no provision in relation to international jurisdiction (sometimes referred to as 'indirect jurisdiction') over civil matters has been expressly stipulated in the Act Governing the Choice of Law in Civil Matters Involving Foreign Elements, the court in which recognition is sought can still apply

[4] Taishangtzu No 232 (2016).
[5] Taikangtzu No 1004 (2015).

domestic law by analogy to determine whether the foreign court had jurisdiction over specific matters. For example, Article 15 of the Code of Civil Procedure on 'issues relating to torts' refers to claims for damage compensation or damage prevention resulting from a tort, or any active or passive declaratory action as a result of a tort. If there are no specific provisions in any special law relating to jurisdiction over special types of torts, Article 15 is applicable. When a plaintiff files a civil lawsuit involving foreign elements and intends to declare the existence of a right to damage prevention, Articles 1, 2, 15(1) and 21 may be applied using the principle of analogy.

Accordingly, any court of the defendant's domicile, main office or principal place of business or any court where the tort is committed or the effect of the tort is felt will have jurisdiction over the case.

In a case on copyright infringement, the plaintiff in the case sought to prevent damage through recourse to a complaint procedure, and the defendant filed a lawsuit against the former for a negative declaration confirming non-existence of the plaintiff's right to damage prevention. The case was considered a tort lawsuit. The civil ruling of the Supreme Court[6] noted that international jurisdiction over foreigners' obligations arising from a tort was not expressly stipulated in the Act Governing the Choice of Law in Civil Matters Involving Foreign Elements. Consequently, Articles 1, 15(1) and 22 of the Code of Civil Procedure should be applied using the principle of analogy, with the result that the courts of the defendant's domicile and the place where the tort was committed will have jurisdiction.

B. The Foreign Judgment was Rendered in Default, Except Where the Notice or Summons had been Legally Served in the Relevant Foreign Country or Through Judicial Assistance Provided under Taiwan Law

This provision's purpose is to protect a defendant's substantive right to present a defence. It does not mean that every application for recognition of default foreign judgments will be rejected by Taiwan courts. This provision does not apply to cases where the notice or summons has been legally served under foreign laws or has been served through judicial assistance in accordance with Taiwan's Law in Supporting Foreign Courts on Consigned Cases, even if the defendant does not appear in court. It is worth noting that, as a result of divergent regulations pertaining to service of legal documents across different countries, a court in Taiwan can use its own discretion to determine whether a defendant's right to present a defence was fully protected in foreign proceedings, particularly when the notice or summons was served in full compliance with the relevant foreign law. A case in point is a 2008 Supreme Court decision[7] which held that the service of legal documents on the parties' statutory agents or advocates instead of the parties to the proceeding was not prohibited. This case was remitted to the High Court as a result of the Supreme Court's finding that it was necessary to conduct a further comprehensive investigation into the facts to determine

[6] Taikangtzu No 185 (2008).
[7] Taishangtzu No 109 (2008).

whether substituted service in the foreign country fully protected the defendant's right to due process and enabled the party to prepare its case. Another example is a civil judgment rendered in 1998 by Banqiao District Court.[8] The District Court concluded that, although the foreign court had considered that it was acceptable for a Taiwanese lawyer to serve legal documents by hand on the counterparty, the method of service did not comply with Article 402(2) of the Taiwan Code of Civil Procedure and the Law Supporting Foreign Courts on Consigned Cases, and consequently the application for recognition of such foreign judgment was rejected. Based on a 2013 civil ruling by the Supreme Court,[9] the response or lack of it by a defendant to a statement of claim should be assessed on the basis of whether a defendant's substantive right to defend one's self was fully secured. If, in light of objective circumstances, the defendant to the foreign proceedings was aware of the initiation of the action and was able to prepare substantially for its response and exercise its right to defend, the condition of due process would be satisfied. Neither the party's personal acceptance of the service nor the party's personal appearance in court would be required in such circumstance. Although an agent's acceptance of service may not be sufficient notice by itself, it can still be considered legal when the agent who was not entitled to accept service, forwards the documents served to a competent representative of the defendant.[10]

C. The Foreign Judgment Violates Taiwan's Public Policy or Morals

As noted above, a foreign court's factual findings and application of laws should not be re-adjudicated by Taiwan courts when reviewing applications for the recognition of foreign judgments. However, Article 402 of the Code of Civil Procedure states that, as an exception, a final and binding foreign judgment can be reviewed to uphold a state's public policy and morals. The purpose of this provision is to ensure that applications for the recognition of foreign judgments do not violate Taiwan's general public policy and morals. In a 2006 civil judgment,[11] the Taiwan High Court defined 'public policy' as the concrete manifestation of a nation's founding spirit or fundamental policy, while defining 'morals' as moral concepts derived from the people. A number of articles in the Civil Code are pertinent here. Some refer to what has been officially translated as 'public policy or morals'. For instance, Article 72 states: 'A juridical act which is against public policy or morals is void'. Similar wording in Article 930 has been officially translated as 'public order and good morals'. In the Code of Civil Procedure, Article 402 has the same wording with the official translation of 'public policy or morals'. The meaning of public policy has always been confusing and controversial, as it differs from place to place, as well as from context to context. Four representative cases are summarised below:

1. A 2011 civil judgment[12] of the Supreme Court noted that, pursuant to Article 402(3) of the Code of Civil Procedure, a foreign judgment should not be recognised if its effect would be contrary to ROC public policy or morals. Under American common

[8] Taishangtzu No 372 (1998).
[9] Taishangtzu No 1367 (2013).
[10] As cited in a summary judgment of the Supreme Court, Kangtzu No 46 (1930).
[11] Chongshangtzu No 525 (2006).
[12] Taishangtzu No 552 (2011).

law, punitive damages serve the purposes of punishing wrongdoing and preventing recidivism, while their calculation depends on the amount of the wrongdoer's total property. By contrast, ROC tort law does not award punitive damages, as the purpose of compensatory damages is to recover damage and restore the *status quo ante* rather than to impose a sanction. Therefore, a Taiwan court may refuse to recognise a foreign judgment granting punitive damages under American law, as recognition would violate Taiwan's fundamental principles or concepts of legal or moral order.

2. A 2008 civil judgment[13] rendered by the Taiwan High Court found that the foreign judgment in question allowed for an award of treble damages in accordance with the California Business and Professions Code, plus punitive damages of US$1 million as determined by the jury. There was effectively a double penalty. As mentioned above, the punitive damages of US$1 million was contrary to Taiwan's legislative policy and legal philosophy and was therefore contrary to Taiwan's public policy.
3. A civil judgment[14] rendered by the Taiwan High Court stressed that US punitive damages awards were contrary to Continental European legal principles of compensatory damages. For example, German provisions expressly refused to recognise the effect of punitive damages. Despite having no such express provisions in Taiwan, a US judgment awarding punitive damages should not be declared enforceable as that would be a violation of Taiwan's fundamental legal principles of legal order and therefore in violation of Taiwan's public policy. This is because such punitive damages awards are akin to criminal sanctions, and may give victims unexpected or excessive compensation, and are therefore contrary to Taiwan's fundamental legal principles that damages should be compensatory, and that private entities should not gain additional benefits by seeking damages compensation in civil proceedings.
4. A civil judgment[15] rendered by the Supreme Court emphasised that a Taiwan court may refuse to recognise a foreign judgment pursuant to Article 402(3) of the Code of Civil Procedure when such recognition would be contrary to Taiwan's fundamental principles or concepts of legal order or moral order. In contrast, when a final and binding judgment rendered by a foreign court violates an imperative provision of Taiwan law but recognition would not violate Taiwan's fundamental principles or concepts of legal order, the Taiwan court should not refuse recognition without reason.

D. There is No Mutual Recognition of Judicial Decisions by the Foreign Court and the Taiwan Court

In view of Taiwan's current diplomatic challenges, mutual recognition does not require formal diplomatic recognition, but rather reciprocal judicial assistance or recognition.[16] That is to say, a formal diplomatic relationship between Taiwan and another country where judgment is delivered is not a prerequisite to mutual recognition of judicial decisions.

[13] Shang-geng (1) tzu No 81 (2008).
[14] Chungshang-geng (2) tzu No 27 (2010).
[15] Taishangtzu No 2213 (2014).
[16] Béligh Elbalti, 'Reciprocity and the Recognition and Enforcement of Foreign Judgments: A Lot of Bark but Not Much Bite' (2017) 13(1) *Journal of Private International Law* 184, 191.

As long as a foreign court recognises the effect of Taiwan judgments, Taiwan courts will recognise judgments rendered by such foreign court. The evidence used to prove the existence of mutual recognition, includes foreign laws, customs, conventions or agreements between the two jurisdictions based on the principle of reciprocity. These bilateral agreements allow one jurisdiction to recognise judgments rendered in another jurisdiction and vice versa. Several cases involving judicial recognition of Taiwanese judgments in a foreign jurisdiction, can be used to evidence reciprocity with that jurisdiction.

In terms of final and binding judgments rendered by a court in mainland China, its application for recognition and enforcement in Taiwan is subject to Article 74 of the Act Governing Relations between the People of Taiwan and Mainland China. When reviewing the application for recognition, the only consideration is whether the judgment violates public policy or morals of Taiwan. In other words, Articles 402(1), 402(2) and 402(4) of the Code of Civil Procedure need not be taken into account in the proceeding for the recognition of final and binding judgment rendered by a court in mainland China. However, such preferential treatment does not extend to judgments rendered by courts in Hong Kong and Macau. A civil ruling rendered by the Supreme Court[17] noted that the so-called 'mutual recognition' under Article 402(4) did not refer to reciprocity between states or jurisdictions in the private international law sense. If a foreign jurisdiction did not expressly refuse to recognise the effect of Taiwan's judgments, Taiwan courts should adopt a more lenient and proactive approach to reciprocity in order to recognise that jurisdiction's judgment.

Although Taiwan is not a party to the 1958 New York Convention[18] due to political reasons, it is worth noting that Taiwan Arbitration Law, particularly Chapter 7 on 'Foreign Arbitral Award', mostly adheres to the fundamental principles adopted in the 1958 New York Convention. It is evident that the legislative explanation of the bill for the Arbitration Law as proposed by the administrative agency, as well as the oral statements of legislators who participated in the legislative process, made several references to the 1958 New York Convention. Article 47(2) of the latest revised Taiwan Arbitration Law provides that 'A foreign arbitral award, after an application for recognition has been granted by the court, shall be binding on the parties and have the same force as a final judgment of a court, and is enforceable'.[19] Furthermore, Article 37(1) of Taiwan Arbitration Law[20] states that the award shall, insofar as relevant, be binding on the parties and have the same force as a final judgment of a court.

IV. Judicial Practice

Taiwan courts do not conduct reviews on the merits of a case when determining applications for recognition of foreign judgments. In short, Taiwan courts will not consider

[17] Taishangtzu No 1367 (2013).

[18] Convention on the Recognition and Enforcement of Foreign Arbitral Awards (New York, 1958).

[19] As promulgated on 2 December 2015, Arbitration Law, Art 47(2) has been amended to read: 'A foreign arbitral award, after an application for recognition has been granted by the court, shall be binding on the parties and have the same force as a final judgment of a court and shall be enforceable'.

[20] Arbitration Law, Art 37(1) stipulates that 'the award shall, insofar as relevant, be binding on the parties and have the same force as a final judgment of a court'. A foreign arbitral award recognised by the court shall have the same legal binding force on the parties as amended.

whether the content of a foreign judgment is appropriate or whether the plaintiff is entitled to file a complaint, but will only consider whether the foreign judgment falls within any of the four exceptional circumstances stipulated in the Code of Civil Procedure for refusing recognition. In the fourth exceptional circumstance, Taiwan courts will not recognise judgments rendered by foreign courts that do not recognise Taiwan's judgments. However, Taiwan courts lean toward a more flexible approach to mutual recognition. In some cases, Taiwan courts are willing to recognise a foreign judgment if that foreign jurisdiction does not explicitly refuse to recognise the effect of judgments in Taiwan. In doing so, mutual recognition occurs when there is an objective expectation that foreign courts will recognise judgments rendered by Taiwan courts in the future. Therefore, mutual recognition of judicial decisions between two jurisdictions should be seen as a principle, and not as an exception. If there is no evidence that the foreign jurisdiction does not recognise judgments rendered by Taiwan courts, Taiwan courts should take a more lenient view towards mutual recognition. In practice, the countries whose judgments are recognised by Taiwan courts include the United States, Canada, United Kingdom, Japan, Singapore, Australia, New Zealand and Malaysia.

Article 4(1) of the Compulsory Enforcement Act stipulates the necessity for an enforceable foreign judgment to meet requirements specified in Article 402 of the Code of Civil Procedure. It seems plausible that the requirements for an enforceable foreign judgment are the same as those for the recognition of a foreign judgment, that is, the prerequisite of an enforceable judgment is compliance with Article 402 of the Code of Civil Procedure. One of the conditions includes a final and binding foreign judgment. Despite the close relationship between a recognition and enforcement of a foreign judgment, recognition is not the same as enforcement. Some recognised foreign judgments can be enforced without a writ of execution. Thus, for example, a divorce judgment need not be declared enforceable and takes effect automatically in Taiwan. On the other hand, some foreign judgments or official documents, which may be regarded as writs of execution in foreign countries, might not be considered final and conclusive, requiring writs of execution to be obtained in Taiwan. Examples include: maintenance without review in judicial proceedings, judgments with respect to employee compensation for sustainable living, or settlements and mediations. It is important to bear in mind that the recognition of foreign judgments should be distinguished from foreign writs of execution. In addition, the scope of recognition for foreign rulings includes injunctions on the maintenance or custody of a child, determination of court fees, and matters with respect to parental rights and responsibilities for children; but it does not include foreign rulings concerning the direction of proceedings, interlocutory judgments irrelevant to the merits of an action, and non-conclusive rulings on security measures such as provisional attachments and provisional injunctions.

V. Recent Cases

Most recent cases concern the recognition of foreign judgments rendered by courts in the US, while others were rendered by courts in Australia, New Zealand, Canada, Japan, Korea, France, the UK and Malaysia. Some recent representative cases are of interest insofar as they illustrate the principles discussed above.

A. Recognition of a Foreign Divorce Judgment

In a 2015 decision,[21] the Supreme Court had to decide whether a foreign divorce judgment had violated public policy or morals. Both parties had migrated to Australia and purchased a residential property. Australia had been the couple's habitual residence for a long time. The respondent argued that the grounds for divorce were irretrievable marriage breakdown and irreconcilable differences, which all took place in Australia. In this context, the Australian court had exclusive jurisdiction over the matter in accordance with the Act Governing the Choice of Law in Civil Matters Involving Foreign Elements. Article 52(1) of the Family Act was applicable. Filing for divorce in Australia required at least 12 months of separation to support the fact that the marriage had broken down and there was no reasonable likelihood of resuming married life. Although the Australian requirements for divorce were different from those of Taiwan law, the divorce judgment rendered in Australia did not violate Taiwan's public policy or morals. The judgment also addressed the issue of the service of legal documents. It noted that the court in Australia served the divorce papers on the appellant. The appellant appeared at the hearing and heard the oral statement of the respondent's representative. Thus, the appellant had not been deprived of the right to present a defence, either through the submission of a written statement or by appearance in court. Finally, the court considered that, under its Foreign Judgments Act 1991, Australia recognised final and conclusive judgments rendered by Taiwan courts in civil cases regarding payment. In addition, the principles for the recognition of final and binding foreign judgments established by the Australian common law system were the same as the principles set out in Article 402 of the Taiwan Code of Civil Procedure. Consequently, the Supreme Court concluded that Australia recognised final and binding judgments in Taiwan civil cases.

B. Recognition of a Foreign Judgment in a Property Dispute

A judgment[22] of the Supreme Court in 2015 addressed several noteworthy issues, including jurisdiction over the issuance of a payment order, due process, conflicts in public policies, and rules governing mutual respect and international comity. The Seoul Central District Court had made a payment order and legally served it on the appellant on 7 January 2010. The order became final and conclusive on 22 January 2010. Hence, the payment order was a ruling in nature and within the meaning of final and binding judgment under Code of Civil Procedure, Article 402(2). The appellant being a company registered in Seoul, it followed that the Seoul district court had jurisdiction over it. Since the Korean Code of Civil Procedure allowed the appellant to answer the claim in 14 days after receiving the payment order, the appellant's procedural rights were sufficiently protected. The process, legal requirements and effect of issuing a payment order under the Korean Code of Civil Procedure were similar to those specified in the Taiwan Code of Civil Procedure. Moreover, the payment order

[21] Taishangtzu No 1998 (2015).
[22] Taishangtzu No 2198 (2015).

related to a contractual dispute. Hence, enforcement did not violate public policy or morals in Taiwan. Lastly, the standards of review of foreign judgments stipulated in Article 217 of the Korean Code of Civil Procedure were consistent with Article 402 of the Taiwan Code of Civil Procedure. On the basis of the principles of mutual respect and international comity, mutual recognition applied to both jurisdictions. It was concluded that the payment order under review did not fall within any of the circumstances prohibited under Article 402 of the Taiwan Code of Civil Procedure.

C. Compensatory Damages for Breach of Contract or Breach of Duty under Tort Law

In recent years, there have been several attempts to have foreign judgments for compensatory damages recognised in Taiwan. The 2014 judgment[23] of the New Taipei District Court is a representative case. Two parties signed a purchase contract on 11 July 2011 requiring the plaintiff seller to supply 500 pieces of motherboards FOB Taiwan. The place of performance of the contract was accordingly Taiwan. It was alleged that defective products were delivered to the defendant in Korea. The plaintiff argued that the Taiwan court had jurisdiction over this matter either in accordance with the maxim *actor sequitur forum rei* or Article 12 of the Code of Civil Procedure. Article 12 specifies that the court in the place of performance of a contract has jurisdiction. The defendant, however, filed a lawsuit in Korea. The defendant contended that, according to Article 15 of the Code of Civil Procedure, an action may be brought in the place where the wrong occurred. Since the defective goods were delivered in Korea, it followed (the defendant submitted) that Korea was an appropriate forum. The Taiwan court held that judgment of the Korean court fell within the exceptional circumstance under Article 402(1) of the Code of Civil Procedure and refused recognition. After reviewing the judgment rendered by the Korean court, the court considered that, the contract being on FOB terms, the delivery of the defective goods in fact had occurred in Taiwan and it was not relevant that the defendant had not appreciated the defective nature of the goods until it had received and examined the same in Korea.

VI. Conclusion

Taiwan courts have demonstrated a more lenient approach when reviewing application for the recognition of foreign judgments, most of which have concerned foreign divorce judgments.[24] Furthermore, most of the reasons for non-recognition have involved procedural defects, such as lack of jurisdiction or non-effective service of legal documents. Overall, there have been no significant difficulties in connection with the recognition

[23] Zonsutzu No 561 (2014).

[24] Yao-Ming Hsu, 'Waiguo Lihun Panjue de Chengren' [Recognition of Foreign Divorce Judgments] (2017) 181 *Taiwan Jurist* 26.

and enforcement of foreign judgments in Taiwan. Outstanding issues, particularly those pertaining to the examination of international jurisdiction and the applicable laws for effective service, which may be subject to relevant regulations in the foreign jurisdiction or to Taiwan regulations on mutual assistance in judicial matters, need to be addressed in follow-up research for the further development of the law. Mutual recognition between Taiwan and foreign jurisdictions assists Taiwan to integrate into the global community. To achieve this objective, it is expected that further effort will be made to facilitate the recognition and enforcement of foreign judgments in Taiwan.

5

Japan

KAZUAKI NISHIOKA*

I. Introduction

With regard to recognition and enforcement of foreign judgments, Japan has concluded three international conventions in specific legal areas (see section III). It has not ratified the 1971 Hague Convention on the Recognition and Enforcement of Foreign Judgments in Civil and Commercial Matters (the 1971 Hague Convention) or the 2005 Hague Convention on Choice of Court Agreements (the 2005 Hague Convention). Therefore, the recognition and enforcement of foreign judgments in civil and commercial matters is mainly subject to domestic law. In this respect, the main sources are the Code of Civil Procedure (CCP)[1] and the Civil Execution Act (CEA).[2] Foreign judgments are automatically recognised in Japan as long as the five requirements in Article 118 of the CCP (see section IV.A) are satisfied. In this regard, it is not necessary to refer to international conventions or treaties. To enforce a foreign judgment, on the other hand, a party seeking enforcement needs to obtain leave from a competent court in Japan under Articles 22(6) and 24 of the CEA (see section IV.B).

II. Background

A. Japan in Brief

Japan is an archipelago of about 6,900 islands in East Asia. As a mountainous country of approximately 3,000 kilometres in length, its climate varies significantly from the snowy north of Hokkaido to the tropical south of Okinawa. The country is a constitutional monarchy with a parliamentary system. The Parliament (called the Diet) is the sole law-making organ of the state (Article 41 of the Japanese Constitution (Constitution)) and the Cabinet is the depositary of the executive power (Article 65 of the Constitution). Japan is also an imperial state, although the emperor (*Tenno*) is just the symbol of the state and of the unity of the people. He does not have any political power (Article 1 of the Constitution).

* The author thanks Dr Béligh Elbalti, Associate Professor at Osaka University in Japan for providing invaluable comments on the draft of this paper.

[1] Act No 109 of 26 June 1996, as amended.

[2] Act No 4 of 1979, as amended.

Economically, Japan is one of the leading industrial countries in Asia and the world. Its GDP (gross domestic product) was worth US$4,940.16 million in 2016, the third highest in the world. The country is a member of the G7 (formerly G8), G20 and Organisation for Economic Co-operation and Development (OECD).

Japan is a secular state. The principle of separation of state and religion is enshrined in the Constitution (Articles 20 and 89). Accordingly, Japan does not have a state religion. But Shinto and Buddhism are the main religions practised by the Japanese population. Japanese culture has many unique aspects in the world, many of which aspects are widely known at a global scale. Examples are Japanese painting and *ukiyo-e*, popular comics (*manga*) and *anime*, Japanese cuisine (including sushi and tempura), and sports (such as *judo* and *sumo*).

The Japanese legal systems can be regarded as a mixture of western elements and East-Asian ethics and customs. From the second half of the nineteenth century, with the Meiji Restoration, the Japanese legal system has drawn heavily from French and German models. After World War II, however, many fundamental reforms were made under a strong American influence. That being said, Japan is generally regarded as belonging to the civil law family, with statutes being the main source of law. Although court decisions are not regarded as law per se in Japan, they play an important role as non-binding guidelines.

B. Private International Law in Japan

The history of Japanese private international law goes back to the mid-nineteenth century.[3] After the Meiji Restoration, one of the first priorities of the new government was to abolish the unequal treaties that Japan had been forced to conclude with a number of foreign countries (such as the US and Russia). One of the purposes of those treaties was to provide foreigners in Japan with legal protection by establishing consular jurisdictions, because the Japanese legal system in those days was feudal in character and deemed to be underdeveloped by the US and Europe. To show its capability to handle cross-border cases, Japan modernised its legal system by modelling the same after the systems in leading states of that time. As part of this endeavour, the codification of private international law (choice of law rules) was deemed necessary, much as the codification of the civil law and civil procedure. This can be regarded as the starting point of Japanese private international law.

In 1898, Japan enacted its first Private International Law (*Horei*) and thereby caught up with Western states in terms of developing the infrastructure of its legal system. The *Horei* had originally been drafted in 1890 based on French, Italian and Belgium laws at the time. This law, however, did not come into force. Eight years later, Japan enacted a revised Private International Law, modelled after the draft German Private International Law prepared by Professor Albert Gebhard. After its enactment, the *Horei* was significantly modernised and modified by two major amendments in 1989 and 2006. In the latter amendment, Japan changed the name of the Law from *Horei* to *Ho no tekiyou ni kansuru tsuu soku hou* (Act on

[3] For details, see eg Masato Dogauchi, 'Historical Development of Japanese Private International Law' in Jürgen Basedow, Harald Baum and Yuko Nishitani (eds), *Japanese and European Private International Law in Comparative Perspective* (Tübingen, Mohr Siebeck, 2008) 27–37; Yoshiaki Sakurada, 'The Origin and Evolution of Private International Law in Japan' (2013) 58 *Japanese Yearbook of International Law* 164.

General Rules for Application of Laws (AGR)).[4] Since then, the AGR has been the primary source of private international law (choice of law rules) in Japan.

With regard to civil procedure, there were no provisions dealing with international (direct) jurisdiction before 2012 except for international conventions. In the absence of such provisions, Japanese courts decided jurisdictional issues based on the notion of *jori*, that is, general principles of law, principle of reason, and justice.[5] In 2011, the CCP was amended and black-letter rules for international (direct) jurisdiction in civil and commercial matters were introduced for the first time (Articles 3-2 to 3-11).[6] The new rules entered into force in 2012. As for international jurisdiction in personal status and family matters, new rules were recently adopted, and promulgated on 25 April 2018. These are expected to enter into force within 18 months following the promulgation date.

Prior to the 1979 amendment, rules on recognition and enforcement of civil judgments[7] were set out together in the CCP. After 1979, the rules were separated. Today, rules on recognition are found in the CCP, while rules on enforcement are in the CEA. Minor amendments were introduced to the rules on recognition as part of the complete revision of the CCP in 1996.[8]

[4] On the 2006 amendment, see eg Koji Takahashi, 'A Major Reform of Japanese Private International Law' (2006) 2(2) *Journal of Private International Law* 311; Yasuhiro Okuda, 'Reform of Japan's Private International Law: Act on the General Rules of the Application of Laws' (2006) 8 *Yearbook of Private International Law* 145; Hironori Wanami, 'Background and Outline of the Modernization of Japanese Private International Law' in Jürgen Basedow, Harald Baum and Yuko Nishitani (eds), *Japanese and European Private International Law in Comparative Perspective* (Tübingen, Mohr Siebeck, 2008); Yoshiaki Sakurada and Eva Schwittek, 'Die Reform des japanischen internationalen Privatrechts' (2012) 76(1) *The Rabel Journal of Comparative and International Private Law* 86.

[5] *Jori* is regarded as a secondary law in Japan. On *jori* generally, see Yoshiyuki Noda, *Introduction to Japanese Law* (Tokyo, University of Tokyo Press, 1976) 222.

[6] On direct jurisdiction rules, see eg Koji Takahashi, 'Japan's Newly Enacted Rules on International Jurisdiction: with a Reflection on Some Issues of Interpretation' (2011) 13 *Yearbook of Private International Law* 146; Masato Dogauchi, 'New Japanese Rules on International Jurisdiction: General Observation' (2011) 54 *Japanese Yearbook of International Law* 260; Shun'ichiro Nakano, 'Agreement on Jurisdiction' (2011) 54 *Japanese Yearbook of International Law* 278; Akira Saito, 'International Civil Jurisdiction Based on the Place of Performance of Obligation Relating to A Contract' (2011) 54 *Japanese Yearbook of International Law* 295; Kazuhiko Yamamoto, 'International Jurisdiction Based on the Location of Property' (2011) 54 *Japanese Yearbook of International Law* 311; Yoshihisa Hayakawa, 'Lis Pendens' (2011) 54 *Japanese Yearbook of International Law* 324; Yoshiaki Nomura, 'Activity-Based Jurisdiction of Japanese Courts – A Bold but Unnecessary Departure –' (2012) 55 *Japanese Yearbook of International Law* 263; Nozomi Tada, 'International Civil Jurisdiction Based on the Place of the Tort' (2012) 55 *Japanese Yearbook of International Law* 287; Tadashi Kanzaki, 'Jurisdiction over Consumer Contracts and Individual Labor-Related Civil Disputes' (2012) 55 *Japanese Yearbook of International Law* 306; Yuko Nishitani, 'International Jurisdiction of Japanese Courts in a Comparative Perspective' (2013) 60(2) *Netherlands International Law Review* 251; Béligh Elbalti and Dai Yokomizo, 'La compétence internationale des tribunaux japonais en matiére civile et commerciale à la lumière de la nouvelle legislation' [2016] 3 *Revue critique de droit international privé* 417; Jun Yokoyama, *Private International Law in Japan* (Alphen aan den Rijn, Kluwer Law International, 2017) 133–48.

[7] For rules on recognition and enforcement of foreign judgments, see also Takao Sawaki, 'Recognition and Enforcement of Foreign Judgments in Japan' (1989) 23(1) *The International Lawyer* 29; Morio Takeshita, 'The Recognition of Foreign Judgments' (1996) 39 *Japanese Annual of International Law* 55; Kono Toshiyuki, 'International Civil Procedure in Japan' (1996) 6 *Asian Yearbook of International Law* 105, 125–32; Nozomi Tada, 'Enforcement of Foreign Judgments in Japan Regarding Business Activities' (2003) 46 *Japanese Annual of International Law* 75; Yuko Nishitani, 'Internationales Privat- und Zivilverfahrensrecht' in Harald Baum and Moritz Bälz (eds), *Handbuch Japanisches Handels- und Wirtschaftsrecht* (Cologne, Carl Heymanns, 2011) 1272–78; Yasuhiro Okuda, 'Recognition and Enforcement of Foreign Judgments in Japan' (2013) 15 *Yearbook of Private International Law* 411; Toshiyuki Kono, 'Country Report: Japan' in Adeline Chong (ed), *Recognition and Enforcement of Foreign Judgments in Asia* (Singapore, Asian Business Law Institute, 2017).

[8] For the history of the rules on recognition of foreign judgments, see Masaaki Haga, *Gaikoku Hanketsu no Shounin [Recognition of Foreign Judgments in Japan]* (Tokyo, Keio University Press, 2018) 11–24.

C. Sources of Private International Law

Private International Law in Japan mainly covers four matters: (1) choice of law; (2) international jurisdiction; (3) recognition and enforcement of foreign judgments; and (4) international arbitration.[9]

i. Major National Legislation

Choice of law issues are mainly dealt with in the AGR, the Act on the Law Applicable to the Obligation of Support, the Act on the Law Applicable to the Form of Wills, Articles 88 to 94 of the Negotiable Instrument Act and Articles 76 to 81 of the Check Act. International jurisdiction is mainly covered by the CCP (for civil and commercial matters), the Personal Status Litigation Act and the Domestic Relations Case Procedure Act (for personal status and family matters respectively). The recognition and enforcement of foreign judgments is regulated by the CCP (for recognition) and the CEA (for enforcement). International arbitration is covered by the Arbitration Act in 2003.[10]

ii. International Conventions

Japan has ratified seven Hague Conventions: (1) the 1954 Hague Convention on Civil Procedure (implemented domestically by the Act on Special Provisions Concerning Civil Procedure Attendant upon Implementation of the Convention on Civil Procedure and Another Convention); (2) the 1956 Hague Convention on the Law Applicable to Maintenance Obligations towards Children; (3) the 1961 Hague Convention on the Conflicts of Laws Relating to the Form of Testamentary Dispositions (implemented domestically by the Act on the Law Applicable to the Form of Wills); (4) the 1961 Hague Convention Abolishing the Requirement of Legalisation for Foreign Public Documents; (5) the 1965 Hague Convention on the Service Abroad of Judicial and Extrajudicial Documents in Civil or Commercial Matters (implemented domestically by the Act on Special Provisions Concerning Civil Procedure Attendant upon Implementation of the Convention on Civil Procedure and Another Convention); (6) the 1973 Hague Convention of the Law Applicable to Maintenance Obligations; and (7) the 1980 Hague Convention on the Civil Aspects of International Child Abduction (implemented domestically by the Act on Implementation of Convention on the Civil Aspects of International Child Abduction).

In addition, there are some international conventions covering choice of law, international jurisdiction, and recognition and enforcement issues. For example, Japan is party to the 1929 Convention for the Unification of Certain Rules Relating to International Carriage by Air (the Warsaw Convention) (international jurisdiction); the 1951 Convention Relating

[9] Items (2), (3), and (4) are parts of so-called 'international civil procedure' which also covers international service of documents, international rules of evidence, and international insolvency. However, this chapter will not cover these matters.

[10] International arbitration in Japan goes back to at least the nineteenth century. The arbitration system was first established by the Code of Civil Procedure of 1890. Since then, Japanese arbitration developed its special laws. In 2003, the Arbitration Act was updated, based primarily on the 1985 UNCITRAL Model Law. International arbitration in Japan is thus similar to the regimes in countries which have adopted the UNCITRAL Model Law.

to the Status of Refugees (choice of law); the 1997 Convention on Supplementary Compensation for Nuclear Damage (choice of law, international jurisdiction, and recognition and enforcement); the 1999 Convention for the Unification of Certain Rules for International Carriage by Air (the Montreal Convention) (international jurisdiction); the 2004 United Nations Convention on Jurisdictional Immunities of States and Their Property[11] (international jurisdiction); the 1992 International Convention on Civil Liability for Oil Pollution Damage (international jurisdiction, and recognition and enforcement); and the 1992 International Convention on the Establishment of an International Fund for Compensation for Oil Pollution Damage (international jurisdiction, and recognition and enforcement).

International arbitration is mainly governed in Japan pursuant to the 1927 Convention on the Execution of Foreign Arbitral Awards (the Geneva Convention), the 1958 New York Convention and the 1965 ICSID Convention. There are also bilateral treaties for the recognition and enforcement of arbitral awards with many countries, including the US, the UK, the People's Republic of China (PRC), Pakistan, Peru, El Salvador, Argentina, Romania, Poland, Bulgaria, and Hungary.

D. Japanese Judicial System in Brief

The judicial system in Japan is a three-tier trial system. The court system consists of two layers of courts: the Supreme Court and the lower courts. The lower courts fall into four groups: eight High Courts (located in Tokyo (including the Intellectual Property High Court), Osaka, Nagoya, Hiroshima, Fukuoka, Sendai, Sapporo and Takamatsu), 50 District Courts, 50 Family Courts and 438 Summary Courts.

Cases relating to the recognition and enforcement of foreign judgments in civil and commercial matters are mainly handled by the following courts (Article 24(1) of the CEA):

1. A District Court having jurisdiction over the general venue of the debtor; or
2. if there is no such general venue, a District Court having jurisdiction over the subject matter of the claim or the seizable property of the debtor are situated.

E. What are Civil and Commercial Matters?

Neither the CCP nor the CEA define 'civil' or 'commercial' matters. According to the Supreme Court,[12] a foreign judgment 'concerning legal relationships in private law' is capable of being recognised and enforced under Article 118 of the CCP and Article 24 of the CEA. It is generally understood in Japan that the term 'private law' includes 'civil and commercial matters'.[13] Although the expression also covers personal status and family

[11] This convention was implemented domestically by the Act on Civil Jurisdiction of Japan with respect to a Foreign State etc (Act No 24 of 24 April 2009).

[12] Judgment of the Supreme Court, 28 April 1998, 52-3 *Minshu* 853 (with English translation available at (1999) 42 *Japanese Annual of International Law* 155).

[13] Okuda (n 7) 413; Yokoyama (n 6) 151.

matters, whether or not contentious, this chapter will not cover the recognition and enforcement of judgments in such matters.

Decisions relating to administrative, criminal or tax matters do not fall within the notion 'civil and commercial matters' and therefore they are not recognisable under the CCP. One of the much-debated questions in Japan is whether judgments awarding punitive damages can be considered as 'foreign judgment concerning private law disputes'. The prevailing opinion is that punitive damages awarded in foreign judgments can be regarded as civil in nature, although their incompatibility with public policy may lead to their being denied recognition or enforcement.[14]

III. Recognition and Enforcement under Treaties

Japan has not entered into any bilateral treaties with other countries for the mutual recognition and enforcement of judgments.

As stated earlier, Japan has concluded three international conventions which provide for the mutual recognition and enforcement of judgments. These are: (1) the 1992 International Convention on Civil Liability for Oil Pollution Damage (Civil Liability Convention); (2) the 1992 International Convention on the Establishment of an International Fund for Compensation for Oil Pollution Damage (Establishment Convention); and (3) the 1997 Convention on Supplementary Compensation for Nuclear Damage (Nuclear Damage Convention).

Typically, under these conventions, a foreign judgment is recognised as long as the rendering court has jurisdiction in accordance with the relevant provisions of a convention and a judgment is no longer subject to ordinary forms of review in the rendering state (see Article X(1) of the Civil Liability Convention; Article 8 of the Establishment Convention; and Article 13(5) of the Nuclear Damage Convention). However, the recognition of judgments may be refused in exceptional cases, such as where the foreign judgment was obtained by fraud or a defendant was not given reasonable notice and a fair opportunity to present one's case (see Article X(1) of the Civil Liability Convention; Article 8 of the Establishment Convention; and Article 13(5) of the Nuclear Damage Convention). In addition, under the Nuclear Damage Convention, the recognition of judgments may be refused where it would be contrary to public policy or not accord with fundamental standards of justice (Article 13(5)(c)).

Once recognised pursuant to a convention, a judgment is enforceable in a Contracting State as long as the formalities required there have been complied with (see Article X(2) of the Civil Liability Convention; Article 8 of the Establishment Convention; and Article 13(6) of the Nuclear Damage Convention). The enforcing state cannot reopen the merits of the case (see Article X(2) of the Civil Liability Convention; Article 8 of the Establishment Convention; and Article 13(6) of the Nuclear Damage Convention).

[14] Judgment of the Supreme Court, 11 September 1997, 51-6 *Minshu* 2573; Akira Takakuwa, 'Gaikoku Saiban no Shounin' [Recognition of Foreign Judgments] in Akira Takakuwa and Masato Dogauchi (eds), *Shin Saiban Jitsumu Taikei (3) – Kokusai Minji Sosho-ho (Zaisanho Kankei) [New Court Practice Series (3) – International Procedural Law (Property Law Matters)]* (Tokyo, Seirin Shoin, 2002) 308–09. *cf* see eg Judgment of Tokyo High Court, 28 June 1993, 1471 *Hanrei Jiho* 89 (with English translation available at (1994) 37 *Japanese Annual of International Law* 155).

In Japan, there have been no cases in which courts have recognised and enforced foreign judgments under the three conventions discussed here.

Japan has not ratified any Hague Conventions which oblige a Contracting State to recognise and enforce the judgments of other Contracting States.

IV. Recognition and Enforcement in the Absence of Treaties or Similar Arrangements

A. Recognition Generally

Conceptually, Japanese law distinguishes recognition from enforcement. Recognition involves the acceptance in Japan of the effects of foreign decisions (for instance, declaratory judgments, judgments determining a legal right or status and judgments ordering the defendant to perform or refrain from a certain action). It is governed by Article 118 of the CCP. Enforcement, on the other hand, concerns the implementation in Japan of the effects of foreign judgments. It is governed by Articles 22(6) and 24 of the CEA. Only judgments ordering the defendant to perform or refrain from a specific action need to be enforced. To enforce such judgments, a successful party needs to obtain an enforcement judgment (*shikko hanketsu*) from a competent court in Japan. Although recognition and enforcement are distinguished conceptually, the requirements of recognition and enforcement are identical. Thus, it can be said that a foreign judgment is enforceable as long as it can be recognised in Japan.

Article 118 of the CCP sets out five requirements for recognition: (1) finality; (2) indirect jurisdiction; (3) service of process; (4) conformity with the public policy of Japan; and (5) reciprocity. Article 118 does not explicitly rule out the possibility of a review of the merits (*révision au fond*) of the foreign judgment. This is in contrast to Article 24 of the CEA which stipulates that there is to be no such review (see section IV.B.i). Nonetheless, it is generally understood that the principle that there is to be no review of the merits also applies at the stage of recognition.[15]

i. Final and Binding Judgment

A foreign judgment is automatically recognised in Japan as long as the five requirements set out in Article 118 of the CCP are satisfied.[16] The parties do not need to go through any formal procedure. Nevertheless, in practical terms, parties can have the benefit of the effects of a foreign judgment when a Japanese court actually recognises it in a proceeding, for instance, by accepting a party's contention on the effect of a foreign judgment as *res judicata*. In theory, foreign judgments have *de plano* effects unless their validity is contested.

In order for a foreign judgment to be recognised in Japan, it must be 'a final and binding judgment rendered by a foreign court' within the meaning of Article 118 of the CCP.

[15] Yoshiaki Sakurada, *Kokusai Shiho [Private International Law]* 6th edn (Tokyo, Yuhikaku, 2012) 385.

[16] There is one exception: a foreign insolvency proceeding is not automatically recognised in Japan. Its recognition is subject to the Act on Recognition of and Assistance for Foreign Insolvency Proceedings (Act No 129 of 29 November 2000). See Yokoyama (n 6) 157–58.

The Supreme Court has held that a 'judgment' covers any judgment, decision, order or decree rendered by a foreign court.[17] Japanese courts have held that default judgments,[18] summary judgments[19] and costs decisions[20] also fall within the notion of a 'judgment'. The Supreme Court in 2014 held that a permanent injunction order can also be recognised.[21] Accordingly, both 'monetary' and 'non-monetary' judgments are recognisable in Japan.

According to the prevailing view,[22] admissions, waiver of claims, authentic instruments or judicial settlements do not fall under the notion of a 'judgment', and therefore they are not recognisable in Japan, even if they have the same effect as a final and binding judgment of the rendering state. But a judgment by a foreign court based on a settlement is recognisable and enforceable as a foreign judgment.[23]

The expression 'final and binding' means that a foreign court judgment is no longer subject to ordinary forms of review in the rendering state. Therefore, non-final and binding judgments such as interlocutory judgments would not be 'judgments' within the meaning of Article 118 of the CCP. The result would be that interlocutory judgments are not recognisable in Japan.[24] By similar token, according to the prevailing view and case law, provisional measures do not qualify as 'final and binding' judgments under Article 118 of the CCP.[25]

Moreover, such 'final and binding' judgments have to be given by a foreign court. Although CCP and CEA do not define a 'foreign court', according to the Supreme Court, a 'foreign court' means a judicial body of a foreign state, regardless of its name, procedures, or form.[26] Accordingly, the term 'court' may include any authority that regularly exercises judicial functions and is empowered to issue binding decisions on the parties.[27] The fact that a rendering state has not been diplomatically recognised by Japan does not affect the

[17] Judgment of the Supreme Court, 28 April 1998 (n 12).

[18] Judgment of Nagoya District Court, 6 February 1987, 1236 *Hanrei Jiho* 113 (with English translation available at (1990) 33 *Japanese Annual of International Law* 189); Judgment of Tokyo District Court, 14 January 1994, 1509 *Hanrei Jiho* 96; Judgment of Tokyo District Court, 31 January 1994, 1509 *Hanrei Jiho* 101.

[19] Judgment of Tokyo District Court, 25 February 1998, 972 *Hanrei Taimuzu* 258.

[20] Judgment of the Supreme Court, 28 April 1998 (n 12).

[21] Judgment of the Supreme Court, 24 April 2014, 68-4 *Minshu* 329 (with English translation available at (2015) 58 *Japanese Yearbook of International Law* 463). On this decision, see Béligh Elbalti, 'The Jurisdiction of Foreign Courts and the Recognition of Judgments Ordering Injunction – The Supreme Court Judgment of April 24, 2014' (2016) 59 *Japanese Yearbook of International Law* 395.

[22] Takakuwa (n 14) 308; Yasunori Honma, Shun'ichiro Nakano and Hajime Sakai, *Kokusai Minji Tetsuduki-ho [International Civil Procedure Law]* 2nd edn (Tokyo, Yuhikaku, 2012) 181. But see Eiji Adachi, 'Wagakuni ni okeru Beikoku Kurasu Akushion jouno Wakai no Shounin Tekikaku' [Recognisability of Judicial Settlement Reached in the Course of Class Action in the US] in Yoshimitsu Aoyama and others (eds), *Gendai Shakai ni okeru Minji Tetsuzuki-ho no Tenkai [Development of Civil Procedure Law in the Modern Society]* (Tokyo, Shojihomu, 2002) 268.

[23] Takakuwa (n 14) 308.

[24] Kono (n 7) 106–07, para 4; Yokoyama (n 6), para 429.

[25] Judgment of the Supreme Court, 26 February 1985, 37-6 *Katei Saiban Geppo* 25 (with English translation available at (1985) 28 *Japanese Annual of International Law* 225). In academic literature, however, there are some opinions for recognising foreign provisional measures in exceptional cases. See eg Shun'ichiro Nakano, 'Gaikoku Hozen Meirei no Kouryoku' [Effectiveness of Foreign Provisional Orders/Measures] in Akira Takakuwa and Masato Dogauchi (eds), *Shin Saiban Jitsumu Taikei (3) – Kokusai Minji Sosho-ho (Zaisanho Kankei) [New Court Practice Series (3) – International Procedural Law (Property Law Matters)]* (Tokyo, Seirin Shoin, 2002) 414.

[26] Judgment of the Supreme Court, 28 April 1998 (n 12).

[27] Tada (n 7) 82.

recognition of judgments of that state.[28] There is, therefore, no doubt that a judgment rendered by a foreign domestic or national court is, in principle, capable of recognition and enforcement in Japan.

ii. Indirect Jurisdiction

Article 118(i) of the CCP requires a foreign rendering court to have jurisdiction (indirect jurisdiction) to render a judgment under Japanese law or treaties.[29] However, there are no provisions dealing with grounds for indirect jurisdiction. In addition, Japan has not ratified any bilateral or multilateral treaties which oblige Member States to recognise and enforce judgments from other Member States (except for the Civil Liability Convention, the Establishment Convention and the Nuclear Damage Convention).

In the absence of specific rules for indirect jurisdiction, the Supreme Court in 1998 held that indirect jurisdiction should be examined in light of *jori*, basically in accordance with the rules on local jurisdiction from the viewpoint of whether it is appropriate to recognise the given foreign judgment, taking into consideration specific circumstances of each case (that is, the criteria for direct jurisdiction at that time). It was unclear from the decision whether the Supreme Court was adopting the so-called 'mirror-image' approach (indirect jurisdiction should be examined in accordance with the identical criteria as those for direct jurisdiction). While the Judicial Research Officer of the Supreme Court (*saiko saibansho chosakan*) explained that the Supreme Court was not adopting the mirror-image approach,[30] the clarification was not binding on Japanese courts and it remained controversial among academics whether the Supreme Court had adopted the mirror-image approach.[31] Nevertheless, since the Supreme Court's judgment, lower courts have followed the Supreme Court's approach when examining the indirect jurisdiction of foreign rendering courts, without mentioning whether or not the mirror-image approach was being followed.[32]

[28] Takakuwa (n 14) 307; Toshiyuki Kono, 'Gaikoku Saibansho' [Foreign Courts] in Akira Takakuwa and Masato Dogauchi (eds), *Shin Saiban Jitsumu Taikei (3) – Kokusai Minji Sosho-ho (Zaisanho Kankei) [New Court Practice Series (3) – International Procedural Law (Property Law Matters)]* (Tokyo, Seirin Shoin, 2002) 318–21; Shun'ichiro Nakano, 'Gaikoku Hanketsu no Shikko' [Enforcement of Foreign judgments] in Hiroshi Takahashi and Shintaro Katou (eds), *Jitsumu Minji Sosho Koza (Dai 3 Ki) Dai 6 Kan – Joso, Saishin, Shogaku Sosho to Kokusai Minji Sosho [Practical Lecture on Civil Procedure (Third Period) Vol 6 – Appeals, Small Claims, and International Civil Litigation]* (Tokyo, Nippon Hyoron Sha, 2013) 445. As for recognisability of judgments given by international courts (such as the Court of Justice of the European Union (CJEU) and International Court of Justice (ICJ)), see Honma (n 22) 180; Kono (n 28) 322–24; Nakano (n 28) 445.

[29] Judgment of the Supreme Court, 28 April 1998 (n 12).

[30] Yoshinori Kawabe, 'Saiko Saibansho Chosakan Kaisetsu' [Explanatory Remarks on the Supreme Court Decisions] in Hoso Kai (ed), *Saiko Saibansho Hanrei Kaisetsu Heisei 10 (1998) Nendo (Jo) [Explanatory Remarks on the Supreme Court Decisions 1998 (1)]* (Tokyo, Hoso Kai, 1998) 339.

[31] Some (eg Kazuhiko Yamamoto, 'Case Notes' (1999) 1157 *Jurist* 299; Yasushi Nakanishi, 'Case Notes' (2003) 169 *Bessatsu Jurist* 253) argue the Supreme Court had adopted the mirror-image approach, while others (eg Kono (n 28) 337; Eiji Adachi, 'Case Notes' (1999) 678 *New Business Law* 65) argue the Supreme Court had not adopted so.

[32] Mari Nagata, 'Wagakuni ni okeru Gaikoku Hanketsu no Shounin Shikko' [Recognition and Enforcement of Foreign Judgments in Japan] in Japan Association of International Economic Law (ed), *Kokusai Keizai-ho Koza 2 – Torihiki, Zaisan, Tetsuduki [International Economic Law II – Transactions, Property and Procedure]* (Kyoto, Horitsu Bunkasha, 2012) 219.

Even after the 2012 amendment which introduced rules on direct jurisdiction, there are still no provisions dealing with indirect jurisdiction and Japan has not ratified any bilateral or multilateral treaties in this area. More recently, the Supreme Court held that:

> [I]t is appropriate to construe that in an action other than those relating to personal status matters, the indirect jurisdiction of the foreign rendering court should be determined in light of *jori*, while basically complying with the provisions on international jurisdiction under the CCP and considering whether or not it is appropriate for Japan to recognise a judgment rendered by the foreign court, in the context of the specific circumstances of the case.[33]

As is evident from the above holding, the Supreme Court does not make clear whether it adopts the mirror-image approach. The Judicial Research Officer of the Supreme Court again explained that following its judgment of 1998, the Supreme Court was not adopting the mirror-image approach.[34] On the other hand, academic opinion remains divided in assessing the Supreme Court's position.[35] Although it is still unclear whether Japan has adopted the mirror-image approach, it can at least be said that the grounds of direct jurisdiction in the CCP are relevant, in principle, to the determination of the indirect jurisdiction of the foreign rendering court.

As a result, Japanese courts may uphold the indirect jurisdiction of a foreign rendering court where the latter has based its jurisdiction on, for instance, one or other grounds which the Japanese court uses to establish direct jurisdiction in situations involving international elements. Such grounds of direct jurisdiction include the respondent's domicile,[36] the respondent's principal place of business,[37] the place of performance of the contractual obligation,[38] the place of the tort[39] and the respondent's submission.[40]

A further question that remains to be considered is whether Article 3-9 of the CCP (which gives the court a discretion to dismiss a claim, taking account of the nature of the case, the burden of the defendant to answer the claim, the location of evidence and any other factors, even if the court may have jurisdiction over the dispute) applies when assessing indirect jurisdiction. There has been no case law on this question and academic opinions are divergent.[41] Some argue that it should apply. Others argue that it should not apply, since it is not a provision conferring jurisdiction on a court, but one setting forth a ground for rejecting direct jurisdiction. In other words, it is not a ground for establishing jurisdiction.

[33] Judgment of the Supreme Court, 24 April 2014 (n 21).

[34] Takashi Hirose, 'Saiko Saibansho Chosakan Kaisetsu' [Explanatory Remarks on the Supreme Court Decisions], (2015) 67(9) *Hoso Jiho [Law Association Journal]* 339.

[35] For the view that the Supreme Court has adopted the mirror-image approach, see Yokoyama (n 6) 151–52. For the view that the criteria for direct and indirect jurisdiction are not necessarily identical, see eg Naoshi Takasugi, 'Nihon Kokunai deno Shingai Koui no Sashitome wo meijita Gaikoku Hanketsu no Nihon deno Shikko' [Enforcement of the Foreign Judgment ordering the Permanent Injunction against Infringement Activities Carried out in Japan] (2014) 1032 *New Business Law* 21–22.

[36] Judgment of the Supreme Court, 28 April 1998 (n 12).

[37] Judgment of the Supreme Court, 26 September 2002, 56-8 *Minshu* 1551 (with English translation available at (2003) 46 *Japanese Annual of International Law* 168).

[38] Judgment of Tokyo District Court, 14 January 1994 (n 18).

[39] Judgment of Tokyo District Court, Hachioji Branch, 13 February 1998, 987 *Hanrei Taimuzu* 282.

[40] Judgment of Nagoya District Court, 6 February 1987 (n 18).

[41] See Eiji Adachi, 'Gaikoku Hanketsu no Shonin Shikko ni okeru Kokusai Saiban Kankatsu' [International Jurisdiction at the stage of Recognition and Enforcement of Foreign Judgments] in Hideyuki Kobayashi (ed), *Kokusai Saiban Kankatsu no Riron to Jitsumu [Theory and Practice of International Jurisdiction]* (Nagoya, Shinnippon-Hoki, 2017) 352.

However, it should be noted that according to the Supreme Court, indirect jurisdiction is determined in light of *jori*. Thus, it seems that a court may be able to take into consideration special circumstances in the framework of *jori*, even if Article 3-9 of the CCP does not apply. If so, special circumstances may play a role, whether Article 3-9 of the CCP applies or not.

iii. Reciprocity

Article 118(iv) of the CCP sets out the reciprocity requirement. According to the Supreme Court, reciprocity exists

> if in the rendering state, judgments of the courts of Japan that are of the same type as the judgment at issue are capable of being recognised in accordance with conditions that are not different in any material respect from those in Article 118 of the CCP.[42]

In deciding whether reciprocity exists between Japan and a foreign state, Japanese courts have taken a liberal approach and have recognised judgments from a wide range of jurisdictions including California,[43] Washington DC,[44] Germany,[45] Hawaii,[46] Hong Kong,[47] Illinois,[48] Minnesota,[49] Maryland,[50] Nevada,[51] New York,[52] Oregon,[53] Queensland,[54] the Republic of Korea,[55] Singapore,[56] Texas,[57] the UK (England and Wales),[58] Virginia[59] and Switzerland.[60]

[42] Judgment of the Supreme Court, 7 June 1983, 37-5 *Minshu* 611 (with English translation available at (1984) 27 *Japanese Annual of International Law* 119).

[43] Judgment of Tokyo District Court, 6 September 1968, 242 *Hanrei Taimuzu* 263; Judgment of Tokyo District Court, 18 February 1991, 760 *Hanrei Taimuzu* 250 (with English translation available at (1992) 35 *Japanese Annual of International Law* 177); Judgment of Tokyo District Court, Hachioji Branch, 13 February 1998 (n 39); Judgment of Tokyo District Court, 19 February 2008, 2008WLJPCA02198003; Judgment of Tokyo District Court, 28 March 2011, 1351 *Hanrei Taimuzu* 241.

[44] Judgment of the Supreme Court, 7 June 1983 (n 42).

[45] Judgment of Nagoya District Court, 6 February 1987 (n 18); Judgment of Tokyo District Court, 24 February 1998, 995 *Hanrei Taimuzu* 271.

[46] Judgment of Tokyo District Court, 24 October 1970, 259 *Hanrei Taimuzu* 254; Judgment of Mito District Court, Ryuugasaki Branch, 29 October 1999, 1034 *Hanrei Taimuzu* 270 (although this judgment held that reciprocity exists between Japan and the US but not the Hawaii state, the judgment sought to be enforced was rendered by a Hawaii Court).

[47] Judgment of the Supreme Court, 28 April 1998 (n 12).

[48] Judgment of Tokyo District Court, 29 January 2016, 2313 *Hanrei Jiho* 67.

[49] Judgment of Tokyo District Court, 2 September 1996, 1608 *Hanrei Jiho* 130.

[50] Judgment of Osaka District Court, 17 January 1996, 956 *Hanrei Taimuzu* 286.

[51] Judgment of Tokyo District Court, 16 December 1991, 794 *Hanrei Taimuzu* 246.

[52] Judgment of Tokyo District Court, 14 January 1994 (n 18); Judgment of Tokyo District Court, Hachioji Branch, 8 December 1997, 976 *Hanrei Taimuzu* 235; Judgment of Tokyo District Court, 29 January 2008, 2008WLJPCA01298006; Judgment of Tokyo District Court, 8 January 2014, 2014WLJPCA01088001.

[53] Judgment of Nagoya District Court, 24 November 1999, 1068 *Hanrei Taimuzu* 234.

[54] Judgment of Tokyo District Court, 25 February 1998 (n 19).

[55] Judgment of Yokohama District Court, 30 March 1999, 1696 *Hanrei Jiho* 120 (although the court is enforcing the divorce decree).

[56] Judgment of Tokyo District Court, 19 January 2006, 1229 *Hanrei Taimuzu* 334 (with English translation available at (2007) 50 *Japanese Annual of International Law* 240).

[57] Judgment of Tokyo District Court, 30 January 1992, 45-9 *Katei Saiban Geppo* 45; Judgment of Tokyo High Court, 15 November 1993, 46-6 *Katei Saiban Geppo* 47 (although in a family matter).

[58] Judgment of Tokyo District Court, 31 January 1994 (n 18).

[59] Judgment of Tokyo District Court, 29 May 1995, 904 *Hanrei Taimuzu* 202.

[60] Judgment of Tokyo District Court, 13 November 1967, 215 *Hanrei Taimuzu* 173.

The Japanese courts, on the other hand, have refused to recognise judgments rendered by the Belgian[61] and Mainland Chinese[62] courts for lack of reciprocity.[63] The Belgian judgment was refused recognition because Belgium at that time allowed *révision au fond* (a review of the merits). But Belgium has since abolished *révision au fond*. Therefore, in principle, it should now be possible for Belgian judgments to be recognised and enforced in Japan.[64] As for Mainland China, according to the precedents, it is impossible for its judgments over civil and commercial disputes to be recognised in Japan due to the reciprocity requirement.

iv. Proper Service

The requirement of proper service is found in Article 118(ii) of the CCP. The Japanese courts examine whether a respondent has been duly served with necessary documents such as the summons initiating the proceedings. On service of process pursuant to the requirement of Article 118 of the CCP, the Supreme Court has held that:

> the serving of process necessary to commence an action against defendants mentioned in Article 118(ii) of the CCP does not have to comply with the laws and rules of our civil procedure. But it is required that the process serving give the defendant actual knowledge of the commencement of an action and not hinder the exercise of his or her right to defence.[65]

The question may consequently arise as to what types of service will be regarded as sufficient. The text of Article 118(ii) explicitly excludes service by public notice or other similar modes of service. Therefore, a foreign judgment is not recognised if the service of process is made in such manner, even if that would comply with the law of the rendering state.[66] As for the manner to be followed, the Supreme Court held that:

> from the viewpoint of ensuring clarity and stability of the procedure of litigation, if there is a treaty of judicial cooperation between the country of judgment and Japan and if this treaty provides that the service of the document required for the commencement of litigation must be effected in a manner set out in this treaty, service of documents not in accordance with the manner set out in the treaty should not be regarded as service which fulfils the requirement of the above provision of the CCP.[67]

[61] Judgment of Tokyo District Court, 20 July 1960, 11-7 *Kaminshu* 1522.

[62] Judgment of Osaka High Court, 9 April 2003, 1141 *Hanrei Taimuzu* 270 (with English translation available at (2005) 48 *Japanese Annual of International Law* 171); Judgment of Tokyo District Court, 20 March 2015, 1422 *Hanrei Taimuzu* 348 (and affirmed by Judgment of Tokyo High Court, 25 November 2015, 2015WLJPCA11256007). For these judgments, see Satoshi Watanabe, 'A Study of a Series of Cases Caused Non-recognition of a Judicial Judgment between Japan and Mainland China – A Cross-border Garnishment Order of the Japanese Court Issued to a Chinese Company as a Third-party Debtor –' (2014) 57 *Japanese Yearbook of International Law* 287. The judgment of Tokyo High Court was appealed to the Supreme Court, but the Supreme Court rejected the appeal. As a criticism to the 2003 Judgment of Osaka High Court, Professor Okuda argues that the Chinese judgment should have been recognised in Japan because 'the recognition rules of China may be milder than Japanese rules. … Decisive for reciprocity is not a precedent but recognition rules of the foreign country. Unless the rules are clearly stricter than the Japanese rules, the reciprocity should be affirmed': Okuda (n 7) 418.

[63] According to Nakano (n 28) 456 at fn 74, there is a judgment in which an Indian Judgment was refused recognition due to a lack of reciprocity (Judgment of Tokyo District Court, 4 July 1960, unreported). However, the same author considers that nowadays reciprocity with India would be upheld.

[64] Nagata (n 32) 227.

[65] Judgment of the Supreme Court, 28 April 1998 (n 12).

[66] However, service by public notice towards a foreign defendant is not prohibited under the CCP (Art 110(1)(iii)).

[67] Judgment of the Supreme Court, 28 April 1998 (n 12).

In addition to some bilateral conventions (with the US and the UK) and judicial assistance agreements or arrangements in this field,[68] Japan has ratified the Hague Service Abroad Convention[69] and the Hague Civil Procedure Convention. Therefore, where one of the said treaties (mostly, the 1965 Hague Service Abroad Convention) is applicable, the service must be conducted in accordance with the manner set out therein. In this regard, the Supreme Court in the above mentioned judgment held that personal service in Japan (service of documents by direct delivery to the recipient by a person who has personally been asked by the plaintiff) is not valid under Article 118(ii) of the CCP due to its non-conformity with the 1965 Hague Service Abroad Convention and the Consular Convention between Japan and the UK.[70] On the other hand, service by post which is allowed under Article 10(a) of the Hague Service Abroad Convention is debatable because Japan has not objected to it, but according to government opinion, service by post 'would not be deemed valid service in Japan in circumstances where the rights of the addressee were not respected'.[71] From the government's position, it follows that service by post to a respondent in Japan would be invalid. Indeed, lower courts have held that service by post without a Japanese translation is not valid.[72] In academic literature, some have argued that, even if service is not effected in a manner which complies with the 1965 Hague Service Abroad Convention, it should be deemed valid as long as it complies with the law of the rendering state and enables a respondent to appreciate that an action has been commenced against him or her in the rendering state.[73] Under this approach, the decisive factor would be whether the respondent is made aware of the commencement of an action abroad.

In such case, would a (Japanese) translation of the relevant documents have to be provided at the time of service? While lower courts have required a translation, academic opinion is divided.[74] Some argue that a translation must be attached unless the addressee voluntarily receives the complaint. Others argue that it is not necessary as long as the addressee is able to appreciate from the complaint that an action has been brought abroad. In a recent case, the Tokyo High Court held that postal service by an American plaintiff to a Japanese respondent living in the US without a Japanese translation met the service requirement in Article 118(ii) of the CCP because the Japanese respondent was capable

[68] For details, see 'Japan – Central Authority & Practical Information' (*Hague Conference on Private International Law*, 7 January 2018), available online: www.hcch.net/en/states/authorities/details3/?aid=261.

[69] On the operation of the 1965 Hague Service Abroad Convention from a Japanese perspective, see Yuko Nishitani, 'The Operation of the 1965 Hague Service Convention in Japan' (2004) 9(17) *Zeitschrift für Japanisches Recht [Journal of Japanese Law]* 215; Keisuke Takeshita, 'Sovereignty and National Civil Procedure: An Analysis of State Practice in Japan' (2016) 9(2) *Journal of East Asia and International Law* 361.

[70] Judgment of the Supreme Court, 28 April 1998 (n 12).

[71] 'Conclusions and Recommendations adopted by the Special Commission on the Practical Operation of the Hague Apostille, Evidence, and Service Conventions' (*Hague Conference on Private International Law*, 28 October–4 November 2003) para 57, available online: assets.hcch.net/docs/0edbc4f7-675b-4b7b-8e1c-2c1998655a3e.pdf.

[72] Judgment of Tokyo District Court, 21 December 1976, 870 *Hanrei Jiho* 96; Judgment of Tokyo District Court, 11 November 1988, 1315 *Hanrei Jiho* 95; Judgment of Tokyo District Court, 26 March 1990, 857 *Kin'yu Shoji Hanrei* 39.

[73] eg Hideyuki Kobayashi, 'Gaikoku Hanketsu no Shounin Shikko ni tsuiteno Ichi Kousatsu' [A Reflection on Recognition and Enforcement of Foreign Judgments] (1982) 467 *Hanrei Taimuzu* 23; Kono (n 7) 111, para 11.

[74] Ichiro Kasuga, 'Sotatsu (Sotatsu Jouyaku 10 Jo (a) ni yoru Chokusetsu Soutatsu)' [Service of Process (Service by Post in Accordance with Art 10(a) of the Hague Service Convention)] in Akira Takakuwa and Masato Dogauchi (eds), *Shin Saiban Jitsumu Taikei (3) – Kokusai Minji Sosho-ho (Zaisanho Kankei) [New Court Practice Series (3) – International Procedural Law (Property Law Matters)]* (Tokyo, Seirin Shoin, 2002) 348.

of understanding English.[75] Following this judgment, whether a translation is necessary should be a matter to be determined on a case-by-case basis.

Although the requirement of proper service must be satisfied, defects in service can be cured by the submission of a defence to the claim. In other words, this requirement will be satisfied if a defendant has voluntarily responded to the claim even where there has not been proper service.

v. *Public Policy*

The public policy requirement is found in Article 118(iii) of the CCP. Japanese courts examine on their own motion whether the enforcement of a foreign judgment would be contrary to *ordre public* (public policy) (that is, public order or the good morals of Japan). Public policy at the stage of recognition and enforcement of foreign judgments is two-pronged: substantive and procedural public policy. Substantive public policy concerns the substance of the judgment, while procedural public policy concerns the litigation proceedings before the rendering court. The criteria for determining whether the recognition would be contrary to public policy are also two-pronged: (1) incompatibility of the effects of the foreign judgment with Japanese legal order (the impact of recognising and enforcing the foreign judgment); and (2) connection of the case in question with Japan (strength of domestic nexus).

By reference to public policy, at what point in time should this requirement be assessed? Some argue that it should be the time when a foreign judgment becomes final in the rendering state, because the judgment is automatically recognised as soon as the requirements in Article 118 of the CCP are satisfied. Others argue that it should be the time when the question of whether the recognition of a foreign judgment conforms with material public policy of Japan is examined by courts, because the material public policy being considered is whether the recognition would give rise to intolerable effects in Japan. There has been one case (although in a family matter) in which a lower court decided this issue, taking into consideration the circumstances which occurred after the foreign judgment had become final in the rendering state.[76]

As in most jurisdictions, one of the typical matters in relation to substantive public policy[77] is whether a foreign judgment awarding punitive damages in addition to compensatory damages and costs may be recognised. In this regard, the Supreme Court has held that the punitive parts of such a judgment cannot be recognised.[78] Only the non-punitive

[75] Judgment of Tokyo High Court, 24 September 2015, 2305 *Hanrei Jiho* 68.

[76] Judgment of Tokyo High Court, 15 November 1993 (n 58). There are some academic views for this approach, see eg Hiroshige Takata, 'Art 200' in Masahiro Suzuki and Yoshimitsu Aoyama (eds), *Chu'u Shaku Minji Sosho-ho (4) [Commentary on Civil Procedure Law (4)]* (Tokyo, Yuhikaku, 1997) 384.

[77] Another typical example is that recognition of a foreign judgment ordering a registration of the mother-child relationship between a mother and twins whom a foreign surrogate mother bore. See Judgment of the Supreme Court, 23 March 2007, 61-2 *Minshu* 619 (with English translation available at (2008) 51 *Japanese Yearbook of International Law* 552).

[78] Judgment of the Supreme Court, 11 July 1997, 51-6 *Minshu* 2573. As for recognition of judgments awarding punitive damages, there have been different views. Some argue that such judgments do not fall within the notion of 'a judgment' in the meaning of Art 118 of the CCP due to its penal nature, others argue that even punitive parts are recognisable and enforceable unless a rendering court awarded punitive damages on discriminatory grounds or its amount is excessive. As for the former approach, see eg Masato Dogauchi, 'Amerika no Choubatasu teki Songai Baisho Hanketsu no Nihon ni okeru Shikko' [Enforcement of American Judgments Awarding Punitive

parts can be recognised and enforced in Japan. Thus, there would only be partial recognition and enforcement. Foreign judgments ordering the payment of debts might be refused recognition if the debts arise from, for instance, drug-dealing, gambling or human trafficking.[79] As far as civil and commercial matters are concerned, lower courts have held that the recognition of the following judgments are not contrary to public policy of Japan. For instance, a Korean judgment ordering a payment calculated on the basis of an agreed interest rate (48 per cent per year in contrast to a maximum of 20 per cent per year permitted by Japanese law) between two individuals,[80] a Korean judgment awarding damages on the basis of the statutory rate (20 per cent per year, in contrast to five or six per cent per year in Japan),[81] and a Californian judgment ordering the payment of an attorney's fee (approximately 1.7 times higher than what would have been payable in Japan)[82] have all been recognised and enforced.[83]

As for procedural public policy, there have been some judgments in which Japanese courts have refused the recognition and enforcement of a foreign judgment on this ground. It is said that procedural public policy will function if a foreign judgment is obtained fraudulently (for instance, falsification of documents)[84] or if there are other procedural defects (apart from defects of service), for instance, where the tribunal was acting in an unfair manner.[85] Foreign judgments may be refused recognition if they conflict with a final Japanese judgment between the same parties on the same dispute or cause of action.[86]

Although foreign judgments are automatically recognised in Japan as long as the requirements in Article 118 of the CCP are met, a party can make a claim for the recognition or non-recognition by courts of a foreign judgment.[87]

Damages in Japan] in Teiichiro Nakano and others (eds), *Minji Tetsuduki Ho-gaku no Kakushin (jou) [Innovation of Civil Procedure Law (1)]* (Tokyo, Yuhikaku, 1991) 423. As for the latter, see eg Toshiyuki Kono, 'Die Anerkennung von US-amerikanischen Urteilen über punitive damages in Japan' in Andreas Heldrich and Toshiyuki Kono (eds), *Herausforderungen des Internationalen Zivilverfahrensrechts* (Tübingen, Mohr Siebeck, 1994) 46–48; Kazuaki Nishioka, 'Kyouso Seikyu'u ni kansuru Gaikoku Hanketsu no Shounin oyobi Shikko' [Recognition and Enforcement of Foreign Judgments in Relation to Competition Law Claims] (2015) 25 *Nihon Kokusai Keizai-ho Gakkai Nenpo [International Economic Law]* 105.

[79] Honma, Nakano and Sakai (n 22) 192.

[80] Judgment of Tokyo District Court, 13 December 2013, 2013WLJPCA12138015.

[81] Judgment of Tokyo District Court, 12 February 2009, 2068 *Hanrei Jiho* 95.

[82] Judgment of Tokyo District Court, 9 September 2003, 2003WLJPCA09090007.

[83] For other reported cases in which foreign judgments were found not to be contrary to public policy, see Tada (n 7) 89–90; Haga (n 8) 203–06.

[84] Although in the case relating to the validity of marriage, Judgment of Tokyo High Court, 27 February 1990, 1344 *Hanrei Jiho* 139 (with English translation available at (1991) 34 *Japanese Annual of International Law* 166). For cases in which the fraud defence was not accepted, see eg Judgment of Tokyo District Court, 14 January 1994 (n 18); Judgment of Tokyo District Court, Hachioji Branch, 13 February 1998 (n 40).

[85] Kono (n 7) p 112, para 13.

[86] Judgment of Osaka District Court, 22 December 1977, 361 *Hanrei Taimuzu* 127. In academic literature, however, there has been no consensus on how Japanese courts should deal with this issue. For details, see Masato Dogauchi, 'Naikoku Hanketsu tono Teishoku' [Conflict with Domestic Judgments] in Akira Takakuwa and Masato Dogauchi (eds), *Shin Saiban Jitsumu Taikei (3) – Kokusai Minji Sosho-ho (Zaisanho Kankei) [New Court Practice Series (3) – International Procedural Law (Property Law Matters)]* (Tokyo, Seirin Shoin, 2002) 365.

[87] Yoshimitsu Aoyama, 'Art 24' in Chu'uichi Suzuki and Akira Mikazuki (eds), *Chu'ukai Minji Shikko-ho (1) [Commentary on Civil Execution Act (1)]* (Tokyo, Daiichi Hoki Shuppan, 1984) 389–90; Takata (n 78) 364–65; Nishitani (n 7) 1273, para 177; Sakurada (n 15) 387.

As far as judgments ordering the defendant to perform a certain action are concerned,[88] it is still debatable whether a party may have foreign judgments 'recognised' by bringing a fresh action in Japan on the merits in relation to the same cause of action (re-litigation), instead of claiming for the enforcement judgment under Article 24 of the CEA. In this regard, some argue that a party who has already obtained a foreign judgment in favour of himself/herself may bring such an action because the *exequatur* proceeding is not necessarily more expeditious or less cumbersome and the requirements for recognition are examined in the *exequatur* proceedings.[89] Others argue that such action is not allowed because the *exequatur* proceedings can be instituted for the purpose of enforcement and such a second claim would violate the prohibition of *révision au fond.*[90]

vi. Interlocutory Judgments

As mentioned above (see section IV.A.i), a foreign judgment must be 'final and binding' within the meaning of Article 118 of the CCP. Although there has been no case law dealing with the recognition and enforcement of interlocutory judgments, they are unlikely to be recognised or enforced in Japan due to their lack of finality.[91] It would therefore seem that there is no way that a party can obtain recognition of interlocutory judgments. Even if they fell within the notion of 'a final and binding judgment' under Article 118 of the CCP, Japanese courts would still apply the requirements in that article to determine whether they were recognisable and enforceable in Japan.

B. Enforcement

In order to enforce a foreign judgment, a successful party must file a suit before a competent court and obtain an enforcement judgment (*shikko hanketsu*) granting the enforcement of the foreign judgment. That serves as a title of debt (*saimu meigi*) necessary to initiate enforcement proceedings (Article 22(6) of the CEA). The CEA does not expressly provide for the jurisdiction of Japanese courts in relation to the execution of foreign judgments that have been recognised in Japan, but it is generally understood that such jurisdiction is justified insofar as the object of dispute or the assets of the debtor are situated in Japan.[92] The competent court for the enforcement of judgments is determined as follows (Article 24(1) of the CEA):

1. A District Court having jurisdiction over the general venue of the debtor; or
2. if there is no such general venue, a District Court having jurisdiction over the subject matter of the claim or the seizable property of the debtor are situated.

[88] With regard to declaratory and constitutive judgments, the academic opinion seems to be settled to deny the possibility for the successful party to bring a fresh action on the basis that the claimant would have no interest in bringing such an action. See Aoyama (n 89) 389.

[89] Aoyama (n 89) 389; Takata (n 76) 365–66; Honma, Nakano and Sakai (n 22) 199; Nakano (n 28) 444.

[90] Kazunori Ishiguro, *Gendai Kokusai Shiho (Jo) [Modern Conflict of Laws in Japan (Vol I)]* (Tokyo, University of Tokyo Press, 1986) 391–404; Sakurada (n 15) 386.

[91] Yokoyama (n 6) 151; Kono (n 7) 106–07, para 4.

[92] Okuda (n 7) 418.

Article 24(2) of the CEA explicitly prohibits *révision au fond* and, therefore, a Japanese court cannot review the merit of the case. The court will dismiss such a suit where it finds that one or more of the requirements in Article 118 of the CCP are not satisfied (Article 24(3) of the CEA). An enforcement judgment must declare that the compulsory execution of the foreign judgment is permitted (Article 24(4) of the CEA).

Possible means of enforcement differ between monetary and non-monetary judgments. For monetary judgments, the following means are available: filing a petition for attachment or seizure; seizure and judicial auction of immovable property, semi-immovable property (such as a car) and movable property; attachment and execution of a respondent's rights against a third party; and conversion of the respondent's assets into money and distribution of the resultant proceeds (Articles 43 to 167(16) of the CEA). As for non-monetary judgments, such means of execution as vacating immovable property to secure a creditor's possession, and delivery of movable property are available (Articles 168 to 179 of the CEA).

As noted above, to enforce a foreign judgment, a party seeking enforcement needs to obtain an enforcement judgment. At that stage, the respondent may object to the enforcement, and the objection may take time to resolve. There are no available statistics on the average time taken to enforce judgments.

V. Special Cases

A. Foreign Judgments Relating to Intellectual Property Rights

Pursuant to Article 3-5(3) of the CCP, disputes concerning the existence/non-existence or the validity of intellectual property rights that are established by registration (Article 2(2) of the Intellectual Property Basic Act)[93] fall under the exclusive jurisdiction of the Japanese courts if the registration was effected in Japan. Therefore, foreign judgments concerning those disputes will not be recognised in Japan. There have been, at least, two judgments dealing with the recognition of foreign judgments relating to intellectual property rights. The Mito District Court[94] refused to recognise a Korean judgment ordering the Japanese respondent to submit a notification of change in the name of the applicant in the proceeding for obtaining a patent in Japan. The Nagoya High Court[95] also did not recognise a Korean judgment ordering the Japanese respondent to complete the transfer registration of a patent registered in Japan and to make a payment of costs relating to patents registered in Taiwan and the US. Both courts so held on a similar basis, that is, that actions relating to the (transfer) registration of a patent should fall under the exclusive jurisdiction of the state of registration and thus the relevant foreign courts lacked jurisdiction over disputes regarding the patents registered in other states.[96] Following these judgments, foreign judgments

[93] Pursuant to Art 2(2) of the Act, the term 'intellectual property right' covers a patent right, a utility model right, a plant breeder's right, a design right, a copy right, a trademark right, a right that is stipulated by laws and regulations on other intellectual property or right pertaining to an interest that is protected by acts.

[94] Judgment of Mito District Court, Shimozuma Branch, 5 November 2012, 2012WLJPCA11056005.

[95] Judgment of Nagoya High Court, 17 May 2013, 2013WLJPCA05176005. For analysis and criticism, see Dai Yokomizo, 'Case Notes' (2015) 1487 *Jurist* 106; Miho Shin, 'Case Notes' (2016) 1492 *Jurist* 305.

[96] In these cases, Art 3-5(3) did not apply because the actions had been initiated before such provision was introduced.

relating to registration of an intellectual property right (at least, a patent right) in other states (Japan and elsewhere) will not be recognised in Japan due to the lack of indirect jurisdiction (for the criteria of indirect jurisdiction, see section IV.A.ii).[97]

On the other hand, actions for damages based on the infringement of intellectual property rights registered in Japan do not fall under the exclusive jurisdiction of Japanese courts.[98] The indirect jurisdiction requirement would not, therefore, prevent such judgments from being recognised. This analysis will also apply to judgments relating to intellectual property rights registered elsewhere. But in order for such judgments to be recognised and enforced, all the other requirements must be satisfied.

B. Foreign Judgments Relating to Immovable Property in Japan

There has been no case law dealing with this situation. According to Japanese rules of international jurisdiction, actions relating to immovable property in Japan (except for those relating to entries in public registers)[99] do not fall under the exclusive jurisdiction of the Japanese courts.[100] Therefore, while foreign judgments concerning entries in public registers of immovable property in Japan are not recognised in Japan due to a lack of indirect jurisdiction, foreign judgments relating to other disputes concerning immovable property in Japan are likely to be recognised in Japan if the requirements in Article 118 of the CCP are satisfied.

C. Foreign Judgments Relating to Environmental Wrongs

There has been no case law dealing with this situation. In the context of an environmental wrong committed in Japan, actions relating to environmental damage do not fall within the exclusive jurisdiction of the Japanese courts under the CCP.[101] Therefore, the indirect jurisdiction requirement would not prevent such foreign judgment from being recognised and enforced. Foreign judgments relating to environmental wrongs are likely to be recognised in Japan as long as the requirements in Article 118 of the CCP are satisfied.

In the case of class action claims for environmental wrongs, an additional question may arise. If class actions follow the 'opt-out' principle as in the US, all the members of the class should in theory have been informed that the action was ongoing and that they would be bound by the outcome unless they opt out of the proceedings. In practice, there are likely to be some class members (mainly from outside the relevant state) who will not

[97] As for a legislative proposal on recognition and enforcement of foreign judgments relating to intellectual property rights, see Toshiyuki Kono (ed), *Chiteki Zaisanken to Shougai Minji Sosho [Intellectual Property and Transnational Civil Litigation]* (Tokyo, Kobundo, 2010) 331.

[98] Nishitani (n 6) 267; Yokoyama (n 6) 142.

[99] CCP, Art 3-5(2).

[100] See Nishitani (n 6) 259–60. As for disputes concerning immovable property, courts of the state where immovable property is situated has international jurisdiction (non-exclusive though) pursuant to Art 3-3(11) of the CCP.

[101] For the matters falling within the exclusive jurisdiction of Japanese courts, see CCP, Art 3-5.

have been informed and would not have had notice of the action and their right to opt out (often referred to as 'absent claimants'). There is no doubt that claimants who participate in the proceedings are bound by the outcome and the resulting judgment is likely to be recognised in Japan. But it would be problematic if absent claimants were also to be treated as bound by the foreign judgment (for example, for the purposes of *res judicata*), even if they did not appear before the court and did not participate in the proceedings because they were unaware of the proceedings. Recognition in the case of absent claimants would instead likely to be deemed by the Japanese courts as a violation of procedural public policy in Article 118(iii) of the CCP,[102] because the right to be heard of the absent claimants will not be necessarily effectively guaranteed. As a result, foreign judgments rendered in class action will not be recognised in Japan insofar as such class members are concerned.[103] On the other hand, if class actions follow an 'opt-in' mechanism, all class members who opted in would be treated by the Japanese courts as bound by the outcome. Nevertheless, there has been, so far, no precedent on the recognition in Japan of foreign class action judgments.

D. Foreign Judgments Relating to Anti-competitive Conduct

There has been no case law dealing with this situation. Under the CCP, actions relating to damages suffered from infringement of Japanese competition law do not fall under the exclusive jurisdiction of the Japanese courts.[104] Foreign judgments given in actions of this sort are likely to be recognised and enforced in Japan insofar as the requirements in Article 118 of the CCP are satisfied. There seems to be no obstacle in terms of indirect jurisdiction. Where competition law claims are concerned, however, the public policy requirement may prevent judgments from being recognised and enforced. It is generally said that competition law constitutes part of public policy. Therefore, foreign judgments relating to the infringement of Japanese competition law may be refused recognition and enforcement on public policy grounds, if recognising such judgments would manifestly distort market order in Japan. In the case of class actions in competition law cases, a similar analysis to that sketched out above in connection with environmental wrongs may also apply. Insofar as judgments concerning breaches of foreign competition law are concerned, the public policy requirement would not seem to be triggered as far as foreign markets are concerned. According to the Supreme Court and the view of a majority of scholars, punitive or exemplary damages (typically granted in the US and other countries' antitrust laws) will be refused recognition in Japan (see section IV.A.v).

[102] Eiji Adachi, 'Kurasu Akushion Hanketsu/Wakai no Chiriteki Han'i' [Territorial Scope of Class Actions Judgments and Settlements] (2014) 86(2) *Horitsu Jiho* 51.

[103] Similarly, see Eiji Adachi, 'Beikoku Kurasu Akushion Hanketsu/Wakai no Shounin Shikko to Koujo' [The Class Action in Japanese Law und Japanese *Ordre Public*] (2002) 69 *Seijo Law Review* 266; Masato Dogauchi, 'Gaikoku Saibansho niyoru Kurasu Akushion Hanketsu (Wakai) no Nihon deno Koryoku' [Effect in Japan of Class Action Judgments/Settlements Given by Foreign Courts] (2010) 925 *New Business Law* 20.

[104] CCP, Art 3-5(2).

VI. The Future

A. Prospects

From a Japanese perspective, one of the most important benefits of acceding to the 2005 Hague Convention would be to enable foreign judgments to be recognised and enforced under a unified legal framework among Member States of a multilateral instrument, with the result that parties' expectations in relation to the effectiveness of judgments will be secured and even enhanced across borders. Nevertheless, foreign judgments are already readily recognised and enforced under the current Japanese system. Therefore, in practical terms, there is no real necessity to accede to the 2005 Hague Convention.

More particularly, there are at least three areas which might be developed further: (1) overcoming the reciprocity requirement by becoming party to the forthcoming Hague Convention on the Recognition and Enforcement of Judgments in Civil and Commercial Matters; (2) clarifying the grounds of indirect jurisdiction also through the forthcoming Hague Convention; and (3) recognising and enforcing judicial settlements. First, if a more liberal regime to the reciprocity requirement in Article 118 of the CCP can be worked out in the forthcoming Hague Convention, judgments from what are currently regarded as non-reciprocating states (such as Mainland China) may be recognised and enforced, provided that such states also have to be Member States of the Convention. Second, grounds for indirect jurisdiction will be clarified. Under the current system, there are no provisions dealing with indirect jurisdiction and therefore, the question whether a foreign rendering court has indirect jurisdiction over a case has to be examined in light of *jori* (presently largely based on rules on direct jurisdiction in the CCP). The forthcoming Hague Convention clearly stipulates grounds for recognition and enforcement, with the result that a party seeking recognition and enforcement can readily assess whether the indirect jurisdiction of the rendering court will be upheld. In addition to identifying grounds of indirect jurisdiction, the forthcoming Hague Convention will also specify grounds for refusal of recognition. Thus, it will be clearer and more transparent when recognition of a foreign judgment may be refused, especially in the context of *lis pendens* and inconsistency with a domestic judgment. Third, judicial settlements will be recognised and enforced in Japan. Under the current domestic rules, judicial settlements do not fall under the notion 'a judgment' and therefore are not recognisable. The forthcoming Hague Convention should open the door to the recognition of judicial settlements. There seems no obvious difficulty to accede to the forthcoming Hague Convention. But, in acceding to such instrument, Japan may need to modify principles and rules on jurisdiction for certain matters (such as jurisdiction relating to rights *in rem* in immovable property situated in Japan) in order to secure the consistency between the Convention and domestic rules.

B. Reform

In the author's view, the following can be pointed out as shortcomings of the current regime. First, the notion of 'a judgment' is relatively narrow (for instance, in excluding judicial settlements). Its scope does not satisfy the needs of modern commercial transactions.

Second, there is no provision dealing with grounds of indirect jurisdiction, thereby introducing uncertainty. Third, the reciprocity requirement has prevented, or is likely to prevent, judgments from certain states from being recognised in Japan. Fourth, it is unclear how Japanese courts deal with the recognition of a foreign judgment which conflicts with a Japanese or third State judgment between the same parties on the same dispute. These shortcomings may be overcome by acceding to the forthcoming Hague convention on the recognition and enforcement of foreign judgments. Nevertheless, reform can also be achieved by domestic legislation.

It may also be profitable to enter into Memorandums of Understanding (MOUs) with judiciaries of other states to share information on recognition and enforcement of foreign judgments. There would seem to be no difficulty in MOUs as a matter of principle. These would be mere guidelines which, although non-binding, would promote transparency. In Japan, it is generally said that judges are not allowed to communicate directly with judges in other States because that would be regarded as an infringement of national sovereignty,[105] although there is no specific statutory provision so providing. Therefore, although MOUs may be viable, the use of technology whereby Japanese judges communicate directly with judges in other states on the resolution of specific cross-border matters is unlikely to be useful in improving the system for recognition and enforcement of foreign judgments.

VII. Conclusion

Japan has been generous in recognising and enforcing foreign judgments. As long as the five requirements in Article 118 of the CCP (final judgment, indirect jurisdiction, proper service, public policy and reciprocity) are satisfied, a foreign judgment is automatically recognised and then enforced under similar conditions (Article 24 of the CEA). It would seem that the indirect jurisdiction and public policy hurdles will often be most difficult requirements to overcome, but those requirements are not unique to Japan (see sections IV.A.ii and IV.A.v for details).

[105] In the context of taking evidence, the General Secretariat of the Supreme Court expressed a similar view: 'Taking of evidence is an execution of judicial authority. Therefore, there must be a treaty, cooperation agreement, or other agreement with that foreign nation to take evidence abroad. Taking evidence abroad when such treaties do not exist is an infringement of national sovereignty': see General Secretariat of the Supreme Court (ed), *Shiho Kyojyo Shitsumu Shiryo [Working Documents on International Judicial Cooperation]* (Tokyo, General Secretariat of the Supreme Court, 1992) 3.

6

South Korea

UNHO LEE

I. Introduction

Foreign judgments are recognised and enforced in South Korea, if they meet requirements under Articles 217 and 217 *bis* of the Civil Procedure Act (CPA) and Articles 26 and 27 of the Civil Execution Act (CEA). The recognition and enforcement of foreign judgments aims to secure the finality of a foreign judgment by acknowledging *res judicata* of the same, while preventing multiple legal proceedings and potential conflicts of legal outcome between the same parties in different jurisdictions. As an Amendment Proposal of Private International Law Act (the Amendment Proposal) was only pre-announced in January 2018,[1] it remains to be seen how the Amendment Proposal will affect the recognition and enforcement of foreign judgments in South Korea.

II. Background

South Korea sits in the centre of northeast Asia, between China and Japan. After declaring independence from Japanese rule (1910–45), the Korean government was established in 1948, upholding the cause of the Provisional Government of Republic of Korea born of the March First Independence Movement of 1919. The Korean War (1950) brought about a division of Korea into South and North Korea that has lasted now for almost 70 years. Nevertheless, the South Korean economy rapidly grew, based on export-oriented development focusing on manufacturing and heavy industries from the 1960s to 1980s. A successful transition in the 1990s and 2000s to the industrial development of shipbuilding, semiconductors, information technology, entertainment, etc made it possible for South Korea to knock on the door of the world's major economies. Politically, efforts at democratisation persisted against military dictatorships and violations of the Constitution leading to the introduction of direct elections in the 1980s and an end to military rule in the 1990s.

The legal system of South Korea is a civil law system. Modernisation of the legal system started autonomously with the Gabo Reform of 1894. But it was later heavily influenced

[1] The proposal for a wholesale amendment of the Private International Act (the Amendment Proposal) was pre-announced on 19 January 2018 and approved by the Council of Ministers on 20 November 2018. As at 30 December 2018, the Amendment Proposal is under review by a Legislative Standing Committee.

by the Japanese legal system, which in turn was modelled after French and German laws. Nevertheless, the fundamental legal principles of South Korean law originated from the 1919 Constitutional Charter of the Provisional Government of the Republic of Korea, the predecessor of the Constitution of the Republic of Korea promulgated in 1948.[2] The Constitution ensures judicial independence based on the separation of legal, administrative, and judicial powers. There is a three-tiered judicial system comprising the Supreme Court (at the apex), five High Courts and 18 District Courts.[3] After abolishing unconstitutional laws and institutions under the Japanese occupation, South Korea established its principal legal codes, such as the Criminal Code (1953), the Criminal Procedure Code (1954), the Civil Code (1958), the Civil Procedure Code (1960) and the Commercial Code (1962). The application of statutory provisions takes precedence over that of customary law or reasoning. Court precedents do not constitute a source of law, but inferior courts are bound by the precedents of superior courts. Court precedents are becoming more important with the increasing number and complexity of today's lawsuits.

The Conflict of Laws Act legislated in 1962 was based on out-dated theories and legislation of the nineteenth century. The Act drew criticism for its inability to accommodate the modern international environment and was completely revised by the Private International Law Act (PILA) in April 2001. The PILA is now the main source of private international law rules in South Korea. It determines governing law and establishes principles of international jurisdiction in matters involving foreign elements. The current PILA consists of nine chapters[4] and 62 provisions. Applicable law is designated on the basis of the rule of 'the most closely connected law' – the law of the country that is most closely connected to the relevant relationships. The PILA further stipulates a general rule of international jurisdiction that requires a party or a case to be substantively related to South Korea. In January 2018 the Amendment Proposal was pre-announced based on cases that have been decided since 2001 and a comprehensive review of jurisdictional rules. The Amendment Proposal provides criteria for determining international jurisdiction, adopting more specific rules in light of global developments in private international law.[5]

South Korea, the 45th Member State of the Hague Conference on Private International Law (HCCH), is currently a contracting party to four Hague Conventions, the 1961 Hague Convention Abolishing the Requirement of Legalisation for Foreign Public Documents,

[2] There have been nine amendments of the Constitution with the last one in 1987. In 2018, the South Korean government began to discuss a tenth constitutional amendment that aims to strengthen direct democracy and decentralisation together with the introductions of a different form of government and the articulation of human rights to life and information.

[3] In addition, there are a Constitutional Court and several other courts of specialised jurisdiction, such as the five Family Courts, the Administrative Court and the Patent Court.

[4] The chapters are: I. General Provisions, II. Persons, III. Juristic Acts, IV. Real Rights, V. Claims, VI. Family, VII. Inheritance, VIII. Notes and Cheques and IX. Maritime Commerce.

[5] The following rules on jurisdiction have been included in the Amendment Proposal: For General Provisions (Ch I): General Jurisdiction (Art 3); Specific Jurisdiction of Office or Business Place (Art 4); Specific Jurisdiction of Location of Property (Art 5); Correlated Jurisdiction (Art 6); Jurisdiction over Counterclaims (Art 7); Jurisdiction by Agreement (Art 8); Jurisdiction by Pleading (Art 9); Exclusive Jurisdiction (Art 10); Concurrent International Jurisdiction (Art 11); Non-exercise of International Jurisdiction (Art 12); Jurisdiction over Preservative Measures (Art 14); and Jurisdiction over Non-contentious Cases (Art 15). For Special Provisions (Chs II–X), newly included are jurisdiction rules on Person (Ch II: Arts 24–25); Real Rights (Ch IV: Art 33); Intellectual Property Rights (Ch V: Arts 39–40); Claims (Ch VI: Arts 42 and 45); Family (Ch VII: Arts 57–63); Inheritance (Ch VIII: Art 77); Note and Check (Ch IX: Art 80); and Maritime Commerce (Ch X: Arts 90–94).

the 1965 Hague Convention on the Service Abroad of Judicial and Extrajudicial Documents in Civil or Commercial Matters (1965 Hague Service Abroad Convention), the 1970 Hague Convention on the Taking of Evidence Abroad in Civil or Commercial Matters (1970 Hague Evidence Abroad Convention) and the 1980 Hague Convention on the Civil Aspects of International Child Abduction.

The making of a judgment and its execution are two different functions in South Korea. The Government does not determine the existence of a right. That is the province of the Judiciary. Consequently, the enforcement of foreign judgments requires a judgment of execution from the South Korean court. Article 26 of CEA provides that compulsory execution based on a foreign judgment can only be effected if a court has so permitted by an execution judgment. A lawsuit seeking an execution judgment should thus normally be filed in the District Court where the debtor is to be found.

III. Recognition and Enforcement under Treaties or Similar Arrangements

South Korea has not signed any bilateral treaties or other arrangements in relation to the recognition and enforcement of foreign judgments.[6] With regards to judicial assistance, the 1965 Hague Service Abroad Convention and the 1970 Hague Evidence Abroad Convention entered into force in 2000 and 2010, respectively. South Korea has signed bilateral agreements for mutual judicial assistance with five states so far. These enable service of judicial documents and the taking of evidence between South Korea and the relevant states respectively.[7] South Korea has not concluded any conventions for the recognition and enforcement of foreign judgments. South Korea has no specific plans to sign or ratify the 2005 Hague Convention on Choice of Court Agreements.

IV. Recognition and Enforcement in the Absence of Treaties or Similar Arrangements

A. Recognition

South Korea distinguishes between the recognition and the enforcement of foreign judgments in terms of conceptualisation as well as legal procedure. Foreign judgments are automatically recognised if they meet certain requirements, but their enforcement requires an execution judgment. The requirements for the recognition and enforcement of foreign

[6] Foreign arbitral awards are recognised and enforced in accordance with the 1958 New York Convention on the Recognition and Enforcement of Foreign Arbitral Awards. Art 39 of the Arbitration Act in South Korea provides that Art 217 of the Civil Procedure Act and Arts 26(1) and 27 of the Civil Execution Act shall apply *mutatis mutandis* to the recognition or execution of a foreign arbitral awards which are not subject to the 1958 New York Convention.

[7] Australia (signed in 1999), China (2003), Mongolia (2008), Uzbekistan (2012) and Thailand (2013).

judgments are provided under Articles 217 and 217 *bis* of the CPA and Articles 26 and 27 of the CEA. Foreign judgments that meet the requirements for recognition are automatically treated as *res judicata*. They do not require any specific proceedings. But, to be recognised, a judgment must be 'final and conclusive or acknowledged to have the same force'.[8] Finality does not require that an instrument be called a 'judgment' or the formality required of a judgment in South Korea. Thus, a ruling or order can constitute a final judgment as long as it gives rise to *res judicata* and finally settles a substantive relationship.

Not all judgments are entitled to recognition. The Supreme Court has held that a judgment following a confession made pursuant to the Code of Civil Procedure of the State of California[9] does not constitute a judgment. The judgment by confession was obtained without judicial scrutiny, but merely upon the plaintiff's application for a confession judgment. A law clerk had merely reviewed the confession and then registered a judgment.[10] The Supreme Court held that the judgment based on the confession failed to meet the definition of a 'judgment' which requires a judicial procedure that safeguards a defendant's entitlement to a court determination.[11] In contrast, according to the Supreme Court, a decision in a discharge trial under a foreign country's bankruptcy procedure can constitute[12] a foreign judgment entitled to recognition.[13] A discharge trial, although conducted under a foreign country's bankruptcy procedure, involves a judicial determination of a party's entitlement to be discharged as a debtor. A dispute as to the existence and scope of such entitlement would need to be resolved by a court on the basis of evidence and submissions from the parties to a suit brought pursuant to the jurisdiction's bankruptcy procedures. The resulting order of the foreign court was therefore in the nature of a judgment and, subject to questions of public order and morals, could be recognised under Article 217 of the CPA.

In order for a foreign judgment to be recognised, all four requirements under Article 217(1) of the CPA must be met. Those requirements are that:

1. The foreign court must have international jurisdiction under South Korean law.
2. The defendant must have been lawfully served and notified of the proceedings in sufficient time to allow one to defend or respond to the lawsuit.
3. Approval of the foreign judgment must not undermine sound morals or other social order of South Korea.
4. There must be a guarantee of reciprocity or, at any rate, the criteria for the recognition of a South Korean final judgment by the rendering state must be similar to those applied by the South Korean court.

The South Korean court is duty-bound to investigate of its own whether the four requirements are satisfied,[14] even in the absence of a request from a party to do so. If a foreign

[8] CPA, Art 217(1); In the 2014 amendment of the CPA, the phrase 'or a judgment acknowledged to have the same force' was added after the pre-existing phrase 'a final and conclusive judgment'.

[9] 'A judgment may be entered without action either for money or become due, or to secure any person against contingent liability …'.

[10] Arts 1132–34 of the former Civil Execution Act (California).

[11] Supreme Court Decision 2009Da68910 (29 April 2010).

[12] The Supreme Court did not recognise the discharge trial for a different reason – undermining the social order of South Korea.

[13] Supreme Court Decision 2009Ma1600 (25 March 2010).

[14] CPA, Art 217(2).

judgment meets the four requirements, the South Korean court will recognise it. The South Korean court will not look into the substantive merits of the foreign judgment.[15]

B. International Jurisdiction

For recognition of a foreign judgment, the foreign court must have international jurisdiction based on the principles of South Korean law.[16] The foreign court's international jurisdiction is subject to the same criteria that a South Korean court applies in deciding whether it would have international jurisdiction if a similar case were brought before it. The criteria for international jurisdiction thus mirror the general principles of international jurisdiction in the PILA[17] while referring to the judicial decisions developed in consideration with venue provisions under the CPA.[18]

The Amendment Proposal aims to provide more rational and specific rules for international jurisdiction based on the past judicial decisions. As briefly introduced above, a number of jurisdiction rules have been added to the Amendment Proposal. Amongst others, the newly established principles of international jurisdiction require the South Korean court to decide whether a party to or the case in a dispute is substantively related to South Korea in accordance with 'the basic idea of ensuring impartiality between the parties, and appropriateness, speediness and economy of the proceedings'[19] in determining whether it can claim international jurisdiction in a case having foreign elements brought before it. With regards to general jurisdiction rules, Article 3(1) of the Amendment Proposal provides that a South Korean court has international jurisdiction in an action against a party whose habitual residence is in South Korea. International jurisdiction also exists when a lawsuit is brought against corporations or other organisations whose principal office or business place, statutory seat or central administration (hereinafter 'principal place of business') is in South Korea.[20] Accordingly, the South Korean court will recognise the international jurisdiction of a foreign rendering court in cases where a respondent has a habitual residence or principal place of business in the state where the rendering court is situated.

There has been criticism that international jurisdiction has been too liberally interpreted in the past, so that courts have simply referred to the 'general forum' of a foreign juristic person[21] without regard to that forum's connection with a cause of action. In 2000 the

[15] CEA, Art 27(1).

[16] CPA, Art 217(1)-1.

[17] PILA, Art 2(1): 'In case a party or a case in dispute is substantively related to the Republic of Korea, a court shall have the international jurisdiction. In this case, the court shall obey reasonable principles, compatible to the ideology of the allocation of international jurisdiction, in judging the existence of the substantive relations'.

[18] CPA, Arts 2–40.

[19] Amendment Proposal of PILA, Art 2(1). This is based on the Supreme Court Decision 2002Da59788 (22 January 2005).

[20] Amendment Proposal of PILA, Art 3(3).

[21] Under CPA, Art 2, an action is 'subject to the jurisdiction of a court at the place where a defendant's general forum is located'. CPA, Art 3 then defines the 'general forum' as 'his/her domicile: provided, that where the person has no domicile in the Republic of Korea or his/her domicile is unknown, it shall be determined pursuant to his/her residence, and if the residence is unfixed or unknown, it shall be determined pursuant to his/her last domicile'. CPA, Art 5(1) states the 'general forum' of the juristic person is to be 'determined pursuant to the place where its principal office or business place is located, and in cases where there exists no office and business place, it shall

Supreme Court held that courts have jurisdiction based on the location of a business office, even if the affairs of that office were not connected with the matters at issue in the lawsuit, unless that would lead to partiality in the treatment of the parties, would be inappropriate for some reason or would affect the efficiency and expeditiousness of proceedings.[22] It was inappropriate to determine jurisdiction generally, on the basis of the location of a business office, without taking into account Article 12 of the CPA, which specifically allows a lawsuit to be brought before the court where the office whose business is actually connected with a cause of action is located. As a result of the PILA's amendment in 2001 and the application of Article 2 thereof, there has been a small change in the Supreme Court's attitude. In a 2010 case the Supreme Court ruled in favour of international jurisdiction of the South Korean court based on the substantive relation between South Korea on the one hand and the case in dispute and the party whose interest was to be protected on the other. Nonetheless, the Supreme Court emphasised the importance of the territoriality principle by noting that the general forum of a foreign business office itself constitutes a basis for determining the existence of a substantive relation.[23]

Article 4(1) of the Amendment Proposal reaffirms that the seat of a business office alone will no longer constitute a basis of general jurisdiction.[24] This means that it will be more difficult for courts to find international jurisdiction merely based on the location of a business office, and what must be sought preferentially is the substantive relation between the matters at issue in a lawsuit and the affairs of a business place. Accordingly, the Korean court will recognise the international jurisdiction of the rendering court in a case (1) where an action concerning the affairs of an office or business place is brought against a person, juristic person or association that keeps the office or business place in the state or territory of the rendering court,[25] or (2) where a lawsuit concerning a business or sales activity is brought against a person, juristic person or association engaging in a continuous and systematic course of business or sales activity in the state or territory of the rendering court.[26]

Article 8 of the Amendment Proposal provides that the South Korean court has international jurisdiction as the result of a choice of court agreement, whether in writing or electronic format.[27] A choice of court agreement is presumed to be exclusive[28] and is treated as separate from other contractual provisions.[29] Accordingly, the Korean court will recognise the international jurisdiction of a rendering state's court in a case where the parties have agreed to confer jurisdiction on the court of the rendering state. A 1997 Supreme

be determined pursuant to the domicile of the person principally in charge of its duties'. CPA, Art 5(2) elaborates that in the case of a foreign juristic person, association, or foundation, their general forum shall be 'determined pursuant to their offices, business places, or the domiciles of the persons in charge of their duties, in the Republic of Korea'.

[22] Supreme Court Decision 98Da35037 (9 June 2000).

[23] Supreme Court Decision 2010Da18355 (15 July 2010).

[24] Ministry of Justice, 'Public Hearing for the Proposal of All Amendments of the Private International Act' (*Ministry of Justice*, 27 February 2018) 27, available online: www.moj.go.kr/bbs/moj/93/385349/download.do.

[25] Amendment Proposal, Art 4(1).

[26] Amendment Proposal, Art 4(2).

[27] Amendment Proposal, Art 8(2).

[28] Amendment Proposal, Art 8(3).

[29] Amendment Proposal, Art 8(4).

Court case requires four conditions for a choice of court agreement conferring exclusive jurisdiction upon a foreign court to be valid.[30] The most controversial requirement is that of a reasonable connection between the case in question and the foreign court. This means that lack of a reasonable connection with the state or territory of the designated court would invalidate a choice of court agreement. Such a condition could deny the jurisdiction of a neutral third country, while taking away the parties' opportunity to settle their dispute in an impartial jurisdiction as agreed. Also, a foreign court that is related to the case in question might not be necessarily the best jurisdiction for dispute resolution. For those reasons, the Amendment Proposal has excluded such requirement.[31] It provides instead that a choice of court is invalid: (1) if the agreement is null and void under the law of the state of the chosen court or the applicable law; (2) if a party lacked the capacity to conclude the agreement; (3) if the lawsuit falls under the exclusive international jurisdiction of a state other than the one chosen by agreement pursuant to Article 10(1) (of PILA) or the statutes or treaties of South Korea; or (4) if giving effect to the agreement would be manifestly contrary to sound morals or other social order of the state of the court seised.[32] Accordingly, a choice of court agreement will be valid and confer international jurisdiction on the designated court, unless it falls under any of the four situations just mentioned.

Article 9 of the Amendment Proposal provides for jurisdiction as the result of the submission of a pleading. The South Korean court will assume international jurisdiction over a case where a defendant has submitted (1) a pleading on the merits or (2) a statement during an interlocutory stage without asserting the non-existence of international jurisdiction.[33] Accordingly, the Korean court will recognise the international jurisdiction of the rendering state's court by reason of the defendant's pleading or statement, unless the defendant has claimed otherwise. Jurisdiction under this head will not arise if it conflicts with the exclusive jurisdiction of another state.[34] However, if jurisdiction by reason of the submission of a pleading is in conflict with a choice of court agreement, it will be accepted as the former takes precedence over the latter.[35]

[30] They are: (1) The case in question should not fall under the exclusive jurisdiction of the South Korean court; (2) the chosen foreign court should have a valid jurisdiction over the case in question under its law; (3) the case in question should have a reasonable connection with the foreign court; and (4) the exclusive choice of court agreement should not constitute a legal act that is contrary to the public policy for being substantially unreasonable and unjust: Supreme Court Decision 96Da20093 (9 September 1997).

[31] Ministry of Justice (n 24) 36. See also Ministry of Justice, *Research on the Proposal of a New Private International Law* (February 2014) 184–85, available online: policy.nl.go.kr/upload/Atch/20140707b04.pdf.

[32] Amendment Proposal, Art 8(1).

[33] The Supreme Court has interpreted 'pleading' or 'making a statement' under Art 30 of the CPA, which corresponds to Art 9 of the Amendment, to mean that a defendant actually appears and argues on the merits of a case before the court. But a defendant's submission of a written response without making an appearance may not amount to a submission to jurisdiction by pleading: Supreme Court Order Ja80Ma403 (26 September 1980).

[34] Amendment Proposal, Art 10(2): 'Article 9 [Jurisdiction by Pleading] shall not apply to a lawsuit that exclusively falls within the international jurisdiction of a foreign court under the principle of international jurisdiction pursuant to the statutes or treaties of South Korea …'.

[35] Amendment Proposal, Art 8(5): 'In the case where a foreign court has been chosen as exclusive international jurisdiction by agreement, … a [Korean] court shall dismiss the lawsuit … unless jurisdiction by pleading invokes in accordance with Article 9'.

C. Reciprocity

Recognition of foreign judgments requires the existence of reciprocity between South Korea and the foreign country. Actual recognition of a South Korean judgment by the state of the rendering court is not required to show reciprocity.[36] Nor is it necessary to rely on a treaty between South Korea and the rendering state. It is sufficient to show that the foreign court is likely to recognise a similar judgment rendered by a South Korean court. Article 217(1)-4 of the CPA provides that a reciprocal guarantee shall be secured or that there should be no substantial difference between the two countries in recognising a foreign judgment. The 'no substantial difference' limb of Article 217(1)-4 was added by a 2014 amendment to the CPA as a result of a Supreme Court decision in 2004 which held that

> the requirements for mutual guarantee … shall be deemed fulfilled inasmuch as the respective requirements for recognition of like judgments in Korea and the other country are not disproportionately off balance, the foreign requirements are not unduly more burdensome overall than those in Korea, and the two sets of requirements are not substantially different in important points.[37]

A comparison of the recognition requirements in South Korea and another state will need to focus on the same kind of judgments. For example, recognition of a South Korean non-monetary judgment in a foreign country will not provide a ground for the recognition of a foreign money judgment in South Korea. Further, recognition of a money judgment will not always assure the reciprocal guarantee for all kinds of money judgments. Different types of money judgment may be subject to different statutory requirements for recognition. The recognition requirements for similar types of judgments will need to be reviewed carefully when determining whether they in fact evidence reciprocity.[38] Similarly, if a judgment involves decisions on two or more claims, it is necessary for the court to examine whether there is reciprocal guarantee for all the claims involved, especially if each claim requires a different set of requirements for recognition.[39]

South Korean courts have in the past recognised the existence of reciprocity with Argentina, China, England, Germany, Hong Kong, Japan, Ontario, Alberta, New York, Minnesota, New Jersey, Texas, California and Washington state. The refusal by a foreign court to recognise a South Korean judgment does not necessarily lead to a reactive refusal

[36] Supreme Court Decision 2002Da74213 (28 October 2004); Supreme Court Decision 2012Da23832 (30 May 2017).

[37] Supreme Court Decision 2002Da74213 (n 36). This is somewhat a relaxed interpretation of the reciprocal guarantee, compared to the 1971 Supreme Court decision which required the requirements for recognition of a foreign country to be equal to or less strict than those in Korea: Supreme Court Decision 71Da1393 (22 October 1971).

[38] For example, if a money judgment is subject to Uniform Foreign Money-Judgments Recognition Act (UFMJRA), the recognition requirements under the CPA should be compared with those under the UFMJRA. If the judgment was for child support payment, requirements for recognition of the like judgment should be the comparison target.

[39] Where the US judgment rendered by the court in the state of Oregon granted the applicant divorce together with a parental right and child custody, the Supreme Court recognised the judgment on the grounds that recognition requirements of the Oregon state do not demand more than those under the CPA and do not differ substantially in major points. This decision can be criticised for having considered only the requirements for recognition of divorce judgments under the Oregon state law – in other words, it failed to consider the recognition requirements under the Oregon state law for custody designation, which should have also been compared with the Korean requirements: Supreme Court Decision 2012Meu66 (15 February 2013).

by the South Korean court. It is uncertain whether South Korean courts will refuse Austrian judgments merely because Austria refused to recognise a South Korean judgment in the past. A comparison between the South Korean and Austrian requirements would indicate no substantial difference on major points. The current position in relation to Chinese judgments is likewise unclear. No mutual guarantee seems to exist between South Korea and China. In 2011 the Chinese court dismissed an application for the enforcement of a South Korean judgment[40] on the ground that there was no treaty or reciprocal relationship between the two States.[41] This was despite the fact that in 1999 a South Korean District Court had recognised the *res judicata* of a Chinese judgment[42] and, until recently, several South Korean courts made decisions based on a presumption that there was reciprocity between China and South Korea[43] despite China's dismissal of a South Korean judgment in 2011. In the case of French judgments, the requirements for recognition of foreign judgments are substantially different from South Korean ones in that France requires applicable law to be determined in accordance with French private international law rules. It is thus unlikely that the South Korean court will recognise French judgments. The Supreme Court once found against reciprocal treatment in relation to an Australian judgment.[44] However, since then, the Australian Foreign Judgments Regulations 1992[45] have been amended by Statutory Rules No 334 of 1999, and the Treaty on Judicial Assistance in Civil and Commercial Matters between Australia and the Republic of Korea was concluded in 1999. The courts of South Korea fall under the category of superior courts for the purpose of the reciprocal enforcement of judgments in Australia. This allows Australian courts to register and enforce judgments rendered by South Korean courts. It is thus also expected that South Korean courts will recognise and enforce Australian decisions.

In summary, South Korean courts have taken a relatively constructive attitude towards the recognition and enforcement of foreign judgments through the lenient interpretation of the conditions for reciprocal guarantee. Nevertheless, where there is no precedent, South Korean courts must individually examine and determine the existence of reciprocity between South Korea and the rendering jurisdiction through a comparison of respective requirements for recognition.

[40] Seoul District Court Western Branch Decision 2009Gahap6806 (14 December 2010).

[41] *Spring Comm v Piao Zonggen* Guangdong Shenzhen Intermediate People's Court Decision (2011) Shen Zhong Fa Min Yi Chu Zi No 45 (30 September 2011) (China).

[42] Despite that there was no precedent of Chinese courts recognising a Korean case at that time, the Korean court dismissed the counterclaim of the Korea Trade Insurance Corporation by recognising the *res judicata* of the Shandong Weifang Intermediate People's Court judgment in China: Seoul District Court Decision 99Gahap26523 (5 November 1999).

[43] For example, the Seoul Central District Court dismissed a counteraction on the ground that a final judgment was made in China: Seoul Central District Court Decision 2015Gahap534482 (9 June 2017). In another case, the Seoul High Court admitted the interest of an action since that Korean judgment can be recognised in China – the court considered that reciprocity exists between China and South Korea based on the similar requirements for recognition of foreign judgments in the two States: Seoul High Court Decision 2017Na2009518 (17 November 2017). This issue is not further disputed in the upper level: Supreme Court Decision 2017Da288757 (26 April 2018).

[44] Supreme Court Decision 85Daka1767 (28 April 1987). However, the decision has been criticised for having denied reciprocal guarantee for the entire nation of Australia while the foreign judgment was in fact only made by the state court of New South Wales.

[45] Statutory Rules No 321 of 1992, under the Foreign Judgments Act 1991.

D. Sound Morals and Social Order as Grounds for Refusal of Recognition

Article 217(1)-3 of the CPA prohibits the recognition of a foreign judgment where it would undermine sound morals or other social order of South Korea. This so-called public policy ground for refusal of recognition should be understood as having an aspect of internationality. It is consequently defined more narrowly than the same expression as used in the Civil Code. For example, it would not constitute a violation of the public policy ground merely because a rendering state applied some law other than South Korean law. It will be contrary to public policy in the narrow sense intended here, if the recognition of a foreign judgment would be against the fundamental principles underpinning Korean law and order or against core legal values that cannot be abandoned.

i. Lack of Due Process

South Korean courts must refuse recognition of a foreign judgment obtained without due process. The Supreme Court held in 2004 that the recognition and enforcement of a foreign judgment should not undermine the sound morals or other social order of South Korea not only in respect of the content of the foreign judgment, but also in respect of the procedure used to obtain such judgment.[46] This interpretation of the law was explicitly adopted in the 2014 amendment to the CPA. Thus, a foreign judgment will not be recognised if it violates South Korean standards of due process. For example, it would be contrary to procedural public policy if a foreign court failed to maintain its judicial independence or impartiality or failed to grant the defendant a reasonable opportunity to defend himself. A foreign judgment obtained by fraudulent means (such as the use of forged or discarded documents or perjury) might also be thought to undermine procedural public policy. However, the Supreme Court has held that such methods should not in principle be a cause for refusing recognition and enforcement. This is because examining whether a foreign judgment is right or wrong, under the pretext of finding whether fraud was used to obtain the judgment, would be contrary to the principle of non-review of the merits (*révision au fond*) in Article 27(1) of the CEA. It would also be contrary to the rationale of South Korean law providing for a system of execution judgments. Instead, the Supreme Court refused recognition in the case on two bases: (1) that the defendant had not been able to raise the question of fraud before the court of the originating jurisdiction; and (2) that there was overwhelming proof that the party seeking enforcement had been accused of forgery and found guilty by the criminal court.[47]

[46] Supreme Court Decision 2002Da74213 (n 36).

[47] Supreme Court Decision 2002Da74213 (n 36). The two bases are found in the CPA provisions regarding grounds for a retrial. Arts 451(1)(6) and 451(1)(7) provide that '[a] petition for a retrial against the final judgment which has become conclusive may be made when falling under any one of the following subparagraphs … 6. [w]hen a document or any other article used as evidence for the judgment has been forged or fraudulently altered; 7. [w]hen the false statements by … a sworn party or legal representative have been adopted as evidence for the judgment'. However, these grounds are applicable only when: a party was not aware of such a cause for retrial and failed to allege it by an appeal (Art 451(1)); and a conviction or a judgment to impose an administrative fine has become final and conclusive against the punishable acts (Art 451(2)).

ii. Violation of Substantive Public Policy

The recognition of a foreign judgment should not undermine public policy insofar as the contents of such judgment are concerned. South Korean courts have held that punitive, treble or excessive damages ordered by a foreign court are contrary to the sound morals or other social order of South Korea.[48] Damages in South Korea are meant to be compensatory. They are a means of recovering the actual loss suffered by a victim, restoring the latter's situation to what it was prior to the occurrence of the wrong. Damages are not intended to impose a punitive element. Thus, any portion of the damages ordered by the foreign court that is grossly beyond a reasonably compensatory sum will not be enforceable in accordance with the rule of proportionality and the principle of compensation in South Korea.[49] Moreover, Article 32(4) of the PILA does not allow compensation for tort-based damages to be recognised 'when the scope of such right is substantially beyond the necessary extent of appropriate compensation for the injured party'. Based on those grounds lower instance courts have only allowed enforcement of 50 per cent of the damages ordered by foreign courts[50] or disapproved interest for delayed payments as well as punitive damages in excess of an appropriate amount of compensation.[51] A 2014 amendment of the CPA stipulated that Korean courts should refuse a foreign judgment for damages that are markedly against the basic order of Korean law.[52] But the Supreme Court has clarified that the amended provision should not be deemed 'to limit the recognition of a foreign ruling even in cases of compensatory damages (not punitive damages) solely on the ground that amount of damages is excessive'.[53]

It is becoming more difficult to limit the recognition of foreign judgment on the ground of damages being excessive, considering legislative trends in Korea. For example, Article 35 of the 2011 Amendment to the Fair Transactions in Subcontracting Act introduced the concept of treble damages, allowing a principal contractor to be liable to compensate for injury to the extent of up to three times the actual amount of loss. Similarly, Article 13(2) of the 2014 Amendment to the Act on the Protection, etc of Fixed-term and Part-time Workers allows the Labor Relation Commission to order monetary compensation up to three times the amount of damages sustained by any fixed-term or part-time workers as a result of discriminatory treatment. These changes demonstrate that the concept of treble damages is not really against the basic order of South Korean law. Therefore, South Korean courts may not be able to refuse the whole or part of punitive or treble damages merely on the ground that such are against the public policy in Korea.

Another example that would be contrary to the substantive public policy of South Korea is when a foreign judgment conflicts with the *res judicata* established by a South Korean case on the same facts and parties. The Supreme Court has held that, where a divorce judgment had previously become final and conclusive in Korea, a foreign judgment in respect of

[48] CPA, Art 217(1)-3; PILA, Art 10.
[49] Seoul District Court Eastern Branch Decision 93Gahap19069 (10 February 1995).
[50] Ibid; Seoul District Court Southern Branch Decision 99Gahap14496 (20 October 2000).
[51] Suwon District Court Pyeongtaek Branch Decision 2007Gahap1076 (24 April 2009).
[52] CPA, Art 217 *bis* (1).
[53] Supreme Court Decision 2015Da1284 (15 October 2015); Supreme Court Decision 2015Da207747 (28 January 2016).

the same case between the same parties as the Korean judgment was null and void as being contrary to the sound morals or other social order of South Korea.[54]

iii. Violation of Mandatory Law

Violation of mandatory provisions of law can constitute a ground for a refusal of recognition. The violation of mandatory provisions will not always lead to a violation of public policy in South Korea. Whether the consequences of recognising or enforcing a foreign judgment would lead to undermining the public policy of South Korea will need to be verified by giving comprehensive consideration to various elements, such as the objective of a particular mandatory provision, the effect of violation of that provision, etc.[55] The Supreme Court refused to recognise two Japanese judgments related to forced mobilisation on the ground that they violated the constitutional values of South Korea.[56] In these cases, South Koreans sued Mitsubishi Heavy Industries Ltd and New Nippon Steel Corporation respectively for forced labour during the Japanese occupation period. The plaintiffs claimed damages and payment of accrued wages. The Supreme Court of Japan dismissed their claims on the basis of the Statute of Limitation and on the ground that the claims had expired under the Agreement between Japan and the Republic of Korea Concerning the Settlement of Problems in Regard to Property and Claims and Economic Cooperation in 1965. Since the Japanese judgment was premised on an understanding that Japan's colonial rule over Koreans and the Korean peninsula was lawful, it was in irreconcilable conflict with South Korean constitutional values, which regards the forced mobilisation of Koreans during the Japanese occupation and Japan's colonial rule as unlawful. The Supreme Court of South Korea held that the recognition of such judgments would be contrary to the sound morals and other social order of South Korea.

iv. Further Examples

Other cases where it was found that the concrete result of recognising a foreign judgment would be contrary to the sound morals and other social order of South Korea are as follows: the Supreme Court affirmed that recognition of the discharging effect of the US court's approval of a rehabilitation plan in US bankruptcy proceeding would be contrary to public policy, because it would unduly breach the right of a creditor who, relying on the territorial principle of the former Company Reorganisation Act, had not participated in the US rehabilitation procedure.[57] The Supreme Court refused recognition of a declaratory judgment of debt repayment rendered by the court of Buenos Aires, where the plaintiff had made repayment by taking advantage of the plummeting currency in Argentina, on the

[54] Supreme Court Decision 93Meu1051 (10 May 1994), 1068.

[55] For example, in the case where the Supreme Court of South Korea approved recognition and enforcement of the arbitral award given by the China International Economic and Trade Arbitration Commission (CIETAC), it was also held that recognition or enforcement of the arbitral award in question may be refused only when the specific outcomes in accepting such arbitral award would be contrary to the sound morals or other social order of the enforcing state: Supreme Court Decision 2000Da35795 (8 December 2000).

[56] Supreme Court Decision 2009Da22549 (24 May 2012); Supreme Court Decision 2009Da68620 (24 May 2012).

[57] Supreme Court Order Ja2009Ma1600 (25 March 2010).

ground that recognition of such judgment would infringe the defendant's property right and undermine the constitutional guarantee of the same.[58]

E. Timely and Legitimate Service of Process

South Korean law further requires timely and legitimate service of notice to allow a defendant fair trial and sufficient opportunity to defend. Article 217(1)-2 of the CPA requires the defendant to have been served with notice of the foreign proceedings by a lawful method in order to give the defendant sufficient time to defend. The Supreme Court denies legitimacy to documentary service that fails to conform to the methods and procedures of the originating State. For example, a judgment rendered by a court in Washington state was regarded as unlawful on the ground that the court had entered a default judgment without correcting a defect to the period for the defendant to respond. The court had issued a writ of summons allowing the defendant 20 days to respond, instead of the statutory period of 60 days.[59] The court should have given a correction order after the lapse of the 20-day response period. Otherwise, it had no jurisdiction to render a default judgment.[60] However, the Supreme Court held in 2016 that a defendant is deemed to have responded to the lawsuit as required under Article 217(1)-2 of the CPA if the defendant actually had the opportunity to defend his or her interests in the foreign court proceedings, regardless of whether the foreign judgment was in conformity with the method or procedure of service in the originating State. In this case, the requirement for lawful service of judicial documents was satisfied, because the defendant had been afforded the opportunity to defend his interests in the US court proceedings 'by being granted the right to retain/change attorneys and by making substantive/procedural claims and requests upon being served litigation-related documents'.[61]

If a defendant located in South Korea is served with judicial documents by a foreign court, the method and procedure of the service must comply with South Korean law. The 1965 Hague Service Abroad Convention applies among Member States as it entered into force in South Korea in August 2000. Since South Korea explicitly objected to the service of judicial documents directly through diplomatic or consular agents or by postal channels,[62] judicial documents may only be effectively served via the Central Authority under the 1965 Hague Service Abroad Convention, that is, the National Court Administration of South Korea (or diplomatic channels in exceptional circumstances).[63] The Seoul High Court has refused recognition of a foreign judgment where judicial documents were delivered to the defendant in South Korea by an international courier service, not through the Central Authority.[64]

[58] Supreme Court Decision 2009Da25944 (11 June 2009) affirmed, by discontinuance of trial, Seoul High Court Decision 2007Na122966 (6 March 2009).
[59] See the service provisions in the Revised Code of Washington, s 4.28.180; Superior Court Civil Rules, r 4.
[60] Supreme Court Decision 2008Da31089 (22 July 2010).
[61] Supreme Court Decision 2015Da207747 (n 53).
[62] 1965 Hague Service Abroad Convention, Arts 8 and 10.
[63] 1965 Hague Service Abroad Convention, Arts 5 and 9.
[64] Seoul High Court Decision 2013Na2012912 (12 March 2015).

F. Partial Recognition

South Korean courts can recognise part of a foreign judgment. As discussed above, a number of lower courts have approved part of punitive damages on the ground that damages in extraordinary excess over a compensatory amount is contrary to public policy. Also, Article 217 *bis* (1) of the CPA explicitly allows 'the whole or part of' a foreign judgment to be approved.

G. Recognition of a Foreign Judgment in a Domestic Action

A final and conclusive judgment rendered by a foreign court is automatically recognised. If the effect of a foreign judgment is at issue or constitutes a preliminary question that needs to be answered in domestic court proceedings, the South Korean court must *ex officio* investigate whether the foreign judgment meets the requirements for recognition.[65] It is also possible to file a separate lawsuit for interlocutory confirmation.[66] This is the case even if a foreign judgment is not bound up with another lawsuit – in this case, a party can file an independent lawsuit to have the foreign judgment confirmed and recognised as such in South Korea. The lawsuit for confirmation is distinguished from the one seeking an execution judgment as the former is not intended for the enforcement of the foreign judgment.[67]

There is no practice of a summary procedure for civil or commercial cases in South Korea. Formal trial proceedings are necessary even when a party seeks a confirmatory judgment for the foreign judgment – a court basically conducts a formal examination as to whether a foreign judgment complies with the requirements for recognition under CPA Article 217 without examining whether the judgment is right or wrong.[68] Since a lawsuit for confirmation is subject to the same requirements as recognition of a foreign judgment, failure to comply with the requirements for recognition in CPA Article 217(1) constitutes a cause for refusal of confirmation.

H. Interlocutory Judgments

A foreign judgment must be final and conclusive, or acknowledged to have the same force, for its recognition in South Korea. The courts will thus refuse interlocutory judgments or

[65] CPA, Art 217(2).

[66] CPA, Art 264(1) (Lawsuit for Interlocutory Confirmation).

[67] Not all judgments require an execution judgment. For example, a judgment dismissing a claim in the originating state does not need to be enforced. Only recognition of such judgment can be an issue – in Seoul District Court Decision 99Gahap26523 (n 42), the defendant argued that the plaintiff's claim should be dismissed, recognising the *res judicata* effect of the Chinese judgment. Divorce judgments also do not require execution judgments. In South Korea, a foreign divorce judgment requires an ex post facto procedure for correction of the family register. This may be distinguished from requiring an execution judgment, although in a broad sense correction of the family register falls within the scope of an execution judgment. In practice, a public official in charge of family relation register examines whether a foreign divorce judgment complies with the requirements for recognition in CPA and decides whether to accept the application for registration. If it is unclear, or if there is a doubt as to the effect of the foreign divorce judgment, the public official is required to make an inquiry and receive a reply from the supervision court in order to process the registration of such a judgment. See Supreme Court Established Rule for Family Relation Register No 173 (10 December 2007) and No 419 (8 January 2015).

[68] CEA, Art 27(1).

provisional measures, including orders for interim relief, provisional attachment or interim injunctions. For instance, interlocutory freezing orders (also known as *Mareva* injunctions in common law jurisdictions) against assets in South Korea will not be recognised and enforced, because these are provisional measures. In this regard, an interlocutory injunction having permanent effect in practical terms can be an exception. Although not formally a final judgment, such injunction may be recognised and enforced so long as it is final and conclusive or acknowledged to have similar force. The subject of recognition is a judgment on the merits of a case.

The recognition of a foreign judgment does not aim to approve the effect of a court ruling that has significance merely within litigation proceedings in the originating state. For example, a court's dismissal of a case due to the lack of some requirement for the bringing of litigation before the foreign court, a ruling on evidence, or a ruling for the preservation of evidence required by the foreign court would not be recognised as final and conclusive judgments. Similarly, anti-suit injunctions issued by an originating State's court to prohibit a party from proceeding with an action in South Korea will not be recognised. Even if a judgment is on the merits of a case, a foreign judgment pending an appeal to a higher instance court cannot be recognised. Should the provisional measure imposed by a foreign court turn out to be final and conclusive or acknowledged to have the same force, it must satisfy all the requirements for recognition under CPA Article 217(1) as is the case with foreign judgments generally.

V. Enforcement

A judgment of execution is necessary for the enforcement of foreign judgments in South Korea. According to the Supreme Court, an execution judgment signifies that a party's right as determined by a foreign judgment should be compulsorily realised in South Korea. The process of obtaining recognition and enforcement is thus ultimately one where the court in South Korea will 'examine the validity of the foreign judgment only and give effect to a foreign-country judgment by rendering the execution judgment to approve the enforcement'.[69] An execution judgment is granted for a final and conclusive judgment that satisfies the requirements for recognition under CPA Article 217(1). Failing to meet such requirements means that an execution judgment will not be issued.[70] In general, the District Court of the defendant's general forum has jurisdiction for a lawsuit seeking a judgment of execution.[71] If there is no general forum, the lawsuit can be brought before the court in the place where the objects of the claim or security for the claim are located or in the place where any seisable property of the defendant is situated.[72]

Once a judgment for execution is granted, the rules for compulsory execution apply in accordance with the CPA and the CEA. That is, compulsory execution of a foreign judgment requires an execution judgment to be exemplified with an execution clause therein that identifies the creditor and the person subject to execution.[73] Compulsory execution

[69] Supreme Court Decision 2009Da68910 (n 11).
[70] CEA, Art 27(2).
[71] CEA, Art 26(2).
[72] CPA, Art 11.
[73] CEA, Arts 28(1) and 39(1).

can be commenced only when the execution judgment has been served – or execution may take place at the same time as service.[74] Execution can be carried out against any seisable property of a debtor by means of compulsory auction or administration of immovables;[75] distraint;[76] garnishment of monetary claims, securities, and other defendant's claims against a third party,[77] etc. A creditor entitled to commence compulsory execution can preserve his or her right by requesting the competent court for specification of the debtor's property,[78] for entry in the defaulter's list,[79] and for an inquiry into the debtor's property.[80] Delay can occur in the two phases of an enforcement process, before and after an execution judgment has been granted. Issuance of an execution judgment takes longer if the court closely examines the requirements for recognition and enforcement. In practice, the majority of disputes concern arguments over the foreign court's international jurisdiction and compliance with the public policy of South Korea. The foreign judgment, once validated by an execution judgment, is treated as any other Korean judgment and readily enforceable. It will thus be subject to the same rule for enforcement as any other South Korean judgment. For example, execution of a foreign judgment must be suspended or restricted when the other party submits any of the documents stipulated by CEA Article 49.[81]

VI. Special Cases

A. Judgments Relating to Intellectual Property Rights (IPRs)

It is generally understood that the state of registration has exclusive international jurisdiction over the disputes regarding establishment of a patent right or a claim for validation, invalidation or revocation of a patent right. This is because a patent right is dependent upon the laws of the country where it has been registered (the territorial principle)[82] and a court cannot rule upon another country's acts to grant patent rights on the validity or invalidity of such act. In a lawsuit where such exclusive jurisdiction has been determined, jurisdiction by agreement is not applicable according to CPA Article 31.

The jurisdiction rule above changed with a 2011 Supreme Court decision. In the case where a dispute regarding a patent registered in Japan was brought before the South Korean court based on the parties' choice of court agreement,[83] the Supreme Court held that issues

[74] CEA, Art 39(1).
[75] CEA, Arts 78–171.
[76] CEA, Arts 188–222.
[77] CEA, Arts 223–51.
[78] CEA, Art 61(1).
[79] CEA, Art 70.
[80] CEA, Art 74.
[81] Art 49 of the CEA allows submission of certain documents such as an exemplification of a judgment revoking the judgment to be executed or ordering suspension of the same; a document attesting that a security has been furnished in order to avert the execution; and an exemplification of a compromise protocol stating that compulsory execution is not to be effected.
[82] As a result, the country of registration is most closely connected in deciding the establishment and validity of a patent right and, at the same time, is likely to be the most convenient in terms of processing a lawsuit relating to a patent right and issuing an effective judgment for enforcing the patent. See Seoul Central District Court Decision 2006Gahap89560 (23 August 2007).
[83] Supreme Court Decision 2009Da19093 (28 April 2011).

related to the interpretation or validity of a contract to transfer patent rights did not necessarily fall under the exclusive jurisdiction of the country of registration. The lawsuit sought performance of the contract for patent transfer. Thus, it was not material whether the patent right was valid or invalid in Japan and the parties' purely contractual dispute could not be subject to the exclusive jurisdiction of the Japanese court. The Supreme Court consequently enforced the parties' jurisdictional agreement. This may be distinguished from the position of the Japanese court. Later, the plaintiff filed a request for an execution judgment in Japan, but the South Korean judgment was refused enforcement. The Supreme Court of Japan affirmed the lower court decision that it was natural for the Japanese court to have exclusive jurisdiction over an action related to the registration of IPRs. Among other reasons, the exclusive jurisdiction of the Japanese court signalled that there was a public interest at stake. Thus, a lawsuit related to the registration of IPRs involved the registration and public notification of a legal relationship in Japan. Further, speedy and reasonable examination of an IPR was possible in courts of the country of registration and legal proceedings in Japan on an IPR were less complicated than recognition and enforcement of a foreign judgment relating to the IPR.[84]

South Korea has further liberalised the types of lawsuits involving cross-border IPR contracts that can be heard by the South Korean court in a new provision under the Amendment Proposal. As a result, it will be possible to bring a lawsuit related to IPR contracts before the court of South Korea as long as the IPR is protected, used, exercised or registered in South Korea.[85] This will broaden the scope of international jurisdiction to be enjoyed by foreign courts. Foreign judgments can satisfy the requirement of international jurisdiction over an action concerning IPR contracts so long as the IPR is protected, used, exercised or registered in that foreign country. A lawsuit may concern the infringement of an IPR. In this regard, the Amendment Proposal has three provisions on international jurisdiction in connection with IPRs: exclusive jurisdiction over an action related to the establishment of IPRs (Article 10(1)-4); special jurisdiction over an action related to IPR contracts (Article 39); and special jurisdiction over a lawsuit related to an IPR infringement (Article 40).[86]

B. Judgments Relating to Land

The current law does not provide whether an action related to immovables located in South Korea falls under the exclusive jurisdiction of the Korean court.[87] However, the Amendment Proposal has adopted exclusive jurisdiction. Article 10(1)-3 provides that the South Korean court has exclusive jurisdiction over an action concerning real rights to immovables in Korea or over an action concerning the right registered in a public record for use of immovables. Applying the same rule, the South Korean court cannot exercise

[84] Judgment of Nagoya District Court, Toyohashi Branch, Heisei 23(Wa) No 561 (29 November 2012).
[85] Amendment Proposal, Art 39.
[86] Amendment Proposal, Art 40(1) allows a lawsuit related to infringement of an IPR to be brought before the court of South Korea in or towards which the conduct occurred or in which the injury occurred.
[87] CPA, Art 20 only allows an action related to immovables to be brought to the court in the place where such immovables are located.

international jurisdiction if the immovable is located abroad. Accordingly, the South Korean court must refuse to recognise a foreign judgment in a dispute over real rights to an immovable located in a different country from that of the rendering court. This is distinguishable from a contractual claim relating to an immovable. For example, a claim for transfer of registration would not fall under the exclusive jurisdiction of the South Korean court, since it is a contractual claim based on a purchase contract for an immovable. Accordingly, the South Korean court should not jump to a conclusion and recognise the international jurisdiction of a rendering state's court over a dispute concerning the transfer of registration merely because the immovable to be transferred is located in the state of the rendering court.

C. Judgments Relating to Environmental Wrongs

For an action in tort, CPA Article 18 is taken into account in determining the question of international jurisdiction. Article 18 provides that an action related to tort can be brought before the court of the place of the tortious act (*lex loci delicti*). This is understood to encompass both the place where the event giving rise to the damage took place and the place where the damage occurred. Thus, it is possible for a court of the country where environmental damage occurred to have international jurisdiction over the tort-related action. In tort-related cases, determination of international jurisdiction is closely related to protection of a party's private interest as well as public interest of fairness, appropriateness, speed and economy in court proceedings.[88] Whether a foreign court in the place where the damage occurred has international jurisdiction, is determined based on the existence of a substantive connection between the court and the parties or the case in dispute. In a 1995 product liability case where a plaintiff sought recognition and enforcement of its successful judgment obtained in Florida, the Supreme Court refused to recognise the judgment due to the lack of substantive connection between Florida and the defendant. It was not reasonable for the defendant to anticipate facing a lawsuit in Florida.[89] Article 45 of the Amendment Proposal has adopted such requirement of reasonable anticipation for a tort action to be tried before a court sitting in the place where damage has occurred. Thus, a tort action can be brought before the court of South Korea if damage has occurred in South Korea *and* damage could reasonably have been anticipated to occur there. Accordingly, in order for a court sitting in the country of damage to have international jurisdiction over an environmental lawsuit, it must have been reasonably capable of anticipation that the environmental damage would have occurred in such a country. A foreign judgment failing to have substantive relation based on such reasonable anticipation will be refused.

D. Judgments Relating to Competition Law

South Korea's competition law is mainly to be found in the Monopoly Regulation and Fair Trade Act (FTA). It is substantially subject to administrative regulation. The Supreme Court

[88] Supreme Court Decision 2010Da18355 (n 23).
[89] Supreme Court Decision 93Da39607 (21 November 1995).

took the view that the FTA (prior to amendment in 2004) permitted for the extraterritorial application of its administrative regulations, thereby effectively protecting domestic competition and treating foreign enterprisers as included in the scope of business operators subject to South Korea's competition regime.[90] With the addition of Article 2-2 of the FTA, the extraterritorial ambit of the FTA became more apparent, as the Supreme Court noted in the same case. Article 2-2 provides that 'in cases where any act performed abroad affects the domestic market, this Act shall apply to such act'. For administrative lawsuits, the court of the country whose law is applicable has international jurisdiction in accordance with the principle of parallelism (*gleichlauf Grundsatz des internationalen Verwaltungsrechts*). This is appropriate in the area of public law, since no country will apply the public law of another country insofar as investigating and ordering corrective measures against an enterprise for causing harm within the country is concerned. The law applicable to an action claiming damages suffered in South Korea for breach of the FTA[91] would thus *ex hypothesi* be South Korean law. On that basis, the court of South Korea should have international jurisdiction based on the extraterritorial application of the FTA, even where the anti-competitive conduct took place abroad. Further, in an action seeking damages suffered in South Korea for breach of the FTA, it would seem that no other court but that of South Korea could have international jurisdiction over the action. Thus, the South Korean court may refuse to recognise a foreign judgment that purported to exercise international jurisdiction over such an action. On the other hand, it is arguable that a claim for damages suffered abroad as a result of the breach of the FTA would purely be an issue of civil liability. In that case, if international jurisdiction is determined pursuant to the jurisdiction rules of the CPA or PILA as with other tort-related actions, the court of the country where the damage was suffered by reason of the breach of the FTA may claim jurisdiction, so long as the defendant ought reasonably to have anticipated facing a lawsuit in that country. In such case, the South Korean court should be able to accept the international jurisdiction of the rendering court. The Amendment Proposal says nothing about the jurisdiction for actions in relation to the violation of competition law. This may be an indication that jurisdiction in competition law cases solely depended on the application of the FTA or that the jurisdiction rules for general torts are regarded as applicable to competition law issues.

VII. Conclusion: Facing the Future

A. Prospects

South Korea has not acceded to the 2005 Hague Convention on Choice of Court Agreements and there seems to be no discussion at governmental or legislative level for accession

[90] The Supreme Court relied on the fact that Art 2 of the former FTA ('Operator of Manufacturing Business, Service Business and Other Businesses') was not limited to domestic operators for committing unfair collaborative activities: Supreme Court Decision 2004Du11275 (24 March 2006).

[91] Before the 2004 amendment, a party was not allowed to claim damages in court before corrective measures under the FTA became final and conclusive. The priority of administrative relief was abolished with the 2004 amendment, allowing a claimant to rely on the court to determine a reasonable amount of damages where it is difficult to establish the facts necessary for the calculation of damages. See FTA, Arts 56(1) and 57.

in the near future. Discussion has focused on the need to prepare more specific statutory rules for international jurisdiction and such effort is reflected in the Amendment Proposal. The current PILA does not provide specific rules for choice of court agreements, though there is no question as to the validity of choice of court agreements for international jurisdiction. Still, statutory provisions can be made more certain and transparent by expressly stipulating for the effectiveness of choice of court agreements and listing the specific requirements for their validity. The most challenging issue is whether a substantive relation between the country or territory in which a court is located and the dispute in question should be required for cases involving exclusive choice of court agreements to the same extent as in cases where no such agreement has been made. The Amendment Committee decided not to include the requirement of a substantive link, reversing the 1997 Supreme Court's precedent,[92] so that the Amendment Proposal would be consistent with the 2005 Hague Convention.

South Korea has not so far expressed any intention to become a party to the forthcoming Hague Convention on the Recognition and Enforcement of Foreign Judgments in Civil and Commercial Matters presently being drafted as part of the Hague Conference's Judgments Project. The fact that not much research has been conducted into the matter may lead to a delay to South Korea signing the finalised convention in the near future. On the other hand, the recent effort to amend the statutory rules for international jurisdiction is expected to function as the groundwork to future accession to PIL conventions, including the forthcoming one on the recognition and enforcement of foreign judgments. An objective of the Amendment Proposal was to enhance consistency among the rules of international jurisdiction in South Korean law, international treaties, and the legislation of other countries. With regards to specific rules under the forthcoming Hague Convention, some provisions relating to the scope of international jurisdiction for consumer or employment contracts may be criticised for being over-protectionist in comparison to South Korean law, although the gap may be narrowed to a certain extent with the enactment of the Amendment Proposal.

B. Reform

Despite the dynamic changes of South Korean PIL legislation over the last several years, the current regime for the recognition and enforcement of foreign judgments still needs improvement in some respects.

For instance, one issue is the maintenance of a requirement of reciprocity. It was welcome that the 2014 amendment of the CPA extended reciprocity to the point where the foreign country's requirements for recognition are not far off balance, while having no substantial difference when compared to the requirements of the enforcing country (in this case, South Korea). However, reciprocity implies that a correspondent action is expected to be taken in response to one's favour or disfavour. Continued refusal by one country can create a

[92] Supreme Court Decision 96Da20093 (n 30).

situation where the other country refuses to recognise, possibly as a form of retaliation, even though enforcement of a judgment would otherwise be unobjectionable. Refusal on the basis of a lack of reciprocity means that private individuals may suffer from the conduct of the courts of a rendering state in cases over which they have not been a party and over which they have no control. Considering that the objective of recognition is to protect parties' private civil or commercial relations as determined by a foreign court, countries should strive to minimise the application of a reciprocity requirement, while at the same time cooperating internationally to conclude an international convention that will command a large number of accessions and thereby make reciprocity obsolete as a requirement for recognition. There have also been a number of difficulties with the requirement of international jurisdiction. International jurisdiction has relied on jurisdiction rules in the CPA as well as decisions of the Supreme Court. Two issues highlighted in this report have been: (1) the mechanical application of the general forum rule; and (2) the undermining of party autonomy by requiring a substantive connection between the state where a court is situated and the case in a dispute despite the designation of that court by agreement between the parties as the neutral forum in which to resolve their disputes. A bold attempt to address issues such as these has been made in the Amendment Proposal. It remains to be seen whether issues of international jurisdiction can be effectively addressed in the forthcoming future.

In general, it takes time and effort to conclude a successful convention with other states. Until a multilateral convention is successfully negotiated, and finalised and a large number of states accede to the same, entry into more bilateral agreements may be a good start, bilateral treaties being good evidence of reciprocity. An even speedier way of addressing reciprocity would be to enhance cooperation with judiciaries in other states, which is essential to minimise the impact of the reciprocal guarantee requirement for recognition. Memorandums of Understanding (MOUs) among judiciaries relating to the procedures for the mutual recognition and enforcement of judgments in their respective jurisdictions may be non-binding. But they would provide some evidence of reciprocity and thereby facilitate the process of recognition and enforcement.

Since the recognition and enforcement of foreign judgments involves transportation and other inconvenience as parties will need to attend court in an enforcing state, use of technology should be developed to improve the recognition and enforcement of judgments across borders. In order to achieve this, it should be legally permitted and effective to conduct court proceedings electronically in both the court of an originating state and that of an enforcing state. The court of execution judgment in an enforcing state should accept the electronic communication of documents in enforcement applications. South Korea was one of the first states to provide a legal basis for the use of electronic documents in civil litigations[93] and communications for a video trial. Oral statements and defences can be conducted via the computer system of the competent court.[94] However, the legislation does

[93] The Act on the Use, etc of Electronic Documents in Civil Litigation, etc requires registration as a user in order to access and use an electronic data processing system (Art 6(1)) and the users' consent to the use of such system for the conduct of civil litigation (Art 8). Its Rules on the Use, etc of Electronic Documents in Civil Litigation, etc of the same Act further provide specific procedures for registration and consent (rr 4 and 10).

[94] Rules on the Use, etc. of Electronic Documents in Civil Litigation, etc, rr 30(1) and 30(2).

not extend to the use of the system across borders.[95] There remains a pressing need for international cooperation on the development and use of technology for the recognition and enforcement of foreign judgments across borders. Once the new Hague Convention has been promulgated, such an initiative could usefully form part of the Hague Judgments Project and the Hague Conference's ongoing technical support for the new convention.

[95] Foreigners are not prevented from registering in the electronic data processing system in South Korea, but the registration requires a digital signature based on an accreditation certificate, which is difficult to obtain in practice without an address or a cell phone registered in Korea. Further, it remains uncertain if the court would recognise electronic documents issued by a foreign court unless the courts have agreed to mutually accept electronic documents of the judiciaries or share the same electronic data processing system. A separate legislation, the Act on Special Cases Concerning Remote Video Trials, provides for a remote video trial, but its use is confined to a limited range of domestic cases (Art 3).

7

Singapore

KENNY CHNG*

I. Introduction

The legal system of modern Singapore owes a significant part of its heritage to English law.[1] As a colony of the British Empire established by Sir Thomas Stamford Raffles, Singapore's laws and legal institutions were from their origins substantively shaped by their English equivalents. To the present day, a strong connection continues to exist between English and Singapore law[2] – English precedents are carefully considered by Singaporean judges, even though they are no longer binding in Singapore. Nevertheless, since independence, Singapore law has advanced in an incrementally autochthonous direction as lawyers, judges and academics have striven to develop a legal system adapted to Singapore's unique circumstances.[3] A significant development highlighting Singapore's push towards a distinctive legal system was the creation of the Singapore International Commercial Court (SICC), established in 2015 as a division of the Singapore High Court to hear cases of an international and commercial nature.[4]

Singapore's private international law reflects this trajectory of development. Historically, it was heavily influenced by English common law. Key common law doctrines that form the core of Singapore's private international law have their origins in English law.[5]

* The author is deeply grateful to Professor Anselmo Reyes, University of Hong Kong, and Associate Professor Yip Man, Singapore Management University, for their helpful suggestions and comments on this chapter. Any mistakes are entirely the author's own.

[1] Yihan Goh and Paul Tan, 'An Empirical Study on the Development of Singapore Law' in Yihan Goh and Paul Tan (eds), *Singapore Law: 50 Years In The Making* (Singapore, Academy Publishing, 2015) 4–5.

[2] Goh and Tan (n 1) 5.

[3] This holds true even where commercial law is concerned: see *Man Financial (S) Pte Ltd (formerly known as E D & F Man International (S) Pte Ltd) v Wong Bark Chuan David* [2008] 1 SLR 663 [133]; Chan Sek Keong, 'Keynote Address' (Singapore, New York State Bar Association Seasonal Meeting, 27 October 2009), available online: www.supremecourt.gov.sg/docs/default-source/default-document-library/media-room/cj-keynote-address-at-nysba-international-seasonal-meeting_27-oct-2009.pdf.

[4] 'Report of the Singapore International Commercial Court Committee' (29 November 2013), available online: www.mlaw.gov.sg/content/dam/minlaw/corp/News/Annex%20A%20-%20SICC%20Committee%20Report.pdf, paras 1, 5–6, the co-chairs being Ms Indranee Rajah SC and Mr V K Rajah SC. See also Kenny Chng, 'The Impact of the Singapore International Commercial Court and Hague Convention on Choice of Court Agreements on Singapore's Private International Law' (2018) 37(1) *Civil Justice Quarterly* 124.

[5] For example, the *forum non conveniens* doctrine in *Spiliada Maritime Corp v Cansulex Ltd* [1987] AC 460 is unquestionably part of Singapore's private international law: see *JIO Minerals FZC v Mineral Enterprises Ltd* [2011] 1 SLR 391.

Singapore's private international law statutes have also been shaped by English statutes[6] – the Reciprocal Enforcement of Commonwealth Judgments Act (RECJA)[7] and the Reciprocal Enforcement of Foreign Judgments Act (REFJA),[8] enacted in 1920 and 1959 respectively,[9] were both modelled after their equivalents in English law.[10] However, Singapore's private international law has since made strides towards legal autochthony. The most significant recent development in this regard is the Choice of Court Agreements Act (CCAA),[11] enacted in Singapore in 2016 to give effect to the 2005 Hague Convention on Choice of Court Agreements (Hague Convention),[12] which Singapore signed in 2015. In tandem with the SICC, the CCAA will be an important boost to Singapore's efforts to become a desirable litigation destination, as commercial parties will be much more inclined to select the SICC as a dispute resolution venue if the SICC's judgments are widely enforceable across jurisdictions around the world.[13] Moreover, on the common law front, the Singapore Court of Appeal has moved away from the position in English law regarding the effect of fraud on the recognition of foreign judgments.[14]

This chapter is intended to provide a survey of the Singapore regime on the recognition and enforcement of foreign civil and commercial judgments. As a broad overview, at present, there are four routes to the recognition or enforcement of a foreign judgment in Singapore: the common law, the RECJA, the REFJA and the CCAA. If the foreign judgment sought to be recognised or enforced belongs to a Contracting State to the Hague Convention, the CCAA applies to the exclusion of the RECJA and REFJA.[15] If not, and if the foreign judgment comes from one of the jurisdictions gazetted in the RECJA or REFJA, the judgment may be registered under these statutes.[16] If neither of the above situations apply, the common law regime can be used to recognise or enforce the foreign judgment. It is worth noting at this juncture that the ambit of the CCAA is drawn even more narrowly than the ordinary meaning of 'civil and commercial' would suggest – section 9 of the CCAA provides a list of matters to which the CCAA does not apply, including consumer agreements,[17] employment matters[18] and matters analogous to bankruptcy or insolvency, among others.[19] In the sections to follow, Singapore's statutory regime will be discussed first, followed by the common law regime.

[6] Adeline Chong, 'Country Report: Singapore' in Adeline Chong (ed), *Recognition and Enforcement of Foreign Judgments in Asia* (Singapore, Asian Business Law Institute, 2017) 163.

[7] Reciprocal Enforcement of Commonwealth Judgments Act (Cap 264, 1985 rev ed) (RECJA).

[8] Reciprocal Enforcement of Foreign Judgments Act (Cap 265, 2001 rev ed) (REFJA).

[9] Tiong Min Yeo, *Halsbury's Laws of Singapore* vol 6(2) Reissue (Singapore, LexisNexis, 2016) para 75.151.

[10] ibid.

[11] Choice of Court Agreements Act 2016 (Act 14 of 2016) (CCAA).

[12] Hague Convention on Choice of Court Agreements (30 June 2005).

[13] Chng (n 4) 126.

[14] *Hong Pian Tee v Les Placements Germain Gauthier Inc* [2002] 1 SLR(R) 515; Chong (n 6) 163.

[15] RECJA, s 2A, REFJA, s 2A. Even though the common law regime remains an open option for the judgment creditor, the CCAA is likely to be a much more advantageous regime for a judgment creditor.

[16] If REFJA applies in this situation, it must be used to the exclusion of the common law regime: REFJA, s 7(1).

[17] CCAA, s 9(1)(a).

[18] ibid, s 9(1)(b).

[19] ibid, s 9(2)(d).

II. Recognition and Enforcement of Judgments in Singapore under Treaties/Statutes

The statutory regime for the recognition and enforcement of foreign judgments in Singapore comprises three main statutes: the RECJA, the REFJA and the CCAA. This section will discuss the RECJA and REFJA together, as they bear many similarities to each other, followed by the CCAA. Nevertheless, the RECJA and REFJA are not identical, and their differences will be highlighted wherever relevant.

A. RECJA and REFJA

The RECJA is a reciprocal judgment recognition regime applying to judgments obtained from superior courts in the United Kingdom, as well as judgments from superior courts of gazetted Commonwealth jurisdictions. The gazetted jurisdictions are New Zealand, Sri Lanka, Malaysia, Windward Islands, Pakistan, Brunei Darussalam, Papua New Guinea, India (except the state of Jammu and Kashmir), the Commonwealth of Australia, the states of New South Wales, Queensland, South Australia, Tasmania, Victoria and Western Australia, the Australian Capital Territory, Norfolk Island and the Northern Territory.[20] The REFJA is a similar regime, with the Hong Kong Special Administrative Region of the People's Republic of China as the only gazetted jurisdiction. Courts of a foreign jurisdiction are gazetted if there is an assurance that judgments from the forum will be treated in a reciprocal manner in that jurisdiction.[21]

The general concept behind both the RECJA and REFJA is that judgments to which these statutes are applicable can be registered under the respective statutes. Once a foreign judgment has been successfully registered under the RECJA or REFJA, the foreign judgment becomes enforceable in Singapore as if it is a Singapore judgment.[22] An important advantage of registration over proceedings under the common law is that a party seeking to enforce a foreign judgment in Singapore does not need to commence fresh proceedings in Singapore to sue on the foreign judgment. In this vein, a point worth noting is that if a jurisdiction is gazetted under the REFJA, the REFJA becomes the exclusive means of recognition and enforcement of that jurisdiction's judgments in Singapore.[23] This, however, does not apply to the RECJA. Under the RECJA, even if a foreign judgment comes from a jurisdiction gazetted under the RECJA, enforcement under the common law remains an option. However, the RECJA itself seeks to discourage a judgment creditor from proceeding under the common law where the RECJA is applicable, by providing that a judgment creditor will be unable to recover for costs if he chooses to proceed under the common law in such circumstances.[24]

[20] Yeo (n 9) para 75.148.
[21] ibid, para 75.151.
[22] RECJA, ss 3(1), 3(3); REFJA, s 4(4); Yeo (n 9) para 75.151.
[23] REFJA, s 7(1).
[24] RECJA, s 3(5).

As a matter of procedure, under the RECJA and REFJA, a judgment creditor of a judgment from a foreign gazetted jurisdiction can apply to the Singapore High Court for registration of the judgment.[25] While the RECJA and REFJA apply only to judgments from superior courts in gazetted jurisdictions, scheduled courts are deemed to be superior courts.[26] The time limitations applicable to registration differ between the RECJA and REFJA. Under the RECJA, the application for registration of the judgment must be within 12 months from the date of the foreign judgment or 'such longer period as may be allowed by the Court'.[27] In contrast, under the REFJA, registration must be within six years from the foreign judgment being handed down.[28] Under both regimes, only money judgments issuing from foreign courts can be registered.[29]

The substantive requirements of registration under the RECJA and REFJA, as well as the defences to such registration, bear close similarities to those of the common law regime for the recognition or enforcement of foreign judgments.[30] As such, the substantive requirements of registration and the defences under the RECJA and REFJA will be elaborated in more detail in the section discussing the common law regime in Singapore. The pertinent differences between the common law regime and the RECJA/REFJA registration regimes will be pointed out in that part of the discussion.

B. The CCAA

The CCAA, as an enactment of the Hague Convention, mirrors the Hague Convention's substantive goal of doing for litigation what the 1958 New York Convention on the Recognition and Enforcement of Foreign Arbitral Awards[31] did for international arbitration. The CCAA enacts in Singapore a scheme for the mutual enforcement of choice of court agreements across the Hague Convention's signatories, ensuring the reciprocal recognition and enforcement of judgments handed down by the chosen courts. At the time of writing, the countries which have ratified the Hague Convention are the Member States of the European Union (including Denmark), Mexico, Montenegro and Singapore.[32] China, the Ukraine and the US have signed the Hague Convention.

[25] The procedural requirements for such registration are set out in Supreme Court of Judicature Act (Cap 322, s 80, 2014 rev ed) Rules of Court, Ord 67.

[26] Yeo (n 9) para 75.156. As noted by Yeo, there is no definition of 'superior courts' in the RECJA and REFJA. In the absence of authority on this issue, the author agrees with Yeo's suggested interpretation in this regard: 'Where the issue does arise, on general principles, a foreign court is likely to be considered an inferior court if it is subject to the supervisory powers of another court, or if its competence is limited geographically within the country itself or if its subject matter jurisdiction is limited to lesser matters within particular subject matters'.

[27] RECJA, s 3(1); *Westacre Investments Inc v The State-Owned Company Yugoimport SDPR (also known as Jugoimport-SDPR)* [2009] 2 SLR(R) 166.

[28] RECJA, s 4(1)(a).

[29] RECJA, s 2(1), REFJA, s 2(1).

[30] RECJA, s 3(2), REFJA, s 3(2), 5(1); Chong (n 6) 164.

[31] United Nations Convention on the Recognition and Enforcement of Foreign Arbitral Awards (New York, 10 June 1958).

[32] The European Union, with the exception of Denmark, originally ratified the Hague Convention. Later, Denmark ratified the Convention on its own. Accordingly, at this point, all the European Union states have ratified the Convention. With the impending exit of the United Kingdom from the European Union, questions may be raised about the United Kingdom's Hague Convention status. It is suggested that in all likelihood, the United Kingdom will ratify the Hague Convention independently after its exit from the European Union.

The CCAA applies to a foreign judgment if the foreign court which handed down the judgment was the designated court in an exclusive choice of court agreement concluded in a civil or commercial matter, and if the agreement was concluded after the Hague Convention entered into force in the Contracting State.[33] If the CCAA applies to a foreign judgment and its requirements are satisfied, the foreign judgment will be recognised or enforced 'in the same manner and to the same extent' as a Singapore judgment.[34] Decisions that count as 'judgments' for the purposes of recognition or enforcement under the CCAA include final decisions on the merits, consent orders, consent judgments or default judgments.[35] Interim measures of protection do not fall under the ambit of the CCAA.[36] Notably, a significant departure of the CCAA from the common law regime and the RECJA/REFJA registration regimes is that it allows the enforcement of non-monetary foreign judgments.[37] This is not possible under the common law or RECJA/REFJA regimes.

As with the RECJA/REFJA regimes, the concept of reciprocity underlies the CCAA regime – judgments from the originating foreign court are entitled to recognition and enforcement, provided that judgments of the enforcing state are entitled to the same treatment by the originating foreign court.[38] The CCAA regime takes the concept of reciprocity further than the RECJA/REFJA regimes; however, under the Hague Convention, jurisdictional rules governing when courts can hear cases are harmonised across Contracting States. Consequently, under the CCAA regime, the issue of international jurisdiction is not determined by Singapore private international law rules, in contrast to the RECJA/REFJA regimes.

In contrast to the RECJA/REFJA regimes, there is no time limit for the registration of foreign judgments. However, a foreign judgment can only be enforced under the CCAA if it still has effect and can be enforced in the state of origin[39] – a requirement that may serve as a time limit in practice. Severance of foreign judgments is recognised as a possibility under the CCAA regime – if only a part of a foreign judgment meets the requirements of the CCAA, the acceptable part of the judgment can be enforced if it is severable from the rest of the foreign judgment.[40]

Several defences to the recognition of foreign judgments exist under the CCAA. These defences fall into two categories – non-discretionary and discretionary bars to recognition. Under the first category, a foreign judgment *must* be refused recognition if there was a breach of natural justice in the foreign proceedings,[41] the foreign judgment was obtained by fraud in connection with a matter of procedure,[42] or if recognition or enforcement of the foreign judgment is manifestly incompatible with Singapore public policy.[43] Under the

[33] Chong (n 6) 176.
[34] CCAA, s 13(1).
[35] CCAA, s 2.
[36] CCAA, s 10.
[37] CCAA, s 2(1).
[38] CCAA, s 13.
[39] CCAA, s 13(2).
[40] CCAA, s 19.
[41] CCAA, s 14(a).
[42] CCAA, s 14(b).
[43] CCAA, s 14(c). It is worth noting that the public policy defence for the purposes of the CCAA might be shaped by an overarching public policy consideration to give effect to the Hague Convention framework. This will be illustrated at the end of this section.

second category, the Singapore court has the discretion to refuse recognition or enforcement under several circumstances;[44] for example, where the exclusive choice of court agreement is null and void under the law of the state of the chosen court,[45] or where the judgment is for exemplary or punitive damages.[46]

As the latest development in Singapore's regime for the recognition and enforcement of foreign judgments, how does the CCAA interact with the existing system of rules? Several points of interaction will be highlighted here. First, as a matter of applicability, where the CCAA is applicable, the RECJA and REFJA no longer apply.[47] With respect to the common law, although the common law regime remains applicable in the wake of the CCAA, it is difficult to imagine why a judgment creditor would prefer to seek recognition of his judgment under the common law regime whenever the CCAA is applicable.[48]

Second, at a substantive level, since the defences to recognition in the CCAA are somewhat analogous to those that already exist in the common law regime, it is an open question whether the Singapore courts will import the common law approaches in their interpretation of the CCAA's provisions. For example, will the Singapore common law distinction between extrinsic and intrinsic fraud[49] be applicable to the CCAA's fraud defence? It is suggested that in view of the theme of reciprocity underlying the CCAA, the interpretation of the CCAA's defences to recognition may not necessarily echo the positions taken by the Singapore common law authorities – the Explanatory Report[50] on the Hague Convention[51] and other similar documents are likely to be of significant influence, to ensure a commonality of approach across Hague Convention signatories.[52]

To illustrate the potential complexities that may arise, one can consider a foreign judgment obtained in breach of an anti-suit injunction as an example. While Singapore courts have found the enforcement of such judgments to be contrary to Singapore public policy at common law,[53] it is less certain whether such judgments would fall foul of the CCAA's public policy defence. On one hand, the CCAA does allow for the grant of anti-suit injunctions by the Singapore courts.[54] On the other hand, the Hague Convention allows a non-chosen court to assume jurisdiction in specific situations.[55] Thus, an anti-suit injunction granted against proceedings in a non-chosen court that the Hague Convention has allowed to assume jurisdiction over proceedings might actually be inconsistent with the framework of the Hague Convention. In such situations, enforcing a judgment obtained

[44] CCAA, s 15(1).
[45] CCAA, s 15(1)(a).
[46] CCAA, s 16.
[47] RECJA, s 2A, REFJA, s 2A.
[48] Chong (n 6) 176.
[49] *Hong Pian Tee* (n 14). See s III.D.ii below for reference.
[50] Trevor Hartley and Masato Dogauchi, 'Explanatory Report on the 2005 Hague Choice of Court Agreements Convention' (*Hague Conference on Private International Law*, 2013), available online: www.hcch.net/index_en.php?act=publications.details&pid=3959&dtid=3.
[51] See especially Hague Convention, Art 23.
[52] See *Shi Wen Yue v Shi Minjiu* [2016] SGHCR 8 as an indication of the approach the Singapore courts may take to the interpretation of the CCAA's provisions. Also, in *Ermgassen & Co Ltd v Sixcap Financials Pte Ltd* [2018] SGHCR 8, it is worth noting that the Assistant Registrar placed heavy emphasis on the Explanatory Report to interpret the substantive requirements on the CCAA.
[53] *WSG Nimbus Pte Ltd v Board of Control for Cricket in Sri Lanka* [2002] 1 SLR(R) 1088.
[54] CCAA, s 10(2).
[55] Hague Convention, Art 6.

in breach of the anti-suit injunction might actually be in accord with the purposes of the Hague Convention – and thus potentially not in contravention of public policy for the purposes of the CCAA. Indeed, in construing the public policy defence for the purposes of the CCAA, the Singapore courts might have regard to an overarching public policy consideration to give effect to the framework of the Hague Convention. Thus, the Singapore court, in determining the applicability of the public policy defence in the CCAA, might be compelled to have regard to the specific circumstances surrounding the proceedings in the non-chosen court to determine if the public policy against the enforcement of judgments obtained in breach of an anti-suit injunction indeed applies to the foreign judgment in question.[56]

III. Recognition and Enforcement of Judgments in Singapore under Common Law

Before proceeding with the discussion of the common law regime, two preliminary points will be made. First, the RECJA/REFJA regimes frequently draw upon common law developments in the interpretation of their statutory provisions. As such, the discussion in this section serves as a description of the substantive rules governing *both* the common law and RECJA/REFJA regimes. Any pertinent differences will be highlighted. Second, the discussion in this section will begin with the rules governing *in personam* civil and commercial judgments. The rules governing *in rem* judgments will be discussed at the end of this section.

A. The Conceptual Basis for Recognition or Enforcement of Foreign Judgments at Common Law

The statutory regimes, as described earlier, rest on the conceptual basis of reciprocity insofar as they apply only to jurisdictions which have promised reciprocal treatment of Singapore's judgments.[57] However, reciprocity in itself is not an independent ground of jurisdiction in any of the statutory regimes' rules. Reciprocity is not a ground of jurisdiction at common law either, and does not serve as the conceptual basis for the recognition or enforcement of foreign judgments at common law.[58] Instead, the conceptual basis of the common law regime in Singapore has been held to be the obligation theory.[59] Under this theory, at common law, foreign judgments do not have direct effect in Singapore law – rather 'any judgment enforced in Singapore (under the common law) is ultimately one given by the Singapore courts'.[60] The reason that a Singapore court will recognise a foreign judgment is the idea that 'where a judgment is issued by a court of competent jurisdiction over the

[56] See Chng (n 4) 133–35 for a fuller discussion of related issues.
[57] Yeo (n 9) para 75.194.
[58] ibid.
[59] *Giant Light Metal Technology (Kunshan) Co Ltd v Aksa Far East Pte Ltd* [2014] 2 SLR 545.
[60] ibid, [60].

parties, that judgment creates an obligation on the parties to abide by it which the courts of other countries ought to recognise and enforce'.[61] Thus, the Singapore court, in recognising or enforcing the foreign judgment, is simply 'holding the parties to their obligation to abide by the foreign judgment'.[62] While the conceptual coherence of the obligation theory may be open to question,[63] it is undeniable that as a matter of precedent, it is the obligation theory that forms the conceptual basis for the recognition or enforcement of foreign judgments in Singapore.

B. The Effect of a Foreign Judgment in Singapore – Recognition versus Enforcement

At common law, a foreign judgment can have different effects in Singapore. First, the doctrine of *res judicata* applies to foreign judgments entitled to recognition.[64] The foreign judgment can be *recognised* for the purposes of raising an issue estoppel with respect to an issue that was decided by the foreign court,[65] or for raising a cause of action estoppel with respect to the plaintiff's claim in the foreign court.[66] For a foreign judgment to be raised for the purposes of issue estoppel, aside from the standard requirements for recognition of foreign judgments that will be discussed later, two more requirements must be met: there must be both identity of parties and identity of subject matter.[67] The foreign judgment can also be recognised for the purpose of the extended *res judicata* doctrine articulated in *Henderson v Henderson*[68] – that is, beyond the scope of the estoppel doctrines, the Singapore court may take it as an abuse of process to commence proceedings or re-argue an issue that has already been decided by a foreign court.[69] This doctrine has its conceptual basis in the public policy of promoting finality of litigation.[70]

Once a foreign judgment has been recognised, subject to the applicability of the defences to recognition, it is taken to be conclusive on the merits.[71] This is a point of some strategic significance. The doctrine of merger, which provides that a cause of action merges into the order handed down by the court which hears the case and thereby loses independent existence, does *not* apply to foreign judgments both at common law and in the RECJA/REFJA regime.[72] Thus, a judgment creditor has the option of ignoring the foreign judgment and

[61] ibid, [61].

[62] ibid.

[63] See Kenny Chng, 'A Theoretical Perspective of the Public Policy Doctrine in the Conflict of Laws' (2018) 14(1) *Journal of Private International Law* 130, 147–48.

[64] *Manharlal Trikamdas Mody v Sumikin Bussan International (HK) Ltd* [2014] 3 SLR 1161 [135]; *Humpuss Sea Transport Pte Ltd (in compulsory liquidation) v PT Humpuss Intermoda Transportasi TBK* [2016] 5 SLR 1322 [65].

[65] *Manharlal Trikamdas Mody* (n 64) [135], *Murakami Takako (exrx of the estate of Takashi Murakami Suroso, decd) v Wiryadi Louise Maria* [2007] 4 SLR(R) 565 [51].

[66] Yeo (n 9) para 75.199.

[67] *The Vasiliy Golovnin* [2007] 4 SLR(R) 277 [38]; *The Bunga Melati 5* [2012] 4 SLR 546 (CA) [80]; *Manharlal Trikamdas Mody* (n 64) [136].

[68] *Henderson v Henderson* (1843) 3 Hare 100. See also *Humpuss Sea Transport* (n 64) [65].

[69] *Ching Mun Fong (exrx of the estate of Tan Geok Tee, decd) v Liu Cho Chit* [2000] 1 SLR(R) 53; *Kwa Ban Cheong v Kuah Boon Sek* [2003] 3 SLR(R) 644.

[70] *Johnson v Gore Wood & Co* [2002] 2 AC 1, 30–31.

[71] *Godard v Gray* (1870) LR 6 QB 139; *Hong Pian Tee* (n 14) [12].

[72] Yeo (n 9) para 75.205. The doctrine of merger also does not apply to the CCAA.

suing afresh in Singapore on his original cause of action, provided that the foreign judgment has not been completely satisfied.[73] If he does so, however, the judgment debtor may seek to have the foreign judgment recognised in Singapore to raise an estoppel against the judgment creditor's fresh claim in Singapore. The judgment debtor may also seek to argue that the judgment creditor's fresh suit amounts to an abuse of process as a re-litigation of a claim that has already been settled in a foreign court, especially if the foreign judgment readily meets the standards of enforcement in Singapore.[74]

Second, foreign judgments can be *enforced* in Singapore. Should a foreign judgment be recognised at common law, beyond its *res judicata* effect, it can also create 'a fresh obligation to pay the judgment debt'[75] which the judgment debtor must obey as a matter of Singapore law.[76] As a matter of procedure, in order to enforce a foreign judgment in this manner, the plaintiff will sue in a fresh action for a debt, often invoking the summary judgment procedure.[77] This action must be commenced within six years of the foreign judgment being handed down.[78] Should this fresh action for a debt be successful, there are several modes of execution available to the judgment creditor. The judgment creditor may apply to the Singapore court to garnish debts owed by garnishees to the judgment debtor.[79] The judgment creditor may also apply to the court for a Writ of Seizure and Sale to seize the property of the judgment debtor to satisfy the judgment debt.[80] Another means of satisfying the judgment debt would be to appoint a receiver by way of equitable execution, acquiring income from the judgment debtor's assets to satisfy the judgment debt.[81] These modes of execution can be performed concurrently. To determine the full extent of the judgment debtor's assets available for enforcement against, the judgment creditor may apply for an order for examination of the judgment debtor.[82]

C. The Substantive Requirements for Recognition and Enforcement

The substantive requirements for a foreign judgment to be *recognised* at common law are as follows: the foreign judgment must be a final and conclusive one, from a court which had international jurisdiction as determined by Singapore's private international law rules, and no defences to recognition must be applicable.[83] For a foreign judgment to be *enforced*,

[73] Yeo (n 9) paras 75.206–75.207.

[74] Yeo (n 9) para 75.208.

[75] *Alberto Justo Rodriguez Licea v Curacao Drydock Co Inc* [2015] 4 SLR 172 [21].

[76] *Poh Soon Kiat v Desert Palace Inc (trading as Caesars Palace)* [2010] 1 SLR 1129 [42].

[77] *Hong Pian Tee* (n 14) [12], *Giant Light Metal Technology* (n 59) [62].

[78] *Poh Soon Kiat* (n 76) [49], [54]; Yeo (n 9) para 75.234.

[79] The procedural requirements for garnishee proceedings are set out in Supreme Court of Judicature Act (Cap 322, S 80, 2014 rev ed) Rules of Court, Ord 49.

[80] The procedural requirements for Writs of Seizure and Sale are set out in Supreme Court of Judicature Act (Cap 322, S 80, 2014 rev ed) Rules of Court, Ord 47.

[81] The procedural requirements for equitable execution are set out in Supreme Court of Judicature Act (Cap 322, S 80, 2014 rev ed) Rules of Court, Ord 51.

[82] The procedural requirements for examination of judgment debtors are set out in Supreme Court of Judicature Act (Cap 322, S 80, 2014 rev ed) Rules of Court, Ord 48.

[83] *Poh Soon Kiat* (n 76) [14]; *Giant Light Metal Technology* (n 59) [13], [17]; *Alberto Justo Rodriguez Licea* (n 75) [22]; *Humpuss Sea Transport* (n 64) [67]; Chong (n 6) 166.

in addition to these requirements, the foreign judgment must be for a fixed or ascertainable sum of money. These requirements will be discussed in turn.

i. *Final and Conclusive*

The foreign judgment must be a final and conclusive one.[84] The Singapore Court of Appeal has described the question of finality as having two aspects.[85] First, a foreign judgment that 'cannot be varied, reopened, or set aside by the court that delivered it' is a final and conclusive one.[86] At common law, a foreign judgment that is subject to appeal or stay of execution remains a final and conclusive one.[87] Notably, however, under the RECJA, a foreign judgment cannot be registered if an appeal is pending, or if the judgment creditor is entitled to and intends to appeal.[88] Similar circumstances entitle a defendant to set aside the registration under the REFJA.[89] Default judgments can qualify as final and conclusive judgments – 'as long as the judgment is intended to be final, it remains final until a defendant takes steps to set it aside'.[90] Interlocutory judgments which provide final judgments on the rights of parties on specific issues can be final and conclusive as well.[91]

Second, finality must be assessed by 'asking whether the foreign court rendering the judgment would itself regard it as final and conclusive'.[92] This is premised on the idea that it would be absurd to regard as conclusive a judgment which the foreign court would itself not regard as conclusive.[93] Thus, in determining the question of finality, the Singapore court will be concerned about the status of the foreign judgment from the perspective of the jurisdiction which issued it.[94]

ii. *International Jurisdiction*

The foreign court issuing the judgment sought to be recognised must have had international jurisdiction. This is a question that is determined by Singapore's private international law rules.[95] This may be said to be a doctrinal expression of the obligation theory – it should be up to the forum in which recognition is sought to determine the circumstances under which it will recognise an obligation of the judgment creditor to obey the foreign judgment.[96]

[84] *Hong Pian Tee* (n 14) [12]; *Eleven Gesellschaft Zur Entwicklung Und Vermarktung Von Netzwerktechonologien MBH v Boxsentry Pte Ltd* [2014] SGHC 210 [89].
[85] *Humpuss Sea Transport* (n 64) [69].
[86] *Murakami Takako* (n 65) [51]; *The Bunga Melati 5* (n 67) [81]; *Manharlal Trikamdas Mody* (n 64) [140]–[142]; *Humpuss Sea Transport* (n 64) [69]; Chong (n 6) 167–68.
[87] *Goh Nellie v Goh Lian Teck* [2007] 1 SLR(R) 453 [28]; *Manharlal Trikamdas Mody* (n 64) [140]–[144]; *Humpuss Sea Transport* (n 64) [69].
[88] RECJA, s 3(2)(e).
[89] REFJA, s 6(1).
[90] *Humpuss Sea Transport* (n 64) [77], Yeo (n 9) para 75.158.
[91] *The Bunga Melati 5* [2011] 4 SLR 1017 (HC). The judgment was overruled in *The Bunga Melati 5* (n 67), but on other grounds. See also Yeo (n 9) paras 75.159, 75.163.
[92] *Humpuss Sea Transport* (n 64) [70].
[93] *Carl Zeiss Stiftung v Rayner & Keeler Ltd* [1967] 1 AC 853, 919; *Humpuss Sea Transport* (n 64) [70].
[94] *The Bunga Melati 5* (n 67) [86].
[95] *Giant Light Metal Technology* (n 59) [20].
[96] ibid.

Accordingly, under Singapore's private international law rules, whether the foreign court had international jurisdiction depends on the concepts of presence or residence in the jurisdiction, and submission to the jurisdiction.

Considering first the concept of presence/residence, the relevant time to determine presence is the date of commencement of foreign proceedings.[97] This is also the position under both the RECJA and REFJA.[98] With respect to persons, at common law, presence in the foreign jurisdiction is sufficient for the foreign court to have international jurisdiction over the judgment debtor.[99] Under the RECJA and REFJA, however, mere presence is insufficient. Residence is required.[100] With respect to corporations, at common law, a corporation's presence/residence for the purposes of international jurisdiction depends on whether the corporation can be said to have 'established and maintained at its own expense a fixed place of business' in the relevant jurisdiction, or if 'a representative has for more than a minimal period of time been carrying on' business in the jurisdiction.[101] The RECJA's requirements for corporations are similar to the common law position.[102] Under the REFJA, a corporation must either have its principal place of business in the foreign country,[103] or have an office or place of business in the foreign country with proceedings in the foreign jurisdictions being in respect of a transaction effected through or at that office or place.[104]

Submission can occur in two principal ways. First, submission can occur by agreement, generally through a choice of court agreement. There is some Singapore authority to the effect that such agreements must be express – they will not be implied by the courts.[105] However, the UK Privy Council has held that this principle is not a bar on implied agreements to submit – the true principle is rather that there must be *actual* agreement, which may be express or implied.[106] While this principle has yet to be considered by the Singapore courts, it is suggested that such an approach would cohere with the common law approach to contractual terms generally. The validity of such agreements is governed by the proper law of the agreement, as directed by Singapore's private international law rules.[107] The REFJA imposes an additional requirement on submission by agreement that does not exist at common law – the agreement must be made before the commencement of foreign proceedings.[108] One should be careful to note that under the CCAA, a choice of the Singapore High Court is taken to include the SICC unless there is an express intention to the contrary,[109] and that such a choice is taken to be an agreement to submit to the jurisdiction of the Singapore High Court (including the SICC).[110]

[97] Yeo (n 9) para 75.174.
[98] Yeo (n 9) para 75.174.
[99] *Adams v Cape Industries plc* [1990] Ch 433; *United Malayan Banking Corp Bhd v Khoo Boo Hor* [1995] 3 SLR(R) 839 [9].
[100] RECJA, s 3(2)(b); REFJA, s 5(2)(a)(iv); Yeo (n 9) para 75.171.
[101] *Adams v Cape Industries* (n 99) 530; *William Jacks & Co (Singapore) Pte Ltd v Nelson Honey & Marketing (NZ) Ltd* [2015] SGHCR 21 [30].
[102] RECJA, ss 3(2)(b), 3(2)(c).
[103] REFJA, s 5(2)(a)(iv).
[104] REFJA, s 5(2)(a)(v).
[105] *Sun-Line (Management) Ltd v Canpotex Shipping Services Ltd* [1985–1986] SLR(R) 695 [23]; *United Overseas Bank Ltd v Tjong Tjui Njuk* [1987] SLR(R) 275 [17].
[106] *Vizcaya Partners Ltd v Picard* [2016] 3 All ER 181 [56]–[61].
[107] Yeo (n 9) para 75.187.
[108] REFJA, s 5(2)(a)(iii).
[109] CCAA, s 2(2).
[110] Supreme Court of Judicature Act (Cap 322, 2007 rev ed), s 18F.

Second, submission can occur by the conduct of the relevant party in the foreign jurisdiction. The Singapore courts will take a nuanced approach to determining whether there was submission for the purposes of international jurisdiction.[111] Whether there was submission depends on what the relevant party did or did not do in the relevant jurisdiction.[112] The overarching inquiry is whether the party, by his actions or omissions, has necessarily waived any objections to the foreign court's jurisdiction with respect to the relevant dispute.[113] The Singapore court will take into account the perspective of the foreign jurisdiction in considering the significance to be accorded to the steps taken by the judgment debtor in the foreign jurisdiction,[114] although the question is ultimately to be determined by Singapore's private international law rules.[115] Filing a counter-claim, defence or a claim for set-off are generally taken as evidence of submission to the foreign court's jurisdiction.[116]

A challenge to the *existence* of the foreign court's jurisdiction, for example, an argument that the writ had been improperly served, without more, does not equate to submission – indeed, it would frustrate the reasonable expectations of commercial parties to hold that such a challenge amounted to a submission to the foreign court's jurisdiction.[117] This is also the position under the REFJA.[118] While the RECJA is silent on this issue, the common law position is likely to be persuasive in interpreting the RECJA's requirements.[119] A more vexed question is whether a challenge to the *exercise* of jurisdiction by the foreign court – for example, an application for a stay of proceedings on *forum non conveniens* grounds – will be taken as submission. The traditional English common law position on this question – that an application to a foreign jurisdiction challenging the exercise of jurisdiction amounts to an implicit acknowledgement of the existence of its jurisdiction, and thus amounts to submission – was heavily criticised and statutorily overruled in the UK.[120] In Singapore, however, the courts have left open the question of whether the traditional English common law approach is good law in Singapore. Nevertheless, the criticisms directed against this approach by the Singapore Court of Appeal in *WSG Nimbus Pte Ltd v Board of Control for Cricket in Sri Lanka*,[121] as well as the Singapore courts' emphasis on giving effect to the reasonable expectations of commercial parties, point towards the Singapore courts being receptive to an argument that a challenge to the exercise of jurisdiction does *not* amount to submission for the purposes of international jurisdiction.[122]

iii. Fixed or Ascertainable Sum of Money

Where the foreign judgment is sought to be *enforced* in Singapore, it must be for a fixed or ascertainable sum of money. This is not a relevant requirement where the plaintiff is merely

[111] *Giant Light Metal Technology* (n 59) [26]–[27].
[112] Yeo (n 9) para 75.176.
[113] *WSG Nimbus* (n 53) [54]; Yeo (n 9) para 75.176.
[114] *Giant Light Metal Technology* (n 59) [26].
[115] Yeo (n 9) para 75.177.
[116] *WSG Nimbus* (n 53); *Giant Light Metal Technology* (n 59).
[117] *WSG Nimbus* (n 53).
[118] REFJA, s 5(2)(a)(i).
[119] Yeo (n 9) para 75.180.
[120] *Henry v Geoprosco International Ltd* [1976] QB 726. See also Yeo (n 9) para 75.181.
[121] *WSG Nimbus* (n 53).
[122] Yeo (n 9) para 75.181.

seeking recognition of the judgment in Singapore.[123] As such, foreign judgments ordering non-monetary relief such as injunctions or specific performance cannot be *enforced*, although they may still be recognised for the purposes of *res judicata* or issue estoppel.[124] As long as there is a monetary component to the foreign judgment, it can be enforced – it is immaterial that the foreign judgment contains other non-monetary relief.[125]

Interest accruing on the foreign judgment from the time of the judgment to the time the judgment becomes enforceable, as determined by the law of the jurisdiction from which the judgment originated, will be enforceable in Singapore.[126] This is the position under the RECJA/REFJA registration regimes as well.[127]

D. Defences to Recognition or Enforcement

The final requirement for successful recognition or enforcement of a foreign judgment in Singapore is that no defences can be raised against such recognition or enforcement. The defences that exist at common law are as follows: enforcement of the foreign judgment would amount to enforcement of a foreign penal, revenue or other public law; the foreign judgment was obtained by fraud; recognition or enforcement of the foreign judgment would be contrary to Singapore's public policy; the foreign judgment was obtained in breach of natural justice; the foreign judgment conflicts with an earlier Singapore or foreign judgment entitled to recognition in Singapore; or the foreign judgment has been completely satisfied. These defences will be discussed in turn, followed by a discussion of the defences specific to the RECJA/REFJA registration regimes.

As a preliminary point, it should be noted that even if a defence applies to the foreign judgment in question, there exists the possibility of severing the objectionable parts of the judgment such that the rest of it can be validly enforced in Singapore if 'the unobjectionable part could be clearly identified and separated from the objectionable part'.[128] For example, a foreign judgment providing for both punitive and compensatory damages can still be enforced in Singapore if the punitive component can be clearly severed from the rest of the judgment.[129] The same position applies under both the RECJA[130] and the REFJA.[131]

i. No Enforcement of Foreign Penal, Revenue or Other Public Law

If enforcement of the foreign judgment in Singapore amounts to an enforcement of a foreign penal, revenue or other public law, whether directly or indirectly, the foreign

[123] *Humpuss Sea Transport* (n 64) [67].
[124] RECJA, s 2(1); REFJA, ss 2(1), 3(2)(b); Yeo (n 9) para 75.169; Chong (n 6) 167.
[125] *Giant Light Metal Technology* (n 59) [72]–[78]. Note that the Singapore courts have taken the position that it is unnecessary to refer to the doctrine of severance in such a situation – the doctrine of severance is better applied to a foreign judgment which is partly objectionable under the terms of one of the defences to recognition/enforcement.
[126] Yeo (n 9) para 75.166.
[127] RECJA, s 3(3)(a); REFJA, ss 4(4)(a), 4(4)(c).
[128] *Alberto Justo Rodriguez Licea* (n 75) [28]; Yeo (n 9) para 75.158.
[129] *Alberto Justo Rodriguez Licea* (n 75) [28].
[130] *Yong Tet Miaw v MBF Finance Bhd* [1992] 2 SLR(R) 549.
[131] REFJA, s 4(7).

judgment will not be enforceable in Singapore.[132] This defence is based on the principle that the common law will not allow its procedure to be used for the purposes of foreign sovereign authorities.[133] Thus, the court's inquiry will be principally directed at determining the extent to which the claim of enforcement is an act of sovereign character or authority. In determining whether enforcement does indeed have such effect, the Singapore court will consider whether the proceedings leading to the foreign judgment were 'in the nature of a suit in favour of the State for the recovery of penalties'.[134] Whether the penal law in question is part of the foreign country's criminal code is not conclusive – the characterisation of a law as penal or not is a matter of Singapore law.[135] A foreign judgment made pursuant to a foreign law that forfeited property of public officials in favour of the State through proceedings instituted by the State has been held to be unenforceable in Singapore, as enforcement would amount to 'an execution and indirect enforcement of a foreign penal law'.[136] While the Singapore court's considerations in this regard have been directed at the issue of foreign penal laws, the same underlying inquiry is likely to be applicable to the issue of foreign revenue or other public laws, ie what is the extent to which the claim of enforcement is an act of sovereign character or authority?

Where the plaintiff has applied for the *recognition* of such a law in Singapore, the relevant question is whether recognition of the foreign law necessarily involves the execution of the foreign penal law.[137] A form of this defence exists expressly in the REFJA.[138] While it is not stated expressly in the RECJA, the substance of this defence will probably fit readily under the public policy defence in the RECJA.[139]

ii. Foreign Judgment Obtained by Fraud

A foreign judgment will not be recognised or enforced in Singapore if it was obtained by fraud. At common law, for the purposes of this defence, a distinction has been drawn in Singapore law between extrinsic and intrinsic fraud. If the fraud in question is extrinsic fraud – fraud that was external to the merits of the case – then fraud can be raised as a defence even if there is no new evidence of fraud and if the foreign court had already considered and dismissed it as an issue.[140] If the fraud in question is intrinsic – fraud going to the merits of the case – then any allegation of fraud must be supported by fresh evidence that was not reasonably attainable at the time of the foreign proceedings, and which would have made a difference in the judgment.[141] This represents a departure in Singapore law from the English position, which does not draw a distinction between extrinsic and intrinsic fraud, allowing fraud to be raised as a defence in both situations even in the absence of

[132] *The Republic of the Philippines v Maler Foundation and other appeals* [2014] 1 SLR 1389; *Alberto Justo Rodriguez Licea* (n 75).

[133] Yeo (n 9) para 75.231.

[134] *Maler Foundation* (n 132) [68].

[135] ibid.

[136] ibid, [69]–[70].

[137] ibid, [68].

[138] REFJA, s 3(2)(b).

[139] RECJA, s 3(2)(f).

[140] *Hong Pian Tee* (n 14) [27]; *Eleven v Boxsentry* (n 84) [89]; Yeo (n 9) paras 75.227–75.228.

[141] ibid.

fresh evidence.[142] This departure was justified on the basis of the principles of finality and international comity.[143] The distinction between extrinsic and intrinsic fraud is a subtle one – the Singapore court has characterised the distinction as depending on whether the fraud occurred within or outside the trial.[144] For example, bribery of a solicitor, counsel or witness would amount to extrinsic fraud, while perjury would be a matter of intrinsic fraud.[145]

Fraud also exists as a defence under the RECJA and REFJA registration regimes.[146] It remains open to question, however, whether the Singapore courts' position on fraud at common law applies to these registration regimes, especially in view of the fact that the English courts have interpreted equivalent provisions in English law as being governed by the traditional English common law position.[147] It has been argued that the Singapore courts should adopt the common law position in interpreting the fraud defence in these registration regimes,[148] and it is suggested that consistency and coherence of doctrine lean in favour of the Singapore courts doing so.[149]

iii. Recognition or Enforcement is Contrary to Singapore Public Policy

A foreign judgment will not be recognised or enforced in Singapore if such recognition or enforcement is contrary to the public policy of Singapore. The public policy doctrine has been described as the only avenue through which the *substance* of the foreign judgment or law can be questioned.[150] In view of the inherent ambiguity in the public policy doctrine, common law courts have approached the doctrine with great caution. As a manifestation of this caution, courts have required a very high threshold to be met before allowing the invocation of the public policy doctrine.

To that end, Singapore judges have drawn distinctions between *types* of public policy. One such distinction is that between domestic public policy and 'international' public policy – domestic public policy expresses the public policy of the forum, while 'international' public policy refers to the 'higher standard of public policy in operation when a forum court is faced with a foreign judgment'.[151] Only foreign judgments or laws which are contrary to 'international' public policy will be denied recognition in the forum. Putting aside the potentially confusing terminology, this simply means that a higher threshold must be met for a foreign judgment to fall foul of the public policy defence, as compared to the standard that would ordinarily apply to a domestic action – for example, enforcement

[142] *Hong Pian Tee* (n 14) [27]; Yeo (n 9) para 75.230.
[143] *Hong Pian Tee* (n 14) [27]–[28].
[144] *Eleven v Boxsentry* (n 84) [103].
[145] ibid.
[146] RECJA, s 3(2)(d), REFJA, s 5(1)(a)(iv).
[147] *Owens Bank Ltd v Bracco* [1992] 2 AC 443.
[148] Yeo (n 9) para 75.230.
[149] Note, however, that the same considerations do not apply to the CCAA regime, as was argued earlier in this chapter.
[150] Alex Mills, 'The Dimensions of Public Policy in Private International Law' (2008) 4(2) *Journal of Private International Law* 201, 209.
[151] *Liao Eng Kiat v Burswood Nominees Ltd* [2004] 4 SLR(R) 690, [32], [36]–[42]; *Poh Soon Kiat* (n 76) [112]–[113]; Ebenezer OI Adodo, 'Enforcement of Foreign Gambling Debts: Mapping the Worth of the Public Policy Defence' (2005) 1(2) *Journal of Private International Law* 291, 315.

of the foreign judgment would have to be offensive to some 'fundamental principle of justice, some prevalent conception of good morals, or some deep-rooted tradition of the forum'.[152]

In the application of the public policy doctrine in Singapore law, the courts draw a distinction between the cause of action in the foreign court and the effect of enforcement of the foreign judgment. The public policy doctrine has generally been held to operate only if the *effect* of the foreign judgment's enforcement in the forum is contrary to public policy, in order to avoid a perception of over-intrusiveness in foreign judicial proceedings. To that end, courts are very careful in their characterisation of the issues before them – if the issue before them is determined to be sufficiently distant from the problematic foreign law or cause of action, the courts may be willing to uphold the foreign judgment or apply the foreign law accordingly.[153] Notably, the English Court of Appeal decision in *Israel Discount Bank of New York v Hadjipateras*[154] has been criticised for failing to draw this distinction by appearing to accept the proposition that a judgment based on an agreement obtained through undue influence is contrary to English public policy.

One example of a foreign judgment falling foul of this doctrine is one obtained in breach of an anti-suit injunction directed against the foreign proceedings. Such a judgment will not be recognised or enforced in Singapore for contravening Singapore's public policy.[155] The recognition or enforcement of foreign judgments based on gambling debts is also likely to be considered as contravening Singapore's public policy.[156] It should be noted, as leading academics in Singapore have observed, that this defence has seldom been successful, especially in the commercial context.[157]

The public policy defence exists in both the RECJA and REFJA.[158] The defence as stated in the RECJA, however, is directed at whether the *cause of action* litigated before the foreign court is against Singapore's public policy – distinct from the common law position as described above. That said, the Singapore courts have in substance treated the public policy defence at common law and in the RECJA as similar in substance.[159] While this position does require one to close one's eyes to the clear wording of the RECJA, a significant advantage of this position is the promotion of coherence and certainty. The articulation of the public policy defence in the REFJA echoes the common law understanding of the defence.

iv. Foreign Judgment Obtained in Breach of Natural Justice

A foreign judgment will not be recognised or enforced in Singapore if it was obtained in breach of natural justice. It has been observed that this defence has not been the subject

[152] *Boardwalk Regency Corp v Maalouf* (1992) 88 DLR (4th) 612 (Ont CA), 616–18, cited in *Liao Eng Kiat* (n 151) [31]; Yeo (n 9) para 75.210.

[153] Lord Collins of Mapesbury (ed), *Dicey, Morris and Collins on the Conflict of Laws* 15th edn (London, Sweet & Maxwell, 2012) [5-006]. This may be viewed as a manifestation of the concept of 'proximity' suggested by Mills (n 150).

[154] *Israel Discount Bank of New York v Hadjipateras* [1984] 1 WLR 137.

[155] *WSG Nimbus* (n 53).

[156] *Poh Soon Kiat* (n 76).

[157] Yeo (n 9) para 75.210.

[158] RECJA, s 3(2)(f), REFJA, s 5(1)(a)(v).

[159] *Liao Eng Kiat* (n 151).

of much attention in Singapore law, and that the Singapore courts are likely to follow the English position on this doctrine.[160] Some examples of situations where a foreign judgment may be considered to be obtained in breach of natural justice include when 'the judgment debtor had not been given notice of the proceedings in the foreign court or had not been given sufficient opportunity to present his case'.[161] Natural justice also includes procedural defects in the foreign proceedings which breach the forum's 'views of substantial justice'.[162] The natural justice defence is indeed a close cousin of the public policy defence, insofar as the public policy defence relates also to fundamental principles of justice. The key difference between the defences may be described as such – the natural justice defence focuses on the issue of justice in the *procedure* leading up to the award of the foreign judgment, while the public policy defence is directed at the *effect of enforcement* of the foreign judgment in Singapore. This defence is applicable in the RECJA/REFJA registration regime too. Under the RECJA, it applies when the defendant was 'not duly served with the process of the original court and did not appear'.[163] Under the REFJA, it applies when the defendant did not receive notice of the foreign proceedings 'in sufficient time to enable him to defend the proceedings and did not appear'.[164]

v. *Foreign Judgment is Inconsistent with Another Judgment*

A foreign judgment will not be recognised or enforced in Singapore at common law if it is inconsistent with a Singapore judgment, in line with the principles underlying the doctrine of *res judicata*.[165] The same position obtains under the REFJA,[166] and arguably as part of the public policy defence under the RECJA.[167] Where the foreign judgment sought to be recognised or enforced is inconsistent with an earlier *foreign* judgment entitled to recognition in Singapore,[168] the position at common law is not settled, although the Singapore courts are likely to give priority to the earlier judgment.[169] Under the REFJA, the Singapore court has the discretion to set aside the later judgment in favour of an earlier foreign judgment.[170] The RECJA is silent on this issue.

vi. *Foreign Judgment has been Wholly Satisfied*

A foreign judgment will not be recognised or enforced in Singapore at common law if it has been wholly satisfied. This coheres with the obligation theory as the conceptual basis for the recognition of foreign judgments – if the foreign judgment has already been wholly

[160] Chong (n 6) 172.
[161] Yeo (n 9) para 75.220.
[162] *Adams v Cape Industries* (n 99) 564.
[163] RECJA, s 3(2)(c).
[164] REFJA, s 5(1)(a)(iii).
[165] Yeo (n 9) para 75.218.
[166] REFJA, s 5(1)(b).
[167] RECJA, s 3(2)(f); Yeo (n 9) para 75.218.
[168] That is, a foreign judgment for which recognition has not actually yet been sought in Singapore, but which would be entitled to be recognised, if an application is made.
[169] *Showlag v Mansour* [1995] 1 AC 431; Yeo (n 9) para 75.219.
[170] REFJA, s 5(1)(b).

satisfied as determined by the law of the foreign court, then there is no reason for the Singapore court to find an obligation on the part of the judgment debtor.[171] Similarly, under the REFJA, a foreign judgment cannot be registered if it has been wholly satisfied.[172] While the RECJA does not expressly deal with this, it is likely that wholly satisfied foreign judgments will not be registrable under the RECJA under either the public policy defence,[173] or the requirement that registration must be 'just and convenient' which we will turn to shortly.[174]

vii. RECJA/REFJA – Specific Defences

We now move to the defences specific to the RECJA/REFJA registration regime. Under the REFJA, a foreign judgment will be refused registration if proceedings were brought in breach of 'an agreement under which the dispute was to be settled otherwise than by proceedings in the courts of the country of that court'.[175] This defence only applies if the defendant had not already submitted to the foreign court's jurisdiction, however.[176]

Under the RECJA, registration of a foreign judgment is subject to the requirement that enforcing the judgment in Singapore is 'just and convenient'.[177] The Singapore Court of Appeal has interpreted this requirement to mean that 'it must be fair and equitable to allow the Commonwealth judgment in question to be enforced in Singapore', and that enforcement of the judgment must also be 'appropriately tailored to meet the exigencies of the circumstances'.[178] The overarching inquiry is directed at determining where 'the interests of justice lie, having regard to the factual matrix of the case'.[179] For example, when faced with a situation where there was a substantial delay between the handing down of the foreign judgment and its registration in Singapore, the Singapore court will consider whether the delay 'has caused prejudice to the judgment debtor', whether the judgment creditor can provide 'a reasonable explanation' for the delay, whether the judgment creditor has been 'reasonably diligent' in his efforts to enforce the foreign judgment and whether the judgment debtor has been 'obstructive'.[180]

E. Foreign Judgments *In Rem*

Foreign judgments *in rem* are subject to a distinct regime for recognition and enforcement. A judgment *in rem* is 'a judgment by a court where the relevant property is situate, adjudicating on its title or disposition as against the whole world (and not merely as between parties or their privies in the litigation before it)'.[181] In determining whether a judgment is

[171] Yeo (n 9) para 75.232.
[172] REFJA, s 4(3)(a).
[173] RECJA, s 3(2)(f).
[174] RECJA, s 3(1).
[175] REFJA, s 5(3)(b).
[176] REFJA, s 5(3)(b), reading together with ss 5(2)(a)(i), 5(2)(a)(ii) and 5(2)(a)(iii).
[177] RECJA, s 3(1).
[178] *Westacre Investments* (n 27) [21].
[179] ibid, [24].
[180] ibid.
[181] *Maler Foundation* (n 132) [64], quoting from *Pattni v Ali* [2007] 2 AC 85 [21]. See also Yeo (n 9) para 75.241.

in rem or *in personam*, the Singapore courts will 'consider the substance of the judgment and its intended effect on the parties'.[182]

For a foreign judgment *in rem* to be recognised in Singapore, the property which was the subject matter of the foreign proceedings must be situated within the foreign jurisdiction at the time of the judgment.[183] If so, the Singapore court will recognise the jurisdiction of the foreign court to bind the whole world with respect to that property.[184] It has been noted that this rule may not be entirely exhaustive – judgments on the beneficial succession to movables may be recognised if granted by the court of the country of domicile of the deceased, for example, as a reflection of the choice of law rule that such property rights are governed by the law of the testamentary domicile.[185] The position under the REFJA with respect to foreign judgments *in rem* is the same as the common law one.[186] The RECJA does not deal with foreign judgments *in rem*. The defences applicable to the recognition or enforcement of foreign judgments *in personam* apply equally to foreign judgments *in rem*, save that fraud in obtaining the foreign judgment would not affect a third party who has acquired title to the property in good faith and for value in reliance upon the foreign judgment.[187]

IV. Reflections on the Future of Singapore's Regime for Recognition and Enforcement

In closing, several thoughts about the future of Singapore's regime for the recognition and enforcement of foreign judgments will be offered. First, as Singapore, in conjunction with the international community, moves towards treaty regimes as a major frontier in the development of the law on the recognition or enforcement of foreign judgments, an area worth paying attention to is the theoretical basis underlying such regimes. The obligation theory described earlier in this chapter has long served as the foundation for the common law regime in this regard. However, the obligation theory is not conceptually without flaw.[188] In particular, *why* should the existence of international jurisdiction give rise to an obligation on a defendant that the forum court should recognise?[189] The obligation theory is hard-pressed to find an answer to this question, beyond saying that the obligation arises because of the existence of international jurisdiction, which would then be a circular argument.

In defence of the obligation theory, Adrian Briggs has suggested that, where international jurisdiction is founded on the concept of presence, this obligation may be justified

[182] *Murakami Takako* (n 65) [30]; *Maler Foundation* (n 132) [64].
[183] *Maler Foundation* (n 132) [66].
[184] ibid; Yeo (n 9) para 75.243.
[185] Yeo (n 9) para 75.243.
[186] REFJA, s 5(2)(b).
[187] *Payna Chettiar v Low Meng Seng* [1998] 1 SLR(R) 657 [24].
[188] See Chng (n 63) 147–48.
[189] This question was also raised in Jonathan Harris, 'Recognition of Foreign Judgments at Common Law – The Anti-suit Injunction Link' (1997) 17(3) *OJLS* 477. See also Ho Hock Lai, 'Policies Underlying the Enforcement of Foreign Commercial Judgments' (1997) 46 *ICLQ* 443, 445.

on the basis of voluntary presence, or on 'the common law understanding of international law principles of territoriality, comity and sovereignty'.[190] Where international jurisdiction is founded on the concept of submission, the obligation is founded on the basis of agreement.[191] Two points will be made in response. First, to the extent that Briggs suggests that consent may be invoked as a justification for the obligation theory even where international jurisdiction is founded on presence, the connection between consent and presence is tenuous.[192] While it *is* a factual possibility, the defendant's presence in the foreign jurisdiction may not necessarily be equated with his consent to the foreign court's jurisdiction over him. Second, and more fundamentally, one still must justify *why* consent to the foreign court's jurisdiction is sufficient to create a binding obligation on the defendant within the forum to obey the foreign judgment.[193] If one were to refer to 'the international law principles of territoriality, comity and sovereignty' in aid of a justification for the obligation theory,[194] this raises the question as to whether it is these higher-order principles which provide the fundamental normative basis for the importance of the concept of consent, and thus provide the true justification for the courts' practice of recognising foreign judgments, rather than the obligation theory. In view of the growing importance of international treaty regimes in this domain of private international law, one wonders whether an alternative, more universalist, theoretical account of the recognition of foreign judgments will become increasingly relevant in times to come.

Second, the Singapore courts' move towards entering into non-legally-binding memorandums with foreign courts around the world is a development that may potentially influence Singapore's regime for the recognition and enforcement of foreign judgments. For example, to date, the SICC has entered into Memorandums of Guidance with the Abu Dhabi Global Market Courts, Bermuda, Dubai International Financial Centre Courts and the State of Qatar, and engaged in an Exchange of Letters with the Supreme Court of Victoria, Australia.[195] These memoranda and letters have no strict legal effect and do not involve any change in substance to any existing legal regime. However, insofar as the enforcement of foreign judgments is related to the concept of reciprocity, the existence of such agreements provides a strong reassurance to commercial parties of the likelihood of

[190] Adrian Briggs, 'Recognition of Foreign Judgments: A Matter of Obligation' (2013) 129(Jan) *LQR* 87, 93–94. See also Adrian Briggs, *The Conflict of Laws* 3rd edn (Oxford, Oxford University Press, 2013) 169–72.

[191] Briggs, 'Recognition of Foreign Judgments' (n 190) 93.

[192] See Richard Frimpong Oppong, 'Mere Presence and International Competence in Private International Law' (2007) 3(2) *Journal of Private International Law* 321, 326. It should also be noted that the obligation theory is even harder to reconcile with approaches to jurisdiction such as that taken by Canada, which rests on a real and substantial connection between the defendant and the foreign jurisdiction: see *Beals v Saldanha* [2003] 3 SCR 416. In such jurisdictions, the forum may find that the foreign court has international jurisdiction over the defendant even where the defendant is not present or has not consented to the foreign court's jurisdiction. The obligation theory applied in the context of such jurisdictions would be significantly hard-pressed to explain the existence of the obligation on the forum to recognise the foreign judgment.

[193] This can be seen from the reasoning of the Court of Appeal in *Adams v Cape Industries* (n 99), where Slade LJ first held that international comity was the overarching rationale for the courts' practice of recognising foreign judgments, and then went on to discuss presence and submission as means of identifying *which* foreign judgments should be recognised.

[194] Briggs, 'Recognition of Foreign Judgments' (n 190) 94.

[195] Singapore International Commercial Court, 'Enforcement of Money Judgments – SICC' (*Singapore International Commercial Court*, 19 November 2018), available online: www.sicc.gov.sg/guide-to-the-sicc/enforcement-of-money-judgments.

reciprocal enforcement by evincing mutual understanding of each jurisdiction's regime. Indeed, while such agreements fall short of registration regimes such as the RECJA/REFJA and the CCAA, the mutual understanding of judicial processes fostered by such agreements is likely to exercise some influence on how Singapore judges perceive judgments originating from these jurisdictions.

Finally, this area of Singapore's private international law is likely to be the subject of considerable attention for the foreseeable future, in view of its indispensability to Singapore's drive to become an internationally-recognised commercial litigation hub. Indeed, the advent of the SICC, closely followed by the enactment of the CCAA, represents the ambition and resolve of Singapore's leaders to place Singapore firmly on the trajectory of becoming an international commercial dispute resolution hub in the region and beyond, as well as the ability of the shapers of Singapore's legal industry to take bold and concrete steps to fully bring this vision into reality. Further, even more developments are potentially on the horizon for Singapore's regime for the recognition and enforcement of foreign judgments. Singapore is an active participant in the Hague Judgments Project, which seeks to lay out a common approach across signatories for the recognition and enforcement of foreign judgments. Significantly, this project goes far beyond the scope of the existing Hague Convention, which is limited to harmonising approaches across signatories to foreign judgments involving exclusive choice of court agreements. At the time of writing, the Special Commission on the Recognition and Enforcement of Foreign Judgments has already produced a draft convention.[196] With Singapore's active role in the Judgments Project, coupled with Singapore's enthusiastic reception of the existing Hague Convention, there is a high likelihood that Singapore will ratify the final product of the Project unless there is grave cause for concern. One potential area of concern, as highlighted by Yeo Tiong Min, is that a broadening of the grounds for the recognition of foreign judgments would lead to the Singapore courts having to more often undertake intrusive review into the circumstances underlying the grant of the foreign judgment, especially when the foreign judgment originates from a nation with a dubious rule of law record.[197] In addition, given the ambitious scope of the draft convention, the final product promises to be a far-reaching reform of Singapore's entire regime of recognition and enforcement. The interaction between this regime and the existing common law, RECJA/REFJA and CCAA regimes will surely raise numerous teething issues calling for clarification. Nevertheless, these issues are certainly not insurmountable. Indeed, these developments in Singapore's private international law present an interesting opportunity for judges, lawyers and legal academics to contribute to the development of a substantive body of case law and commentary directed towards the coherent harmonisation of all the different regimes for the recognition and enforcement of foreign judgments in Singapore.

[196] Special Commission on the Recognition and Enforcement of Foreign Judgments, '2018 Draft Convention' (*Hague Conference on Private International Law*, 24–29 May 2018), available online: assets.hcch.net/docs/23b6dac3-7900-49f3-9a94-aa0ffbe0d0dd.pdf.

[197] Tiong Min Yeo, 'Common Law Developments Relating to Foreign Judgments' (Singapore, Ninth Yong Pung How Professorship of Law Lecture, 18 May 2016) paras 69–72, available online: cebcla.smu.edu.sg/sites/law.smu.edu.sg/files/law/Paper2016_YPH.pdf.

8

Malaysia

SITPAH SELVARATNAM

I. Introduction

The need for cross-border co-operation in the enforcement of judgments for civil and commercial matters has long been recognised in Malaysia. The primary statutory source of recognition and enforcement of foreign judgments in Malaysia is the Reciprocal Enforcement of Judgments Act 1958 (REJA), which carves out, from the common law approach of an action on a foreign judgment, a simpler method of recognition and enforcement of foreign judgments under specified circumstances, substantially founded on reciprocity between countries.

The process of recognition can accordingly take two forms. First, an action under common law on the foreign judgment or based on the original cause of action; and second, pursuant to the process prescribed by REJA. There are similarities in the defences that may be raised under each method of recognition, and the significant difference lies in the procedure to be adopted and the relative ease of recognition. The REJA process, although faster and simpler, is circumscribed in its application by statute. Where a judgment does not fall within the ambit of REJA, an action on the judgment may be considered for commencement.

II. Background

Malaysia is a union of 13 States that came together in her present form in 1963, comprising 11 States in Peninsula Malaysia, and two States that are on the island of Borneo. Singapore, once the 14th State, left this union in 1965. Peninsula Malaysia is situated on the ancient silk route of trade between the Far East and the Middle East. Her West Coast lines the Straits of Malacca; and her East Coast, the South China Sea. The history of this trade route dictates her cultural, social and economic heritage; having been under Portuguese, Dutch and English rule at various points in time. As a colony of the British Empire from 1824 until her independence in 1957, and as a part of the Commonwealth, Malaysia's legal system is strongly influenced by English law. Despite Malaysia's unique cultural and religious mix of races, predominantly Malay, Chinese, Indian, Iban and Kadazan in ethnicity, shaped by her historic trade and migrant narrative, the English legal system is entrenched in the administration of justice in Malaysia.

The pre-eminence of English law within the Malaysian legal system is marked by the Civil Law Act 1956 that enacts for the application of English law in respect of commercial matters as administered in England on 7 April 1956, unless particular legislation in that regard has been passed in Malaysia. In the States of Malacca, Penang, Sabah and Sarawak, the application of English law is not limited in time to 1956, but shall be administered as if the case had arisen in the corresponding period of time in England, unless relevant provision has been made by Malaysian enactment.

The private international law of Malaysia adopts much of the principles of English conflicts of law, adjusted to suit local circumstances. Some of the early reported judgments capture the struggle with questions of jurisdiction exercised by one sovereign province over property and persons that are the subject matter of judgment of another sovereign province, both provinces of which are now within Malaysia. The Penang Court had to consider if it could interfere with a judgment of the Kedah Court, by ordering the return of property taken in execution under a Kedah Court judgment. Principles of comity featured.[1] The judgment in *Ho Hong Bank Ltd v Ho Kai Neo*[2] of the Johor Court traces its history of reciprocal enforcement of foreign judgments to the Statute of George III in 1800, passed in order to facilitate in one part of the United Kingdom decrees of the court of another, and the Judgment Extension Act 1868 that introduced the machinery of registration of money judgments as between England, Scotland and Ireland. That Johor Court judgment discerns the application of the latter enactment through the Administration of Justice Act 1920 to the British Empire at large, by providing that each Dominion, Colony or Protectorate seeking admission into this comity should first pass reciprocal legislation. Hence, the Johor Judgments (Reciprocity) Enactment 1922 was effected.

The REJA was passed in 1958, a year after independence, to consolidate the various enactments relating to reciprocal enforcement of foreign judgments operating in the Federated Malay States of Perak, Selangor, Negeri Sembilan, Pahang, and the individual enactments of Johor and Kedah; replaces the Foreign Judgments (Reciprocal Enactment) Act 1933 of the United Kingdom that was then in force in the Straits Settlement of Penang and Malacca; and further extends REJA to all States in the Federation of Malaya.[3]

The hierarchy of the Malaysian court system provides for subordinate courts and superior courts. The Magistrates' and Sessions Courts afford redress for matters within a limited monetary value, except for motor vehicle accidents, and landlord and tenant claims, which are all heard before the Sessions Court regardless of the quantum claimed. The High Court, the Court of Appeal and the Federal Court form the superior courts of Malaysia. Appeals from the Federal Court to the Privy Council ceased in 1985. The Federal Court is, accordingly, the court of final appeal in Malaysia, and hears appeals from the Court of Appeal only with leave, save in prescribed circumstances. The High Court is a court of first instance;

[1] *Tankam and Shina Tamby v RMKA Mootoopalany Chetty* [1899] 6 SSLR 11, cited in RH Hickling and Min Aun Wu, *Conflict of Laws in Malaysia* (Kuala Lumpur, Butterworths Asia, 1995).

[2] *Ho Hong Bank Ltd v Ho Kai Neo* [1932] 1 MLJ 76.

[3] Legislative Council, Federation of Malaya, *Hansard* (Second Meeting of the Fourth Session of the Second Legislative Council, 4 December 1958) 5442, on the Second Reading of the Foreign Judgments (Reciprocal Enforcement) Bill 1958. REJA was revised in 1972.

the others being appellate in jurisdiction. The recognition and enforcement of foreign judgments fall within the jurisdiction of the High Court for first instance determination.

The supreme source of this court structure is the Federal Constitution. The Courts of Judicature Act 1964 and the Subordinate Courts Act 1948 stipulate the jurisdiction of each court. The Sessions Court has unlimited jurisdiction to try all actions of a civil nature in respect of motor vehicle accidents, landlord and tenant, and distress. Its jurisdiction to try all other suits of a civil nature is limited to where the amount in dispute or the value of the subject matter does not exceed RM1 million, unless parties have entered into a written agreement to have the Sessions Court try the matter. Where the amount at stake exceeds RM1 million, the High Court assumes jurisdiction to try the matter. The Admiralty jurisdiction, however, can only be exercised by the High Court. Similarly, the dissolution of marriages, custody of infants, grant of representation of the estate of deceased persons, enforcement of trust or for accounts, and questions of ownership of immovable property all fall to be determined by the High Court. There are two High Courts in Malaysia: the High Court of Malaya with branches throughout the Peninsula Malaysia, and the High Court of Sabah and Sarawak located in North Borneo.[4] Both High Courts are of co-ordinate jurisdiction. Each High Court and its branches exercise jurisdiction over the land, territorial waters and air space above them.[5] The jurisdiction of the court is divided into civil and criminal jurisdictions, with the extent of each division of the High Court jurisdiction demarcated by the Courts of Judicature Act 1964.[6] The courts exercising criminal jurisdiction are distinct from the courts exercising civil jurisdiction. Commercial proceedings are a sub-set of the civil jurisdiction. In the High Court of Malaya at Kuala Lumpur however, civil and commercial divisions within the civil courts have been administratively established through Practice Directions,[7] with selected courts hearing either civil or commercial matters.[8] The recognition and enforcement of foreign judgments are to be commenced in the civil courts.

The REJA, read together with Order 67 of the Rules of Court 2012, stipulates for the statutory jurisdiction and procedure for the recognition and enforcement of foreign judgments. Case law and precedent feature strongly in Malaysian judicial findings. The principle of stare decisis is applied to provide certainty in judicial determination. Judicial pronouncements on principles of private international law, particularly from the Commonwealth, are of persuasive value and often adopted for their resonance with the underlying ethos of the Malaysian judicial system.

Malaysia, as an active trading nation, adopts many international conventions and is a party to numerous bilateral treaties. There is, however, no specific bilateral treaty on the recognition and enforcement of judgments. Although Malaysia is a Member State to the Hague Conference on Private International Law (HCPIL), Malaysia is not a party to any of

[4] Federal Constitution, Art 121(1).

[5] Courts of Judicature Act 1964, s 3.

[6] Courts of Judicature Act 1964, s 22 for criminal jurisdiction; Courts of Judicature Act 1964, ss 23 and 24 for civil jurisdiction.

[7] Practice Directions 6 and 7 of 2013.

[8] The matters that fall within the Kuala Lumpur commercial courts are admiralty (*in rem* and *in personam*), banking, bankruptcy, registration of businesses, companies, contracts of agency, finance, insurance, intellectual property, laws of the sea, partnership, sale of goods and *muamalat* (Islamic financing).

the HCPIL Conventions. The 2005 Hague Convention on Choice of Court Agreements is therefore not applicable in Malaysia.

III. Recognition and Enforcement under REJA

The recognition and enforcement of foreign judgments under REJA may be considered in two parts: first, the recognition of the foreign judgment from a reciprocating country by registration of the judgment as a judgment of the Malaysian court; and second, the enforcement of the registered foreign judgment as a judgment of the Malaysian court.

A. Recognition

REJA is premised on reciprocity, although it is also a means to honour comity, and the principle of obligations. It is the confluence of all three principles that permits a foreign judgment to be readily recognised within Malaysia, as observed from the following three characteristics underpinning REJA.

First, the country, whose judgment is to be recognised under REJA, must recognise a judgment issued by a superior court of Malaysia in substantially equal terms. Second, the foreign judgment must have been made within the jurisdiction of the foreign court. In recognition of judicial comity, the precise manner of exercise of the foreign jurisdiction, whether based on the procedure or merits of the case, is not open for challenge in the registration of the judgment before the court in Malaysia. Third, the foreign judgment must impose a monetary obligation that remains unsatisfied.

As a broad checklist, the foreign judgment must meet the following criteria under REJA in order to be registered as a judgment of a Malaysian court:

1. The judgment is from a country that grants reciprocity to judgments of the Malaysian High Court. The list of countries recognised as affording reciprocity is prescribed in the First Schedule to REJA;[9]
2. The judgment is of the superior court of that reciprocating country, as identified in the First Schedule of REJA. Most often, it is the High Court of that country;
3. The judgment is final and conclusive as between the parties, and given in civil proceedings; or if in criminal proceedings, is for payment of a sum of money in compensation or damages to an injured party;[10]
4. The judgment must be for a monetary sum, not being a sum payable as taxes, fine or other penalty;[11]
5. The judgment, or a part thereof, remains unsatisfied;[12]

[9] REJA, ss 3(2), 3(3).
[10] ibid, s 2, definition of 'judgment'.
[11] ibid, s 3(3).
[12] ibid, s 4(1), proviso (a).

6. The judgment must be capable of enforcement by execution in the country of the original court;[13]
7. The judgment must have been made within the jurisdiction of the original court;[14]
8. The judgment is *in personam*. If it is *in rem*, the property must have been situated within the jurisdiction of the original court at the time of the proceedings;[15]
9. The judgment *in personam* cannot be in respect of any matrimonial cause, administration of the estate of deceased persons, bankruptcy, winding-up of companies, lunacy or guardianship of infants;[16]
10. The enforcement of the judgment would not be contrary to public policy;
11. The judgment was not obtained by fraud or in breach of natural justice;[17]
12. The application for registration of the judgment in Malaysia is made by the person in whom the rights under the foreign judgment vest;[18]
13. The procedures established under Order 67 of the Rules of Court 2012 have been complied with, particularly with regard to due service on the judgment debtor of the Order of registration, and due notice to the judgment debtor of the right to set-aside the registration of the foreign judgment within a specified time;
14. The application for registration is made within six years of the date of the foreign judgment;[19] and
15. The matter in dispute before the original court had not been the subject of a final and conclusive judgment of another court having jurisdiction in the matter, before the judgment in the original court was made.[20]

Where REJA applies, the recognition process is simple. It is commenced in court by way of an originating summons, supported by an affidavit affirming as to matters prescribed by Order 67 of the Rules of Court 2012.[21] The application for registration is filed in the High

[13] ibid, s 4(1), proviso (b).
[14] ibid, ss 5(1)(a)(ii), 5(2), 5(3).
[15] ibid, ss 5(2)(a), 5(2)(b).
[16] ibid, s 2, definition of 'action in personam'.
[17] ibid, ss 5(1)(a)(iii), 5(1)(a)(iv), 5(1)(a)(v).
[18] ibid, s 5(1)(a)(vi).
[19] ibid, s 4(1).
[20] ibid, s 5(1)(b).
[21] Rules of Court 2012, Ord 67 r 3(1) provides that:

An application for registration shall be supported by an affidavit—

(a) exhibiting the judgment or a verified or certified or otherwise duly authenticated copy thereof, and where the judgment is not in the English language, a translation thereof in that language certified by a notary public or authenticated by affidavit;
(b) stating the name, trade or business and the usual or last known place of abode or business of the judgment creditor and the judgment debtor respectively, so far as known to the deponent;
(c) stating to the best of the information or belief of the deponent-
    (i) that the judgment creditor is entitled to enforce the judgment;
    (ii) as the case may require, either that at the date of the application the judgment has not been satisfied, or the amount in respect of which it remains unsatisfied;
    (iii) where the application is made under REJA, that the judgment does not fall within any of the cases in which a judgment may not be ordered to be registered under subsection 4(2) of REJA;

Court on an ex parte basis, without the need for service of the cause papers on the judgment debtor. The Order of Court granting leave to register the foreign judgment as a judgment of the Malaysian court will stipulate that the judgment debtor has a specified period of time within which he could apply to court to set aside the Order, and that judgment will not be executed until that period (or any extended period of time) expires.[22] A register of judgments ordered to be registered is maintained by court.[23] Upon service of the Order, as required under Order 67 rules 5(1) and 5(7) of the Rules of Court 2012, the judgment debtor may apply to set aside the Order. Execution of the judgment is then suspended by operation of the Rules of Court 2012 until the setting aside application is determined by the High Court.[24]

Subject to the provision for setting aside, a registered judgment shall for the purposes of execution have the same force and effect as a local judgment entered on the date of registration.[25] The sum payable under the judgment registered is expressed in the Malaysian currency, on the basis of the rate of exchange prevailing at the date of judgment of the original court.[26] Where the foreign judgment bears different matters, some of which are not capable of registration, the judgment may be registered in respect of parts capable of being registered as a separate judgment.[27] If partly satisfied, the judgment shall not be registered for the whole sum payable under the judgment of the original court, but only in respect of the balance remaining payable at the date of the application for registration.[28]

Premised on reciprocity, section 3(2) of REJA provides that the list of countries (whose judgments may be registered) may be expanded by amendment to the First Schedule. Countries in that list accord substantial reciprocity of treatment to judgments of the High Court of Malaysia. Conversely, section 9(1) of REJA provides for the removal of countries from the First Schedule, if substantially less favourable treatment is afforded to Malaysian judgments than that accorded by Malaysia. The First Schedule to REJA currently provides for the High Court of United Kingdom,[29] Hong Kong (Special Administrative Region of the People's

(iv) where the application is made under REJA, that at the date of the application the judgment can be enforced by execution in the country of the original Court and that, if it were registered, the registration would not be, or be liable to be, set aside under section 5 of REJA;

(d) specifying, where the application is made under REJA, the amount of the interest, if any, which under the law of the country of the original Court has become due under the judgment up to the time of registration.

There are also other requirements in Rules of Court 2012, Ord 67 rr 3(2), 3(3), 3(4).

[22] Rules of Court 2012, Ord 67 r 5(2).

[23] ibid, Ord 67 r 6.

[24] REJA, s 4(2), proviso; Rules of Court 2012, Ord 67 r 10(2).

[25] REJA, s 4(2).

[26] ibid, s 4(3). Where the sum payable under a judgment sought to be registered is expressed in a currency other than the currency of Malaysia, Rules of Court 2012, Ord 67 r 3(2) requires that the affidavit shall state the amount which that sum represents in the currency of Malaysia calculated at the rate of exchange prevailing at the date of the judgment.

[27] REJA, s 4(5). Where a judgment sought to be registered under REJA is in respect of different matters, and some, but not all, of the provisions of the judgment are such that if those provisions had been contained in separate judgments, those judgments could properly have been registered, Rules of Court 2012, Ord 67 r 3(3) requires that the affidavit shall state the provisions in respect of which it is sought to register the judgment.

[28] REJA, s 4(4).

[29] The superior courts being recognised are: the High Court in England; the Court of Session in Scotland; the High Court in Northern Ireland; the Court of Chancery of the County Palatine of Lancaster; and the Court of Chancery of the County Palatine of Durham.

Republic of China),[30] Singapore,[31] New Zealand,[32] Sri Lanka,[33] India[34] and Brunei.[35] Brunei was added to the First Schedule on 31 March 2000[36] and Australia was removed from the list with effect from 27 June 1993.[37] Reciprocity is, therefore, fundamental.

The status as a superior court of the original court from which the foreign judgment emanates is a critical element. In *Charles Priya Marie v Koshy Cherian*,[38] the judgment of the subordinate court of Singapore, although registered in the High Court of Singapore, was refused from registration in Malaysia.

The judgment must be final and conclusive to qualify for registration. An order granting parties the liberty to vary its terms is not final.[39] Interlocutory orders are not registrable under REJA. A default judgment is accepted as a final judgment, and has been registered by the Malaysian court pursuant to REJA.[40] An appeal does not affect the finality of the judgment.[41] However, under section 6(1) of REJA, the Malaysian court retains the discretion to set aside the registration pending an appeal, without prejudice to the judgment creditor's right to apply afresh for registration after the appeal is disposed of.

The judgment must remain unsatisfied, or part thereof must be outstanding, to enable registration for enforcement in Malaysia. In *Malayan Banking Bhd v Paxelent Corporation Bhd*,[42] an order granting registration for the full judgment sum granted by the original court was set aside, notwithstanding that a partial amount remained payable. The court held that it had no jurisdiction to amend the order granting registration to reflect the reduced amount. Whether a fresh application for registration of the reduced sum by the judgment creditor in these circumstances would be barred under the wider principle of issue estoppel remains open for consideration. Satisfaction of the judgment may take the form of the transfer of property to the judgment creditor, thereby denying a right to having the judgment registered in Malaysia.[43]

A common challenge to registration is the lack of jurisdiction of the original court. Section 5(2) provides for circumstances where jurisdiction is presumed. This is where the judgment debtor:

1. Submitted by voluntary appearance in the original court;[44]

[30] The superior court being the High Court.
[31] The superior court being the High Court. Note that the Singapore subordinate court was not recognised as a superior court for the purposes of REJA in *Excelmore Trading Pte Ltd v Excelmore Classics Sdn Bhd* [1996] 1 LNS 392 (HC) and *Charles Priya Marie v Koshy Cherian* [2010] 6 CLJ 693 (HC).
[32] The superior court being the High Court.
[33] The superior court being the High Court and the District Courts.
[34] Excluding the State of Jammu and Kashmir, the State of Manipur, the Tribal Areas of the State of Assam, and Scheduled Areas of the States of Madras and Andhra. The superior court being the High Court.
[35] The superior court being the High Court.
[36] See Reciprocal Enforcement of Judgments (Extension of Part II) Order 2000, PU(A) 122/2000.
[37] See Reciprocal Enforcement of Judgments (Application of Section 9) Order 1994, PU(A) 73/1994.
[38] *Charles Priya Marie* (n 31). See also REJA, s 3(3); *Excelmore Trading Pte Ltd* (n 31); *Zhang Jing v Ng Fong Yong* [2014] 10 CLJ 841 (HC).
[39] *Charles Priya Marie* (n 31).
[40] *Bank of New Zealand v Wong Kee Tat* [1990] 2 MLJ 435 (HC).
[41] REJA, s 3(4).
[42] *Malayan Banking Bhd v Paxelent Corporation Bhd* [2007] 3 CLJ 247 (HC).
[43] *KS Das v P Suppiah* [1988] 2 MLJ 445 (SC).
[44] REJA, s 5(2)(a)(i). The defendant shall not be deemed to have submitted to the jurisdiction of the court if its appearance is for the purpose of protecting, or obtaining the release of property seized, or threatened with seizure, in the proceedings or of contesting the jurisdiction of that court.

2. Counter-claimed in the original court;[45]
3. Agreed before the commencement of the foreign proceedings to submit to the jurisdiction of the original court;[46]
4. Had its principal place of business in the country of the original court at the time proceedings were instituted;[47] or
5. Had an office in the country of the original court and the proceedings in that court are in respect of a transaction effected through or at that office.[48]

Jurisdiction of the original court is also presumed if it is 'recognised by the law of Malaysia'.[49] The test in this regard is not readily ascertained. The High Court in *Chan Hak Foon v Sutera Harbour Sdn Bhd* suggested that a reading of section 5(2)(c) with the First Schedule of REJA offers a basis for finding that the Hong Kong court had jurisdiction to determine the matter by its placement in the First Schedule to REJA as a reciprocating country.[50] It is however, discerned by the author that the requirement for reciprocity of the original court by listing in the First Schedule, is distinct from the requirement for the original court to have jurisdiction over the particular matter. Whether the original court has jurisdiction over a matter is irrelevant to the reason why a country is listed in the First Schedule. On the other hand, the mere fact that a country is listed in the First Schedule does not lead to the conclusion that the original court has jurisdiction over every matter. It is currently unclear whether the jurisdiction of the original court is assessed according to Malaysian domestic law or private international laws. If the latter applies, the prescription of those laws is also unclear.

In *Malayan Banking Bhd v Ng Man Heng*,[51] the court held that the deeming provision on jurisdiction in section 5(2) of REJA is not exhaustive. Jurisdiction may additionally be conferred by other statute of the foreign country, similar to section 23 of the Malaysian Courts of Judicature Act 1964. The statutory provision of the foreign country conferred jurisdiction on the original court over a judgment debtor who was not a resident in that foreign jurisdiction but was one of several defendants in the foreign proceedings and the other defendants were resident within that jurisdiction.[52] By drawing a parallel with a similar Malaysian jurisdictional provision in section 23(1) of the Courts of Judicature Act 1964, the Malaysian court accepted the original court's connection with the dispute as endowing the original court with jurisdiction over the judgment debtor. Malaysian courts have considered if submission to jurisdiction may be implied by conduct,[53] but there is currently no definitive position on this issue.

[45] REJA, s 5(2)(a)(ii).
[46] ibid, s 5(2)(a)(iii).
[47] ibid, s 5(2)(a)(iv).
[48] ibid, s 5(2)(a)(v).
[49] ibid, s 5(2)(c).
[50] *Chan Hak Foon v Sutera Harbour Sdn Bhd* [2010] 9 CLJ 995 (HC).
[51] *Malayan Banking Bhd v Ng Man Heng* [2005] 1 MLJ 470 (HC). See also *United Malayan Banking Corp Bhd v Soo Lean Tooi* [1984] 1 MLJ 47 (HC); *Bank of New Zealand* (n 40).
[52] See further the discussion on the Courts of Judicature Act 1964, s 23 by the Federal Court in *Goodness For Import And Export v Phillip Morris Brands Sarl* [2016] 5 MLJ 171 and the Court of Appeal in *Siti Nur Aishah bt Ishak v Golden Plus Holdings Bhd* [2017] 3 MLJ 701.
[53] *Wong Teck Lim v Sim Lim Finance Ltd* [2001] 2 CLJ 685 (CA); cf *United Overseas Bank Ltd v Tjong Tjui Njuk* [1987] 2 MLJ 295 (Singapore HC).

A large number of challenges to the registration of foreign judgments in Malaysia are on the grounds of public policy. The public policy considered is the public policy of Malaysia, and has been held to be wider than illegality.[54] The facts giving rise to illegality or infringement of public policy may need to have been raised before the original court.[55] Foreign judgments relating to gambling debts had, in the past, given rise to significant concern for public policy reasons. In preservation of comity, it is now judicially regarded that it is the recognition of a valid foreign judgment which is the subject matter of the Malaysian registration proceedings; rather than the enforcement of the underlying cause of action for recovery of the gambling debt.[56] Viewed in this manner, it has been held not to contravene public policy to register a foreign judgment relating to a gaming transaction lawfully obtained in accordance with the relevant *lex loci* and *lex fori* of the original court. This approach, however, leaves uncertain whether a common law action on the judgment or original cause of action for recovery of a gambling debt may be treated differently, and considered to infringe public policy, where the judgment is not from a REJA reciprocating country.

The courts before 2000 regarded the manner of service of foreign process on a Malaysian judgment debtor as a matter falling within public policy. They viewed service of foreign process by an agent, as opposed to service through the governmental channel, as a transgression of the sovereignty of Malaysia and hence, contrary to public policy. By amendments introduced to the Rules of the High Court in the year 2000, service of Malaysian court process abroad through agents is now permitted. The Court of Appeal in *Commerzbank (South East Asia Ltd) v Tow Kong Liang*[57] clarified by analogy, that service through the Malaysian government of foreign process was only one method of service provided by Order 65 of the Rules of the High Court 1980, which method was only engaged if a request was made for such manner of service by the foreign court. Where no such letter of request is received, Order 65 had no application since Order 65 is not exclusive; adopting the reasoning in the Singapore case of *Fortune Hong Kong Trading Ltd v Cosco Feoso (Singapore) Pte Ltd*.[58] Service of foreign process by agents was accordingly not treated as an infringement of Malaysian sovereignty, and did not render the registration of the foreign judgment contrary to public policy. Irregularity of service is, on recent developments, considered to be a matter that had to be addressed by setting aside the judgment in the original court.[59]

The absence of assets in the foreign country does not render the foreign judgment incapable of execution in the foreign State, within the meaning of section 4(1), proviso (b). Such incapacity is not inherent within the foreign judgment, but due to practical circumstances. The foreign judgment remains eligible for registration under REJA.[60]

[54] *Banque Nasionale De Paris v Wuan Swee May* [2000] 3 MLJ 587 (HC).

[55] *Ralli v Angullia* (1917) 15 SSLR 33 (Straits Settlements CA); *Bank of India v Trans Continental Commodity Merchants Ltd* [1986] 2 MLJ 342 (Singapore HC), adopted by the Malaysian High Court in *Commerzbank (South East Asia) Ltd v Dennis Ling Li Kuang* [2000] 2 CLJ 57 (HC); *Ng Man Heng* (n 51).

[56] *Marina Bay Sands Pte Ltd v Wong Kar Hin* [2017] 1 LNS 680 (HC) which confirmed that High Court decision in *The Ritz Hotel Casino Ltd v Seri Osu Hj Sukam* [2005] 3 CLJ 390 (HC) was set aside on appeal by the Court of Appeal. See also *The Aspinall Curzon Ltd v Khoo Teng Hock* [1991] 2 MLJ 484 (HC); *Ng Man Heng* (n 51); *Jupiters Ltd (trading as Conrad International Treasury Casino) v Gan Kok Beng* [2007] 7 MLJ 228 (HC).

[57] *Commerzbank (South East Asia Ltd) v Tow Kong Liang* [2011] 3 CLJ 127 (CA).

[58] *Fortune Hong Kong Trading Ltd v Cosco Feoso (Singapore) Pte Ltd* [2000] 2 SLR 717 (CA).

[59] *Marina Bay Sands Pte Ltd v Ng Kong Seong* [2016] 1 LNS 1007 (HC).

[60] *Standard Chartered Bank (Singapore) Ltd v Pioneer Smith (M) Sdn Bhd* [2015] 7 CLJ 677 (HC).

Where the procedures of REJA are not complied with, the registration or subsequent execution issuing on that judgment are vulnerable to challenge. A winding-up petition presented on the strength of a foreign judgment, without seeking the prior registration of the foreign judgment in Malaysia, has been declared bad in law.[61] This raises a separate question within the insolvency regime. A petition to wind-up a company on a deemed inability to pay a debt, upon issuance of a 21-day statutory demand for payment that remains unsatisfied, without any prior judgment is permissible under corporate insolvency laws in Malaysia. The court in *The Bank of East Asia Ltd Singapore Branch v Axis Incorporation Bhd (No 1)*[62] held that where REJA applies, that is the only means by which recognition and enforcement of a foreign judgment can be pursued, precluding the presentation of a winding up petition without prior registration of the foreign judgment. Section 7 of REJA stipulates that:

> No proceedings for the recovery of a sum payable under a judgment of a superior court, being a judgment to which this Part applies, other than proceedings by way of registration of the judgment, shall be entertained by any court in Malaysia.

To the extent the foreign judgment to which section 7 applies is the only means by which the debt is evidenced, prior registration under REJA appears mandatory before winding-up proceedings are commenced.

Section 8 of REJA deserves mention in this context for it provides that a judgment to which REJA applies or would have applied, if a sum of money had been payable thereunder, whether it can be registered or not and whether (if it can be registered) it is registered or not, shall be recognised in any court in Malaysia as conclusive between the parties thereto in all proceedings founded on the same cause of action and may be relied on by way of defence or counterclaim in any such proceedings. The exceptions to such reliance are: the judgment had been set aside on grounds other than that a sum of money was not payable under the judgment; the judgment had been wholly or partly satisfied; at the date of the application, the judgment could not be enforced by execution in the country of the original court. The precise effect of section 8 in giving rise to issue estoppel without registration has not been considered in reported decisions of the courts of Malaysia.

The issuance of a bankruptcy notice before the expiry of the time prescribed to set aside the Order registering the foreign judgment was held to be premature in failing to comply with the procedures under REJA.[63]

Applications to set aside the registration of the foreign judgment must be made within the time allowed by the Order of registration, or any extended time. An application to extend time must, however, be sought within the time while the court remains competent to set aside the registration, and it must be supported by reasons for the delay.[64]

[61] *The Bank of East Asia Ltd Singapore Branch v Axis Incorporation Bhd (No 1)* [2009] 6 MLJ 587 (HC); *The Bank of East Asia Ltd Singapore Branch v Axis Incorporation Bhd (No 2)* [2009] 6 MLJ 564 (HC).

[62] *The Bank of East Asia Ltd Singapore Branch (No 1)* (n 61).

[63] *Re Raju Jayaraman Kerpaya ex p Associated Asian Securities (Pte) Ltd* [1999] 5 CLJ 23 (HC).

[64] Rules of Court 2012, Ord 67 rr 5(2), 5(3), 9(1); *International Factors Leasing Pte Ltd v Winds Cruises Pte Ltd* [1999] 4 MLJ 165 (HC). See also *Saeed U Khan v Lee Kok Hooi* [2001] 5 MLJ 416 (HC).

B. Enforcement

Upon registration, a foreign judgment is enforceable as if it was a Malaysian judgment. The ordinary processes of execution include writ of seizure and sale,[65] garnishee,[66] order of committal[67] and charging order.[68] Bankruptcy and winding-up proceedings[69] may also be initiated based on the registered judgment. Enforcement may be effected within six years of the registration of the foreign judgment, and for another six years with leave of court.[70]

IV. Recognition and Enforcement in Common Law

Where the REJA pre-conditions cannot be met, the Malaysian courts have accepted jurisdiction to entertain an action on the foreign judgment, or on the original cause of action.[71] This jurisdiction relies heavily on principles of comity of nations and *res judicata* in acknowledging the judgment and the obligation created thereunder. In *PNG Oxygen Limited v Lim Kok Chuan*,[72] this jurisdiction was reaffirmed. Recognition would take longer if the foreign judgment is not admitted – a trial may be necessitated for the Malaysian courts to hear evidence from witnesses. In that case, the benefits under REJA are not available and one has to establish jurisdiction over the defendant.[73] Therefore, section 23 of the Courts of Judicature Act 1964 in respect of jurisdiction over the defendant has to be met.[74] Where necessary, the requirement for service out of jurisdiction of the Malaysian court process has additionally to be satisfied.[75]

Where the foreign judgment is not denied, the common law action on the judgment may be commenced by an originating summons, supported by affidavit evidence.

[65] Rules of Court 2012, Ord 47.

[66] ibid, Ord 49.

[67] ibid, Ord 52.

[68] ibid, Ord 50.

[69] Note that bankruptcy and winding-up proceedings are not treated as execution proceedings in Malaysia: see *Maril-Rionebel (M) Sdn Bhd v Perdana Merchant Bankers Bhd and other Appeals* [2001] 4 MLJ 187 (CA) and *Juara Aspirasi (M) Sdn Bhd v Tan Soon Ping* [2012] 1 MLJ 50 (CA).

[70] Rules of Court 2012, Ord 46 r 2(1)(a).

[71] *Kader Nina Merican v Kader Meydin* (1876) 1 SSLR 3; *JM Lyon & Co v Meyer & Goldenberg* (1891) 1 SSLR 19; *Ralli v Angullia* (n 55).

[72] *PNG Oxygen Ltd v Lim Kok Chuan* [2018] 1 LNS 237 (HC).

[73] *See Hua Daily News Bhd v Tan Thien Chien & Ors* [1986] 2 MLJ 107 (SC); *PNG Oxygen Ltd* (n 72).

[74] Courts of Judicature Act 1964, s 23 provides that:

> (1) Subject to the limitations contained in Article 128 of the Constitution the High Court shall have jurisdiction to try all civil proceedings where—
>
> (a) the cause of action arose; or
>
> (b) the defendant or one of several defendants resides or has his place of business; or
>
> (c) the facts on which the proceedings are based exist or are alleged to have occurred; or
>
> (d) any land the ownership of which is disputed is situated, within the local jurisdiction of the Court and notwithstanding anything contained in this section in any case where all parties consent in writing within the local jurisdiction of the other High Court.

[75] Rules of Court 2012, Ord 11.

Alternatively, one can commence action by a writ of summons, followed by an application for summary judgment. However, the precise application of the concept of merger of the original cause of action into the foreign judgment remains unclear.[76]

Recognition by the common law action on the foreign judgment may be refused on grounds of lack of jurisdiction, fraud, public policy or breach of natural justice, in the same vein as the REJA defences. Public policy as a ground is sparingly used, in embracing the belief that it can be an 'unruly horse'.[77] The recognition of interlocutory orders, such as a worldwide *Mareva* injunction, may need to resort to this process.[78] It is conceivable that an action on the interlocutory foreign order may be brought, if the subject matter of such order is within the jurisdiction of the Malaysian court, to merit a corresponding order granted in Malaysia. This could be framed as an interlocutory order, coupled with a prayer seeking a substantive declaration for the recognition of the potential final foreign judgment. A similar approach is used to arrest ships within Malaysian waters as security to satisfy a potential judgment of a foreign court where the merits of the dispute are to be ultimately determined.[79]

V. Special Cases

A. Matrimonial Causes

The Maintenance Orders (Facilitation for Enforcement) Act 1949 (Maintenance Act) provides for enforcement in Malaysia of maintenance orders made in reciprocating countries listed in the Schedule to the Maintenance Act. These countries are not identical to the First Schedule of REJA. Australia, Pakistan and South Africa, which are not within the First Schedule to REJA, can be found in the Maintenance Act.

Section 3 of the Maintenance Act provides for a certified copy of an order of a foreign court to be transmitted to the Minister charged with the responsibility for the judiciary. The Minister shall cause a copy of that order to be sent to the appropriate Sessions Court or Magistrate Court in the district where the person against whom the maintenance order is made resides, having jurisdiction to try suits relating to maintenance of wife or children for registration. The order shall be registered in the prescribed manner, and shall from the date of registration have the same force and effect and be subject to the Maintenance Act, as if the order had been an order made in the local court, with the power to enforce the order accordingly.

Section 6 of the Maintenance Act provides also for orders that are of a provisional nature to be processed, in a matter that allows the local court to call the person against whom it is made to show cause as to why the foreign order should not be confirmed.[80]

[76] *JM Lyon & Co* (n 71); *Ralli v Angullia* (n 55).

[77] *The Aspinall Curzon Ltd v Khoo Teng Hock* (n 56); *PNG Oxygen Ltd* (n 72).

[78] For a discussion generally on *Mareva* injunctions, see *Metrowangsa Asset Management Sdn Bhd v Ahmad b Hj Hassan* [2005] 1 MLJ 654.

[79] Rules of Court 2012, Ord 70 r 12(11).

[80] REJA, ss 6(1)–6(7). See also *Charles Priya Marie* (n 31) [37].

B. Probate and Administration

Part IV of the Probate and Administration Act 1959 empowers the High Court to re-seal a Grant of Probate or Letters of Administration issued by a Court of Probate of a Commonwealth Country. The Malaysian court will not re-seal the grant of probate or letter of administration if at the time of death, the deceased was not domiciled in the jurisdiction of the foreign court from which the grant was issued, unless the grant was such that the High Court in Malaysia would have issued it. The effect of re-sealing is to render the grant having the same force as if it were a grant of the Court of Malaysia. If a foreign probate has not been re-sealed in the Malaysian court in accordance with section 52 of the Probate and Administration Act 1959, it has no legal effect in Malaysia.[81]

C. Bankruptcy

Section 104 of the Insolvency Act 1967 provides that the Malaysian court shall in all matters of bankruptcy and insolvency act in aid of and be auxiliary to the courts of the Republic of Singapore or any designated country having jurisdiction in bankruptcy and insolvency. Reciprocity features prominently, as such aid by the Malaysian court is to be given 'as long as the law [of the Republic of Singapore or any designated country] requires its courts to act in aid of and be auxiliary to the courts of Malaysia'. There are only two designated countries thus far, the United Kingdom and Australia.[82]

By virtue of these reciprocal provisions on bankruptcy and insolvency, plaintiffs who are adjudged bankrupt by the Singaporean courts were held not to have the necessary locus standi to commence civil proceedings in Malaysia without the sanction of the Official Assignee.[83]

D. Employment

Section 83 of the Employment Act 1955 provides that if the Minister of Human Resources is satisfied that arrangements have been made by or under any legislation in force in the Republic of Singapore for the service, execution or enforcement in the Republic of Singapore of summonses, warrants or orders issued or made under the Employment Act 1955, the said Minister may make regulations to prescribe the procedure for sending such summonses, warrants and orders to the Republic of Singapore for service, execution or enforcement, and make reciprocal provisions for the service, execution or enforcement in Malaysia of summonses, warrants and orders issued or made in the Republic of Singapore. The Employment (Procedure-Reciprocal Provisions) Regulations 1957 (revised 1983) (PU(A) 334/1983) was subsequently made by the Minister, and provides for, inter alia, the

[81] *Issar Singh v Samund Singh* (1941) 10 MLJ (FMSR) 28; *Lim Kang Hai v Lim Chik Lock* [2013] 1 LNS 539 (HC).

[82] See Insolvency Act 1967, s 104(7); the 'designated country' is appointed by PU(B) 2/1989.

[83] *Amos William Dawe v Development & Commercial Bank (Ltd) Bhd* [1981] 1 MLJ 230 (FC); *Kuah Tian Nam v Lee Siok Poh* [2009] 1 LNS 703 (HC).

mechanism of registration of orders made by the Commissioner for Labour of the Republic of Singapore in the Malaysian Sessions Court.[84]

E. Merchant Shipping, Liability and Compensation for Oil and Bunker Oil Pollution

By section 24 of the Merchant Shipping (Liability and Compensation for Oil and Bunker Oil Pollution) Act 1994 (MSO-Oil Pollution Act), the REJA applies to any judgment given by a court in a Liability Convention Country, Fund Convention Country or a Bunker Convention Country[85] to enforce a claim in respect of liability incurred by a shipowner for pollution damage caused by the ship. However, the deeming provisions regarding jurisdiction, sections 5(2) and 5(3) of the REJA, are not incorporated. The reference to First Schedule of REJA is to be construed as a reference to Second Schedule of the MSO-Oil Pollution Act.

F. Hague Convention on the Choice of Court Agreement

Although Malaysia is a Member State to the HCPIL, the 2005 Hague Convention on Choice of Court Agreements (Choice of Court Convention) has not been adopted by Malaysia. The Choice of Court Convention seeks to replicate the success of the 1958 New York Convention on the Reciprocal Recognition and Enforcement of Arbitral Awards. The benefits of adoption of the Choice of Court Convention would include recognising party autonomy in choosing the forum for the dispute resolution, and having State courts honour such choice. In the absence of the Choice of Court Convention, a Malaysian court when presented with a dispute which bears a choice of jurisdiction clause would apply the common law principles of *forum non conveniens* to determine whether to stay the Malaysian court proceedings brought contrary to the choice of jurisdiction agreement. A discretion is retained by the court when determining such application for a stay, although a heavy burden rests with the plaintiff to displace strict compliance with the choice of court agreement when the choice of court clause is held to be an exclusive choice of forum. In contrast, a mandatory stay would ensue if the Choice of Court Convention was adopted in Malaysia, and all choice of court agreements would be deemed to be an exclusive choice of forum.

The comparative value of a discretion vested in court, in contrast with the strict application of the Choice of Court Convention rules, is worthy of consideration. It is additionally useful to contemplate whether replicating the position in arbitration is advantageous.

[84] Employment (Procedure-Reciprocal Provisions) Regulations 1957 (revised 1983) (PU(A) 334/1983), rr 5, 6.

[85] The Liability Convention Country is a country in respect of which the International Convention on Civil Liability for Oil Pollution Damage signed in London on 27 November 1992, is in force. The Fund Convention Country is a country in respect of which the International Convention on the Establishment of an International Fund for Compensation for Oil Pollution Damage signed in London on 27 November 1992, is in force. The Bunkers Convention Country is a country in respect of which the International Convention on Civil Liability for Bunker Oil Pollution Damage signed in London on 23 March 2001, is in force.

Arbitrations do encounter difficulty when multi-party or multi-contracts are involved. A system that recognises the court's discretion to retain jurisdiction where such facets are anticipated, would allow parties a healthy selection of dispute resolution mechanisms. It is also conceivable that one contracting party's dominant position could override the other party's free will in the choice of forum, and may dilute the neutrality of the dispute resolution process before the chosen State court. The comfort derived in arbitration from the parties' appointment of the tribunal is absent in State court litigation. Arbitration has further evolved into a quasi-commercial enterprise. Whether the State court system should replicate the arbitration process is a matter requiring significant reflection, particularly in terms of access to justice. To replicate so by mandatorily staying court proceedings on account of a choice of court agreement may have the effect of removing protection against subtle economic coercion, which could undermine the ultimate principles of fairness and equality that underpin a justice system, even if in practice this is a rare encounter.

The benefits of the Choice of Court Convention lies in the certainty and harmonisation of dispute resolution practices surrounding choice of forum. These are recognised pillars that facilitate trade and reduce transactional costs. It would reduce duplication of proceedings, avoid re-litigation of the merits of the case and discourage interlocutory anti-suit injunctions, rendering greater predictability in the law. Nevertheless, there is now a greater mindfulness that reduced costs is not the only end desired. Intending for a degree of flexibility, to maintain the independence and integrity amidst a variety of dispute resolution systems is a sound aspiration. Exactly which side of the evaluation process Malaysia will weigh down on remains to be seen. Perhaps the draft Convention on the Recognition and Enforcement of Judgments in Civil and Commercial Matters, drawn by the working group on the Judgments Project of HCPIL, without the element on the recognition of a choice of court agreement, may be the acceptable middle ground. It would facilitate enforcement of foreign judgments once issued, whilst retaining the flexibility of discretion on the selection of the forum that determines the dispute. This would promote ease in enforcement of non-monetary judgments, subject to the number of countries ultimately adopting this draft Convention and thereby, affording reciprocity.

VI. Reform

The REJA recognition and enforcement of foreign judgment would benefit from greater particularisation surrounding the principles of jurisdiction of foreign courts recognised in Malaysia, where the deeming provisions do not apply. The concept of merger of the original cause of action needs to be clarified by the Malaysian courts in relation to the recognition of non-REJA judgments. Wider reciprocity would be welcomed, by expanding the list of countries under the First Schedule of REJA.

Memorandum of understanding or guidance between judiciaries on the recognition and enforcement of foreign judgments may be beneficial, as observed in the realm of cross-border insolvency through the Judicial Insolvency Network (JIN). These efforts encourage communication and collaboration between judges of various jurisdictions without compromising independence. For instance, joint hearings are now possible with the help of technology. This will help reduce multiplicity of disputes in different forums. At the very least, mutual understanding and appreciation across judicial systems can be enhanced. It could prompt the application of laws to be streamlined further, particularly surrounding issues of jurisdiction and public policy considerations.

VII. Conclusion

The REJA, coupled with the common law right of action on the judgment or on the original cause of action, provide an adequate structure for the recognition and enforcement of foreign judgments in Malaysia. The public policy exception, which is now in accordance with international practices, shows Malaysia's globalised and integrated value system. Together with the principles of comity and reciprocity, Malaysia has adopted a balanced approach to the recognition and enforcement of foreign judgments.

9

Vietnam

NGUYEN NGOC MINH, TRAN HA HAN
AND NGUYEN THI THU TRANG

I. Introduction

Foreign judgments may be recognised and enforced in Vietnam in two main circumstances. The first is where they fall within the ambit of one of a number of bilateral treaties on civil judicial assistance to which Vietnam is a signatory. The second is where recognition and enforcement is sought on a reciprocal basis. Foreign judgments, however, may only be executed through civil enforcement procedures after having been recognised by a competent local court in accordance with the 2015 Civil Procedure Code (CPC). Even if there is no challenge against recognition, the court has to be satisfied that all statutory prerequisites are met. Other mechanisms also exist to enable proactive refusal of recognition and enforcement to be sought on a foreign court judgment, even if no request for refusal has been made. In any case, the underlying substantive legal grounds are similar and there are two levels of consideration, ie first instance and appeal. Recognised foreign judgments or orders carry the same final and binding effect as their Vietnamese court equivalents. That is, they are qualified for execution under the 2008 Law on Enforcement of Civil Judgments by an enforcement agency, which is an administrative authority under the Ministry of Justice and separate from the judiciary. The Vietnamese legal framework on recognition and enforcement of foreign judgments is not very sophisticated, but the process of recognition and enforcement can still be significantly complicated and time-consuming in practice. This may be why Vietnam has not developed a large body of case law on the subject.

II. Background

The Socialist Republic of Vietnam is a country with a special geo-political position on the eastern Indochina peninsula, covering an area of approximately 331,210 km^2, sharing a border with China to the north, Laos to the northwest, Cambodia to the southwest, Thailand across the Gulf of Thailand and the Philippines, Malaysia and Indonesia across the Southeast Asia Sea. The population of Vietnam in 2018 was more than 96 million.[1] Vietnam is a one-party state, led by the Communist Party. The political system is

[1] 'Vietnam Population 2019' (*World Population Review*, 25 September 2018), available online: worldpopulationreview.com/countries/vietnam-population/.

underpinned by the principle of centralised democracy and, in theory, there is no separation of powers. All state powers are centralised in one supreme body, the National Assembly, which delegates authority to lower bodies in the hierarchy. Accordingly, the executive authority lies with the Government, which is assisted by various ministries such as the Ministry of Foreign Affairs, the Ministry of Planning and Investment, the Ministry of Finance and the Ministry of Industry and Trade. At the local level, each province, city, district or ward is administered by a People's Council, an elected body similar to the National Assembly, and a People's Committee, an executive body analogous to the national government. Each People's Committee is assisted by a number of departments corresponding to the Ministries at the central level, such as the Department of Planning and Investment.

Vietnam has adopted a civil law system, which originated from French civil law. The system has also been influenced by other legal systems, notably Soviet and Chinese laws. The main source of law is written legislation. Court judgments are not binding in subsequent cases except for some judgments selected by the Judges Council of the Supreme People's Court as precedents. There is a hierarchy of regulations in Vietnam, with laws being passed by the National Assembly, their implementing decrees issued by the government, and circulars by ministries. A large number of other legal instruments and guidelines have also been issued by various other authorities. Vietnam is party to a large number of international treaties. Under Vietnamese law, in case of inconsistency, international treaties take precedence over domestic legislation.

After a long period of closure, in 1986 Vietnam introduced the Đổi Mới (or 'economic renovation') policy which transformed Vietnam from a centrally planned economy to a socialist-oriented market economy. However, it was not until the US ended its trade embargo of Vietnam that the country had a chance to develop rapidly as seen today. It finished the first-half of 2018 with GDP growth of 7.08 per cent, towards which the service sector contributed 42 per cent (the largest share), followed by the industry and construction sectors at 34 per cent.[2] The major trading partners of Vietnam in terms of exports and imports include China, Japan, Korea and the US.[3] According to the latest statistics of the Ministry of Planning and Investment, by 20 December 2018, Vietnam had attracted 27,353 registered foreign investment projects, with a total registered capital of around US$340 billion. These investments ranged across a variety of sectors, with manufacturing, real estate, hospitality and construction being the key sectors attracting large amounts of direct foreign investment.[4]

A. Development of Private International Law

Vietnamese private international law (PIL) was established late due to several reasons. In the past, legal issues relating to foreign elements seldom arose in Vietnam. That was

[2] 'The socio-economic situation in the first 6 months of 2018' (*General Statistics Office of Vietnam*), available online: www.gso.gov.vn/default.aspx?tabid=621&ItemID=18864.

[3] The World Bank, 'Vietnam Trade at a Glance: Most Recent Values' (*World Integrated Trade Solution*, 20 February 2019), available online: wits.worldbank.org/CountrySnapshot/en/VNM.

[4] 'The situation of foreign investments in 2018' (*Ministry of Planning and Investment Foreign Investment Agency*, 25 December 2018), available online: dautunuocngoai.gov.vn/tinbai/6110/Tinh-hinh-thu-hut-Dau-tu-nuoc-ngoai-nam-2018.

because transport networks were undeveloped, so it was difficult to travel from one place to another within the country, not to mention travelling abroad. Vietnamese people had a tradition of living within their village or province and not venturing far from those places. Further, Vietnamese dynasties did not want to establish relations with foreign countries and even forbade immigrants.[5] As a result, it was not until the nineteenth century that some PIL regulations came into force in Vietnam including 'Hoang Viet laws and regulations' or 'Gia Long Code'. Those provided that Vietnamese law would apply to Vietnamese citizens even if domiciled abroad. On the other hand, Vietnamese law would apply to foreign citizens in Vietnam.[6] Today, much like other countries, Vietnam has not established or developed a separate code of PIL. Instead, it regulates PIL through provisions in various codes, laws, decrees, circulars and other legal instruments or guidance. The 1995 Civil Code is a high point in the development of PIL in that it has a specific part governing matters having foreign elements. This part for the first time provided basic principles for determining applicable law (whether Vietnamese, foreign or international law and practice) in relationships having foreign elements. These principles have been developed in the 2005 and 2015 Civil Codes.

The first legislation dealing with the recognition and enforcement of foreign judgments was Circular No 11/TATC dated 12 July 1974, in which the Supreme People's Court gave guidance on foreign divorces. Part IV of the Circular acknowledges, in the context of divorce, certain principles in recognition and enforcement of foreign judgments. Examples are that the requested court should not review the substance of the foreign judgment, but only consider whether the judgment contradicts the fundamental principles of Vietnamese law and whether there has been an effective previous judgment rendered by either a Vietnamese or foreign court on the same subject. Concurrently, Vietnam started signing bilateral treaties on mutual judicial assistance in which provisions on the recognition and enforcement of foreign judgments featured. On 17 April 1993 the National Assembly passed the Ordinance on Recognition and Enforcement of Civil Judgments and Decisions of Foreign Courts dealing exclusively with this matter. This Ordinance is complemented by Joint Circular No 04/TTLN dated 24 July 1993 issued by the Ministry of Justice, the Supreme People's Court and the Supreme People's Procuracy. These two documents comprehensively deal with issues arising out of the recognition and enforcement of foreign judgments, including types of foreign judgments, the principles of recognition and enforcement, and the procedure to be followed by the Vietnamese court. Based on these principles, the 2004 and 2015 Civil Procedure Codes provided a more thorough regulation of the recognition and enforcement of foreign judgments and arbitral awards in Vietnam.

B. Sources of Private International Law

There are two sources of private international law of Vietnam: international and domestic sources.

[5] Le Tai Trien (ed), *Commentary on Vietnamese Commercial Law* vol 1 (Bach Dang Publishing House, Saigon, 1959) 6.

[6] Hoang Viet laws and regulations (Gia Long Code) (1815) Art 195.

By way of international sources, there are international treaties and international practice.[7] Currently, Vietnam is a party to numerous PIL-related multilateral treaties or conventions. For instance, Vietnam is a Contracting State to the 1958 New York Convention on Recognition and Enforcement of Foreign Arbitral Awards. PIL regulations may also be found in bilateral treaties between Vietnam and other countries. For instance, the Mutual Legal Assistance Treaty on Civil, Family, Labour, and Criminal Matters between Vietnam and Belarus has a number of regulations on the choice of law. Article 18 of the Mutual Legal Assistance Treaty on Civil and Criminal Matters between Vietnam and China stipulates a rule for determining which court has jurisdiction to hear a dispute in specified circumstances. For example, if a respondent has its representative office in one state at the commencement of proceedings, the court of that state will have jurisdiction to hear the dispute. On international practice, Article 666 of the 2015 Civil Code allows the parties in a relationship having foreign elements to choose to apply international practice to the extent that the parties have the right to choose the applicable law to their relationship, unless the consequence of such choice will violate the fundamental principles of Vietnamese law. Article 5(2) of the 2015 Maritime Code provides that, in a contract for maritime operations, in which one party is foreign, there is a right to choose which foreign law or international maritime practice will govern the contracts. In practice, the courts have used international practice to decide the merits of a case. In Decision No 02/2005/KT-ST (22 August 2005) of the People's Court of Khanh Hoa, the court applied the ICC Uniform Customs and Practice for Documentary Credits (UCP 500) to settle a dispute between two parties on a letter of credit. Although whether UCP 500 was actually applicable in the situation remains an open question in Vietnamese law, it is interesting that the court was prepared to consider not just foreign law, but also international practice.

By way of domestic sources, Vietnamese PIL provisions may be found in the codes and laws passed by the National Assembly. Both the 2015 Civil Code and the CPC have parts on matters having foreign elements. For example, Part 5 of the 2015 Civil Code contains a general rule on the application of treaties, international practice and foreign law in specified circumstances, as well as choice of laws rules applicable in cases of contract, tort, intellectual property, etc. Part 8 of the CPC includes general rules for civil cases with foreign elements, such as on the general and exclusive jurisdictions of the courts, stays of proceedings in support of arbitration or choice of court agreement, etc. PIL regulations can also be found in laws and bye-laws, such as the 2014 Law on Marriage and Family, the 2012 Labour Code, etc.

C. Judicial System

The framework for the judicial system is found in the CPC and the 2014 Law on Organisation of People's Courts, where the District Courts have jurisdiction to resolve most civil cases at first instance. The Provincial Courts have jurisdiction to resolve civil disputes which do not fall within the jurisdiction of the District Courts as well as disputes in which the litigants or assets are abroad or there is need for a legal mandate. The Provincial Courts also

[7] See 2015 Civil Code, Art 664; Civil Procedure Code, Art 2(3).

have jurisdiction to review certain judgments of the District Courts. The High Courts have jurisdiction to review certain judgments of the Provincial Courts and the District Courts. There are three High Courts. They are akin to circuit courts in other jurisdictions in the sense that each of them has geographical jurisdiction over a number of provinces. The Supreme Court has jurisdiction to review specified judgments of the lower courts. A court's jurisdiction may be determined by territory, usually the place where a respondent has a domicile, the place where a contract is to be performed, and so on. By Articles 37(1)(b) and 39(2)(d) of the CPC, the Provincial Court of the place where a judgment debtor resides or works has jurisdiction to consider application for a foreign judgment to be recognised and enforced. For instance, if the judgment debtor has a registered office in District 1 of Ho Chi Minh City, the court having jurisdiction to resolve an application for recognition and enforcement would be the court of Ho Chi Minh City. The court having jurisdiction to hear the matter on appeal would be the High Court in Ho Chi Minh City.

D. Types of Enforceable Judgments

By Articles 27(5), 29(9), 31(4) and 33(3) of the CPC, foreign judgments on civil, matrimonial, commercial and labour matters may be recognised and enforced in Vietnam. Thus, the scope for recognition and enforcement appears to be wide. Article 423 of the CPC confirms this. Chapter XXXIV of the CPC is entitled Procedure to Consider the Application for the Recognition and Enforcement of Foreign Civil Judgments. Although the chapter name does not include marital, family, commercial and labour judgments, from the content of the chapter (including Article 423), it is clear that it should be understood as applying to such judgments. The meaning of civil, matrimonial, commercial and labour judgments can be found in the legislation. Article 3 of the 2012 Labour Code reads that 'labour dispute means a dispute over rights, obligations or interests which arise between the parties in employment relation'. This article also provides the definition of employment relation as 'a social relation arising from the hiring or employment and wage payment between an employee and an employer'. Regarding civil relations, Article 1 of the 2015 Civil Code states that civil relations are 'relations established on the basis of equality, freedom of will, independence of property and self-responsibility'. Under Article 3 of the 2014 Law on Marriage and Family, 'marriage means the relation between husband and wife after they get married' and 'family means a group of persons closely bound together by marriage, blood ties or raising relations, thus giving rise to obligations and rights among them as prescribed in this Law'. Article 3 of the 2005 Commercial Law defines commercial activities as 'activities for the purpose of generating profits, including: sale and purchase of goods, provision of services, investment, commercial promotion and other activities for the profit purpose'.

III. Recognition and Enforcement under Treaties or Similar Arrangements

Pursuant to Article 423(1)(a) of the 2015 Civil Procedure Code, there should be recognition and enforcement of foreign judgments in compliance with the treaties to which Vietnam is a signatory. Where there is a difference between the treaties and national law on the same subject, the treaties are to prevail.[8] Therefore, when receiving an application for the recognition and enforcement of a foreign judgment, the Vietnamese competent authorities will first have to check whether the judgment was rendered in a jurisdiction with which Vietnam has a treaty.[9] As at July 2017, Vietnam had concluded bilateral treaties on mutual judicial assistance in civil matters which include the provisions on the recognition and enforcement of foreign judgments as follows:[10]

Table 1 Bilateral treaties on mutual judicial assistance in civil matters which include the provisions on the recognition and enforcement of foreign judgments concluded between Vietnam and other countries

	Country	Treaty	Date of signature
1	Algeria	Treaty on Mutual Judicial Assistance in Civil and Commercial Matters between the Socialist Republic of Viet Nam and the People's Democratic Republic of Algeria	14 April 2010
2	Belarus	Treaty on Mutual Legal Assistance in Civil, Family, Labour and Criminal Matters between the Socialist Republic of Vietnam and the Republic of Belarus	14 September 2000
3	Bulgaria	Treaty on Mutual Legal Assistance in Civil, Family and Criminal Matters between the Socialist Republic of Vietnam and the People's Republic of Bulgaria	03 October 1986
4	Cambodia	Treaty on Mutual Legal Assistance in Civil Matters between the Socialist Republic of Vietnam and the Kingdom of Cambodia	21 January 2013
5	China	Treaty on Mutual Assistance on Civil and Criminal Matters between the Socialist Republic of Vietnam and the People's Republic of China	19 October 1998
6	Cuba	Treaty on Mutual Legal Assistance in Civil, Family, Labour and Criminal Matters between the Socialist Republic of Vietnam and the Republic of Cuba	30 November 1984
7	Czech Republic & Slovakia	Treaty on Mutual Assistance on Civil and Criminal Matters between the Socialist Republic of Vietnam and the Socialist Republic of Czechoslovakia	12 October 1982
8	France	Treaty on Mutual Assistance on Civil Matters between the Socialist Republic of Vietnam and the French Republic	24 February 1999
9	Hungary	Treaty on Mutual Assistance on Civil, Family and Criminal Matters between the Socialist Republic of Vietnam and the People's Republic of Hungary	18 January 1985

(continued)

[8] 2016 Law on Treaties, Art 6(1).

[9] See spc.toaan.gov.vn/portal/pls/portal/docs/701340.PDF, 24.

[10] See lanhsuvietnam.gov.vn/Lists/BaiViet/B%C3%A0i%20vi%E1%BA%Bft/DispForm.aspx?List=dc7c7d75-6a32-4215-afeb-47d4bee700eee&ID=414.

Table 1 *(Continued)*

	Country	Treaty	Date of signature
10	Kazakhstan	Treaty on Mutual Judicial Assistance in Civil Matters between the Socialist Republic of Viet Nam and the Republic of Kazakhstan	31 October 2011
11	Laos	Treaty on Mutual Assistance on Civil and Criminal Matters between the Socialist Republic of Vietnam and the Lao People's Democratic Republic	06 July 1998
12	Mongolia	Treaty on Mutual Assistance on Civil, Family and Criminal Matters between the Socialist Republic of Vietnam and the Mongolian People's Republic	17 April 2000
13	North Korea	Treaty on Mutual Assistance on Civil and Criminal Matters between the Socialist Republic of Vietnam and the Democratic People's Republic of Korea	04 May 2002
14	Poland	Treaty on Mutual Legal Assistance in Civil, Family and Criminal Matters between the Socialist Republic of Vietnam and the Republic of Poland	22 March 1993
15	Russia	Treaty on Mutual Assistance on Civil and Criminal Matters between the Socialist Republic of Vietnam and the Russian Federation	25 August 1998
		Protocol to the Agreement on Mutual Assistance on Civil and Criminal Matters between the Socialist Republic of Vietnam and the Russian Federation	23 April 2003
16	Taiwan	Agreement between Vietnam Economic and Cultural Office in Taipei and Taipei Economic and Cultural Office in Vietnam on mutual legal assistance in civil matters	12 April 2010
17	Ukraine	Treaty on Mutual Assistance on Civil and Criminal Matters between the Socialist Republic of Vietnam and the Ukrainian Republic	06 April 2000

Vietnam is presently negotiating agreements on mutual judicial assistance in civil matters with Thailand and South Korea.[11] Vietnam is not party to the 2005 Hague Convention on Choice of Court Agreements or any multilateral treaty on the recognition and enforcement of foreign judgments.

Normally, the conditions set out under the foregoing bilateral treaties are not stricter or higher than the conditions set out under national law.[12] Most of the treaties have at least one provision clarifying the types of judgments that can be recognised and enforced,

[11] 'Press Release: Joint Press Statement on the Official Visit of His Excellency Mr Nguyen Xuan Phuc, Prime Minister of the Socialist Republic of Viet Nam to the Kingdom of Thailand 17–19 August 2017, Bangkok' (*Ministry of Foreign Affairs of the Kingdom of Thailand*, 18 August 2017), available online: www.mfa.go.th/main/en/news3/6886/80416-Joint-Press-Statement-on-the-Official-Visit-of-His.html; 'Việt-Hàn thúc đẩy ký kết hiệp định tương trợ tư pháp trong thương mại' (Vietnam and South Korea Promote the Signing of Judicial Assistance Agreement in Commercial Matters), 21 November 2017, available online: vietnam.vnanet.vn/vietnamese/viet-han-thuc-day-ky-ket-hiep-dinh-tuong-tro-tu-phap-trong-thuong-mai/358312.html [in Vietnamese].

[12] See spc.toaan.gov.vn/portal/pls/portal/docs/701340.PDF [in Vietnamese], 12.

but the provisions are not always identical. Generally, the judgments must concern civil, family or labour matters.[13] Such judgments are categorised into two groups: monetary and non-monetary judgments. Each group is subject to different recognition and enforcement procedures. None of the treaties defines or differentiates between 'monetary' and 'non-monetary' judgments. Under some treaties, 'monetary judgments' include both judgments rendered by the court and mediated agreements recognised by the court,[14] whereas under some others they are limited to court judgments only.[15] Similarly, some treaties provide that 'non-monetary judgments' can be issued by courts or other authorities (such as judicial authorities, registrars of births, marriages and deaths).[16] But other treaties narrow them down to the ones rendered by the courts only.[17]

It is a mandatory requirement of Vietnamese law that a foreign judgment be rendered by a competent court (that is, the court should have 'indirect jurisdiction'). However, the grounds to determine whether a rendering court had jurisdiction to decide a matter are not consistent among treaties. More specifically, depending on the treaty, a requested court can determine the indirect jurisdiction of the rendering court based on the law of the enforcing state, the law of the rendering state or the requirements set out under a treaty itself.[18] Moreover, while some treaties explicitly state that a requested court shall not make a substantive review of a foreign judgment,[19] under some treaties a requested court will have to review the substance of the foreign judgment to make sure that it is proper to be recognised and enforced in the requested state. In such cases, the substance of the foreign judgment must typically not infringe one or more of the exclusive jurisdiction,[20] public policy[21] or previous judgments[22] of the requested state. For foreign judgments to be recognised and enforced,

[13] Agreement between Vietnam and Cuba, Art 46; Agreement between Vietnam and Laos, Art 44(1); Agreement between Vietnam Economic and Cultural Office in Taipei and Taipei Economic and Cultural Office in Vietnam, Art 19.

[14] For example, Agreement between Vietnam and the Russian Federation, Art 52(2); Agreement between Vietnam and Mongolia, Art 43; Agreement between Vietnam and Belarus, Art 57(2).

[15] For example, Agreement between Vietnam and Cuba, Art 46; Agreement between Vietnam and Kazakhstan, Art 24(1); Agreement between Vietnam and Cambodia, Art 21.

[16] For example, Agreement between Vietnam and Cuba, Art 47; Agreement between Vietnam and Hungary, Art 51(2); Agreement between Vietnam and Bulgaria, Art 47.

[17] For example, Agreement between Vietnam and Kazakhstan, Art 23; Agreement between Vietnam and Cambodia, Art 20.

[18] For example, Agreement between Vietnam and Czechoslovakia, Art 47(1)(b); Agreement between Vietnam and Laos, Art 45(2); Agreement between Vietnam and France, Art 21(1).

[19] For example, Agreement between Vietnam and Algeria, Art 18(2); Agreement between Vietnam and Kazakhstan, Article 27(2).

[20] For example, Agreement between Vietnam and Poland, Art 45(a); Agreement between Vietnam and Kazakhstan, Art 25(i). The treaties rarely specify the issues that fall within the exclusive jurisdiction of a Contracting State. Under 2015 Civil Procedure Code, Art 470, the Vietnamese courts have exclusive jurisdiction over a case which: (1) relates to immovable property in Vietnam; (2) involves a divorce between a Vietnamese citizen and a foreigner or a stateless person if their long-term domicile is Vietnam; or (3) the Vietnamese court has been chosen by the parties.

[21] For example, Agreement between Vietnam and France, Art 21(5); Agreement between the Vietnam and North Korea, Art 30(1)(2). Both treaties require that the substance of judgments, rather than their recognition and enforcement, must not infringe the fundamental principles and public order of Vietnam. But, under Vietnamese law, the concepts of 'fundamental principles' and 'public order' are ambiguous and controversial.

[22] For example, Agreement between Vietnam and Hungary, Art 55(2); Agreement between Vietnam and Bulgaria, Art 54(c). These treaties provide that foreign judgments will be refused recognition and enforcement if

almost all treaties prescribe a condition of due process. Accordingly, a judgment may not be recognised if the defendant was not given a reasonable opportunity to be heard by the rendering court. To that end, the enforcing court will review the service of process in the original proceedings. If the defendant was not properly served with the document instituting a claim, the application for recognition and enforcement will be denied.

The treaties usually differentiate between recognition and enforcement procedures. Accordingly, recognition of a foreign judgment can be sought separately or as a preliminary to enforcement proceedings. The question of whether a party will seek recognition of a foreign judgment only or both recognition and enforcement of the judgment depends on the nature and the content of the judgment. Non-monetary judgments are not usually enforceable, since the treaties only regulate recognition. Those judgments will be recognised provided that the authorities of the requested state: (1) have not rendered or recognised another judgment on the same matter parties; and (2) do not have exclusive jurisdiction over the dispute. In contrast, for monetary judgments, the treaties provide for both recognition and enforcement procedures. A majority of these treaties identify the authority which has the jurisdiction to decide on recognition and enforcement to be the judicial authority where the judgment is to be recognised and enforced.[23] But that authority is not always the place where the application is filed by the judgment creditor. According to the treaties, judgment creditors may make an application for recognition and enforcement to the competent authority in the enforcing state, the first instance court which rendered the judgment, or both. When the rendered court receives the application, they are to transfer it to the competent authority in the enforcing state. The treaties do not provide a specific limitation period for the enforcement of a foreign judgment. Some treaties stipulate that the foreign judgment must have been made within the limitation period for enforcement under the laws of the rendering state and an application for recognition and enforcement of a foreign judgment must be submitted within that period. At the same time, pursuant to CPC Article 432(1), the statute of limitation to request a Vietnamese authority to recognise and enforce a foreign judgment is three years from the time when the judgment became effective.

A special form is required for all applications for recognition and enforcement. Almost all treaties specify the documents that need to be submitted together with the form. The documents that are frequently required under the treaties include (1) a copy of the foreign judgment; (2) a document certifying that the judgment is effective; (3) a document certifying that a copy of the judgment has been served on the judgment debtor; and (4) a document certifying that the judgment debtor was summoned properly. Otherwise, if the treaty does not specify the necessary documents for recognition and enforcement, the judgment creditor will need to submit the documents required under CPC Article 434.

the substance or merits of a judgment contradict an effective judgment on the same subject matter between the same parties rendered or recognised by the judicial authorities of the requested state. Thus, even when a judicial authority of a requested state has rendered an effective judgment on the same subject matter between the same parties, the foreign judgment may still be recognised if the two judgments are reconcilable.

[23] For example, Agreement between Vietnam and Bulgaria, Art 48(2); Agreement between Vietnam and Ukraine, Art 42(1).

IV. Recognition and Enforcement in the Absence of Treaties or Similar Arrangements

Recognition and enforcement are different procedures under Vietnamese law. Before a foreign judgment can be enforced in Vietnam, it must be recognised by the Vietnamese court under the procedure for recognition of foreign judgment in Chapters XXXV and XXXVI of the CPC. Once a foreign judgment has been recognised, it has the same effect as a domestic judgment and is eligible for enforcement or execution by the State Agency for Enforcement of Civil Judgments. The enforcement procedure is regulated by the 2008 Law on Enforcement of Civil Judgments as amended in 2014. Besides the procedure for recognition of foreign judgments, the CPC also provides separate procedures for requests for the denial of recognition to foreign judgments.

A. Recognition Generally

A foreign judgment will only be exempted from the procedure of recognition if it is expressly stipulated by a judicial assistance treaty that such type of judgment can automatically be enforced in Vietnam and there is no request for the denial of recognition to such judgment. In the absence of judicial assistance treaties, the formal procedure for recognition by the local court will be applicable to a foreign judgment. Judgment creditors are entitled to request recognition of a foreign judgment if (1) the judgment debtor is an individual residing or working in Vietnam or an agency or organisation headquartered in Vietnam or (2) the judgment debtor's property against which is sought exists in Vietnam at the time when an application is filed. To request recognition, the judgment creditors are required to submit an application. The application must identify the judgment creditor and debtor and the specific request of the judgment creditors. It must include: (1) an original or copy of the foreign judgment; and (2) documents issued by competent foreign authorities certifying that the foreign judgment has taken legal effect and has not expired and that due process has been followed. All documents must be duly notarised, legalised and accompanied by Vietnamese translations. The court having jurisdiction to consider the application for recognition of foreign judgments at first instance is the city and provincial court where a judgment debtor resides or works in Vietnam in the case of individuals or is headquartered in the case of agencies or organisations, or where the property relating to the enforcement is situated. The decision of the first instance court may be subject to review by the High Court upon appeal by either party or as a result of the protest of the procuracy. The first instance proceedings should take up to seven months in theory.[24] However, judging from the actual

[24] CPC, Art 436 states:

> Within *05 working days* from the day on which the dossiers transferred from the Ministry of Justice are received or from the day on which the dossiers sent from the applicants are received, the Courts shall rely on Articles 363, 364 and 365 of this Code to consider and accept the dossiers and notify such to the applicants, the judgment debtors or their lawful representatives in Vietnam, the Procuracies of the same levels and the Ministry of Justice.'

practice of Vietnamese courts, the proceedings take around one year on average. The appellate proceedings can take up to four months in theory.[25] But the actual time for an appeal decision to be issued can be from six months to a year.

The key provision on the recognition of foreign civil judgments is found in CPC Article 439. The provision lists the types of judgments that will not be recognised in Vietnam, namely:

1. Judgments that do not satisfy the conditions for recognition set out in treaties to which Vietnam is a signatory;
2. Judgments that have not taken legal effect under the law of the rendering state;
3. Default judgments resulting from the debtor not having been duly summoned or court documents not having been delivered in reasonable time under the law of the rendering state, thereby preventing the debtor from exercising the right to self-defence;
4. Judgments issued by a rendering court that lacked jurisdiction as prescribed by CPC Article 440;
5. Judgments in matters that:
   (a) have been settled by legally effective decisions of the Vietnamese courts;
   (b) were brought before the Vietnamese courts prior to being litigated in the rendering state and that remain ongoing before the Vietnamese courts; or
   (c) have been settled by judgments of the courts of third countries which have been recognised by the Vietnamese courts;
6. Judgments for which the time limit for enforcement as prescribed by the law of the rendering state has expired;
7. Judgments that have been set aside or terminated in the rendering state; and
8. Judgments for which recognition would be contrary to the fundamental principles of Vietnamese law.

CPC, Art 437 states:

> …
>
> 3. Time limit for preparation for consideration of an application shall be *04 months* from the day on which it is accepted. Within such time limit, on a case-by-case basis, the Court shall issue one of the following decisions:
>
> (a) To suspend the consideration of the application;
> (b) To terminate the consideration of the application;
> (c) To open a hearing for considering the application.
>
> If the Court requests for explanation as provided for in clause 1 of this Article, time limit for consideration of the application *may be extended but not for over 02 months*. …
>
> The Court shall have to open a hearing for considering the application within *01 month* after issuing a decision to open a hearing for considering the application. (emphasis added)

[25] CPC, Art 442 states:

> 1. Within … *15 days* after the day on which the Court renders a decision to recognize and enforce or a decision not to recognize and enforce a judgment, decision of a foreign court, the litigants and their lawful representatives shall have the right to appeal against that decision … (emphasis added)

CPC, Art 443 states:

> 1. High People's Court shall consider the decision of the provincial People's Court which is appealed against within its jurisdiction within *01 month* from the day on which the documents are received; if explanation is required as prescribed in clauses 1 and 2 Article 437 of this Code, such time limit *may be extended but not for over 02 months*. (emphasis added)

Reference should also be made to CPC Article 440. That stipulates when, under Vietnamese law, a rendering court will be treated as having jurisdiction to settle a civil case. A foreign court will have such jurisdiction where:

1. The civil case does not fall within the exclusive jurisdiction of Vietnam's courts as specified in CPC Article 470;[26]
2. The civil case falls within CPC Article 469[27] but at least one of the following conditions is satisfied:
   (a) The defendant has participated in oral argument without appeal against the jurisdiction of the foreign court;
   (b) There is no judgment by the court of a third country for such civil case that has been recognised and enforced by the Vietnamese court; or
   (c) The civil case was accepted by the rendering court before being accepted by the Vietnamese court.

i. Recognition Based on Reciprocity

CPC section 423(1)(b) specifies that, in the absence of an express provision in a treaty, the recognition and enforcement of foreign judgments shall be considered based on the principle of reciprocity. But there is no detailed guidance on how reciprocity is to be determined. On the basis of international practice, the Ministry of Justice has unofficially suggested[28] that reciprocity should be applied in consideration of the following elements: (1) diplomatic and economic relations between Vietnam and the originating country; (2) the sovereignty and interests of Vietnam; (3) the particular relations of each case; (4) the rights and interests of the relevant parties, especially any Vietnamese parties. It is expected that the Supreme Court will issue official guidance on this issue in the future taking into consideration the suggestions of the Ministry of Justice.

ii. Recognition will be Refused Due to Lack of Due Process

One of the grounds for refusal of recognition of foreign judgments would seem to be violation of due process. This may be inferred from CPC Article 439 which expressly stipulates that recognition may be refused if the judgment debtor was absent from or unrepresented at hearings because he or she had not been duly summoned or the documents of the foreign court had not been properly served as prescribed by the law of the originating state. Judgment creditors are thus required to prove that judgment debtors were duly summoned to attend the hearing in the originating state. Furthermore, in case the judgment debtor was

[26] For example, under CPC Art 470, the Vietnamese courts have exclusive jurisdiction over cases which: (1) relate to immovable property in Vietnam; (2) involves a divorce between a Vietnamese citizen and a foreigner if their long-term domicile is Vietnam; or (3) the Vietnamese court has been chosen by the parties.

[27] CPC Art 469 sets out the situations when a Vietnamese court has 'common jurisdiction' to resolve civil cases involving foreign elements. For instance, the Vietnamese courts have common jurisdiction in cases with foreign elements where (1) the defendant is an individual who resides, works or has lived for a long period in Vietnam; (2) the defendant is an agency or organisation headquartered in Vietnam or the defendant is an agency or organisation that has a branch or a representative office in Vietnam; or (3) the defendant owns property in Vietnam.

[28] Letter No 4609/BTP-PLQT of the Ministry of Justice to the Supreme People's Court dated 3 October 2017 on the application of the reciprocity principle.

absent from a hearing, the judgment creditor must prove that the relevant court notices were served in an appropriate manner and in sufficient time to enable the debtor to present a defence. Such proof must be made through an official letter of the court certifying that the service of documents was duly conducted in accordance with the law of the originating state.

iii. Recognition should not be Contrary to 'Public Policy'

The concept of 'public policy' in Vietnam is treated as equivalent to the 'fundamental principles of Vietnamese laws'.[29] Accordingly, recognition will be denied if that would be contrary to the fundamental principles of Vietnamese laws. Nevertheless, the precise ambit of the 'fundamental principles of Vietnamese laws' has never been clarified in legislation. The concept of the 'fundamental principles of Vietnamese laws' has only ever been discussed in Resolution No 01/2014/NQ-HDTP of the Council of Judges of the Supreme People's Court Guiding the Implementation of Certain Provisions of the 2010 Law on Commercial Arbitration (Resolution No 01). By Article 14(2)(dd) of Resolution No 01, the 'fundamental principles of Vietnamese law' is defined as 'the effective basic rules for the formulation and implementation of Vietnamese laws'. Under the same provision, the following actions are characterised as examples of contraventions of the fundamental principles of Vietnamese laws:

1. The parties concerned have an agreement that does not contravene the law or social ethics, but the arbitral tribunal does not recognise such agreement in an award. In such case, the award violates the right to enter into free and voluntary business agreements prescribed by Article 11 of the Law on Commerce and Article 4 of the Civil Code. The court should thus consider setting aside the arbitral award because it contravenes a basic rule of Vietnam's law which is prescribed in the Law on Commerce and the Civil Code.
2. A party to a dispute provides evidence that an award was obtained through coercion, fraud, threats or bribery. In such case, the award would violate the rule that arbitrators must be independent, objective, and impartial prescribed by Article 4(2) of the 2010 Law on Commercial Arbitration.

Such guidance is still unclear and arguably only applies to arbitral awards. It is unsure whether Resolution No 01 can be applied generally in the context of the recognition and enforcement of foreign judgments. At the moment, it may only provide a point of reference for foreign judgments.

iv. Partial Recognition

There is no provision under Vietnamese law providing for the recognition of only part of a judgment. That means that if any one of the grounds for refusal has been made out, recognition of the whole judgment will be refused. Note further that, although not expressly set out in Vietnamese law, it will not be possible to have a foreign judgment 'recognised'

[29] Resolution No 01/2014/NQ-HDTP of the Council of Judges of the Supreme People's Court Guiding the Implementation of Certain Provisions of the 2010 Law on Commercial Arbitration.

by bringing a claim for debt as evidenced by the judgment before the Vietnamese court. If such a claim were brought, the court will likely dismiss it on the ground that the matter has already been settled by an effective judgment. The proper and only course would be to go through the recognition and enforcement procedures described above.

v. Interlocutory Judgments

There is no specific procedure applicable to the recognition of interlocutory judgments. Foreign interlocutory judgments (such as an order for interim relief) must also undergo the formal procedures set out here for recognition in Vietnam. In practice, it would be impractical to request recognition of interlocutory judgments as the formal procedures take time, ranging from six months to a year, so that the urgency called for in applications for interim relief would be defeated.

B. Enforcement

The procedure for enforcement is totally separate from the procedure for recognition and is conducted by the State Agency for Enforcement of Civil Judgments, which is under the Ministry of Justice. The time limit for a request for enforcement of an effective judgment is five years from the date when the judgment takes effect. In order to enforce a foreign judgment once recognised by the court, the judgments creditor must file an application to the competent enforcement agency. The head of the enforcement agency will then issue a decision for enforcement of the judgment and notify the judgments debtor about such decision. Upon the receipt of the decision, the judgment debtor will have 10 days to voluntarily execute the judgment. Within 10 days from the expiry of the period for voluntary execution, the enforcement agency will conduct a verification of the debtor's ability to execute a judgment. If the debtor is assessed as having capacity to execute the judgment, the enforcement agency will execute the judgment against the debtor. In case the judgment debtor does not have capacity, the enforcement shall be postponed and the enforcement agency will review its assessment of the debtor's capacity every six months. The enforcement will be terminated in certain circumstances, such as where the judgment debtor is an organisation which has been dissolved and which has no assets. The time for enforcement cannot be anticipated with accuracy as it will depend on the judgment debtor's capacity for execution. It can take considerable time, years in some cases, from the submission of the request for enforcement until completion of execution. Enforcement is often delayed due to one or more of the following reasons: (1) the judgments debtor is incapable of executing the judgments; (2) it is impossible to identify the debtor's assets or the debtor has dissipated assets; and/or (3) the debtor has become involved in insolvency proceedings or there are disputes with other creditors.

V. Special Cases

According to some local judges, the number of foreign judgments relating to civil matters with an application made for recognition and enforcement in Vietnam is minimal, especially foreign judgments relating to intellectual property rights (IPRs), land situated in Vietnam, environmental wrongs and competition law. The local courts have mainly dealt with the recognition and enforcement of foreign judgments relating to marriage and family. To illustrate, in 2017, the judges of the Ho Chi Minh City Court only handled two cases on recognition and enforcement of foreign judgments. They were related to the disposal of mortgaged assets under a foreign loan, and both cases were accepted. Thus, much of what will be said below about the recognition of judgments in specific situations can only be speculative, in light of current provisions of Vietnamese law.

A. Enforcement of Foreign Judgments on IPRs

According to the laws of Vietnam, IPRs are governed by substantive laws including the 2015 Civil Code (general legislation) and the 2005 Law on Intellectual Property as amended in 2009 (specialised legislation). The Civil Code provides: 'The intellectual property rights shall be determined in accordance with the laws of the country in which the objects of the intellectual property rights are required to be protected'.[30] The expression 'the laws of the country in which the objects of the intellectual property rights are required to be protected' may be construed as including the laws of Vietnam (the enforcing state) where IPRs are registered for the first time or the laws of a foreign jurisdiction where IPRs are required to be registered for their protection after a first time registration in Vietnam. As a result, if a judgment relates to IPRs registered in Vietnam, the recognition and enforcement of the foreign judgments shall be considered in accordance with the laws of Vietnam, possibly even in terms of the merits of a case. The Law on Intellectual Property does not provide for jurisdiction and procedure to resolve IPR disputes. These matters shall instead be considered in accordance with the CPC and the international treaties to which Vietnam is a party.

By CPC Article 30(2), the courts of Vietnam have jurisdiction to resolve IPR disputes in accordance with the procedures in the CPC. The registration of IPRs in Vietnam may also be considered as 'acts performed in Vietnam' or 'civil relations which are established, changed or terminated in Vietnam'. Therefore, by CPC Article 469(1)(dd), the Vietnamese courts would have common jurisdiction to resolve disputes over IPRs registered in Vietnam. On that basis, foreign judgments relating to such IPRs may be refused recognition and enforcement, especially if the Vietnamese party challenged the rendering court's jurisdiction in accordance with CPC Articles 439(4) and 440(2). The international treaties to which Vietnam is a party, such as the TRIPS Agreement[31] (Article 64), the Berne Convention[32] (Article 33), the Paris Convention (Article 28) and the 2000 Bilateral Agreement between Vietnam and the United States of America (Chapter II), do not stipulate a jurisdiction for the resolution of IPR disputes between the courts of Member States. Therefore, where a foreign court issues a judgment relating to IPRs registered in Vietnam, such judgment may be refused recognition and enforcement if it falls among the exceptions in CPC Articles 439(4) and 440(2). Article 679 of the 2015 Civil Code provides that '[t]he intellectual

[30] 2015 Civil Code, Art 679.

[31] Vietnam became a party to the TRIPS Agreement on 7 November 2006.

[32] Vietnam acceded to the Berne Convention on 26 October 2004 in accordance with Presidential Resolution No 332/2004/QD-CTN (7 June 2004).

property rights shall be determined in accordance with the laws of the country in which the objects of the intellectual property rights are required to be protected'. If IPRs are registered elsewhere, foreign laws may govern them. In such case, judgments relating to IPRs registered in a foreign country may be considered for recognition and enforcement in Vietnam if they satisfy the general conditions that have been already discussed.

B. Judgments Relating to Land

As land is a valuable asset and its ownership may affect the security, politics and sovereignty of a country, it is strictly regulated under the laws of Vietnam. Under CPC Articles 439(4), 440(1) and 470(1)(a), disputes relating to land in Vietnam fall within the exclusive jurisdiction of the Vietnamese courts. If a foreign court issues a judgment in a dispute relating to Vietnamese land, the judgment will not be recognised. This is also reflected in the treaties between Vietnam and other states (for example, China and Russia).[33] If a foreign judgment relates to land outside Vietnam, the courts will not have exclusive jurisdiction on such property.

C. Judgments Relating to Environmental Damage

Environmental wrongs may seriously affect the interests of the country as well as harm the public. The matter is therefore specially regulated by the Law on Environmental Protection No 55/2014/QH13 (23 June 2014). Article 161(4) of that law states:

> Environmental disputes that take place within the Socialist Republic of Vietnam in which either or both of the parties are foreign organization or individual shall be settled in accordance with the law of the Socialist Republic of Vietnam except otherwise as stipulated in the international treaty of which the Socialist Republic of Vietnam is a member.

The Law on Environmental Protection also defines the environmental disputes to include: (1) disputes over rights and responsibility for environmental protection insofar as concerns the exploitation and use of environmental components; and (2) disputes over responsibility for handling and remedying the consequences of and compensating for environmental pollution and degradation. The CPC does not particularly provide for the jurisdiction of the Vietnamese courts to resolve disputes relating to environmental wrongs. But such disputes are likely to be considered as civil in nature. Where an environmental incident happens in Vietnam, it may then be regarded as 'acts performed in Vietnam' or 'civil relations which are established, changed or terminated in Vietnam', so the courts will have ordinary jurisdiction to resolve the dispute under CPC Article 469(1)(dd). The Vietnamese court may then refuse to recognise a foreign judgment on the dispute in accordance with CPC Articles 439(4) and 440(2), especially if a Vietnamese party has challenged the jurisdiction of the foreign court in proceedings there. But, as damage caused by an environmental wrong may affect the public interest of Vietnam, it is also possible that the

[33] Agreement between Vietnam and China, Arts 17(1), 18(1), 18(2); Agreement between Vietnam and the Russian Federation, Arts 35 and 53(2).

Vietnamese court will apply Article 3(4) of the 2015 Civil Code[34] and refuse recognition outright on the basis that the foreign judgment violates the fundamental principles or public policy of Vietnamese law.

The court will consider recognition and enforcement of a judgment relating to damage from an environmental wrong committed in a foreign country in the same way that it deals with foreign judgments on other matters.

D. Judgments Relating to Competition Law

Vietnamese courts may refuse to recognise foreign judgments relating to Vietnamese competition law for the reason that they contradict the fundamental principles of Vietnamese law. An important point that may influence the courts' attitude is that the procedure to resolve a competition case under Vietnamese law is different from the procedure to resolve other civil cases. According to Article 58 of the 2004 Law on Competition and Decree No 116/2005/ND-CP providing guidance on provisions of that law, if organisations and individuals (including foreign organisations in Vietnam) consider that their rights and interests have been infringed as a result of anti-competitive practices, they should lodge a complaint to resolve the complaint in accordance with Chapter 5 of the 2004 Law and Chapter III of Decree No 116/2005/ND-CP. The resolution of the complaint will then be handled by the Administrative Body for Competition and the Competition Council. The courts will not have jurisdiction to resolve the complaint. The courts will only have jurisdiction if (1) the complainant disagrees with the decision of the Administrative Body for Competition and the Competition Council or (2) the application of administrative preventive measures do not conform with the regulations on competition. This practice may lead to a perception among Vietnamese judges that a foreign decision involving the violation of Vietnamese competition law is by nature not a court judgment and so does not qualify for recognition in Vietnam. So far there has not been an application for recognition of such foreign decision to verify what the courts' attitude will be.

A foreign judgment in respect of a breach of foreign competition law may still be refused recognition and enforcement if it contradicts Vietnamese competition law. In addition, the judgment might not be regarded as a court judgment qualifying for recognition.

VI. The Future

A. Prospects

Vietnam has not ratified the 1971 Hague Convention on the Recognition and Enforcement of Foreign Judgments in Civil and Commercial Matters (1971 Hague Convention) or the 2005 Hague Convention on Choice of Court Agreements (2005 Hague Convention).

[34] Art 3(4) of the 2015 Civil Code states: 'The establishment, exercise and termination of civil rights and/or obligations may not infringe national interests, public interests, lawful rights and interests of other persons.'

There is some prospect that Vietnam may consider acceding to these Conventions. First, Vietnam became a member of the Hague Conference on Private International Law on 10 April 2013.[35] As a member, Vietnam has enjoyed the support and network of Central Authorities, the provision of assistance to Member States, and the training and support services provided by the Hague Conference's Permanent Bureau. This has contributed to raise awareness of the benefits of accession to Hague Conventions generally. Second, comparing the number of states with which Vietnam has concluded treaties in civil and commercial matters with and the number of foreign civil judgments likely to be enforced in Vietnam in the future as its economy grows, Vietnam will need a multilateral regime for cross-border civil legal assistance to avoid the difficulties in resolving transnational and international disputes, including the enforceability of foreign civil judgments in Vietnam and vice versa. As has been seen, Vietnam has only concluded treaties dealing with the recognition and enforcement of judgments with 17 jurisdictions.[36] Meanwhile, from 1994 to 2011, the Ministry of Justice of Vietnam received about 220 applications for the recognition and enforcement of foreign civil judgments or decisions in Vietnam out of which almost no foreign civil judgment has been recognised and enforced in Vietnam.[37] Third, Vietnamese law recognises choice of court agreements between parties in civil relations with foreign-related elements.[38] The CPC's chapter on the recognition and enforcement of foreign judgments in Vietnam is itself in line with the 1971 Hague Convention. Fourth, becoming members of the two Conventions can be advantageous in terms of attracting foreign trade and investment. International commercial realities have called for the establishment of international commercial courts, for example, in Singapore and China. Having the legal framework to ensure the effectiveness and enforceability of judgments rendered by such courts will make Vietnam more attractive as a destination for trade and investment.

On the other hand, Vietnam will also have to face difficulties when acceding to these Conventions. The Ministry of Justice has studied the prospect of joining in detail, but has expressed caution. First. the majority of the mutual legal assistance treaties which Vietnam has concluded involve criminal or marital matters. This illustrates a high demand for mutual legal assistance in criminal or marital, rather than commercial, matters. In contrast, the 1971 Hague Convention has excluded from its scope the status or capacity of persons, compositions and analogous proceedings, and questions of family law, succession, bankruptcy and social security.[39] Meanwhile, commercial matters involving foreign entities are now often resolved through arbitration or mediation. Therefore, in the short term, Vietnamese may not see a strong need to accede to the 1971 Hague Convention. Second, if Vietnam becomes a party to the 1971 and 2005 Hague Conventions, it will have to review, amend and revise

[35] 'Details: Viet Nam' (*Hague Conference on Private International Law*), available online: www.hcch.net/en/states/hcch-members/details1/?sid=230.

[36] According to statistics as at July 2017: lanhsuvietnam.gov.vn/Lists/BaiViet/B%C3%A0i%20vi%E1%BA%BFt/DispForm.aspx?List=dc7c7d75-6a32-4215-afeb-47d4bee70eee&ID=414.

[37] Le Hong, 'Not Easy to Recognise and Enforce Foreign Judgments and Decisions' (*Pháp Luật* 12 November 2017), available online: baophapluat.vn/tu-phap/khong-de-de-cong-nhan-va-thi-hanh-ban-an-quyet-dinh-dan-su-cua-toa-an-nuoc-ngoai-365544.html.

[38] CPC, Art 472. See also 2014 Law on Investment, Art 14.

[39] 1971 Hague Convention, Art 1.

its legislation in accordance with their provisions. This will need time to complete with support from international experts. Vietnamese judges also lack experience in dealing with choice of court agreements and resolving applications for the recognition and enforcement of foreign judgments. According to a report from the People's Court of Ho Chi Minh City – one of two main courts in Vietnam – among the 14 concluded applications for the recognition and enforcement of foreign judgments from 2014 to 2016, only six (42 per cent) were accepted.[40] Plainly, local judges and lawyers will need to be trained on the interpretation and application of the Conventions. As the number of judges and lawyers in Vietnam who are fluent in English is limited, it would be difficult for most to access relevant information. Third, Vietnam still has a significant concern that acceding to the Conventions will open the floodgates for foreign parties to sue local companies in foreign courts. Vietnamese companies may perceive themselves as becoming easy prey for foreign companies by reason of the Conventions. This seems to be the foremost reservation underlying the Ministry of Justice's reluctance to recommend joining the Conventions. Fourth, with regard to the rise of international commercial courts, Vietnam may alternatively choose to negotiate bilateral treaties with its strategic partners in which such courts have been established. This will eliminate the need for an umbrella legal regime together with all the associated risks, while still making Vietnam attractive to investors from specific countries.

B. Reform

As mentioned above, the number of foreign judgments recognised and enforced in Vietnam has been extremely low. This suggests that the current regime for the recognition and enforcement of foreign judgments may be problematic.

CPC Article 425[41] provides that only judgment creditors (or their legal representatives) have the right to request the Vietnamese court to recognise and enforce foreign civil judgments. Similarly, only judgment debtors and parties having related rights and interests can apply for the refusal of recognition and enforcement of foreign civil judgments. However, there are no guidelines on who is to be considered as a judgment creditor or debtor, especially in divorce cases where there is no dispute on property. This provision is not consistent with Article 13 of the 1971 Hague Convention which uses the phrase 'the party seeking recognition or applying for enforcement' rather than 'the judgment creditor'.[42] Further, by excluding parties with related rights and interests from the class of parties able to apply for recognition and enforcement, the CPC has introduced a novel ground for refusing recognition and enforcement when compared to international law. Further, the court can only accept an application for recognition and enforcement if the judgment debtor (1) resides in Vietnam; (2) has its headquarters in Vietnam; or (3) has assets in Vietnam. In practice, for example, in a divorce case where there is no claim for asset division and the foreign court

[40] See www.tand.hochiminhcity.gov.vn/web/guest/118?p_p_id=EXT_ARTICLEVIEW&p_p_lifecycle=0&p_p_col_id=column-2&p_p_col_pos=3&p_p_col_count=9&_EXT_ARTICLEVIEW_groupId=10217&_EXT_ARTICLEVIEW_articleId=728331&_EXT_ARTICLEVIEW_version=1.0&_EXT_ARTICLEVIEW_redirect=%2Fweb%2Fguest%2Fhome.

[41] See also CPC, Art 192.

[42] 1971 Hague Convention, Art 13.

only declares the parties' divorce, an application can be refused enrolment on the ground that a party is not resident in Vietnam.[43]

In the absence of a bilateral treaty, the Vietnamese court will need to consider whether reciprocity exists with the state of a rendering court. To date, there have been no official guidelines on how to apply the principle of reciprocity. Nor has data been provided on countries that have recognised Vietnamese judgments. Thus, there is little or no information on how to apply reciprocity in practice where no treaty exists. In practice, the court will have to request clarification from Ministry of Foreign Affairs, the Ministry of Justice, or the Supreme People's Court on a case-by-case basis. Meanwhile, in theory, the time period for a court to consider an application for recognition and enforcement of foreign judgments is only from four to six months.[44] As a result, this could lead to a violation of procedure, if the competent authority takes too much time to reply to the court or the court has to suspend the proceedings to wait for clarification from a competent authority.[45]

CPC Chapter XXXV provides for three different procedures in relation to the enforcement of foreign civil judgments in Vietnam, in particular there are: (1) a procedure for recognition (Articles 432 to 443); (2) a procedure for pre-emptive refusal of recognition (Articles 444 to 446); and (3) a procedure for pre-emptive refusal when recognition is not being sought in Vietnam (Articles 447 to 450). These constitute a redundant and cumbersome regime. There is actually no system whereby local courts can ascertain whether or not an application has been made for recognition of a judgment in Vietnam. Therefore, when receiving an application, it will be difficult for a court to decide which procedure to apply. There are no guidelines on how the court should resolve the situation where a judgment debtor submits an application for pre-emptive refusal and a judgment creditor requests for recognition in Vietnam at a later stage. The classification of applications just described has logical defects and is plainly inconsistent with the 1971 Hague Convention, which provides for a single procedure for the recognition of civil judgments.[46]

CPC Article 439 sets out eight grounds for non-recognition of foreign civil decisions and judgments in Vietnam. Of these, the ground most likely to give rise to disputes is the last one, in which recognition would be 'contrary to the fundamental principles of the law of the Socialist Republic of Vietnam'. As mentioned above, the concept of 'fundamental principles of Vietnamese law' may be considered as a local adaptation of what in other jurisdictions is referred to as 'public policy' or *ordre public*.[47] The concepts may be somewhat similar in scope and content, but they are not identical. There has been no document, whether official or unofficial, which attempts to identify those provisions of Vietnamese law

[43] See, for example, Decision No 133/2010/QDST-HN (26 January 2010) where the People's Court of Ho Chi Minh City held that, since the respondent (Mr Hieu) was domiciled in Canada, the applicant (Ms Ha) was not entitled to request the court to deal with her application for recognition.

[44] See the legislative provisions reproduced in n 24.

[45] See, for example, Decision No 302/2011/QD-TDC-DSST (22 June 2011) where, when considering an application for the recognition and enforcement of Judgment HCA No 302/2008 of the Hong Kong Court of First Instance, the People's Court of Ho Chi Minh City sent Correspondence No 1247 (26 May 2011) requesting confirmation on the existence or otherwise of reciprocity between Vietnam and Hong Kong. Since the time for resolving the application under Vietnamese law expired without the court having received a reply from the Ministry of Foreign Affairs, the court had to suspend the resolution of the matter in June 2011.

[46] 1971 Hague Convention, Art 13.

[47] Bui Thi Thu, *Textbook on Private International Law* (Hanoi, Vietnam Education Publisher, 2012) 175–76.

that can be regarded as 'fundamental principles'. The application of this ground is thus open to interpretation on a case by case basis by local judges. Reference has already been made to Resolution No 01. But it is unclear that it applies to the recognition of foreign judgments, as opposed to arbitral awards. It is rarely referred to or applied by local judges in a more general context, as on its terms it is applicable only to the setting aside of arbitral awards. In any event, the guidance and explanations provided remain vague and can cause confusion as to which principles of law have an overriding effect on the development and implementation of Vietnamese laws or which and what violations of those laws are to be regarded as 'serious'. At worst, by referring directly to a number of general principles in specific laws as examples, Resolution No 01 can give rise to a misleading impression that, insofar as a legal provision is labelled as a principle of a particular law, the provision can be deemed to be a 'fundamental principle of Vietnamese law'. Such a view would broaden the circumstances in which a foreign judgment may be refused recognition in Vietnam. In addition, in conjunction with the lack of express recognition of the principle of *res judicata*, the 'fundamental principles of Vietnamese law' test could make foreign judgments open to review on their merits by the Vietnamese court.

Under CPC Article 432, applications for recognition may be submitted to (1) the Ministry of Justice in accordance with international treaties to which Vietnam is a party; or (2) a competent Vietnamese court. There is no single central authority to which applications may be submitted. This can cause difficulty for a requesting party who will need to ascertain to which body an application for recognition should be submitted.

How might the defects highlighted in the preceding paragraphs be rectified? Vietnamese laws should be amended or supplemented so as to clarify matters such as the reciprocity principle or the fundamental principles of Vietnamese law. The Supreme People's Court, the Ministry of Justice and other relevant authorities should issue guidelines on these. In addition, the government should consider acceding to the 1971 and 2005 Hague Conventions and should enter into bilateral treaties on judicial assistance with countries which have a high demand for recognition of their judgments, such as Germany, the US and Canada. These treaties will establish a framework for recognition and enforcement of foreign judgments in Vietnam, as well as limit the cases needed to be considered under the reciprocity principle. In the meantime, it is necessary to review and re-negotiate existing legal assistance treaties to improve efficiency in the mutual recognition and enforcement. At the very least, improvement can be obtained through adopting a more consistent interpretation to the various existing bilateral treaties.

When considering applications for recognition and enforcement of foreign judgments, foreign law will be applicable to different issues such as the capacity of parties, the legal effect of judgments and the nature and fairness of the procedures followed by foreign courts. Even though CPC Article 481 sets out a mechanism for determining foreign laws for the Vietnamese court to apply in the settlement of civil cases involving foreign elements, it is still important for the courts and other authorities such as the Ministry of Justice and Ministry of Foreign Affairs to be up-to-date in their information on international and foreign laws and to improve their familiarity and skills in handling cases involving foreign elements. The Vietnamese judiciary has cooperated with other judiciaries in the region, for example those in ASEAN states, China, Japan and South Korea. However, this has so far only been for the purpose of capacity building and exchanging experience. It may be beneficial for the Vietnamese court to establish a network with judiciaries in the region for the purpose of facilitating the obtaining of information on foreign law and the mutual recognition and enforcement of judgments.

As far as disseminating information on Vietnamese case law is concerned, since July 2017 the judgments and decisions of Vietnamese courts have been made available through the official website of the Supreme People's Court.[48] A limited number of precedents considered to be important legal sources are now also being published by the Supreme People's Court.[49] The information provided there will be an important source for local courts when resolving applications for recognition, as well as for applicants planning to submit such applications. For the future, the Supreme Court should consider listing Vietnamese decisions on recognition and enforcement together with the recognised foreign judgments or decisions.

The Supreme People's Court can cooperate with the Ministry of Justice and the Ministry of Foreign Affairs to provide regularly updated lists of mutual legal assistance agreements providing regimes for recognition and enforcement. This will avoid the time-consuming exercise of determining the proper procedure to use in making an application to a competent court for recognition. Additionally, electronic filing can be implemented and relevant databases set up to expedite applications. The use of technology will furnish a means for courts to keep track of whether applications to enforce particular judgments have been made and possibly whether there has been a prior or ongoing Vietnamese judgment or case on the same matter and between the same parties as in the foreign decision.

VII. Conclusion

It can be difficult to seek recognition and enforcement of a foreign judgment in Vietnam owing to the lack of an official guidance on a number of key conditions. Even judgments originating from countries with which Vietnam have bilateral judicial assistance treaties can face obstacles owing to uncertainties in the current legal framework under the CPC. This is perhaps why there is a lack of jurisprudence from Vietnamese courts on applications to recognise and enforce foreign judgments. As Vietnam does not have any plans to join the Hague Conventions in the near future, the immediate way forward should be trying to develop and promote a unified and harmonious reading of the existing bilateral treaties. More importantly, current gaps in legislation should be filled by guidance from the Supreme People's Court and the Ministry of Justice. In this regard, certain principles from international conventions and practice may provide good points of reference. Lessons, for example, can be drawn from Vietnam's experience with the 1958 New York Convention.[50]

[48] See congbobanan.toaan.gov.vn.

[49] See anle.toaan.gov.vn.

[50] The 1958 New York Convention remains a topical issue even though Vietnam has been a signatory since 1995.

10

Cambodia

ALEX LARKIN AND POTIM YUN

I. Introduction[1]

The rapid development of Cambodia's economy over the past two decades has brought with it a demand for codified laws and regulations. This has driven the development of the nation's legal framework including its very first foreign judgment recognition and enforcement treaty, the Agreement on Mutual Judicial Assistance in Civil Matters between the Kingdom of Cambodia and the Socialist Republic of Vietnam (2013) (the Cambodia–Vietnam Treaty). That treaty provides for Vietnamese and Cambodian courts to take into account and enforce judgments in connection with civil and commercial matters from the other jurisdiction. Despite the treaty having been in force for more than half a decade, to the author's knowledge, Cambodia has yet to see a Vietnamese court judgment brought to a local court for recognition and enforcement. Nevertheless, the fact that the two jurisdictions have entered into this treaty is viewed as a favourable development.

II. Background

Cambodia, a former French colony, retains a measure of colonial influence in its legal framework. During the Khmer Rouge period (1975–79), the nation suffered major setbacks in its legal system, under which the regime abolished civil laws and the rule of law, replacing them with a centralised dictatorship. The regime implemented agrarian socialism and perceived any ideal of intellect other than the regime's as a threat to the nation; hence, the regime took extreme measures in eliminating intellectualism, including destroying the previous regime's laws, and imprisoning and executing legal practitioners and academics. The nation lost most of its written laws and persons who were well-versed in the law, causing a vacuum and crippling the nation's legal system. 1979 marked the invasion of the nation by Vietnam, which began a gradual process towards a de-centralised government[2]

[1] Cambodian courts generally do not publish case reports and certain relevant rules and regulations may not be publicly available. The authors have therefore only relied on information available from public sources in preparing this chapter.

[2] Local (*sangkat*/commune level) authorities in Cambodia were granted powers over their respective administrative territories during the Vietnamese occupation, through laws such as the Sub-decree on Recognition of Private Ownership of Cambodian Citizens No 25 (22 April 1989).

until the 1991 Paris Peace Accords officially ended the Vietnamese–Cambodian war.[3] The Paris Peace Accords led to the installation of the United Nations Transitional Authority in Cambodia during 1992–93, which provided assistance in the creation of the sovereign state of Cambodia, with a separation of powers in administration. From this period onwards, the nation's legislators, together with the delegated power of the ministries, enacted and published various private and public laws and regulations. Cambodian law does not distinguish between international or domestic law; hence, in the context of commercial and civil disputes between parties from different jurisdictions, the private law of Cambodia will apply.[4]

The Civil Code (2007) and Civil Procedure Code (2006) comprise a substantial portion of private law in Cambodia. Since Cambodian law can mean both international law and domestic law, the Civil Code and Civil Procedure Code play major roles in private international disputes. In addition, the Civil Code applies to Cambodians and foreigners without discrimination. The Civil Code sets out the general principles governing legal relations that apply to property-related matters, contracts and family relations, among others.[5] The Civil Procedure Code sets out the procedures for civil disputes to be brought to court for trial and resolution in respect of the protection of private parties' rights and enforcement of their obligations.

The judicial system of Cambodia is divided into three levels of courts in hierarchical order. At the first level are the Phnom Penh Municipal Court of First Instance and the Provincial Courts of First Instance, one in each province. The middle level consists of a single Appeals Court, and the highest level is the Supreme Court. In addition, there are two special courts – the Military Court, which hears military disputes, and the Extraordinary Chambers of the Courts of Cambodia, which exclusively hears the Khmer Rouge war crimes and crimes against humanity trials. The three levels of courts just mentioned hear civil and criminal disputes, including all disputes of a commercial nature, since Cambodia is yet to have a separate commercial court. The limited amount of specific commercial court and commercial law expertise in the judicial system is a significant challenge that the nation is facing with regard to its judicial and legal development.[6] Hence the courts' methodology of resolving the blurred line between civil and commercial matters is to rely on the principle of freedom of contract. Litigation of disputes arising from contracts are generally decided in accordance with the provisions of the agreement, unless the agreement violates any law or public order and good customs.[7] In addition, an agreement to submit such a dispute to commercial arbitration would be respected by the court and recognises the arbitration tribunal's jurisdiction to resolve the dispute. It is notable that any commercial dispute in respect of ownership of land in Cambodia will be resolved under civil law and the Civil Code will be applicable regardless of a different choice of law clause in the commercial

[3] The Paris Peace Accords are formally known as the Agreements on a Comprehensive Political Settlement of the Cambodia Conflict.

[4] The Constitutional Council Case No 131/003/2007 of 26 June 2007, Decision No 092/003/2007 CC.D of 10 July 2007.

[5] Civil Code (2007), Art 1.

[6] The National Assembly Commission 6 on Legislation and Justice, 'Briefing Note of Legal and Judicial Reform in Cambodia' (*Parliamentary Institute of Cambodia*, February 2016), available online: www.pic.org.kh/images/2016Research/20170505_Legal_Judicial_Reform_Eng.pdf.

[7] Civil Code (2007), Art 354.

agreement, as in Cambodia only Cambodian citizens (natural persons and business entities) have the right to own land – an instrument of protection of national rights and public policy.[8]

III. Recognition and Enforcement under Treaties or Similar Arrangements

The Cambodia–Vietnam Treaty is the only bilateral treaty for recognition and enforcement of foreign civil and commercial judgments to which Cambodia is a party.[9] The treaty was ratified by Cambodia on 17 July 2014.[10] Cambodia is not a contracting or signatory state of any multilateral foreign judgment conventions, such as the 2005 Hague Convention on Choice of Court Agreements. A party wishing to have a Vietnamese court judgment recognised and enforced in Cambodia must apply to the Ministry of Justice of Cambodia, requesting that the Ministry of Justice correspond with the Ministry of Justice of Vietnam to invoke the treaty.[11]

Under Article 22 of the Cambodia–Vietnam Treaty, there are five conditions to be met in order for a Vietnamese judgment to be recognised and enforced in Cambodia:[12]

1. The case does not fall into the exclusive jurisdiction of the courts of the requested party[13] (here, Cambodia) under the national law of the requested party.
2. The litigants or their legal representatives were duly summoned before the court of the requesting party (here, Vietnam) or declared absent in accordance with the national law of the requested party.
3. The judgment or decision has entered into legal effect and the statutes of limitation for execution of such judgment or decision have not expired under the national law of the requested party.
4. There has not been a legally effective civil court judgment or decision on the same case that has been made by the court of the requested party or there is no judgment or decision by the court or a third party that has been recognised for enforcement by the court of the requested party, or at the time of recognition of that judgment or decision, the court of the requested party has not registered or heard the same case.
5. The recognition and enforcement of the court judgment or decision and the consequences of the recognition and enforcement of such judgment or decision will not contradict the fundamental principles of law and public order of the requested party.

[8] Constitution of the Kingdom of Cambodia, Art 44.

[9] Agreement on Mutual Judicial Assistance in Civil Matters between the Kingdom of Cambodia and the Socialist Republic of Vietnam (2013) (the Cambodia–Vietnam Treaty).

[10] Royal Kram No NS/RKM/0714/018 dated 17 July 2014 on the Promulgation of the Law approving the Agreement on Mutual Judicial Assistance in Civil Matters between the Kingdom of Cambodia and the Socialist Republic of Vietnam.

[11] The Cambodia–Vietnam Treaty (n 9), Art 23.

[12] ibid, Art 22.

[13] Under the provisions of the treaty, the 'requesting party' is the nation state that submits a request to the other nation state, the 'requested party', for the requested party to take such action as is necessary and appropriate under the treaty to achieve recognition and enforcement of a court judgment issued by a court in the jurisdiction of the requesting party.

Under the Cambodia–Vietnam Treaty, the procedures for recognition and enforcement of the court judgments and decisions are subject to the national law of the requested party,[14] hence the Civil Procedure Code is the applicable law in Cambodia.

The conditions set out in the Cambodia–Vietnam Treaty and the requirements set out under Cambodian law, ie the Civil Procedure Code, are similar in respect of recognition and enforcement of foreign judgments, such as the fifth condition under the treaty, which overlaps with Civil Procedure Code Article 199(c), both of which require that the foreign judgment not violate the public order of the intended jurisdiction of enforcement.

IV. Recognition and Enforcement in the Absence of Treaties or Similar Arrangements

A. Sources and Development of Private International Law

The Cambodian courts do not distinguish between recognition and enforcement of a foreign judgment. A foreign judgment that is recognised will be enforced by the court, as the Cambodian court is prohibited from examining the merits of the foreign judgment.[15] However, the complexity and heavy burden of proof for recognising and enforcing a foreign judgment may create a barrier for any party intending to do so. As an overview, before any foreign judgment (apart from a Vietnamese judgment) can be enforced in Cambodia, there are four requirements to satisfy and one consideration to take into account under the Civil Procedure Code.[16] Together the five requirements to be met by a foreign judgment are analogous to the criteria for enforcement under the abovementioned treaty.[17] Again, to our knowledge Cambodia has yet to see a foreign judgment recognised and enforced in the local courts. This is mainly due to a lack of conventions and treaties to which Cambodia is a party in respect of reciprocal recognition between contracting or signatory states.[18] As the Cambodia–Vietnam Treaty was ratified relatively recently, it remains to be seen how the Cambodian courts will interpret the relevant provisions of the Civil Procedure Code on enforcing foreign judgments, in light of any future practical application of the treaty in relation to Vietnamese judgments.

B. Final Judgments

Under the legal framework set out by the Civil Procedure Code, in no circumstances can a foreign judgment be recognised and enforced without meeting all the requirements set out

[14] The Cambodia–Vietnam Treaty (n 9), Art 24.
[15] Civil Procedure Code (2006), Art 352(4).
[16] ibid, Arts 199, 352(3).
[17] The Cambodia–Vietnam Treaty (n 9), Art 22.
[18] Civil Procedure Code (2006), Art 199(d).

under the law.[19] A party who wishes to enforce a foreign judgment should file and obtain an execution judgment through a motion to the competent court. Such competent court must either have territorial jurisdiction over the debtor or the property of the claim.[20] The court will decide whether the submission satisfies the requirements and conditions under the law.[21]

The four requirements for execution of recognition and enforcement of foreign judgments are set out in Article 199 of the Civil Procedure Code and may be summarised as follows:[22]

1. Jurisdiction must be properly conferred on the foreign court by law or by treaty.
2. The losing party must have received a service of summons or any other order necessary to commence the action or responded without receiving such summons or order.
3. The contents of the judgment and the procedures followed in the foreign action do not violate the public order or morals of Cambodia.
4. There is a guarantee of reciprocity between Cambodia and the foreign country in which the court is based.

The first requirement is whether there is any Cambodian law, treaty or convention to which Cambodia is a signatory or Contracting State, recognising the jurisdiction of the court where the foreign judgment is issued. The foreign judgment that the party intends to enforce in the Cambodian court must have the right conferred by Cambodian law, state treaty or convention. As mentioned, the principle of freedom of contract is well respected by the Cambodian courts. Hence, in a situation where an agreement gives rise to the subject matter of the dispute, if the foreign judgment which the party wishes to enforce conflicts with the jurisdiction conferred by the choice of court clause in the agreement, the court may uphold the principle of freedom of contract and decide that the foreign judgment violates the public order of Cambodia under Article 199(c) of the Civil Procedure Code. The second requirement is whether the losing party received proper notice in the pre-trial stage or during the proceedings, such as whether a summons was served on the party, or the party responded even without being served and thereby waived service. A procedural defect in this regard would render the party that wishes to enforce the foreign judgment unable to fulfil such requirement. This is to essentially guarantee due process such that both claimant and respondent have an opportunity to provide their statements and conduct cross-examination of each party by their respective attorney and are treated as equal in the eyes of the law and in the presence of the court. The third requirement is whether the enforcement of the foreign judgment is contradictory to the public order and morals of Cambodia. Public order and morals are not explicitly defined in Cambodian law and the authors are not aware of any court interpretation of these terms. The fourth requirement relates to reciprocity; specifically, whether Cambodian court decisions are recognised or able to be recognised by the state or territory in which rendering court is situated. The most common mechanism of reciprocal recognition of judgments would be found in a treaty or convention. It is unlikely

[19] ibid, Art 199.
[20] ibid, Art 352(2).
[21] ibid, Art 352(3).
[22] ibid, Art 199.

that Cambodia will recognise and enforce a foreign judgment voluntarily without a satisfactory reciprocity provision in a bilateral treaty or convention with the jurisdiction of the rendering court, as recognition and enforcement in the absence of such instrument would bypass the Article 199(d) requirement.[23] This is partly due to the nature of the judiciary system in Cambodia, where precedents are enforceable but are not favoured by the courts and the courts rarely refer to precedents in deciding cases.[24] As such, for the time being, Cambodian courts may not recognise or enforce foreign judgments voluntarily without a public policy reason to do so or an amendment of the Civil Procedure Code to change such practice.

As noted above, in addition to the four requirements under Article 199,[25] there is an additional consideration under the Civil Procedure Code. That is that the Cambodian court must look into whether the foreign judgment is final and binding in its respective jurisdiction under Article 352(3).[26]

C. Interlocutory Judgments

The Civil Procedure Code expressly states that only a final and binding foreign judgment may be enforced in Cambodia. Therefore, a foreign interlocutory judgment issued by a court at an intermediate stage of proceedings is likely to be unenforceable in Cambodia.

D. Enforcement

If a foreign judgment satisfies (1) (in the case of a Vietnamese judgment) all five conditions under the Cambodia–Vietnam Treaty[27] or (2) (in the case of any other foreign judgment) the four requirements and one consideration under the Civil Procedure Code,[28] the court should issue an execution order of the judgment. The available executions of judgment are set out under the Civil Procedure Code and categorised as follows:

1. Monetary claims: executions against attached property, movables, immovables, property rights, and vessels.[29]
2. Additional rules for security interest enforcement: enforcement against movables, immovables, property rights, and vessels.[30]
3. Non-monetary claims.[31]

[23] ibid, Art 199(d).

[24] Hor Peng, Kong Phallack and Jorg Menzel, *Introduction to Cambodian Law* (Cambodia, Konrad-Adenauer-Stiftung, 2012) 8.

[25] Civil Procedure Code (2006), Art 199.

[26] ibid, Art 352(3).

[27] The Cambodia–Vietnam Treaty (n 9), Art 21.

[28] Civil Procedure Code (2006), Arts 199, 352(3).

[29] ibid, Book 6, ch 2.

[30] ibid, Book 6, ch 3.

[31] ibid, Book 6, ch 4.

V. The Future

A. Prospects

As mentioned, Cambodia is not a signatory of the 2005 Hague Convention on Choice of Court Agreements. We are not aware of any information with respect to the Cambodian government's intention to enter into the Convention.

B. Reform

The current legal framework in Cambodia has an element of deterrence against enforcing foreign judgments. Undefined legal terms such as 'public order' and 'morals' in the provisions of requirements on recognition and enforcement of foreign judgments[32] confer on the courts broad discretion in interpreting such terms. The issue of undefined legal terms can be resolved by the issuance of explanatory notes or supplementary legal instruments. To date, no foreign judgments have been enforced in Cambodia. As such, the relevant provisions of the Civil Procedure Code have yet to be tested.[33]

VI. Conclusion

Given that the Cambodia–Vietnam Treaty is the only instrument for enforcing foreign judgments in Cambodia, no foreign court judgments, other than those issued by Vietnamese courts, may currently be enforced in Cambodia. Further, to the best of our knowledge, there have been no attempts to enforce a Vietnamese court judgment in Cambodia to date. Thus, the application of the treaty and relevant provisions of the Civil Procedure Code by the Cambodian courts is untested and it is not known exactly how the Cambodian courts will construe and apply such provisions.

[32] ibid, Art 199(c).
[33] ibid, Art 199.

11

Myanmar

ZAW THURA

I. Introduction

For much of the twentieth century and the early part of the twenty-first century, Myanmar has had a troubled legal history.[1]

On 4 January 1948 the Union of Burma[2] gained independence from the British under a Constitution drafted the year before. Chapter VIII (Articles 133 to 153) of the 1947 Constitution established a Supreme Court and a High Court (each headed by a Chief Justice), with Article 141 providing for an independent judiciary subject only to the Constitution and the law. This common law-style court system was abrogated on 2 March 1962 when the military under General Ne Win took over the government, ruling through a Revolutionary Council. The judicial system was replaced by a Council of People's Justice, a Chief Court and Special Criminal Courts. A new Constitution was put into effect by the military on 3 January 1974, ostensibly signalling the transition to a civilian government with Ne Win as president. He remained in that position until July 1988 at a time of protracted student unrest. The new president, Sein Lwin, resigned not long after to be followed by Maung Maung. On 18 September 1988, following continuing protests, military rule was re-established under the State Law and Order Restoration Council (SLORC). The SLORC created a new Supreme Court on 27 September 1988, but shut down all courts in November 1988 with retrospective effect from 1 June 1988. Under domestic and international pressure,

[1] For a detailed account of Myamar's legal history, see Melissa Crouch, 'The Layers of Legal Development in Myanmar' in Melissa Crouch and Tim Lindsey (eds), *Law, Society and Transition in Myanmar* (Oxford, Hart Publishing, 2014).

[2] To all intents and purposes, the names 'Myanmar' and 'Burma' are interchangeable in the English language. In the Burmese language, the two are pronounced in nearly the same way. The more formal expression 'Myanmar' is the official designation currently used by its government. The change in name from Socialist Republic of the Union of Burma to the Union of Myanmar was instigated by the SLORC when it came into power in September 1988. In the 1947 Constitution, the 'Union of Burma' was defined in Art 2 as comprising 'the whole of Burma, including (i) All the territories that were heretofore governed by His Britannic Majesty through the Governor of Burma, and (ii) the Karenni States'. Within the Union, Art 5 renamed what had been known as the Federated Shan States and the Wa States as 'the Shan State'; Art 6 renamed the territories previously known as the Myitkyina and Bhamo Districts as 'the Kachin State'; and Art 7 renamed the territories known as the Karenni States (that is, Kantarawaddy, Bawlake and Kyebogyi) as 'the Kayah State'. The Union is consequently constituted by seven states (Mon, Kayin, Rakhine, Kayah, Shan, Chin and Kachin) and seven divisions (Thaninthayi, Yangon, Ayeyarwaddy, Bago, Magwe, Mandalay and Sagaing). The states and divisions are made up of districts. The districts are in turn sub-sub-divided into townships.

in 2011 the SLORC (now known as the State Peace and Development Council (SPDC)) promulgated a fresh Constitution, which had been put to a referendum in May 2008 and under which the SPDC was to hand over power to a civilian government under a president. Chapter VI (Articles 293 to 336) of the 2008 Constitution dealt with the judiciary. It set up a court system for the Union, including an apex Supreme Court of the Union (headed by a Chief Justice of the Union), High Courts of the Region, High Courts of the State, Courts of the Self-Administered Division and Courts of the Self-Administered Zone, District Courts and Township Courts. It also established a new Constitutional Tribunal of the Union. That system remains in force today.

With the return to civilian government, Myanmar has been gradually opening up to foreign direct investment as part of national economic development. It is anticipated that over time there will be an increasing number of commercial contracts (and disputes arising out of such contracts) between foreign and Myanmar nationals. It is more than likely that, as a consequence, the Myanmar courts will have to consider more and more applications for the recognition and enforcement of foreign judgments, if only for the purposes of establishing *res judicata* where a Myanmar national has successfully defended a claim abroad or of enabling foreign investors to enforce their commercial rights against assets of defendants in Myanmar. The question is how the Myanmar courts are to tackle such applications for recognition and enforcement and where the law on the same is to be found.

In answering such questions, it should be borne in mind that, despite the tumult of recent history, the ordinary civil law in Myanmar has formally remained the same from post-colonial to present times.[3] Thus, codes, statutes and commentaries on the same from the British colonial era which remained in effect after independence still apply in the Union today, albeit as amended by subsequent legislation passed from time to time. This is not dissimilar from the situation in many other former British colonies that (like Myanmar) have, since acquiring independence, maintained a common law system. In Myanmar's case in particular, the Civil Procedure Code (CPC) which was originally enacted by the British as India Act V of 1908 and which came into effect for Burma on 1 January 1909, continues to govern civil procedure in the Myanmar courts. This means that Myanmar law on the recognition and enforcement of foreign judgments can legitimately be derived from the sections and Orders of the CPC. Myanmar has not entered into any bilateral or multilateral treaties for the mutual recognition and enforcement of judgments. Nor has it passed laws on that specific subject. Therefore, read and understood in the context of decided cases, the CPC should be regarded as a primary source of Myanmar law relating to the recognition and enforcement of judgments.

This chapter concentrates on Myanmar law on the recognition and enforcement of foreign judgments in commercial matters.[4] But it should be noted at the outset that the expression 'commercial' is not a term of art in Myanmar law.[5] For the purposes of the

[3] See Crouch (n 1) 41, 44. For example, SLORC Declaration 6/88 (24 September 1988) provided: 'All laws existing on 18th September 1988, the date on which the State Law and Order Restoration Council took charge of the sovereign powers of the State, shall remain in effect until and unless repealed'. *cf* the earlier State Revolutionary Council Declaration 14/62 (7 March 1962) to similar effect.

[4] On the recognition and enforcement of foreign judgments in Myanmar generally, see Adrian Briggs, *Private International Law in Myanmar* (Oxford, Oxford University Press, 2015), ch 3.

[5] There are ongoing discussions on the establishment of a specialised commercial court in Myanmar.

exposition here, 'commercial' will be taken as encompassing the matters listed in footnote 2 to Article 1 of the UNCITRAL Model Law on International Commercial Arbitration, that is, 'all relationships of a commercial nature, whether contractual or not'. Such relationships include, but are not to be taken as limited to

> any trade transaction for the supply or exchange of goods or services; distribution agreement; commercial representation or agency; factoring; leasing; construction of works; consulting; engineering; licensing; investment; financing; banking; insurance; exploitation agreement or concession; joint venture and other forms of industrial or business cooperation; carriage of goods or passengers by air, sea, rail or road.

II. Recognition and Enforcement of Judgments in the Absence of Treaties or Similar Arrangements

Myanmar is not currently party to any treaty or multilateral instrument providing for the mutual recognition and enforcement of foreign judgments. Nor does Myanmar law have any special enactment for the recognition and enforcement of foreign judgments. But the CPC offers ways and means to achieve this purpose.

A. Recognition of Foreign Judgments

i. Use of CPC Sections 13 and 14 and Order XV

CPC section 2(5) defines 'foreign Court' as 'a Court situate beyond the limits of the Union of Myanmar which has no authority in the Union of Myanmar and is not established or continued by the President of the Union'. Section 2(6) defines 'foreign judgment' as 'the judgment of a foreign Court'. Section 13 then provides that foreign judgments shall be conclusive in Myanmar courts on 'any matter thereby directly adjudicated upon between the same parties, or between parties under whom they or any of them claim litigating under the same title'. The foreign judgment will, however, not be regarded as conclusive in the six situations specified in section 13. Those situations are:

1. Where the foreign judgment has not been pronounced by a foreign court of competent jurisdiction;
2. Where the foreign judgment has not been given on the merits of the case;
3. Where it appears on the face of the proceedings that the foreign judgment was founded on an incorrect view of international law or a refusal to recognise the law of the Union of Myanmar in cases in which such law is applicable;
4. Where the proceedings in which the judgment was obtained were opposed to natural justice;
5. Where the foreign judgment was obtained by fraud; and,
6. Where the foreign judgment sustains a claim that is not founded on a breach of any law in force in the Union of Myanmar.

Situation (1) is essentially a condition of indirect jurisdiction (sometimes also called 'international jurisdiction'). Grounds of indirect jurisdiction that should be acceptable under

Myanmar law are discussed in section II.A.ii below. Situation (2) requires that a foreign judgment be final and conclusive in order to be recognised. An interlocutory judgment would therefore not be enforceable, as it may be subject to change following trial and cannot be said to have been made 'on the merits'.[6] Situations (3) (4), (5) and (6) in effect mean that recognition of a foreign judgment should not contravene public policy. Recognition of the foreign judgment should instead accord with what might be called 'international public policy'. In other words, the foreign judgment should not be contrary to international law or tainted by fraud and should have been obtained in accordance with natural justice. Moreover, the foreign judgment should be consonant with what might be referred to as 'domestic public policy'. This means that recognition should not lead to the contravention of Myanmar law, including presumably that recognition should not lead to inconsistency with a prior decision of the Myanmar court in a case between the identical parties on the same subject matter as the foreign judgment.[7] Where Myanmar law is unclear and (say) allows for two plausible interpretations A or B, it is an unresolved question whether a foreign judgment applying interpretation A should be refused recognition insofar as the Myanmar judge hearing an application for the recognition or enforcement of that judgment, believes that interpretation A is wrong and interpretation B right. This specific situation is discussed further in section II.A.iii below. But howsoever such a case might be decided in the future by the Myanmar court, the point here is that CPC section 13 essentially provides for most (if not all) of the elements that a special law on the recognition of foreign judgments would cover.

As for the procedure to be followed to have a foreign judgment recognised and then converted into an enforceable judgment of the Myanmar court, it is submitted that this may be accomplished through Order XV of Rules of Procedure in the First Schedule to the CPC,[8] in particular where the foreign judgment is for a sum of money to be paid by a defendant to the plaintiff.

Order XV states:

> 1. Where at the first hearing of a suit it appears that the parties are not at issue on any question of law or of fact, the Court may at once pronounce judgment.
>
> 2. Where there are more defendants than one, and any one of the defendants is not at issue with the plaintiff on any question of law or of fact, the Court may at once pronounce judgment for or against such defendant and the suit shall proceed only against the other defendants.
>
> 3. (1) Where the parties are at issue on some question of law or of fact, and issues have been framed by the Court as hereinbefore provided, if the Court is satisfied that no further argument or evidence than the parties can at once adduce is required upon such of the issues as may be sufficient for the decision of the suit, and that no injustice will result from proceeding with the suit

[6] In *K B Walker v Gladys P Walker* [1935] AIR (Rangoon) 284 (Mya Bu J and Dunkley JJ), the District Court (Magwe) distinguished (at [285]) between two types of default judgment insofar as recognition and enforcement is concerned. Where judgment is given in default without a hearing of the merits, as a sanction for the defendant's non-appearance, the Myanmar court will regard the same as a penalty and not as a final and conclusive judgment. But, where judgment is given in default only after a consideration of the evidence, the judgment will be taken as one on the merits. In the latter circumstance, there will be *res judicata* between the parties.

[7] Under CPC s 10, the mere fact that a cause of action is pending before a foreign court will not prevent a court in Myanmar from adjudicating upon that matter.

[8] CPC s 121 stipulates that the Rules in the First Sch 'shall have effect until annulled or altered …'.

forthwith, the Court may proceed to determine such issues, and, if the finding thereon is sufficient for the decision, may pronounce judgment accordingly, whether the summons has been issued for the settlement of issues only or for the final disposal of the suit:

Provided that, where the summons has been issued for the settlement of issues only, the parties or their pleaders are present and none of them objects.

(2) Where the finding is not sufficient for the decision, the Court shall postpone the further hearing of the suit, and shall fix a day for the production of such further evidence, or for such further argument as the case requires.

4. Where the summons has been issued for the final disposal of the suit and either party fails without sufficient cause to produce the evidence on which he relies, the Court may at once pronounce judgment, or may, if it thinks fit, after framing and recording issues, adjourn the suit for the production of such evidence as may be necessary for its decision upon such issues.

Order XV offers the possibility of obtaining summary judgment of a debt established by the foreign judgment as due and owing from the defendant to the plaintiff. The plaintiff can first commence domestic proceedings before the relevant Myanmar court, pleading an action in debt (that is, money due and owing) against the defendant based on the foreign judgment. The plaintiff would produce the foreign judgment to the Myanmar court as evidence of the debt. In this connection, CPC section 14 states:

The Court shall presume upon the production of any document purporting to be a certified copy of a foreign judgment, that such judgment was pronounced by a Court of competent jurisdiction, unless the contrary appears on the record; but such presumption may be displaced by proving want of jurisdiction.[9]

The plaintiff can thereafter apply for summary judgment to be granted at the first substantive hearing of the suit under the procedure in Order XV. At that hearing, it is difficult to see how the existence of the foreign judgment can be denied or be at issue. Subject only to the Myanmar court satisfying itself as to the finality of the foreign judgment, the jurisdiction (that is, indirect jurisdiction) of the rendering court, and the absence of a public policy impediment, the Myanmar court should recognise the foreign judgment and, in so doing, establish the existence of the pleaded debt. Where the criteria for recognition have

[9] Cf Ord XIII r 10 which provides, in the case of Myanmar (as opposed to foreign) judgments:

(1) The Court may of its own motion, and may in its discretion upon the application of any of the parties to a suit, send for, either from its own records or from any other Court, the record of any other suit or proceeding and inspect the same.
(2) Every application made under this rule shall (unless the Court otherwise directs) be supported by an affidavit showing how the record is material to the suit in which the application is made, and that the applicant cannot without unreasonable delay or expense obtain a duly authenticated copy of the record or of such portion thereof as the applicant requires, or that the production of the original is necessary for the purposes of justice.
(3) If the Court thinks fit to send for the record, it shall do so by sending a formal proceeding to the Court whose record is required. No summons to produce any record shall be issued to any record-keeper, chief clerk or official of any Court.
(4) Whenever a Judge sends for the record of another suit or case, or other official papers, and uses any part of such record or papers as evidence in a trial before him, he shall direct that an authenticated copy of the part so used shall be put up with the trial record, and shall further direct at the expense of which party such copy shall be made.

been met, the Myanmar court can pursuant to Order XV accordingly grant summary judgment at the first substantive hearing for the debt due and owing under the foreign judgment. The resulting judgment may be enforced in the same way as any other judgment of the Myanmar court.[10]

ii. Indirect Jurisdiction

As a condition for recognition of a foreign judgment, CPC sections 13 and 14 stress the importance of establishing that the foreign court rendering the judgment was one of 'competent jurisdiction'. How precisely does the Myanmar court evaluate whether a foreign court is one of 'competent jurisdiction'? Myanmar has no special enactment concerning indirect jurisdiction. But there are provisions on domestic jurisdiction in CPC sections 15 to 24.[11] By analogy with those provisions, it should in principle be possible for the Myanmar court to develop criteria for assessing whether a foreign court properly assumed jurisdiction (was 'competent') in a given case. It would be anomalous if the Myanmar court could claim jurisdiction in the situations identified in CPC sections 15 to 24, but Myanmar law denies jurisdiction to foreign courts in analogous circumstances. The Myanmar courts' approach to indirect jurisdiction should mirror the CPC's rules on

[10] See s II.B below. The possibility of bringing domestic proceedings in Myanmar based on a foreign judgment was acknowledged by the High Court in *VAS Arogya Odeyar v VR RM N S Sathappa Chettiar* [1951] *Burma Law Reports* 211 (HC) [218], where U Tun Byu CJ observed: 'It is true that the decree which the defendant respondent obtained in India was based on the decree which he obtained in Burma, but this is matter which the law allows him to do. A foreign decree can also form the basis of a suit in Burma'. See also remarks in n 14.

[11] CPC s 15 stipulates that '[e]very suit shall be instituted in the Court of the lowest grade competent to try it'. CPC s 16 states that suits in relation to immovable property are to be instituted where the subject matter is situated. CPC s 17 deals with the case where immovable property is situated within the jurisdictions of different domestic courts. CPC s 18 concerns cases where the local limits of a domestic court's jurisdiction are uncertain. CPC s 19 states:

> Where a suit is for compensation for wrong done to the person or to moveable property, if the wrong was done within the local limits of the jurisdiction of one Court, and the defendant resides, or carries on business, or personally works for gain within the local limits of the jurisdiction of another Court, the suit may be instituted at the option of the plaintiff in either of the said Courts.

CPC s 20 states:

> Subject to the limitations aforesaid, every suit shall be instituted in a Court within the local limits of whose jurisdiction: (a) the defendant, or each of the defendants where there are more than one, at the time of the commencement of the suit, actually and voluntarily resides, or carries on business, or personally works for gain; or (b) any of the defendants, where there are more than one. at the time of the commencement of the suit, actually and voluntarily resides, or carries on business, or personally works for gain, provided that in such case either the leave of the Court is given, or the defendants who do not reside, or carry on business, or personally work for gain, as aforesaid, acquiesce in such institution; or (c) the cause of action, wholly or in part, arises.

Explanation II to CPC s 20 clarifies that: 'A corporation shall be deemed to carry on business at its sole or principal office in the Union of Burma or. in respect of any cause of action arising at any place where it has also a subordinate office, at such place'. CPC s 21 provides that an objection to jurisdiction will not be allowed on appeal or review, unless the objection was taken in the court of first instance at the 'earliest possible opportunity and in all cases where issues are settled at or before such settlement, and unless there has been a consequent failure of justice'. CPC s 22 enables a judge, upon application by a defendant, to transfer a suit that may be instituted in more than one court. CPC s 23 specifies to which court an application under s 22 should be made. CPC s 24 provides a general power to the High Court and the District Court to transfer or withdraw suits or proceedings.

domestic jurisdiction. Thus, for example, by analogy with CPC section 20 Explanation II,[12] where the rendering court has assumed jurisdiction on the basis that a defendant company has its place of principal business in the rendering state, the condition of competent jurisdiction (that is, indirect jurisdiction) under CPC sections 13 and 14 should be regarded by the Myanmar court as met.

Guidance on the likely approach of Myanmar courts today to indirect jurisdiction may also be obtained from previously decided cases. For instance, in *VAS Arogya Odeyar v VR RM N S Sathappa Chettiar*[13] the High Court held that, where a person appears by one's self or through an agent to contest proceedings before a court (whether in Burma or elsewhere), that person is to be treated as having submitted to the court's jurisdiction. Accordingly, if a defendant has contested proceedings before a foreign court, the latter forum should be treated by Myanmar law as having had competent or indirect jurisdiction to render judgment against the defendant. The defendant will have submitted to the foreign court's jurisdiction.[14] In *Steel Brothers & Co Ltd v Y A Ganny Sons and Two*[15] the question was whether, when two courts (in that case, the English and Burmese courts) have jurisdiction to try a suit, the jurisdiction of one court could be ousted by agreement of the parties. The judge answered the question:

> The authorities are in favour of the view that they can. The consensus of opinion of the Courts in Burma as well as in India is that when two Courts have jurisdiction to try a suit the parties by agreement can choose the forum. The choice of a forum in such a case is left open to the parties by agreement which is not considered illegal.[16]

Steel Brothers accordingly supports the proposition that, where a foreign court has assumed jurisdiction on the basis of the parties' choice of court agreement, then in the absence of illegality or some objection of public policy, Myanmar law should treat the rendering court as having indirect jurisdiction by reason of the parties' agreement. In other words, the parties should be viewed as having submitted to the jurisdiction of the parties' designated court.

An interesting question is the extent to which the Myanmar court would recognise a foreign judgment dealing with land in Myanmar. CPC section 16 provides that, as a basic rule, the suits should be instituted in the court where immovable property is located.[17]

[12] See n 11 for the text of Explanation II.

[13] *VAS Arogya Odeyar* (n 10).

[14] *VAS Arogya Odeyar* (n 10) is also authority (at [218]) for the proposition that the Myanmar court will not issue an injunction to prevent a party resident in another country from enforcing a judgment obtained in that country, where the subject matter of the judgment is wholly within the jurisdiction of the courts of that other country.

[15] *Steel Brothers & Co Ltd v Y A Ganny Sons and Two* [1965] *Burma Law Reports* 449 (CC) (U Kyaw Zan U J).

[16] *Steel Brothers & Co Ltd* (n 15) [456]. Interestingly, the judge observed (at [463]) that

> It is not necessary that every order of a Court should be supported by a specific statutory provision and when there is neither provision nor prohibition it has to be guided by ordinary principles of common sense, justice, equity and good conscience. Since the laws are general rules, they cannot regulate for all time to come so as to make express provisions against all the cases that may possibly happen. The inherent power of the Court to act *Ex Debito Justitiae* is expressly recognised in section 151 of the Code of Civil Procedure.

Echoing the judge, it is submitted that by section CPC s 151 the Myanmar court has an inherent power to develop principles of indirect jurisdiction 'as may be necessary for the ends of justice or to prevent abuse of the process of the Court'.

[17] Contrast *SPS Chokkappa Chetty v ISPSRM Raman Chetty* (1917) 9 *Lower Burma Rulings* 103 (Ormond Offg CJ, Parlett J), where the Burmese court refused to recognise a Pudukkottai (Indian) judgment dealing with property (a money-lending business) in Pegu (Bago).

This is the same as the general limb of the *Moçambique* rule.[18] But section 16 includes a proviso that reflects one of the exceptions to the *Moçambique* rule. The proviso states:

> Provided that a suit to obtain relief respecting, or compensation for wrong to, immoveable property held by or on behalf of the defendant may, where the relief sought can be entirely obtained through his personal obedience, be instituted either in the Court within the local limits of whose jurisdiction the property is situate, or in the Court within the local limits of whose jurisdiction the defendant actually and voluntarily resides, or carries on business, or personally works for gain.

According to the proviso, where title to immovable property only arises as an incidental question, the court of the place where the defendant (say) is resident or carries on business may assert jurisdiction. Consequently, if (for example) a plaintiff sues a defendant for overdue rent on property situated in Myanmar and the defendant alleges by way of defence for non-payment that the relevant parcel of land does not belong to the plaintiff, the question of title to land is only incidentally related to the parties' dispute. The main issue is whether the defendant has a personal obligation to pay rent to the plaintiff. If a foreign court in country X hears such case on the basis that the defendant carries on substantial business in country X, the Myanmar court may well accept, on the basis of section 16, that the foreign court has met the condition of indirect jurisdiction in CPC sections 13 and 14. This would be despite the relevant parcel of land being in Myanmar and title to land being at issue.

CPC section 16 may be further generalised. Consider, for instance, the case where an intellectual property right (IPR) is registered in Myanmar. The plaintiff owner of the IPR licenses the defendant to make use of that right in country X, where the defendant conducts its business. The plaintiff sues the defendant in country X for non-payment of royalties. The defendant pleads a defence that the registration of the IPR in Myanmar is invalid. A judgment by the court of country X in the plaintiff's favour may be recognised in Myanmar by analogy with CPC section 16 because the dispute between the parties is essentially whether the defendant owes the plaintiff a personal obligation to pay royalties. The question of the validity of the IPR registration in Myanmar only arises as an incidental question. In the example, neither party was asking that the IPR registration be vacated or amended in some way and the judgment does not purport to order a change to the IPR registration.

In brief, although Myanmar has no legislation specifically dealing with indirect jurisdiction, there is sufficient material in CPC sections 15 to 24 and existing case law to enable judges to identify rudimentary principles of indirect jurisdiction. Such activism by judges would be consistent with the power and duty under CPC section 151 to make such orders as may be necessary to serve the ends of justice and prevent the abuse of a litigant seeking to re-open substantive issues that have previously been determined by a foreign court of competent jurisdiction.[19]

[18] Named after the case *British South Africa Co v Companhia de Moçambique* [1893] AC 602 (HL).

[19] See also *Mohamed Khan v Damayanthi Parekh* [1952] *Burma Law Reports* 356 (U Aung Tha Gyaw J) [373], for obiter remarks on when a foreign court may claim international jurisdiction, in which the judge concludes that 'cause of action is not a general ground of jurisdiction recognised by International Law'. However, the latter principles were inapplicable in the case, since there was domestic legislation explicitly authorising the Burmese court to exercise jurisdiction over an absent foreigner.

iii. Public Policy

Myanmar has no enactment defining 'public policy'. But, in light of CPC section 13, if a foreign judgment is to be recognised by the Myanmar court, it must not have been obtained by fraud and must accord with international law, natural justice and Myanmar law. Accordingly, one can deduce that those requirements essentially delineate the bounds of 'public policy' as far as the Myanmar court is concerned. On the one hand, foreign judgments must conform with international law and natural justice, that is, with international public policy or international standards of fairness and due process.[20] On the other hand, they must comply with domestic public policy which, on the basis of section 13, means that recognition of a foreign judgment should not lead to a contravention of Myanmar law.

One may ask what it means for a foreign judgment to conform with (and not contravene) Myanmar law. Take the case where Myanmar law is plainly applicable in a matter, because of (say) the close connection between the matters in dispute and Myanmar, but the foreign court by reference to its conflict of law rules applies a different law. There is a possibility that the Myanmar court will not recognise the judgment on the ground that (in the words of section 13) there has been 'a refusal to recognise the law of the Union of Burma in cases in which such law is applicable'. Nonetheless, it is submitted that not every failure to apply Myanmar law should be taken as falling within the proscription in section 13. Thus, for instance, in *SPSN Kasivisvanathan Chettiar v SS Khrishnappa Chettiar*, the Court of Appeal observed:[21]

> There is yet another aspect to this case. Section 13 of the [CPC] lays down that 'a foreign judgment shall be conclusive as to any matter thereby directly adjudicated upon between the same parties', except under certain specified circumstances. Assuming for the sake of argument that the plaintiff-appellant's claim was time-barred [under Burmese law as the *lex fori*], the learned Counsel for the respondent has argued that the foreign Court's decree is 'a claim founded on a breach of law in force in Burma'. It is difficult to appreciate this argument as a claim to recover monies in deposit is hardly an illegal claim. Had the suit been on for the recovery of a gambling debt or in respect of an immoral contract then clearly such a claim would be 'founded on a breach of a law in force in the Union of Burma'. In *Ganga Prasad and another v Ganesh Lal and others* [56 All 119] it

[20] For an example of the court looking into the due process of a proceeding, see *C Burn v D T Keymer* (1913) 7 *Lower Burma Rulings* 56 (Parlett J), involving an English default judgment that the Burmese court held was enforceable as the defendant (who was resident in Burma) had been afforded a reasonable opportunity to defend himself. The defendant had filed an affidavit setting out his defence and the plaintiff had put in an affidavit in reply. Leave to defend had been given on condition that the defendant made a payment into court by a certain date. The defendant claimed not to have received notice of the condition in time to remit the payment by post. He did not telegraph the requisite payment on account of expense. Accordingly, default judgment was entered against the defendant. The Burmese judgment notes that '[i]nstead of taking steps to get the judgment in default set aside and to obtain leave to defend the action in accordance with the rules of the Supreme Court, the appellant did nothing, again, he says, on the score of expense'. See also *A N Abdul Rahiman v J M Mahomed Ali Rowther* (1928) 6 AIR (Rangoon) 552, doubting the correctness of *C Burn v D T Keymer* (at [556]) and refusing to enforce a Singapore default judgment entered 'as a matter of course in favour of the plaintiff without the plaintiff being called upon to prove his case'. Chari J was of the view (at [557]) that what was needed to be enforceable in Burma was 'a decision on the merits [which] involves the application of the mind of the Court to the truth or falsity of the plaintiff's case'. Consequently, 'though a judgment passed after a judicial consideration of the matter by taking evidence may be a decision on the merits even though passed *ex parte* [that is, the defendant being in default], a decision passed without evidence of any kind cannot be held to be a decision on the merits'.

[21] *SPSN Kasivisvanathan Chettiar v SS Khrishnappa Chettiar* [1951] *Burma Law Reports* 399 (U On Pe and U San Maung JJ) [402].

> was laid down by a Bench of the Allahabad High Court that where a foreign Court merely applies its own law of Limitation in respect of a matter before it that Court cannot be said to have refused to recognise the laws of India simply because the law of Limitation may be different in the two countries …

Suppose instead that the foreign court applies Myanmar law, but does so incorrectly. Will the judgment be refused recognition on the ground that there has been a contravention of Myanmar law? It is submitted that the Myanmar court should exercise caution in the handling of such situations and should not automatically refuse recognition merely because in the view of the Myanmar judge the foreign court has wrongly applied Myanmar law. The actual wording of CPC section 13 is that a foreign judgment 'shall be conclusive … except … (f) where it sustains a claim founded on a breach of any law in the Union of Burma'. Not every error as to the content of Myanmar law will have the consequence that the underlying claim founded on such error breaches Myanmar law. For instance, the foreign court may have incorrectly applied the Myanmar law relating to offer and acceptance when concluding that a commercial contract came into existence between the plaintiff and the defendant. It is difficult to see how recognising the foreign judgment in such circumstance would mean sustaining a claim that is in breach of Myanmar law. The Myanmar judge dealing with an application for the recognition of the relevant foreign judgment must evaluate whether recognition of the judgment would mean the breach (as opposed to the mere mis-application) of some Myanmar law. It is submitted that it would not be enough for the Myanmar judge to say that the foreign court erred in its application of Myanmar law and, on that basis alone, there is a breach of Myanmar law.

The foregoing discussion is not a mere quibble with words. There is a danger, if any error of Myanmar law (whether trivial or otherwise) automatically leads to a foreign judgment being refused recognition, that applications for the recognition of foreign judgments will become occasions for unscrupulous defendants to re-open and re-litigate decided cases by taking unmeritorious or overly-technical points of Myanmar law. This (it is submitted) would be an abuse of process by such defendants. The Myanmar court will need to be vigilant against such practice. An enforcing court should refrain from going into the merits of a foreign judgment.[22]

iv. Restriction to Money Judgments?

The Order XV procedure discussed above is at heart a means of obtaining recognition of a foreign judgment and converting the same into a domestic judgment of the Myanmar court. The focus has been on a claim for debt due to the plaintiff by the defendant as the result of the foreign judgment. It might be asked whether the Order XV procedure can be used in connection with foreign judgments granting specific performance or injunctions or whether the Order XV procedure is limited to foreign judgments for the payment of a sum of money. On its terms, Order XV is not limited to money claims. Therefore, in theory, it can also be used to convert orders for specific performance or injunctions by a foreign court into analogous orders by the Myanmar court. But, in practical terms, the process of conversion into a Myanmar judgment in such cases is unlikely to be as automatic as

[22] ibid, [403].

where the claim is simply for the payment of a sum of money due and owing. The reason is that, in keeping with most common law systems, the remedies of specific performance and injunctions in Myanmar law are equitable remedies that are subject to the court's discretion. Therefore, although the Myanmar court may recognise the judgment as giving rise to some right in the plaintiff applicant under the Order XV procedure, the mere fact of the foreign judgment will not absolve the Myanmar judge from having to determine whether in the exercise of one's own discretion it would be appropriate to grant specific performance or an injunction in the particular situation before the Myanmar court. In deciding whether to exercise its discretion, the Myanmar judge will have to consider all relevant circumstances at the time of the Order XV application. Such circumstances may or may not be the same as those existing at the time of the original judgment by the rendering court.

B. Enforcement of Foreign Judgments

i. Use of CPC Section 44A

The procedure for the enforcement (as opposed to mere recognition) of foreign judgments is set out in CPC section 44A:[23]

> (1) Where a certified copy of a decree of any of the superior courts of the United Kingdom or any reciprocating territory has been filed in a District Court, the decree may be executed in the Union of Myanmar as if it had been passed by the District Court.
>
> (2) Together with the certified copy of the decree shall be filed a certificate from such superior Court stating the extent, if any, to which the decree has been satisfied or adjusted and such certificate shall, for the purpose of proceedings under this section, be conclusive proof of the extent of such satisfaction or adjustment.
>
> (3) The provision of section 47[24] shall as from the filing of the certified copy of the decree apply to the proceedings of a District Court executing a decree under this section, and District Court shall refuse execution of such decree, if it is shown to the satisfaction of the Court that the decree falls within any of the exceptions specified in clauses (a) to (f) of section 13.
>
> Explanation 1 – 'Superior Court', with reference to the United Kingdom, means the High Court in England, the Court of Session in Scotland, the High Court in Northern Ireland, the Court of Chancery of the Country Palatine of Durham.
>
> Explanation 2 – 'Reciprocating territory' means any country or territory, which the President may, from time to time, by notification in the Gazette declare to be reciprocating territory for the purposes of this section: and 'superior Courts', with reference to any such territory means such Courts as may be specified in the said notification.

[23] Inserted into the CPC by the Code of Civil Procedure (Amendment) Act 1937 (India Act VIII of 1937). CPC s 44A was purportedly amended by the Code of Civil Procedure (Amendment) Act 1956 (enacted on 9 October 1956), so as to delete the references to the courts of the United Kingdom. But it does not appear that the 1956 amendment ever came into effect. This is because s 1(2) of the 1956 Act provided that 'It shall come into force on such date as the President of the Union may, by notification, appoint' and no date ever seems to have been notified.

[24] CPC s 47 specifies the questions to be determined by the court executing a decree.

> Explanation 3 – 'Decree', with a reference to a superior Court, means any decree or judgment of such Court under which a sum of money is payable, not been a sum payable in respect of taxes or other charges of a like nature or in respect of a fine or other penalty, and
>
> (a) with reference to the superior Courts in the United Kingdom includes judgments given and decrees made in any Court in appeal against such decrees or judgment, but
>
> (b) shall in no case includes an arbitration award, even if such award is enforceable as a decree or judgment.

Consequently, as a curious vestige of colonial times, only UK judgments may be directly enforced in Myanmar under section 44A. Otherwise, no reciprocating territory having ever been notified or gazetted by any Myanmar government, the judgments of no other country can be enforced pursuant to the procedure in section 44A. The provision is thus of extremely limited use at present.

Section 44A refers to the gazettal of 'reciprocating territories'. The term 'reciprocating' is not defined. In actuality, it is unclear what would constitute a 'reciprocating territory' as a matter of Myanmar law. Nonetheless, as Myanmar's economy opens up to the outside world and foreign direct investment, consideration may be given in the future to the identification and notification of more and more countries as 'reciprocating territories'. It is submitted that guidance may be obtained on the meaning of 'reciprocating' or 'reciprocity' from the liberal approach spelled out in the Nanning Statement issued by the 2nd China–ASEAN Justice Forum on 8 June 2017. The Statement was a consensus reached at the Forum among Chief Justices and senior judges from China, ASEAN and other Asian countries, including Chief Justice of the Union of Myanmar Htun Htun Oo. Article VII of the Nanning Statement reads:

> Regional cross-border transactions and investments require a judicial safeguard based on appropriate mutual recognition and enforcement of judicial judgments among countries in the region. Subject to their domestic laws, Supreme Courts of participating countries will keep good faith in interpreting domestic laws, try to avoid unnecessary parallel proceedings, and consider facilitating the appropriate mutual recognition and enforcement of civil or commercial judgments among different jurisdictions. If two countries have not been bound by any international treaty on mutual recognition and enforcement of foreign civil or commercial judgments, both countries may, subject their domestic laws, presume the existence of their reciprocal relationship, when it comes to the judicial procedure of recognizing or enforcing such judgments made by courts of the other country, provided that the courts of the other country had not refused to recognise or enforce such judgments on the ground of lack of reciprocity.

In the absence of evidence to the contrary, it is suggested that reciprocity can be presumed for the purposes of the mutual recognition and enforcement of judgments across borders.

ii. Enforcement of Foreign Judgments as Myanmar Judgments under Order XV

General provisions have been enacted in CPC section 36 to 74 and the Rules of Procedure, Order XXI Rules 1 to 103 for the enforcement or execution of the decrees (judgments) of the Myanmar court, including those resulting from a foreign judgment through the Order XV procedure discussed above. In gist, the Myanmar court in a relevant geographical area may execute a decree on the application of the decree-holder in the following ways:[25] (1) by delivery of any property specifically decreed; (2) by attachment and sale or by sale without attachment of any property; (3) by arrest and detention in prison; (4) by appointing a receiver under Order XL Rules 1 to 5; and (5) by any other manner as the nature of the relief granted may require.

III. Conclusion

This chapter has suggested that the Myanmar court can recognise and enforce foreign judgments on the basis of existing sections and Orders in the CPC. The chapter has argued that, by analogy with such provisions and guided by previously decided cases, it should be possible for the Myanmar court to fashion principles of indirect jurisdiction and public policy for the purposes of evaluating whether a foreign judgment should be recognised. Through the summary procedure in Order XV, foreign judgments that meet the conditions of finality, indirect jurisdiction and that do not contravene public policy may be converted into readily enforceable judgments of the Myanmar court, especially where the foreign decree has given rise to a debt due from defendant to the plaintiff. The Order XV procedure will make up for the limited utility of CPC section 44A whereby currently only UK judgments can be directly enforced in Myanmar.

Nonetheless, in conjunction with the gradual opening up of the Myanmar economy to foreign direct investment, it is envisaged, especially following on the approach to 'reciprocity' on the Nanning Statement of 2017 as signed by the Chief Justice of the Union of Myanmar, that the government will be notifying more and more countries as 'reciprocating territories' within the terms of section 44A. This would further facilitate the recognition and enforcement of foreign judgments in Myanmar.

Other developments that might be considered, although more likely in the middle- to long-term, rather than in the immediate future, would be for Myanmar to become party to the 2005 Hague Convention on Choice of Court Agreements[26] and the forthcoming Convention of the Recognition and Enforcement of Judgments in Civil and Commercial Matters currently being drafted as part of the Hague Conference on Private International Law's Judgments Project. Accession to those two conventions would assist in (1) identifying the types of foreign judgments that should be recognised and enforced under Myanmar law; and (2) clarifying the principles of indirect jurisdiction and public policy that should apply to such process.

[25] For limitation periods on the execution of a Burmese decree, see CPC s 48 (imposing a general limit of 12 years) and para 183 of the First Sch to the Limitation Act (India Act IX of 1908), which came into force in Burma on 1 January 1909 and remains in effect today. Under para 117 of the First Sch, the time for bringing suit upon a foreign judgment is six years.

[26] As at 1 April 2019, there were 32 Contracting States to the 2005 Hague Convention, including one Regional Economic Integration Organization (REIO) (namely, the European Union). In addition, the US, Ukraine and China have signed the 2005 Convention, but have not to date acceded to it.

12

The Philippines

ARVIN A JO AND JOCELYN P CRUZ

I. Introduction

No other body of law is more completely judge-made than the law on the recognition and enforcement of foreign judgments.[1] With almost no statute or treaty basis from the political branches of government about foreign court orders, the case law and court rules of procedure in the Philippines have developed under the principles of *ex comitate* and *ex debito justitiae* (principles of comity). Instead of reciprocity, focus is placed on the persuasiveness of foreign judgments in enunciating legal obligations. The Supreme Court's emerging characterisation of the obligation to recognise or enforce foreign judgments as part of generally accepted principles of international law, coupled with recent legislation and developments that bolster the extra-territorial commercial and civil interests of Filipino firms and nationals, should militate towards the adoption of a more seamless framework for giving effect to judgments from foreign courts.

II. Background

Up until the late nineteenth century, the mainstream Philippine society could be readily characterised as Hispanicised, following Spanish colonial rule beginning from the mid-sixteenth century. The Philippines though was not directly administered from the monarch's court in Madrid, as it was only a part of the vast Spanish domains at the time that included territories in Central and South America.[2] Rather, for administrative purposes, Spain ruled through a type of jurisdiction known as the viceroyalty, one of which was the viceroyalty of New Spain under which the Philippines was a *gobernacion* (provincial government).[3] The import of this was that, while the laws governing the colonies emanated from the Spanish monarch's council, the viceroy or governor running affairs in the Philippines implemented the laws from Madrid through an impressive assortment of decrees (eg *cedulas, decretos, resoluciones, ordenamientos, reglamentos, pragmaticas*)[4] which were essentially different from the laws in Spain and other Spanish colonies.

[1] Ronald H Graveson, *Conflict of Laws: Private International Law* 7th edn (London, Sweet & Maxwell, 1974).
[2] Ruben F Balane, 'The Spanish Antecedents of the Philippine Civil Code' (1979) 54 *Philippine Law Journal* 1, 37.
[3] ibid.
[4] Horacio de la Costa, *Asia and the Philippines* (Manila, Solidaridad Publishing House, 1967).

Spain codified its laws several decades after the Napoleonic occupation in 1812, and the *Codigo Civil* was extended to the Philippines in 1889.[5] That legislation already contained provisions addressing the conflict of laws. These same legal provisions[6] have been carried on and adopted in the present Civil Code and have gained greater relevance following the Philippines' attainment of full sovereignty in 1946. Thus, when a Filipino national contracts a marriage or pursues any other act concerning his personal status while in a foreign country, the Civil Code provisions on conflict of laws provides for the nationality principle[7] (that is, Filipino nationals are always governed by Philippine personal and family laws even when residing in another county with different laws). Other conflict of laws principles in the Philippine Civil Code that remain applicable today include the use of the *lex loci rei sitae*[8] (the law of the place where property is situated) to govern immovables and the *lex loci celebrationis*[9] (the law of the place of celebration) to govern the formalities of a marriage.

At the turn of the nineteenth century, as Spanish global empire was waning, control over the Philippines was taken over by the US. American colonial administrators wasted no time in introducing elements of the common law system. They specifically created a novel trial and appellate court system in the Philippines, manned by full-time judges.[10] The Second Philippine Commission was a legislative cum executive body created by US President William McKinley. Composed of five American administrators, it enacted a law in 1901 providing for the establishment of a set of courts, the apex of which later became the Supreme Court of the Philippines.[11] By 1914 the Philippine Commission had evolved into the Philippine Legislature (with a lower chamber consisting of elected representatives) and promulgated the Code of Civil Procedure of the Philippine Islands, essentially providing for more explicit rules of procedure before the courts created earlier.[12] The Code of Civil Procedure was copied from the Californian Code of Civil Procedure,[13] making it a definite progeny of the American common law system.

This set the backdrop of *Ingenohl v Olsen*,[14] a trademark dispute between a German and American company. The German company sought to enforce a Hong Kong judgment in the Philippines, where the American company's assets were located. The Philippine Supreme Court decided this case in 1925 and introduced the concept of 'comity', which had first been articulated in the landmark US Supreme Court case of *Hilton v Guyot*:

> The extent to which the law of one nation, as put in force within its territory, whether by executive order, by legislative act, or by judicial decree, shall be allowed to operate within the dominion of another nation, depends upon what our greatest jurists have been content to call 'the comity of nations'. Although the phrase has been often criticised, no satisfactory substitute has been suggested. 'Comity', in the legal sense, is neither a matter of absolute obligation, on the one hand,

[5] Balane (n 2).
[6] An Act to Ordain and Institute the Civil Code of the Philippines, Republic Act No 386 (1950) (Civil Code).
[7] Civil Code, Art 15.
[8] ibid, Art 16.
[9] ibid, Art 17.
[10] 'A Constitutional History of the Supreme Court of the Philippines' (*Supreme Court of the Philippines*, 2013), available online: sc.judiciary.gov.ph/aboutsc/history/index.php.
[11] ibid.
[12] ibid.
[13] *Mijares v Ranada* GR No 139325 (2005).
[14] *Ingenohl v Olsen* GR No L-22288 (1925).

> nor of mere courtesy and good will, upon the other. But it is the recognition which one nation allows within its territory to the legislative, executive, or judicial acts of another nation, having due regard both to international duty and convenience, and to the rights of its own citizens, or of other persons was are under the protection of its laws.[15]

III. Recognition and Enforcement under Treaties or Similar Arrangements

The principle of comity has been consistently applied in subsequent cases since its early adoption in the 1920s.[16] Despite this, the government has never seized the opportunity to articulate the principles underlying recognition and enforcement in any detail. Further, the executive, the principal architect of foreign relations under the Philippine Constitution, has never signed a treaty or international convention regarding the enforcement and recognition of foreign judgments. In particular, the Philippines has acceded to neither the 1971 Hague Convention on the Recognition and Enforcement of Foreign Judgments in Civil and Commercial Matters nor the 2005 Hague Convention on Choice of Court Agreements. However, the Philippines became a member of the Hague Conference on Private International Law in July 2010 and membership has borne fruit in terms of removing a significant hurdle in the procedure for recognition and enforcement of foreign judgments. In September 2018 the Philippines deposited its instrument of accession to the 1961 Hague Apostille Convention. The instrument will become legally binding in the Philippines (which is a monist state) from May 2019.[17] That will facilitate the process of recognition and enforcement of foreign judgments, because at present a foreign public document (such as a judgment) has to be certified by both its foreign custodian and the Philippine embassy or consular officer of the foreign country in order to be admissible before the Philippine court.[18] This requirement of double notarisation may be costly and time-consuming.

IV. Recognition and Enforcement in the Absence of Treaties or Similar Arrangement

In the absence of treaties and international conventions, the recognition and enforcement of foreign judgments hinges on national law. In contrast to the American approach (as shown in the *Hilton* case where the US Supreme Court refused to enforce a French judgment on the ground that there was no reciprocity), the Philippine court does not tie up the principle of comity with reciprocity. As commonly understood in international relations, reciprocity pertains to the exchange of mutual favours or treatment.[19] Understood in that sense,

[15] *Hilton v Guyot* 159 US 113 (1895) 163–64.
[16] See eg *St Aviation Services Co Pte Ltd v Grand International Airways Inc*, GR No 140288 (2006).
[17] ibid.
[18] Revised Rules on Evidence, as Amended per Supreme Court Resolution Adopted on 14 March 1989 (1989) (Rules of Evidence), r 132, s 24.
[19] Robert O Keohane, 'Reciprocity in International Relations' (1986) 40(1) *International Organization* 1.

reciprocity has never been specifically considered by the Philippine Supreme Court in cases of recognition or enforcement of foreign judgments. While a Philippine court may favourably take into account the existence of reciprocity in deciding whether to recognise and enforce foreign judgments, the absence of it is not a ground for denial.

Rule 39, Section 48 of the 1997 Rules of Civil Procedure (Rules of Court) is the sole relevant provision in this regard. It provides:

> Sec. 48. Effect of foreign judgments or final orders
>
> The effect of a judgment or final order of a tribunal of a foreign country, having jurisdiction to render the judgment or final order is as follows:
>
> (a) In case of a judgment or final order upon a specific thing, the judgment or final order, is conclusive upon the title to the thing, and
>
> (b) In case of a judgment or final order against a person, the judgment or final order is presumptive evidence of a right as between the parties and their successors in interest by a subsequent title.
>
> In either case, the judgment or final order may be repelled by evidence of a want of jurisdiction, want of notice to the party, collusion, fraud, or clear mistake of law or fact.

Rule 39 is almost identical, save for the addition of the phrases 'or tribunal' and 'in either case', to the equivalent proviso in the 1914 Code of Civil Procedure. However, it should be mentioned that the present Rules of Court was issued under the constitutional authority of the Philippine Supreme Court to 'promulgate rules concerning the … procedure in all courts'[20] and is therefore not a legislative creation. It is also worth mentioning that the use of the more inclusive term 'tribunal' implies that Rule 39 is not limited to foreign court judgments. It may also be applied to foreign decisions made by quasi-juridical institutions such as foreign arbitral panels (especially arbitral awards rendered in states which are not parties to the 1958 New York Convention and which do not extend comity or reciprocity to arbitral awards rendered in the Philippines), as was done by the Philippine Supreme Court in *Oil and Natural Gas Commission v Court of Appeals*.[21] Nowhere does Rule 39 requires reciprocity. Instead, the principle of comity that has long been part of Philippine case law has led to courts focusing on the existence, finality, specificity and possibility of repeal of a foreign judgment when deciding whether or not to recognise and enforce the same. In the authors' view, the absence of grounds for repeal (especially on the basis of clear mistake of law or clear mistake of fact) as well as the extrinsic grounds of want of jurisdiction or notice, fraud and collusion, go towards the persuasiveness of the foreign judgment as an instrument giving rise to an obligation on the part of the Philippines to recognise and enforce it *ex comitate et ex debito justitiae*. One leading American decided case succinctly put it this way:

> Comity is not a rule of law, but it is a rule of practice, convenience and expediency. It is something more than mere courtesy, which implies only deference to the opinion of others, since it has a substantial value in securing uniformity of decision and discouraging repeated litigation of the same question. It, therefore, rests, not on the basis of reciprocity, but rather upon the persuasiveness of the foreign judgment.[22]

[20] 1987 Constitution of the Republic of the Philippines, Art VIII, s 5(5).

[21] *Oil and Natural Gas Commission v Court of Appeals* GR No 114323 (1998).

[22] *Johnston v Compagnie Generale Transatlantique* 242 NY 381 (1926).

Thus, a legal obligation to recognise or enforce is not owed to an individual plaintiff. The obligation that stems from the existence of a qualifying foreign judgment is owed to the community of nations pursuant to generally accepted notions of international law.[23]

A. Initiating the Process of Recognition and Enforcement

Although the dispute in *Ingenohl*[24] was entirely commercial in nature, the law that figured prominently in the ruling of the Philippine Supreme Court was the 1914 Code of Civil Procedure which applies to all civil actions. The Philippine courts are generally indifferent as to the nature of specific transactions between parties. They are all classified as civil cases, whereas cases which may lead to imprisonment are classified as criminal in nature. For purposes of recognising or enforcing foreign court judgments, the Philippines does not make any distinction between 'civil' and 'commercial'. There is however a tangential way of identifying matters that are deemed by Philippines law as 'commercial', by reference to the sorts of cases that trial court branches designated by the Supreme Court as special commercial courts can hear. These are cases pertaining to an alleged violation of Philippine laws on: (1) financial rehabilitation and insolvency; (2) intra-corporate and securities disputes; (3) intellectual property (including alleged civil or criminal wrongs, as well as application for temporary relief); (4) admiralty and maritime; and (5) dissolution of business partnerships.[25] Notably absent from the special commercial courts' jurisdiction are: (1) cases involving the enforcement of international commercial arbitration awards from non-parties of the 1958 New York Convention, which do not extend comity or reciprocity to the Philippines; (2) Philippine anti-trust or competition law matters; and (3) certain disputes arising from the Philippine foreign investments law. These special commercial courts have merely been 'designated' as such from among the multiple branches of regional trial courts (RTCs). The designation does not create exclusive jurisdiction. In the absence of a designated commercial court (which is not uncommon in some regions), other branches of an RTC may take cognisance of the commercial cases just enumerated. This is unlike tax cases, which in the Philippines are exclusively handled by a separate trial court system (although ultimately appealable to the same Supreme Court). Hence, tax disputes as well as anti-graft or government corruption cases are handled by specialised courts. Decisions of the RTCs are appealed to the Court of Appeals. The Court of Appeals' decision may then be brought for review before the Supreme Court.

There is no separate process for the recognition and enforcement of foreign court judgments. If the goal of bringing a foreign judgment before a Philippine court is 'for the enforcement or protection of a right', then it is properly initiated through a civil action.[26] Such civil action can be further classified into personal or real actions. A real action is one which may affect title to or possession of land or an interest therein. Actions other than that

[23] *Mijares v Ranada* (n 13).

[24] *Ingenohl v Olsen* (n 14).

[25] See eg *Re Consolidation of Intellectual Property Courts with Commercial Courts*, Supreme Court of the Philippines Administrative Matter No 03-03-03-SC.

[26] ibid.

(such as a claim for damages) are deemed to be personal actions.[27] One the other hand, if a party's purpose is merely the recognition of a foreign judgment to 'establish a status, a right, or a particular fact', then one has to initiate a 'special' proceeding before the Philippine court to recognise the foreign judgments.[28] This process is 'special' in the sense that the plaintiff's case will be challenged by some public or governmental authority (eg the Civil Registrar who issues and maintains birth certificate records), instead of the defendant in the original action.

The enforcement of a foreign judgment necessarily presupposes prior recognition. Hence, there is an implied plea for 'recognition' in an enforcement action relating to a foreign judgment. One should not, however, take the silence of Rule 39, Section 48 of the Rules of Court as to a distinction between 'recognition' or 'enforcement' to mean that they are the same process. A special proceeding for 'recognition' of foreign judgment would only amount to a plea for the establishment of a 'status, a right, or a particular fact' before a pertinent government functionary. Enforcement does not follow from such recognition of a foreign judgment. The special proceeding for the recognition of the foreign judgment is governed by a separate section of the Rules of Court and will normally conclude upon the public functionary's acknowledgement or rejection of such status. On the other hand, a claim for enforcement or protection of a right must be brought as a civil action against a person or against real property under a different section of the Rules of Court. It is often accompanied by an application for affirmative relief or an active measure from the Philippine court.

The latter was precisely the situation in *Hang Lung Bank Ltd v Saulog*,[29] a case involving a sum of money adjudged by a Hong Kong court in favour of the plaintiff bank. The Philippine Supreme Court there characterised the petitioner bank's action as thus:

> In its pleadings before the court, petitioner appears to be in a quandary as to whether the suit below is one for enforcement or recognition of the Hong Kong judgment. … The complaint therefore appears to be one of enforcement of the Hong Kong judgment because it prays for the grant of the affirmative relief given by said foreign judgment.
>
> …
>
> However, a foreign judgment may not be enforced if it is not recognised in the jurisdiction where affirmative relief is being sought. Hence, in the interest of justice, the complaint should be considered as a petition for the recognition of the Hong Kong judgment under Section 50(b), Rule 39 [now Section 48, Rule 39] of the Rules of Court in order that the defendant, private respondent herein, may present evidence of lack of jurisdiction, notice, collusion, fraud or clear mistake of fact and law, if applicable.

It bears emphasis that *Hang Lung Bank* ruling does not mean that 'enforcement' should first be sought, so that 'recognition' by the same court will be proper. Rather, the jurisprudential lesson here is that the way or manner by which a foreign judgment is presented before the Philippine court dictates whether it will be treated as a mere 'recognition' issue or as an 'enforcement' matter requiring affirmative relief. Attention should be focused on the fact

[27] Willard B Riano, *Civil Procedure: A Restatement for the Bar* (Manila, Rex Book Store, 2009).
[28] 1997 Rules of Civil Procedure of the Philippines (1997) (Rules of Court), r 4, ss 1–2.
[29] *Hang Lung Bank Ltd v Saulog* GR No 73765 (1991).

that the plaintiff bank, in its original action before the Philippine trial court, adduced the following evidence:

1. Copies of two continuing guarantees (ie credit line documents) executed between the plaintiff bank and the defendant debtor;
2. A mere photocopy of the judgment of the Hong Kong court ordering the defendant to pay a certain sum of money to the plaintiff; and,
3. Copies of demand letters written by the bank's counsel and the documents that were received in defendant's place of business after issuance of the Hong Kong judgment.

The foregoing demonstrate that what the plaintiff was seeking to prove before the Philippine court was the fact of breach of contract giving rise to a cause of action, and not the fact and existence of the foreign court judgment itself. This distinction between proving the facts that evince a cause of action as opposed to proving the existence of the foreign judgment was further elucidated by the Supreme Court in *Mijares v Ranada*:[30]

> There are distinctions, nuanced but discernible, between the cause of action arising from the enforcement of a foreign judgment, and that arising from the facts or allegations that occasioned the foreign judgment. They may pertain to the same set of facts, but there is an essential difference in the right-duty correlatives that are sought to be vindicated. For example, in a complaint for damages against a tortfeasor, the cause of action emanates from the violation of the right of the complainant through the act or omission of the respondent. On the other hand, in a complaint for the enforcement of a foreign judgment awarding damages from the same tortfeasor, for the violation of the same right through the same manner of action, the cause of action derives not from the tortious act but from the foreign judgment itself.

In other words, proving the underlying facts or allegations that occasioned a foreign judgment amounts to no more than an exercise to establish a 'status, right, or particular fact' which is tantamount to seeking recognition of the status or right declared in the foreign judgment. In the *Hang Lung Bank* case, had the plaintiff bank presented its case in such a way that it proved the existence of the foreign judgment, it would have been a matter of enforcing such foreign judgment for affirmative relief from the Philippines court. In short, depending on how a case has been pleaded, the Philippine court can determine whether a matter will be treated as one requiring mere recognition or one calling for enforcement of a foreign judgment.

B. Existence of the Foreign Judgment

The Rules of Court provision on foreign court judgments clearly does not provide for its recognition or enforcement by a mere motion for execution. Rather, the non-satisfaction of the foreign court judgment will give rise to a cause of action by which a case for enforcement or recognition may be filed before a Philippine trial court. A petition or action for the recognition or enforcement of a foreign judgment should be filed before an appropriate RTC.[31] The reason for this is that, under the statute delineating jurisdiction

[30] *Mijares v Ranada* (n 13).

[31] Judiciary Reorganization Act of 1980 (Batas Pambansa Blg 129), s 19.

among the various courts, in all cases not falling within the exclusive jurisdiction of any court or body (such as a petition for foreign judgment recognition), it is the RTC that shall have jurisdiction.[32] Specifically, this would be the RTC in the city or province where the plaintiff or defendant is situated or where the subject real property is to be found. It is not necessary to have an action for enforcement of foreign judgment directed to an RTC that is designated as a special commercial court.

The first step in enforcement will be to establish the existence of the foreign judgment. Following Rule 132, Section 24 of the Rules of Evidence, court judgments emanating from a foreign country need to be authenticated through official publication in the originating state or through production of a copy of the court judgment as certified by its legal custodian in the foreign country, who must likewise certify to be the official custodian. The Philippine embassy or consular official in the rendering state must certify the foreign judgment, if the latter is to be accorded probative value by the Philippine court.[33] Following this double authentication, the foreign judgment will be regarded as valid by the Philippine court.[34] Left uncontradicted, this will be satisfactory proof that the foreign court which rendered the relevant judgment acted within its jurisdiction. Rule 39, Section 48 of the Rules of Court states that, in such circumstance, the Philippine court is duty-bound to accord conclusive effect to the foreign judgment as far as title to property is concerned or presumptive effect as far as personal actions are concerned.

Nonetheless, foreign judgments that are authenticated, uncontroverted or (in the case of real rights) conclusive may still be refused recognition and enforcement by the Philippine court. Rule 39, Section 48 of the Rules of Court provides that, in actions against persons or property, if there is evidence of the following, the foreign judgment will be rendered nugatory: (1) lack of jurisdiction; (2) lack of notice to a defendant; (3) collusion; (4) fraud; (5) clear mistake of law; or (6) clear mistake of fact. These grounds of review are considered in the next two sections.

C. External Grounds for Review of Foreign Judgments

The Philippines, as the enforcing state, and its courts may undertake a limited review of authenticated foreign judgments. Review is limited in the sense that the specific grounds that may be considered are external to the merits of the case.

Jurisdiction refers to a court's power to try and decide cases. In the absence of jurisdiction, the proceedings and the subsequent court judgment are void. In determining whether a foreign court lacks jurisdiction, the foreign law upon which the rendering court's jurisdiction was based should be proved by the plaintiff before the Philippine court. This was the underlying issue in the case of *Northwest Orient Airlines v Court of Appeals*[35] wherein a Japanese court's summons was not served on the defendant corporation's office in Japan, but was later coursed through diplomatic channels to its headquarters in the Philippines.

[32] ibid.

[33] This process will be simplified by the 1961 Hague Apostille Convention coming into force, when certification of a judgment through the affixing of an apostille issued by the Competent Authority of the Contracting State in which the judgment was issued will suffice.

[34] Rules of Evidence, r 131.

[35] *Northwest Orient Airlines v Court of Appeals* GR No 112573 (1995).

When the enforcement of the final judgment by the Japanese court was sought in the Philippines, the defendant corporation raised the defence of a lack of jurisdiction. The Philippine Supreme Court ruled:

> A foreign judgment is presumed to be valid and binding in the country from which it comes, until the contrary is shown. It is also proper to presume the regularity of the proceedings and the giving of due notice therein.
>
> …
>
> Also, under Section 3 of Rule 131, a court, whether of the Philippines or elsewhere, enjoys the presumption that it was acting in the lawful exercise of jurisdiction and has regularly performed its official duty.
>
> It is settled that matters of remedy and procedure such as those relating to the service of process upon a defendant are governed by the lex fori or the internal law of the forum. In this case, it is the procedural law of Japan where the judgment was rendered that determines the validity of the extraterritorial service of process on [defendant corporation]. As to what this law is, is a question of fact, not of law. It may not be taken judicial notice of and must be pleaded and proved like any other fact. Sections 24 and 25, Rule 132 of the Rules of Court provide that it may be evidenced by an official publication or by a duly attested or authenticated copy thereof. It was then incumbent upon [defendant corporation] to present evidence as to what that Japanese procedural law is and to show that under it, the assailed extraterritorial service is invalid. It did not. Accordingly, the presumption of validity and regularity of the service of summons and the decision thereafter rendered by the Japanese court must stand.
>
> Alternatively, in the light of the absence of proof regarding Japanese law, the presumption of identity or similarity or the so-called processual presumption may be invoked. Applying it, the Japanese law on the matter is presumed to be similar with the Philippine law on service of summons on a private foreign corporation doing business in the Philippines.

Two points stand out from this ruling. First, that Philippine courts will assume that foreign judgments are valid on their face based on the statutory presumption of regularity and lawful exercise of jurisdiction. Second, that a party challenging the jurisdiction of the foreign court must present evidence to prove that under laws of the foreign country jurisdiction was wanting. Otherwise, the Philippine court will apply the doctrine of processual presumption which holds that in case of failure to establish the foreign law, the law of the forum shall be assumed to be similar to that of the foreign country and will be applied.

Want of notice to a party is another ground for impeaching a foreign judgment. In *Boudard v Tait*,[36] the enforcement of a Hanoi court judgment was denied by the Philippine Supreme Court. It inquired why the foreign judgment was issued in default or without any participation from the defendant. It turned out that:

> The evidence adduced at the trial conclusively proves that neither the appellee [the defendant] nor his agent or employees were ever in Hanoi, French Indo-China … The appellee's first intimation of his having been sued and sentenced to pay a huge sum by the civil division of the Court of First Instance of Hanoi was when he was served with summons in the present case.
>
> …
>
> Moreover, the evidence of record shows that the appellee was not in Hanoi during the time mentioned in the complaint of the appellants, nor were his employees or representatives. The rule

[36] *Boudard v Tait* GR No L-45193 (1939).

> in matters of this nature is that judicial proceedings in a foreign country, regarding payment of money, are only effective against a party if summons is duly served on him within such foreign country before the proceedings.

There is wisdom in making 'want of notice to party' a separate ground from 'lack of jurisdiction'[37] as the two do not necessarily have a causal relationship. In the Philippines, since the crux of procedural due process is the provision of 'a reasonable opportunity [for a defendant] to be heard and to present any evidence he may have in support of his defence', it is easy to see how the lack of notice to the defendant is inseparable from the constitutional requirements of procedural due process.[38]

Philippine courts are likewise wary of fraud (more specifically known as 'extrinsic fraud') that may have prevented a party to the foreign judgment from presenting evidence or fully participating in the trial. In *Philippine Aluminum Wheels v FASGI Enterprises*, the Philippine Supreme Court had the opportunity to explain why extrinsic fraud, as opposed to intrinsic fraud, is determinative in the enforcement of foreign judgments:[39]

> Fraud, to hinder the enforcement within this jurisdiction of a foreign judgment, must be extrinsic, i.e., fraud based on facts not controverted or resolved in the case where judgment is rendered, or that which would go to the jurisdiction of the court or would deprive the party against whom judgment is rendered a chance to defend the action to which he has a meritorious case or defence. In fine, intrinsic fraud, that is, fraud which goes to the very existence of the cause of action – such as fraud in obtaining the consent to a contract – is deemed already adjudged, and it, therefore, cannot militate against the recognition or enforcement of the foreign judgment.

Related to external fraud is 'collusion' upon which the enforcement of foreign judgment may also be denied. The collusion, however, must be some form of acting in concert that is prohibited by law. Such was the finding in *Asiavest Merchant Bankers v Court of Appeals* in which an allegation of collusion between the Malaysian plaintiff and the Malaysian lawyers representing a Philippine defendant before the Malaysian court, was rejected by the Philippine Supreme Court:[40]

> On the matter of alleged lack of authority of the law firm of Allen and Gledhill to represent private respondent … of greater significance is the fact that petitioner offered in evidence relevant Malaysian jurisprudence to the effect that (a) it is not necessary under Malaysian law for counsel appearing before the Malaysian High Court to submit a special power of attorney authorizing him to represent a client before said court, (b) that counsel appearing before the Malaysian High Court has full authority to compromise the suit, and (c) that counsel appearing before the Malaysian High Court need not comply with certain pre-requisites as required under Philippine law to appear and compromise judgments on behalf of their clients before said court.

Thus, in *Asiavest Merchant Bankers*, although the actions of the Malaysian law firm were characterised by the Philippine trial court as 'intriguing', the plaintiff's evidence that the Malaysian law authorised such actions, was taken into consideration to rule out collusion.

[37] Note that, in the Philippines, personal service of summons is required to establish jurisdiction over a person.

[38] Ruben E Agpalo, *Conflict of Laws (Private International Law)* (Manila, Rex Book Store, 2004).

[39] *Philippine Aluminum Wheels v FASGI Enterprises* GR No 137378 (2000). Case citations have been omitted from the quoted passage.

[40] *Asiavest Merchant Bankers v Court of Appeals* GR No 110263 (2001). Case citations have been omitted from the quoted passage.

D. Merit-based Review of Foreign Judgments

With respect to the other two grounds for impeaching a foreign court judgment – clear mistake of law or clear mistake of fact – whether a review by a Philippine court on these grounds can still be characterised as external to the merits of the case is disputed.[41] This is because while it had been decided in *Fujuki v Marinay* where the Supreme Court forcefully stated that:[42]

> Courts are not allowed to delve into the merits of a foreign judgment. Once a foreign judgment is admitted and proven in a Philippine court, it can only be repelled on grounds external to its merits, i.e., 'want of jurisdiction, want of notice to the party, collusion, fraud, or clear mistake of law or fact'.

Such statement has been criticised for being overly general.[43] The opposite school of thought is that when a Philippine court examines whether clear mistake of law or clear mistake of fact have been committed in a foreign court judgment, such scrutiny will inevitably delve into the merits of the foreign judgment.[44] There are two leading cases in which the Philippine Supreme Court denied recognition and enforcement to a foreign judgment on account of clear mistake of law and clear mistake of fact. The first one, *Ingenohl v Olsen*,[45] involved a Hong Kong Supreme Court decision which essentially construed a phrase in a contract ('wheresoever situate in the Philippine Islands') and on that basis ruled in favour of the plaintiff. When enforcement of the Hong Kong court's decision was sought and challenged in the Philippines, the defendant raised the issue of clear mistake of fact and law. The Philippine Supreme Court decided the case by identifying three issues. The first was 'the construction that should be placed upon the conveyance'. The Philippine Supreme Court answered that issue thus:

> We have read and reread with care the exhaustive opinion rendered by the Hong Kong court, which had before it all of the evidence now before this court, except as to the proof of the defendant in the instant action on its counterclaim for damages. The Hong Kong court was construing the deed of conveyance made to the defendant founded upon the proceeding which the United States took as a war measure against the plaintiff and his company, as alien enemies, under its Trading with the Enemy Act. For the purposes of this opinion, all of such proceedings must be construed as legal and valid, the scope and nature of which is very apparent from the record.
>
> …
>
> We frankly concede that the authorities cited in that opinion are good law, but they are not in point, for the simple reason that they are founded upon other and different facts. The purpose and intent of the whole transaction is apparent upon the face of the deed of conveyance, the stipulated facts and the nature of the proceedings.
>
> …

[41] See Elizabeth Aguiling-Pangalangan, 'Country Report: Republic of the Philippines' in Adeline Chong (ed), *Recognition and Enforcement of Foreign Judgments in Asia* (Singapore, Asian Business Law Institute, 2017) 157–58; *cf* Agpalo (n 38); Ranhilio Callangan Aquino, *Elements of Private International Law* 2nd edn (Quezon, Central Book Supply, 2006).

[42] *Fujuki v Marinay* GR No 196049 (2013).

[43] Aquino (n 41).

[44] ibid.

[45] *Ingenohl v Olsen* (n 14).

> The judgment which is here sought to be enforced is clearly a mistake of both law and fact and was rendered in direct conflict with that comity between nations, which should exist among those which were allies in the world war.

The Supreme Court concluded that the Hong Kong court's decision was based on a misapprehension of the law and facts.[46] It did so, not by evaluating documents or acts that happened outside the foreign judgment, but by finding that the Hong Kong court's judgment was mistaken in its interpretation of the contract and law involved.

The second case of *Nagarmull v Binalbagan-Isabela Sugar Co*[47] concerned a judgment rendered by the Calcutta High Court in India. The dispute came up because the Indian plaintiff was delayed by a few months in shipping to the Philippines certain goods bought by the defendant. By the time the goods were shipped to the Philippines, higher export taxes were already in effect which the defendant refused to pay. It contended that, had the shipment been made on time, there would have been no higher taxes imposed. Here, the Philippine Supreme Court agreed with the foreign court's finding that the plaintiff breached the contract and that the defendant refused to pay damages. However, it held that the defendant could not be held liable for the damages claimed:

> … We are constrained to hold that the decision sought to be enforced was rendered upon a 'clear mistake of law' and because of that it makes appellant – an innocent party – suffer the consequences of the default or breach of contract committed by appellee [the plaintiff].
>
> …
>
> The breach of contract committed by appellee gave appellant, under the law and even under general principles of fairness, the right to rescind the contract or to ask for its specific performance, in either case with right to demand damages. Part of the damages appellant was clearly entitled to recover from appellee growing out of the latter's breach of the contract consists precisely of the amount of the increase decreed in the export tax due on the shortage – which, because of appellee's fault, had to be delivered after the effectivity of the increased export tax.
>
> …
>
> We can not sanction a clear mistake of law that would work an obvious injustice upon appellant.

Mistake of law is one which involves a misconception of the law applicable to a given state of facts or a wrong legal inference drawn from the facts. In *Nagarmull*, the Supreme Court drew a different conclusion of law from the facts found by the Indian court. It confined itself to considering acts and allegations already considered in the foreign judgment.

In both *Ingenohl* and *Nagarmull*, the Philippine Supreme Court's consideration was limited to the four corners of the foreign judgment. It touched on the fundamental issues of the cases, and not mere technicalities. What emerges is that 'clear mistake of law' and 'clear mistake of fact' may give rise to merit-based reviews. However, the nature of such reviews is not tantamount to a full-blown scrutinisation. In *Mijares v Ranada*, the Supreme Court provided the public policy justification for this:[48]

> The limitations on review is in consonance with a strong and pervasive policy in all legal systems to limit repetitive litigation on claims and issues. Otherwise known as the policy of preclusion,

[46] The US Supreme Court eventually reversed the Philippine Supreme Court's ruling (as Philippines was a US colony at the time), but even that decision was a review on the merits.

[47] *Nagarmull v Binalbagan-Isabela Sugar Co* GR No L-22470 (1970).

[48] *Mijares v Ranada* (n 13). Case citations have been omitted from the quoted passage.

> it seeks to protect party expectations resulting from previous litigation, to safeguard against the harassment of defendants, to insure that the task of courts not be increased by never-ending litigation of the same disputes, and – in a larger sense – to promote what Lord Coke in the Ferrer's Case of 1599 stated to be the goal of all law: 'rest and quietness'. If every judgment of a foreign court were reviewable on the merits, the plaintiff would be forced back on his/her original cause of action, rendering immaterial the previously concluded litigation.

Another way of looking at the *Ingenohl* and *Nagarmull* decisions is that, despite admittedly, the foreign courts involved had 'cited good law' or 'applied facts', there were public policy grounds for the Philippine court to refuse recognition and enforcement. In *Ingenohl*, for example, the Philippine Supreme Court, which at that time had American judges, was adamant in insisting that US law (namely, the Trading with the Enemy Act) should be treated as overriding legislation during World War I for the simple reason that its 'primary purpose … was to wipe them [that is, foreign enemies] out of existence and put them out of business'. While in *Nagarmull*, the Philippine Supreme Court absolved the defendant from liability because not doing so 'would work an obvious injustice' based on 'known principles of fairness and justice'. That a court of law in the Philippines can make policy choices or decide policy outcomes in relation to foreign court judgments is not without legal basis. Article 17(3) of the Philippine Civil Code, a private international law proviso, states that: 'Prohibitive laws … which have for their object public order, public policy and good customs shall not be rendered ineffective by laws or judgments promulgated, or by determinations or conventions agreed upon, in a foreign country …'

Consequently, it can be argued that, in providing for 'clear mistake of law or fact' as a ground for refusing recognition to a foreign judgment, Rule 39, Section 48 did so in the context of public order, public order and good customs. Although the legal norms relied on by the Philippine Supreme Court in *Ingenohl* (that is, comity among nations during the war) and *Nagarmull* (that is, known principles of fairness and justice) cases may not on their face be 'prohibitive laws', they can be formulated as injunctions to refrain from engaging in certain types of conduct.

Further, in *Mijares*, the Philippine Supreme Court observed that public policy was a consideration in the recognition and enforcement of foreign judgments:[49]

> The viability of the public policy defence against the enforcement of a foreign judgment has been recognized in this jurisdiction. This defence allows for the application of local standards in reviewing the foreign judgment, especially when such judgment creates only a presumptive right, as it does in cases wherein the judgment is against a person. The defence is also recognized within the international sphere, as many civil law nations adhere to a broad public policy exception which may result in a denial of recognition when the foreign court, in the light of the choice-of-law rules of the recognizing court, applied the wrong law to the case. The public policy defence can safeguard against possible abuses to the easy resort to offshore litigation if it can be demonstrated that the original claim is noxious to our constitutional values.

The Supreme Court had previously elaborated on public policy as a way of impeaching a foreign judgment in *Querubin v Querubin*:[50]

> The Court could not, without satisfactory evidence, dispose without remorse of conscience the delivery of the girl to the appellant's lawyer … It is not just about resolving the preferential right

[49] ibid. Case citations have been omitted from the quoted passage.
[50] *Querubin v Querubin* GR No L-3693 (1950). The judgment is originally in Spanish.

> of the father and mother in custody. The vital and transcendental question of the future of the girl is superior to any consideration. The State watches over its citizens. Article 171 of the Civil Code provides that 'Courts may deprive parents of parental authority, or suspend the exercise of this, if they treat their children with excessive harshness, or if they give them orders, advice or corrugated examples'. In Cortes v. Castillo and another, this Court declared that the Court of First Instance did not err in appointing the grandmother, as guardian of two minors, instead of her mother who was convicted of adultery.
>
> ...
>
> The judgments of foreign courts cannot be effective in the Philippines if they are contrary to laws, customs and public order. If such decisions, by the simple theory of reciprocity, judicial courtesy and international civility are sufficient basis for our courts to decide in accordance with them, then our courts would be in the poor position of having to issue sentences contrary to our laws, customs and public order. This is absurd.

The use of public policy, in the context of Article 17(3) of the Philippine Civil Code (formerly Article 11(a) of the *Codigo Civil*), was proper in the *Querubin* case because it involved prohibitive law, namely, Article 171 of the *Codigo Civil* which provides for deprivation of parental custody in certain instances.

Another case on public policy in the domain of private international law was *Pakistan International Airlines v Ople*,[51] concerning a choice of court agreement. Under Philippine law, jurisdiction over subject matter is conferred by law. Non-exclusive stipulations of forum by the parties will not oust such jurisdiction.[52] Moreover, even if the foreign judgment sought to be enforced in the Philippines is alleged to have been secured in breach of an exclusive choice of court agreement, the Philippine court will only look into the jurisdiction of the rendering state.[53] In *Pakistan International Airlines*, the Philippine Supreme Court contrasted the foreign choice of court agreement and Philippine public policy considerations in this manner:

> Petitioner PIA cannot take refuge in the [choice of court clause] of its employment agreement which specifies, firstly, the law of Pakistan as the applicable law of the agreement and, secondly, lays the venue for settlement of any dispute arising out of or in connection with the agreement '*only* [in] courts of Karachi Pakistan'. The [choice of court clause] cannot be invoked to prevent the application of Philippine labor laws and regulations to the subject matter of this case, i.e., the employer-employee relationship between petitioner and private respondents. We have already pointed out that the relationship is much affected with public interest and that the otherwise applicable Philippine laws and regulations cannot be rendered illusory by the parties agreeing upon some other law to govern their relationship. Neither may petitioner invoke [the choice of court clause], specifying the Karachi courts as the sole venue for the settlement of dispute between the contracting parties. Even a cursory scrutiny of the relevant circumstances of this case will show the multiple and substantive contacts between Philippine law and Philippine courts, on the one hand, and the relationship between the parties, upon the other: the contract was not only executed in the Philippines, it was also performed here, at least partially; private respondents are Philippine citizens and respondents, while petitioner, although a foreign corporation, is licensed to do business (and actually doing business) and hence resident in the Philippines; lastly, private respondents were based in the Philippines in between their assigned flights to the Middle

[51] *Pakistan International Airlines v Ople* GR No 61594 (1990).
[52] *Hongkong and Shanghai Banking v Sherman* GR No 72494 (1989).
[53] Aguiling-Pangalangan (n 41) 160.

> East and Europe. All the above contacts point to the Philippine courts and administrative agencies as a proper forum for the resolution of contractual disputes between the parties. Under these circumstances, [the choice of court clause] cannot be given effect so as to oust Philippine agencies and courts of the jurisdiction vested upon them by Philippine law.[54]

From this ruling in *Pakistan International Airlines*, the Philippine Supreme Court carried out an expansive consideration of public interest matters in addressing the foreign elements of the case. It is submitted that such exercise is functionally equivalent to the Court's consideration of whether there has been a clear mistake of law or fact by a foreign court. The line of distinction (if any) between public policy and clear mistake of law or fact is a thin one. The public policy ground hinges on the violation of a statutory provision, whereas the test of clear mistake of law or fact is possibly more flexible in that it may relate to the violation of some fundamental legal, social or other norm. Nonetheless, it is accepted that the distinction sought to be drawn here may be vague and difficult to articulate in practice. On the assumption that there is some distinction to be drawn, it would be best if the respective ambits of public policy and of clear mistake of law and fact are to be clarified.

The Philippine Supreme Court in *Mijares v Ranada* explained the theoretical basis for recognising and enforcing foreign judgments in the Philippines by reference to the Philippine Constitution.[55] The case concerned the filing fees charged for enforcing multi-million dollar judgments in favour of human rights abuse victims. The explanation was later cited in *Bank of the Philippine Islands Securities v Guevara*:

> There is no obligatory rule derived from treaties or conventions that requires the Philippines to recognize foreign judgments or allow a procedure for the enforcement thereof. However, generally accepted principles of international law, by virtue of the incorporation clause of the Constitution, form part of the laws of the land even if they do not derive from treaty obligations. The classical formulation in international law sees those customary rules accepted as binding result from the combination two elements: the established, widespread, and consistent practice on the part of States; and a psychological element known as the opinion juris sive necessitatis (opinion as to law or necessity). Implicit in the latter element is a belief that the practice in question is rendered obligatory by the existence of a rule of law requiring it.
>
> While the definite conceptual parameters of the recognition and enforcement of foreign judgments have not been authoritatively established, the Court can assert with certainty that such an undertaking is among those generally accepted principles of international law. As earlier demonstrated, there is a widespread practice among states accepting in principle the need for such recognition and enforcement, albeit subject to limitations of varying degrees. The fact that there is no binding universal treaty governing the practice is not indicative of a widespread rejection of the principle, but only a disagreement as to the imposable specific rules governing the procedure for recognition and enforcement.
>
> … Certainly, the Philippine legal system has long ago accepted into its jurisprudence and procedural rules the viability of an action for enforcement of foreign judgment, as well as the requisites for such valid enforcement, as derived from internationally accepted doctrines. Again, there may be distinctions as to the rules adopted by each particular state, but they all prescind from the premise that there is a rule of law obliging states to allow for, however generally, the recognition

[54] *Pakistan International Airlines* (n 51). Emphasis as original.
[55] *Mijares v Ranada* (n 13).

> and enforcement of a foreign judgment. The bare principle, to our mind, has attained the status of opinio juris in international practice.
>
> … Rules of procedure are promulgated by the Supreme Court and could very well be abrogated or revised by the high court itself. Yet the Supreme Court is obliged, as are all State components, to obey the laws of the land, including generally accepted principles of international law which form part thereof, such as those ensuring the qualified recognition and enforcement of foreign judgments.[56]

The court considered that the generally accepted principles of international law impel the Philippines to promote recognition or enforcement of foreign judgments. The court effectively suggested that a state owes a legal obligation to the international community (and not to the individual plaintiff) to recognise and enforce a foreign judgment, because other states are increasingly doing the same out of a sense of legal obligation. However, this idea is based on comity and is not to be constricted to reciprocity.

From the foregoing, it is possible to use the notion of generally accepted principles of international law to circumscribe the scope of a clear mistake of law or fact. Doing so addresses the uncertainty that will inevitably arise whenever the Philippine court reviews foreign judgments for an alleged clear mistake. Ultimately, it is submitted that the clear mistake of law or fact review should mirror the public policy ground and foreign judgments should be rejected only when recognition would go against some overriding or mandatory statutory provision or fundamental legal principle.

E. Finality and Specificity of the Foreign Judgment

Since Rule 39, Section 48 of the Rules of Court speaks of 'foreign judgments or final orders' and the entire provision deals with either the conclusive (as to property title) or presumptive (as to personal sections) 'effects' of foreign judgments, it may be inferred that only judgments which are final, specific and rendered as to the merits of a case can be recognised or enforced in the Philippines. Interlocutory orders by foreign courts cannot therefore be enforced. This has been affirmed in the *Querubin* case[57] where the Philippine Supreme Court denied an interlocutory order from a US court mandating the transfer of custody of a child:

> The decree is by no means final. It is subject to change with circumstances. The first decree awarded the custody to the father, prohibiting the mother from taking the child to her home because of her adulterous relationships with another man. The decree was amended when [the child] was not in Los Angeles. Because the decree is interlocutory, it cannot be implemented in the Philippines. Where judgment is merely interlocutory, the determination of the question by the Court which rendered it did not settle and adjudge finally the rights of parties.

To put it in another way, a foreign judgment must be one that goes into the merits of a case and therefore has the effect of *res judicata* with the result that the parties are barred from

[56] *Bank of the Philippine Islands Securities v Guevara* GR No 167052 (2015). Case citations have been omitted from the quoted passage.

[57] *Querubin v Querubin* (n 50).

re-litigating the same dispute. In *Philsec Investment v Court of Appeals*,[58] the Philippine Supreme Court qualified the *res judicata* effect of foreign judgments:

> … While this Court has given the effect of res judicata to foreign judgments in several cases, it was after the parties opposed to the judgment had been given ample opportunity to repel them on grounds allowed under the law.
>
> …
>
> In the case at bar, it cannot be said that petitioners were given the opportunity to challenge the judgment of the US court as basis for declaring it res judicata or conclusive of the rights of private respondents. The proceedings in the trial court were summary. Neither the trial court nor the appellate court was even furnished copies of the pleadings in the US court or apprised of the evidence presented thereat, to assure a proper determination of whether the issues then being litigated in the U.S. court were exactly the issues raised in this case such that the judgment that might be rendered would constitute res judicata.

Closely related to the idea of finality on the merits, is the technical requirement of specificity – that the foreign court judgment must specify the rights or obligations of the parties or, in case of money judgment, a specific amount (or specified basis for computation) must have been fixed.

V. Special Cases

Among the category of properties and rights that may require extra-territorial recognition or enforcement, intellectual property rights (IPRs) would probably be foremost. As early as 1925 there was a Philippine Supreme Court case[59] concerning the enforcement of a foreign judgment dealing with trademark and tradename. In 1980 the Philippines acceded to the Paris Convention for the Protection of Industrial Property,[60] paving the way for same level of protection accorded to nationals from other Paris Convention state parties, with respect to patents, trademarks, industrial designs, utility models, service marks, trade names and geographical indications. The protection of intellectual property was expanded to cover copyright and related rights, as well as confidential information (eg trade secrets), with the enactment of the Intellectual Property Code of the Philippines (IP Law) in 1997. Section 3 of the IP Law provides that:

> Any person who is a national or who is domiciled or has a real and effective industrial establishment in a country which is a party to any convention, treaty or agreement relating to intellectual property rights or the repression of unfair competition, to which the Philippines is also a party, or extends reciprocal rights to nationals of the Philippines by law, shall be entitled to benefits to the extent necessary to give effect to any provision of such convention, treaty or reciprocal law, in addition to the rights to which any owner of an intellectual property right is otherwise entitled by this Act.

[58] *Philsec Investment v Court of Appeals* GR No 103493 (1997).

[59] *Ingenohl v Olsen* (n 14).

[60] 'Contracting Parties to the Paris Convention' (*World Intellectual Property Organisation*), available online: www.wipo.int/treaties/en/ShowResults.jsp?lang=en&treaty_id=2.

Therefore, under the IP Law the benchmark for protection of IPRs of foreigners is no longer just based on nationality, but also on a real and effective connection with or domicile in a country with which the Philippines has entered into a convention, treaty or agreement for the protection of IPRs. It bears stressing though that the benefits that may be accorded to qualified foreign nationals are similar to those accorded to Philippine nationals and include the right to obtain provisional remedies (eg injunctions) and damages in connection with the protection of IPRs. However, a qualified foreign party would still need to commence an original action under the IP Law and cannot merely ask for the execution of a foreign court judgment.

In relation to private international law disputes concerning land and certain nationalised (or partly nationalised) industries in the Philippines, there would be a need to adhere to the limitations imposed by the Philippine Constitution on foreign ownership.[61] Land, for example, cannot lawfully be fully owned by a foreigner except through inheritance. Hence, a foreign judgment awarding title to land situated in the Philippines will not be enforced by the Philippine court on the basis of the public policy objection (ie, recognition of the judgment would be unconstitutional).

In relation to foreign judgments in matters of competition law, it will be interesting to see how the recently enacted Philippine Competition Act[62] (Competition Law), a piece of anti-trust legislation, will play out in private international law court cases. The Competition Law is: '[a]pplicable to international trade having direct, substantial, and reasonably foreseeable effects in trade, industry, or commerce in the Republic of the Philippines, including those that result from acts done outside the Republic of the Philippines'.[63]

By defining 'relevant geographic market' as that which 'comprises the area in which the entity concerned is involved in the supply and demand of goods and services, in which the conditions of competition are sufficiently homogenous and which can be distinguished from neighboring areas because the conditions of competition are different in those areas',[64] it is foreseeable that a civil or criminal action under the Competition Law will be brought against foreign parties. The unavoidable question therefore is whether a Philippine court judgment imputing liability to a foreign entity would be enforced or recognised in the foreign entity's home state.

VI. Conclusion: The Future in ASEAN and the World

As an archipelago, the Philippines is notable in the Southeast Asian region in that it has no land border with another country. All maritime countries in the region, including the neighbouring archipelago of Indonesia, have had to deal with complications arising from land borders, but not the Philippines. Possibly as a result of this, a survey of ASEAN students indicates that those from the Philippines have a significantly lower ability to list the names of other ASEAN countries, a weak cartographic knowledge of the region, and

[61] Aguiling-Pangalangan (n 41) 161.

[62] Republic Act No 10667 (21 July 2015) (Competition Law).

[63] See Competition Law, s 3. The Competition Law also stipulates that it 'shall be enforceable against any person or entity engaged in any trade, industry and commerce in the Republic of the Philippines'.

[64] See Competition Law, s 4(k)(2).

the least awareness of ASEAN as a regional group.[65] While this is indicative of a lack of international and regional consciousness among the younger generation of Filipinos, the move towards ASEAN regional integration is inevitable. Part of ASEAN's transformation into a cohesive economic community is its ASEAN Comprehensive Investment Agreement (ACIA). ACIA Article 13 deals with the transfer of investments, including payments made by a private investor in an ASEAN state to a party in another ASEAN state:

> Article 13 Transfers
>
> 1. Each Member State shall allow all transfers relating to a covered investment to be made freely and without delay into and out of its territory. Such transfers include:
>
> …
>
> (f) payments arising out of the settlement of a dispute by any means including adjudication, arbitration or the agreement of the Member States to the dispute.

Certainly, an order of payment arising out of a court judgment and relative to foreign investment can be contemplated within Article 13(1)(f) which mandates ASEAN states to allow and fast-track the effecting of such payment. Since the ACIA is a multilateral international agreement, Article 13 could be a legal basis to facilitate the recognition or enforcement of foreign judgments (relating to covered investments) rendered in one ASEAN state in favour of parties in another ASEAN state with the development of a simple motion for execution process. Against this backdrop, with the globalisation of markets, emphasis on regional integration and the Philippine Supreme Court's emerging use of customary international law to uphold foreign judgments, it is further submitted that it is time for the Philippines in conjunction with other ASEAN countries seriously to consider accession to the 2005 Hague Convention on Choice of Court Agreements.[66]

The Philippine experience on the recognition or enforcement of foreign judgments has been largely developed by judges' rulings, which in turn have become part of the domestic law. While there is nothing objectionable about this, the Philippines should progressively look at the issue from a more transnational viewpoint in an increasingly borderless world. The Philippine Supreme Court has provided the cue by enforcing foreign court judgments as a matter of customary international law. It is now for the government to build on this foundation by entering into bilateral treaties with economic partners for the mutual recognition and enforcement of judgments and by acceding into multilateral conventions such as the 2005 Hague Convention.

[65] Eric C Thompson and Chulanee Thianthai, 'Attitudes and Awareness toward ASEAN: Findings of a Ten Nation Survey' (*ASEAN Foundation*), available online: www.aseanfoundation.org/documents/Attitudes%20and%20Awareness%20Toward%20ASEAN.pdf.

[66] At present, among ASEAN countries, only Singapore is a party to the 2005 Hague Convention.

13

Indonesia

AFIFAH KUSUMADARA

I. Introduction

As a matter of general principle, foreign judgments are not enforceable in Indonesia. This is because Article 436 of the *Reglement op de Burgerlijke Rechtsvordering* (Rv)[1] stipulates that:

> (1) All judgments delivered by foreign courts are unenforceable in Indonesian territory, except in the matters mentioned in Article 724 of Commercial Code[2] and in other regulations.
> (2) Those [other] matters can be brought again in front of and be judged by Indonesian courts.
> …

The reason underlying Indonesia's refusal to enforce foreign judgments is sovereignty. Indonesian legal scholars adopt the view espoused by the Dutch Supreme Court during the colonial era that foreign judgments should not be enforced based on reasons of judicial and territorial sovereignty.[3] This principle could only be waived in the case of foreign judgments by the courts of states with reciprocal agreements with Indonesia for the mutual enforcement of judgments.[4] However, until now, Indonesia has not established any agreements with other states regarding the enforcement of judgments. Thus, in the absence of a treaty with Indonesia, where an Indonesian party and its foreign counterpart designate the court of some state as the forum for the settlement of disputes arising out of an international commercial contract, the judgment of such court will not be enforceable in Indonesia.

[1] The Rv was the Code of Civil Procedure for European inhabitants during the Dutch colonial rule in Indonesia. The Rv was adopted into the Indonesian legal system, following independence from the Dutch, under Article II of the Transitional Provisions of Indonesian Constitution. That allowed existing laws and regulations (including those of the Dutch colonial government) to remain in effect until substituted by new laws and regulations. Rv Art 436 has never been amended.

[2] Art 724 of the Commercial Code (*Wetboek van Koophandel voor Nederlandsch-Indie*) (1847) concerns foreign judgments in matters of maritime general average. Art 724(5) provides that foreign authorities may make judgments in general average situations involving Indonesian parties. Consequently, foreign judgments relating to maritime general average are enforceable in Indonesia.

[3] Sudargo Gautama, *Hukum Perdata Internasional Indonesia Jilid III Bagian 2 Buku Ke-8* 4th edn (Bandung, Alumni, 2002) 277–92.

[4] Sudargo Gautama, 'Recognition and Enforcement of Foreign Judgments and Arbitral Awards in the ASEAN Region' (1990) 32 *Malaya Law Review* 171, 172–73; M Yahya Harahap, *Hukum Acara Perdata Tentang Gugatan, Persidangan, Penyitaan, Pembuktian, dan Putusan Pengadilan* 16th edn (Jakarta, Sinar Grafika, 2016) 136.

Insofar as the recognition of foreign judgments is concerned, certain legal theories are prevalent. Although as a rule foreign judgments cannot be enforced in Indonesia, it has been said that they may be accepted as prima facie evidence, in particular as written evidence of the sort referred to in Article 1902 of the *Burgerlijk Wetboek voor Nederlandsch-Indie* (1846) (BW), Indonesia's Civil Code.[5] R Subekti, the fourth Chief Justice of the Indonesian Supreme Court, has gone further and argued that foreign judgments are equivalent to authentic deeds as mentioned in BW Article 1868.[6] On that basis, pursuant to BW Article 1870, a foreign judgment should be accepted as near-unimpeachable evidence of its content and a party challenging such judgment bears the heavy burden of establishing that the foreign judgment is faulty. A former justice of the Indonesian Supreme Court, M Yahya Harahap, has expressed the view that, in hearing matters that have been decided outside Indonesia, the Indonesian court has a discretion whether or not to accept the foreign judgment as prima facie evidence or to treat it as an authentic deed.[7] Nonetheless, the Indonesian court may also ignore the foreign judgment completely on the basis that foreign judgments are neither enforceable nor recognizable in Indonesia.

For certain types of judgments, namely, those which are declaratory and constitutive in nature, Indonesian legal scholars agree that the same should be recognised in Indonesian territory.[8] A declaratory judgment is usually made to confirm a legal status or legal position (for example, the validity of a contract, ownership of a property or a decree of heirship), while a constitutive judgment is made to create a new legal condition or abolish an existing legal condition (for example, a divorce, an adoption or an annulment of a contract). The recognition of declaratory and constitutive judgments in Indonesia is in line with the acceptance of the acquired (vested) rights doctrine in Indonesian private international law.

But in practice, the Indonesian court has a wide discretion whether or not to apply the legal theories just summarised. For example, in 2007 the South Jakarta District Court recognised a judgment of the Administrative Tribunal of Western Australia.[9] The Australian tribunal had held that the applicant's elderly father, who was an Indonesian citizen but who lived and owned properties in Australia as well as in Indonesia, was legally incompetent to manage his properties. The tribunal thus put those properties under an administrator. The tribunal reached its judgment in light of, among other matters, an assessment by a medical doctor in Western Australia. The applicant, who lived in Indonesia, applied for a decree of guardianship over her father and his properties on the basis of the Western Australian decision and witness evidence. The South Jakarta District Court accepted the applicant's request and appointed her as guardian. The father appealed against both the decree of the South Jakarta District Court and the decision of the Administrative Tribunal respectively.[10] In his appeal to the Indonesian Supreme Court, the father argued that a foreign judgment was not enforceable in Indonesia (Rv Article 436) and the South Jakarta District Court

[5] Gautama (n 4) 172–73.

[6] R Subekti, *Arbitrase Perdagangan* (Jakarta, Binacipta, 1981) 28.

[7] Harahap (n 4) 136.

[8] Gautama (n 3) 282.

[9] Decision of the South Jakarta District Court No 258/Pdt.P/2007/PN.JAK.SEL (25 September 2007).

[10] 'MA Batalkan Penetapan Pengampuan Prof. Sudargo' (*hukumonline.com*, 29 March 2008) available online: www.hukumonline.com/berita/baca/hol18857/ma-batalkan-penetapan-pengampuan-prof-sudargo. See also 'Ketika Profesor Digugat Sang Putri' (*Gatra.com*), available online: arsip.gatra.com/2008-04-07/majalah/artikel.php?pil=23&id=113936.

had to examine and hear him before delivering a decree of guardianship (BW Article 439). The Supreme Court found that the South Jakarta District Court had neither examined nor heard from the Appellant. The lower court had therefore violated BW Article 439. As a result, in March 2008, the Supreme Court annulled the decree of guardianship.[11]

In short, save in limited cases (such as maritime general average cases or where Indonesia has entered into a treaty with another state for the mutual recognition and enforcement of judgments), foreign judgments are neither enforceable nor recognizable in Indonesia under Rv Article 436. There are legal theories suggesting that foreign judgments, especially declaratory and constitutive judgments, may be recognised. However, despite such theories, the Indonesian court may still refuse to recognise those judgments.

II. Background

A. Overview of the Indonesian Legal System

After gaining independence from Dutch colonial rule in 1945, Indonesia became a republic. It was a federal state until 1949. But since 1950 it has been a unitary state with its central government, parliament and Supreme Court in its capital Jakarta. To avoid a legal vacuum, Article II of the Transitional Provisions of the Indonesian Constitution 1945 provided that all previous Dutch colonial laws would be adopted into the Indonesian legal system until superseded by new legislation. Dutch law therefore co-exists with the other legal systems, namely *adat* law (customary law) and Islamic law (as compiled by the Ministry of Religious Affairs and the Supreme Court).[12] There are two different court systems for settling dispute cases in civil and commercial matters. Non-Islamic cases are brought before the general court or the commercial court, while Islamic cases are brought before the religious court. The appellate court of the highest instance for all matters (except constitutionality matters) is the Court of Cassation (also known as the Supreme Court). The fall of the military government in 1998 ushered in the Reform Era (*Reformasi*), in which a civilian government has passed many new laws and revoked some Dutch laws as part of wide-ranging legal reforms. Indonesia has at the same time acceded to more international conventions.

The Indonesian government has granted special status to Aceh province, allowing it to implement its own law (*Qanun*) based on shari'a law.[13] *Qanun* is applicable to the entire population of Aceh[14] and is implemented by the syariah court. Aceh's special status and the implementation of *Qanun* in Aceh were the result of the 2005 Peace Accord between the Indonesian government and the Free Aceh Movement (an Acehnese separatist group). Notwithstanding this, Indonesia being a unitary state, the judgment of a court in one city or province will be recognised and enforced all over the country. International conventions to which Indonesia has acceded will also be applicable to all regions of Indonesia.

[11] ibid.

[12] See Joint Decree between the Chief Justice of the Supreme Court and the Minister of Religious Affairs No 07/KMA/1985 and No 25 of 1985. See also President Instruction No 1 of 1991 on the Dissemination of the Compilation of Islamic Law.

[13] Act No 11 of 2006 on the Governing of Aceh.

[14] Qanun Aceh No 8 of 2014 on Basic Islamic Sharia.

B. Historical Development of Private International Law in Indonesia

From the colonial era through to independence and the present day, Indonesia has never had a codified private international law. Matters relating to private international law are instead governed by different acts and regulations. There has been some effort by the Indonesian Ministry of Law to draft a Code of Indonesian Private International Law. But the draft has not to date reached the parliament.

i. Before Independence

In 1847, the Dutch colonial government passed the General Provisions of Legislation for the Dutch East Indies (*Algemene Bepalingen van Wetgeving voor Nederlandsch Indie*) (AB). It was the first law that divided the population into different groups: (1) the Dutch; (2) indigenous; and (3) resident foreigners (neither Dutch nor Indigenous) (AB Article 4). AB Articles 3, 11, 12, 15 stipulated the applicable law was for each group. Later, the 1926 Dutch Colonial Constitution (*Indische Staatsregeling*) (IS) maintained the same groups and added the foreign Oriental group (IS Article 163). Each group had its personal law for private matters: Dutch law for Europeans; customary law for indigenous and foreign Oriental groups; and selected Dutch law for foreign Chinese Orientals (IS Article 131). Faced with legal pluralism in its colony, the Dutch colonial government did not pursue unification in the field of private law, but instead maintained the legal traditions of the different communities in Indonesia.[15] The colonial government developed interpersonal laws that governed private relations or transactions among persons of different groups with different legal systems. AB Articles 16, 17, and 18(1) governed the applicable law for interpersonal relations and private matters having foreign elements. The foreign or external elements could come from groups outside the Dutch East Indies or from groups of inhabitants within the country. AB Articles 16, 17 and 18(1) are explained further below.

As a consequence of the plural legal system, the Dutch colonial government established plural court systems for the different groups of the population. Court precedent became increasingly important as a source of interpersonal law. As pointed out by Ratno Lukito, '[t]he Dutch preference for a jurisprudential solution to cases of interpersonal conflicts seems to reflect the fact that the variety of private law in the colony was too complicated to resolve by means of state legislation'.[16] Dutch colonial legislation in interpersonal relations and court decisions settling interpersonal law conflicts thus laid the foundation for the development of Indonesian private international law.

ii. After Independence

A unified law for all Indonesian citizens and inhabitants was important for the unity of the newly independent country. Unlike the Dutch colonial government which maintained

[15] Ratno Lukito, *Legal Pluralism in Indonesia: Bridging the Unbridgeable* (London, Routledge, 2013) 126.
[16] ibid, 132.

legal pluralism especially in the field of private law, the Indonesian government preferred legal uniformity. Article 26 of the Indonesian Constitution abolished the grouping system that the Dutch had established, so that Indonesian law now only recognises Indonesian citizens and non-Indonesian citizens (foreigners). As already noted, Article II of the 1945 Transitional Provisions of the Indonesian Constitution stipulated: 'All existing state institutions and regulations shall remain effective, as long as new ones have not yet been provided for pursuant to this Constitution'. Through this expedient, the new Indonesian government adopted most of the Dutch colonial legislation previously in force. The colonial legislation served (and continues to serve) as national law unless and until replaced or revised by new statutes enacted by the government.

Since the Indonesian Constitution only recognises Indonesian citizens and foreigners, AB Articles 16, 17 and 18(1) no longer govern interpersonal matters among different groups of the population. Instead, those articles now only govern interpersonal matters between Indonesian citizens and foreigners. Consequently, the articles have become a source of Indonesian private international law. Case precedents (jurisprudence) on interpersonal matters decided during the colonial era are also accepted as a source of Indonesian private international law.

Over time, the government has gradually promulgated codes containing provisions regulating relations between Indonesians and foreigners. Examples are the Basic Agrarian Act (No 5 of 1960), the Marriage Act (No 1 of 1974), the Citizenship Act (No 12 of 2006), and the Investment Act (No 25 of 2007). These statutes complement AB Articles 16, 17 and 18(1). However, this body of private international law acts is insufficient to regulate the increasing number of conflict of law cases in Indonesia.[17] There has been an effort by the government to replace the present regime with a private international law code. The first effort to draft such a code was in 1983. For unknown reasons, the 1983 draft never reached the parliament. The second effort was in 2014 when the Ministry of Law and Human Rights commissioned a team to write an academic paper for an Indonesian private international law bill. The team submitted the paper and a draft bill on Indonesian private international law to the Ministry of Law and Human Rights in 2015. The bill has yet to be placed before the parliament. Thus, in fact, the Dutch colonial private international law system is essentially still applied even today, albeit supplemented by the provisions of a few Indonesian codes.

C. Sources of Indonesian Private International Law

Since private international law is part of the national law, its sources are the same as the sources of other fields of law, namely: (1) legislation (written laws enacted by state authorities); (2) customary laws or usages; (3) jurisprudence (court decisions recommended as

[17] Supancana, IBR, Basuki, Zulfa Djoko, Kusumadara, Afifah, Soeriaatmadja, Arvianto, Hikmah, Mutiara, Oppusunggu, Yu Un, Panjaitan, Roki, Iriani, Sukesti, Wahyu, Isthining, Besturen, Maretta, Puspitasari, Anggriana, and Junaidi, Haris Ahmad, *Naskah Akademik Rancangan Undang-Undang tentang Hukum Perdata Internasional (lanjutan)* (Jakarta, Badan Pembinaan Hukum Nasional Kementerian Hukum dan Hak Asasi Manusia RI, 2015), www.bphn.go.id/data/documents/na_ruu_ttg_hukum_perdata_internasional_(lanjutan).pdf.

binding by the Supreme Court or classified as *yurisprudensi tetap* (stable jurisprudence) by the Supreme Court;[18] (4) treaties or international conventions that have been ratified either by a Presidential Decree or through the passing of an Act;[19] and (5) doctrines (legal theories that are regularly used referred to and applied in court judgments and which are commonly referred to by legal practitioners in support of their arguments before the court).[20]

The sources of Indonesian private international law date from both the Dutch colonial and post-independence eras. It must be admitted, however, that the sources of Indonesian private international law mostly originate from the colonial period, as legitimated by Article II of the Transitional Provisions of the Indonesian Constitution 1945. Although, strictly speaking, those provisions of the Constitution only validate state institutions and regulations of the colonial period, other sources of law from those times, including Dutch jurisprudence and doctrine, remain effective in practice unless they violate public policy or have been overruled by more recent cases.

In keeping with the civil law tradition introduced by the Dutch, the Indonesian legal system places a premium on codified and written law, and so treats legislation as the main source of law. Other sources of law (such as case law) are deployed to support the legislation or fill in legal gaps, as (for instance) where legislation is silent on a particular subject.

Given that there is no Code of Private International Law currently in force in Indonesia, conflict of laws questions are governed by provisions scattered in different acts and regulations. This means that, in effect, AB Articles 16, 17 and 18(1) have become and remain the principal sources of Indonesian private international law. These three articles identify the applicable law in private matters relating to the status of persons, family matters, real property, and formalities in transactions involving international elements. For instance, statutory provisions governing the status and capacity of persons remain binding on Indonesian citizens[21] even when abroad (AB Article 16). As for immovable property, the applicable law is that of the country or place where the property is located (AB Article 17). Formality in respect of a legal act is to be determined in accordance with the law of the country or place where the act is performed (AB Article 18(1)).

The other source of private international law (namely, jurisprudence) is used to regulate matters that are not dealt with by AB Articles 16, 17 and 18(1). The case law is supplemented by the application of doctrines such as *renvoi*, acquired/vested rights theory, proper law (that is, the law of closest connection to a transaction), and public policy (*ordre public*).

Following independence, the government passed several acts that contain provisions relating to private international law matters. Thus, the Basic Agrarian Act (No 5 of 1960) has

[18] See 'Bahasa Hukum: Sumber Hukum Formal Bernama "Yurisprudensi"' (*hukumonline.com*, 7 February 2018), available online: www.hukumonline.com/berita/baca/lt5a7ad95871d1a/bahasa-hukum--sumber-hukum-formal-bernama-yurisprudensi. The Supreme Court issues a Yearly Report with a list of cases (together with annotations) classified as 'stable jurisprudence': Alamo D Laiman, Dewi Savitri Reni, Ronald Lengkong and Sigit Ardiyanto, 'The Indonesian Legal System and Legal Research' (*GlobaLex*, July 2011), available online: www.nyulawglobal.org/globalex/Indonesia.html#sourcesoflaw.

[19] Indonesia is a dualist state as in practice, a treaty or convention may not be implemented by Indonesian authorities until transformed into domestic legislation by a Presidential Decree or through the passing of an Act or another type of regulation. See Act No 24 of 2000 on Treaties, Arts 9 and 10.

[20] Laiman and others (n 18).

[21] Originally referred to in colonial legislation as 'inhabitants of the Dutch East Indies'.

several sections regulating the rights of foreigners over Indonesian land and the Marriage Act (No 1 of 1974) includes rules regulating marriages between Indonesians and foreigners. The government has also issued regulations that have become important sources of private international law. For instance, Government Regulation No 54 of 2007 governs inter-country adoption, while Presidential Decree No 34 of 1981 and Supreme Court Regulation No 1 of 1990 govern the recognition and enforcement of foreign arbitral awards. These post-Independence Acts and regulations complement AB Articles 16, 17 and 18(1) and the pre-independence jurisprudence and doctrines.

Apart from 1958 Convention on the Recognition and Enforcement of Foreign Arbitral Awards (popularly known as the 1958 New York Convention), Indonesia has not acceded to any other multilateral instruments. Indonesia's reluctance to join international conventions has contributed to the limited sources of private international law principles in Indonesia.

D. Relevant Authorities in Indonesia for the Recognition of Foreign Judgments

As explained above, foreign judgments are not enforceable but may be recognised in Indonesia. The authorities or institutions that deal with applications involving the recognition of foreign judgments are identified in this section.

i. The Court

Although by Rv Article 436 foreign judgments are not enforceable, jurists maintain that they can serve as prima facie evidence before the court. It would then be for the court whether or not to place any weight on the foreign judgment as prima facie evidence of relevant facts. The Indonesian courts that may admit foreign judgments as evidence in civil and commercial matters are the Civil Court, the Commercial Court, and the Religious Court. Under the Religious Court Act,[22] the latter court deals with Islamic civil and commercial matters.

ii. The Civil Registry

A foreign declaratory or constitutive judgment which confirms or creates a legal status is generally recognised in Indonesia, unless it offends against Indonesia's public policy. If the declaratory or constitutive judgment involves an Indonesian party, the judgment will be recognised by the civil registry office that registers the judgment. The recognition of foreign declaratory or constitutive judgments by a civil registry office is governed by Act No 23 of 2006, as amended by the Act No 24 of 2013, on Population Administration.

[22] Act No 7 of 1989, as amended by Act No 3 of 2006 and as amended by Act No 50 of 2009, on Religious Court.

E. Civil and Commercial Matters in Indonesian Law

i. Civil Matters

After independence, civil matters have been basically regulated under the Civil Code. There is also the compilation of Islamic law and customary law (*adat* law). The latter co-exists with the Civil Code in Indonesia, but do not characterise matters as civil, commercial or procedural in nature. Therefore, to ascertain what should be categorised as civil matters, reference is usually made to the Civil Code or to statutes[23] that amend the Civil Code's provisions. Such matters include: status and legal capacity of natural persons; marriage and family matters; inheritance; things and ownership; collaterals and liens; obligations (contracts and torts).

ii. Commercial Matters

Commercial matters are generally governed by the Commercial Code in 1847 and other post-independence legislation. In contrast to civil matters which have not changed much since the colonial era, the scope of commercial matters has expanded following changes and developments in business practices. Commercial matters that are dealt with in the Civil or Commercial Code include trading; middlemen; commercial partnership and limited liability entities; negotiable instruments for payment of money; shipping; and insurance. In line with the development of commercial practice domestically and internationally, matters classified as commercial are growing in Indonesian law. The Elucidation to Article 66(b) of Act No 30 of 1999 on Arbitration and Alternative Dispute Resolution (Arbitration Act) notes that within the 'scope of commercial law' are (among others) activities in the fields of trading, banking, finance, investment, industry and intellectual property rights.

The matters just identified from the Civil Code, the Commercial Code and the Arbitration Act are not exhaustive. There will always be newer business activities that can be characterised as commercial. Examples are negotiable instruments, warehouse receipts, unfair trade, bankruptcy and insolvency, and Islamic financing (including instruments such as *mudarabah*,[24] *murabahah*[25] and *sukuk*[26]). Conversely, matters that are ostensibly civil and commercial in nature may fall into the category of activities regulated by public law. These activities (such as trading with end-buyers, real-property ownership and employment contracts) may be governed by (say) the Consumer Protection Act (No 8 of 1999), the Basic Agrarian Act (No 5 of 1960) and the Labour Act (No 13 of 2003). They are considered to involve public law and mandatory provisions. They are not, therefore, treated as civil or commercial matters in Indonesian law.

[23] For example, Marriage Act (No 1 of 1974), Basic Agrarian Act (No 5 of 1960), and Mortgage Act (No 4 of 1996).

[24] An arrangement whereby parties share in the profit and loss of a venture.

[25] A transaction whereby one buys property and then re-sells the same to a third party at a higher price. For example, a finance company may buy a car from a dealer at a discounted price and then re-sell the car to a consumer end-user at a higher price.

[26] A certificate entitling a person to ownership of identified assets and the rent generated by those assets. As a country with a majority Muslim population, Indonesia also categorises some Islamic practices as commercial matters, even though they may not be commonly known in non-Muslim countries.

III. Recognition and Enforcement of Judgments under Treaties or Similar Arrangements

Indonesia is not a party to any international treaty or convention requiring the recognition and enforcement of judgments. Rv Article 436, which renders foreign judgments unenforceable, remains applicable.

IV. Recognition and Enforcement in the Absence of Treaties or Similar Arrangements

In the absence of treaties and conventions, the recognition and enforcement of foreign judgments in Indonesia is governed by Rv Article 436 and the jurisprudence explained above. Rv Article 436 emphasises that recognition and enforcement of condemnatory judgments cannot be sought in Indonesia. The dispute must be retried in (and determined by) an Indonesian Court (Rv Article 436(2)). In hearing matters that have been determined outside Indonesia, an Indonesian Court may use its discretion to accept a foreign judgment as prima facie evidence or treat the foreign judgment as equivalent to an authentic deed.[27]

Regarding declaratory judgments that do not require enforcement such as judgments in status of person, Indonesian jurists agree that it can be recognised in Indonesia, insofar it does not offend Indonesia's public policy.

An exception to the rule is that foreign judgments in respect of maritime general average are capable of recognition and enforcement in Indonesia by Rv Article 436(1). To enforce such judgment, the interested party should bring the judgment before the Indonesian court to obtain an execution order (Rv Article 436(3)).

As the only law that governs the recognition and enforcement of foreign judgments in Indonesia, Rv Article 436 does not say whether the judgment on general average must be final (that is, it can no longer be appealed or reviewed in the originating jurisdiction) before it can be executed in Indonesia. The Indonesian Civil Procedural Law[28] allows for the execution of a judgment that is still being appealed to a higher court. But the Civil Procedural Law is only applicable to judgments rendered by a domestic, not a foreign, court. Therefore, in the author's opinion, it is up to the enforcing court in Indonesia to decide whether or not to execute a foreign judgment on general average that is subject to appeal in the rendering state.

Rv Article 431 further provides that Indonesian judgments are valid and enforced only within Indonesia, not outside Indonesia. M Yahya Harahap, a former justice of the Indonesian Supreme Court, has suggested that the principle in Rv Article 431 may be waived

[27] Harahap (n 4) 136.

[28] Renewed Indonesian Code (*Het Herziene Indonesisch Reglement*) Art 180(1); Code of Procedure for Areas Outside Java and Madura) (*Rechtsreglement Buitengewesten*) Art 191(1); Code of Civil Procedure (*Reglement op de Rechtvordering*) Arts 54–57; Supreme Court Regulation (*Surat Edaran Mahkamah Agung*) No 3 of 2000 and No 4 of 2001 on *Putusan Serta Merta (Uitvoerbaar bij voorraad) dan Provisionil* [Judgment with Immediate Execution and Provisional Judgment].

when Indonesia establishes a reciprocal agreement with another country on the recognition and enforcement of judgments.[29]

V. The Future

A. Prospects

There is a prospect of Indonesia becoming a party to bilateral or multilateral instruments with other countries, insofar as the mutual recognition and enforcement of judgments is concerned. However, the prospect is limited to commercial matters or cases that arise out of or in relation to commercial transactions. For civil matters unconnected with commercial transactions, there seems to be little possibility. Commercial matters are regarded as more neutral than civil matters, because civil matters strongly relate to the culture and beliefs of the Indonesian society. There is a strong feeling in Indonesia that such norms should be respected by other states and should not be exposed to outside interference by foreign courts. For example, in some sessions for the public dissemination of the 2014 Bill on Indonesian private international law, judges of the religious court and officials of the Office of Religious Affairs insisted on preserving the religious rules and beliefs embraced by Indonesians. Therefore, it will be easier to accept foreign judgments on purely commercial matters, subject always to the same not being in conflict with Indonesian public policy.

In terms of multilateral instruments, since the 1971 Hague Convention on the Recognition and Enforcement of Foreign Judgments in Civil and Commercial Matters has not entered into force, the only viable option for Indonesia at present would be to join the 2005 Hague Convention on Choice of Court Agreements (2005 Hague Convention) in the future. Pending the promulgation of the draft Convention for the Recognition and Enforcement of Judgments in Civil and Commercial Matters currently being worked on by the Judgments Project of the Hague Conference, there is no other regional or international convention that deals with the recognition and enforcement of foreign judgments. The 2005 Hague Convention is a likely possibility for accession by Indonesia, especially given that the scope of this instrument is limited to commercial or civil matters that arise out of or in relation to international commercial transactions. Article 2 of the 2005 Hague Convention excludes civil matters such as family, personal status, inheritance, and succession that would potentially involve the culture and beliefs of Indonesian society. In addition, the 2005 Hague Convention also excludes areas that touch on Indonesian public policy, such as consumer contracts, employment contracts, and rights in immovable properties.

Like the 1958 New York Convention and 1965 ICSID Convention that have been ratified by the Indonesian government to attract foreign investors to Indonesia, the 2005 Hague Convention may come into effect in Indonesia in the near future to complement the 1958 and 1965 Conventions to improve the ease of doing business in Indonesia.

In the meantime, in the absence of treaties or conventions, the Indonesian court could follow the practice in the Netherlands which has a similar provision to Rv Article 436.

[29] M Yahya Harahap, *Ruang lingkup permasalahan eksekusi bidang perdata* 2nd edn (Jakarta, Sinar Grafika, 2005) 356.

The Dutch court abides by Article 431 of the Dutch Code of Civil Procedure, which is equivalent to Rv Article 436. Accordingly, the Dutch court must judge anew matters that have been decided by the courts of countries that do not have mutual treaties with the Netherlands for the recognition and enforcement of judgments. However, Dutch jurisprudence and doctrine allow the court to simplify trial proceedings, if all criteria for the recognition of a foreign judgment are met: Those criteria are: (1) the foreign judgment must be the result of proceedings compatible with Dutch concepts of due process or fair trial; (2) the judgment should not contravene the public policy of the Netherlands; (3) the foreign court must have assumed jurisdiction on grounds which are internationally accepted; and (4) the foreign judgment is enforceable or has not been revoked in the jurisdiction from which it originated. If all those criteria are met, in general there will be no further litigation in the Dutch court on the merits of the foreign judgment. The Dutch court will instead summarily grant a decree of execution and thereby enforce the foreign judgment as a judgment of the Dutch court.[30] In other words, although the practical effect is that the Dutch court will be 'recognising' and 'enforcing' a foreign judgment, in actuality what is enforced is a judgment of the Dutch court which is subject to appeal and cassation in the ordinary way as any other judgment of the Dutch court.

This approach may be adopted in Indonesia to help speed up the settlement of business litigation in the absence of treaties and conventions on the recognition and enforcement of judgments. As indicated earlier, Indonesian doctrine recognises foreign judgments as prima facie evidence or as authentic deeds. Therefore, once an Indonesian court takes a foreign judgment as prima facie evidence or as an authentic deed, it may simplify the trial proceedings, without a review of the merits of the case, enabling de facto recognition and enforcement of a foreign judgment, as long as it meets the international standards and criteria for recognition and enforcement. To make such practice acceptable in all Indonesian courts, the Indonesian Supreme Court should formulate a comprehensive set of criteria for the recognition of foreign judgments where no treaty applies, that is, the Supreme Court (much as the Dutch court has done) will need to identify and make explicit what the international standards and criteria for the recognition and enforcement of foreign judgments are in the absence of treaties. This would certainly help the Indonesian court deal with matters that have been judged by courts outside Indonesia and speed up the settlement of litigation in Indonesia.

B. Reform

i. Deficiency in the Current Regime

Accession to the 2005 Hague Convention may speed up the settlement of commercial cases that face delays due to the backlog in the Indonesian judiciary system. However, there is uncertainty regarding the position of a treaty or international convention in Indonesian law.

[30] Supreme Court of the Netherlands Decision NJ 2004, 615, LJN: AF7005 (27 June 2003). See also Bird & Bird, 'Enforcement of Foreign Judgments in the Netherlands' (*Birdbuzz*), available online: birdbuzz.nl/wp-content/uploads/2015/01/Enforcement-of-Foreign-Judgements-in-the-Netherlands.pdf; 'Jurisdiction: National Rules of International Jurisdiction of Dutch Courts' (*Dutchcivillaw.com*), available online: www.dutchcivillaw.com/jurisdiction/internatjuris044.htm.

Although Article 11 of the Indonesian Constitution recognises treaties, it does not stipulate whether a treaty shall become law in Indonesia after being approved by the parliament. The government passed Act No 24 of 2000 on Treaties. Like the Constitution, the Act does not specify whether a treaty or convention shall become a part of Indonesian law after being ratified or approved. The Act only governs the process of entering into international agreements and related formalities. This omission raises questions on the status of ratified treaties or conventions within the Indonesian legal system.

For example, after the ratification of the 1958 New York Convention on Recognition and Enforcement of Foreign Arbitral Awards by Presidential Decree No 34 of 1981, the Supreme Court maintained its refusal to enforce foreign arbitral awards. In *PT Nizwar v Navigation Maritime Bulgare*,[31] the Supreme Court acknowledged the ratification of the 1958 New York Convention, but held that Indonesian courts could not enforce foreign arbitral awards due to the lack of implementing regulations identifying the court to which applications for the enforcement of foreign awards should be made and stating whether the Supreme Court had jurisdiction to determine whether foreign awards violated Indonesian public policy. Thus, *PT Nizwar* suggests that a ratified convention may not be part of Indonesian Law until there is a statute or regulation implementing the convention. It could take years to pass such an act or regulation. As a matter of fact, it took nine years for the 1958 New York Convention to become a law in Indonesia. It was not until 1990 that the Supreme Court issued Regulation No 1 of 1990 dealing with the procedure for enforcing foreign arbitral awards. The uncertain status of a treaty or convention, even after ratification, may hinder the effectiveness of the 2005 Hague Convention in Indonesia.

Another issue in relation to the 2005 Hague Convention is that its effectiveness might be impeded by Indonesian lawyers and judges who may not pay heed to choice of court agreements between the parties or who may disregard judgments made by foreign courts. There have been cases in which Indonesian judges have ignored choice of forum clauses in business contracts or have decided cases brought to court by a party in breach of an arbitration agreement.[32]

In addition, Indonesian courts do not consistently recognise or enforce foreign arbitral awards.[33] This may also be the case in relation to foreign judgments that are supposed to be recognised and enforced in Indonesia. To prevent such an occurrence in relation to the recognition and enforcement of foreign judgments, there will need to be a change of attitude

[31] *PT Nizwar v Navigation Maritime Bulgare* No 2944K/PDT/1983 (20 August 1984) (Supreme Court).

[32] See eg *PT Tempo v PT Roche Indonesia* No 454/Pdt.G/1999/PN.JAK.SEL (25 January 2000) (South Jakarta District Court); *Bankers Trust Co v PT Mayora Indah Tbk* No 46/Pdt.G/1999 (9 December 1999) (South Jakarta District Court). In *PT Perusahaan Listrik Negara (PLN) v PT Paiton Energy* No 517/Pdt.G/1999/PN.JKT.PST (13 December 1999) (Central Jakarta District Court), the court disregarded the separability principle of arbitration clauses and held that an arbitration clause in the parties' Power Purchase Agreement (PPA) was invalid because the PPA violated Indonesian law and public policy. The practice of setting aside choice of forum clauses and ignoring the separability principle may continue even after Indonesia accedes to the 2005 Hague Convention on Choice of Court Agreements. See also Gatot P Soemartono, *Arbitrase dan mediasi di Indonesia* (Jakarta, Gramedia Pustaka Utama, 2006) 41; George A Bermann (ed), *Recognition and Enforcement of Foreign Arbitral Awards: The Interpretation and Application of the New York Convention by National Courts* (Cham, Springer, 2017) 30.

[33] See eg *Karaha Bodas Co LLC v Perusahaan Pertambangan Minyak dan Gas Bumi Negara (Pertamina)* Nos 001 and 002/Pdt/Arb.Int/1999/PN.JKT.PST and 002/Pdt.P/2000/PN.JKT.PST (3 February 2000) (Central Jakarta District Court); *Bankers Trust Co v PT Jakarta International Hotel and Development Tbk* No 46/Pdt.G/1999 (9 December 1999) (South Jakarta District Court).

among Indonesian judges in terms of upholding party autonomy in commercial contracts, as manifested in the parties' choice of forum. Accession to the 2005 Hague Convention must immediately be followed by issuance of implementing regulations and guidelines to transform the Convention into part of Indonesian law. Otherwise, the Convention will be on paper only and not be properly implemented, much as what happened previously with the New York Convention.

ii. Reforms to be Implemented

Accession to the 2005 Hague Convention would be useful for Indonesian judgments, as they will be recognised and enforced in Contracting States. This will benefit Indonesian businesses that prefer (and are more familiar with the practices of) the Indonesian court as the forum to resolve their cross-border commercial disputes. This must particularly be the case in light of the establishment of the ASEAN Economic Community on 31 December 2015. But, for Indonesian judgments to be recognised and enforced internationally, there must be an improvement in the domestic judiciary system that unfortunately has a reputation for rampant corruption. Judgments influenced by corruption and bribery will simply not be recognised and enforced by other Member States of the 2005 Hague Convention on the basis of the public policy or due process exceptions in that instrument.

Furthermore, there needs to be capacity building. The international implications of the 2005 Hague Convention will need to be communicated to Indonesian judges, since a practice of not recognising or enforcing foreign judgments in contravention of the Convention could trigger widespread complaint from Contracting States. This may have an impact on Indonesian business abroad and ultimately on the Indonesian economy.

When acceding to the 2005 Hague Convention, the Indonesian government will need to declare that Rv Articles 436 and 431 are no longer valid. Otherwise, there will be a conflict between the Convention and Rv Articles 436 and 431. The Supreme Court as the supervising body of all Indonesian courts should have a regulation to determine which courts are to hear applications for the enforcement of foreign judgments, including the jurisdiction to issue exequaturs in relation to foreign judgments. Specialist courts for that purpose would be important to speed up the process of enforcement, especially because District Court judges in remote areas of Indonesia may be unfamiliar with the handling of foreign judgments. A Supreme Court regulation is also needed to govern how courts at district level are to execute foreign judgments in their territories. Since there are three kinds of courts that can execute judgments in commercial matters, the Supreme Court must decide in their regulation whether the General Court, Commercial Court and Religious Court all have the authority to execute foreign judgments, or only the General Court has the authority to execute, like in the case of foreign arbitral awards.[34] Without this kind of directives, when the government accedes to the 2005 Hague Convention, there will be confusion and a lack of clarity in what courts should be doing in respect of foreign judgments.

The introduction of advanced technology for Indonesian judges to communicate directly with their colleagues in other judiciaries is also important. Their oral or written

[34] See Act No 30 of 1999 on Arbitration and Alternative Dispute Resolution, Art 69.

communication supported by advanced technology may help increase the efficiency of recognizing and enforcing both Indonesian judgments abroad and foreign judgments in Indonesia.

In summary, the reforms that must be carried out to prepare the way to accession to the 2005 Hague Convention are: (1) to address the public perception in Indonesia and abroad of rampant corruption in the judiciary; (2) to educate judges to respect choice of court agreements and foreign judgments; (3) to abolish Rv Article 436; and (4) to issue clear directives to all district and other relevant courts in Indonesia on the proper approach to the enforcement of foreign judgments.[35] The task is not easy. But the quid pro quo is that with such reform, the Indonesian judiciary will gain experience and reputation, and its judgments will be recognised and enforced internationally as well. Greater confidence by international investors in the Indonesian judiciary, and in the enforcement of judgments generally, should also assist in bringing increased foreign direct investment (FDI) into Indonesia, thereby benefitting the economy and the entire population.

iii. Cooperation with Judiciaries in Other States

The 2005 Hague Convention may improve the business climate in Indonesia if more countries join the Convention. Indonesian judgments could be recognised and enforced in other states, and vice versa. This may standardise judgments in commercial matters and lead to increased legal certainty in doing business in Indonesia. Cooperation with judiciaries in other countries, both at the regional level (for instance, ASEAN countries) and beyond would be important to support such a system. The cooperation would establish an understanding among judges in Indonesia and abroad and help to develop a procedural standard for the recognition and enforcement of judgments in commercial matters. This kind of cooperation will help reduce the level of mistrust in one state of judgments by courts of other states. In this connection, it is worth noting that Professor Sudargo Gautama, a leading private international law scholar in Indonesia, suggested that the 1978 Agreement on Judicial Cooperation between the Republic of Indonesia and the Kingdom of Thailand could be used as a model for closer judicial cooperation among ASEAN Member States.[36] Professor Gautama argued further that the ASEAN judicial cooperation should not be limited to procedural matters but should also cover the reciprocal recognition and enforcement of court judgments within the ASEAN countries.[37]

[35] Insofar as accession to the 2005 Hague Convention may oblige Indonesian courts to recognise and enforce judgments against state-owned enterprises (SOEs), the government may have to clarify the position of Art 50 of Act No 1 of 2004 concerning State Treasury. Art 50 prohibits the seizure of properties belonging to the Indonesian state and to SOEs, including their properties in the possession of third parties. This provision may prevent the enforcement of foreign judgments against Indonesian SOEs that fail in their commercial contracts with foreign partners.

[36] On the 1978 Agreement, see further Yu Un Oppusunggu, 'Country Report: The Republic of Indonesia' in Adeline Chong (ed), *Recognition and Enforcement of Foreign Judgments in Asia* (Singapore, Asian Business Law Institute, 2017) 100. The 1978 Agreement relates to cooperation in the service of judicial documents and in the taking of evidence in civil or commercial matters. It does not cover cooperation the recognition and enforcement of judgments. In any event, until now no cooperation of any sort has been carried out between Indonesia and Thailand pursuant to the 1978 Agreement. For the text of the 1978 Agreement in Indonesian and Thai, see treaty.kemlu.go.id/apisearch/pdf?filename=THA-1978-0009.pdf.

[37] Gautama (n 4) 172.

VI. Conclusion

This chapter has analysed Indonesia's practice in relation to the recognition and enforcement of foreign judgments in civil and commercial matters and sought to explain the reasons underlying the unenforceability and unrecognisability of foreign judgments in Indonesia. It has also considered the prospect and benefits of recognising and enforcing of foreign judgments in Indonesia as well as the legal reform that must be implemented to achieve such an outcome.

In principle, foreign judgments are neither enforceable nor recognisable in Indonesia. Regarding the enforcement of foreign judgments, Rv Article 436 stipulates that all foreign judgments are unenforceable in Indonesian territory, except in the matter of maritime general average. As for the recognition of foreign judgments, there have been some legal theories supporting the recognition of foreign judgments in Indonesia, especially declaratory and constitutive judgments. But in practice the Indonesian court has a wide discretion whether or not to apply these legal theories.

Despite this overarching principle, Indonesian legal scholars agree that Indonesia may enforce and recognise foreign judgments by the courts of states that have entered into reciprocal agreements with Indonesia regarding the enforcement of judgments. This suggests that there is a future for the recognition and enforcement of judgments in Indonesia. This chapter has thus considered the prospect of Indonesia joining the 2005 Hague Convention on Choice of Court Agreements that deals with the recognition and enforcement of judgments by the court designated in the parties' commercial contract. Accession to the 2005 Hague Convention could complement the 1958 New York Convention and the 1965 ICSID Convention, both of which have been ratified by Indonesia to attract foreign investors and to improve the ease of doing business in Indonesia. In addition, accession to the 2005 Hague Convention would be useful for Indonesian judgments, as they will then be recognised and enforced by other Contracting States to the Convention.

To realise the benefits of the 2005 Hague Convention or of bilateral treaties with other states for the recognition and enforcement of judgments, this chapter has proposed certain legal reforms that need to be implemented in Indonesia. These suggested reforms are to address the problem of corruption in the Indonesian judiciary; to educate Indonesian judges to respect choice of court agreements and foreign judgments; to abolish Rv Article 436; and to issue a clear regulation to all district courts in Indonesia concerning the enforcement of foreign judgments. Greater cooperation with judiciaries in other states is also advocated. The aim of this cooperation would be to establish an understanding among judges and authorities in Indonesia and other states and to develop a procedural standard for the recognition and enforcement of judgments across borders.

14

Thailand

AKAWAT LAOWONSIRI

I. Background

In Thailand private international law (PIL) is a legal discipline that may be described as an uncertain area. Code and legislation, which are the main sources of the civil law system, play a limited role in this context, and wide discretion has been left to Thai judges when ruling in individual cases and laying down jurisprudence. Conflict of laws in this country also involves conflicts of methodologies and approaches among Thai legal scholars. In short, the law in this area is unsettled.

Within this fascinating discipline, no subject is more uncertain than the recognition and enforcement of foreign judgments, which is not governed by the Conflict of Laws Act BE 2481 (1938) (1938 Act) or the Civil Procedure Code. The exclusion of this aspect of Thai PIL from the written law was not accidental, but rather attributable to the country's maintenance of its sovereignty. The exclusion was part of efforts to shield the country from colonisation by the superpowers of the day.[1] Since the development of Thai PIL has been occurring in the pre- and post-colonial contexts, one cannot fully understand this aspect of PIL (that is, the recognition and enforcement of foreign judgments) without appreciation of Thailand's history, which may influence Thai judges when they contemplate whether to recognise and enforce foreign legislation or judgments. Postcolonial explanations[2] are also of relevance since PIL rules involve a derogation from domestic law, which could trigger resistance from the Thai judiciary.

In Thailand, resistance is not confined to the courts. Judicial resistance has usually influenced the legislature, the government and diplomats. The legislature and government are mindful of the judicial view when they propose and draft legislation. The diplomats

[1] For the history of the drafting of the 1938 Act, see Prasit Piwawatanapanich, *Lecture on Private International Law* (Bangkok, Thammasat University Press, 2013) 28.

[2] The author concurs with Bhabha's characterisation of the term post-colonial as 'a form of social criticism that bears witness to the unequal and uneven process of representation by which the historical experience of the once colonized Third World comes to be framed in the West', as quoted and rephrased by Mongia: see Homi K Bhabha, 'Freedom's Basis in the Indeterminate' (1992) 61 *October* 46; Padmini Mongia, *Contemporary Postcolonial Theory: A Reader* (Oxford, Oxford University Press, 1997) 1. Even though Thailand was never colonised by a western power, it has undergone a similar process insofar as it was confronted by its colonised neighbours. One of these processes was the legal transplant of European laws. Modernisation of the Thai legal system cannot be deemed a process of self-identification or self-determination, but rather an emulation of western legal wisdom at a certain degree.

similarly take account of judicial views when deciding whether to ratify international agreements relating to PIL. A brief review of Thai legal history will enable one to understand the attitude of the Thai judiciary.

The post-colonial complexity of Thailand is tied to its current PIL in a number of ways. First, the enactment of the 1938 Act prompted the revocation of British extraterritorial jurisdiction in Thailand.[3] In brief, the 1938 Act had the objective of preventing the country from falling into the colonial sphere. It was a successful attempt, Siam (as Thailand was then known) having pledged to England at that time to enact the PIL codification in return for England revoking its extraterritorial jurisdiction over Siamese territory.[4] Second, the process of developing jurisprudence on aspects of the Thai PIL under the 1938 Act as well as other legislation[5] has been fuelled to an extent by postcolonial and nationalist ideologies. When these ideologies are espoused with conflicts rules, the reasoning of judges has often revolved around the notion of sovereignty.[6] However, judges are not unanimous in their views and a factor that plays a critical role in distinguishing views of the judges from one another is the generation to which they belong. Adherence to reasoning by reference to sovereignty and conservatism on PIL aspects insofar as issues of sovereignty are concerned is less apparent among the younger generation of Thai judges.[7]

The more conservative judges, for example, adhere closely to the law of the forum and to precedent and have expressed reservations about (and cautioned against) the consequences of recognising and enforcing foreign laws and judgments. This inclination has also affected how public policy has been defined in connection with the recognition and enforcement of foreign law and judgments. It is submitted that Thai judges have a clear preference for upholding international arbitration. Foreign arbitral awards thus have a higher likelihood of being recognised and enforced in Thailand, judges there having less frequently invoked public policy to strike down foreign awards.

The ideologies of Thai judges have, however, been changing. Their attitude has shown a gradual shift towards liberalism and functionalism. But the spectrum of judicial attitudes still varies. This means that currently counsel must tailor their arguments to the viewpoint of the judge before whom a case has been assigned. In time, as the younger generation of judges move up in seniority, Thai PIL, especially in relation to the recognition and enforcement of foreign judgments, may become more transparent.

One of the factors mitigating the resistance of the Thai judiciary has been the emergence of global norms of international economic law and international human rights law that have influenced the articulation of conflict of law rules in many countries. Conflict rules can facilitate economic development in a given state and such development will be governed at a higher level by the imperatives of international economics. On the one hand,

[3] Piwawatanapanich (n 1) 28.

[4] ibid.

[5] These are, for example, the Civil and Commercial Code and Civil Procedure Code which contain some PIL rules.

[6] Please see a similar remark in Piwawatanapanich (n 1) 319.

[7] The author distinguishes postcolonialism from sovereign conservatism. Postcolonialism which is a derived form of postmodernism involves deconstruction of mainstream approaches. Logically, it does not necessarily lead to sovereign conservatism, but rather to approaches that can strike a balance against the mainstream. Generalisation of postcolonialism as conservatism, protectionism, or any similar characterisation would (in the author's view) constitute a one-sided understanding.

systems of conflict of law rules can resonate with international human rights law, but on the other hand they can also be challenged by them. In contrast to nearby countries, however, Thailand is a state that allows international human rights law scope for operation in the private sphere to a large extent.[8] In short, one cannot simply look at the black letter of the law when ascertaining the rules applicable to the recognition and enforcement of foreign judgments in Thailand. There are surrounding factors to consider.

II. Sources of Law

There are two sources of law to consider in the context of recognition and enforcement of foreign judgments, namely, international and domestic sources.

A. International Sources

International sources consist of two types of instruments, legally and non-legally binding international instruments.

i. Legally Binding Instruments

Thailand has ratified a couple of international agreements directly relating to the recognition and enforcement of foreign judgments. These are the 1992 International Convention on Civil Liability for Oil Pollution Damage[9] and the 1971 International Convention on the Establishment of an International Fund for Compensation for Oil Pollution Damage.[10] Certain international agreements that are not directly relevant have been ratified and they may affect certain stages in the enforcement of foreign judgments. These are the 1989 United Nations Convention on the Rights of the Child, the 1980 Hague Convention on the Civil Aspects of International Child Abduction, and the 1993 Hague Convention on Protection of Children and Co-operation in Respect of Intercountry Adoption.

[8] The comparison is clear-cut when made between Thailand and its ASEAN neighbours. Despite being currently a military regime, the Thai authorities have been more active in proposing adoption of human rights legislation, as compared to their counterparts in the region. Thailand has thus been keeping pace with the ongoing global development universal of human rights norms. These norms have had an impact on the operation of administrative or criminal rules. These norms can likewise interact with PIL, insofar as the norms may be characterised as laws of public order (*loi d'ordre public*) or as laws of immediate application (*loi d'application immediate*) and regarded as reflecting public policy within the scope of s 5 of the 1938 Act.

[9] See Art X of the 1992 International Convention on Civil Liability for Oil Pollution Damage which contains the obligation of a Contracting State to recognise and enforce foreign judgments rendered in accordance with the requirements of the treaty. After ratification of this Convention, Thailand enacted the Civil Liability for Oil Pollution Damage Act BE 2560 (2017). Art X of the Convention is reflected in s 36 of the Act.

[10] See Art 8 of the 1971 International Convention on the Establishment of an International Fund for Compensation for Oil Pollution Damage which contains the obligation of a Contracting State to recognise and enforce foreign judgments rendered in accordance with the requirements of the treaty. In light of this Convention, Thailand enacted the Requirement of Contributions to the International Fund for Compensation to the International Fund for Compensation for Oil Pollution Damage Caused by Ships Act BE 2560 (2017). Art 8 of the Convention is reflected in s 34 of the Act.

At the regional level, ASEAN does not have a regional instrument that would be applicable in this context. ASEAN is unlikely to come up with any relevant treaty in the foreseeable future, because unlike the European Union, ASEAN is not a Regional Economic Integration Organisation (REIO); ASEAN Member States have largely retained their sovereignty.[11] ASEAN Member States may enter into bilateral agreements on PIL matters either with each other or third party states. In addition, as evidenced in regional instruments and practice,[12] bilateral arrangements have been pursued by individual ASEAN states on PIL matters and it is likely that, in the future, there will be an increasing number of bilateral treaties among ASEAN countries. Currently, Thailand has ratified bilateral agreements on judicial cooperation relating to civil and commercial matters with six countries.[13] But these bilateral agreements do not have an impact on the recognition and enforcement of foreign judgments.

The lack of treaties relating to the recognition and enforcement of judgments does not mean that international agreements do not play a role in the context of recognition and enforcement of foreign judgments. The author is of the view that some international norms can influence conflict of laws rules if the objects to be protected by these norms are perceived to call for sensitive treatment by the Thai judiciary. Thus, these norms may be applied as general principles of Thai PIL. By their nature, rules of international economic law inevitably interact with conflict of laws rules since, depending on how the latter are applied, economic well-being and foreign investment in a country may be facilitated or hindered. However, insofar as Thai jurisprudence is concerned, the link between international economic law and PIL has yet to be fully articulated. Rules of international human rights law might also be of value. Thus, a foreign judgment that violates some aspect of human rights law may be subject to judicial scrutiny on that basis.[14] For example, in Supreme Court Judgment No 585/2461 (SCJ 585/2461) rendered in 1918, the Thai Supreme Court refused to enforce a Vietnamese default judgment on the basis that the plaintiff had failed to adduce sufficient evidence to establish that the judgment was final and conclusive and could no longer be revoked.[15] Some commentators have focused on the issue of finality of the Vietnamese judgment.[16] Nonetheless, although the Thai court certainly focused on the apparent lack of

[11] On 31 December 2015 the 10 ASEAN states inaugurated the ASEAN Economic Community (AEC). For legal aspects of the AEC, see Stefano Inama and Edmund W Sim, *The Foundation of the ASEAN Economic Community* (Cambridge, Cambridge University Press, 2015) 197. For a political point of view, see Donald E Weatherbee, *International Relations in Southeast Asia: The Struggle for Autonomy* (New York, Rowman & Littlefield, 2015) ch 4.

[12] See, for example, Art 9 of the ASEAN Framework Agreement on Services and Art 12 of the Framework Agreement on the ASEAN Investment Area, allowing member states to ratify other treaties with one another or a third party state on the same matter.

[13] The countries are Australia, China, Indonesia, Laos, Spain and Vietnam.

[14] This statement should not be taken to imply that the violation of any rule of international human rights law by a foreign judgment ought to be the subject to scrutiny. The scope for interaction between human rights norms and Thai PIL remains an open question and awaits further jurisprudence to clarify. Thailand became a Contracting State to the International Covenant on Civil and Political Rights (ICCPR) on 29 October 1996.

[15] SCJ 585/2461, where reference was made to the old Thai Civil Procedure Act RE 127 (BE 2451, 1908), in which s 50 provided: 'In any case in which the court has rendered final judgment in a defendant's absence, the defendant may declare justifiable reasons for one's absence and request the court to resume the proceedings. The defendant shall make such request within 15 days'. The defendant does not appear to have made any such request within the 15 days stipulated. Nonetheless, the Thai court ruled in favour of the defendant, possibly applying the spirit of s 50, rather than its letter.

[16] See Kamol Sontikasetrin, *Private International Law* (Bangkok, Nitibannagarn, 1996) 310; Vichai Ariyanuntaka, 'Jurisdiction and Recognition and Enforcement of Foreign Judgments and Arbitral Awards: A Thai Perspective' (*Court of Justice*) 9–10, available online: www.coj.go.th/en/pdf/AlternativeDisputeResolution04.pdf.

finality of the Vietnamese judgment, the case may also be read as one in which the court's underlying concern was as to whether due process had been observed and the defendant had been afforded a reasonable opportunity to present one's case.[17] The author submits that, in similar cases brought before the Thai Court today, it would be appropriate refer to ICCPR Article 14, dealing with the right to a fair hearing in a suit of law.[18]

To summarise, there are two types of legally binding instruments that could have legal effect on the recognition and enforcement of foreign judgments: (1) instruments directly relating to recognition and enforcement of foreign judgments; and (2) instruments the underlying principles of which may be said to apply as internationally recognised norms to aspects of the recognition and enforcement of foreign judgments. It should be noted that, if in the future, Thailand ratifies international or bilateral agreements on the subject, the second type of international instruments may play less of a role since the Thai court may then only consult ratified international instruments directly relating to the recognition and enforcement of foreign judgments.

ii. Non-legally Binding Instruments

There are a number of non-legally binding instruments (sometimes referred to as 'soft law instruments') that may have implications on the functioning of the Thai judiciary, insofar as the recognition and enforcement of judgments is concerned. In the absence of legally binding instruments, this type of instruments could play a significant role.

For example, the 'Asian Principles of Private International Law' (APPIL)[19] should, once published, provide guidance among others on general principles and best practice in relation to the recognition and enforcement of foreign judgments. APPIL's underlying methodology of identifying PIL rules common to Asian jurisdictions could complement the postcolonial values of Thai law professors, lawyers, legislators and judges. The APPIL, being the product of Asian legal academics (including Thai law professors), should thus reflect Asian and Thai perspectives on suitable ways of developing PIL in light of the historical, political, cultural, religious and legal traditions and conditions encountered in Asia.

The Hague Judgments Project should also be a source of guidance. The functional rules and principles that have emerged and will emerge from the Hague Judgments Project can be adopted by the Thai judiciary. In this respect, the lack of ratification of (say) the 2005 Hague Convention on Choice of Court Agreements or the forthcoming Convention on the Recognition and Enforcement of Judgments in Civil and Commercial Matters currently being worked on by the Hague Conference's Judgment Project, would not prevent Thailand from adopting the principles reflected by those instruments insofar as they embody good or best practice. The adoption of principles or rules contained in non-ratified treaties can be done through the process of lobbying the national authorities that are competent to propose draft legislation.

[17] Panthip Karnjanachittra-Saisoontorn, 'Problems in the Requirements for Recognition of Foreign Judgments' (1992) 22(2) *Thammasat Law Journal* 213. Karnjanachittra-Saisoontorn has been working as PIL scholar and human rights activist.

[18] Thailand became a Contracting State to the International Covenant on Civil and Political Rights (ICCPR) on 29 October 1996.

[19] See Weizuo Chen and Gerald Goldstein, 'The Asian Principles of Private International Law: Objectives, Contents, Structure and Selected Topics on Choice of Law' (2017) 13(2) *Journal of Private International Law* 411.

Non-binding Memorandums of Understanding (MOUs) between Thai and foreign courts have been adopted to facilitate certain forms of judicial cooperation and collaboration. But so far, no MOU has set out the principles by which the Thai judiciary will recognise and enforce the judgments of particular courts.

In brief, even though there is an absence of legally and non-legally binding instruments regarding recognition and enforcement of foreign judgments, the law is not in vacuum. It is possible for counsel to refer to international soft law instruments by way of guidance on the practices that the Thai courts should follow.

B. Domestic Sources

When it comes to domestic sources, discussion should start from the applicability of the 1938 Act to the recognition and enforcement of foreign judgments. If this Act is applicable, a foreign judgment can be recognised or enforced in the light of section 3 of this PIL codification. Although it does not directly address this subject, the statute contains universally recognised rules of private international law. There are two possible approaches.[20] One approach maintains that section 3 of Act applies in the context of the recognition and enforcement of judgments. Another approach holds a negative view on this issue. The second approach seems to prevail as the majority view. The validity of this approach is backed by the drafting history of the Act. There was a communication among the drafters that the scope of the statute should be limited to choice of law problems and should not extend to procedural matters.[21] In effect, the recognition and enforcement of foreign judgments is principally subject to the review of the Thai judiciary. In practice, the rulings of the Supreme Court have strong persuasive effect in setting down the principles to be followed in a matter. Often, sound rulings may emanate from the lower courts. But, as a legal tradition, they do not constitute binding jurisprudence. Nonetheless, there have been several decisions of the lower courts that have contributed to jurisprudential development (as will be discussed in the next section).

Legislation and codes can also serve as domestic sources, even though none directly regulate the recognition and enforcement of judgments. Although they do not provide instructions for judges, the court may consult them as providing guiding rules and principles. Legislation, for instance, may be used by the court as an aid to ascertain Thai public policy. The Thai Civil Procedure Code can also be a source from which the court infers PIL principles by analogy.[22] The process of inferring principles from the Code, however, will inevitably have a subjective element, since the court has the discretion as to whether and (if so) in what manner to deduce rules that would be appropriate when (say) deciding whether to recognise and enforce foreign judgments.

Moreover, the exercise of inferring applicable principles is not necessarily limited to Thai jurisprudence, legislation and codes. On occasion the court can take a comparative

[20] Piwawatanapanich (n 1) 320–21.

[21] ibid.

[22] This is comparable to what was done in SCJ 585/2461 (n 15), where reference was made to s 50 of the Thai Civil Procedure Act 1908 in determining whether a Vietnamese judgment was final and conclusive.

approach by referring to principles of other jurisdictions that reflect good or best practice.[23] This may especially be the case where judges have studied law abroad and have been influenced by the legal system of the country in which they have studied. While foreign legal principles obviously cannot be regarded as a source of Thai law, they can inspire the direction in which Thai jurisprudence is developed.

III. Requirements for the Recognition and Enforcement of Foreign Judgments

Although Thai law has generally followed the civilian law approach since the modernisation of its legal system in the nineteenth century, Thai law on the recognition and enforcement of foreign judgments has also been influenced by the common law. Accordingly, one should not ascertain the relevant rules and principles by simply referring to practice in civil law jurisdictions.

A. What Qualifies as a 'Foreign Judgment'?

Foreign judgments are not defined in Thai law. Neither are foreign judicial acts defined. Clear cases are namely SCJ 585/2461 and Central Juvenile and Family Court Judgment No 2351/2548. The first involved a money judgment that was rendered in Vietnam. The plaintiff requested that the Thai court enforce the judgment. The second involved a family judgment rendered by the Swedish court relating to the custody of a child. The Thai court accepted that the Swedish judgment was a foreign one.

Judicial settlements (*transactions judiciaires*) that would be treated as foreign judgments in other jurisdictions are not considered as judgments by the Thai court. Such are not even considered as judicial acts. SCJ 15066/2555, for example, involved a judicial settlement by the New York family court. Instead of treating the judicial settlement as a foreign judgment, the Thai court characterised the matter as one involving a contractual performance and surprisingly applied section 13 of the Conflict of Laws Act 1938 to the case.

Since the number of cases concerning the characterisation of foreign judgments or other judicial acts is limited, a number of questions remain unanswered. An anti-suit injunction granted by a foreign court, for example, is likely to be unenforceable in the Thai court. This, in the view of the author, is because the enforcement of an anti-suit injunction granted by a foreign court would likely be regarded by Thai judges as contravening judicial sovereignty. Although this may mean an increase in the caseload of Thai judges, the jurisdiction of the Thai court has always been interpreted as largely inclusive. The court has accordingly developed a particular way of interpreting the concept of *forum non conveniens*.[24]

[23] See, for instance, in SCJ 585/2461 (n 15), the presiding judge, Phrya Debvidura (Boonchuay Vanikkul), President of the Supreme Court, studied law in England. This has prompted commentators to suggest that the judge's ruling was influenced by English law: see Piwawatanapanich (n 1) 325–26. See also Ariyanuntaka (n 16) 10.

[24] Supranee Ajjit and Vichai Ariyanuntaka, 'Agreements Relating to Dispute Settlement in International Commercial Matters: Arbitration Agreement and Choice-of-Court Agreement' (*Dhurakij Pundit University*) 240–45, available online: libdoc.dpu.ac.th/mtext/article/487038.pdf.

Regardless of whether a foreign court has exclusive jurisdiction by reason of the parties' agreement, as long as the Thai court deems itself to be a *forum conveniens*, it is unlikely to dismiss a case on the ground that it has been decided by a foreign court. In SCJ 3882/2549, the parties designated the Hong Kong court in their contract as the forum to settle any disputes. Nevertheless, the Thai court affirmed its jurisdiction with reference to domestic legislation and proceeded to hear the case in full.

Foreign judgments are not necessarily regarded as 'judgments'. It may depend on how a party characterises the foreign judgment. For example, a party may refer to a foreign judgment as simply a piece of evidence to be presented to the court. In SCJ 937/2476, a judgment rendered in Indonesia related to a case being heard in Thailand. The court affirmed that the Indonesian judgment could be admitted as a piece of evidence in the Thai proceedings,[25] provided that the party seeking to adduce the judgment make it available in the Thai language.

While the distinction between commercial cases and other types of cases may be significant, the meaning of 'commercial' has not been addressed in a case. It remains to be seen how Thai judges will approach the recognition and enforcement of commercial cases and whether Thai judges will be more or less willing to recognise and enforce foreign judgments in purely commercial cases, as opposed to foreign judgments in the area of family, intellectual property and insolvency law. The absence of an established practice may be a blessing in disguise as counsel can then play a significant role in steering the development of the Thai jurisprudence on recognition and enforcement.

B. Procedural Requirements

Procedural requirements are currently non-exhaustive. There are at least three elements that have been stipulated in Thai case law, namely indirect jurisdiction, due process and *res judicata*. Since the only relevant case (SCJ 585/2461)[26] was decided a long time ago, these elements may be subject to revision in the future. Readers should therefore be mindful of possible significant changes in the future. Lawyers should therefore be conscious of a degree of freedom in how they construct their arguments.

i. Jurisdiction of the Rendering Court

For a century, on the basis of the ruling in SCJ 585/2461, the existence of international (also known as 'indirect') jurisdiction has been regarded as a criterion for recognition and enforcement of foreign judgments without an exhaustive definition of what constitutes international jurisdiction ever having been given by the court. Many decades later, the Supreme Court was confronted with the problem of international jurisdiction, but did not use this chance to substantiate the jurisdiction criterion. In SCJ 6565/2544, it only recognised that the rendering Court had international jurisdiction to hear the case but did not

[25] See also Panthip Karnchanachittra-Saisoontorn, 'Referencing Foreign Judgments in Thai Court' (1990) 20(3) *Thammasat Law Journal* 147.

[26] SCJ 585/2461 (n 15).

clarify substantive details of international jurisdiction. The matter is hence subject to future formulations by other judges.

There are a number of options as to how the Thai court might define international jurisdiction. For instance, the Thai court may follow the *Spiegelbildprinzip* (mirror principle) of German law[27] or the 'characteristic link' of French law.[28] In the author's view, *Spiegelbildprinzip* is least likely to be transplanted into the Thai system. The doctrine is unnecessarily complicated and thus contrary to the Thai legal tradition that prefers an economical, effective and practical approach. In addition, the *Spiegelbildprinzip* requires the enforcing court to see whether its national rules on jurisdiction are mirrored at the enforcement stage. That entails the enforcing court looking into whether the rendering Court would have had jurisdiction under the law of the requested state. These requirements do not seem to be a useful consideration in the author's view. Criteria for jurisdiction vary from one state to another. That is precisely why it is necessary to seek recognition and enforcement of foreign judgments. If indirect jurisdiction depends on the grounds by which a claimant can establish direct jurisdiction before the courts of an enforcing state, then the enforceability of a judgment will vary from state to state. There will be no consistent, over-arching principle as to why a judgment is enforceable in one state, but not another. On the other hand, the test of a characteristic link between a rendering court and the facts of a case that has been developed by the French Supreme Court seems to be a better starting point and an advocacy of this should be more welcome by Thai judges. A widespread application of the characteristic link doctrine would lead to the judgment of a rendering court in a state or territory having a connection with the facts of a case being more consistently enforced in other countries.

ii. Due Process[29]

Although not directly dealing with due process when refusing to recognise or enforce the judgment rendered by the Vietnamese court, as discussed above, the Supreme Court in SCJ 585/2461 may well have been concerned about a possible lack of due process in the obtaining of the Vietnamese judgment.[30] Provisions in the Civil Procedure Code may be applied by analogy in determining whether or not a foreign judgment was obtained through due process. A regard by the Thai court to the due process by which a foreign judgment was obtained would enhance transnational governance. However, at the same time there is likely to be potential uncertainty until the development of a settled jurisprudence, since the Thai court may apply any one of a myriad of procedural rules relating to due process under Thai law. Lawyers in their arguments before the court should not simply cite SCJ 585/2461,

[27] Rolf A Schütze, '§328' in Bernhard Wieczorek and Rolf A Schütze (eds), *Zivilprozessordnung und Nebengesetze: Grosskommentar*, 3. Teilband, 1. Teil (Berlin, De Gruyter Recht, 2007) s 462; Tanja Domej, 'Recognition and Enforcement of Judgments (Civil Law)' in Jürgen Basedow, Giesela Rühl, Franco Ferrari and Pedro de Miguel Asensio (eds), *Encyclopaedia of Private International Law* (Cheltenham, Edward Elgar Publishing, 2017) 1474.

[28] According to this approach, the French Court can examine whether there is a characteristic link between the case and the State of the rendering court. The French Court can also look into whether the rendering Court has interfered with the jurisdiction of the French Court. See Cass le civ, Simitch [1985] Rev crit DIP 369, cited in Domej (n 27) 1475.

[29] It is also possible to describe due process as a procedural dimension of public policy. See s III.B.v below.

[30] Karnchanachittra-Saisoontorn (n 17). Different Thai commentators have put forward different readings of this judgment.

but can also refer to rules of international human rights law especially as evidenced in the treaties to which Thailand is Contracting State or in customary international law.[31]

iii. Res Judicata

The ruling in SCJ 585/2461 refers to *res judicata* as a criterion for the recognition and enforcement of foreign judgments. This requirement is a classical one and applies to all types of cases. Importantly, the requesting party is required to show to the Thai court that the judgment of the rendering court has acquired *res judicata* status. In other words, it must be established that the judgment of the rendering court is final and conclusive. Failure to demonstrate this can lead to the refusal to recognise or enforce the judgment. Moreover, it follows that there will be problems in obtaining recognition or enforcement of judicial acts other than final judgments, that is, decisions that can be challenged at any time or that are merely interlocutory. Thai jurisprudence has yet to clarify what foreign judicial acts will be enforced as final and conclusive judgments and what will not.

iv. Reciprocity

Whether reciprocity is or should be counted as a requirement for recognition and enforcement of foreign judgments by the Thai court is a fascinating topic. Reciprocity has so far been scarcely mentioned in judgments[32] and so cannot be deemed as a settled rule contained in the Thai jurisprudence. Reciprocity is thus not yet a criterion within the Thai legal system. Some authors have proposed including reciprocity as a requirement.[33] But the author is of the view that it will be hard to accommodate reciprocity within the Thai legal system. The concept of reciprocity is at odds with modern trends in private international law. There has been greater focus on the role of the individual in cross-border transactions. The individual's rights have become increasingly disengaged from the sanctions of states in their dealings with each other. The concept of reciprocity posits that a state is entitled to retaliate against another state in situations where the latter has failed to enforce a judgment of the former, by punishing individuals of the former state seeking to enforce their rights in the latter state. It is submitted that it does not make sense for an individual to bear the burden for perceived wrongs done by that individual's home country.[34]

v. Public Policy

Courts will normally consider public policy in the sense of *ordre public atténué*. This is to be contrasted with *ordre public plein* that normally involves a consideration of whether a foreign law is contrary to public policy of the forum. *Ordre public atténué*, on the other

[31] Discussion on the possible way to construct arguments has been made in s II.A.i above.

[32] It was mentioned in SCJ 585/2461 (n 15), as it reads, 'the principle underlying recognition and enforcement of foreign judgments is one of mutual respect among nations'.

[33] Karnchanachittra-Saisoontorn (n 17) 218; Patanawanich (n 1) 329.

[34] Ralf Michaels, 'Recognition and Enforcement of Foreign Judgments' in Rüdiger Wolfrum (ed), *Max Planck Encyclopedia of Public International Law* (Oxford, Oxford University Press, 2009) para 7.

hand, simply examines whether a foreign judgment is contrary to the fundamental norms of the enforcing state. The employment of *ordre public atténué* can lead to the maintenance of judicial economy, since the scrutiny is more limited. An example of the application of *ordre public atténué* by the Thai court may be found in a case on the recognition of an administrative act done in China. This was SCJ 45/2524, which involved a request to recognise the marriage between minors of 10 and 12 years of age. Applying the attenuated test of public policy, the Thai court felt that as the marriage had been validly entered into abroad, there was no compelling reason of Thai public policy to refuse recognition to the same.

Where then is Thai public policy to be found? One possibility is to look at relevant legislation. These are sometimes called *lois d'ordre public* (laws of public policy). They can provide guidance to Thai judges on how they might apply notions of public policy to a foreign judgment and on how they may tolerate effects of a foreign judgment. A second method, albeit not as ideal, because it would introduce a subjective element into the process of recognition and enforcement, is to found public policy on what a judge would regard as contrary to Thai fundamental norms. The burden of proof in showing inconsistency with public policy, as the Supreme Court has made clear in SCJ 6565/2544, can belong to the defendant or judgment debtor.

IV. The Future Development of Thai PIL

In 2015 when core ASEAN treaties on economic integration came into effect among Member States,[35] Thai policy makers began to appreciate the importance of PIL as a way of facilitating regional economic integration. The project 'Thai PIL reform' was accordingly initiated by the Ministry of Justice in conjunction with the International Law Association of Thailand. The project was temporarily suspended when Thailand returned to military rule. Efforts then resumed in 2017, when there was discussion in government and academic circles on the possibility of Thailand joining the Hague Conference and acceding to the 2005 Hague Convention on Choice of Court Agreements. The discussions are still ongoing. It remains to be seen whether the discussions will mature into something concrete. There is a risk that acceding to the 2005 Hague Convention will lead to a PIL backlash in Thailand, especially among more conservative senior judges. Judicial resistance to, and suspicion of, reforms that may lead (or be perceived as leading) to a curtailment of judicial autonomy is still strong and potentially pervasive in Thailand. Thus, future developments in PIL, including as regards the law relating to the recognition and enforcement of foreign judgments, are likely to be introduced by the Thai government and courts only gradually over an extended period of time.

[35] These include ASEAN Trade in Goods Agreement (ATIGA), ASEAN Framework Agreement on Services (AFAS), and ASEAN Comprehensive Investment Agreement (ACIA).

15

Sri Lanka

KANKANI TANTRI CHITRASIRI, SAJINI FERNANDO
AND ASLESHA WEERASEKARA

I. Introduction

International trade and commerce and related matters have shown an exponential growth over the past few decades. In an increasingly interconnected and globalised world, the rapidity of transportation, human migrations and technological advancements has brought about questions that transcend political boundaries. Contrary to these rapid developments, we are to admit that the law, in many circumstances, has failed to develop at a similar or desirable pace.

Legal systems within and among countries are diverse in nature and the inherent complexities that are unique to each of these systems have resulted in the absence of political will and commitment on the part of governments to reinforce new or existing international legal principles within their domestic legal systems.

The process of recognising and enforcing a foreign judgment in civil and commercial matters before a domestic court, requires a state to take appropriate legislative and other measures to facilitate such recognition and enforcement. Further, this involves a degree of judicial activism and calls on the judiciary to have confidence, both in the authority and competence of a foreign legal system and in the independent and efficient manner in which the matter in question has been adjudicated.

The statutory law relating to the recognition and enforcement of foreign judgments in Sri Lanka is governed by the Reciprocal Enforcement of Judgments Ordinance (No 41 of 1921) (Reciprocal Enforcement of Judgments Ordinance) and the Enforcement of Foreign Judgments Ordinance (No 4 of 1937) (Enforcement of Foreign Judgments Ordinance).[1] Notably, the former is the only instrument presently in force, although limited in terms of its scope of application, as opposed to the latter which has not been made operative.

[1] The main difference between the two ordinances may be seen from their long titles. The Reciprocal Enforcement of Judgments Ordinance was enacted 'to provide for the enforcement in Ceylon of judgments obtained in the superior courts of the United Kingdom and of other parts of Her Majesty's realms and territories'. In contrast, the Enforcement of Foreign Judgments Ordinance was enacted 'to make provision for the enforcement in Ceylon of judgments given in countries which accord reciprocal treatment to judgments given in Ceylon, for facilitating the enforcement in other countries of judgments given in Ceylon and for other purposes in connection with the matters aforesaid'. Otherwise, the requirements in both ordinances for the enforcement of judgments are broadly similar and reflect the common law principles discussed in this chapter.

Since the nineteenth century, the judiciary has attempted to fill this lacuna by employing common law principles in its interpretive process.

This chapter discusses at length the overall legal framework pertaining to the recognition and enforcement of foreign judgments in Sri Lanka and the nature of Sri Lanka's international legal obligations in this regard. This chapter also proposes key reforms and recommendations that may enable swifter, less costly and viable mechanisms for the recognition and enforcement of foreign judgments in Sri Lanka.

II. Background

Sri Lanka is home to a community of people belonging to diverse faiths and ethnicities. Located in the Indian Ocean, off the southern end of the Indian subcontinent, the island of Sri Lanka is geo-strategically located in an enviable position, adjacent to the Indian Ocean shipping route that connects the West with the East. Sri Lanka is a lower middle-income country with a GDP per capita of US$4,073 (2017) and a total population of 21.4 million people.[2] With a history that goes back more than 2,500 years, Sri Lanka is one of the oldest constitutional democracies in the region, presently governed by an executive President operating within a parliamentary democracy.

The legal, political and administrative fabric of the republic reveals its colonial underpinnings and the plurality of laws in the country. The personal and territorial legal systems of the country include the Kandyan law, *Tesawalamai* law and Muslim law which are reflective of the inherent diversity in the country. Persons who are governed by these personal laws are governed in other respects by Roman-Dutch law, which is the common law of the country applicable to everyone. Additionally, the laws of Sri Lanka have been influenced greatly by English law as well as the Indian and Anglo-American legal systems, particularly in relation to commercial litigation.

Sri Lanka is in the process of recovering from the ramifications of two insurrections and a 30-year civil war and is working towards achieving lasting peace and reconciliation through its robust transitional justice framework.

A well-functioning and independent judiciary is the cornerstone of a democracy. An independent, efficient and apolitical judicial system helps to build trust among the public, especially among locals and foreign nationals who are engaged in cross-border commercial activities and involuntarily turn to the law to settle disputes.

The 19th Amendment to the Constitution in 2015 reinstated the Constitutional Council, which was originally established with the intention of creating a system of checks and balances when making certain Presidential appointments to positions of power and influence.[3] The Constitutional Council consists of the following members: the Prime Minister; the Speaker; the Leader of the Opposition; a Member of Parliament appointed by the President; five persons appointed by the President on the nomination of the Prime Minister and the Leader of the Opposition of whom two persons shall be Members of

[2] The World Bank, 'The World Bank in Sri Lanka: Outline' (*The World Bank*, 17 October 2017), available online: www.worldbank.org/en/country/srilanka/overview.

[3] Constitution of the Democratic Socialist Republic of Sri Lanka (Constitution of Sri Lanka), Sch to Art 41B and Sch to Art 41C.

Parliament; and a Member of Parliament appointed by the President, nominated by agreement of the majority of Members of Parliament belonging to political parties or independent groups other than the respective political parties or independent groups to which the Prime Minister and the Leader of the Opposition belong.[4]

The Constitutional Council has been vested with the power to make recommendations that the President is bound by, when appointing chairpersons and members of independent commissions.[5] Further the Constitutional Council has the authority to approve (or reject) individuals who have been nominated by the President to certain positions, including that of Chief Justice and judges of the Supreme Court, the President and judges of the Court of Appeal, the members of the Judicial Service Commission, and the Attorney General.[6]

The 19th Amendment has further ushered in reasonable checks and balances and reinforces the principle that sovereignty lies with the people. This Amendment affirmed the peoples' right to access information by enshrining the same as a fundamental right protected under the Constitution[7] and a separate statutory framework has been created to facilitate the exercise of this right.[8]

When determining the broad parameters relevant to the recognition and enforcement of foreign judgments in civil and commercial matters in Sri Lanka, an examination of private international law in the country becomes vital.

Private international law (interchangeably used with the term 'conflict of laws') relates to rules applied by domestic courts to determine which laws apply to cases that involve people of different countries or of different nationalities or transactions which transcend international boundaries.[9] The sources of private international law in Sri Lanka are primarily national legislation, treaties and agreements to which Sri Lanka is a party, and decisions of courts. In ascertaining the application of private international law rules, a court will essentially consider jurisdiction, choice of law and the possibility of the enforcement of foreign judgments. In this regard, the enactment of the Reciprocal Enforcement of Judgments Ordinance and the Enforcement of Foreign Judgments Ordinance and the subsequent association with the Hague Conference on Private International Law are important steps taken towards the development of private international law in Sri Lanka.

The court system of Sri Lanka consists of the Magistrate's Courts, the District Courts, the High Courts, the Court of Appeal and the Supreme Court, as well as various tribunals and specialised courts established by law. A Magistrate's Court has original criminal jurisdiction[10] and conducts non-summary proceedings before indictment to the High Court. Any party aggrieved by any conviction, sentence or order entered or imposed by a Magistrate's Court may, subject to the provisions of any law, appeal therefrom to the High Court in the first instance or the Court of Appeal or Supreme Court in the second instance.

[4] ibid, Art 41A(1).

[5] ibid, Art 41B.

[6] ibid, Art 41C.

[7] ibid, Art 14A.

[8] Right to Information Act (No 12 of 2016).

[9] David P Stewart, 'Private International Law: A Dynamic and Developing Field' (2009) 30(4) *University of Pennsylvania Journal of International Law* 1121.

[10] Judicature Act (No 2 of 1978) (Judicature Act), s 30.

District Courts have unlimited original jurisdiction in all civil, revenue, trust, matrimonial, insolvency and testamentary matters.[11] Any person who is dissatisfied with any judgment, decree or order delivered and made by a District Court or a Family Court within a particular Province may prefer an appeal to the Civil Appellate High Court of that Province for the correction of all errors in fact or in law[12] and an appeal therefrom may lie to the Supreme Court.[13]

High Courts of Sri Lanka ordinarily exercise the power and authority to hear, try and determine in the manner provided for by written law all criminal prosecutions on indictment.[14] A High Court trial can be heard by the judge alone or with a jury or may be held as a trial-at-bar, with three judges appointed by the Chief Justice. In 1987, the 13th Amendment to the Constitution introduced a devolved system of governance with the creation of Provincial Councils to administer the provinces in accordance with the law and established High Courts for each of the Provinces. The High Courts are empowered to exercise original criminal jurisdiction in respect of offences committed within the Province; appellate and revisionary jurisdiction in respect of convictions, sentences and orders entered or imposed by Magistrate's Courts and Primary Courts within the Province; and the writ jurisdiction of the High Court.[15]

The High Court of the Provinces (Special Provisions) Act (No 19 of 1990) provides for the procedure in respect of exercising the right of appeal to a High Court; the exercise of the writ jurisdiction of the High Court; appeals to the Supreme Court in certain cases; and references to the Supreme Court involving the infringement of fundamental rights.

The specialised High Court for the Western Province (also known as the Commercial High Court) was established in terms of the High Court of the Provinces (Special Provisions) Act (No 10 of 1996). This Act provides for the civil jurisdiction of the High Courts established by Article 154P of the Constitution. The Commercial High Court in particular has the jurisdiction to hear cases above a particular monetary threshold determined by the Minister of Justice. This is currently five million Sri Lankan rupees, for causes of action which have arisen within the Western Province. Cases involving commercial transactions below that value, fall outside the statutory parameters in the Act and are heard in District Courts.

The jurisdiction of the Commercial High Court under Act No 10 of 1996 is set out in the First Schedule to the Act, the contents of which are as follows:

1. All actions where the cause of action has arisen out of commercial transactions (including causes of action relating to banking, the export or import of merchandise, services affreightment, insurance, mercantile agency, mercantile usage, and the construction of any mercantile document) in which the debt, damage or demand is for a sum exceeding twenty million rupees or such other amount as may be fixed by the Minister from time to time, by notification published in the gazette, other than actions instituted under the Debt Recovery (Special Provisions) Act (No 2 of 1990).[16]

[11] ibid, s 19.
[12] High Court of the Provinces (Special Provisions) Act (No 54 of 2006), s 5A.
[13] ibid, s 5C.
[14] Judicature Act, s 9.
[15] Constitution of Sri Lanka, Art 154P.
[16] The twenty million rupees threshold applied to actions filed in the High Court on or after 15 March 2019. The threshold had been five million rupees, before it was amended by Gazette No 2112/33 (28 February 2019).

2. All applications and proceedings under sections 31, 51, 131, 210 and 211 of the Companies Act (No 17 of 1982).[17]
3. All proceedings under the Code of Intellectual Property Act (No 52 of 1979).

Further, enforcement of arbitration awards and admiralty matters are also heard in the Commercial High Court. District Courts in general do not have the jurisdiction in relation to arbitration, intellectual property, companies and admiralty matters. Hence, the jurisdiction given to the High Courts through the aforesaid Act is indicative of the areas that may be considered when constructing a definition of 'commercial matters'. Courts have in fact observed that wider interpretations need to be considered[18] when determining the commercial nature of matters that come before the courts.

III. Recognition and Enforcement of Foreign Judgments in Sri Lanka

The direct enforcement of foreign judgments by statute or alternatively at common law are the two modes by which foreign judgments may be recognised and enforced in Sri Lanka.

A. Recognition and Enforcement by Statute

The Reciprocal Enforcement of Judgments Ordinance and the Enforcement of Foreign Judgments Ordinance were introduced with the aim of facilitating the process of recognition and enforcement of foreign judgments.

The Enforcement of Foreign Judgments Ordinance which provides for a system of registration in order to enforce foreign judgments has not been brought into operation in terms of section 2, which provides that this Ordinance comes into operation on such date as the Minister may appoint by Order published in the Gazette.

The Reciprocal Enforcement of Judgments Ordinance is the only legislative enactment presently in force in this regard. The Ordinance enables the Minister by Order published in the Gazette, to extend the application of the Ordinance to judgments obtained in a superior court in any part of Her Majesty's Realm and Territories outside the UK, where the Minister is satisfied that reciprocal legislative provisions have been made in any part of such Realm and Territories outside the UK to enforce judgments obtained in any District Court or in the Supreme Court of Sri Lanka.[19]

[17] Companies Act (No 17 of 1982), s 31 (actions to relieve a company of the consequences of noncompliance with the conditions constituting it a private company); s 51 (actions to make irregular allotments void and actions to recover loss, damage or costs incurred as a result of such irregular allotments); s 131 (actions for a court to order a meeting of a company to be held as specified where compliance with the articles of the company or the provisions of the Companies Act is impracticable); s 210 (applications complaining against oppression in the conduct of the affairs of a company); s 211 (applications complaining of mismanagement). The equivalent of these provisions can be found in the current Companies Act (No 7 of 2007).

[18] *Cornel & Co Ltd v Mitsui and Co Ltd* [2000] 1 Sri LR 57 (Fernando J).

[19] Reciprocal Enforcement of Judgments Ordinance, s 6.

This Ordinance is of limited geographical application, as it extends only to the UK and other parts of Her Majesty's Realm and Territories outside the UK. Ministerial Orders published in accordance with section 6 extended the application of the Ordinance to Hong Kong, Mauritius, New South Wales, Straits Settlement, Tanganyika, Uganda, Victoria, Federation of Malaya, Australian Capital Territory, Northern Territory of Australia, New Zealand (including the Cook and Niue Islands) and the Trust Territory of Western Samoa, Queensland, Western Australia, South Australia and Tasmania. Despite its limitations, the conditions that need to be met in order to register a foreign judgment under the Reciprocal Enforcement of Foreign Judgments Ordinance set out in section 3 are notably in line with the principles applied when enforcing foreign judgments at common law.

Section 3(2) provides that:

> No judgment shall be ordered to be registered if:
> (a) the original court acted without jurisdiction; or
> (b) the judgment-debtor, being a person who was neither carrying on business nor ordinarily resident within the jurisdiction of the original court, did not voluntarily appear or otherwise submit or agree to submit to the jurisdiction of that court; or
> (c) the judgment-debtor, being the defendant in the proceedings, was not duly served with the process of the original court and did not appear notwithstanding that he:
>   (i) was ordinarily resident, or
>   (ii) was carrying on business within the jurisdiction of that court, or
>   (iii) agreed to submit to the jurisdiction of that court; or
> (d) the judgment was obtained by fraud; or
> (e) the judgment-debtor satisfies the registering court either that an appeal is pending, or that he is entitled and intends to appeal against the judgment; or
> (f) the judgment was in respect of a cause of action which for reasons of public policy or for some other similar reason could not have been entertained by the registering court.

In *Associated Newspapers of Ceylon Limited v Prins Gunasekera*, Jayasinghe J considered section 3(1) of the Reciprocal Enforcement of Judgments Ordinance which provides, inter alia, that the court may only order a foreign judgment to be registered 'if in all the circumstances of the case they think it is just and convenient that the judgment should be enforced in Ceylon'. The court upheld the restrictions in sections 3(1) and 3(2)(b) which limit the registration of a judgment for enforcement only against a judgment debtor who is an ordinary resident of the country in which the judgment was delivered.[20] The impact of the principle of reciprocity on jurisdiction was considered by the court in *Lalwani v Indian Overseas Bank*[21] which held that the rights of the parties is to be determined as at the date of the action and that, since the requirement of reciprocity only needs to be established as at the time when a foreign judgment is registered under the Ordinance, the disappearance of reciprocity by the repeal of legislation in the rendering state would not affect the validity of the original registration.

[20] *Associated Newspapers of Ceylon Limited v Prins Gunasekera* [2000] 2 Sri LR 323.

[21] *Lalwani v Indian Overseas Bank* [1998] 2 Sri LR 197. In the case, the judgment debtor argued that, there has been a severance of reciprocity, as Hong Kong had ceased to be a 'part of Her Majesty's Realm and Territories outside the UK' with effect from 1 July 1997 and that registration proceedings in terms of the Reciprocal Enforcement of Judgments Ordinance would have to be terminated.

It is evident that the statutory regime for recognition and enforcement, despite mostly being in line with accepted general principles, has scope for further improvement in its operation. With relevant amendments, these instruments have the potential to further the development of private international law in the country.

B. Recognition and Enforcement at Common Law

The jurisdictional bases on which an action may be instituted in Sri Lanka in respect of a civil or commercial matter is provided for in section 9 of the Civil Procedure Code which reads as follows:

> [S]ubject to the pecuniary or other limitations prescribed by any law, action shall be instituted in the court within the local limits of whose jurisdiction (a) a party defendant resides; or (b) the land in respect of which the action is brought lies or is situate in whole or in part; or (c) the cause of action arises; or (d) the contract sought to be enforced was made.

Other statutory enactments may also refer to special grounds of jurisdiction or grounds which are complimentary to those set out in section 9, for instance the specialised jurisdictional clauses concerning the aforementioned Commercial High Court.

For the purposes of discussion, it is important to note the interpretation assigned to a foreign court and foreign judgment in section 5 of the Civil Procedure Code. A foreign court is defined as 'a court situate beyond the limits of, and not having authority in, Sri Lanka' and a foreign judgment is 'a judgment of a foreign court'.

In the absence of a comprehensive legislative framework which is operational and not limited in application, the alternative approach has been to enforce foreign judgments in Sri Lanka in accordance with the common law. In *Narayanaswami v Marimuttupillai*, the Supreme Court referring to the shortcomings of the Enforcement of Foreign Judgments Ordinance stated that:

> [T]his does not dispose of the matter. The Judgment of a Foreign Court of Competent Jurisdiction is in accordance with the Principles of Private International Law regarded in other Courts as prima facie evidence of a debt at common law. This rule has been recognised in Ceylon and an action lies for the recovery of the debt so adjudged, subject to such defences as they may be raised at the trial by the alleged debtor.[22]

i. Requirements for Registration

The enforcement of foreign judgments *in personam* is subject to the fulfillment of several conditions.

a. The Judgment Must have been Given by a Court of Competent Jurisdiction

One of the primary questions considered by a court called upon to enforce a foreign judgment is whether the court of the country from which the judgment proceeds had the

[22] *Narayanaswami v Marimuttupillai* [1949] XLI CLW 12.

jurisdiction and necessary competence to deal with the matter considered in the judgment. A frequently cited statement of Buckley LJ in *Emanuel v Symon*[23] provides that:

> In actions *in personam* there are five cases in which the courts of this country will enforce a foreign judgment.
>
> 1. Where the defendant is a subject of the foreign country in which the Judgment has been obtained.
> 2. When he was resident in the foreign country when the action began.
> 3. Where the defendant in the character of plaintiff has selected the forum in which his is afterwards sued.
> 4. Where he has voluntarily appeared.
> 5. Where he has contracted to submit himself to the forum, in which the judgment was obtained.[24]

In essence, where jurisdiction exists, residence and submission are the most common bases for conceding jurisdiction to foreign courts in actions *in personam*. First, if the defendant was resident in the country of the foreign court on the date on which the proceedings commenced, such court has jurisdiction to deliver a judgment *in personam*. In *Worman & Co v Noorbhai*,[25] the court decided that the judgment of a foreign court is not binding on a defendant if the latter is not resident or domiciled in the territory where the foreign court is situated. Similarly, a defendant would not be bound by the judgment of a foreign court if one does not appear in the case or otherwise submit to the jurisdiction of the court.

Second, if one voluntarily invokes the jurisdiction of a foreign court by initiating a claim there as plaintiff, one renders one's self liable to a judgment of that court in respect of costs or counterclaims. Notably, in the case of *Vaitalingam v Murugesu*[26] where the plaintiff was ordered by the foreign court to pay the costs of the successful defendant, the Sri Lankan court held in an enforcement action that the costs of the foreign proceedings were payable by the plaintiff according to the terms of the foreign decree.

Courts have adopted the view that domicile alone may not suffice as a ground of jurisdiction. For instance, in *Shamji Gordhandas & Co v Ramanathan & Co* Wood Renton CJ stated:

> [T]hat a man's domicile of origin or where that has been acquired, his domicile of choice governs his civil status, does not appear to me to justify the conclusion that, where he is resident in another country, a judgment passed against him *in absentem*, and without notice, by a court of the country of his domicile, to the jurisdiction of which he has not in any way submitted himself, can be enforced against by an action in the country of his residence.[27]

However, dicta contrary to this position may also be found.

[23] *Emanuel v Symon* [1908] 1 KB 302.
[24] ibid, 309.
[25] *Worman & Co v Noorbhai* 15 NLR 355.
[26] *Vaitalingam v Murugesu* [1931] 34 NLR 79.
[27] *Shamji Gordhandas & Co v Ramanathan & Co* [1917] 20 NLR 129, 134.

b. The Judgment Must be Final and Conclusive

The foreign judgment that is sought to be recognised and enforced in Sri Lanka must be final and conclusive, whereby the rights and liabilities of the parties to the action are determined and the case is fit to be disposed.

In *Siriwardene v Air Ceylon Ltd*,[28] the plaintiff obtained an ex parte judgment against the defendant and a decree was entered. An application was filed by the defendant under section 189 of the Civil Procedure Code to amend the judgment and decree. The decree was amended by the District Court accordingly. The plaintiff moved the Court of Appeal under section 754(1) of the Civil Procedure Code for leave to appeal against that order of the District Court. Section 754(1) provides that when preferring an appeal, a 'judgment' means any judgment or order having the effect of a final judgment made by any civil court and 'order' means the final expression of any decision in any civil action, proceeding or matter which is not a judgment. Sharvananda J referred to the test laid down in *Bozson v Altrincham Urban District Council*[29] to determine whether an order has the effect of a final judgment. By that test, to be regarded as final, an order must comply with certain requirements:

1. It must be an order finally disposing of the rights of the parties.
2. The order cannot be treated to be a final order if the suit or action is still left a live suit or action for the purpose of determining the rights and liabilities of the parties in the ordinary way.
3. The finality of the order must be determined in relation to the suit.
4. The mere fact that a cardinal point in the suit has been decided or even a vital and important issue determined in the case is not enough to make an order, a final one.

In *Fernando v Chittambaram Chettiar*,[30] the court referred to dicta in the Indian judgment *Abdul Rahman v Cassim & Sons* to similar effect:

> [T]he test of finality is whether the order finally disposes of the rights of the parties. Where [the] order does not finally dispose of those rights but leaves them to be determined by the Courts in the ordinary way, the order is not final. That the order went to the root of the suit, namely, the jurisdiction of the Court to entertain it is not sufficient. The finality must be a finality in relation to the suit. If, after the order, the suit is still a live suit in which the rights of the parties have still to be determined, no appeal lies against it.[31]

c. The Judgment Must be for a Definite Sum

The foreign judgment must be for a definite sum. An order for the payment of costs is not enforceable until the costs have been taxed.[32] This is to ensure that the decreed amount is quantifiable by way of a simple arithmetical process.

[28] *Siriwardene v Air Ceylon Ltd* [1982] 2 Sri LR 544.
[29] *Bozson v Altrincham Urban District Council* [1903] 1 KB 547 (CA), 548–49.
[30] *Fernando v Chittambaram Chettiar* [1949] 49 NLR 217.
[31] *Abdul Rahman v Cassim & Sons* [1933] AIR PC 58, 60.
[32] *Sadler v Robins* [1808] 1 Camp 253.

ii. Defences to Actions on Foreign Judgments

In actions for the enforcement of a foreign judgment, parties may plead various defences – that the foreign court lacked jurisdiction; that the original judgment was obtained by fraud; that the foreign judgment was delivered in contravention of public policy and natural justice.

The defence that the foreign court had no jurisdiction to adjudicate the matter and the defence that the foreign judgment is contrary to natural justice were considered in *Shamji Gordhandas & Co v Ramanathan & Co* which held that:

> In an action on a foreign judgment it is not necessary for a plaintiff to aver that the foreign court had jurisdiction over the parties … Jurisdiction is presumed and when that presumption has not been rebutted, the court in which the action on the foreign judgment is brought will not review the competency of or an irregularity of the proceeding in the foreign court or even the correction of the foreign judgment itself, unless there has been something in the nature of a violation of the rule of natural justice.[33]

Fraud on the part of a party to the suit or on the part of the foreign court or fraud by way of suppressing material evidence may be pleaded as a defence in an action to enforce a foreign judgment.

Although it is common for parties to plead the aforementioned defences, parties are precluded from taking the position that fresh evidence has been discovered since a judgment was delivered or that there are errors of fact or law. In the case of *Denoon v Northway*[34] this stance was reinforced by Clarence J who stated: 'I am not aware of any decided cases in which an action on a foreign judgment has been resisted on the ground of fresh evidence discovered since the judgment'.[35] Parties to the original action pertaining to the foreign judgment are not afforded an opportunity to lead evidence or cross-examine, in the event fresh evidence were to be admitted by a court in support of a defence. This would contravene the principle of *audi alteram partem* and forms part of the rationale precluding parties from pleading such a defence.

C. Mechanics of Enforcement

The procedure relating to the administration of civil proceedings is provided for in the Civil Procedure Code of 1889 (No 2 of 1889) (as amended) (CPC), while other statutory instruments may provide for specialised procedures in respect of specific areas of the law. In order to ascertain the procedural legal framework created statutorily for the enforcement of judgments and decrees domestically, it is important to examine the relevant provisions in the CPC.

According to the CPC, a judgment shall contain a concise statement of the case, the points for determination, the decision thereon and the reasons for such decision; and if there

[33] *Shamji Gordhandas & Co* (n 26) 134.
[34] *Denoon v Northway* [1883] 5 SCC 133.
[35] ibid, 134.

are any assessors to the said judgment, their opinions shall be prefixed to the judgment and signed by the assessors respectively.[36]

As soon as the judgment is pronounced, a formal decree bearing the same date as the judgment shall be drawn up by court in the format provided in the CPC or in a similar manner, specifying the order which is made by the judgment in regard to the relief granted or other determination of the action. It will also specify the parties and the proportion by which costs are to be paid. In the case of the Primary Courts, the amount of the costs shall also be stated.[37] Upon application for the execution of a decree being made, the court shall satisfy itself that the application is substantially in conformity with, and the applicant is entitled to obtain the execution of, the decree or order. The court shall direct a writ of execution to issue to the Fiscal.[38]

Upon receiving the writ, if the debtor resides within five miles of the office of the Fiscal, the latter shall within 48 hours require the debtor to settle the amount in accordance with the writ. In the event that the debtor is absent or the demand is not complied with, the Fiscal shall forthwith proceed to seize and sell, or otherwise realise in money, the debtor's property (either property of the judgment debtor that is not subject to a claim or property specified by the judgment creditor or in the writ). Provided that when the debtor is out of Sri Lanka, it shall not be necessary to require the debtor to pay the amount of the writ before execution is carried into effect.[39]

Seizure of movable property shall be done manually and, in the instance of perishable property, the Fiscal may sell it immediately, if keeping it in custody would exceed its value.[40] If the property is a negotiable instrument, it shall be brought to court and held subject to further orders of the court.[41] Seizure of debts, shares and movable property not in the possession of the debtor and not deposited in court, is to be by written notice of prohibition signed and served by the Fiscal.[42] Seizure of immovable property is to be by written notice of prohibition.[43] The Fiscal or other officer shall make a list of the property seized and sign it provide the same to the judgment debtor and any other person claiming possession of such property. Copies shall be deposited in the Fiscal's office.[44]

IV. Special Cases

A. Intellectual Property Rights (IPRs)

Intellectual property (IP) has a direct co-relation to economic growth in both developed and developing economies, as innovation and technological progress contribute immensely

[36] CPC, s 187.
[37] CPC, s 188.
[38] CPC, s 225.
[39] CPC, s 226.
[40] CPC, s 227.
[41] CPC, s 228.
[42] CPC, ss 229, 233.
[43] CPC, s 237.
[44] CPC, s 240.

towards ensuring productivity. Further, the protection of IPRs by the enactment of comprehensive legislative instruments is crucial for the enhancement of cross-border trade relationships. Sri Lanka is a signatory to the Trade Related Intellectual Property Rights (TRIPS) Agreement and this association has ushered in reforms to the IP law of the country, by replacing the Code of Intellectual Property Act (No 52 of 1979) with the Intellectual Property Act (No 36 of 2003) (IP Act), which is consistent with the TRIPS Agreement, as well as settled law in other countries and case law development in Sri Lanka and other jurisdictions.

The IP Act codifies the law relating to intellectual property. It provides an efficient procedure for the registration, control and administration of IP matters and protects IPRs such as copyright, patents, marks and trade names, trade secrets, industrial designs, layout designs of integrated circuits, and geographical indications. It also deals extensively with unfair competition and undisclosed information in relation to the same.[45] In terms of section 2 of the High Court of the Provinces (Special Provisions) Act (No 10 of 1996), all island jurisdiction with regard to IP matters is vested in the Commercial High Court.

Both emerging and well-established companies need to formulate comprehensive strategies for the protection of IPRs and these must align with their core business strategies. The Companies Act (No 7 of 2007) and the IP Act in conjunction, provide a favourable environment for local and foreign companies to invoke the jurisdiction of the Commercial High Court in respect of IP matters. Further, it is observed that judgments concerning such matters are being successfully enforced in Sri Lanka. Thus, creating the platform to recognise and enforce foreign judgments in Sri Lanka would undoubtedly facilitate the protection of IPRs in a more efficient and meaningful manner.

B. Environmental Law

The relationship between the environment and the economy may be understood in terms of the resource input function of the environment and the economy's role in environmental degradation. Over the last few decades, there has been a heightened level of awareness and consciousness of the effects of climate change and the irreversible damage caused to the environment as a result of economic activities and pollution. Therefore, policies and procedures relating to trade and commerce are to be informed by principles such as sustainable development and transboundary harm. Sri Lanka is a signatory to multilateral environmental agreements[46] and there have been attempts to incorporate into Sri Lankan law the principle of sustainable development. Although not expressly provided for by statute, Part IV (Environmental Management) of the National Environmental Act[47] reflects this principle.

Usually, cases relating to the environment are filed as fundamental rights applications in the Supreme Court in terms of Article 12 of the Constitution which provides for the equality of the law and the equal protection of the law to citizens. This is the most frequently invoked

[45] Intellectual Property Act (No 36 of 2003).

[46] See eg the 1973 Convention on International Trade in Endangered Species of Wild Fauna and Flora; the 1982 United Nations Convention on the Law of the Sea; the 1992 Convention on Biological Diversity.

[47] National Environmental Act (No 47 of 1980) (as amended).

article either on its own or in conjunction with other provisions. Parties may also invoke the writ jurisdiction of the Court of Appeal in terms of Article 140 of the Constitution and the writ jurisdiction of the High Courts of the Provinces in terms of Article 154P(4)(b) of the Constitution.

These provisions empower these respective courts to grant and issue, according to law, orders in the nature of writs of *certiorari*, prohibition, *procedendo*, mandamus and *quo warranto*. In *Weragama v Eksath Lanka Wathu Kamkaru Samithiya*[48] the Supreme Court held that the writ jurisdiction of the Provincial High Courts is concurrent with that of the Court of Appeal.

The judiciary has, on many occasions, referred to international legal principles or instruments in the interpretation of cases, especially in relation to environmental law. In the *Eppawela Phosphate Mining* case discussed below,[49] the court was of the view that the organs of the state and the public at large were jointly responsible for the guardianship of resources. In *Watte Gedera Wijebanda v Conservator General of Forests*,[50] Tilakawardane J referred to the Stockholm Declaration 1972 and the Rio Declaration 1992 as soft law and stated that the importance and relevance of these instruments must be recognised when reviewing executive action vis-à-vis the environment, despite the instruments not being binding on the state. The Constitution provides that it is the fundamental duty of every Sri Lankan citizen to protect nature and conserve its riches.[51] It also provides that state policy must be informed by the duty of the state to protect, preserve and improve the environment for the benefit of the community.[52]

V. Recognition and Enforcement under Treaties or Similar Arrangements

Sri Lanka is a dualist state, which recognises the distinction between international law and municipal law and, based on the doctrine of transformation, requires international law to be explicitly incorporated into the domestic sphere by way of an enabling legislation. In terms of the Directive Principles of State Policy, the Constitution provides that 'the State shall promote international peace, security and co-operation, and the establishment of a just and equitable international economic and social order and shall endeavour to foster respect for international law and treaty obligations in dealings among nations'.[53] However, Directive Principles of State Policy 'do not confer or impose legal rights or obligations and are not enforceable in any court or tribunal'.[54] Article 33(h) of the Constitution empowers the President of Sri Lanka 'to do all such acts and things, not inconsistent with the provisions of the Constitution or written law, as by international law, custom or usage the President is authorised or required to do'. This may be interpreted to suggest that the President can take

[48] *Weragama v Eksath Lanka Wathu Kamkaru Samithiya* [1994] 1 Sri LR 293.
[49] *Bulankulama v Secretary of Industrial Development* [2000] 3 Sri LR 243 (the *Eppawala Phosphate Mining* case).
[50] *Watte Gedera Wijebanda v Conservator General of Forests* [2009] 1 Sri LR 337, 358.
[51] Constitution of Sri Lanka, Art 28(f).
[52] Constitution of Sri Lanka, Art 27(14).
[53] Constitution of Sri Lanka, Art 27(15).
[54] Constitution of Sri Lanka, Art 29.

measures to incorporate international legal principles into domestic law, provided it is not in contravention of the provisions of the Constitution.

Further, Article 157 of the Constitution pertaining to international treaties and agreements states as follows:

> Where Parliament by resolution passed by not less than two-thirds of the whole number of Members of Parliament (including those not present) voting in its favour, approves as being essential for the development of the national economy, any Treaty or Agreement between the Government of Sri Lanka and the Government of any foreign State for the promotion and protection of the investments in Sri Lanka of such foreign State, its nationals, or of corporations, companies and other associations incorporated or constituted under its laws, such Treaty or Agreement shall have the force of law in Sri Lanka and otherwise than in the interests of national security no written law shall be enacted or made, and no executive or administrative action shall be taken, in contravention of the provisions of such Treaty or Agreement.

In the 2005 case of *Nallaratnam Singarasa v Attorney General*, an application was made to the Supreme Court, for the exercise of the Court's inherent power of revision of a conviction and sentence carried out in 1995. This was pursuant to the United Nations Human Rights Committee expressing its views that Singarasa's right to a fair trial had been breached. The Divisional Bench of five judges of the Supreme Court stated the following, reinforcing the dualist nature of the state:

> As noted in the preceding analysis, the [International Covenant on Civil and Political Rights] is based on the premise of legislative or other measures being taken by each State Party 'accordance with its constitutional processes … to give effect to the rights recognised in the … Covenant' (Article 2). Hence the act of the then President in 1980 in acceding to the Covenant is not per se inconsistent with the provisions of the Constitution or written law of Sri Lanka. The accession to the Covenant binds the Republic qua state. But, no legislative or other measures were taken to give effect to the rights recognised in the Convention as envisaged in Article 2. Hence the Covenant does not have internal effect and the rights under the Covenant are not rights under the law of Sri Lanka.[55]

Despite the precedent set by the *Singarasa* judgment, courts have taken into consideration international norms and principles on numerous occasions, both in the absence of applicable domestic law or as an accessory to further substantiate the domestic law. In *Sepala Ekanayake v Attorney General* the court referred to an article of the 1970 Hague Convention for the Suppression of Unlawful Seizure of Aircraft.[56] In *Bulankulama v Secretary of Industrial Development* (the *Eppawala Phosphate Mining* case)[57] the Supreme Court made extensive reference to international environmental principles to arrive at the decision that an agreement between a multinational company and the government constituted an imminent infringement of the fundamental rights of the petitioners. The Court's interpretation of the law was essentially expansive and progressive and enabled the tacit recognition of international legal principles which were otherwise not part of the domestic law.

Similarly, though Sri Lanka is not a Contracting State to many of the Hague Conventions relating to private international law, recognition and enforcement of foreign judgments in

[55] *Nallaratnam Singarasa v Attorney General* SC Spl (LA) No 182/99 (SC) (15 September 2006).
[56] *Sepala Ekanayake v Attorney General* [1988] 1 Sri LR 46.
[57] *Bulankulama* (n 48).

particular, courts may take on the role of interpreting the law in an expansive manner. In any event, the state may consider what conventions have already been ratified and incorporated through relevant enabling legislation and, in light of that, continue its efforts at ratifying further treaties and passing enabling legislation which could provide a more complete and robust legal framework for matters related to commercial transactions. It will be apparent that a number of conventions which do not have a direct bearing on commercial matters have to date been incorporated into the domestic law by way of enabling legislation. This precedent can spur the government to continue ratifying conventions that will facilitate cross-border commercial transactions and to incorporate the same into domestic law.

A. Conventions which Oblige States to Recognise and Enforce Judgments

Sri Lanka's association with the Hague Conference on Private International Law has resulted in the ratification of certain conventions by Sri Lanka and the introduction of domestic legislation to give effect to such international obligations. Sri Lanka is a contracting party to the following conventions of the Hague Conference: (1) the 1965 Hague Convention on the Service Abroad of Judicial and Extrajudicial Documents in Civil or Commercial Matters; (2) the 1970 Hague Convention on the Taking of Evidence Abroad in Civil or Commercial Matters; (3) the 1980 Hague Convention on the Civil Aspects of International Child Abduction; and (4) the 1993 Hague Convention on the Protection of Children and Co-operation in Respect of Intercountry Adoption. The Mutual Assistance in Civil and Commercial Matters Act (No 39 of 2000) reinforces the international obligations under the first two Conventions mentioned above.[58] The objects of the Act are to

> facilitate the provision of, and the obtaining by Sri Lanka of assistance in civil and commercial matters, including (a) the service of judicial and extra judicial documents; (b) the examination of witnesses and the obtaining of evidence, documents and other articles; (c) the provision of documents and other records.[59]

However, the Act does not deal with the enforcement of judgments as it explicitly provides that a 'judicial act [under the Act] does not include the issue of a writ or other process for the enforcement or execution of an order or judgment or an order for provisional or protective measures'.[60]

The Civil Aspects of International Child Abduction Act (No 10 of 2001) gives effect to the obligations arising under the 1980 Hague Child Abduction Convention. The Act provides for the return of children wrongfully removed to or retained in Sri Lanka or other

[58] The Preamble of the Mutual Assistance in Civil and Commercial Matters Act (No 39 of 2000) states 'An Act to provide for the rendering of mutual assistance in civil and commercial matters between Sri Lanka and other countries, and to give effect to, the Hague Convention on the Service Abroad of Judicial and Extra Judicial Documents in Civil and Commercial Matters, and the Hague Convention on the Taking of Evidence Abroad in Civil and Commercial Matters'.

[59] Mutual Assistance in Civil and Commercial Matters Act (No 39 of 2000), s 2.

[60] Mutual Assistance in Civil and Commercial Matters Act (No 39 of 2000), s 16.

country of habitual residence and empowers the High Court of the Western Province as the designated court to hear applications for return. Notably, the Act provides that

> for the purpose of determining whether the removal to, or retention in Sri Lanka of a child is wrongful within the meaning of section 3, the High Court may, at the hearing of an application under section 9 for the return of the child, take judicial notice of the relevant law and judicial decisions of the specified country in which that child has his or her habitual residence.[61]

In *Suhada Gamlath, Secretary to the Ministry of Justice and Law Reform v Kristina Ivasauskaite-Rosairo*, the court recognised that

> the prime concern of the Hague Convention is the restoration of children who have been wrongfully removed, whether or not this is in breach of a custody order in one of the contracting states. It is wider in scope as it goes beyond the mere recognition and enforcement of custody orders and protects rights to custody even where there has been no order.[62]

This decision shows that courts have the potential to interpret statutes of this nature in their entirety in consideration of the underlying purposes and objectives and treat like cases in a like manner.

VI. Reform

A. Ratification of International Conventions Related to Private International Law

Article 157 of the Constitution (cited earlier in this chapter) reflects the state's express willingness to take on international legal obligations. Acting in terms of the Constitution and the relevant laws of the country, Sri Lanka has ratified many international treaties, including certain conventions of the Hague Conference on Private International Law. However, a brief survey of the process of passing enabling legislation and the time taken to do so in the past, would reveal that, in many instances, domestic laws incorporating international legal obligations have not been passed at all or have been passed after a considerable amount of time.

Further, the non-ratification of international treaties which are progressive and timely in nature, could stall the overall development of the domestic legal systems. For instance, although the Hague Conference on Private International Law is a forum that seeks to further the progressive development of the law in respect of civil and commercial matters, Sri Lanka is still not a Contracting State to some of the core Hague Conventions in those areas. Therefore, with a view to developing domestic law in this area, the state must make a conscientious effort to ratify conventions that are related to the recognition and enforcement of foreign judgments and civil and commercial matters in general.[63] Further, the

[61] Civil Aspects of International Child Abduction Act (No 10 of 2001), s 15(2).

[62] *Suhada Gamlath, Secretary to the Ministry of Justice and Law Reform v Kristina Ivasauskaite-Rosairo* No (PHC) APN 3/2010 (CA Revision) (1 June 2011) 7, citing PM North and JJ Fawcett, *Private International Law* 12th edn (London, Butterworths, 1992) 733–34.

[63] 'Conventions, Protocols and Principles' (*Hague Conference on Private International Law*), available online: www.hcch.net/en/instruments/conventions.

state must accordingly pass enabling legislation to give effect to progressive and salutary provisions of such conventions with the aim of facilitating the availability of swift and cost-effective remedies to aggrieved parties.

B. Ensure that Present Legal Instruments are Rendered Effective and Operational

The legal framework pertaining to the recognition and enforcement of foreign judgments in Sri Lanka is in its infancy at present and the Enforcement of Foreign Judgments Ordinance and the Reciprocal Enforcement of Foreign Judgments Ordinance form the basis of the statutory framework in this area. It is imperative to acknowledge their salutary provisions and make necessary amendments to these instruments. As the Reciprocal Enforcement of Foreign Judgments Ordinance is limited in terms of its scope of application, it is recommended that the Enforcement of Foreign Judgments Ordinance be brought into operation duly, with amendments as may be necessary in order to enable the registration of foreign judgments in accordance with procedures provided by law.

Both the Enforcement of Foreign Judgments Ordinance and the Reciprocal Enforcement of Foreign Judgments Ordinance enable the rule-making function of the courts for the purposes of the two ordinances and for the purpose of regulating the practice and procedure (including evidence) in respect of the proceedings of any kind under those ordinances.[64] The formulation of requisite rules, practice directions and procedures is essential to fully operationalise these instruments. Broadly, in terms of reforming the law in general, a state must enact, amend and repeal national legislation to facilitate greater integration, especially within the region, in terms of trade and commerce, transportation, tariffs, human capital, etc. The legal framework created thus ought to facilitate and be on par with developments that continue to take place globally in terms of information and communication technology, e-commerce, trade and other related matters.

C. Build Judicial Capacity

A judge plays a vital role in the recognition and enforcement of a foreign judgment. Judicial activism should be motivated by the willingness and commitment to develop the law, to apply principles of natural justice and the rule of law, and to facilitate the provision of remedies to aggrieved parties by treating cases with similar facts in a similar manner.

From the outset, it is important to enhance public trust and confidence in the judicial system, as an institution that provides procedural justice defined by the availability of accessible procedural channels and fair and predictable outcomes. Further, appropriate measures must be taken to ensure that cases are heard and resolved within established time frames in a way that would not impede economic progress.

[64] Enforcement of Foreign Judgments Ordinance, s 4; Reciprocal Enforcement of Foreign Judgments Ordinance, s 5.

A state must thus invest in training and capacity building among judges, prosecutors, legal practitioners and the subordinate staff of the court to ensure that they are aware of the latest legal developments in terms of domestic, regional and international law relating to civil and commercial matters. Further, they must be adequately remunerated, and reasonable measures should be adopted to mitigate corruption that may be present in the judicial system.

The judicial system should be modernised to simplify and expedite administration and to manage the judicial process efficiently and more cost-effectively. This would include the digitisation of court rooms to include the use of computer devices directly to assist judges and court clerks, the use of computerised databases for the registration and management of cases, and the use of technology in court rooms to present cases across borders, through use of video-conferencing, electronic evidence presentation software, overhead projectors, scanning devices, digital audio technology and real-time transcription. In *Ruhunu Ware Pvt Ltd v Freight Links International and Direx Corp*, a commercial matter that came before the Commercial High Court when it was presided over by Justice KT Chitrasiri, the court admitted electronic evidence obtained through the examination of a witness who gave evidence from New York through Skype technology.[65] An e-filing system was introduced a few years ago as an initial step towards modernising the judicial system. Regrettably, however, this system is not being utilised at present and it is incumbent upon the authorities to take steps to create a conducive environment to facilitate the use of the e-filing system by litigants.

Capacity building of the judiciary must be accompanied by efforts to make available all relevant information concerning applicable laws, regulations and government policy decisions in the public domain. This would include the publication of court decisions, guides, booklets and reviews relating to applicable procedural and substantive laws in civil and commercial matters, etc. Providing information centres and maintaining websites which are up-to-date and blogs concerning the law that operates in a particular country, can facilitate greater knowledge-sharing among the different countries in a region.

D. Creation of a Special Regional Court

A well-functioning judicial system underpins economic development as it creates a climate of certainty and reliability. The relationship between justice and the economy is most explicit in the areas of contract enforcement, settlement of disputes, protection of investors, intellectual property rights, land ownership and related disputes, employment rights, labour market operations, insolvency proceedings as well as family related disputes.

Asia, as a region which is characteristically diverse and complex in nature, is deeply integrated as a result of its international trade routes. Many of the states in the region tend to face similar issues and challenges in relation to population, climate, governance and economy, and creating a special court to adjudicate on commercial matters arising within the region in particular may be a desirable step forward. Further, the establishment of a special court has the potential to overcome the difficulties faced by litigants when enforcing a judgment across borders.

[65] Bandula Sirimanna, 'Sri Lanka Takes Historic Step in Evidence Through Video Conferencing' (*The Sunday Times*, 26 October 2008), available online: www.sundaytimes.lk/081026/FinancialTimes/ft3020.html.

VII. Conclusion

The recovery of money has become a key consideration when aggrieved parties file an action in respect of civil and commercial matters. The question that is often asked is whether a party to an action can easily and in a cost-effective manner recover money upon a judgment being delivered, if an action is filed in a particular jurisdiction. The difficulties in getting a foreign judgment recognised and enforced due to inadequacies in the legal framework, inordinate administrative delays, judicial passivism and complex and cumbersome procedures, will prompt aggrieved parties to exercise caution when filing actions. In this context, it is safe to state that, in the minds of a party that wishes to file action, the recognition and enforcement of a foreign judgment becomes a concern, given the systematic challenges involved in the registration of a foreign judgment in Sri Lanka.

This chapter has closely analysed the nature of the current domestic legal framework relating to the recognition and enforcement of foreign judgments in Sri Lanka and related limitations and challenges. It has recommended several reforms to develop the law in this area. Taking the necessary steps to address the challenges, limitations and gaps in the legal framework and thereby creating an environment that favours the recognition and enforcement of foreign judgments would further the development of private international law in the country.

Additionally, the policies of a state in relation to commercial matters should be informed by its international obligations as well as best practices under private international law. To this end, genuine and robust measures should be adopted in order to facilitate the recognition and enforcement of foreign judgments, as this would contribute largely towards the promotion of trade and commerce, greater regional cooperation and in turn, the development of a country's economy.

16

India

SAI RAMANI GARIMELLA

I. Introduction

India gained independence from the British[1] on 15 August 1947 after being directly ruled from England for nearly a century. The British arrived in the east of India as traders and later gained territorial rights from the rulers of the princely States through *firman* (royal sanction) issued by those rulers in territories across India. In 1857, the princely States formed into a consortium to fight the British East India Company that had acquired territorial control and was ruling through the governments in the three presidency towns of Calcutta, Madras and Bombay (modern day Kolkata, Chennai and Mumbai respectively). The mutiny of 1857 failed to usher independence but marked the end of the rule of the East India Company. The Indian territories of the company were annexed as the overseas territory of England through a royal charter of 1858, directly ruled by the laws of the Parliament of England for a period of 90 years. Much of the legislation in India as it exists today is derived from its colonial antecedents, especially in matters of private law, procedure and evidence. Within private law, the British allowed diversity to prevail in matters related to family law based on religion, while commercial law has been uniform and secular.

The principles of Indian private international law, including the recognition of foreign judgments, have been largely founded upon colonial law. The connecting factors for establishing jurisdiction of a forum court have typically been habitual residence and domicile. Party autonomy remains the primordial feature for jurisdiction, although the principle of objective choice is known to Indian law. Colonial Indian law has examples of recognising and enforcing foreign judgments provided that they are not against mandatory rules or public policy.[2]

[1] The British Raj included the territories of native princes, otherwise called princely States, and the chief territories under the suzerainty of Her Majesty the Queen of Great Britain. Though the exact number of princely States differed over time, immediately after independence, the new national government of India recorded a final figure of 584 states, including those that had seceded to Pakistan. *cf* Bimalkumar Natvarlal Patel, 'The State Practice of India and The Development of International Law: Selected Areas' (PhD thesis, Leiden University, 2015). Prior to 1857, India or substantial parts of it had been governed by the British East India Company. The latter had been in India since 1600.

[2] See eg *Ram Coomar Condoo v Chunder Canto Mookerjee* (1876) ILR 2 Cal 233; *Achal Ram v Kazim Hussain Khan* (1905) ILR 27 All 271.

II. Background

A. General Considerations

India, a South Asian nation, is the seventh largest country by area, the second most populous country with over 1.33 billion people, and the most populous democracy in the world. Located on 8° 4' to 37° 6' north, and 68° 7' to 97° 25' east, India is nestled as a part of the Indian subcontinent by Pakistan and Afghanistan with whom India shares political borders on the West, while Bangladesh and Myanmar stand adjacent on the Eastern borders. The northern boundary comprises Xinjiang province of China, Tibet, Nepal and Bhutan. Sri Lanka is another neighbouring country which is separated by a narrow channel of sea formed by the Palk Strait and the Gulf of Mannar. The Indian peninsula is enclosed by a long coastline spread over 7,517 km, including the mainland, the coastlines of the Andaman and Nicobar Islands in the Bay of Bengal and the Lakshadweep Islands in the Arabian Sea.

The country's uniqueness stems from its diversity and hence has adapted itself to international changes with poise and comfort. While the economy has increasingly engaged with international investment since liberalisation in the 1990s, Indians have been actively participating in international economic trends (especially through its membership in the WTO and regional and multilateral groups such as the South Asian Association for Regional Cooperation (SAARC), BRICS and G20). Indians have also been pro-active in adopting global approaches and skills. Indian villagers proudly take up farming, advanced agriculture and unique handicrafts as their profession. India's major economic activities offer a mix of agriculture and industry, with professional service sectors upcoming in a significant way. In 2018 India was positioned as the world's sixth largest economy in terms of nominal GDP and the third largest economy by purchasing power parity. The India Brand Equity Foundation projected a GDP increase of 7.3 per cent in the 2018–19 fiscal year from 6.6 per cent in the 2017–18 one.[3] In the April to June quarter of the 2018–19 fiscal year, GDP grew by 8.2 per cent, allowing room for faith in such growth predictions.

Following independence in 1947, India remained a truncated State. British India (the territory ruled by the British through laws passed by Parliament in London) was partitioned, following political uprising, along religious lines into India and Pakistan. Hindus constitute the majority of the population in India (79.2 per cent), while 14.8 per cent follow Islam and six per cent are believers in other faiths including Christianity, Sikhism and Zoroastrianism.

B. Development of Private International Law

Modern private international law rules in India (since independence in 1947) trace their origin to colonial history and law. Jurisdiction has been the terrain on which the notion of British imperial sovereignty was understood and interpreted. The political conception of India encompassed British India (the areas within the jurisdiction of the Presidency towns)[4]

[3] 'Indian Economy: About Indian Economy Growth Rate & Statistics' (*Indian Brand Equity Foundation*, January 2019), available online: www.ibef.org/economy/indian-economy-overview.

[4] These included the *mofussil*, that is, areas outside the Presidency towns, but within their jurisdiction.

and the territories that were ruled by the princely States (at the time of Independence their count stood at more than 560).[5] Over these princely States, the British had exercised indirect sovereignty that extended to supervisory role over their military, external affairs and revenue administration.

There were few attempts by the British Parliament to legislate rules for the settlement of disputes arising among princely States and between princely States and individuals. The Regulating Act 1773 and the Charter of 1774 empowered the newly established Supreme Court at Calcutta to apply English law insofar as the latter was suited to Indian conditions. The Supreme Court had various jurisdictions, which involved private and public law and norms. Above its original jurisdiction, it had an equity jurisdiction, an Admiralty jurisdiction, a probate and ecclesiastical jurisdiction, and a jurisdiction to supervise. The Act of Settlement 1781 amended the Regulating Act 1773 to provide clarity in certain areas of legal relationship. The Supreme Court of Calcutta had a diversified *lex fori* and applied the personal laws of Hindus and Muslims in matters relating to inheritance, succession and matters of status. This regulation was re-adopted in 1793 in the Calcutta Presidency, in the Bombay *mofussil* in 1799, in the Madras *mofussil* in 1802 and in Oudh in 1803. The Regulation of 1793 had difficulties and defects, such as: (1) the jurisdiction of the court over Indians was vague; (2) the jurisdiction of the court over government actions was unclear; (3) procedures could be oppressive and harsh; and (4) European British subjects could use the jurisdiction of the Supreme Court to their advantage, while Indians in distant parts of Bengal, Bihar and Orissa could not avail themselves of the jurisdiction of the Supreme Court. European British subjects could choose to sue Indians either in the *adalats* or in the Supreme Court.[6] The mergers of princely States themselves presented questions related to the execution of ex parte decrees of the British India courts in the merged states and vice versa. Ultimately, the principle guiding indirect jurisdiction was that articulated by Lord Selborne in *Sirdar Gudyal Singh v The Rajah of Faridkote*[7] to the effect that 'in a personal action … a decree pronounced in absence by a foreign court, to the jurisdiction of which the defendant has not in any way submitted himself, is by international law an absolute nullity'.[8]

The period of colonial rule and its immediate aftermath in respect of the integration of the princely States, also yields insights into the treatment of law and jurisdiction in interpersonal conflicts. There is anecdotal evidence of an innovative development in relation to dispute settlement in the domain of private international law during early colonial rule. With regard to execution of a decree, it was observed that execution by the court of one country could be directed not only against property in one dominion, but also against property in another. Thus, when an English person died leaving property in India without appointing a legal representative, the practice was for the Governor-in-Council of a relevant Presidency town to sell the property by public auction. The sale proceeds were deposited for the benefit of the deceased's estate in England. In English proceedings in relation to the estate, the East India Company would then often have to pay damages by order of the English court for the wrongful handling of an estate. The Company very much desired to avoid

[5] 'Princely States' (*GlobalSecurity.org*, 2018), available online: www.globalsecurity.org/military/world/india/princely-states.htm.

[6] Patel (n 1).

[7] *Sirdar Gudyal Singh v The Rajah of Faridkote* [1894] AC 670.

[8] ibid, 684.

such complication. The Company accordingly requested, and was granted by the Crown, such powers as were conducive to the punishment of vice, the administration of justice and the better governance of estate settlement abroad. The current regime on recognition of foreign decrees in India bears no trace of this feature.[9]

C. Sources of Private International Law

A key source of Indian private international law is the doctrine of 'equity, justice and good conscience'. The application of that doctrine has been marked by two features. First, the application of personal laws to Hindus and Muslims was limited to certain areas of the law, namely, inheritance, succession, marriage, and religious usages and institutions. Still other cases were decided according to the customs of the community to which the parties belonged. Second, the practice followed by the British courts and that of the East India Company's courts were not identical. Both courts applied personal laws to Hindus and Muslims. However, the former judged all other persons in accordance with English law, the law of the Presidency towns. The latter courts decided the cases of persons other than Hindus and Muslims in accordance with the customs and usages followed by the community to which those persons belonged. The cumulative effect of the two features just identified was the development of law, including private international law, through judicial activism. This situation was unique to the Indian sub-continent and remains valid today.[10] Modern private international law rules are thus largely to be discerned from judicial opinions and are woven around the principle of party autonomy in choice of forum and governing law, the use of domicile and habitual residence as connecting factors and the maintenance of comity. Jurisdiction based upon a cause of action is not a feature of Indian law. Instead, all jurisdiction is territorial. There are, however, a few instances where Indian courts have refused to recognise foreign judgments as a matter of public policy, because the rendering courts did not apply Indian law. This is despite the fact that jurisdiction was properly founded on the basis of the parties' domicile.[11] In this connection, it might be noted that Indian law on indirect jurisdiction is largely to be found in judicial opinions interpreting sections 2(2), 2(9), 13 and 44A of the Code of Civil Procedure (CPC). Apart from such judicial dicta, the law relating to the enforcement of foreign judgments may also be derived from the bilateral treaties on legal assistance and judicial cooperation that India has entered into with other countries.

D. The Judicial System and Enforcement of Judgments

The Indian Constitution of 1950 envisaged a three-tier dispute resolution mechanism, with the Supreme Court of India at the apex. Immediately below, there are the High Courts of the 29 states and seven Union Territories. Some states may have more than one High Court bench, while a High Court may address work from more than one state. But civil and

[9] SK Agrawala, 'Law of Nations as Interpreted and Applied by Indian Courts and Legislatures' (1962) 2 *Indian Journal of International Law* 431.

[10] Rama Jois, *Legal and Constitutional History of India* (Bombay, NM Tripathi, 1985) 16.

[11] *Y Narasimha Rao v Y Venkata Lakshmi* [1991] 2 SCR 821; [1991] 3 SCC 451.

commercial dispute resolution is, in large measure, handled by the civil and commercial courts that have been established in India's 719 districts. The jurisdiction of the District Courts is founded upon territorial and pecuniary reasons.

CPC section 2 defines 'commercial' disputes as encompassing those arising in connection with a wide range of matters:

> (i) ordinary transactions of merchants, bankers, financiers and traders ...; (ii) export or import of merchandise or services; (iii) issues relating to admiralty and maritime law; (iv) transactions relating to aircraft, aircraft engines, aircraft equipment and helicopters, including sales, leasing and financing of the same; (v) carriage of goods; (vi) construction and infrastructure contracts, including tenders; (vii) agreements relating to immovable property used exclusively in trade or commerce; (viii) franchising agreements; (ix) distribution and licensing agreements; (x) management and consultancy agreements; (xi) joint venture agreements; (xii) shareholders agreements; (xiii) subscription and investment agreements pertaining to the services industry ...; (xiv) mercantile agency and mercantile usage; (xv) partnership agreements; (xvi) technology development agreements; (xvii) intellectual property rights relating to registered and unregistered trademarks, copyright, patent, design, domain names, geographical indications and semiconductor integrated circuits; (xviii) agreements for sale of goods or provision of services; (xix) exploitation of oil and gas reserves or other natural resources including electromagnetic spectrum; (xx) insurance and re-insurance; (xxi) contracts of agency relating to any of the above; and (xxii) such other commercial disputes as may be notified by the Central Government.

Matters not included in the foregoing list would be considered as civil matters. They might include matters relating to status and inheritance, claims relating to trusts, public law claims (including actions relating to competition law), intellectual property law, insolvency law and environmental law.

CPC section 44A provides that an application for the enforcement of a foreign judgment should be presented to a relevant District Court in accordance with the procedure prescribed therein. The section further provides that, if the foreign decree is to be capable of execution in India, it must be 'the decree of any of the superior Courts of any reciprocating territory'. Explanation I to section 44A defines a 'reciprocating territory' as 'any country or territory outside India which the Central Government may, by notification in the Official Gazette, declare to be a reciprocating territory for the purposes of this section'.

Explanation II defines a 'decree' as 'any decree or judgment of [a foreign superior Court] under which a sum of money is payable, not being a sum payable in respect of taxes or other charges of a like nature or in respect to a fine or other penalty'. Explanation II expressly states that 'arbitration awards' are not to be regarded as 'decrees', even when the awards are enforceable as judgments.

III. Recognition and Enforcement under Treaties or Similar Arrangements

India is not a signatory to the 1971 Hague Convention on the Recognition and Enforcement of Foreign Judgments in Civil and Commercial Matters or the 2005 Hague Convention on Choice of Court Agreements. India is a member of the Hague Conference, but it has not participated in the latter's Judgments Project, which is currently working on a new convention for the general recognition and enforcement of judgments in civil and commercial problems. Nor has the Indian government given any indication that it is likely to accede to the forthcoming Hague Conventions. India has instead signed bilateral treaties with a number of countries. Some of the latter countries have been notified by the Indian government as a reciprocal territory, while a few have yet to be notified within the official gazette. The reciprocal territories that have been gazetted are the UK,[12] Fiji,[13] Aden,[14] New Zealand,[15] Singapore,[16] Malaysia,[17] Trinidad and Tobago,[18] Hong Kong,[19] Papua New Guinea[20] and Bangladesh. Treaties with Afghanistan, Azerbaijan, Bahrain, Bulgaria, France, Kazakhstan, Mongolia, Turkey, Oman, the United Arab Emirates (UAE) and the Ukraine have not yet been gazetted and consequently remain as non-reciprocal territories. Judgments from gazetted territories are enforceable through an execution petition, whereas judgments of non-reciprocating territories may be enforced by initiating a civil suit before the competent court in India.

The Agreement between India and Afghanistan on Juridical and Judicial Cooperation in Civil and Commercial Matters for the Service of Summons, Judicial Documents, Commission and Execution of Judgments and Arbitral Awards was signed at New Delhi on 14 September 2016. Jurisdiction is founded upon two connecting factors: (1) domicile (a feature of Indian law); and (2) nationality (a feature of Afghan law).[21] Claims relating to status and capacity are subjected to rules founded on nationality[22] and claims relating to immovable property are to be decided in accordance with the *lex situs*.[23] The Treaty between the Republic of Azerbaijan and the Republic of India on Legal and Judicial Cooperation in Civil and Commercial Matters was signed on 4 April 2013 and ratified on 12 August 2014. It came into force on 29 February 2016. The provisions on recognition and execution of judgments and arbitral awards are similar to the treaty provisions with Afghanistan.[24] The connecting factors for the determination of jurisdiction are domicile and habitual residence, while the treaty adopts the *lex situs* for disputes involving immovable property.[25] While Indian private international law rules allow party autonomy through exclusive and non-exclusive forum selection clauses, the treaty goes one step further and recognises the possibility of the parties' choice of forum being either express or implied.[26]

[12] Ministry of Law Notification No SRO 399 (1 March 1953); Ministry of Law Amended Notification No GSR 201 (13 March 1958).

[13] Ministry of Law Notification No SRO 1959 (2 March 1954).

[14] Ministry of Law Notification No SRO 183 (18 January 1956).

[15] Ministry of Law Notification No SRO 3282 (15 October 1957).

[16] Ministry of Law Notification No F12(4)/68J (17 June 1968).

[17] Ministry of Law Notification No SRO 4 (3 January 1956).

[18] Ministry of Law Notification No F12(3)/68J (31 July 1968).

[19] Ministry of Law Notification No GSR 2096 (18 November 1968).

[20] Ministry of Law Notification No GSR 1720 (26 September 1970).

[21] Wali Mohammed Naseh, 'Conflict of Laws – State Practice in Afghanistan' in Sai Ramani Garimella and Stellina Jolly (eds), *Private International Law: South Asian States' Practice* (Singapore, Springer, 2017).

[22] Agreement between the Republic of India and the Islamic Republic of Afghanistan on Juridical and Judicial Cooperation in Civil and Commercial Matters for the Service of Summons, Judicial Documents, Commission and Execution of Judgments and Arbitral Awards (2016), Art 16.

[23] ibid, Art 17.

[24] Treaty between the Republic of India and the Republic of Azerbaijan on Legal and Judicial Cooperation on Civil and Commercial Matters 2013, Art 14.

[25] ibid, Art 17.

[26] ibid.

India and the UAE agreed a Treaty on Juridical and Judicial Cooperation in Civil and Commercial Matters on 25 October 1999.[27] The provisions on jurisdiction are similar to those in the treaty with Azerbaijan. Ratified on 29 May 2000, the instrument has yet to be notified in the official gazette. In a case,[28] enforcement was sought of a judgment rendered by the Sharjah Federal Court of First Instance. But the application was dismissed by the District Court in Kasargod (Kerala). The court noted the debtor had not been present within the jurisdiction of the rendering court when proceedings were commenced or when the judgment was pronounced. The Indian court also found a lack of due process before the UAE court. The dismissal was appealed to the Kerala High Court through a civil revision petition based on the argument that there was a bilateral treaty between India and the UAE. The creditor, however, could not prove the notification of the UAE as a reciprocal territory within the official gazette. In light of CPC section 44A, the Kerala High Court emphasised the importance of a rendering court being notified in the Official Gazette as the superior Court of a 'reciprocating territory', before a judgment of the rendering court could be enforced in India. Hence the appeal failed. In another case,[29] execution in India was sought of a judgment of the Dubai court whereby probate was granted. Evidence was presented of a notification in the Official Gazette on 23 November 2000. But closer perusal of the alleged notification established that it was in the context of service of foreign summons in the UAE.[30] The Bombay High Court refused to hold such notification[31] as equivalent to the declaration of a reciprocating territory for purposes of CPC section 44A.

In 1968 the Indian government notified Hong Kong in the Official Gazette as a reciprocating territory under section 44A.[32] The notification provided a list of superior courts in Hong Kong.[33] Indian courts could therefore execute judgments rendered by those Hong Kong courts. In a 2008 case,[34] it was contended that, since on 1 July 1997 the PRC had resumed sovereignty over Hong Kong and there had been no new notification in the Official Gazette in respect of Hong Kong's courts thereafter, Hong Kong judgments could not be executed in India under section 44A. The Bombay High Court rejected the argument, pointing out that the legislation had deliberately referred to the courts of a 'country' or 'territory' so that it was sufficient for the superior Courts of a 'territory' outside of India to have been gazetted.

Many treaties have yet to be notified in the Official Gazette. While the absence of a treaty is not of itself a bar to recognition, it would mean that a foreign judgment will be the subject of much more judicial scrutiny. It will consequently be more expensive for a creditor to

[27] Agreement between the Republic of India and the United Arab Emirates on Juridical and Judicial Cooperation in Civil and Commercial Matters for the Service of Summons, Judicial Documents, Judicial Commissions, Execution of Judgments and Arbitral Awards.

[28] *Super General Co v Suresh Thonikkadavu Veedu* [2017] CRP No 506/2016 (D) (21 February 2017) (Kerala High Court).

[29] *Dr Devika Damji Shah v Rashmi Mukesh Shah* (2012) 114(5) Bom LR 2757 (Bombay High Court).

[30] CPC s 29(c) provides that 'any other Civil or Revenue Court outside India to which the Central Government has, by notification in the Official Gazette, declared the provisions of this section to apply may be sent to the Courts in the territories to which this Code extends, and served as if they were summonses issued by such Courts'.

[31] Ministry of Law Justice and Company Affairs Notification No F12(1)/98-Judl (23 November 2000).

[32] Notification No F12(3)/68J (n 18).

[33] Supreme Court, Victoria District Court, Kowloon District Court, and Fanling District Court.

[34] *Sumikin Bussan International (Hong Kong) Ltd v King Shing Enterprises Ltd (in liq)* [2008] 5 Bom CR 464. See also *Kevin George Vaz v Cotton Textiles Exports* [2006] 5 Bom CR 555.

enforce a foreign judgment in India. The process for obtaining recognition of and enforcing a foreign judgment in the absence of a treaty is considered in the next section.

IV. Recognition and Enforcement in the Absence of Treaties or Similar Arrangements

A. Recognition in General

Recognition is a distinct process and a precursor to enforcement. It is accorded as a result of a pre-existing treaty with the country in which the rendering court is located. It involves the acceptance of a decision by the rendering courts on the merits of a case as having a similar effect to a domestic decree of the enforcing state. The re-litigation of the same issues in a domestic proceeding is thus precluded on the basis of *res judicata*. Enforcement, on the other hand, envisages (1) the filing of a petition for the execution in India of a judgment rendered in a reciprocating territory (as defined in CPC section 44A); or (2) the initiation of proceedings in India based on the foreign judgment in the case where the latter was obtained from a non-reciprocating territory.

B. Reciprocity

As mentioned, under CPC section 44A, the decree of any superior court of a reciprocating territory may be executed in India as a decree of a District Court. A 'reciprocating territory' is any country or territory outside India which the Central Government has, by notification in the Official Gazette, declared to be a 'reciprocating territory' for the purposes of section 44A. A 'superior court' means such courts as have been identified in the notification as superior courts of the relevant country or territory.[35] A judgment of the court of a reciprocating territory can be directly enforced in India by filing an execution petition in a District Court. Thereafter, if the petition is approved, the decree may be executed in India as if it had been made by the District Court. When filing the petition, it will be necessary to annex a certified copy of the decree along with a certificate from the foreign superior court stating the extent to which the decree has been satisfied.

The judgment of a court in a non-reciprocating territory is not directly executable in India. A civil action will need to be initiated before a court in accordance with the jurisdiction of the CPC. Within the resulting civil action before the Indian court, the foreign court's judgment will be of evidentiary value.[36] In *Marine Geotechnics LLC v Coastal Marine Construction & Engineering Ltd*,[37] the Bombay High Court observed that, in the case of a decree from a non-reciprocating foreign territory, the decree-holder should file, in a domestic Indian court of competent jurisdiction, a suit based on the judgment debt created by the foreign decree, or based on the original underlying cause of action, or based on both.

[35] CPC s 44A, Explanation I.
[36] *Maloji Rao Narsingh Rao v Sankar Saran* [1955] AIR 1955 All 490 (Allahabad High Court).
[37] *Marine Geotechnics LLC v Coastal Marine Construction & Engineering Ltd* [2014] 2 Bom CR 769.

Although the foreign decree is not by itself executable in India, a domestic decree obtained in a civil action based on the foreign judgment can be executed. The Indian court will treat the foreign judgment as conclusive of the matters decided therein provided that the requirements of CPC section 13 are met.

C. Conclusiveness of a Foreign Judgment

Under CPC section 13 a foreign judgment will be regarded as conclusive on any matter adjudicated by it, provided that: (1) the judgment has been pronounced by a court of competent jurisdiction; (2) the judgment has been given on the merits of a case; (3) the judgment does not appear on its face to be founded on an incorrect view of international law or a refusal to recognise the law of India in cases in which such law is applicable; (4) the proceedings in which the judgment was obtained were not opposed to natural justice; (5) the judgment has not been obtained by fraud; and (6) the judgment does not sustain a claim founded on a breach of any law in force in India.

The requirement in CPC section 13(a) that a rendering court be of competent jurisdiction, will be discussed in section IV.D below. Under CPC section 13(b) foreign judgments that are not on the merits are not conclusive. The following are illustrative of the Indian jurisprudence on whether a foreign judgment has been pronounced on merits. An ex parte judgment where the plaintiff did not lead evidence to prove a claim is not a judgment on the merits.[38] A decree entered following summary process in the absence of an appearance by the defendant or the filing of a defence and without consideration of the plaintiff's evidence is not conclusive within section 13(b).[39] The Bombay High Court in *Gajanan Sheshadri Pandharpurkar v Shantabai*[40] held that determinations on whether a decision was on merits should examine whether the decision was given on a proper appreciation of the plaintiff's claim and evidence or whether the decision was rendered as a penalty for the defendant's conduct. Where a defendant appeared before the foreign court and submitted a written statement, but was not present or represented in the court on the date of the hearing, the foreign court's decree was on merits insofar as the court entered judgment after hearing the plaintiff's case and considering the evidence.[41]

Under CPC section 13(c), the failure by a rendering court to apply Indian law in a matter where Indian law is applicable, will result in a decision being unenforceable in India. In probate proceedings before the foreign court, the refusal to recognise the Indian law applicable to the deceased's immovable property meant that foreign judgment could not be executed in India.[42]

As for the requirement in CPC section 13(d) that foreign judgments should not have been obtained contrary to natural justice, Indian courts have insisted upon adherence to the principles of natural justice for the execution of all decrees, including foreign judgments. The expression 'contrary to natural justice' in section 13(d) refers only to procedural defects

[38] *Gurdas Mann v Mohinder Singh Brar* [1993] AIR P&H 92.
[39] *Middle East Bank Ltd v Rajendra Singh Sethia* [1991] AIR Cal 335.
[40] *Gajanan Sheshadri Pandharpurkar v Shantabai* [1939] AIR Bom 374.
[41] *Trilochan Choudhury v Dayanidhi Patra* [1961] AIR Ori 158.
[42] *Panchpakesa Iyer v K N Husain* [1934] AIR Mad 145.

leading to a party being denied a reasonable opportunity to present a defence before the foreign court.[43] Section 13(d) is not supposed to be a window to revisit the evidence or reasoning of a foreign decision. If the defendant was afforded a reasonable opportunity to defend one's self before the foreign court and yet made no effort to pursue a defence, the foreign court's decision will not be perceived as vitiated by a failure to observe natural justice.[44]

Under CPC section 13(e), a foreign judgment obtained by fraud is unenforceable in India. The Supreme Court in *Satya v Teja Singh*[45] has interpreted section 13(d) as referring to the way in which the foreign judgment was obtained from the foreign court (extrinsic fraud), rather than fraud in relation to the merits of a case (intrinsic fraud). The Supreme Court in *S P Chengalvaraya Naidu v Jagannath*[46] highlights the sensitivity of Indian courts to allegations of fraud in the obtaining of foreign judgments:

> [A] litigant who approaches the court is bound to produce all the documents executed by him which are relevant to the litigation. If he withholds a vital document in order to gain an advantage on the other side, then he would be guilty of playing fraud on the court as well as on the opposite party.[47]

In *Hindupur v Bellur*[48] the Delhi High Court reaffirmed that section 13(e) requires that a foreign judgment is recognised in India only if it conforms with public policy (ie, good conscience and equity as reflected by the grounds in CPC section 13.

D. Indirect Jurisdiction

Indirect jurisdiction refers to an evaluation carried out by the enforcing or requested court of a rendering or requesting court's jurisdiction to make the foreign judgment sought to be enforced. The requested court will not recognise or enforce the decision of the rendering court unless it is satisfied that the rendering court properly exercised jurisdiction in accordance with internationally accepted principles.[49] For this reason, indirect jurisdiction is also referred to as 'international jurisdiction'.

Regulations dealing with the recognition and enforcement of foreign judgments in India are minimal, essentially existing in the few public international law treaties to which India is a signatory. These bilateral treaties do not deal with indirect jurisdiction, leaving the enforcing court to assess the competency of the rendering court in accordance with principles developed under Indian case law. Indirect jurisdiction rules in India are thus similar to those established under English case law, given the colonial influence on the legal system. They are premised upon an understanding that the competency of the rendering court is not to be determined according to the law of the foreign state, but according to the jurisdictional rules of the enforcing state. Thus, for instance, in personal actions jurisdiction may be established if the defendant: (1) was a subject of the foreign state in which the relevant

[43] *Sankaran Govindam v Lakshmi Bharathi* [1975] 1 SCR 57; [1974] AIR SC 1764.
[44] *ABN v Satish Dayalal Choksi* [1990] AIR Bom 170.
[45] *Satya v Teja Singh* [1975] 2 SCR 97.
[46] *S P Chengalvaraya Naidu v Jagannath* [1994] 1 SCC 1; [1994] AIR SC 853.
[47] ibid, [6].
[48] *Hindupur v Bellur* (2015) SCC OnLine Del 7484.
[49] Ralf Michaels, 'Jurisdiction, Foundations' in Jürgen Basedow, Giesela Rühl, Franco Ferrari and Pedro de Miguel Asensio (eds), *Encyclopaedia of Private International Law* (Cheltenham, Edward Elgar Publishing, 2017).

judgment was made; (2) was habitually resident in that foreign state when the action was begun; (3) had sued as the plaintiff in the rendering court in relation to the same cause of action; (4) voluntarily appeared before the rendering court or submitted to its jurisdiction; or (5) had contracted to submit to the jurisdiction of the rendering court.[50] However, the order of a foreign court in a personal action over which it would otherwise have possessed jurisdiction will remain unenforceable, if it creates a charge over immovable property in India.

On habitual residence, Indian law has held that such residence confers jurisdiction on the courts of an originating state. The Indian court has held that the legal representatives of a defendant (deceased after institution of the suit) although themselves non-residents, are bound by the decree of the rendering court, the important factor for establishing jurisdiction being the defendant's residence at the date of institution of the suit.[51] The defendant's physical presence in a foreign country (albeit not a resident of the same) or the latter's conduct of a business in a representative manner within the jurisdiction at the time of entering into a contract will not by themselves support an inference that the defendant had agreed to be bound by the judicial pronouncements of the foreign country.[52] On the bringing of suit in relation to the same cause of action, dicta in *Ramanathan Chettyar*[53] suggest that, if a defendant has in a previous case filed a suit in the same forum that has granted the foreign decree, then the foreign court's indirect jurisdiction will be upheld and the defendant is precluded from challenging the rendering court's jurisdiction in enforcement proceedings. According to *Chormal Balchand*,[54] if a defendant appears before the rendering court and challenges its jurisdiction as well as argues on the merits, such defendant is regarded as having submitted to the jurisdiction of the rendering court. Similarly, filing a counterclaim will be considered as submitting to the rendering court's jurisdiction. In *Shalig Ram v Firm Daulatram Kundanmal*[55] the court held that applying for leave in the rendering court to defend a summary suit would be considered as a voluntary submission to the jurisdiction of such court.

Where the parties have agreed to confer jurisdiction on the rendering court, it should be noted that agreements that restrict the parties from enforcing their rights before ordinary Indian tribunals are void.[56] But, in *ABC Laminart Pvt Ltd v AP Agencies, Salem*[57] the court outlined the following rules for forum selection clauses:

1. The ouster by contract of the jurisdiction of an Indian court which would otherwise have jurisdiction will be void.
2. The conferral by contract of jurisdiction on a court which would otherwise not have jurisdiction is void.
3. Where two or more courts have jurisdiction to try a matter, the limitation by contract of jurisdiction to a particular court is valid.

[50] *Chormal Balchand Firm v Kasturi Chand Seraoji* [1938] AIR Cal 511.
[51] *The Andhra Bank Ltd v R Srinivasan* [1962] 3 SCR 391; [1962] AIR SC 232.
[52] *RMV Vellachi Achi v RMA Ramanatha Chettiar* [1973] AIR Mad 141.
[53] *Ramanathan Chettyar v Kalimuthu Pillay* (1912) 18 Ind Cas 189.
[54] *Chormal* (n 50).
[55] *Shalig Ram v Firm Daulatram Kundanmal* [1963] 2 SCR 574; [1967] AIR SC 739. See also *Lalji Raja and Sons v Firm Hansraj Nathuram* [1971] 3 SCR 815; [1971] AIR SC 974.
[56] Indian Contract Act 1872, s 28.
[57] *ABC Laminart Pvt Ltd v AP Agencies, Salem* [1989] 2 SCR 1; [1989] AIR SC 1239.

The decision also emphasised the need for semantic clarity in order to prevent interpretational ambiguity.[58] In *Kumarina Investment Ltd v Digital Media Convergence Ltd*,[59] the court held that the question of jurisdiction is to be determined as in accordance with the jurisdictional clauses of a contract, especially when the petitioner is a foreigner and the parties have chosen a specific law as the law governing their contract and the resolution of their disputes. The court also identified the following situations when a non-designated court can nonetheless exercise jurisdiction: (1) where the contracting parties are subject to the domestic law of a country with which the case has a close connection or where the cause of action has arisen; (2) where the governing law clause of the contract is contrary to the public policy of the designated court and the contract does not confer exclusive jurisdiction on the latter; and (3) where it is possible according to the governing law to override the designated forum.[60]

The Indian court has also addressed the issue of subject matter jurisdiction for pronouncing upon the validity of a forum selection clauses. In *Patel Roadways v Prasad Trading Co*[61] the Supreme Court of India decided that parties cannot agree to confer jurisdiction on a court that does not have jurisdiction over the subject matter. Indian case law suggests that, where contracting parties choose a neutral forum in preference to the natural forum (that is, the court of a state that is closely conencted to a contract or dispute) for the hearing of disputes arising out of a contract, they will normally be bound by the jurisdiction of the neutral forum. The exception is where there are extraordinary and unforeseen circumstances justifying a party's claim to be relieved from being bound by the jurisdiction clause. Such circumstances will need to be much more than mere inconvenience, arising out of (say) the expense and hardship of getting a witness to the agreed forum.[62] While parties may not be able to confer jurisdiction on a court when it would not otherwise exist, the restriction does not prevent them from agreeing to submit to the exclusive or non-exclusive jurisdiction of a foreign court. Thus, under Indian law, the parties to a contract may agree to have their disputes resolved by a foreign court which is a 'neutral court' or 'court of choice', conferring an exclusive or non-exclusive jurisdiction on that forum. Thus, for example, in a recent decision, the Delhi High Court ruled in favour of the validity of a forum selection clause where the contracting parties agreed to confer jurisdiction on the London Commercial Court.[63]

E. Severability of Judgments

The doctrine of severability is settled law in India. Severability means that portions of a foreign judgment that are unenforceable or invalid may be severed and the remaining

[58] ibid, [3]. See also *Hakam Chand v Gammon India Ltd* [1971] 1 SCC 286; [1971] AIR SC 740; *Angile Insulations v Davy Ashmore India Ltd* [1995] 4 SCC 153; [1995] AIR SC 1766; *Hanil Era Textiles Ltd v Puromatic Filters (P) Ltd* [2004] 4 SCC 671; [2004] AIR SC 2432.

[59] *Kumarina Investment Ltd v Digital Media Convergence Ltd* (2010) SCC Online TDSAT 641.

[60] ibid, 69.

[61] *Patel Roadways v Prasad Trading Co* [1991] 3 SCR 391; [1992] AIR SC 1514.

[62] *Modi Entertainment Network v WSG Cricket Pte Ltd* [2003] AIR SCW 733.

[63] *Bharat Heavy Electricals v Electricity Generation Incorporations* [2017] CS (Comm) 190/2017 (Delhi High Court).

part may be enforced provided that it is not so intertwined with the severed part as to make execution impractical. In *Shin Satellite Public Co Ltd v Jain Studios Ltd*[64] the Supreme Court of India held that severability ought to be based upon substantial severability and not mere 'textual divisibility'. The court may thus sever trivial and merely technical parts of a judgment, while retaining substantive those parts of a judgment that are otherwise enforceable.

V. Interlocutory Judgments

A variety of interlocutory orders issued by foreign courts are enforceable in Indian law in matters relating to costs, jurisdiction, divorce decrees, monetary judgments, mandatory injunctions and anti-suit injunctions. The general rules in CPC sections 13 and 44A remain applicable, while injunctive relief may require initiation of a suit in India with a domestic cause of action for civil damages or injunctive relief.

The Supreme Court in *M/S Alcon Electronics Pvt Ltd v Celem SA of Fos 34320 Roujan, France*[65] enforced a foreign court order that awarded costs with interest in an interlocutory order. The court explained that the foreign court's order was 'conclusive' and 'on the merits' and the quantification of the costs could be characterised as a money decree. Interestingly, the court noted that while the CPC does not provide for interest on costs, Indian courts are not prevented from recognising and enforcing an order for the payment of interest made by a foreign court. The court consequently upheld the plaintiff's right to have its entitlement interest at eight per cent under the UK Judgments Act 1838 recognised in India. The court further opined that the term 'decree' included orders. In *Surya Vadanan v State of Tamil Nadu*,[66] the Supreme Court showed much reluctance in disregarding an interlocutory order of a foreign court. In writ proceedings before the apex court, it was held that comity requires courts in India to respect and enforce orders of a foreign court, including interlocutory orders or orders for interim relief. In the case, the court ordered repatriation of the children to the UK on the basis of a custody order made by the Family Court there. In *Dr V Ravi Chandran v Union of India*,[67] hearing a writ application, the Supreme Court discussed the enforcement of a foreign custody order. It considered a report that the mother, pending litigation in the US Court, had returned to India in violation of a US court's custody order. The court held that the US court was the only competent court to adjudicate upon disputes relating to the child so that, if the mother had any grievance, she should seek modification of the consent order before the US court.

As for freezing orders, the Madras High Court in *BMIC Ltd v Chinnakannan Sivasankaran*[68] admitted an execution petition based on a worldwide freezing order and ordered the respondent not to alienate property without the court's permission. The court took notice of the freezing order issued by the English High Court and ordered its execution under CPC section 44A. There are no reported instances of *Babanaft* orders being enforced

[64] *Shin Satellite Public Co Ltd v Jain Studios Ltd* (2006) 2 SCC 628.
[65] *M/S Alcon Electronics Pvt Ltd v Celem SA of Fos 34320 Roujan, France* [2017] 2 SCC 253; [2017] AIR SC 1.
[66] *Surya Vadanan v State of Tamil Nadu* [2015] AIR SC 2243.
[67] *Dr V Ravi Chandran v Union of India* [2010] 1 SCC 174.
[68] *BMIC Ltd v Chinnakannan Sivasankaran* [2016] Execution Petition No 6 of 2016 (Madras High Court).

in India. But Indian parties successfully requested a worldwide freezing order from the UK's court in *State Bank of India v Dr Vijay Mallya*[69] in order to enforce an Indian tribunal's order on a personal guarantee for the debts incurred by the defendant's businesses. The enforcement process of this UK decision in India is likely to clarify India's position on the recognition of foreign freezing orders.

In claims related to intellectual property rights (IPRs), there has been a tendency for foreign courts to issue interlocutory injunctions. However, the law requires that a plaintiff show a local cause of action to obtain corresponding relief in India. In such situation, the foreign court order may have evidentiary value. Indian law on *Mareva* injunctions (referred to as 'attachments before judgment' in Indian law) is contained in CPC Order 38 Rule 5. Applications for such injunctions should be based on the following criteria: (1) an arguable claim; (2) a real risk that final judgment in an applicant's favour will remain unsatisfied; (3) full and frank disclosure of all the material facts; and (4) the exercise of discretionary power by the court.[70] The procedure for the recognition and enforcement of foreign interlocutory orders is the same as for the final judgments. The foreign interlocutory orders will have to fulfil the requirements in CPC sections 13 and 44A.

VI. Special Cases

The legal regime related to IPRs in India is diverse and largely in consonance with its obligations under the Trade-Related Aspects of Intellectual Property Rights Agreement (TRIPS) and other treaties generally. The Indian regime on IPRs can be understood under the heads of protection and remedial jurisdiction. Regarding protection, Indian law offers rights of protection in respect of a variety of foreign and domestic intellectual property. But protection is dependent upon the international obligations to which India has acceded. In the area of patent, the law offers protection, but requires registration to be enforceable in India. In the area of copyright and trademark, India allows for multiple protection and does not require a separate registration in India for such rights to be enforceable before the Indian courts. On remedial jurisdiction, the law on IPRs being related to public law, a foreign judgment creditor would have to bring a domestic cause of action against the judgment debtor through a civil suit or an application for injunctive relief. The foreign judgment upholding the creditor's IPRs will be of evidentiary value, although it may not operate as a *res judicata*. Indian law on IPRs allows injunctive relief in the form of *Anton Piller* orders, *Mareva* injunctions and *John Doe* orders. Relief may be sought before the Commercial Courts and Commercial Divisions of the High Courts, depending upon the pecuniary value of the claim.

A foreign court's determination on title to immovable property within its jurisdiction will be conclusive between parties in India provided the decision has been made by a competent court and does not contravene CPC section 13. But a foreign court's decision would not be effective in respect of immovable property situated outside its jurisdiction,

[69] *State Bank of India v Dr Vijay Mallya* [2018] EWHC 1084 (Comm).

[70] See generally *M/S Rite Approach Group Ltd v M/S Rosoboronexport Ltd* [2007] 2 Arb LR 443 (Delhi); (2007) 139 DLT 55; [2007] AIR Delhi 145.

even though title to properties in both suits is founded on an identical cause of action, since succession is governed by the *lex situs* in the case of immovable property and, therefore, title must be adjudicated by the court of the country where the property is situated.[71]

Claims relating to environmental law are regarded as matters of public law. There has so far been no instance of the recognition and enforcement of a foreign judgment relating to an environmental wrong. In 1984, following the methyl isocyanate (MIC) gas-leak at the Union Carbide factory at Bhopal, the Indian government approached the New York District Court with a representative suit against the American subsidiary Union Carbide Corporation. The claim was rejected for jurisdictional reasons of *forum non conveniens*.[72] Following this, the Government of India entered into a negotiated settlement with Union Carbide. There have been related claims presented before the US court[73] under the Alien Torts Claims Act which have not seen much success.

Competition law is considered as a public law matter. Hence, claims have to be grounded within a local cause of action under the Competition Act 2002. Claims for violation of competition law are presented to the Competition Commission of India (CCI) and appeals are referred to the National Company Law Appellate Tribunal (NCLAT). District Courts do not have jurisdiction in competition law claims. The Competition Act does not empower the CCI or NCLAT to direct parties to arbitration or other dispute resolution mechanism. The High Court of Delhi in *Union of India v Competition Commission of India*[74] has held that the existence of an arbitration agreement is irrelevant for the purposes of proceedings under the Competition Act. The general rule prevalent in India regarding arbitration is that, although issues *in personam* may be arbitrable, rights *in rem* should not be. Given the specific provision for adjudication of private antitrust claims in section 53N of the Competition Act, competition law disputes are not arbitrable under Indian law.

VII. Enforcement

The procedure for enforcement of a decree from a court of a reciprocating territory is in brief as follows:

1. An application for execution is filed by the judgment creditor before the competent District Court.
2. A notice is issued to the judgment debtor to show cause why the foreign decree should not be executed.
3. If the judgment debtor does not contest the decree, the court orders execution of the decree.
4. If the judgment debtor wishes to contest the decree under CPC sections 13 or 44A, the latter must show cause why the decree should not be executed.
5. If the judgment debtor is unable to make out a case under CPC sections 13 or 44A, the decree is executed. In that case, the decree holder can apply to the court for directions

[71] *Duggamma v Ganeshayya* [1964] ILR Kar 609; [1965] AIR Kant 97.

[72] *In Re Union Carbide Corp Gas Plant Disaster* [1986] 634 F Supp 842 (SDNY).

[73] *Sahu v Union Carbide Corp* [2008] No 06-5694-cv (2d Cir) (3 November 2008), available online: caselaw.findlaw.com/us-2nd-circuit/1418341.html.

[74] *Union of India v Competition Commission of India* [2012] AIR Del 66 (Delhi High Court).

that the judgment debtor disclose its assets. The court may then proceed with the attachment and sale of such assets.

6. The judgment creditor can apply for attachment or similar orders to prevent the alienation or encumbrance of the judgment debtor, pending execution.[75]

Bankruptcy-related disputes are treated as a matter of public law.

VIII. The Future

A. Prospects

There has been no position paper from the Indian government setting out its views on the 2005 Hague Convention. Possible obstacles to India's accession would relate to an absence of clarity on the ambit of the excluded areas in Articles 2(2)(a) to 2(2)(p) of the 2005 Hague Convention. The interpretation of those articles could create practical difficulties, especially when national courts are seised of matters that are addressing claims that are incidentally related to the excluded areas and incidental claims arise before the court designated by the parties to the choice of court agreement. For instance, among the excluded areas, insolvency is considered as part of public law in India. The absence of guidance on the scope of incidental claims raising questions of insolvency could accordingly be a major problem.[76]

The concern is heightened by the fact that India has not so far actively engaged in the drafting or adoption of harmonised law instruments, whether conventions or model laws, except in relation to international arbitration. The Hague Conference could help address this and other concerns, especially in the context of states making declarations (pursuant to Article 19) by providing guidance through supplementary Explanatory Reports or Guides to Good Practice. That would ensure that one of the main purposes of the 2005 Hague Convention, upholding the validity of forum selection clauses and facilitating parties' choice of a neutral forum, is not placed at risk. The author is of the opinion that India's efforts at reforming the law and the institutions relating to the enforcement of contracts could immensely gain from increased engagement with harmonised law, including the 2005 Hague Convention and the draft Hague Convention on the Recognition and Enforcement of Judgments in Civil and Commercial Matters by the Hague Conference's Judgments Project.

B. Reform

The current regime on enforcement is deficient in a few significant aspects, especially given the fact of India's non-accession to relevant international law instruments. These are: (1) the absence of clarity on enforcement of ex parte decrees; and (2) the cumbersome notification

[75] *BMIC* (n 68).

[76] Sai Ramani Garimella and Poomintr Sooksripaisarnkit, 'Jurisdiction under the Hague Convention on Choice of Court Agreements: A Critique' (2017) 57(3–4) *Indian Journal of International Law* 309.

process. The law on the treatment of ex parte decrees needs to be clarified with regard to the following: (1) the enforceability of such decrees without more; (2) their enforceability when the defendant has submitted to the jurisdiction of the rendering court, but does not participate in further proceedings; and (3) their enforceability when the defendant has alleged a denial of natural justice within the terms of CPC section 13(d) and does not participate in the foreign proceedings despite having been afforded a reasonable opportunity to present its defence. The bilateral reciprocity mechanism in CPC section 44A requires multiple steps to activate the recognition process envisaged in a treaty. The result is that, because many of the treaties in which India is a party have not yet been notified within the Official Gazette, the process of recognition is affected. Recognition through the reciprocity mechanism needs to be revised for greater efficiency and flexibility. Gazettal pursuant to CPC section 44A should be treated as evidence of reciprocity and not a barrier to establishing reciprocity in some other way. Enabling legislation enacted by parliament is required only for conventions (multilateral agreements) that India has signed to become effective in domestic law. Bilateral treaties are simply subject to executive ratification. Insofar as reciprocity is concerned, reform should provide for notification merely as an enabling feature, with persuasive value being accorded to evidence of ratification.

C. Judicial Cooperation

Indian courts have taken inspiration from the judgments of foreign courts in matters ranging from family law to IP law. It would help to enter into Memorandums of Understanding (MOUs) with foreign courts, as MOUs can further an enhanced understanding on foreign law, as well as provide evidence of reciprocity between Indian and foreign courts in relation to the recognition and enforcement of judgments, to the mutual benefit of all.

D. Use of Technology

While the Supreme Court, the High Courts and a few District Courts have dedicated electronic portals, access to their decisions is limited in the case of District Courts, where foreign judgments are normally presented for recognition and enforcement. The procedure for such recognition and enforcement in India is also through the traditional paper method. The process can gain immensely through accepting digital transcripts of foreign judgments and their e-registration. Further in proceedings related to the enforcement of foreign judgments, District Courts could also allow submission of evidence through electronic means. India's first systematic engagement with technology within the judicial process was in 2015 with the enactment of Commercial Courts Act 2015.

IX. Conclusion

Indian law on recognition and enforcement of foreign judgments is minimal and scattered in decided cases. While courts have on the whole been faithful to habitual residence and voluntary submission by the defendant as factors establishing indirect jurisdiction in enforcement proceeding, there is still confusion with regard to features like competent jurisdiction and conclusiveness. Importantly, there has been a lack of clarity on the role (if any) of public policy in the recognition and enforcement of foreign judgments, given the absence of a specific provision on public policy in CPC section 13.

India's lack of participation in initiatives for the harmonisation of law across borders is also a matter of concern. While there is an increased transnational commercial and interpersonal engagement of Indian people and businesses, the present legal regime has yet to provide full support for such engagement. It is suggested that India should participate in and ratify the 2005 Hague Convention, especially because there is an alignment among all stakeholders in India and elsewhere in respect of the fundamental belief that parties' choice of forum selection clauses should be recognised as much as possible in commercial matters. Further, India needs to participate in the ongoing Hague Judgments Project and incorporate the 2015 Hague Principles on Choice of Law into Indian law. Ideally, in due course, India should enact comprehensive legislation on matters of private international law, including the recognition and enforcement of foreign judgments.

17

Conclusion: Towards an Asia of Judgments without Borders

ANSELMO REYES

The Introduction set out a no-frills framework for the recognition and enforcement of civil and commercial judgments. That framework will be referred to here as the 'rudimentary system'. Fifteen Asian jurisdictions having been surveyed, this Conclusion will now test out the extent to which a money judgment in a commercial matter can be enforced throughout the 15 jurisdictions. This chapter will evaluate the test results to assess the degree to which something like a rudimentary system for recognition and enforcement is already in place among the 15 jurisdictions. In light of the test, can it be claimed that general civil and commercial judgments are readily portable throughout Asia, conceived as a region of which the 15 jurisdictions are representative? The chapter will end by suggesting how national systems for recognition and enforcement within Asia might be improved to transform the region into one of judgments without borders. On which components of the rudimentary system should efforts at improvement be directed?

I. A Practical Test

A. The Parameters of the Test

This section will test the robustness of the recognition and enforcement regimes within the 15 jurisdictions as a whole by examining the extent to which a judgment of the Singapore International Commercial Court (the SICC) will be enforceable in each of them.[1]

[1] In Anselmo Reyes, 'Recognition and Enforcement of Interlocutory and Final Judgments of the Singapore International Commercial Court' (2015) 2(2) *Journal of International and Comparative Law* 337, the author attempted to map the extent to which SICC judgments would be recognised and enforced around the world. But the approach was embarrassingly crude, amounting to little more than totting up the states with which Singapore had bilateral arrangements (for example, other Commonwealth countries and Hong Kong) and the Contracting States to the 2005 Hague Convention on Choice of Court Agreements (2005 Hague Convention). In the course of the author's seminars on the 2005 Hague Convention and the recognition and enforcement of judgments at Doshisha University's Law Faculty in December 2015, Dr Béligh Elbalti (now Associate Professor in the Graduate School of Law and Politics at Osaka University) pointed out that the author's method was outmoded and insufficiently rigorous. He observed that it was necessary to consider each jurisdiction on a case-by-case basis to understand whether the domestic law of a given state allowed foreign judgments to be recognised and enforced and (if so)

Recent years have seen the rise of the international commercial courts.[2] Within the Asian region, there are at least three: the SICC established in Singapore in January 2015,[3] the Astana International Financial Centre Court (the AIFC Court) established in Kazakhstan in December 2017,[4] and the China International Centre Court (the CICC) established in China in June 2018 and currently situated in Xi'an and Shenzhen.[5] The SICC derives its principal jurisdiction from choice of court agreements designating the SICC as the forum in which disputes arising in relation to an international commercial contract are to be resolved.[6] The most frequently asked question of the SICC (and no doubt the same is true of the AIFC Court and CICC) is whether its judgments can be enforced elsewhere. If recourse to international commercial courts such as the SICC is to be perceived by businesses as a viable alternative to international commercial arbitration, it will be necessary to have a degree of reassurance that their judgments will be recognised and enforced in key jurisdictions. Presently, because of the 1958 New York Convention's success internationally, an arbitral award issued in a Contracting State in connection with a commercial dispute should, at any rate theoretically,[7] be readily recognised and enforced in the other 158 jurisdictions that are currently party to the 1958 New York Convention. While no one is saying that judgments should be enforceable in a like number of jurisdictions, the public may understandably be reluctant to enter into choice of court agreements designating the SICC, unless they have some confidence that the SICC's judgments will be enforceable in places where the counterparties to their commercial transactions are likely to have assets. Thus, the question being explored here has practical utility: to what extent are judgments of the SICC in cross-border commercial disputes enforceable in the jurisdictions surveyed in this book.

At the outset of this test exercise, it should be noted that the SICC is a division of the Singapore High Court. An SICC judgment is therefore to be treated as equivalent to a judgment rendered in Singapore as originating state. For the purposes of the discussion here, it will be assumed that the judgment to be enforced has arisen because the parties designated the SICC under an exclusive choice of court agreement as the forum to resolve their disputes in relation to a particular transaction. Thus, the operative ground of indirect jurisdiction under the rudimentary system in the Introduction would be submission

on what conditions. At the time, Dr Elbalti kindly provided the author with a copy of his article on 'Spontaneous Harmonization and the Liberalization of the Recognition and Enforcement of Foreign Judgments' (2014) 16 *Japanese Yearbook of Private International Law* 264. The author would like to acknowledge his indebtedness to Dr Elbati's scholarship on recognition and enforcement as that has profoundly influenced the author's thinking on the subject.

[2] On the rise of international commercial courts and the rationale underlying their establishment, see the discussion in Marta Requejo Isidro, 'International Commercial Courts in the Litigation Market' (2019) MPILux Research Paper Series 2019 (2), available online: www.mpi.lu/research/woking-paper-series/2019/wp-2019-2/. See also Janet Walker, 'Specialised International Courts: Keeping Arbitration on Top of Its Game' (2019) 85(1) *Arbitration* 2.

[3] For general information on the SICC, see www.sicc.gov.sg.

[4] For general information on the AIFC Court, see aifc-court.kz.

[5] For general information on the CICC, see cicc.court.gov.cn/html/1/219/193/195/index.html.

[6] See Singapore Rules of Court (Cap 322, s 80, 2014 rev ed) Ord 110 r 7.

[7] In practice, it may not be so easy to enforce foreign arbitral awards in numerous countries, even though they are parties to the 1958 New York Convention. In respect of enforcement of arbitral awards in a number of Asian jurisdictions and efforts in those states to reform their arbitration regimes to facilitate the enforcement of arbitral awards, see Anselmo Reyes and Weixia Gu (eds), *The Developing World of Arbitration: A Comparative Study of Arbitration Reform in the Asia Pacific* (Oxford, Hart Publishing, 2018).

to the SICC's jurisdiction by way of an express choice of court agreement. It will be further assumed that: (1) the SICC decision to be recognised and enforced is a final and conclusive money judgment reached following trial on the merits wherein a plaintiff proved its case and (2) being commercial in nature and not relating to land situate in an enforcing state, intellectual property rights (IPRs) or antitrust (competition), the judgment does not contravene the public policy of a relevant state. It should be borne in mind that, while Singapore is a party to the 2005 Hague Convention, the other Asian jurisdictions in this study are not. China has signed the 2005 Hague Convention, but has yet to ratify it. Given the foregoing assumptions, in terms of the rudimentary system, the key elements to check would be whether the SICC's judgment meets the criteria of indirect jurisdiction and reciprocity in a particular jurisdiction.

B. China

There is no bilateral treaty for the mutual recognition and enforcement of judgments between Singapore and China.[8] But on 31 August 2018 the Chief Justices of the Supreme Court of Singapore and the Supreme People's Court of China signed a Memorandum of Guidance on Recognition and Enforcement of Money Judgments in Commercial Cases.[9] The document describes the criteria to be applied by the Chinese and Singapore courts when considering whether to recognise and enforce each other's judgments. According to the Memorandum, where there is an application to enforce a Singapore judgment (including one from the SICC), the Chinese court will essentially consider whether finality and indirect jurisdiction have been met. The Memorandum also sets out non-exhaustive grounds of refusal of recognition and enforcement. The criteria and grounds for refusal are similar to those in the no-frills regime.

The Memorandum has no binding legal effect. Nonetheless, insofar as it has been signed by the Chief Justices of the respective countries and authoritatively sets out the procedures for recognising enforcing money judgments in each jurisdiction, it can be regarded as compelling evidence of reciprocity.[10] Given that in the normal course of events SICC judgments will be money judgments in commercial matters, it follows from the foregoing that the courts in China will generally recognise SICC money judgments.

On indirect jurisdiction there may be situations requiring clarification. Article 9 of the Memorandum states that 'the courts of Singapore must have had jurisdiction to determine the subject matter of the dispute, as determined by the courts of the People's Republic of China, in accordance with Chinese law'. It would consequently appear that, with Singapore judgments, China applies a mirror principle in determining indirect jurisdiction. Where the Singapore court has founded jurisdiction on a basis analogous to a ground of direct jurisdiction that the Chinese court would apply, the Chinese court will treat

[8] See in this book, Weixia Gu, ch 2, s III.A.

[9] For the text, see www.supremecourt.gov.sg/docs/default-source/default-document-library/spc-mog-english-version---signed.pdf.

[10] Independently of the Memorandum, the Nanjing Intermediate People's Court had accepted that there was reciprocity between China and Singapore: *Kolma Group AG v Jiangsu Textile Industry (Group) Import and Export Co Ltd* (2016) Su-01 Xie Wai Ren No 3 Civil Judgment.

the Singapore court as having indirect jurisdiction. Once the 2005 Hague Convention is ratified by China, jurisdiction founded on an exclusive choice of court agreement designating the SICC will plainly be an accepted ground of indirect jurisdiction under Chinese law, as both Singapore and China would then be parties to the Convention.[11] But, for the moment, what is the position? Article 25 of China's Civil Procedure Law stipulates that parties:

> may agree to choose in their written contract the People's Court of the place where the defendant has his domicile, where the contract is performed, where the contract is signed, where the plaintiff has his domicile or where the object of the action is located to exercise jurisdiction over the case, provided that the provisions of this Law regarding jurisdiction by forum level and exclusive jurisdiction are not violated.[12]

This suggests that, if (1) a plaintiff or a defendant has a domicile in Singapore; (2) the relevant contract was performed or signed in Singapore; or (3) the subject matter of the originating action was located in Singapore, China will accept jurisdiction based on an exclusive choice of court agreement designating the SICC as a valid ground of indirect jurisdiction. What is unclear is whether a choice of court agreement designating the SICC will be regarded as a legitimate basis for indirect jurisdiction in a case where, apart from the choice of court agreement, there is no connection with Singapore.

C. Hong Kong

Singapore judgments are enforceable in Hong Kong under the Foreign Judgments (Reciprocal Enforcement) Ordinance (Cap 319) (FJREO).[13] A Singapore judgment (including that of the SICC) qualifies for registration pursuant to FJREO. To be registered, a judgment must be for a money payment and meet certain conditions (including falling within specified bases of indirect jurisdiction). FJREO also lists grounds for refusal of recognition. The condition for registration and the grounds for refusal of recognition are similar to those in the rudimentary system. There would be indirect jurisdiction in the Hong Kong court's view where a defendant has agreed to submit to the SICC by an exclusive choice of court agreement.[14]

[11] Attention, however, is drawn to Art 20 of the 2005 Hague Convention which states:

> A State may declare that its courts may refuse to recognise or enforce a judgment given by a court of another Contracting State if the parties were resident in the requested State, and the relationship of the parties and all other elements relevant to the dispute, other than the location of the chosen court, were connected only with the requested State.

When China signed the 2005 Hague Convention, it did not make a declaration in terms of Art 20. Nevertheless, the author understands that there is an ongoing debate in China as to whether a foreign judgment in the situation posited by Art 20 should or should not be recognised. Thus, it is conceivable that China may at the time of ratification also make a declaration in terms of Art 20.

[12] The provisions on jurisdiction at forum level and exclusive jurisdiction are respectively to be found in the Civil Procedure Law, Arts 19–21, 34. The provisions on forum level specify when a case is to come before the Basic People's Court, the Intermediate People's Court, the High People's Court and the Supreme People's Court. For the three grounds of exclusive jurisdiction in Art 34, see this book, Weixia Gu, ch 2, s III.A.i.a.

[13] See this book, James YP Wong, ch 3, s III.C.

[14] FJREO, s 6(2)(a)(iii).

D. Taiwan

Taiwan operates criteria along the lines of the rudimentary system. On indirect jurisdiction, the Taiwan chapter in this book indicates that the courts will apply a mirror principle.[15] If the Taiwan court would have direct jurisdiction under the Code of Civil Procedure in an analogous case, the rendering court will be treated as having indirect jurisdiction. Article 24 of the Code of Civil Procedure states:

> Parties may, by agreement, designate a court of first instance to exercise jurisdiction, provided that such agreement relates to a particular legal relation.
>
> The agreement provided in the preceding paragraph shall be evidenced in writing.

It follows that, in our example, the SICC would have indirect jurisdiction by analogy in light of the parties' choice of court agreement.

There is also a requirement of reciprocity.[16] However, just as any other foreign judgment, a money judgment in a commercial matter can be recognised and enforced in Singapore at common law. In other words, the plaintiff to the Taiwan judgment can sue the defendant in Singapore on the basis of the judgment debt and apply for summary judgment.[17] Having satisfied itself that (1) the Taiwan court delivering the judgment has indirect jurisdiction; (2) the Taiwan judgment is final and conclusive; (3) the Taiwan judgment was obtained through due process; and (4) the Taiwan judgment does not contravene Singapore public policy, the Singapore court will recognise the Taiwan judgment as giving rise to a debt and enforce the judgment. There will be no review of the merits of the original judgment. It will instead be treated as giving rise to a *res judicata* binding on the defendant. Accordingly, there should be no difficulty in establishing that in practical terms there is reciprocity between Singapore and Taiwan in relation to the recognition and enforcement of money judgments in commercial matters.

E. Japan

Japan has a sophisticated and liberal system for the recognition and enforcement of foreign judgments. The kernel of the Japanese system may be something along the lines of the rudimentary system. But the Japanese Code of Civil Procedure constitutes a much more developed version of that simple regime. Reciprocity is a requirement for the initial recognition and subsequent enforcement of a foreign judgment. As noted in the Japan chapter, a Japanese court has found that there is reciprocity between Singapore and Japan.[18] The Japan chapter suggests, although it is by no means absolutely clear, that the Japanese courts will apply a mirror-image approach when determining indirect jurisdiction. On that basis, since a Japanese court will have direct jurisdiction on the basis of a party's submission,[19] it should by analogy find indirect jurisdiction where there has been a submission to the SICC as a result of a choice of court agreement.

[15] See this book, Fuldien Li and Yen-Te Wu, ch 4, s III.A.
[16] ibid, s III.D.
[17] For the summary judgment procedure, see Singapore Rules of Court (Cap 322, s 80, 2014 rev ed), Ord 14.
[18] See this book, Kazuaki Nishioka, ch 5, s IV.A.iii, fn 56.
[19] ibid, s IV.A.ii, fn 40.

F. South Korea

Like Japan, South Korea's law on recognition and enforcement is highly developed. At heart it follows principles similar to those underlying the rudimentary system. But it has gone further and, with the recent Private International Law Act Amendment Proposal, additional reforms are in store. Article 8 of the Amendment Proposal provides that there will be indirect jurisdiction where parties have entered into a choice of court agreement.[20] In the absence of indication to the contrary, the choice of court agreement will be presumed to be an exclusive jurisdiction clause. Reciprocity will similarly be assumed provided it can be shown that there is a likelihood that South Korean judgments of the same type will be recognised by an originating state or that there is no significant difference between the laws of the originating state and South Korea in respect of the recognition of judgments. In terms of the practical test here, there would accordingly be indirect jurisdiction, the SICC having been designated by the parties' agreement. There would also be reciprocity, as South Korean judgments can be recognised and enforced in Singapore at common law using the summary procedure outlined above.

G. Singapore

Obviously, an SICC judgment will be enforceable in Singapore. Suppose, however, that what is sought to be enforced in Singapore is a money judgment of the CICC or the AIFC Court in a commercial matter. In either case, the judgments can be recognised and enforced in Singapore at common law through the summary procedure described above. CICC judgments have the benefit that the procedure for the enforcement of Chinese judgments has been set out in the Memorandum signed by the Chief Justices of Singapore and China. The Memorandum gives transparency to the requirements for the recognition and enforcement of Chinese judgments in Singapore. There is no bilateral treaty between Kazakhstan and Singapore for the mutual recognition and enforcement of judgments. Nor is there a Memorandum of Guidance between the courts of Kazakhstan and Singapore. But, as pointed out in the Singapore chapter, where foreign judgments are being enforced in Singapore under the common law, reciprocity is not a condition for recognition. Instead, recognition and enforcement under the common law of Singapore is founded on obligation theory, namely, the notion that 'where a judgment is issued by a court of competent jurisdiction over the parties, that judgment creates an obligation on the parties to abide by it which the courts of other countries ought to recognise and enforce'.[21] Thus, the absence of a treaty or a Memorandum of Guidance is not an impediment to the recognition of judgments of the AIFC Court as a matter of common law.

H. Malaysia

The enforcement of Singapore judgments in Malaysia is covered by the Reciprocal Enforcement of Judgments Act 1958 (REJA). Singapore appears in the First Schedule to REJA as

[20] See this book, Unho Lee, ch 6, s IV.B.
[21] See this book, Kenny Chng, ch 7, s III.B.

a jurisdiction which accords reciprocity of treatment to Malaysian judgments.[22] It is clear that, in the eyes of the Malaysian court, a choice of court agreement designating the SICC will amount to a submission to the SICC and so would meet the requirement of indirect jurisdiction in REJA. Accordingly, an SICC judgment will be recognised and enforced in Malaysia. It should be noted in this connection that the requirements in REJA very much reflect the principles underlying the rudimentary system.

I. Vietnam

Although both are members of the Association of Southeast Asian Nations (ASEAN),[23] there is no treaty for the mutual recognition and enforcement of judgments between Singapore and Vietnam. Nor is there any mulitilateral convention for the recognition and enforcement of judgments among ASEAN states.[24] This is despite the fact that on 31 December 2015 ASEAN inaugurated the ASEAN Economic Community (AEC) with the goal of promoting freedom of movement of trade and services among ASEAN states. The AEC can be expected to generate an increased number of cross-border disputes, leading to an urgent need for transparent mechanisms to ensure the speedy and cost-effective enforcement of judgments in commercial matters within ASEAN.

For the moment, SICC judgments will have to be enforced pursuant to Vietnam's Civil Procedure Code of 2015 (CPC). Reciprocity is a requirement under the CPC.[25] But the Vietnam chapter observes that it is unclear how reciprocity will be ascertained by the Vietnamese court in the absence of a bilateral agreement with the originating state.[26] In 2017 the Ministry of Justice proposed, albeit unofficially, that reciprocity might be determined on the basis of four factors: (1) diplomatic and economic relations between Vietnam and the originating country; (2) the sovereignty and interests of Vietnam; (3) the particular relations of each case; and (4) the rights and interests of the relevant parties, especially any Vietnamese parties.[27] While it is unclear how such factors are to be applied in practical terms, it is submitted that, given that Singapore and Vietnam are part of ASEAN and given their common interest as such Member States in developing the AEC, an application of factors (1), (3) and (4) identified by the Ministry of Justice should strongly point to a presumption of reciprocity between Singapore and Vietnam in the absence of evidence to the contrary. Certainly, Vietnamese money judgments in commercial matters can be recognised and enforced in Singapore at common law through the summary procedure described above. It should also be noted that the Deputy Chief Justice of the Supreme People's Court of Vietnam and a Justice of Appeal of the Singapore Supreme Court were among the attendees

[22] See this book, Stipah Selvaratnam, ch 8, s III.A. It should be noted that the judgments of the State Court (formerly called 'the Subordinate Court') of Singapore will not be recognised in Malaysia under REJA, because such decisions are not regarded in Malaysia as the judgments of a 'Superior Court' within the terms of REJA. The SICC is, in contrast, a division of the Supreme Court of Singapore, which is a 'Superior Court' within REJA. There is accordingly no corresponding problem in relation to SICC judgments.

[23] The 10 states comprising ASEAN are Singapore, Malaysia, Brunei, Vietnam, Cambodia, Laos, Thailand, Myanmar, Indonesia and the Philippines.

[24] There is the ASEAN Comprehensive Investment Agreement (ACIA) of 26 February 2009. But that merely establishes a mechanism for dealing with disputes between investors and ASEAN member states. See ACIA, s B.

[25] See this book, Nguyen Ngoc Minh, Tran Ha Han and Nguyen Thi Thu Trang, ch 9, s IV.A.i.

[26] ibid.

[27] ibid, fn 28.

endorsing the liberal approach to reciprocity set out in Article VII of the Nanning Statement of June 2017.[28] Thus, taken in the round, it is suggested that reciprocity between Singapore and Vietnam should at least be presumed by the Vietnamese courts, there being no evidence to the contrary.

As for indirect jurisdiction, it is likewise unclear what criteria will be applied to determine the same in the absence of a treaty.[29] CPC Article 440 stipulates that a foreign court will have jurisdiction in a civil case when two requirements are met. First, there is the negative requirement in Article 440(1) that a case not fall within the exclusive jurisdiction of the Vietnamese courts as provided in CPC Article 470.[30] Second, there is the positive requirement in Article 440(2) that a case fall among the situations having foreign elements in which the Vietnamese court would have 'common jurisdiction' pursuant to CPC Article 469.[31] But the requirement in Article 440(2) is then subject to three provisos, namely that: (a) the defendant has participated in oral argument before the foreign court without appealing against its jurisdiction; (b) there is no judgment in the same matter by the court of a third country that has been recognised and enforced by the Vietnamese court; and (c) the case was accepted by the foreign court before being accepted by the Vietnamese court.[32] Where does that leave our hypothetical SICC judgment? On the assumption that Article 440(2) provides for a mirror approach to indirect jurisdiction, it will be noted that an agreement to confer jurisdiction on a Vietnamese court is not one of the grounds of common jurisdiction listed in Article 469. Thus, on one reading, unless a defendant has not only submitted to the jurisdiction of the SICC by a choice of court agreement but has also appeared before it to argue the merits of a case, the requirement in Article 440(2) will not be met. A mere choice of court agreement would not be enough to confer indirect jurisdiction on the SICC under Article 440. Nonetheless, this result is far from certain,

[28] See this book, Anselmo Reyes, ch 1, fn 28.

[29] See this book, Nguyen Ngoc Minh, Tran Ha Han and Nguyen Thi Thu Trang, ch 9, ss III, IV.A.

[30] CPC Art 470(1) lists the civil lawsuits involving foreign elements which fall under the exclusive jurisdiction of the Vietnamese courts. Those lawsuits are:

> (a) Civil lawsuits involving rights to properties being immovables in the Vietnamese territory; (b) Divorce case between a Vietnamese citizen and a foreign citizen or a stateless person if both spouses reside, work or live permanently in Vietnam; (c) Other civil lawsuits where parties are allowed to choose Vietnamese Courts to settle according to Vietnamese law or International treaties to which the Socialist Republic of Vietnam is a signatory and parties agreed to choose Vietnamese Courts.

Art 470(2) lists the civil cases involving foreign elements that fall under the exclusive jurisdiction of the Vietnamese courts. Those civil cases are:

> (a) Claims without dispute arising from civil legal relationships specified in clause 1 of this Article; (b) Claims for determination of a legal events occurring in Vietnam; (c) Declaration of a Vietnamese citizen or a foreigner residing in Vietnam missing or death if such declaration is related to the establishment of their rights and obligations in Vietnam, except for cases where International treaties to which the Socialist Republic of Vietnam is a signatory otherwise prescribe; (d) Declaration of foreigner residing in Vietnam having limited civil act capacity or lacking legal capacity if such declaration is related to the establishment of their rights and obligations in Vietnam; (dd) Recognition of a property in Vietnam to be derelict, recognition of the right to ownership of the current manager over derelict immovables in Vietnam.

[31] CPC Art 469 sets out the situations when a Vietnamese court has 'common jurisdiction' to resolve civil cases involving foreign elements.

[32] It is unclear whether the three conditions in CPC Art 440(2)(a)–(c) are meant to apply cumulatively or in the alternative. The text reads: 'The civil case falls in a case specified in Article 469 of this Code *but has one of the following conditions*: …' (emphasis added). The highlighted words literally mean that it is enough if one of the conditions in sub-paragraphs (a), (b) or (c) is met. But the sense of the three conditions suggest that they are meant to apply cumulatively.

because Article 440(1) refers to the exclusive jurisdiction of the Vietnamese court under Article 470. One of such grounds of exclusive jurisdiction is that in Article 470(1)(c) wherein the parties have chosen the Vietnamese court for the resolution of their disputes in a civil lawsuit. If the Vietnamese court can assert direct jurisdiction where it has been designated by the parties as the forum for the resolution of their disputes, then it should find that there is indirect jurisdiction in an analogous situation before a foreign court. Accordingly, if Vietnam essentially adopts a mirror approach to indirect jurisdiction, it is not apparent why it should not also accept a foreign court such as the SICC claiming jurisdiction in a commercial matter on the basis of a choice of court agreement.

It is accepted that the law in Vietnam on recognition of foreign judgments is still in a state of flux. According to the Vietnam chapter, guidance from the Supreme People's Court is awaited on questions such as indirect jurisdiction, reciprocity and public policy.[33] In this context, it is submitted that the development of a regime for recognition and enforcement along the lines of the rudimentary system would be of benefit to Vietnam, especially as a means of attracting more FDI and building on the significant gains achieved since 1986 through *Đổi Mới* (economic renovation).

J. Cambodia

The law on recognition and enforcement in Cambodia is likewise uncertain, being still in the process of development. The Cambodia chapter observes that, in the absence of a binding treaty or convention regulating the recognition and enforcement of judgments, the Civil Procedure Code will regulate the subject. There being no treaty between Cambodia and Singapore, one must therefore look to the provisions of the Civil Procedure Code. The latter requires evidence of reciprocity and indirect jurisdiction. On reciprocity,[34] Cambodian judgments in commercial matters may be enforced in Singapore at common law using the summary judgment procedure mentioned earlier. Further the approach of presuming reciprocity suggested by Article VII of the Nanning Statement should normally be applicable, the Vice-President of the Supreme Court of Cambodia and a Judge of the Singapore Court of Appeal having been part of the consensus embodied by the Nanning Statement. As for indirect jurisdiction,[35] the Cambodia chapter points out that the principles of freedom of contract and party autonomy are familiar to Cambodia judges. They are likely to regard the SICC as having jurisdiction on the basis of a choice of court agreement. Indeed, according to the Cambodia chapter, where a foreign judgment is obtained from a court other than the one designated by the parties' contract for the resolution of disputes, the Cambodian court will probably refuse recognition on the ground that the same would be contrary to the public order of Cambodia. Thus, it would seem that the Cambodia court will accept the SICC as having indirect jurisdiction in a matter where jurisdiction is based on a choice of court agreement.

In short, given reciprocity and indirect jurisdiction, the SICC's judgment should be recognised and enforced.

[33] See this book, Nguyen Ngoc Minh, Tran Ha Han and Nguyen Thi Thu Trang, ch 9, ss III, IV.A.i, IV.A.iii, VII.
[34] See this book, Alex Larkin and Potim Yun, ch 10, s IV.B.
[35] ibid.

K. Myanmar

The law on recognition and enforcement in Myanmar is still developing and so the fate of any foreign judgment (let alone those of the SICC) before the Myanmar court today would still be a matter of conjecture. However, the Myanmar chapter demonstrates that there is a solid foundation of case law from the colonial period to the early 1960s upon which the current law (still based on the Civil Procedure Code of 1908 (CPC)) can build and which, if followed as precedent, would imbue Myanmar law on recognition and enforcement with a reasonable degree of transparency and certainty.

From CPC sections 13 and 14 it is apparent that the courts in Myanmar must be satisfied that a rendering court had competent jurisdiction.[36] On this, case law suggests that, in our hypothetical situation, the Myanmar court will find indirect jurisdiction, the Myanmar court having stated in *Steel Brothers & Co Ltd v Y A Ganny Sons*:

> The consensus of opinion of the Courts in Burma as well as in India is that when two Courts have jurisdiction to try a suit the parties by agreement can choose the forum. The choice of a forum in such a case is left open to the parties by agreement which is not considered illegal.[37]

Further, in contrast to the procedure under CPC section 44A (which currently only applies to certain courts in the UK),[38] the CPC First Schedule Order XV summary procedure for the recognition of a foreign judgment does not require that the originating state be a 'reciprocating territory'. Accordingly, if the Order XV procedure[39] is used for the recognition of an SICC judgment, it should not be necessary for the SICC judgment to meet a condition of reciprocity. Nevertheless, if it were somehow necessary by analogy with section 44A or otherwise for reciprocity to be established, the reality is that Singapore courts will recognise and enforce Myanmar commercial judgments at common law through the Singapore summary judgment procedure already mentioned. There is in addition the presumed reciprocity approach advocated by the Nanning Statement to which Singapore and Myanmar were party. It follows that reciprocity should not be a problem and SICC money judgments in commercial matters stand a good chance of being recognised and enforced in Myanmar through the CPC Order XV procedure.[40]

It should be noted that the system for recognition and enforcement posited in the Myanmar chapter is essentially the rudimentary system.

L. The Philippines

The Philippines is unique among the jurisdictions surveyed here, because its case law emphasises 'comity', rather than 'reciprocity', as the basis for recognition and enforcement

[36] See this book, Zaw Thura, ch 11, s II.A.i.
[37] [1965] *Burma Law Reports* 449 (CC) (U Kyaw Zan U J), 456.
[38] See this book, Zaw Thura, ch 11, s II.B.i.
[39] ibid, s II.A.i.
[40] CPC Ord XV in Myanmar is in fact analogous to Singapore's Ord 14 summary judgment procedure. This is hardly surprising, both being common law jurisdictions and the summary judgment procedure being one of the ways in which common law countries typically recognise and enforce foreign judgments.

of judgments.[41] Further, it does not seem to apply any test of indirect jurisdiction to foreign judgments. This may be because a foreign decision that is final and conclusive is simply presumed by the Philippine court to be valid and binding on a defendant in the absence of proof to the contrary.[42]

The Philippines is also unique in that it permits its courts to review of the merits of a foreign judgment when a defendant alleges that the judgment should not be recognised due to 'clear mistake' of law or fact.[43] The Philippines chapter has argued that any merits review should be regarded as functionally equivalent (and thus limited) to assessing whether a foreign judgment should be refused recognition as being contrary to 'public order, public policy and good customs'.[44] But it is unclear whether this latter argument will be accepted by the Philippine courts.

Given comity, the Philippine court will therefore likely recognise an SICC money judgment in a commercial matter as valid, binding and enforceable. There may be a review of the merits in some cases where a defendant alleges that there is 'clear mistake' of law or fact. But it is submitted that any such review should be brief. It should be confined to ascertaining whether there is an obvious mistake on the face of a judgment. The review should not be a pretext for prolonged scrutiny of a judgment, potentially including a hearing of oral evidence and cross-examination on the same. That sort of examination would undermine the principle of comity which the Philippine courts have repeatedly upheld. In the guise of looking for 'clear mistake', a detailed and protracted review of the merits would actually be re-opening substantive matters already decided by the rendering court. It would be a second bite at the cherry for a defendant and contrary to the doctrine of *res judicata*. From an economic standpoint, foreign investors will be reluctant to deal with Philippine parties, if there is a prospect that foreign judgments against the latter will be routinely re-opened by the Philippine court and effectively re-litigated because an obstructive and tactically astute defendant has pleaded 'clear mistake' at the recognition and enforcement stage.[45]

M. Indonesia

It does not seem that the posited SICC judgment will be recognised and enforced in Indonesia. By Article 436 of the *Reglement op de Burgerlijke Rechtsvordering* (Rv), with the exception of matters relating to maritime general average, all foreign judgments are unenforceable in the absence of a bilateral treaty.[46] There is no treaty between Singapore and Indonesia for the mutual recognition and enforcement of judgments.

[41] See this book, Arvin A Jo and Jocelyn P Cruz, ch 12, s IV.

[42] ibid, fn 22. But it does not logically follow from the principle of comity that there is no need to check for indirect jurisdiction. There should at least be some link between the rendering court and one or other or both of the parties or the subject matter of an action. Otherwise, the plaintiff could simply find some advantageous jurisdiction, convenient for the plaintiff but not to the defendant, where the plaintiff can easily obtain judgment.

[43] ibid, s IV.D.

[44] ibid.

[45] It is submitted that the Philippine system requires further development along the lines of the rudimentary system. While the emphasis on comity is laudable, it is insufficient without indirect jurisdiction to support an effective and fair system. It may be possible to have a workable system by treating adherence to due process as a matter of public policy and good order. But the scope of the merits review for 'clear mistake' needs to be more precisely circumscribed.

[46] See this book, Afifah Kusumadara, ch 13, s I.

The Indonesia chapter has argued that foreign judgments can be treated as authentic deeds and, as such, they may be accepted as unimpeachable evidence of a claim.[47] The chapter has also suggested that the Indonesian courts can follow the approach taken by the Dutch courts to Article 431 of the Dutch Code of Civil Procedure (which is similar terms to Rv Article 436).[48] The Dutch courts have held that, provided criteria similar to those of the rudimentary system are met, then a foreign judgment can be de facto 'recognised' by recourse to a summary procedure without need for further trial. The summary procedure would result in the grant of a domestic decree of execution which would be enforceable just like any other decree of the enforcing court. This summary procedure would thus be similar to the summary procedures under Order 14 in Singapore and Order XV in Myanmar. The Indonesian chapter nonetheless acknowledges that it is unknown whether the Indonesian court will accept any of these proposed methods of circumventing the apparently blanket prohibition against the enforcement of foreign judgments in Rv Article 436.

N. Thailand

Like Indonesia, Thailand also has a reputation of not enforcing foreign judgments. Despite this, the Thailand chapter is optimistic that changes will be forthcoming as younger judges succeed the older generation.[49] On the basis of the single case on the matter (SCJ 585/2461, decided in 1908), the Thailand chapter posits that indirect jurisdiction, due process and finality are the minimum criteria that the Thai court will apply when considering whether or not to recognise a judgment.[50] There may be other requirements, although (if so) these have yet to be articulated in cases. In terms of indirect jurisdiction, it is unknown whether the Thai court takes a mirror approach or one predicated on the existence of a 'characteristic link' between an action and the rendering court. As for reciprocity, the Thai courts have barely mentioned it in the few decided cases on recognition and enforcement. The Thailand chapter argues that a requirement of reciprocity would be out of sync with modern trends in private international law.[51] The upshot of all this is that it is unknown whether the Thai court will recognise an SICC money judgment in a commercial matter.

O. Sri Lanka

As Sri Lanka and Singapore both belong to the Commonwealth, Singapore money judgments (including those of the SICC) may be recognised and enforced in Sri Lanka by registration pursuant to the Reciprocal Enforcement of Judgments Ordinance (No 41 of 1921).[52] To be registered, it must be shown that the rendering court was one of competent

[47] ibid.
[48] ibid, s V.A and fn 31.
[49] See this book, Akawwat Laowonsiri, ch 14, s I.
[50] ibid, s III.B.
[51] ibid, s III.B.iv.
[52] See this book, Kankani Tantri Chitrasiri, Sajini Fernando and Asiesha Weerasekara, ch 15, ss I, III.

jurisdiction.[53] That requirement of indirect jurisdiction will be met by an SICC judgment arising out of the parties choice of court agreement.[54]

P. India

Singapore has been gazetted in India as a reciprocating territory.[55] Thus, SICC judgments are enforceable by filing an execution petition.[56] It appears that, under this procedure, the competency of the rendering court will still have to be assessed by the Indian court. Submission by reason of a choice of court agreement is regarded as sufficient to bestow indirect jurisdiction on the rendering court. Accordingly, where the SICC has asserted jurisdiction pursuant to the parties' choice of court agreement, there would be indirect jurisdiction.

Consider now the situation envisaged in Article 20 of the 2005 Hague Convention. The author is aware[57] that there is uncertainty among Indian lawyers as to what will happen where (say) two Indian parties agree to confer exclusive jurisdiction on the SICC on a matter that the SICC would consider as 'international' in nature.[58] Will the Indian courts recognise the exclusive jurisdiction clause as conferring indirect jurisdiction on the SICC or will the Indian courts refuse to recognise any SICC decision in such case on (say) the public policy ground? In other words, would the exclusive jurisdiction clause be treated as invalid in India on the basis, for example, that it seeks to evade the jurisdiction of Indian courts. According to the India chapter, the Indian parties will normally be bound by an exclusive or non-exclusive jurisdiction clause in favour of a foreign court. Exceptionally, an jurisdiction clause will not be binding where rare and extraordinary circumstances justify relieving a party from its obligations under the clause.[59] It would seem then that, in the situation

[53] ibid, s III.B.i.a. The requirements for registration are in fact similar to those for recognition and enforcement in the rudimentary system.

[54] ibid, s III.B.i.a, relying on the 'frequently cited' judgment of Buckley LJ in *Emanuel v Symon* [1908] 1 KB 302.

[55] See this book, Sai Ramani Garimella, ch 16, s III, fn 16.

[56] ibid, s III.

[57] It seems that the standard advice given by Indian lawyers in the situation posited is for the Indian plaintiff suing the Indian defendant abroad pursuant to an exclusive jurisdiction clause, to join a foreign party (preferably one resident in the same territory as the court having exclusive jurisdiction) as a 'necessary or proper party' to the legal proceedings in order to justify resort to a court outside India.

[58] By Singapore's Supreme Court of Judicature Act (Cap 322, 2007 rev ed) s 18D(1)(a), the SICC has jurisdiction to try cases that are international and commercial in nature'. See Singapore Rules of Court (Cap 322, s 80, 2014 rev ed), Ord 110, r 7(1)(a) to similar effect. 'International' and 'commercial' are defined in Ord 110, rr 1(2)(a) and (b) respectively. However, under Ord 110, r 8(2) the SICC 'must not decline to assume jurisdiction in an action solely on the ground that the dispute between the parties is connected to a jurisdiction other than Singapore, if there is a written jurisdiction agreement between the parties'. Consequently, where two Indian parties to a commercial transaction confer jurisdiction on the SICC by a choice of court agreement, the SICC must accept jurisdiction in the absence of some other ground for refusing to hear the case.

[59] See this book, Sai Ramani Garimella, ch 16, s IV.D, citing *Modi Entertainment Network v WSG Cricket Pte Ltd* [2003] AIR SCW 733, *Bharat Heavy Electricals v Electricity Generation Incorporations* [2017] CS (Comm) 190/2017 (Delhi High Court). *Modi* involved a contract whereby the respondent granted to the appellant the right to broadcast an International Cricket Conference tournament taking place in Kenya on Doordarshan (an Indian broadcasting service). The contract contained a non-exclusive jurisdiction clause in favour of the English court. The appellant commenced proceedings before the Bombay High Court. The respondent started proceedings in England. The appellant applied for an anti-suit injunction from the Bombay High Court. An injunction was initially granted by a single judge, but was overturned by the Division Bench of the Bombay High Court.

posited, the Indian courts would as a general rule regard the SICC as having indirect jurisdiction and an SICC money judgment in such matter would be recognised and enforced by the Indian court.

II. The Test Results

The practical test suggests that there is a likelihood that the SICC's judgment will be recognised in all but two of the 15 Asian jurisdictions. The two exceptions are Indonesia and Thailand. Even then, the position with Thailand is not wholly clear. Ignoring Singapore, among the remaining 12 Asian jurisdictions, one finds a spectrum. In China, Hong Kong, Taiwan, Japan, South Korea, Malaysia, the Philippines, Sri Lanka and India, SICC judgments will generally be recognised and enforced, either pursuant to a bilateral arrangement, a Memorandum of Guidance, principles in a code of civil procedure, the common law, or international comity. In Vietnam, Cambodia and Myanmar there is a good chance that SICC money judgments in commercial matters will be recognised and enforced, but there is uncertainty because the relevant law in those jurisdictions is still in the process of articulation and development by the legislature and the courts.

Overall, the test indicates that there is a nascent regime of recognition and enforcement in Asia, to the extent that the 15 jurisdictions may be said to represent the region. That regime is along the lines of the rudimentary system, with a number of states (China, Hong Kong, Taiwan, Japan, South Korea, Singapore, Malaysia, Sri Lanka and India) having more or less fully-developed laws (albeit in the case of China requiring clarification in some instances), while others (Vietnam, Cambodia, Myanmar and the Philippines) are in the process of developing their laws to the level of the rudimentary system, and yet others (Thailand and Indonesia) have still some distance to go to bring their laws up to the level of the rudimentary system.

On appeal, the Supreme Court (Syed Shah Quadri and Arijit Pasayat JJ), holding that the injunction had rightly been discharged, stated:

> In regard to jurisdiction of courts under the Code of Civil Procedure (CPC) over a subject matter one or more courts may have jurisdiction to deal with it having regard to the location of immovable property, place of residence or work of a defendant or place where cause of action has arisen. Where only one Court has jurisdiction it is said to have exclusive jurisdiction; where more courts than one have jurisdiction over a subject matter, they are called courts of available or natural jurisdiction. The growing global commercial activities gave rise to the practice of the parties to a contract agreeing beforehand to approach for resolution of their disputes thereunder, to either any of the available courts of natural jurisdiction and thereby create an exclusive or non-exclusive jurisdiction in one of the available forums or to have the disputes resolved by a foreign court of their choice as a neutral forum according to the law applicable to that court. It is a well-settled principle that by agreement the parties cannot confer jurisdiction, where none exists, on a court to which CPC applies, but this principle does not apply when the parties agree to submit to the exclusive or non-exclusive jurisdiction of a foreign court; indeed in such cases the English Courts do permit invoking their jurisdiction. Thus, it is clear that the parties to a contract may agree to have their disputes resolved by a Foreign Court termed as a 'neutral court' or 'court of choice' creating exclusive or non-exclusive jurisdiction in it.

One might ask what would be an exceptional circumstance justifying the grant of relief from the consequences of an exclusive jurisdiction clause. It is submitted that one example might be where an overriding statute or mandatory law confers exclusive jurisdiction in a matter to an Indian court. It may be contrary to Indian public policy to allow Indian parties to avoid the Indian court's exclusive jurisdiction by a choice of court agreement designating a foreign court as the forum in which their disputes should be brought.

The test was run on certain assumptions (for example, a money judgment in a commercial matter obtained through due process in the rendering court (the SICC) pursuant to a choice of court agreement). Similar tests can be run on other assumptions (for instance, assuming habitual residence of a defendant as the basis upon which a rendering court has accepted jurisdiction). It is submitted that the results thrown up by different scenarios will not be too different overall from those obtained here.[60]

III. An Agenda for the Future

The test results suggest that efforts at improving the nascent system of recognition and enforcement in the Asian jurisdictions might usefully be directed in a number of areas.

First, indirect jurisdiction needs to be clarified. At a minimum it is suggested that states adopt the grounds of indirect jurisdiction put forward in the rudimentary system. Insofar as submission by a choice of agreement designating a court is accepted as a ground of indirect jurisdiction by a state, the latter should make clear how it will deal with the situation envisaged in Article 20 of the 2005 Hague Convention. In other words what will be the outcome where two parties resident in the enforcing state have designated a foreign court as the forum for the resolution of a dispute, but the relationship of the parties and all other elements relevant to the dispute, other than the location of the chosen court, are only connected with the enforcing state? In such case, will the enforcing court recognise the designated rendering court as not having indirect jurisdiction at all or only in limited circumstances and (if so) in what circumstances? Further, it appears from the practical test that many countries follow something like a mirror approach to indirect jurisdiction, but the extent to which they do so is not made explicit in their codes of civil procedure or case law. Consideration should be given to clarifying the position by adopting a mirror approach such as that proposed by Professor Brand and discussed in the Introduction.[61]

Second, reciprocity needs to be thought through. It will probably take too long if a country wishes to establish reciprocity by negotiating bilateral treaties or entering into multilateral conventions such as the forthcoming Hague Convention. If it is deemed urgent for the purposes of attracting FDI and spurring economic growth, countries might consider simply entering into Memorandums of Guidance on a judiciary-to-judiciary basis as evidence of reciprocity. Consideration might be given to whether reciprocity remains meaningful as a requirement in this day and age or whether it should be replaced by a general principle of international comity. If reciprocity is retained, then a liberal approach to that concept, along the lines of the Nanning Statement of June 2017, may be advisable. From the practical test conducted here, it is obvious that, although non-binding, the Nanning Statement of 2017 is

[60] There is an interesting scenario that readers may additionally want to consider. Suppose that there is a bilateral treaty between States X and Y providing for the mutual recognition and enforcement of their respective judgments in commercial matters. Suppose further that an SICC judgment will be recognised and enforced under the law of State X, but it is uncertain whether an SICC judgment will be recognised and enforced under the law of State Y. Will it be possible indirectly to enforce an SICC judgment in State Y by first having the SICC judgment recognised in State X and converted into a judgment of State X, and then enforcing the resulting State X judgment in State Y?

[61] See this book, Anselmo Reyes, ch 1, ss III.C and fn 20.

important not just as a mere statement of aspiration, but as hard evidence of the approach that Asian judiciaries should and will be taking in the future on reciprocity.

Third, it was assumed in the practical test that the hypothetical SICC judgment sought to be enforced did not breach due process and was not contrary to public policy. This does not mean that due process and public policy can be ignored. States need to focus on reaching a consensus on just what adherence to 'due process' involves. It is acknowledged that this may not be an easy task. Due process has many angles and queries over the propriety of procedures may arise in myriad ways. Nonetheless, experience in the field of international commercial arbitration and arbitral awards indicates that many Asian states are prone to take far too narrow a view of due process (that is, one that stresses strict adherence to the letter of a procedural requirement), rather than considering a matter overall and asking whether a defendant was substantially afforded a reasonable opportunity to present a case and defend itself before the rendering court. A narrow approach has led in international arbitration to so-called 'due process paranoia' among arbitrators. If the fairness of the procedure in the rendering court is merely one over which different judges properly advised might reasonably differ, then it is submitted that enforcing courts should not refuse recognition by reason of a failure to follow due process. The lack of due process should be blatant or egregious (for example, fraud in the obtaining of a judgment or the failure to give any or any sufficient notice of proceedings before the rendering court) before it would merit the refusal of recognition to a judgment. Similarly, it should not be every mistake in the application by a foreign court of the law of the enforcing state that will automatically mean that a judgment is contrary to public policy or the fundamental norms or laws of a given Asian state. It is submitted that it is only where recognition would be wholly repugnant to the public order or the legal, social, cultural or religious norms of a state that refusal would be justified. The test for public policy in the recognition and enforcement of foreign judgments should be assimilated with and made identical to the test for public policy in the recognition and enforcement of foreign arbitral awards. Countries should be astute to ensure that challenges based on the due process (especially allegations of fraud) and public policy grounds do not become pretexts for essentially relitigating the substantive merits of foreign judgments. Consideration should be given to enforcing parts of judgments, where judgments are severable and some but not all parts are contrary to a state's public policy or fundamental norms.

Fourth, procedures for enforcement within a state should be streamlined. It is disheartening for litigants when, having won a legal battle in one state, they effectively have to start all over again in another state with the prospect of being tied up there for years in seeking to enforce their judgments. It is suggested that states institute simple processes of registration or summary adjudication as means for converting foreign judgments into domestic decrees capable of ready execution against a defendant's assets within the enforcing state.

Fifth, once an efficient and cost-effective rudimentary regime for recognition and enforcement is in place, a country might consider refinements. For instance, to what extent should foreign judgments relating to IPRs, competition law, immovables or environmental wrongs be enforceable? Should a country countenance the possibility of enforcing judgments where such matters merely arise as preliminary or incidental questions and the rendering court's principal decision essentially deals with the substantive rights of the parties as among themselves? A current hot topic in the Hague Conference's Judgments Project is the extent to which the judgments of 'common courts' (that is, the regional court of an association of countries such as the European Court of the European Union) should be recognised.[62] How should requirements such as reciprocity be applied (if at all) to the recognition and enforcement of the judgments of common courts, where (say) some but not all countries within the relevant association have reciprocal arrangements with the enforcing state?

Sixth, consideration should be given to joining the 2005 Hague Convention and the forthcoming Hague Convention. Although it will take time for these instruments to have a membership that even approaches that of the 1958 New York Convention, in due course a large number of Contracting States for each would greatly assist towards rationalising the system for recognition and enforcement not just in Asia, but all over the world.

This book has advocated implementation and development of a rudimentary system for the recognition and enforcement of judgments throughout Asia. It has attempted to do so in a practical, as opposed to a theoretical, manner. The issue boils down to an economic question. If a state is persuaded that a liberal regime of recognition and enforcement will help to attract FDI and assist in improving the welfare of its citizens, then a rudimentary system at least should be implemented sooner rather than later. One cannot and should not delay.

Currently, as a result of the 1958 New York Convention's success, international commercial arbitration is perceived as more reliable insofar as enforcement is concerned. There is a belief that it will be significantly easier to enforce foreign arbitral awards in (say) Asian countries than to enforce foreign judgments. The nascent system that has become apparent as a result of running the practical test in this chapter, suggests that the belief is unjustified. The reality is that in many Asian countries, even when they are parties to the 1958 New York Convention, there are problems in enforcing arbitral awards that are similar to those encountered in enforcing foreign judgments. One may not have to contend with indirect jurisdiction in the case of arbitral awards, but one has to deal instead with challenges to the validity of an arbitration agreement and an arbitral tribunal's jurisdiction. One also has to contend with questions of due process and public policy. These last two matters in international commercial arbitration are not much different from their counterparts in cross-border commercial litigation.

Whether or not one thinks that arbitration is preferable to litigation, a reason why it is vital and urgent to facilitate the recognition and enforcement of foreign judgments, especially foreign commercial judgments, is that international commercial arbitration is universally regarded today as having become overly technical, overly long and overly expensive.[63] At the very least, by developing improved systems for the recognition and enforcement of foreign judgments across Asia, countries give commercial businesses an option. If they find international commercial arbitration too expensive, they can instead opt for choice of court agreements designating a court as the forum to resolve their dispute. On the other hand, if they think that cross-border litigation is too expensive, they can put

[62] See The Permanent Bureau, Hague Conference on Private International Law, 'Note on "common courts" in Article 22 of the February 2017 Draft Convention', Document No 9 of 2017 (*Hague Conference on Private International Law*, 13–17 November 2017), available online: assets.hcch.net/docs/c168c7c4-e790-4551-993e-fe791ee0a1a6.pdf.

[63] See Anselmo Reyes, *The Practice of International Commercial Arbitration: A Handbook for Hong Kong Arbitrators* (Oxon, Informa Law from Routledge, 2017) 11–12, 201–03.

an arbitration agreement into their commercial contract instead. The competition between the two modes of dispute resolution, arbitration on the one side and litigation on the other, will help to bring down the cost of cross-border commercial dispute resolution down across the board. Hopefully, that will mean that everyone is better off at the end of the day.[64] It is respectfully submitted that giving the public this choice between modes of dispute resolution is at heart what the recognition and enforcement of judgments and this book are about.

[64] See James Spigelman, 'The Hague Choice of Court Convention and International Commercial Litigation' (2009) 83(6) *Australian Law Journal* 386. See also Louise Ellen Teitz, 'The Hague Choice of Court Convention: Validating Party Autonomy and Providing an Alternative to Arbitration' (2005) 53(3) *American Journal of Comparative Law* 543.

BIBLIOGRAPHY

Chapter 1. Introduction

Brand, Ronald A, 'The Circulation of Judgments under the Draft Hague Convention' University of Pittsburgh School Law Legal Studies Research Paper Series Working Paper No 2019-02 (February 2019), University of Pittsburgh School of Law, papers.ssrn.com/sol3/papers.cfm?abstract_id=3334647.
Elbalti, Béligh, 'Reciprocity and the Recognition and Enforcement of Foreign Judgments: A Lot of Bark But Not Much Bite' (2017) 13(1) *Journal of Private International Law* 184–218.
—— 'Spontaneous Harmonization and the Liberalization of the Recognition and Enforcement of Foreign Judgments' (2014) 16 *Japanese Yearbook of Private International Law* 264–88.
Jacobs, Philips, 'Auswirkungen des Brexits auf internationale Finanzierungsyerträge' Londoner Kreis Research Paper Series 2018 No 1 (8 June 2018), London Kreis, www.londoner-kreis.org/deutsch/wp-content/uploads/sites/2/2018/06/20180608_LK_NO1_Studie_zu_Auswirkungen_von_Brexit_Vertragsrecht_vF.pdf.
Nanning Statement of the 2nd China–ASEAN Justice Forum adopted on 8 June 2017, Article VII, www.chinajusticeobserver.com/nanning-statement-of-the-2nd-china-asean-justice-forum.
Paul, Joel R, 'The Transformation of International Comity' (2008) 71 *Law and Contemporary Problems* 19–38, scholarship.law.duke.edu/cgi/viewcontent.cgi?article=1477&context=lcp.
Reed, Lucy, 'Ab(use) of Due Process: Sword vs Shield' (2017) 33(3) *Arbitration International* 361–77.
Tu, Guangjian, *A Study on a Global Jurisdiction and Judgments Convention* (Hong Kong, Sweet & Maxwell, 2009).

Chapter 2. China

Alférez, Francisco J Garcimartín, and Saumier, Geneviève, 'Judgments Convention: Revised Preliminary Explanatory Report', *Hague Conference on Private International Law*, assets.hcch.net/docs/7cd8bc44-e2e5-46c2-8865-a151ce55e1b2.pdf, 24–29 May 2018.
Brand, Ronald A, and Herrup, Paul M, *The 2005 Hague Convention on Choice of Court Agreement: Commentary and Documents* (New York, Cambridge University Press, 2008).
Chen, Albert, *An Introduction to the Legal System of the People's Republic of China* (Hong Kong, LexisNexis, 2011).
Chen, Tung-Pi, 'Private International Law of the People's Republic of China: An Overview' 35(3) *American Journal of Comparative Law* (1987) 445–86.
Elbalti, Béligh, 'Reciprocity and the Recognition and Enforcement of Foreign Judgments: A Lot of Bark But Not Much Bite' (2017) 13(1) *Journal of Private International Law* 184–218.
Ferdinand, Peter, 'Westward Ho – The China Dream and "One Belt, One Road": Chinese Foreign Policy Under Xi Jinping' (2016) 92(4) *International Affairs* 941–57.
Gu, Weixia, 'Courts in China: Judiciary in the Economic and Societal Transition' in Jiunn-Rong Yeh and Wen-Chen Chang (eds), *Asian Courts in Context* (Cambridge, Cambridge University Press, 2014) 487–527.
Guo, Yujun, 'Country Report: The People's Republic of China' in Adeline Chong (ed), *Recognition and Enforcement of Foreign Judgments in Asia* (Singapore, Asian Business Law Institute, 2017) 49–69.
Han, Depei, *Guoji Sifa [Private International Law]* (Beijing, China Higher Education Press, 2000).
Huang, Jie (Jeanne), 'The Partially Modernized Chinese Conflicts System: Achievements and Challenges – Review of Zheng Sophia Tang, Yongping Xiao, and Zhengxin Huo, Conflict of Laws in the People's Republic of China' (2017) 13(3) *Journal of Private International Law* 633–54.
Huang, Jin, *Guoji Sifa [Private International Law]* (Beijing, Beijing Law Press, 2005).
Huo, Zhengxin, *Guoji Sifa [Private International Law]* 2nd edn (Beijing, Foreign Trade University Press, 2015).
Juan, Shen, *Guoji Sifa [Private International Law]* (Beijing, China Social Science Press, 2006).

Luo, Haocai, and Sun, Wanzhong (eds), *Yushi Jujin de Zhongguo Faxue [The Developing Legal Science of China]* (Beijing, Chinese Legal System Press, 2001).

Moser, Michael J, and Yeoh, Friven, 'Arbitrating China Business Disputes' in Michael J Moser (ed), *Dispute Resolution in China* (New York, JurisNet, 2012) 1–44.

Nanning Statement of the 2nd China–ASEAN Justice Forum adopted on 8 June 2017, Article VII.

Reyes, Anselmo, 'ASEAN and The Hague Conventions' (2014) 22(1) *Asia Pacific Law Review* 25–44.

Ruan, Yicheng, 'Zhongguo Guoji Sifa Zhidu De Jianli' [The Establishment of the Chinese Private International Law System] in Hanbao Ma (ed), *Guoji Sifa Lunwen Xuanji* (Taipei, Wu-nan Book, 1984) 1–29.

Tang, Zheng Sophia, Xiao, Yongping, and Huo, Zhengxin, *Conflict of Laws in the People's Republic of China* (Cheltenham, Edward Elgar, 2010).

The Ministry of Foreign Affairs, 'The Present Situation of China's Judicial Assistance and Extradition Treaties', *Ministry of Foreign Affairs*, www.fmprc.gov.cn/web/ziliao_674904/tytj_674911/wgdwdjdsfhzty_674917/t1215630.shtml, February 2018.

The World Bank, 'GDP Per Capital (Current US$)', *The World Bank*, 919 data.worldbank.org/indicator/NY.GDP.PCAP.CD?locations=CN.

Tsang, King Fung (Dicky), 'Chinese Bilateral Judgment Enforcement Treaties' (2017) 40(1) *Loyola of Los Angeles International and Comparative Law Review* 1–49.

Tu, Guangjian, *Private International Law in China* (Singapore, Springer, 2016).

—— 'The Hague Choice of Court Convention: A Chinese Perspective' (2007) 55(2) *The American Journal of Comparative Law* 347–65.

Wolff, Lutz-Christian, 'China's Private International Investment Law: One-Way Street into PRC Law?' (2008) 56 *American Journal of Comparative Law* 1039–73.

Wuhan University Institute of International Law, 'Model Law on Recognition and Enforcement of Foreign Judgments in China' (Model Law), presented in the 2nd China Private International Law Society Research Committee Seminar in the National Justice and Chinese International Civil Procedure Law Reform Forum.

Xiao, Yongping, 'Pizhun Xuanze Fayuan Xieyi Gongyue de Libi Fenxi Ji Woguo de Duice' [An Analysis of Ratifying the Convention on Choice of Court Agreements and China's Way to Deal with it] (2017) 1(5) *Wuhan University International Law Review* 1–16.

Xu, Qingjun, 'The Codification of Conflicts of Laws in China: A Long Way to Go' (2017) 65(4) *The American Journal of Comparative Law* 919–62.

Yuen, Peter, and Choong, John, 'The Enforcement of Domestic and Foreign Court Judgments in the PRC' in Michael J Moser (ed), *Dispute Resolution in China* (New York, JurisNet, 2012) 381–408.

Zhang, Huang, 'International Jurisdiction under the 2005 Hague Convention on Choice of Court Agreements: Implications for China' (2017) 47 *Hong Kong Law Journal* 555–84.

Zhang, Wenliang, 'Sino-Foreign Recognition and Enforcement of Judgments: A Promising "Follow-Suit" Model?' (2017) 16 *Chinese Journal of International Law* 515–45.

—— 'Recognition and Enforcement of Foreign Judgments in China: A Call for Special Attention to Both the "Due Service Requirement" and the "Principle of Reciprocity"' (2013) 12(1) *Chinese Journal of International Law* 143–74.

Chapter 3. Hong Kong

'2018 Draft Convention', *Hague Conference on Private International Law*, assets.hcch.net/docs/23b6dac3-7900-49f3-9a94-aa0ffbe0d0dd.pdf, 24–29 May 2018.

Cameron, Camille, and Kelly, Elsa, *Principles and Practice of Civil Procedure in Hong Kong* 2nd edn (Hong Kong, Sweet & Maxwell, 2008).

Clarke, WS, *Hong Kong Civil Court Practice: Desk Edition 2019* (Hong Kong, LexisNexis, 2019).

Department of Justice, 'Consultation Paper No. 2 on 2018 Draft Convention on the Recognition and Enforcement of Foreign Judgments', *Department of Justice*, www.doj.gov.hk/eng/public/pdf/2019/consultation_ild.pdf, February 2019.

—— 'Proposed Arrangement Between Hong Kong and the Mainland on Reciprocal Recognition and Enforcement of Judgments in Civil and Commerical Matters: Consultation Paper', *Department of Justice*, www.doj.gov.hk/eng/public/pdf/2018/lpdpapere.pdf, July 2018.

—— 'Proposed Arrangement on Reciprocal Recognition and Enforcement of Judgments in Civil and Commercial Matters between Hong Kong and the Mainland', *Legislative Council*, www.legco.gov.hk/yr18-19/english/panels/ajls/papers/ajls20181126cb4-230-3-e.pdf, November 2018.
'Enforcement of Judgments and Arbitral Awards Global Guide', *Practical Law*, uk.practicallaw.thomsonreuters.com/Browse/Home/International/EnforcementofJudgmentsGlobalGuide?transitionType=Default&contextData=(sc.Default)&firstPage=true&comp=pluk&bhcp=1, 2019.
Fox, Hazel, and Webb, Philippa, *The Law of State Immunity* 3rd edn (Oxford, Oxford University Press, 2013).
Ghai, Yash, *Hong Kong's New Constitutional Order* 2nd edn (Hong Kong, Hong Kong University Press, 1999).
'Hong Kong in Figures (Latest Figures)', *Census and Statistics Department*, www.censtatd.gov.hk/hkstat/hkif/index.jsp, 22 February 2019.
'International Convention on Civil Liability for Bunker Oil Pollution Damage (BUNKER)', *International Maritime Organisation*, www.imo.org/en/About/Conventions/ListOfConventions/Pages/International-Convention-on-Civil-Liability-for-Bunker-Oil-Pollution-Damage(BUNKER).aspx.
'International Convention on the Establishment of an International Fund for Compensation for Oil Pollution Damage (FUND)', *International Maritime Organisation*, www.imo.org/en/About/Conventions/ListOfConventions/Pages/International-Convention-on-the-Establishment-of-an-International-Fund-for-Compensation-for-Oil-Pollution-Damage-(FUND).aspx.
Johnston, Graeme, and Harris, Paul, *The Conflict of Laws in Hong Kong* 3rd edn (Hong Kong, Sweet & Maxwell, 2017).
Law Society of Hong Kong Circular 12–883.
'LCQ15: The Hague Convention on Choice of Court Agreements', *gov.hk*, www.info.gov.hk/gia/general/201406/25/P201406240828.htm, 25 June 2004.
Leung, Allan, and Clark, Douglas, *Civil Litigation in Hong Kong* 5th edn (Hong Kong, Sweet & Maxwell, 2017).
'List of Treaties in Force and Applicable to the Hong Kong Special Administrative Region', *Department of Justice*, www.doj.gov.hk/eng/laws/interlaw.html, 14 November 2018.
Lord Collins of Mapesbury (eds), *Dicey, Morris & Collins on the Conflict of Laws* 15th edn (London, Sweet & Maxwell, 2012).
Premti, Anila, 'Liner Shipping: Is There a Way for More Competition?' UNCTAD Discussion Papers No 224, *United Nations Conference on Trade and Development*, unctad.org/en/PublicationsLibrary/osgdp2016d1_en.pdf, March 2016.
Wilkinson, Michael, Cheung, Eric TM, and Meggitt, Gary, *A Guide to Civil Procedure in Hong Kong* 6th edn (Hong Kong, LexisNexis, 2017).

Chapter 4. Taiwan

Elbalti, Béligh, 'Reciprocity and the Recognition and Enforcement of Foreign Judgments: A Lot of Bark But Not Much Bite' (2017) 13(1) *Journal of Private International Law* 184–218.
Hsu, Yao-Ming, 'Waiguo Lihun Panjue de Chengren' [Recognition of Foreign Divorce Judgments] (2017) 181 *Taiwan Jurist* 26.

Chapter 5. Japan

Adachi, Eiji, 'Beikoku Kurasu Akushion Hanketsu/Wakai no Shounin Shikko to Koujo' [The Class Action in Japanese Law und Japanese *Ordre Public*] (2002) 69 *Seijo Law Review* 255–72.
—— 'Case Notes' (1999) 678 *New Business Law* 62–67.
—— 'Gaikoku Hanketsu no Shonin Shikko ni okeru Kokusai Saiban Kankatsu' [International Jurisdiction at the stage of Recognition and Enforcement of Foreign Judgments] in Hideyuki Kobayashi (ed), *Kokusai Saiban Kankatsu no Riron to Jitsumu [Theory and Practice of International Jurisdiction]* (Nagoya, Shinnippon-Hoki, 2017) 347–64.
—— 'Kurasu Akushion Hanketsu/Wakai no Chiriteki Han'i' [Territorial Scope of Class Actions Judgments and Settlements] (2014) 86(2) *Horitsu Jiho* 50–54.

—— 'Wagakuni ni okeru Beikoku Kurasu Akushion jouno Wakai no Shounin Tekikaku' [Recognisability of Judicial Settlement Reached in the Course of Class Action in the US] in Yoshimitsu Aoyama and others (eds), *Gendai Shakai ni okeru Minji Tetsuzuki-ho no Tenkai [Development of Civil Procedure Law in the Modern Society]* (Tokyo, Shojihomu, 2002) 245–74.

Aoyama, Yoshimitsu, 'Art 24' in Chu'uichi Suzuki and Akira Mikazuki (eds), *Chu'ukai Minji Shikko-ho (1) [Commentary on Civil Execution Act (1)]* (Tokyo, Daiichi Hoki Shuppan, 1984) 362–436.

'Conclusions and Recommendations adopted by the Special Commission on the Practical Operation of the Hague Apostille, Evidence, and Service Conventions', *Hague Conference on Private International Law*, assets.hcch.net/docs/0edbc4f7-675b-4b7b-8e1c-2c1998655a3e.pdf, 28 October–4 November 2003.

Dogauchi, Masato, 'Amerika no Choubatasu teki Songai Baisho Hanketsu no Nihon ni okeru Shikko' [Enforcement of American Judgments Awarding Punitive Damages in Japan] in Teiichiro Nakano and others (eds), *Minji Tetsuduki Ho-gaku no Kakushin (jou) [Innovation of Civil Procedure Law (1)]* (Tokyo, Yuhikaku, 1991) 423–39.

—— 'Gaikoku Saibansho niyoru Kurasu Akushion Hanketsu (Wakai) no Nihon deno Koryoku' [Effect in Japan of Class Action Judgments/Settlements Given by Foreign Courts] (2010) 925 *New Business Law* 20–27.

—— 'Historical Development of Japanese Private International Law' in Jürgen Basedow, Harald Baum and Yuko Nishitani (eds), *Japanese and European Private International Law in Comparative Perspective* (Tübingen, Mohr Siebeck, 2008) 27–60.

—— 'Naikoku Hanketsu tono Teishoku' [Conflict with Domestic Judgments] in Akira Takakuwa and Masato Dogauchi (eds), *Shin Saiban Jitsumu Taikei (3) – Kokusai Minji Sosho-ho (Zaisanho Kankei) [New Court Practice Series (3) – International Procedural Law (Property Law Matters)]* (Tokyo, Seirin Shoin, 2002) 365–71.

—— 'New Japanese Rules on International Jurisdiction: General Observation' (2011) 54 *Japanese Yearbook of International Law* 260–77.

Elbalti, Béligh, 'The Jurisdiction of Foreign Courts and the Recognition of Judgments Ordering Injunction – The Supreme Court Judgment of April 24, 2014' (2016) 59 *Japanese Yearbook of International Law* 395–419.

Elbalti, Béligh, and Yokomizo, Dai, 'La compétence internationale des tribunaux japonais en matiére civile et commerciale à la lumière de la nouvelle legislation' [2016] 3 *Revue critique de droit international privé* 417–52.

General Secretariat of the Supreme Court (ed), *Shiho Kyojyo Shitsumu Shiryo [Working Documents on International Judicial Cooperation]* (Tokyo, General Secretariat of the Supreme Court, 1992).

Haga, Masaaki, *Gaikoku Hanketsu no Shounin [Recognition of Foreign Judgments in Japan]* (Tokyo, Keio University Press, 2018).

Hayakawa, Yoshihisa, 'Lis Pendens' (2011) 54 *Japanese Yearbook of International Law* 324–32.

Hirose, Takashi, 'Saiko Saibansho Chosakan Kaisetsu' [Explanatory Remarks on the Supreme Court Decisions], (2015) 67(9) *Hoso Jiho [Law Association Journal]* 339–64.

Honma, Yasunori, Nakano, Shun'ichiro, and Sakai, Hajime, *Kokusai Minji Tetsuduki-ho [International Civil Procedure Law]* 2nd edn (Tokyo, Yuhikaku, 2012).

Ishiguro, Kazunori, *Gendai Kokusai Shiho (Jo) [Modern Conflict of Laws in Japan (Vol I)]* (Tokyo, University of Tokyo Press, 1986).

'Japan – Central Authority & Practical Information', *Hague Conference on Private International Law*, www.hcch.net/en/states/authorities/details3/?aid=261, 7 January 2018.

Judgment of Nagoya District Court, 6 February 1987, 1236 *Hanrei Jiho* 113, (1990) 33 *Japanese Annual of International Law* 189–95.

Judgment of Osaka High Court, 9 April 2003, 1141 *Hanrei Taimuzu* 270, (2005) 48 *Japanese Annual of International Law* 171–75.

Judgment of the Supreme Court, 7 June 1983, 37–5 *Minshu* 611, (1984) 27 *Japanese Annual of International Law* 119–26.

Judgment of the Supreme Court, 26 February 1985, 37–6 *Katei Saiban Geppo* 25, (1985) 28 *Japanese Annual of International Law* 225–32.

Judgment of the Supreme Court, 28 April 1998, 52–3 *Minshu* 853, (1999) 42 *Japanese Annual of International Law* 155–60.

Judgment of the Supreme Court, 26 September 2002, 56–8 *Minshu* 1551, (2003) 46 *Japanese Annual of International Law* 168–74.

Judgment of the Supreme Court, 23 March 2007, 61–2 *Minshu* 619, (2008) 51 *Japanese Yearbook of International Law* 552–55.

Judgment of the Supreme Court, 24 April 2014, 68–4 *Minshu* 329, (2015) 58 *Japanese Yearbook of International Law* 463–65.

Judgment of Tokyo District Court, 18 February 1991, 760 *Hanrei Taimuzu* 250, (1992) 35 *Japanese Annual of International Law* 177–83.

Judgment of Tokyo District Court, 19 January 2006, 1229 *Hanrei Taimuzu* 334, (2007) 50 *Japanese Annual of International Law* 240–43.

Judgment of Tokyo High Court, 27 February 1990, 1344 *Hanrei Jiho* 139, (1991) 34 *Japanese Annual of International Law* 166–69.

Judgment of Tokyo High Court, 28 June 1993, 1471 *Hanrei Jiho* 89, (1994) 37 *Japanese Annual of International Law* 155–57.

Kanzaki, Tadashi, 'Jurisdiction over Consumer Contracts and Individual Labor-Related Civil Disputes' (2012) 55 *Japanese Yearbook of International Law* 306–22.

Kasuga, Ichiro, 'Sotatsu (Sotatsu Jouyaku 10 Jo (a) ni yoru Chokusetsu Soutatsu)' [Service of Process (Service by Post in Accordance with Art 10(a) of the Hague Service Convention)] in Akira Takakuwa and Masato Dogauchi (eds), *Shin Saiban Jitsumu Taikei (3) – Kokusai Minji Sosho-ho (Zaisanho Kankei) [New Court Practice Series (3) – International Procedural Law (Property Law Matters)]* (Tokyo, Seirin Shoin, 2002) 343–50.

Kawabe, Yoshinori, 'Saiko Saibansho Chosakan Kaisetsu' [Explanatory Remarks on the Supreme Court Decisions] in Hoso Kai (ed), *Saiko Saibansho Hanrei Kaisetsu Heisei 10 (1998) Nendo (Jo) [Explanatory Remarks on the Supreme Court Decisions 1998 (1)]* (Tokyo, Hoso Kai, 1998) 450–96.

Kobayashi, Hideyuki, 'Gaikoku Hanketsu no Shounin Shikko ni tsuiteno Ichi Kousatsu' [A Reflection on Recognition and Enforcement of Foreign Judgments] (1982) 467 *Hanrei Taimuzu* 18–26.

Kono, Toshiyuki (ed), *Chiteki Zaisanken to Shougai Minji Sosho [Intellectual Property and Transnational Civil Litigation]* (Tokyo, Kobundo, 2010).

—— 'Country Report: Japan' in Adeline Chong (ed), *Recognition and Enforcement of Foreign Judgments in Asia* (Singapore, Asian Business Law Institute 2017) 105–16.

—— 'Die Anerkennung von US-amerikanischen Urteilen über punitive damages in Japan' in Andreas Heldrich and Toshiyuki Kono (eds), *Herausforderungen des Internationalen Zivilverfahrensrechts* (Tübingen, Mohr Siebeck, 1994) 35–48.

—— 'Gaikoku Saibansho' [Foreign Courts] in Akira Takakuwa and Masato Dogauchi (eds), *Shin Saiban Jitsumu Taikei (3) – Kokusai Minji Sosho-ho (Zaisanho Kankei) [New Court Practice Series (3) – International Procedural Law (Property Law Matters)]* (Tokyo, Seirin Shoin, 2002) 318–25.

Nagata, Mari, 'Wagakuni ni okeru Gaikoku Hanketsu no Shounin Shikko' [Recognition and Enforcement of Foreign Judgments in Japan] in Japan Association of International Economic Law (ed), *Kokusai Keizai-ho Koza 2 – Torihiki, Zaisan, Tetsuduki [International Economic Law II – Transactions, Property and Procedure]* (Kyoto, Horitsu Bunkasha, 2012) 213–30.

Nakanishi, Yasushi, 'Case Notes' (2003) 169 *Bessatsu Jurist* 252–53.

Nakano, Shun'ichiro, 'Agreement on Jurisdiction' (2011) 54 *Japanese Yearbook of International Law* 278–94.

—— 'Gaikoku Hanketsu no Shikko' [Enforcement of Foreign judgments] in Hiroshi Takahashi and Shintaro Katou (eds), *Jitsumu Minji Sosho Koza (Dai 3 Ki) Dai 6 Kan – Joso, Saishin, Shogaku Sosho to Kokusai Minji Sosho [Practical Lecture on Civil Procedure (Third Period) Vol 6 – Appeals, Small Claims, and International Civil Litigation]* (Tokyo, Nippon Hyoron Sha, 2013) 441–58.

—— 'Gaikoku Hozen Meirei no Kouryoku' [Effectiveness of Foreign Provisional Orders/Measures] in Akira Takakuwa and Masato Dogauchi (eds), *Shin Saiban Jitsumu Taikei (3) – Kokusai Minji Sosho-ho (Zaisanho Kankei) [New Court Practice Series (3) – International Procedural Law (Property Law Matters)]* (Tokyo, Seirin Shoin, 2002) 414–19.

Nishioka, Kazuaki, 'Kyouso Seikyu'u ni kansuru Gaikoku Hanketsu no Shounin oyobi Shikko' [Recognition and Enforcement of Foreign Judgments in Relation to Competition Law Claims] (2015) 25 *Nihon Kokusai Keizai-ho Gakkai Nenpo [International Economic Law]* 94–110.

Nishitani, Yuko, 'International Jurisdiction of Japanese Courts in a Comparative Perspective' (2013) 60(2) *Netherlands International Law Review* 251–77.

—— 'Internationales Privat- und Zivilverfahrensrecht' in Harald Baum and Moritz Bälz (eds), *Handbuch Japanisches Handels- und Wirtschaftsrecht* (Cologne, Carl Heymanns, 2011) 1211–85.

—— 'The Operation of the 1965 Hague Service Convention in Japan' (2004) 9(17) *Zeitschrift für Japanisches Recht [Journal of Japanese Law]* 215–36.

Noda, Yoshiyuki, *Introduction to Japanese Law* (Tokyo, University of Tokyo Press, 1976).

Nomura, Yoshiaki, 'Activity-Based Jurisdiction of Japanese Courts – A Bold but Unnecessary Departure –' (2012) 55 *Japanese Yearbook of International Law* 263–86.

Okuda, Yasuhiro, 'Recognition and Enforcement of Foreign Judgments in Japan' (2013) 15 *Yearbook of Private International Law* 411–20.

—— 'Reform of Japan's Private International Law: Act on the General Rules of the Application of Laws' (2006) 8 *Yearbook of Private International Law* 145–68.

Saito, Akira, 'International Civil Jurisdiction Based on the Place of Performance of Obligation Relating to A Contract' (2011) 54 *Japanese Yearbook of International Law* 295–310.

Sakurada, Yoshiaki, *Kokusai Shiho [Private International Law]* 6th edn (Tokyo, Yuhikaku, 2012).

—— 'The Origin and Evolution of Private International Law in Japan' (2013) 58 *Japanese Yearbook of International Law* 164–95.

Sakurada, Yoshiaki, and Schwittek, Eva, 'Die Reform des japanischen internationalen Privatrechts' (2012) 76(1) *The Rabel Journal of Comparative and International Private Law* 86–130.

Sawaki, Takao, 'Recognition and Enforcement of Foreign Judgments in Japan' (1989) 23(1) *The International Lawyer* 29–36.

Shin, Miho, 'Case Notes' (2016) 1492 *Jurist* 304–05.

Tada, Nozomi, 'Enforcement of Foreign Judgments in Japan Regarding Business Activities' (2003) 46 *Japanese Annual of International Law* 75–94.

—— 'International Civil Jurisdiction Based on the Place of the Tort' (2012) 55 *Japanese Yearbook of International Law* 287–305.

Takahashi, Koji, 'A Major Reform of Japanese Private International Law' (2006) 2(2) *Journal of Private International Law* 311–38.

—— 'Japan's Newly Enacted Rules on International Jurisdiction: with a Reflection on Some Issues of Interpretation' (2011) 13 *Yearbook of Private International Law* 146–70.

Takakuwa, Akira, 'Gaikoku Saiban no Shounin' [Recognition of Foreign Judgments] in Akira Takakuwa and Masato Dogauchi (eds), *Shin Saiban Jitsumu Taikei (3) – Kokusai Minji Sosho-ho (Zaisanho Kankei) [New Court Practice Series (3) – International Procedural Law (Property Law Matters)]* (Tokyo, Seirin Shoin, 2002) 306–12.

Takasugi, Naoshi, 'Nihon Kokunai deno Shingai Koui no Sashitome wo meijita Gaikoku Hanketsu no Nihon deno Shikko' [Enforcement of the Foreign Judgment ordering the Permanent Injunction against Infringement Activities Carried out in Japan] (2014) 1032 *New Business Law* 18–24.

Takata, Hiroshige, 'Art 200' in Masahiro Suzuki and Yoshimitsu Aoyama (eds), *Chu'u Shaku Minji Sosho-ho (4) [Commentary on Civil Procedure Law (4)]* (Tokyo, Yuhikaku, 1997) 354–92.

Takeshita, Keisuke, 'Sovereignty and National Civil Procedure: An Analysis of State Practice in Japan' (2016) 9(2) *Journal of East Asia and International Law* 361–62.

Takeshita, Morio, 'The Recognition of Foreign Judgments' (1996) 39 *Japanese Annual of International Law* 55–77.

Toshiyuki, Kono, 'International Civil Procedure in Japan' (1996) 6 *Asian Yearbook of International Law* 105–34.

Wanami, Hironori, 'Background and Outline of the Modernization of Japanese Private International Law' in Jürgen Basedow, Harald Baum and Yuko Nishitani (eds), *Japanese and European Private International Law in Comparative Perspective* (Tübingen, Mohr Siebeck, 2008) 61–76.

Watanabe, Satoshi, 'A Study of a Series of Cases Caused Non-recognition of a Judicial Judgment between Japan and Mainland China – A Cross-border Garnishment Order of the Japanese Court Issued to a Chinese Company as a Third-party Debtor –' (2014) 57 *Japanese Yearbook of International Law* 287–304.

Yamamoto, Kazuhiko, 'Case Notes' (1999) 1157 *Jurist* 297–99.

—— 'International Jurisdiction Based on the Location of Property' (2011) 54 *Japanese Yearbook of International Law* 311–23.

Yokomizo, Dai, 'Case Notes' (2015) 1487 *Jurist* 106–09.

Yokoyama, Jun, *Private International Law in Japan* (Alphen aan den Rijn, Kluwer Law International, 2017).

Chapter 6. South Korea

Ministry of Justice, 'Public Hearing for the Proposal of All Amendments of the Private International Act', *Ministry of Justice*, www.moj.go.kr/bbs/moj/93/385349/download.do, 27 February 2018.

Ministry of Justice, *Research on the Proposal of a New Private International Law*, policy.nl.go.kr/upload/Atch/20140707b04.pdf, February 2014.

Chapter 7. Singapore

Adodo, Ebenezer OI, 'Enforcement of Foreign Gambling Debts: Mapping the Worth of the Public Policy Defence' (2005) 1(2) *Journal of Private International Law* 291–321.
Briggs, Adrian, 'Recognition of Foreign Judgments: A Matter of Obligation' (2013) 129(Jan) *LQR* 87–100.
—— *The Conflict of Laws* 3rd edn (Oxford, Oxford University Press, 2013).
Chan, Sek Keong, 'Keynote Address', Singapore, New York State Bar Association Seasonal Meeting, www.supremecourt.gov.sg/docs/default-source/default-document-library/media-room/cj-keynote-address-at-nysba-international-seasonal-meeting_27-oct-2009.pdf, 27 October 2009.
Chng, Kenny, 'The Impact of the Singapore International Commercial Court and Hague Convention on Choice of Court Agreements on Singapore's Private International Law' (2018) 37(1) *Civil Justice Quarterly* 124–47.
—— 'A Theoretical Perspective of the Public Policy Doctrine in the Conflict of Laws' (2018) 14(1) *Journal of Private International Law* 130–59.
Chong, Adeline, 'Country Report: Singapore' in Adeline Chong (ed), *Recognition and Enforcement of Foreign Judgments in Asia* (Singapore, Asian Business Law Institute, 2017) 163–78.
Goh, Yihan and Tan, Paul, 'An Empirical Study on the Development of Singapore Law' in Goh Yihan and Paul Tan (eds), *Singapore Law: 50 Years In The Making* (Singapore, Academy Publishing, 2015).
Harris, Jonathan, 'Recognition of Foreign Judgments at Common Law – The Anti-suit Injunction Link' (1997) 17(3) *OJLS* 477–98.
Hartley, Trevor and Dogauchi, Masato, 'Explanatory Report on the 2005 Hague Choice of Court Agreements Convention', *Hague Conference on Private International Law*, www.hcch.net/index_en.php?act=publications.details&pid=3959&dtid=3, 2013.
Lai, Ho Hock, 'Policies Underlying the Enforcement of Foreign Commercial Judgments' (1997) 46 *ICLQ* 443–62.
Lord Collins of Mapesbury (ed), *Dicey, Morris and Collins on the Conflict of Laws* 15th edn (London, Sweet & Maxwell, 2012).
Mills, Alex, 'The Dimensions of Public Policy in Private International Law' (2008) 4(2) *Journal of Private International Law* 201–36.
Oppong, Richard Frimpong, 'Mere Presence and International Competence in Private International Law' (2007) 3(2) *Journal of Private International Law* 321–32.
'Report of the Singapore International Commercial Court Committee', www.mlaw.gov.sg/content/dam/minlaw/corp/News/Annex%20A%20-%20SICC%20Committee%20Report.pdf, 29 November 2013.
Singapore International Commercial Court, 'Enforcement of Money Judgments – SICC', *Singapore International Commercial Court*, www.sicc.gov.sg/guide-to-the-sicc/enforcement-of-money-judgments, 19 November 2018.
Special Commission on the Recognition and Enforcement of Foreign Judgments, '2018 Draft Convention', *Hague Conference on Private International Law*, assets.hcch.net/docs/23b6dac3-7900-49f3-9a94-aa0ffbe0d0dd.pdf, 24–29 May 2018.
Yeo, Tiong Min, *Halsbury's Laws of Singapore* vol 6(2) Reissue (Singapore, LexisNexis, 2016).
—— 'Common Law Developments Relating to Foreign Judgments' (Singapore, Ninth Yong Pung How Professorship of Law Lecture, cebcla.smu.edu.sg/sites/law.smu.edu.sg/files/law/Paper2016_YPH.pdf, 18 May 2016.

Chapter 8. Malaysia

Hickling, RH and Wu, Min Aun, *Conflict of Laws in Malaysia* (Kuala Lumpur, Butterworths Asia, 1995).
Legislative Council, Federation of Malaya, *Hansard* (Second Meeting of the Fourth Session of the Second Legislative Council, 4 December 1958).

Chapter 9. Vietnam

Bui, Thi Thu, *Textbook on Private International Law* (Hanoi, Vietnam Education Publisher, 2012).
Correspondence No 1247 (26 May 2011).

'Details: Viet Nam', *Hague Conference on Private International Law*, www.hcch.net/en/states/hcch-members/details1/?sid=230.
Le, Hong, 'Not Easy to Recognise and Enforce Foreign Judgments and Decisions', *Pháp Luật*, baophapluat.vn/tu-phap/khong-de-de-cong-nhan-va-thi-hanh-ban-an-quyet-dinh-dan-su-cua-toa-an-nuoc-ngoai-365544.html, 12 November 2017.
Le, Tai Trien (ed), *Commentary on Vietnamese Commercial Law* vol 1 (Bach Dang Publishing House, Saigon, 1959).
Letter No 4609/BTP-PLQT of the Ministry of Justice to the Supreme People's Court, 3 October 2017.
'Press Release: Joint Press Statement on the Official Visit of His Excellency Mr. Nguyen Xuan Phuc, Prime Minister of the Socialist Republic of Viet Nam to the Kingdom of Thailand 17–19 August 2017, Bangkok', *Ministry of Foreign Affairs of the Kingdom of Thailand*,www.mfa.go.th/main/en/news3/6886/80416-Joint-Press-Statement-on-the-Official-Visit-of-His.html, 18 August 2017.
'The Situation of Foreign Investments in 2018', *Ministry of Planning and Investment Foreign Investment Agency*, dautunuocngoai.gov.vn/tinbai/6110/Tinh-hinh-thu-hut-Dau-tu-nuoc-ngoai-nam-2018, 25 December 2018.
'The Socio-economic Situation in the First 6 Months of 2018', *General Statistics Office of Vietnam*, www.gso.gov.vn/default.aspx?tabid=621&ItemID=18864.
The World Bank, 'Vietnam Trade at a Glance: Most Recent Values', *World Integrated Trade Solution*, wits.worldbank.org/CountrySnapshot/en/VNM, 20 February 2019.
'Vietnam Population 2019', *World Population Review*, worldpopulationreview.com/countries/vietnam-population/, 25 September 2018.
'Việt-Hàn thúc đẩy ký kết hiệp định tương trợ tư pháp trong thương mại' (Vietnam and South Korea Promote the Signing of Judicial Assistance Agreement in Commercial Matters), vietnam.vnanet.vn/vietnamese/viet-han-thuc-day-ky-ket-hiep-dinh-tuong-tro-tu-phap-trong-thuong-mai/358312.html, 21 Nbvember 2017.

Chapter 10. Cambodia

Peng, Hor, Phallack, Kong, and Menzel, Jorg, *Introduction to Cambodian Law* (Cambodia, Konrad-Adenauer-Stiftung, 2012).
The National Assembly Commission 6 on Legislation and Justice, 'Briefing Note of Legal and Judicial Reform in Cambodia', *Parliamentary Institute of Cambodia*, www.pic.org.kh/images/2016Research/20170505_Legal_Judicial_Reform_Eng.pdf, February 2016.

Chapter 11. Myanmar

Briggs, Adrian, *Private International Law in Myanmar* (Oxford, Oxford University Press, 2015).
Crouch, Melissa, 'The Layers of Legal Development in Myanmar' in Melissa Crouch and Tim Lindsey (eds), *Law, Society and Transition in Myanmar* (Oxford, Hart Publishing, 2014) 39–58.
Nanning Statement of the 2nd China–ASEAN Justice Forum adopted on 8 June 2017, Article VII.

Chapter 12. Philippines

'A Constitutional History of the Supreme Court of the Philippines', *Supreme Court of the Philippines*, sc.judiciary.gov.ph/aboutsc/history/index.php, 2013.
Agpalo, Ruben E, *Conflict of Laws (Private International Law)* (Manila, Rex Book Store, 2004).
Aguiling-Pangalangan, Elizabeth, 'Country Report: Republic of the Philippines', in Adeline Chong (ed), *Recognition and Enforcement of Foreign Judgments in Asia* (Singapore, Asian Business Law Institute 2017) 146–62.
Aquino, Ranhilio Callangan, *Elements of Private International Law* 2nd edn (Quezon, Central Book Supply, 2006).
Balane, Ruben F, 'The Spanish Antecedents of the Philippine Civil Code' (1979) 54 *Philippine Law Journal* 1–44.
'Contracting Parties to the Paris Convention', *World Intellectual Property Organisation*, www.wipo.int/treaties/en/ShowResults.jsp?lang=en&treaty_id=2.

de la Costa, Horacio, *Asia and the Philippines* (Manila, Solidaridad Publishing House, 1967).
Graveson, Ronald H, *Conflict of Laws: Private International Law* 7th edn (London, Sweet & Maxwell, 1974).
Keohane, Robert O, *Reciprocity in International Relations* (1986) 40(1) *International Organization* 1–27.
Riano, Willard B, *Civil Procedure: A Restatement for the Bar* (Manila, Rex Book Store, 2009).
Thompson, Eric C, and Thianthai, Chulanee, 'Attitudes and Awareness toward ASEAN: Findings of a Ten Nation Survey', *ASEAN Foundation*, www.aseanfoundation.org/documents/Attitudes%20and%20Awareness%20Toward%20ASEAN.pdf.

Chapter 13. Indonesia

'Bahasa Hukum: Sumber Hukum Formal Bernama "Yurisprudensi"', *hukumonline.com*, www.hukumonline.com/berita/baca/lt5a7ad95871d1a/bahasa-hukum--sumber-hukum-formal-bernama-yurisprudensi, 7 February 2018.
Bermann, George A (ed), *Recognition and Enforcement of Foreign Arbitral Awards: The Interpretation and Application of the New York Convention by National Courts* (Cham, Springer, 2017).
Bird & Bird, 'Enforcement of Foreign Judgments in the Netherlands', *Birdbuzz*, birdbuzz.nl/wp-content/uploads/2015/01/Enforcement-of-Foreign-Judgements-in-the-Netherlands.pdf.
Gautama, Sudargo, *Hukum Perdata Internasional Indonesia Jilid III Bagian 2 Buku Ke-8* 4th edn (Bandung, Alumni, 2002).
—— 'Recognition and Enforcement of Foreign Judgments and Arbitral Awards in the ASEAN Region' (1990) 32 *Malaya Law Review* 171–88.
Harahap, M Yahya, *Hukum Acara Perdata Tentang Gugatan, Persidangan, Penyitaan, Pembuktian, dan Putusan Pengadilan* 16th edn (Jakarta, Sinar Grafika, 2016).
—— *Ruang lingkup permasalahan eksekusi bidang perdata* 2nd edn (Jakarta, Sinar Grafika, 2005).
'Jurisdiction: National Rules of International Jurisdiction of Dutch Courts', *Dutchcivillaw.com*, www.dutchcivillaw.com/jurisdiction/internatjuris044.htm.
'Ketika Profesor Digugat Sang Putri', *Gatra.com*, arsip.gatra.com/2008-04-07/majalah/artikel.php?pil=23&id=113936.
Laiman, Alamo D, Reni, Dewi Savitri, Lengkong, Ronald, and Ardiyanto, Sigit, 'The Indonesian Legal System and Legal Research', *GlobaLex*, www.nyulawglobal.org/globalex/Indonesia.html#sourcesoflaw, July 2011.
Lukito, Ratno, *Legal Pluralism in Indonesia: Bridging the Unbridgeable* (London, Routledge, 2013).
'MA Batalkan Penetapan Pengampuan Prof. Sudargo', *hukumonline.com*, www.hukumonline.com/berita/baca/hol18857/ma-batalkan-penetapan-pengampuan-prof-sudargo, 29 March 2008.
Oppusunggu, Yu Un, 'Country Report: The Republic of Indonesia' in Adeline Chong (ed), *Recognition and Enforcement of Foreign Judgments in Asia* (Singapore, Asian Business Law Institute, 2017) 91–104.
Soemartono, Gatot P, *Arbitrase dan mediasi di Indonesia* (Jakarta, Gramedia Pustaka Utama, 2006).
Subekti, R, *Arbitrase Perdagangan* (Jakarta, Binacipta, 1981).
Supancana, IBR, Basuki, Zulfa Djoko, Kusumadara, Afifah, Soeriaatmadja, Arvianto, Hikmah, Mutiara, Oppusunggu, Yu Un, Panjaitan, Roki, Iriani, Sukesti, Wahyu, Isthining, Besturen, Maretta, Puspitasari, Anggriana, and Junaidi, Haris Ahmad, *Naskah Akademik Rancangan Undang-Undang tentang Hukum Perdata Internasional (lanjutan)* (Jakarta, Badan Pembinaan Hukum Nasional Kementerian Hukum dan Hak Asasi Manusia RI, 2015), www.bphn.go.id/data/documents/na_ruu_ttg_hukum_perdata_internasional_(lanjutan).pdf.

Chapter 14. Thailand

Ajjit, Supranee, and Ariyanuntaka, Vichai, 'Agreements Relating to Dispute Settlement in International Commercial Matters: Arbitration Agreement and Choice-of-Court Agreement', *Dhurakij Pundit University*, libdoc.dpu.ac.th/mtext/article/487038.pdf.
Ariyanuntaka, Vichai, 'Jurisdiction and Recognition and Enforcement of Foreign Judgments and Arbitral Awards: A Thai Perspective', *Court of Justice*, www.coj.go.th/en/pdf/AlternativeDisputeResolution04.pdf.
Bhabha, Homi K, 'Freedom's Basis in the Indeterminate' (1992) 61 *October* 46–57.

Chen, Weizuo and Goldstein, Gerald, 'The Asian Principles of Private International Law: Objectives, Contents, Structure and Selected Topics on Choice of Law' (2017) 13(2) *Journal of Private International Law* 411–34.
Domej, Tanja, 'Recognition and Enforcement of Judgments (Civil Law)' in Jürgen Basedow, Giesela Rühl, Franco Ferrari and Pedro de Miguel Asensio (eds), *Encyclopaedia of Private International Law* (Cheltenham, Edward Elgar Publishing, 2017) 1472–79.
Inama, Stefano and Sim, Edmund W, *The Foundation of the ASEAN Economic Community* (Cambridge, Cambridge University Press, 2015).
Karnjanachittra-Saisoontorn, Panthip, 'Problems in the Requirements for Recognition of Foreign Judgments' (1992) 22(2) *Thammasat Law Journal* 213–14.
—— 'Referencing Foreign Judgments in Thai Court' (1990) 20(3) *Thammasat Law Journal* 147–53.
Michaels, Ralf, 'Recognition and Enforcement of Foreign Judgments' in Rüdiger Wolfrum (ed), *Max Planck Encyclopedia of Public International Law* (Oxford, Oxford University Press, 2009).
Mongia, Padmini, *Contemporary Postcolonial Theory: A Reader* (Oxford, Oxford University Press, 1997).
Piwawatanapanich, Prasit, *Lecture on Private International Law* (Bangkok, Thammasat University Press, 2013).
Schütze, Rolf A, '§328' in Bernhard Wieczorek and Rolf A Schütze (eds), *Zivilprozessordnung und Nebengesetze: Grosskommentar*, 3. Teilband, 1. Teil (Berlin, De Gruyter Recht, 2007) s 462.
Sontikasetrin, Kamol, *Private International Law* (Bangkok, Nitibannagarn, 1996).
Weatherbee, Donald E, *International Relations in Southeast Asia: The Struggle for Autonomy* (New York, Rowman & Littlefield, 2015).

Chapter 15. Sri Lanka

'Conventions, Protocols and Principles', *Hague Conference on Private International Law*, www.hcch.net/en/instruments/conventions.
North, PM, and Fawcett, JJ, *Private International Law* 12th edn (London, Butterworths, 1992).
Sirimanna, Bandula, 'Sri Lanka Takes Historic Step in Evidence Through Video Conferencing', *The Sunday Times*, www.sundaytimes.lk/081026/FinancialTimes/ft3020.html, 26 October 2008.
Stewart, David P, 'Private International Law: A Dynamic and Developing Field' (2009) 30(4) *University of Pennsylvania Journal of International Law* 1121–32.
The World Bank, 'The World Bank in Sri Lanka: Outline', *The World Bank*, www.worldbank.org/en/country/srilanka/overview, 17 October 2017.

Chapter 16. India

Agrawala, SK, 'Law of Nations as Interpreted and Applied by Indian Courts and Legislatures' (1962) 2 *Indian Journal of International Law* 431–78.
Garimella, Sai Ramani, and Sooksripaisarnkit, Poomintr, 'Jurisdiction under the Hague Convention on Choice of Court Agreements: A Critique' (2017) 57(3–4) *Indian Journal of International Law* 309–36.
'Indian Economy: About Indian Economy Growth Rate & Statistics', *Indian Brand Equity Foundation*, www.ibef.org/economy/indian-economy-overview, January 2019.
Jois, Rama, *Legal and Constitutional History of India* (Bombay, NM Tripathi, 1985).
Michaels, Ralf, 'Jurisdiction, Foundations' in Jürgen Basedow, Giesela Rühl, Franco Ferrari and Pedro de Miguel Asensio (eds), *Encyclopaedia of Private International Law* (Cheltenham, Edward Elgar Publishing, 2017) 1043–51.
Naseh, Wali Mohammed, 'Conflict of Laws – State Practice in Afghanistan' in Sai Ramani Garimella and Stellina Jolly (eds), *Private International Law: South Asian States' Practice* (Singapore, Springer, 2017) 63–88.
Patel, Bimalkumar Natvarlal, 'The State Practice of India and The Development of International Law: Selected Areas' (PhD thesis, Leiden University, 2015).
'Princely States', *GlobalSecurity.org*, www.globalsecurity.org/military/world/india/princely-states.htm, 2018.

Chapter 17. Conclusion

Elbalti, Béligh, 'Spontaneous Harmonization and the Liberalization of the Recognition and Enforcement of Foreign Judgments' (2014) 16 *Japanese Yearbook of Private International Law* 264–88.
Isidro, Marta Requejo, 'International Commercial Courts in the Litigation Market' (2019) MPILux Research Paper Series 2019 (2), www.mpi.lu/research/woking-paper-series/2019/wp-2019-2/.
Memorandum of Guidance on Recognition and Enforcement of Money Judgments in Commercial Cases, www.supremecourt.gov.sg/docs/default-source/default-document-library/spc-mog-english-version---signed.pdf.
Nanning Statement of the 2nd China–ASEAN Justice Forum adopted on 8 June 2017, Article VII.
Reyes, Anselmo, 'Recognition and Enforcement of Interlocutory and Final Judgments of the Singapore International Commercial Court' (2015) 2(2) *Journal of International and Comparative Law* 337–58.
—— *The Practice of International Commercial Arbitration: A Handbook for Hong Kong Arbitrators* (Oxon, Informa Law from Routledge, 2017).
Reyes, Anselmo, and Gu, Weixia, *The Developing World of Arbitration: A Comparative Study of Arbitration Reform in the Asia Pacific* (Oxford, Hart Publishing, 2018).
Spigelman, James, 'The Hague Choice of Court Convention and International Commercial Litigation' (2009) 83(6) *Australian Law Journal* 386–94.
Teitz, Louise Ellen, 'The Hague Choice of Court Convention: Validating Party Autonomy and Providing an Alternative to Arbitration' (2005) 53(3) *American Journal of Comparative Law* 543–58.
The Permanent Bureau, Hague Conference on Private International Law, 'Note on "common courts" in Article 22 of the February 2017 Draft Convention', Document No 9 of 2017, *Hague Conference on Private International Law*, 13–17 November 2017, assets.hcch.net/docs/c168c7c4-e790-4551-993e-fe791ee0a1a6.pdf.
Walker, Janet, 'Specialised International Courts: Keeping Arbitration on Top of Its Game' (2019) 85(1) *Arbitration* 2.

INDEX

Aden
India and 296
Afghanistan
India and 296
Algeria
Vietnam and 184
anti-suit injunction
generally 19
Hong Kong 64, 82
India 303
Malaysia 177
Singapore 146–147, 156
South Korea 133
Thailand 265
arbitration/arbitral awards
comity principle 27–28
Draft Hague Convention 2018 11
due process and 324
generally 27, 29, 325–326
Geneva Convention 101
Hague Convention 1971 6
Hague Convention 2005 10
Hong Kong 76
Indonesia 249, 254
Japan 100, 101
New York Convention 1958 24, 27, 310, 325
Philippines 226, 227
South Korea 121n
Thailand 260
Argentina
Japan and 101
South Korea and 126, 130–131
Association of Southeast Asian Nations (ASEAN)
Asian Principles of Private International Law (APPIL) 263
Comprehensive Investment Agreement (ACIA) 241
Economic Community (AEC) 315
Indonesia 255, 256
Nanning Statement 27, 27n, 45–46, 220, 316, 318, 323–324
People's Republic of China and 45–46
Philippines 240–241
Thailand 262, 263, 269
Astana International Financial Centre Court (AIFC Court) 310, 314
***audi alteram partem* principle** 280
Australia
Hong Kong and 59–64, 79–80
Japan and 107
Malaysia and 169
Singapore and 143, 160
South Korea and 127
Sri Lanka and 276
Taiwan and 92, 93
Austria
Hong Kong and 59–64, 79–80
South Korea and 127
Azerbaijan
India and 296

Bahrain
India and 296
Bangladesh
India and 296
bankruptcy proceedings
Hong Kong 73–74
India 306
Malaysia 167, 172, 175
South Korea 122, 130
Belarus
Vietnam and 182, 184
Belgium
Hong Kong and 59–64, 79–80
Japan and 108
Belt and Road Initiative (BRI)
ASEAN 45
generally 16, 32
Hague Convention 2005 47
purpose 32
reciprocity principle 43, 45
Bermuda
Hong Kong and 59–64, 79–80
Berne Convention 193
bilateral agreements/treaties
Cambodia-Vietnam Treaty 201, 203–204, 206, 207
generally 16
Hong Kong 52, 53, 54, 84
India 296–298
Japan 101
People's Republic of China 31, 36, 38–41

South Korea 121
Taiwan 86–87
Thailand 262–263
Vietnam 179, 180, 181, 182, 183–188, 193, 194, 196, 201, 203–204, 206, 207
Brunei Darussalam
Hong Kong and 59–64, 79–80
Malaysia and 169
Singapore and 143
Bulgaria
India and 296
Japan, bilateral treaty 101
Vietnam and 184

Cambodia
background, generally 201–203
Civil Code 202
civil disputes 202
Civil Procedure Code 202, 204–206, 207, 317
commercial disputes 202–203
due process 205
final and binding, judgment must be 204–206
freedom of contract 202, 205
future prospects and reforms 207
immovable property 206
indirect jurisdiction 317
interlocutory judgments 206
judicial system 202–203
legal system 201–202
monetary judgments 206
morals, judgment violating 205, 207
non-monetary judgments 206
private international law 204
public order and good customs, violation 202, 203, 205, 207
reciprocity principle 205, 317
recognition and enforcement 203–206
requirements to be met 203–207
security interests 206
separation of powers 202
Singapore and 317
test for rudimentary system 317, 322
vessels 206
Vietnam and 184, 201, 203–204, 206, 207
Canada
Taiwan and 92
capacity of party
Hague Convention 2005 10
cause of action estoppel
Singapore 148
charging order
Hong Kong 72–73
China *see* **People's Republic of China**
class actions
Hong Kong 78
Japan 114–115
comity principle
generally 27–28, 30, 322
Hong Kong 76, 80
India 238, 294, 303
Malaysia 164, 166, 171, 173, 178
People's Republic of China 48
Philippines 27, 223, 224–225, 226–227, 234, 235, 238, 318–319
Singapore 155, 160
Taiwan 93
commercial matters
generally 3–4, 15, 16–17, 29
common law system
action brought in originating state 28–30
direct jurisdiction over third party 21, 23
fair procedure, principle of 63
final injunctions 17–18
Hong Kong 51, 52, 53, 63, 66–71, 79, 80, 84
Malaysia 163, 165, 173–174
mirror principle 22n
Philippines 224
res judicata 28–29, 51, 52, 54–55, 63, 64, 66–71, 148–149
Singapore 141, 142, 143, 146, 147–158, 159–160, 314
specific performance 17–18
Sri Lanka 272, 277–281
competition law
class actions 78
generally 18
Hong Kong 78
India 295, 305
Japan 115
Philippines 227, 240
South Korea 136–137
Vietnam 195
Convention Relating to the Status of Refugees
Japan 100–101
Convention on Supplementary Compensation for Nuclear Damage
Japan 101
costs
Hong Kong 57, 70, 71
India 303
Japan 104, 110, 113
Malaysia 177
Singapore 143
Sri Lanka 278, 279, 281
Cuba
Vietnam and 184
Czech Republic
Vietnam and 184

damages
generally 18, 20
Hong Kong 64, 73, 77–78, 82–83
India 293, 303
Japan 102, 110–111, 114, 115
Malaysia 166
People's Republic of China 46, 48
Philippines 228, 229, 233–234, 240
Singapore 146, 153
South Korea 129, 130, 132, 137
Taiwan 88, 90, 94
default judgment
Hague Convention 1971 7
Hague Convention 2005 11
Hong Kong 63, 67, 69
Japan 104
Malaysia 169
Myanmar 212n, 217
Singapore 150
Taiwan 85, 87, 88–89
Vietnam 189
digital technology
India 307
Indonesia 255–256
Japan 117
Malaysia 177
South Korea 139–140
Sri Lanka 288
Vietnam 200
Draft Hague Convention 2018
commercial matters 15, 16–17
common elements with other Hague Conventions 14–15
decision no longer subject to review 23
earlier decision on same facts 14
excluded matters 11, 15, 17–18
fair opportunity to present case 23
final and conclusive, judgment must be 15
fraud, judgments obtained by 14, 15, 23
generally 5–6, 6n, 11–18, 325
grounds of indirect jurisdiction 12–14, 15, 19–20, 22
grounds for refusal of recognition or enforcement 13–14, 15, 23
Hong Kong 51, 53, 81, 83–84
immovable property 12, 13, 20, 21
in rem actions 12
India 306
indirect jurisdiction 15, 19, 23
Indonesia 252
Japan 116, 117
lack of due process 14, 15, 23
Malaysia 177
Myanmar 221
notification of defendant 13–14
partial recognition or enforcement 14, 15
People's Republic of China 49
public policy, judgments incompatible with 14, 15, 20, 23
ratification or accession 15
recognition and enforcement, generally 11–12
res judicata 14, 15, 23
residence/place of business 12, 13, 15, 19–20
Singapore 161
South Korea 138, 140
due process
arbitration/arbitral awards 324
Cambodia 205
denial of 30
generally 26, 27, 28, 30, 323, 324, 325
grounds for refusal, lack of 23–25
Hague Conventions 6, 14, 15, 23
Hong Kong 70
India 297
Indonesia 253, 255
Myanmar 217
People's Republic of China 39, 40
Philippines 232
South Korea 128
Taiwan 89, 93, 313
Thailand 263, 266, 267–268, 320
Vietnam 187, 188, 190–191

earlier decision on same facts
Draft Hague Convention 2018 14
Hague Convention 1971 6, 25–26
Hague Convention 2005 10
El Salvador
Japan and 101
employment contract
Hague Convention 2005 9
enforcement
economic benefits 4
recognition distinguished 2–3, 42, 54
enforcing court
generally 6n
enforcing state
proceedings in 30
English cases
Hong Kong 52, 79, 80
Singapore 141
environmental wrong
see also pollution
class actions 114
generally 18
Hong Kong 64, 77–78
India 295, 305
international conventions 64, 77–78, 101
Japan 101, 102–103, 114–115
South Korea 136

Sri Lanka 282–283
Vietnam 194–195

fair opportunity to present case
Hague Conventions 6, 23
Federation of Malaya
Sri Lanka and 276
***fieri facias*, writ of**
Hong Kong 71–72
Fiji
India and 296
final and conclusive, judgment must be
generally 17–19, 29
Hague Conventions 15
France
Hong Kong reciprocal enforcement 59–64, 79–80
India and 296
People's Republic of China and 38, 41
South Korea and 127
Taiwan and 92
Vietnam and 184
fraud, judgment obtained by
Draft Hague Convention 2018 14, 15, 23
generally 23, 24, 30
Hague Convention 1971 6, 15, 23
Hague Convention 2005 10, 15, 23
Hong Kong 58, 63, 70
India 299, 300
Japan 102, 111
Malaysia 167, 174
Myanmar 211, 217
Philippines 226, 228, 230, 232, 233
Singapore 142, 145, 146, 153–155
South Korea 128
Sri Lanka 276, 280
freezing order
see also Mareva injunction
India 303–304

garnishee order
Hong Kong 72
garnishment
South Korea 134
Geneva Convention 1927
Japan 101
Germany
Chinese judgments 45–46
Hong Kong and 59–64, 79–80
Japan and 107
South Korea and 126
globalisation
conflict of law rules and 4, 27, 260–261, 271

Hague Conference on Private International Law
Draft Convention *see* Draft Hague Convention 2018
generally 3, 5–6
Hong Kong 51, 53, 79, 81
India 295, 306, 308
Judgements Project *see* Hague Judgments Project
Malaysia 165–166
membership 5
Philippines 225
South Korea 120–121
Sri Lanka 273, 284–286
Hague Convention 1971
commercial matters 15, 16–17
common elements with other Hague Conventions 14–15
competency of rendering court 6, 7–8
decision no longer subject to review 6, 7, 23
default judgments 7
direct jurisdiction 7
domicile or habitual residence/place of business 8–9, 13, 15, 19–20
earlier decision on same facts 6, 25–26
excluded matters 6, 15, 17–18
fair opportunity to present case 6, 23
final and conclusive, judgment must be 15
fraud, judgments obtained by 6, 15, 23
generally 6–9, 14–18, 19, 20, 22, 23, 23n, 25
grounds for refusal of recognition or enforcement 6, 15, 23, 25–26
immovable property 13, 20, 21
indirect jurisdiction 7–8, 13, 15, 19–20, 23
Japan 97
lack of due process 6, 15, 23
partial recognition or enforcement 8, 15
parties to 8, 16
procedures for recognition and enforcement 8
public policy, judgments incompatible with 6, 15, 20, 23
ratification or accession 15
recognition or enforcement refused 6
requirements to be met for recognition or enforcement 6–7, 19–20
Supplementary Agreements between contracting states 8–9, 16
Supplementary Protocol 8–9, 20
Vietnam 195–197, 198, 199
writ of execution 6
Hague Convention 2005
Belt and Road Initiative 47
capacity of party 10
commercial matters 15, 16–17
common elements with other Hague Conventions 14–15
court of neutral third-party state chosen 11
decision no longer subject to review 23
default judgments 11
earlier decision on same facts 10

excluded matters 9–10, 15, 17–18
exclusive choice of court agreement, meaning 9
fair opportunity to present case 6, 23
final and conclusive, judgment must be 15
fraud, judgments obtained by 10, 15, 23
generally 5, 9–11, 14–18, 325
grounds for refusal of recognition or enforcement 10–11, 15, 20, 23
Hong Kong 51, 53, 80–81, 83–84
immovable property 9, 20, 21
indirect jurisdiction 15, 19–20, 23, 323
Indonesia 252, 254–256, 257
intellectual property rights 46
Japan 97
judgments of, recognition 9
jurisdiction of designated court 10
jurisdiction of rendering court 20–21
lack of due process 23
Malaysia 166, 176–177
null and void agreements 10
partial recognition or enforcement 11, 15
parties to 9, 16, 47, 144, 311
People's Republic of China 9, 31, 40, 41, 46, 47, 48, 49–50, 81, 311
Philippines 241, 311
public policy, judgments incompatible with 10, 15, 20, 23
ratification or accession 15
reciprocity principle 47
requirements to be met for recognition or enforcement 10–11, 19–20
residence/place of business 15, 19–20
Singapore 142, 144–147, 161
South Korea 137–138
Thailand 269
United Kingdom 144n
Vietnam 185, 195–197, 199
Hague Convention Abolishing the Requirement of Legalisation for Foreign Public Documents 1961 100, 120–121, 225
Hague Convention on Civil Aspects of International Child Abduction 1980 261, 285–286
Japan 100
South Korea 121
Sri Lanka 285–286
Hague Convention on Civil Procedure 1954 100, 109
Hague Convention on the Conflicts of Laws Relating to the Form of Testamentary Dispositions 1961 100
Hague Convention on the Law Applicable to Maintenance Obligations 1973 100
Hague Convention on the Law Applicable to Maintenance Obligations Towards Children 1956 100
Hague Convention on Protection of Children and Co-operation in Respect of Intercountry Adoption 1993 261, 285
Hague Convention for the Suppression of Unlawful Seizure of Aircraft 1970 284
Hague Evidence Abroad Convention 1970
South Korea 121
Sri Lanka 285
Hague Judgments Project
see also Hague Conference on Private International Law
Draft Convention *see* Draft Hague Convention 2018
generally 5–6, 324–325
Hong Kong 81
India 308
Malaysia 177
People's Republic of China 49
Singapore 161
Thailand 263
Hague Principles on Choice of Law in International Commercial Contracts 2015 5n
India 308
Hague Service Abroad Convention 1965
Japan 100, 109
People's Republic of China 41
South Korea 121, 131
Sri Lanka 285
Hague Statute 5n
Hong Kong
anti-suit injunctions 64, 82
Application of English Law Ordinance 52–53
arbitration 76
background, generally 51–52
bankruptcy procedure 73–74
Basic Law 52, 53
bilateral agreements 51, 53, 54, 84
Brunei Darussalam and 59–64, 79–80
case law 52, 64, 79, 80
charging orders 72–73
civil and commercial judgments 53–54
class actions 78
comity principle 76, 80
Commercial List 54
committal proceedings 75
common law system 51, 52, 53, 63, 66–71, 79, 80, 84
competition law, breach of 78
conflict of law rules 65
contempt of court 75
costs 57, 70, 71
Crown immunity 67

damages 64, 73, 77–78, 82–83
default judgments 63, 67, 69
deficiencies of judicial regime 79–81
diplomatic immunity 67
Draft Hague Convention 2018 53, 81, 83–84
due process 70
enforcement 54–55, 62–64, 71–75, 78–79
English case law 52, 79, 80
environmental wrongs 64, 77–78
execution 71–75
fair procedure, principle of 63, 65, 67, 78–79
fieri facias, writ of 71–72
final and conclusive, judgment must be 55, 56, 57, 62, 63, 65, 67–70, 79
Foreign Judgments (Reciprocal Enforcement) Ordinance (Cap 319) 59–64, 77–78, 79–80, 81, 83, 312
Foreign Judgments (Restriction on Recognition and Enforcement) Ordinance (Cap 46) 63
fraud, judgments obtained by 58, 63, 70
garnishee order 72
grounds for refusal of recognition or enforcement 63–64, 66–70
Hague Conference 51, 53, 79, 81
Hague Convention 2005 53, 80–81, 83–84
Hague Judgments Project 81
identification of debtor's assets 74–75
immovable property 76–77
immunity 67
impeachable on other grounds 70
in personam actions 66
in rem actions 66
India and 59–64, 79–80, 296, 297
indirect jurisdiction 59, 61–62, 63, 65, 66–67
insolvency proceedings 73–74
intellectual property rights 75–76
interest 57, 62, 71, 72–73
interlocutory judgments 70
international conventions 64–65, 67, 77–78
issue estoppel 55, 66
Japan and 107
judgments incapable of enforcement 54
judicial system 53, 78–81
liner conferences 64–65, 78
Macau and 51, 59
mainland China and 37, 53, 55–59, 60, 67–70, 79, 81–83
Mainland Judgments (Reciprocal Enforcement) Ordinance (Cap 597) 55–59, 79, 81–83
Malaysia, reciprocal enforcement 59–64, 79–80, 168–169
Merchant Shipping (Liner Conferences) Ordinance (Cap 482) 64–65, 78
Moçambique rule 75, 76–77
notice of proceedings 63
Nuclear Material (Liability for Carriage) Ordinance (Cap 479) 78
'One Country, Two Systems' principle 52, 79
oral examination of debtor 74
order *nisi* 72
partial registration 57
private international law 52, 79
procedures and timing for enforcement 71–75
prohibition order 75
proposed reforms 81–84
'protest' (review/trial supervision) system in People's Republic of China 67–70
receiver, appointment 73
reciprocity principle 59–64, 79–80, 81
recognition 54–55, 66–67, 78–79
registration of eligible judgments 51, 56–57, 58, 62, 63
requirements to be met 56–57, 58, 62, 67, 75
res judicata 54–55, 64, 66, 70
separation of powers 52, 78
sequestration, writ of 75
service of documents 58
setting aside registration 58, 63
Singapore and 59–64, 79–80, 143, 312
South Korea and 126
sovereign immunity 67, 67n
special administrative region of China 51, 52
Sri Lanka and 59–64, 79–80, 276
statutory regime 51, 54–65, 71
stop notice 74–75
stop order 74–75
submission 61–62, 66, 76
summary judgment procedure 65–66
Taiwan and 51, 59, 91
test for rudimentary system 312, 322
time limit for registration application 57
unrecognised jurisdictions 59
voluntary compliance 61, 71
winding up procedure 73–74

human rights, international law
conflict of law rules 260–261, 262
fair trial, right to 284

Hungary
Japan and 101
Vietnam and 184

ICSID Convention
Indonesia 252, 257
Japan 101

immovable property
Cambodia 206
Draft Hague Convention 2018 12, 13, 20, 21
generally 18, 29
Hague Convention 1971 13, 20, 21

Hague Convention 2005 9, 20, 21
Hong Kong 76–77
India 301, 304–305
Indonesia 248, 249
Japan 114, 116
Myanmar 215–216
People's Republic of China 39
Philippines 227, 240
South Korea 134, 135–136
Sri Lanka 281
Vietnam 194
***in personam* actions**
Hong Kong 66
India 300–301, 305
Malaysia 167
Singapore 147–158, 159
Sri Lanka 277–278
***in rem* actions**
Draft Hague Convention 2018 12
Hague Convention 2005 9
Hong Kong 66
India 305
Malaysia 167
Singapore 158–159
India
anti-suit injunctions 303
Anton Piller orders 304
application for enforcement 295
attachment before judgment 304
attachment orders 306
background, generally 291–294
bankruptcy proceedings 306
bilateral treaties 296–298, 300
BRICS 292
case law 300, 302
civil matters 295
Code of Civil Procedure (CPC) 294, 295, 299, 303
comity principle 238, 294, 303
commercial disputes 295
competency of rendering court 299, 300, 301–302, 308
Competition Act 305
competition law 295, 305
conclusive, judgment must be 299–300, 308
Constitution 294
costs 303
damages 293, 303
digital technology 307
domicile 291, 294
due process 297
enforcement 294–295, 298–299, 305–306
English law, influence 291, 292–294, 300, 303
environmental law 295, 305
equity, justice and good conscience doctrine 294, 300
ex parte decrees 293, 299, 306–307
fraud, judgments obtained by 299, 300
freezing orders 303–304
future prospects and reforms 306–308
G20 292
Hague Conference 295, 306, 308
Hong Kong and 59–64, 79–80, 296, 297
immovable property 301, 304–305
in personam actions 300–301, 305
in rem actions 305
indirect jurisdiction 283, 293, 294, 300–302
insolvency law 295
intellectual property rights 295, 304
interest 303
interlocutory judgments 303–304
international treaties 295–296
John Doe orders 304
judgments founded on breach of law in India 299
judicial system 294–295
Malaysia and 169, 296
Mareva injunctions 304
natural justice, judgments contrary to 299–300, 307
private international law 291, 292–294
public policy, judgments contrary to 300
reciprocity principle 295, 296–299, 305, 307
recognition 298–299
requirements to be met 299–300
res judicata 298, 304
residence 291, 294, 301, 307
SAARC 292
severability, doctrine of 302–303
Singapore and 143, 296, 321
submission 301, 308, 321
test for rudimentary system 321, 322
TRIPS agreement 304
Union Carbide gas-leak 305
World Trade Organization 292
indirect (international) jurisdiction
Cambodia 317
characteristic link 267
Draft Hague Convention 2018 12–13, 15, 19, 22, 23
future reforms 323
generally 7–8, 19–23, 30
grounds for 19–23, 29
Hague Convention 1971 7–8, 13, 15, 19–20, 23
Hague Convention 2005 15, 19–20, 23, 323
Hong Kong 59, 61–62, 63, 65, 66–67
India 283, 293, 294, 300–302
Japan 99, 100–101, 103, 105–107, 114, 116, 117
jurisdiction gap problem 22, 25

lack of, grounds for refusal 23–25, 30
mirror principle 22–23, 22n, 30, 267, 311, 316, 320, 323
Myanmar 211–212, 213, 214–216, 221
People's Republic of China 39–40, 311
Singapore 145, 150–152, 159–160
South Korea 120, 122, 123–125, 134–137
Sri Lanka 283–285
Taiwan 87–88
Thailand 266–267, 320
Vietnam 186, 316–317

Indonesia
Aceh province, *Qanun* 245
acquired (vested) rights doctrine 244
adat (customary) law 245, 246, 247, 250
adoption, inter-country 249
Algemene Bepalingen van Wetgeving voor Nederlandsch Indie (AB) 246, 248, 249
appeal, judgments subject to 251
arbitral awards 249, 254
Arbitration Act 250
ASEAN 255, 256
authentic deeds, judgments accepted as 244, 251, 253, 320
background, generally 245–247
Basic Agrarian Act 247, 248–249, 250
Burgerlijk Wetboek voor Nederlandsch-Indie (BW) 244
case law 247–248
Citizenship Act 247
Civil Code 250
civil law tradition 248
civil matters 250, 252
civil registry 249
Commercial Code 243, 250
commercial matters 250, 252
Constitution 247, 248, 254
constitutive judgments 244, 249
Consumer Protection Act 250
corruption and bribery 255, 257
declaratory judgments 244, 249
doctrines 248, 249
due process 253, 255
Dutch law 245, 246–247, 248, 252–253
enforcement 251–252
evidence, judgments accepted as 244, 249, 251, 253, 320
future prospects and reforms 252–257
Hague Convention 2005 252, 254–256, 257
ICSID Convention 252, 257
immovable property 248, 249
intellectual property rights 250
international treaties and conventions 253–255
Investment Act 247
Islamic law 245, 250, 252
judicial system 245, 246, 255–256
Labour Act 250
legal system 245
maritime general average, foreign judgments 251, 319
Marriage Act 247, 249
New York Convention 1958 248, 252, 254, 257
non-enforcement of foreign judgments 243–245, 249, 251, 257, 319
ordre public 248
private international law 246–249
public law 250
public policy, judgments contrary to 248, 249
recognition of foreign judgments 244–245, 249–250, 257, 319
Reglement op de Burgerlijke Rechtsvordering (Rv) 243, 249, 251, 255–256, 257, 319–320
renvoi 248
sovereignty, principle of 243
statute law 247, 248, 250
test for rudimentary system 319–320, 322
yurisprudensi tetap 248

insolvency proceedings
Draft Hague Convention 2018 11
Hague Convention 2005 9
Hong Kong 73–74
India 295
Judicial Insolvency Network (JIN) 177
Philippines 227

intellectual property rights
Berne Convention 193
generally 18
Hague Convention 2005 10, 46
Hong Kong 75–76
India 295, 304
Indonesia 250
Japan 113–114
Myanmar 216
Paris Convention 193, 239
People's Republic of China 46
Philippines 224–225, 227, 239–240
South Korea 134–135
Sri Lanka 281–282
TRIPS agreement 193, 282, 304
Vietnam 193–194

interest
Hong Kong 57, 62, 71, 72–73
India 303
Singapore 153
South Korea 129

interlocutory judgments
Cambodia 206
generally 19
Hague Conventions 15

Hong Kong 70
India 303–304
Japan 112
Malaysia 169, 174
Myanmar 212
Philippines 238
Singapore 150
South Korea 132–133
Vietnam 192
International Covenant on Civil and Political Rights (ICCPR) 263
international jurisdiction *see* **indirect jurisdiction**
Israel
Hong Kong and 59–64, 79–80
People's Republic of China and 45–46
issue estoppel
generally 25n
Hong Kong 55
Malaysia 172
Singapore 148
Italy
Hong Kong and 59–64, 79–80

Japan
Act on General Rules for Application of Laws (AGR) 98–99, 100
Act on the Law Applicable to the Form of Wills 100
Act on the Law Applicable to the Obligation of Support 100
admissions 104
arbitral awards 100, 101
authentic instruments 104
background, generally 97–98
bilateral treaties 101, 102
case law 104, 106
Check Act 100
choice of law 100
civil and commercial matters 99, 101–102
Civil Execution Act (CEA) 97, 99
class actions 114–115
Code of Civil Procedure (CCP) 97, 99, 100, 103, 313
competition law 115
Constitution 97–98
Convention Relating to the Status of Refugees 100–101
Convention on Supplementary Compensation for Nuclear Damage 101, 102–103
costs 104, 110, 113
damages 102, 110–111, 114, 115
default judgments 104
Domestic Relations Case Procedure Act 100
enforcement 99, 100, 103, 112–113
environmental wrongs 101, 102–103, 114–115
fair opportunity to present case 102
fairness of court procedures 111
final and binding, judgment must be 11, 103–105, 117
fraud, judgments obtained by 102, 111
future prospects and reforms 116–117
Geneva Convention 1927 101
Hague Conventions 97, 100, 103, 109, 116, 117
Hong Kong and 107
Hōrei 33, 98–99
ICSID Convention 101
immovable property 114, 116
indirect jurisdiction 99, 100–101, 103, 105–107, 114, 116, 117
injunctions 104
intellectual property rights 113–114
interlocutory judgments 112
international conventions 100–101, 102–103, 105
international jurisdiction 100
jori 99, 105–107, 116
judgment, meaning 104, 116–117
judicial settlements 104
judicial system 101
legal system 98
Memorandums of Understanding 117
mirror-image approach 105–106, 311
monetary judgments 104, 113
Montreal Convention 101
morals, judgments contrary to 110–112, 117
Negotiable Instrument Act 100
New York Convention 1958 101
non-monetary judgments 104, 113
non-recognition of judgment, claim for 111–112
personal status and family matters 99
Personal Status Litigation Act 100
People's Republic of China and 44, 101, 108, 116
precedent, role 98
private international law 98–101
public policy, judgments contrary to 110–112, 117
re-litigation 112
reasonable notice 102
reciprocity principle 44, 103, 107–108, 116, 117, 313
recognition 99, 100, 103–112
requirements to be met 97, 103–113, 117
res judicata 103, 115
révision au fond 103, 112, 113
saimu meigi 112
service of documents 103, 108–110, 111, 117
shikko hanketsu 112
Singapore and 107, 313
South Korea and 107, 113–114, 126, 130, 134–135
sovereignty, principle of 117

submission 106, 313
summary judgments 104
Taiwan and 92
test for rudimentary system 313, 322
Vietnam and 199
voluntary response to claim 109
waiver of claims 104
Warsaw Convention 100
jurisdiction gap problem 22, 25

Kazakhstan
AIFC Court 310, 314
Vietnam and 185
India and 296

land *see* **immovable property**
Laos
China-Laos Treaty 39
Vietnam and 185
lex loci delicti
South Korea 136
liner conferences
Hong Kong 64–65, 78
United Nations Convention on a Code of Conduct for 64–65

Macau
Hong Kong and 51, 59, 91
PRC jurisprudence and 37
Malaysia
anti-suit injunctions 177
appeal, foreign judgments subject to 169
background, generally 163–166
bankruptcy proceedings 167, 172, 175
Brunei Darussalam and 169
case law 165
choice of law 176–177
civil and commercial judgments 163, 165
Civil Law Act 164
comity principle 164, 166, 171, 173, 178
common law system 163, 165, 173–174
Constitution 165
costs 177
damages 166
default judgments 169
defences to actions on foreign judgments 163
employment, proceedings as to 175–176
enforcement 165, 173–174
English law, influence 164
ex parte decrees 168
final and conclusive, judgment must be 166, 169
fraud, judgments obtained by 167, 174
future prospects and reforms 177–178
gambling debts 171
guardianship of infants 167
Hague Convention 2005 166, 176–177
Hague Judgments Project 177
Hong Kong and 59–64, 79–80, 168–169
in personam actions 167
in rem actions 167
India and 169, 296
interlocutory orders 169, 174
international jurisdiction 166, 169–170, 174
issue estoppel 172
judicial system 164–165
lunacy 167
matrimonial causes 167
merchant shipping, liability for pollution 176
monetary judgments 166
natural justice, judgments contrary to 167, 174
notice 167
obligation theory 166, 173
partial registration 168
private international law 164
probate and administration 167, 175
public policy, judgments contrary to 167, 171, 174
Reciprocal Enforcement of Judgments Act (REJA) 163, 164, 165, 166–173, 177, 178, 314
reciprocity principle 163, 164, 166–173, 177, 178, 314–315
recognition 163, 165, 166–174
registration of foreign judgments 166–168
requirements to be met 166–172, 173
res judicata 173
service of documents 167, 171
setting aside registration 168, 169
Singapore and 143, 169, 314–315
sovereignty, principle of 171
Sri Lanka and 169
stare decisis 165
submission 170, 315
Taiwan, Malaysian judgments recognised by 92
test for rudimentary system 314–315, 322
time limit for applications 167, 172
unsatisfied, judgment must be 166, 168
winding-up petitions 167, 172
writ of summons 174
***Mareva* injunction**
India 304
Malaysia 174
South Korea 133
matrimonial causes
Hague Convention 2005 9
Malaysia 167
Philippines 224
South Korea 129–130, 132n
Taiwan 92, 93, 94
Vietnam 183, 193, 197–198

Mauritius
Sri Lanka and 276
Memorandums of Guidance (MOGs)
generally 16–17, 160, 177, 311, 314, 322, 323
Memorandums of Understanding (MOUs)
generally 177, 307
Japan 117
South Korea 139
Thailand 264
mirror principle
generally 22–23, 22n, 30, 267, 323
Japan 105–106, 311
People's Republic of China 311
Taiwan 313
Thailand 267, 320
Vietnam 316–317
mistake of law or fact
Philippines 226, 228, 230, 233–238, 319
***Moçambique* rule**
Hong Kong 75, 76–77
Myanmar 216
monetary judgments
generally 17
rudimentary system, suggested 309
Mongolia
Vietnam and 185
India and 296
Montreal Convention
Japan 101
Myanmar
background, generally 209–210
case law 318
Civil Procedure Code (CPC) 210, 211–218, 219–220, 221, 318
commercial disputes 210–211
competency of rendering court 211, 213, 214–215, 216, 318
Constitution 210
default judgments 212n, 217
due process 217
enforcement 210, 219–221
English law, influence 210, 219
final and conclusive, judgment must be 212
foreign court, definition 211
fraud, judgments obtained by 211, 217
future prospects 221
immovable property 215–216
indirect jurisdiction 211–212, 213, 214–216, 221
injunctions 219
intellectual property rights 216
interlocutory judgments 212
international law, judgments must conform with 217
judicial system 209, 210
Moçambique rule 216
monetary judgments 218–219
natural justice, proceedings opposed to 211, 212, 217
Order XIII, Rules of Procedure 213n
Order XV, Rules of Procedure 212–214, 218–219, 220–221, 318
public policy, judgments contrary to 212, 216–218
reciprocity principle 220, 318
recognition 210, 211–219
res judicata 210, 212n
Singapore and 318
specific performance 219
summary judgments 213–214
test for rudimentary system 318, 322
United Kingdom judgments 219–220, 219n, 221

Nanning Statement 27, 27n, 45–46, 220, 316, 318, 323–324
natural justice, breach
India 299–300, 307
Malaysia 167, 174
Myanmar 211, 212, 217
Singapore 145, 153, 156–157
Sri Lanka 280, 287
Netherlands
Hong Kong reciprocal enforcement 59–64, 79–80
New York Convention 1958
generally 24, 47, 91, 310, 325
Indonesia 248, 252, 254, 257
Japan 101
Vietnam 182, 200
New Zealand
Chinese judgments 45–46
Hong Kong reciprocal enforcement 59–64, 79–80
India and 296
Malaysia and 169
Singapore and 143
Sri Lanka and 276
Taiwan, New Zealand judgments recognised by 92
non-contractual obligation
generally 29
non-monetary judgments
generally 17, 18
North Korea
Vietnam and 185
notice of proceedings
sufficient 23, 30, 63
nuclear damage
international conventions 9, 11, 64, 78, 101, 102–103

obligation theory
Malaysia 166, 173
Philippines 223, 238
Singapore 147–148, 149, 150, 157–158, 159–160, 160n, 314
oil pollution
international conventions 64, 77–78, 101, 102–103, 176, 261
Oman
India and 296
order *nisi*
Hong Kong 72, 73
originating court
generally 6n
re-hearing in 30
originating state
action brought in 28–30

Pakistan
Japan, bilateral treaty 101
Singapore and 143
Papua New Guinea
India and 296
Singapore and 143
Paris Convention for the Protection of Industrial Property 193, 239
partial recognition or enforcement
Draft Hague Convention 2018 14, 15
generally 30, 324
Hague Convention 1971 8, 15
Hague Convention 2005 11, 15
People's Republic of China (PRC)
Anti-Monopoly Law 2008 37
applicable law rules 34
application for recognition and enforcement 35
ASEAN and 45–46
background, generally 32–34
Belt and Road Initiative 16, 32, 43, 45, 47
bilateral treaties 31, 36, 38–41
China International Centre Court (ICCC) 310
Civil Aviation Law 1995 34
Civil Code 37
civil law system 31
civil matters 37
Civil Procedure Law (CPL) 2012 35–36, 42, 44, 49, 312
commercial matters 37
common elements (grounds of refusal) 39–41
Company Law 37
competence clause 39
Conflict of Laws Code 2010 34–35
copyright 46
court system 36–37
damages 46, 48
de facto reciprocity 41, 43–45
de jure reciprocity 41, 45–46
development of private international law 32–36
domestic law, application of 41
Draft Hague Convention 2018 49
due process 39, 40
economic development 31, 32, 34, 47, 49
enforcement 42
exclusive jurisdiction of Chinese courts 39
finality of judgment 39, 40
foreign court, enforcement application by 35
foreign court, enforcement application to 35–36
foreign element, what constitutes case with 36–37
General Principles of Civil Law (GPCL) 33–34
Hague Convention 2005 9, 31, 40, 41, 46, 47, 48, 49–50, 81, 311
Hague Judgments Project 49
Hague Service Abroad Convention 41
Hong Kong and 51, 52, 53, 55–59, 67–70, 79, 81–83
immovable property 39
indirect jurisdiction 39–40, 311
intellectual property rights 46
Japan and 44, 101, 108, 116
Judicial Interpretation 2012 34–35
Judicial Interpretation 2015 35–36, 42
jurisdiction of rendering court 39–40
Maritime Law 1992 34
mirror principle 311
Negotiable Instruments Law 1995 34
port operations 39
previous decisions 37
proposed Model Law 48
proposed reforms 48–49
protectionism 35
'protest' (review/trial supervision) system 67–70
public policy exception 37, 39, 40, 46
reciprocity principle 31, 39, 41–46, 47, 48–49, 50
recognition 42
refusal to recognise and enforce judgment 36, 40
requirements to be met 39–41, 44, 49
res judicata 42, 43
Securities Law 37
service of documents 39, 40–41
Singapore and 143, 311–312
South Korea and 126, 127
sovereignty-oriented approach 35, 39, 41, 42
succession and inheritance disputes 39
Taiwan and 37, 91
test for rudimentary system 311–312, 322
time limit for the enforcement application 36
Vietnam and 39, 182, 184, 194, 199
World Trade Organization 34
Peru
Japan, bilateral treaty 101
Philippines
admiralty and maritime disputes 227

anti-trust matters 227, 240
arbitral awards 226, 227
ASEAN 240–241
background, generally 223–224
case law 223, 226
choice of court 236–237
civil cases 227–228
Civil Code 224, 234, 235–236
Code of Civil Procedure 224, 226, 227
collusion, judgment repelled by 226, 228, 230, 232, 233
comity principle 27, 223, 224–225, 226–227, 234, 235, 238, 318–319
commercial disputes 227
common law system 224
competition law 227, 240
conflict of law rules 224
Constitution 225, 237, 240
damages claims 228, 229, 233–234, 240
dissolution of business partnerships 227
due process 232
enforcement 227–229, 238
ex debito justitiae principle 223, 226–227
ex loci celebrationis 224
ex loci rei sitae 224
existence of foreign judgment 229–230
fairness and justice, known principles of 234, 235
finality of judgment 226, 238–239
financial rehabilitation proceedings 227
fraud, judgments obtained by 226, 228, 230, 232, 233
future prospects and reforms 240–241
Hague Conference 225
Hague Conventions 225, 241, 311
immovable property 227, 240
indirect jurisdiction 319
insolvency proceedings 227
intellectual property rights 224–225, 227, 239–240
interlocutory orders 238
intra-corporate disputes 227
lack of jurisdiction 226, 228, 230–231, 233
matrimonial causes 224
mistake of law or fact 226, 228, 230, 233–238, 319
nationalised industries 240
nationality principle 224
notice to party 226, 228, 230, 231–232, 233
obligation theory 223, 238
Paris Convention 239
personal actions 227–228
public order, public policy and good customs 235–237
real actions 227
reasonable opportunity to be heard 232
reciprocity principle 27, 223, 225–226
recognition 227–229, 238
res judicata 238–239, 319
review, external grounds for 226, 228, 230–232
review, merit-based 233–238, 319
Rules of Civil Procedure 226
securities disputes 227
special proceedings 228
specificity of judgment 226, 238–239
test for rudimentary system 318–319, 322
validity of judgments, presumption 231

Poland
Japan and 101
Vietnam and 185

pollution
see also environmental wrong
international conventions 9, 11, 64, 77–78, 101, 102–103, 176, 261

preliminary questions
Hague Conventions 10, 15

probate and administration
Malaysia 167, 175

prohibition order
Hong Kong 75

protectionism
People's Republic of China 35

public policy, judgment incompatible with
Draft Hague Convention 2018 14, 15, 20, 23
generally 324, 325
grounds for refusal 23–25, 30
Hague Convention 1971 6, 15, 20, 23
Hague Convention 2005 10, 15, 20, 23
international and domestic policies 24–25

reciprocity principle
Cambodia 205, 317
de facto 41, 43–45
de jure 41, 45–46, 48
establishing reciprocity 26–28, 30
future reforms 323–324
Hong Kong 59–64, 79–80, 81
India 295, 296–299, 305, 307
Japan 44, 103, 107–108, 116, 117, 313
Malaysia 163, 164, 166–173, 177, 178, 314–315
Myanmar 220, 318
Nanning Statement 27, 27n, 45–46, 220, 316, 318, 323–324
People's Republic of China 31, 39, 41–46, 47, 48–49, 50
Philippines 27, 223, 225–226
Singapore 143–144, 145, 147–148, 314
South Korea 122, 126–127, 138–139, 314
Sri Lanka 271, 276
Thailand 268
Vietnam 179, 190, 198, 315–316

recognition
automatic 2–3
economic benefits of increased recognition 4
enforcement distinguished 2–3, 42, 54
registration procedure
generally 28
rendering court
generally 6n
Republic of China (ROC) 33
see also People's Republic of China; Taiwan
res judicata
cause of action 25n
generally 2, 28–29
grounds for refusal of recognition or enforcement 15, 23, 25, 30
Hague Conventions 12, 13, 14, 15, 23
Hong Kong 54–55, 64, 66, 70
India 298, 304
issue estoppel 25n
Japan 103, 115
Malaysia 173
Myanmar 210, 212n
narrow and extended applications 55
People's Republic of China 42, 48
Philippines 238–239, 319
Singapore 148–149, 153, 157
South Korea 119, 122, 127, 129–130, 132n
Taiwan 86, 313
Thailand 266, 268
Vietnam 199
residence/place of business 7, 8–9, 12, 13, 15, 19–20, 29
review
generally 6, 7, 23, 24, 30
révision au fond
Japan 103, 112, 113
South Korea 128
Rio Declaration 283
Romania
Japan, bilateral treaty 101
rudimentary system, suggested
comity principle 30
commercial matters 29, 309
due process 30
excluded matters 17–18
final and conclusive, judgment must be 18–19, 29
fraud, judgment obtained by 30
generally 16–17, 29–30, 323–326
grounds for refusal of recognition or enforcement 23–26, 30
immovable property 29
indirect jurisdiction 19–23, 29, 30
jurisdictions tested for 309–323
mirror principle 30
monetary judgments 309
non-contractual obligations 29
notice of proceedings 30
procedure 28–29
public policy, judgments incompatible with 30
reciprocity principle 26–28, 30
res judicata 30
residence/place of business 29
submission to jurisdiction 29
Russian Federation
Vietnam and 185, 194

Samoa
Sri Lanka and 276
separation of powers
Hong Kong 52
service of documents
Hong Kong 58
Japan 103, 108–110, 111, 117
People's Republic of China 39, 40–41
Singapore 152
South Korea 121, 122, 131
Sri Lanka 276
Taiwan 88–89, 93, 94–95
Singapore
anti-suit injunctions 146–147, 156
appeal, judgments subject to 150
Australia and 143
background, generally 141
Brunei Darussalam and 143
Cambodia and 317
cause of action estoppel 148
Choice of Court Agreements Act (CCAA) 142, 144–147, 151, 161
comity principle 155, 160
common law system 141, 142, 143, 146, 147–158, 159–160, 314
costs 143
counter-claim, filing 152
damages, exemplary or punitive 146, 153
default judgments 150
defences to actions on foreign judgments 145–146, 152, 153–159
Draft Hague Convention 2018 161
enforcement 142, 149–150, 152–153
English law, influence 141–142
fair and equitable, allowing enforcement must be 158
final and conclusive, judgment must be 148, 149, 150
foreign penal, revenue or other public law 153–154
forum non conveniens 152
fraud, judgments obtained by 142, 145, 146, 153, 154–155
future prospects and reforms 159–161

Hague Convention 2005 142, 144–147
Hague Judgments Project 161
Hong Kong and 59–64, 79–80, 143, 312
in personam actions 147–158, 159
in rem actions 158–159
India and 143, 296, 321
indirect jurisdiction 145, 150–152, 159–160
interest 153
interlocutory judgments 150
international jurisdiction of foreign court 149, 150–152
issue estoppel 148
Japan and 107, 313
judgment, meaning 145
judgment recognised in Singapore, conflict with 153–154, 157
just and convenient, enforcement in Singapore must be 158
legal system 141–142
Malaysia and 143, 169, 314–315
Memorandums of Guidance 160
merger doctrine not applicable 148–149
monetary judgments 143, 150, 152–153
morals, judgment offensive to 156
Myanmar and 318
natural justice, breach of 145, 153, 156–157
non-court proceedings, agreement to settle by 158
non-monetary judgments 145
obligation theory 147–148, 149, 150, 157–158, 159–160, 160n, 314
Pakistan and 143
People's Republic of China and 143, 311–312
presence/residence, concept of 151, 159–160
private international law 141–142
public policy, judgments contrary to 145, 153, 155–156, 157
re-arguing issue decided by foreign court 148
receiver, appointment of 149
Reciprocal Enforcement of Commonwealth Judgments Act (RECJA) 142, 143–144, 146, 147–159
Reciprocal Enforcement of Foreign Judgments Act (REFJA) 142, 143–144, 146, 147–159
reciprocity principle 143–144, 145, 147–148, 314
recognition 142, 148–152
registration of judgments 142, 143–144, 145, 158
requirements to be met 149–153
res judicata 148–149, 153, 157
service, improper 152
set-off claim 152
severance, doctrine of 145, 153n
Singapore International Commercial Court (SICC) 141, 142, 151, 161, 309–323
sovereignty, principle of 160
Sri Lanka and 143, 320
statutory regime 142, 143–147
stay of execution, judgments subject to 150
submission to jurisdiction 151–152, 160
summary judgment procedure 149
Taiwan, Singapore judgments recognised by 92
test for rudimentary system 314
time limit for commencement of action 149
tradition, judgment contrary to 156
Vietnam and 315–316
Windward Islands and 143
writ of seizure and sale 149
Slovakia
Vietnam and 184
South Asian Association for Regional Cooperation (SAARC) 292
South Korea
Act on the Protection, etc of Fixed-term and Part-time Workers 129
Amendment Proposal of Private International Law Act 119, 120, 123, 124, 135, 138, 139, 314
anti-suit injunctions 133
appeal, foreign judgment pending 133
arbitral awards 121n
background, generally 119–121
bankruptcy procedure, foreign 122, 130
bilateral agreements 121
Civil Execution Act (CEA) 119, 122, 128, 133
Civil Procedure Act (CPA) 119, 122, 123, 124, 128, 133, 136
competition law 136–137
confession, judgment following 122
confirmatory judgments 132
damages 129, 130, 132, 137
divorce 129–130, 132n
domestic actions 132
due process, lack of 128
electronic documents 139–140
enforcement 119, 121, 133–134
environmental wrongs 136
evidence 121
execution judgments 121, 132n, 133–134
Fair Transactions in Subcontracting Act 129
final and conclusive, judgment must be 122, 132, 133
fraud, judgments obtained by 128
future prospects and reforms 137–140
garnishment 134
Hague Conventions 120–121, 131, 137–138, 140
immovable property 134, 135–136
indirect jurisdiction 120, 122, 123–125, 134–137
intellectual property rights 134–135
interest 129
interlocutory confirmation 132
interlocutory judgments 132–133

international jurisdiction of foreign court 122, 123–125
Japan and 107, 113–114, 126, 130, 134–135
judgment, failure to meet definition of 122
legal system 119–121
lex loci delicti 136
mandatory law, violation 130
Memorandums of Understanding 139
money judgments 126, 134
Monopoly Regulation and Fair Trade Act 136–137
morals, judgment undermining 122, 128–131
most closely connected law rule 120
parallelism principle 137
partial recognition 132
Private International Law Act (PILA) 120, 123, 124
public policy exception 122, 128–131
reciprocity principle 122, 126–127, 138–139, 314
recognition 119, 121–133
requirements to be met 119, 121–123, 125–127, 132–134, 138–139
res judicata 119, 122, 127, 129–130, 132n
révision au fond 128
service of documents 121, 122, 131
social order, judgment undermining 122, 128–131
substantive relation to South Korea 123–124
Taiwan and 92, 93–94
test for rudimentary system 314, 322
two or more claims, judgments involving 126
Vietnam and 185, 199
sovereignty, principle of
generally 14, 28
Japan of 117
Malaysia 171
People's Republic of China 35, 39, 41, 42
Singapore 160
Sri Lanka 273
Thailand 259, 260, 265
Vietnam 190, 194, 315
specific performance 17–18, 219
Sri Lanka
appeal, judgments subject to 276
background, generally 272–273
case law 273, 277–281
Civil Aspects of International Child Abduction Act 285–286
Civil Procedure Code (CPC) 277, 279, 280–281
Code of Intellectual Property Act 275
Commercial High Court 274–275, 277, 282
common law principles 272, 276, 277–281
Companies Act 275, 275n, 282
competency of rendering court 277–279, 280
Constitution 283–284, 286
Constitutional Council 272–273
costs 278, 279, 281
court system 273–275, 288
Debt Recovery (Special Provisions) Act 274
defences to actions on foreign judgments 280
definite sum, judgment must be for 279–280
Directive Principles of State Policy 283
dualist nature of state 283, 284
enforcement 280–281
Enforcement of Foreign Judgments Ordinance 271, 271n, 273, 275–277, 287
English law, influence 272
environmental law 282–283
ex parte decrees 279
final and conclusive, judgment must be 279
fraud, judgments obtained by 276, 280
future reforms 286–289
Hague Conventions 273, 284–286
Hong Kong and 59–64, 79–80, 276
immovable property 281
in personam actions 277–278
indirect (international) jurisdiction 283–285
Intellectual Property Act 282
intellectual property rights 281–282
international treaties 282, 283–287
Islamic law 272
judicial system 272, 287–288
Kandyan law 272
legal system 272
Malaysia and 169
National Environmental Act 282–283
natural justice, judgments contrary to 280, 287
perishable property 281
private international law 273
public policy, judgments contrary to 276, 280
Reciprocal Enforcement of Judgments Ordinance 271, 271n, 273, 274–277, 287, 320
reciprocity principle 271, 276
requirements to be met 276, 277–279
residence 276, 277, 278
Roman-Dutch law 272
service of documents 276
Singapore and 143, 320
sovereignty, principle of 273
statute law 273, 275–277, 281–283, 287
submission to jurisdiction 278
Tesawalamai law 272
test for rudimentary system 320–321, 322
transformation, doctrine of 283
TRIPS agreement 282
writ of execution 281
stare decisis
Malaysia 165

Stockholm Declaration 283
stop notice
Hong Kong 74–75
stop order
Hong Kong 74–75
Straits Settlement
Sri Lanka and 276
submission
choice of court agreement, by 151, 311, 321, 323
generally 29, 310–311, 323
Hague Conventions 15, 19–20
Hong Kong 61–62, 66, 76
implied 152, 170
India 301, 308, 321
Japan 106, 313
Malaysia 170, 315
Singapore 151–152, 160
Sri Lanka 278
voluntary 15, 20–21
summary judgment procedure 28–29
Hong Kong 28n, 65–66
Japan 104
Myanmar 213–214, 318n
Singapore 149, 313n
Switzerland
Japan, reciprocity with 107

Taiwan
Act Governing Choice of Law in Civil Matters Involving Foreign Elements 87–88, 93
Arbitration Law 91
automatic recognition system 85, 86
breach of contract or duty 88, 94
Code of Civil Procedure 85, 86, 87, 88, 89–90, 92, 313
comity principle 93
Compulsory Enforcement Act 86, 87, 92
damages 88, 90, 94
declaratory judgments confirming enforceability 86
default judgments 85, 87, 88–89
divorce judgments 92, 93, 94
due process 89, 93, 313
exceptions to automatic recognition system 85–86
final and binding, judgment must be 86
foreign court lacking jurisdiction 85, 87–88
foreign judgments recognised by 91–92
Hong Kong and 51, 59, 91
indirect jurisdiction 87–88, 311, 313
international treaties 86–87
Japanese judgments 92
Law Supporting Foreign Courts on Consigned Cases 89
mainland China and 37, 91
mirror principle 313
morals, judgment violating 85, 89–90, 93
mutual recognition of judicial decisions 85, 87, 90–91, 92, 95
property disputes 93–94
public policy, judgments violating 85, 89–90, 93
requirements to be met 86
res judicata 86, 313
service of documents 88–89, 93, 94–95
status 86, 90
test for rudimentary system 313, 322
Vietnam and 87, 185
Tanganyika
Sri Lanka and 276
Thailand
anti-suit injunctions 265
arbitral awards 260
ASEAN 262, 263, 269
background, generally 259–261
bilateral agreements 262–263
civil law 259, 265
Civil Procedure Code 259, 264
common law influence 265
comparative law 264–265
Conflict of Laws Act (1938 Act) 259, 264, 265
domestic sources of law 264–265
due process 263, 266, 267–268, 320
finality of judgment 262, 320
foreign judgment, qualification as 265–266
forum non conveniens 265–266
future development of PIL 269
Hague Judgments Project 263
indirect jurisdiction 266–267, 320
international agreements 261–262, 263
legal system 260
Memorandums of Understanding 264
mirror principle 267, 320
non-legally binding instruments 263–264
ordre public atténué 268–269
ordre public plein 268
precedent 260, 264
private international law 259–260, 264
public policy, judgments contrary to 268–269
reciprocity principle 268
requirements to be met 265–269
res judicata 266, 268
sovereignty, principle of 259, 260, 265
test for rudimentary system 320, 322
transactions judiciaires 265
Vietnam and 185
Trinidad and Tobago
India and 296
TRIPS agreement 193, 282, 304
Turkey
India and 296

Uganda
Sri Lanka and 276
Ukraine
Vietnam and 185
India and 296
Uniform Customs and Practice for Documentary Credits 182
United Arab Emirates
India and 296, 297
United Kingdom
Hague Convention 2005 144n
India and 296
Japan and 101, 107, 109
Malaysia and 168
Myanmar and 219–220, 219n, 221
Singapore and 143–144
South Korea 126
Taiwan and 92
United Nations
Convention on a Code of Conduct for Liner Conferences 64–65, 78
Convention on Jurisdictional Immunities of States and Their Property 101
Convention on the Recognition and Enforcement of Foreign Arbitral Awards *see* New York Convention 1958
Convention on the Rights of the Child 261
United States
India and 305
Japan and 101, 107
South Korea and 126
Taiwan and 92
Vietnam and 193

Vietnam
appellate proceedings 189
application for recognition 188–189, 197–199
background, generally 179–180
Berne Convention 193
bilateral treaties 179, 180, 181, 182, 183–188, 193, 194, 196
Cambodia and 184, 201, 203–204, 206, 207
case law 179, 200
centralised state powers 180
China-Vietnam Treaty 39
choice of law 182, 196
Civil Code 181, 182, 183
civil and commercial judgments 183, 190
civil law tradition 180
Civil Procedure Code (CPC) 179, 181, 182, 183, 189, 193–194, 196, 197–199, 315–316
competition law 195
default judgments 189
due process 187, 188, 190–191
enforcement 179, 183, 187, 188, 192, 198
environmental damage 194–195
fairness of court procedures 199
future prospects and reforms 195–200
Hague Conventions 185, 195–197, 198, 199, 200
indirect jurisdiction 186, 316–317
intellectual property rights 193–194
interlocutory judgments 192
Japan and 199
judicial system 182–183
labour matters 183
land 194
Laos and 185
Law on Competition and Decree 195
Law on Environmental Protection 194
Maritime Code 182
matrimonial causes 183, 193, 197–198
mirror principle 316–317
monetary judgments 186, 188
New York Convention 1958 182, 200
non-monetary judgments 186, 187
North Korea and 185
partial recognition 191–192
People's Republic of China and 182, 184, 199
private international law 180–182
public policy, judgments contrary to 24, 189, 191, 195, 198–199
reciprocity principle 179, 190, 198, 315–316
recognition 179, 183, 187, 188–192, 198–199
requirements to be met 186, 189–192
res judicata 199
Singapore and 315–316
South Korea and 185, 199
sovereignty, principle of 190, 194, 315
Taiwan and 87, 185
test for rudimentary system 315–317, 322
Thailand and 185
time limit for applications 187, 189, 192
TRIPS agreement 193
Uniform Customs and Practice for Documentary Credits 182
voluntary execution 192

Warsaw Convention
Japan 100
winding up proceedings
Hong Kong 73–74
Malaysia 167, 172
World Trade Organization (WTO)
India 292
People's Republic of China 34

www.ingramcontent.com/pod-product-compliance
Ingram Content Group UK Ltd.
Pitfield, Milton Keynes, MK11 3LW, UK
UKHW050649200926
475560UK00005BA/348

9 781509 924257